1,138 GMAT® Practice Questions

3rd Edition

The Staff of The Princeton Review

PrincetonReview.com

Penguin
Random
House

The Princeton Review
24 Prime Parkway, Suite 201
Natick, MA 01760
E-mail: editorialsupport@review.com

Published in the United States by Penguin Random House LLC, New York, and in Canada by Random House of Canada, a division of Penguin Random House Ltd., Toronto.

ISBN: 978-0-375-42748-0
ISSN: 1946-3073

Editor: Aaron Riccio
Production Editor: Jim Melloan
Production Artist: Deborah A. Silvestrini

10 9 8 7 6 5 4 3 2 1

3rd Edition

Editorial

Rob Franek, Senior VP, Publisher
Casey Cornelius, VP Content Development
Mary Beth Garrick, Director of Production
Selena Coppock, Managing Editor
Meave Shelton, Senior Editor
Colleen Day, Editor
Sarah Litt, Editor
Aaron Riccio, Editor
Orion McBean, Editorial Assistant

Random House Publishing Team

Tom Russell, Publisher
Alison Stoltzfus, Publishing Manager
Melinda Ackell, Associate Managing Editor
Ellen Reed, Production Manager
Andrea Lau, Designer

Acknowledgements

A special thanks to John Fulmer and Kyle Fox for their dedication to reviewing, updating, and adding to the content of this book.

Contents

Register Your

1 Go to **PrincetonReview.com/cracking**

2 You'll see a welcome page where you can register your book using the following ISBN: 9780375427480.

3 After placing this free order, you'll either be asked to log in or to answer a few simple questions in order to set up a new Princeton Review account.

4 Finally, click on the "Student Tools" tab located at the top of the screen. It may take an hour or two for your registration to go through, but after that, you're good to go.

NOTE: If you are experiencing book problems (potential content errors), please contact EditorialSupport@review.com with the full title of the book, its ISBN number (located above), and the page number of the error.

Experiencing technical issues? Please e-mail TPRStudentTech@review.com with the following information:

- your full name
- e-mail address used to register the book
- full book title and ISBN
- your computer OS (Mac or PC) and Internet browser (Firefox, Safari, Chrome, etc.)
- description of technical issue

Book Online!

Once you've registered, you can access...

- an additional 70 Integrated Reasoning problems, designed to help provide a mastery of the question type and format

- additional mixed practice drills for the other sections of the test

- a list of any updates to this title, or of information on any changes to the GMAT

The **Princeton** Review®

Introduction

SO YOU'VE DECIDED TO GO TO BUSINESS SCHOOL...

The GMAT, or the Graduate Management Admission Test as it is officially known, is required for admission to most MBA programs. Business schools use the GMAT to predict the performance of students applying to their programs. The admissions staff will consider your GMAT score, undergraduate GPA, work experience, recommendation letters, and application essays in making admissions decisions.

Who Writes the GMAT?

The Graduate Management Admission Council (GMAC), an association of business schools, oversees the GMAT and contracts with ACT to develop the exam. ACT is an independent, nonprofit organization that also writes the ACT college admission exam and other educational and workplace tests. Neither GMAC nor ACT is supervised by the government or any other body. What gives them the right to administer the GMAT? The fact that they give the test.

The Test—Overview

There are four sections on the GMAT: an essay section (Analytical Writing Assessment or AWA), a multiple-choice Quantitative (or Math) section, a multiple-choice Verbal section, and the brand new Integrated Reasoning section. The GMAT is only offered on a computer. The 3.5 hour test is administered at a secure computer terminal at an approved testing center. You enter your multiple-choice answers on the screen with a mouse; you must compose your essay for the Writing Assessment section on the computer as well. Here is how the sections break down by time and number of questions:

1. One 30-minute essay to be written on the computer using a generic word processing program.

2. One 30-minute, 12-question, multiple-choice Integrated Reasoning section. Some integrated reasoning questions can have multiple parts.

   (optional break)

3. A 75-minute, 37-question, multiple-choice Math section

   (optional break)

4. A 75-minute, 41-question, multiple-choice Verbal section

You must answer a question in order to get to the next question—which means that you can't skip a question and come back to it. And while you are not required to finish any of the sections, your score will be adjusted downward to reflect questions you did not complete.

On each of the Math and Verbal sections, approximately one quarter of the questions you encounter will be experimental and will not count toward your score. These questions, which will be mixed in among the regular questions, are there so the test company can try out new questions for future tests. There is no way to identify which questions are experimental, though. They are sprinkled randomly throughout the Math and Verbal sections.

Integrated Reasoning

For 2012, the GMAT gains a new section called the Integrated Reasoning section. If you are taking your GMAT on or after June 5, 2012, you'll need to prepare for the Integrated Reasoning section because it will be part of your test! The new IR section is 30 minutes long and you'll see it as the second section of your test. Officially, there are only 12 questions, which sounds pretty great. However, most of those questions have multiple parts. So, your answer to the question really consists of four separate responses. For the entire section, you'll actually need to select approximately 30 different responses. Note, however, that there is no partial credit on the Integrated Reasoning. Even though we have distinguished between the various sub-questions (such as 1-1, 1-2, 1-3, and 1-4), you will have to get all parts of a question correct in order to earn points for that question. Unlike the Math section, the Integrated Reasoning gives you access to a calculator (on your computer), so keep that in mind when you're practicing.

We've prepared some resources to help you get ready for this new section. This book includes 25 Integrated Reasoning items so that you can practice the new question types. In addition, we have created an Online Companion Tool to accompany this book. This will allow you to practice these four new Integrated Reasoning question types on a computer, just like you will see when you take the real GMAT. Just go to **www.PrincetonReview.com/cracking** to register your book and access this Integrated Reasoning practice content.

WHAT INFORMATION IS TESTED ON THE GMAT?

You will find several different types of multiple-choice questions on the GMAT.

Math (37 questions total)
- Problem Solving—approximately 19 questions
- Data Sufficiency (a strange type of problem that exists on no other test in the world)—approximately 18 questions

Verbal (41 questions total)
- Reading Comprehension (tests your ability to answer questions about a passage)—approximately 13 questions
- Sentence Correction (a grammar-related question type)—approximately 17 questions
- Critical Reasoning (a logic-based question type recycled from the LSAT)—approximately 11 questions

Integrated Reasoning (12 questions total)
- Table Analysis (data is presented in a sortable table, like an Excel spreadsheet; each question usually has four parts)
- Graphics Interpretation (a chart or graph is used to display data; each question usually has three parts; answers are selected from drop-down boxes)
- Multi-Source Reasoning (information—a combination of charts, text, and tables—is presented on two or three tabs; each set of tabbed information is usually accompanied by three questions)
- Two-Part Analysis (each question usually has six options and you need to pick two)

Noteboards

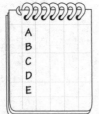

Because the GMAT is presented on a computer screen, you will not have the luxury of solving problems right on the page or marking up passages. Instead, you are required to do all of your work on the erasable noteboards provided at the test center. Do not try to work out problems in your head! That is a surefire way to make careless mistakes.

You will be provided with a blank ten-page booklet and a fine-tipped black marker for scratch work. The pages of the booklet are laminated and printed with a faint grid pattern that is useful for drawing math diagrams. You cannot get additional noteboards until you turn in the ones you have. To avoid having to raise your hand during the test to get replacement boards from the test administrator, turn in your noteboards after the math section. That way you'll have a fresh set for each section of the test.

Start practicing your scratch work now. When you work problems in this book, do not circle words or write notes directly on the problem. Instead, write everything off to the side or get a separate notebook. Set up each page of your notebook just as you would your noteboard during the exam: divide it into sections to organize your work and write A, B, C, D, and E to represent the answer choices for each problem. Cross off answers, using Process of Elimination (POE). Do all of your work in the notebook and label the problems so that you can review them easily once you have finished.

How Is the GMAT Scored?

As soon as you've finished taking the GMAT, your computer will calculate and display your unofficial results, not including your Writing Assessment score. You can print out a copy of your unofficial results to take with you. Within 20 days, you will receive your score report online; a written report will be available only by request.

Most people think of the GMAT score as a single number, but in fact there are five separate numbers:

1. Math score (reported on a scale that runs from 0 to 60)
2. Verbal score (reported on a scale that runs from 0 to 60)
3. Total score (reported on a scale that runs from 200 to 800 and based only on the results of Math and Verbal sections)
4. Analytic Writing Assessment score (reported on a scale of 0 to 6, in half point increments; 6 is the highest score)
5. Integrated Reasoning score (reported on a scale that runs from 1–8)

The report will look something like this:

Math	%	Verbal	%	Total	%	AWA	%	Integrated Reasoning	%
36	42	30	56	550	48	4.5	38	6	75

Your GMAT scores are good for five years. They're also risk-free. There's a Score Preview feature now offered on the GMAT that allows you to review how you did before choosing whether to pass this information on to your prospective schools.

How a CAT Works

The Verbal and Math sections of the GMAT are computer adaptive tests (CAT). The level of difficulty of the test questions adapts to match your performance. In other words, when you answer a question correctly, the next question will be harder. When you answer a question incorrectly, the next question will be easier.

A CAT looks at several things to calculate your score for a section.

- Number of questions you answer correctly
- Difficulty of the questions you answer
- Number of questions you complete

You start the section with a medium score, and the first question you see is of medium difficulty. Every time you answer a question correctly, the computer raises your score and gives you a more difficult question. Every time you answer a question incorrectly, the computer lowers your score and gives you an easier question.

The computer recalculates your score after every question. The difficulty level of the next question generally matches your current score; however, the computer also has to meet certain requirements for the types of questions in a section. For example, the Math section has to have a balance of problem solving and data sufficiency questions and also has to have the proper mix of arithmetic, algebra, and geometry. Thus, the difficulty of a particular question may not always exactly match your current score. There are a couple of other things you should know about how the CAT works.

- Questions at the beginning of each section count more than those at the end.
- You cannot skip a question or go back to a question once you've answered it.
- There is a penalty if you run out of time and leave questions blank.

Remember: The Math and Verbal sections of the GMAT are adaptive, but the new Integrated Reasoning section is not.

Pacing

Because of the way that the Math and Verbal sections of the GMAT are scored, proper pacing is essential to success.

The most important guidelines to remember include the following:

- Start slowly and carefully. Eliminate careless mistakes.
- Gradually pick up speed so you can finish the section.
- Don't waste time on killer questions. Guess and move on.

At the beginning of the section your score can fluctuate dramatically depending on how many questions you get right or wrong. By the end of each section, however, the computer has already made up its mind about you. Your score will fluctuate only within a narrow range. That's why you need to slow down and do your best on the early questions; the early questions are the most important.

To maximize your score, however, you cannot focus solely on the early questions. Your score is also based on the total number of questions you answer correctly. That means you can't just work the first half of the questions, guess on the second half, and get a great score. The GMAT confronts you with more questions than most people can comfortably complete in the time allowed. Expect to feel pressed for time when you take the test. Know that this is normal and stay calm.

Because the penalty for leaving any question blank is quite severe, finish the section, even if it means you have to guess randomly at the end of the section. You may think that guessing on the test automatically dooms you to a bad score, but you can guess on a few questions and still score in the 700s (and many do).

If you answer questions correctly, the subsequent questions get increasingly harder. You are virtually guaranteed to see a few questions that you will not be able to solve. For those killer questions, don't waste your valuable time staring at the screen. Take your best guess and move on. Spend time on questions you can solve.

RESOURCES

In addition to this book, you have some other worthwhile resources to consider.

Cracking the GMAT—While this book is primarily about providing additional practice items for each subject, *Cracking the GMAT* is like a full course in your hands. It contains all of the strategies, tips, and advice that have made The Princeton Review the best standardized test preparation company in the world.

GMATPrep—This is test-preparation software that can be downloaded for free from **www.mba.com**. This software includes two computer-adaptive tests plus additional practice sets, all of which feature real GMAT questions.

PrincetonReview.com/cracking is where you can register this book in order to access the 70 online Integrated Reasoning practice items.

The Official Guide for GMAT Review 2016—This is another ACT publication. It contains 800 previously administered GMAT questions as well as a miniature diagnostic test.

The Official Guide for GMAT Verbal Review and *The Official Guide for GMAT Quantitative Review*—These books each contain 300 additional previously administered verbal and math questions.

Verbal Workout for the GMAT and *Math Workout for the GMAT*—The Princeton Review's *Verbal Workout for the GMAT* and *Math Workout for the GMAT* give you everything you need to tackle the verbal and math portions of the GMAT test. They include hundreds of practice exercises to sharpen your skills.

HOW TO USE THIS BOOK

This book is about building good test taking habits.

Over three and a half hours of testing, your brain will get tired and you will begin to do things by habit without thinking about them actively. If your habits are good, they will help carry you through, even when your brain starts to check out. If you have not taken the time to create good test taking habits, you will get sloppy, and sloppiness kills your score.

The creation of habits requires repetition, and that's where this book comes in. Use *Cracking the GMAT* and GMAC's *Official Guide* to establish your approach to different question types. Then work your way through this book to cement those approaches into habit. When you do this, time and large score fluctuations will cease to be an issue. There will be no such thing as having a good or bad test day. You will be in control, and you will have your scores right where you want them.

If you want to change your score, you must change the way you take the test.

Diagnostic

If you are under a time crunch or just need to shore up some weaknesses, this is your first step. Take the math and verbal diagnostic tests provided at the beginning of the book. Check your scores and find your areas of weakness.

Practice

Each question type begins with a brief synopsis of the basic approach. Read these sections carefully. These approaches have been tried, tested, and refined by hundreds of test takers over the years. They are here because they work and represent good habits. How does the approach described by this book differ from your own? Can yours be improved?

Use questions in the *Official Guide* to work out your approach. Remember that the practice items don't count. No one will ever see how you did. Now is the time to take some risks and try out some different ways to solve these problems. It's not about answers; it's about approach. Some of the new techniques may feel awkward at first, but they're there because they work. Stick with it.

Once you have found some patterns that work for you, move on to the drills in this book. Use your scratch paper, stick to your approach, and drill until the patterns become habit. By the time you are done, every time a question of that type pops up, you will know instinctively what to do, no matter how tired you get. This is a powerful tool.

The One-Two Punch

If you are just starting your GMAT prep, need to add more than 50 to 60 points to your score, or don't yet have an approach, this book is not the place to start. This book is not for teaching. It is a workbook for practice and drilling. *Cracking the GMAT, 2016 Edition* describes the test and the techniques in much more depth. It breaks down the approach to each question in a step-by-step manner with plenty of examples. *Cracking the GMAT, 2016 Edition* is where you go to learn *how* to take the test; in this book you *practice* taking it.

You Can Do It

If you are frustrated that the skills you need for the GMAT bear little resemblance to the subjects you will be studying in business school, remember three things:

- First, the GMAT is not a content test. It does not test a body of knowledge, such as U.S. History or French. It is designed to test a very specific way of thinking.
- Second, the GMAT is only one factor of many that will be considered for admission, and it is often the easiest to change.
- Finally, taking the GMAT is a skill, and like any other skill, it can be learned. That is what this book and *Cracking the GMAT* are all about. With diligence and practice, you can learn everything you need to know for the GMAT in a surprisingly short period of time.

Diagnostic

Analytical Writing Assessment
ANALYSIS OF AN ARGUMENT

Directions: In this section you will be asked to write a critique of the argument presented below. Note that you are not being asked to present your own views on the subject. Instead, you may need to consider what questionable assumptions underlie the thinking, what alternative explanations or counterexamples might weaken the conclusion, or what sort of evidence could help strengthen or refute the argument.

Read the argument and the instructions that follow it, and then make any notes that will help you plan your response. Type your response, using a word-processing program.

The federal government often provides subsidies to certain traditional industries, such as agriculture. However, our economy has grown far more recently from the development of technology-based industries. The federal government should not subsidize traditional industries because it may prevent workers in these traditional industries from moving to technology-based industries that can offer greater benefits to the whole country.

Discuss how well reasoned you find this argument. In your discussion, be sure to analyze the line of reasoning and the use of evidence in the argument. For example, you may need to consider what questionable assumptions underlie the thinking and what alternative explanations or counterexamples might weaken the conclusion. You can also discuss what sort of evidence would strengthen or refute the argument, what changes in the argument would make it more logically sound, and what, if anything, would help you better evaluate its conclusion.

GO ON TO THE NEXT PAGE.

INTEGRATED REASONING
12 Items
Time Limit: 30 minutes

This section is a full practice Integrated Reasoning section. Please note that some questions are laid out slightly differently in this book than what you'll see on the GMAT. Many of the new question formats are interactive. Hence, only approximations can be printed. Specifically,

- Table Analysis questions are shown with a main sort and several alternate sorts. You may not need every sort.
- Graphics Interpretation questions include drop-down boxes. In this book, the box is shown as a fill-in blank and the answers printed below the blank.
- For Multi-Source Reasoning questions, we've printed what's on each tab consecutively on the page.
- For some questions, you'll see things like Question 1-1, Question 1-2, Question 1-3, or (A), (B), (C), appear next to answer choices. These are included only to make it easier to check your work. These do not appear on the real GMAT.

We've included answers to this section starting on page 49.

Item 1:

Exotic Animals		Residential Holdings			Medical Incidents			
	Number	% Change	Rank	Number	% Change	Fatal	% Change
Tigers	2,050	1.1	10	15	0	2	100
Chimpanzees	12,075	–12	9	248	–2.5	8	–37.5
Crocodiles	18,680	–2.69	8	72	–25	15	–9.75
Kinkajou	64,890	–0.27	7	124	–1.59	1	0
Ostriches	95,424	–15.6	6	25,688	16.44	105	–30.48
Pythons	110,150	13.57	5	512	11.3	10	0
Constrictors	250,050	8	4	22,045	6.82	83	12.5
Scorpions	285,335	20.55	3	165,458	27.27	17	41.67
Tarantulas	300,652	8.55	2	120,898	14.45	32	–46.8
Turtles	325,412	12.7	1	105,045	2.8	0	–100

The table above gives information for 2011 on residential holdings and associated medical incidents (totals based on U.S. figures) for 10 types of exotic animals. In addition to the numbers of total residential holdings and medical incidents, the table also gives the percent of increase or decrease over the numbers for 2010 and the rank of the animal for total residential holdings.

Each column of the table can be sorted in ascending order by clicking on the word "Select" above the table and choosing, from the drop-down menu, the heading of the column on which you want the table to be sorted.

GO ON TO THE NEXT PAGE.

Alternate Sort 1: *% Change, Residential Holdings*

Exotic Animals		Residential Holdings			Medical Incidents			
	Number	% Change	Rank	Number	% Change	Fatal	% Change
Scorpions	285,335	20.55	3	165,458	27.27	17	41.67
Pythons	110,150	13.57	5	512	11.3	10	0
Turtles	325,412	12.7	1	105,045	2.8	0	−100
Tarantulas	300,652	8.55	2	120,898	14.45	32	−46.8
Constrictors	250,050	8	4	22,045	6.82	83	12.5
Tigers	2,050	1.1	10	15	0	2	100
Kinkajou	64,890	−0.27	7	124	−1.59	1	0
Crocodiles	18,680	−2.69	8	72	−25	15	−9.75
Chimpanzees	12,075	−12	9	248	−2.5	8	−37.5
Ostriches	95,424	−15.6	6	25,688	16.44	105	−30.48

Alternate Sort 2: *Number of Medical Incidents*

Exotic Animals		Residential Holdings			Medical Incidents			
	Number	% Change	Rank	Number	% Change	Fatal	% Change
Scorpions	285,335	20.55	3	165,458	27.27	17	41.67
Tarantulas	300,652	8.55	2	120,898	14.45	32	−46.8
Turtles	325,412	12.7	1	105,045	2.8	0	−100
Ostriches	95,424	−15.6	6	25,688	16.44	105	−30.48
Constrictors	250,050	8	4	22,045	6.82	83	12.5
Pythons	110,150	13.57	5	512	11.3	10	0
Chimpanzees	12,075	−12	9	248	−2.5	8	−37.5
Kinkajou	64,890	−0.27	7	124	−1.59	1	0
Crocodiles	18,680	−2.69	8	72	−25	15	−9.75
Tigers	2,050	1.1	10	15	0	2	100

Consider each of the following statements about exotic animals. For each statement indicate whether the statement is true or false, based on the information provided in the table.

	True	False	
Question 1-1	○	○	In 2011, approximately 25% of all medical incidents involving crocodiles were fatal.
Question 1-2	○	○	The average residential holding of the top 3 ranking exotic animals, based on the total number of residential holdings, is approximately 303,800.
Question 1-3	○	○	The exotic animal that experienced the greatest percent decrease in total residential holdings from 2010 to 2011 also experienced the second greatest increase in the percent of reported medical incidents.
Question 1-4	○	○	The exotic animal ranked fifth based on the total number of reported medical incidents is the same as the exotic animal that experienced no change in fatal medical incidents.

Item 2:

Country A currently has 2 million people, and Country B currently has 1.5 million people. The population of both countries is growing rapidly and both countries anticipate having 3 million people next year.

In the table below, identify the approximate percent increase of the current population that will be necessary for each of the countries to reach the 3 million people anticipated next year. Make only one selection in each column.

	Country A	Country B	Percent Increase
(A)	○	○	25
(B)	○	○	33
(C)	○	○	50
(D)	○	○	66
(E)	○	○	75
(F)	○	○	100

GO ON TO THE NEXT PAGE.

Item 3:

Andre is buying gifts for his office staff. He wants to spend exactly $280 and he can buy either sweatshirts, which cost $22, or baseball caps, which cost $26.

In the table below, choose the number of sweatshirts and the number of baseball caps that Andre should buy.

	Sweatshirts	Baseball Caps	Number to Buy
(A)	○	○	4
(B)	○	○	5
(C)	○	○	6
(D)	○	○	7
(E)	○	○	8
(F)	○	○	9

Data for Items 4, 5, and 6

| Table | Proposal | Pie Chart |

City A wants to analyze the flow of traffic for the various means of transportation the city has available. The table below gives the average number of bus commuters (in hundreds) for each weekday in City A during selected months.

	Monday	Tuesday	Wednesday	Thursday	Friday
February	12	13	11	10	13
April	15	14	13	16	15
June	17	16	17	18	15
August	21	20	22	19	23
October	13	15	14	9	11
December	9	11	12	8	10

| Table | Proposal | Pie Chart |

Proposal from city official regarding the price of bus fare in City A.

During the summer months, the height of tourist season in our city, there is a noticeable increase in the amount of traffic of all types. In order to decrease congestion on our highways, this city needs to increase the portion of the commuters who ride on our city's bus services. In order to encourage this, I propose that we decrease our current $2 bus fare by 50 cents during July and August. Our analysis suggests that the numbers of people who ride the train or ferry or who walk are unlikely to be significantly affected by this measure. However, it also suggests that enough people would ride the bus rather than commute by automobile to increase bus ridership by 20%. This will, in part, make up for the lost revenue.

| Table | Proposal | Pie Chart |

The pie chart below gives the breakdown of City A's total number of weekday (Monday through Friday) commuters by method of transportation for an average week during the month of August.

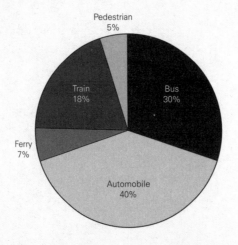

GO ON TO THE NEXT PAGE.

Item 4:

Assuming that the analysis presented by the city official is correct, what is the ratio of the current bus revenue in August to what the bus revenue in August would be if the proposal were to be implemented?

- (A) 3 to 4
- (B) 4 to 5
- (C) 10 to 9
- (D) 4 to 3
- (E) 5 to 2

Item 5:

Consider each of the following statements. Does the information in the tabs support the inference as stated?

	Yes	No	
(A)	○	○	The number of weekday commuters in an average week in February is greater than that in October.
(B)	○	○	The ratio of the number of weekday automobile commuters to that of weekday bus commuters during the average week in August is 3 to 4.
(C)	○	○	In August, the total number of people who travel by ferry and the total number of people who travel by train is less than the number of those who travel by bus.
(D)	○	○	During each of the five weekdays, the average number of bus commuters is greater in August than in any of the other months listed.

Item 6:

Consider each of the following statements. Does the information in the tabs support the inference as stated?

	Yes	No	
(A)	○	○	If the analysis presented by the city official is correct, then increasing the bus fare by 50 cents would decrease ridership by 20%.
(B)	○	○	There are fewer bus commuters in December than there are in any other month of the year.
(C)	○	○	If the analysis presented by the city official were correct, then decreasing the bus fare by 50 cents would decrease the number of automobile commuters by 20%.
(D)	○	○	There are 35,000 total commuters in the average work week during August.

Item 7:

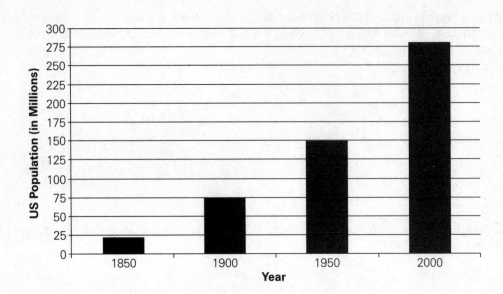

The bar chart above displays the population of the United States according to official census figures every fifty years over a 150 year period.

Use the drop-down menus to fill in the blanks in each of the following statements based on the information given by the graph.

Question 7-1:

The ratio of the U.S. population in 2000 to the U.S. population in 1900 is closest to _____.

(A)   1 to 4
(B)   2 to 7
(C)   2 to 1
(D)   3 to 1
(E)   11 to 3

Question 7-2:

The U.S. population in 1950 was approximately _____ of the U.S. population in 1850.

(A)   800%
(B)   600%
(C)   200%
(D)   85%
(E)   15%

GO ON TO THE NEXT PAGE.

Question 7-3:

The U.S. population increased by approximately _____ from 1900 to 1950.

    (A)   25%

    (B)   33%

    (C)   50%

    (D)   100%

    (E)   200%

Integrated Reasoning

Data for Items 8, 9, and 10

Tab #1   Tab #2

E-mail from chief operating officer to factory manager

March 27, 7:21 a.m.

One of our computers crashed – the one that stored the secret recipe for our soft drink that we've used for over 50 years. We've been able to reconstruct most of the recipe from a partial hard drive recovery, but we still can't find the number of ounces of ingredients X and Y that need to be added to each batch. I think the crash was the result of industrial espionage: one of our competitors must have discovered we've been storing the recipe on that same computer for the last 10 years. It is very important that we recover that information.

Tab #1   Tab #2

E-mail from factory manager to chief operating officer

March 27, 9:03 a.m.

I found a cost analysis report that includes the following: two years ago ingredients X and Y both cost the same amount, 6 cents per ounce, and the total cost of ingredients X and Y per batch was $1.20. Trend analysis showed that four years earlier, X cost twice as much, Y cost half as much, and the total cost of ingredients X and Y per batch was 3 cents higher.

GO ON TO THE NEXT PAGE.

Item 8

For each of the following statements, select *Yes* if, based on the information provided, the statement is an assumption on which the chief operating officer's argument depends. Otherwise, select *No*.

	Yes	No	
(A)	○	○	This is the first time the company has been the victim of industrial espionage.
(B)	○	○	The number of ounces of ingredients X and Y was kept secret by having a different employee add each ingredient to the batch.
(C)	○	○	The computer that stored the secret recipe did not crash purely due to age.
(D)	○	○	The secret recipe could not be reverse-engineered through spectral analysis of the final soft drink product.

Item 9

For each of the following statements, select *Yes* if, based on the information provided, the inference is supported by the information in the two emails. Otherwise, select *No*.

	Yes	No	
(A)	○	○	A computer crash does not always result in the loss of all data contained in the computer.
(B)	○	○	Ingredients X and Y are the most important ingredients in the company's secret recipe.
(C)	○	○	The prices of ingredients X and Y are not directly related to the level of inflation.
(D)	○	○	If the company cannot recover the complete secret recipe, the company will likely incur a large financial loss.

Item 10

Based on the information in the two emails, approximately how many ounces of Ingredient X are used in the secret recipe?

(A)	4
(B)	7
(C)	10
(D)	13
(E)	16

Item 11

Student Score at XYZ College

Class	Number of Students	Average Score on Test 1	Average Score on Test 2	Average Score on Test 3	% Change from Test 2 to Test 3
Basket Weaving	2	69	66.2	65.4	–2.3%
Physics	8	88	78.9	79.5	0.80%
Calculus	10	90.2	86.2	88.4	2.60%
English	12	79.4	86.6	88.8	2.50%
History	14	88.7	89.4	89.6	0.20%
Engineering	14	81.3	86.6	88.2	1.80%
Algebra	15	82.8	89.1	89.5	0.40%
Chemistry	16	70.2	78.5	81.8	4.20%
Geography	20	86.9	83	85.6	3.10%
Economics	23	78.2	84.5	86	1.80%
Literature	25	86.1	79.9	81.3	1.80%
Physical Education	26	86.3	80.4	81.4	1.30%
Biology	37	76.1	75.8	74.8	–1.3%

The table above shows information on how many students are in each class at XYZ College and the average of each class on standardized tests 1, 2, and 3. In addition, the table also shows the percent change in the average scores from test 2 to test 3. Each column of the table can be sorted in ascending order by clicking on the word "Select" above the table and choosing, from the drop-down menu, the heading of the column on which you want the table to be sorted.

Alternate Sort 1: *Average Score on Test 1*

Class	Number of Students	Average Score on Test 1	Average Score on Test 2	Average Score on Test 3	% Change from Test 2 to Test 3
Basket Weaving	2	69	66.2	65.4	–2.3%
Chemistry	16	70.2	78.5	81.8	4.20%
Biology	37	76.1	75.8	74.8	–1.3%
Economics	23	78.2	84.5	86	1.80%
English	12	79.4	86.6	88.8	2.50%
Engineering	14	81.3	86.6	88.2	1.80%
Algebra	15	82.8	89.1	89.5	0.40%
Literature	25	86.1	79.9	81.3	1.80%
Physical Education	26	86.3	80.4	81.4	1.30%
Geography	20	86.9	83	85.6	3.10%
Physics	8	88	78.9	79.5	0.80%
History	14	88.7	89.4	89.6	0.20%
Calculus	10	90.2	86.2	88.4	2.60%

GO ON TO THE NEXT PAGE.

Alternate Sort 2: *Average Score on Test 2*

Class	Number of Students	Average Score on Test 1	Average Score on Test 2	Average Score on Test 3	% Change from Test 2 to Test 3
Basket Weaving	2	69	66.2	65.4	−2.3%
Biology	37	76.1	75.8	74.8	−1.3%
Chemistry	16	70.2	78.5	81.8	4.20%
Physics	8	88	78.9	79.5	0.80%
Literature	25	86.1	79.9	81.3	1.80%
Physical Education	26	86.3	80.4	81.4	1.30%
Geography	20	86.9	83	85.6	3.10%
Economics	23	78.2	84.5	86	1.80%
Calculus	10	90.2	86.2	88.4	2.60%
English	12	79.4	86.6	88.8	2.50%
Engineering	14	81.3	86.6	88.2	1.80%
Algebra	15	82.8	89.1	89.5	0.40%
History	14	88.7	89.4	89.6	0.20%

Consider each of the following statements about the student scores at XYZ College. For each statement indicate whether the statement is true or false, based on the information provided in the table.

	True	False	
Question 11-1	○	○	The class with the median rank based on number of students is the same as the class with the median based on test 1.
Question 11-2	○	○	The smallest percent increase in average score from test 1 to test 2 was by the students in History.
Question 11-3	○	○	The total points scored by the students on test 2 in Chemistry is more than the total points scored by students on test 2 in History.
Question 11-4	○	○	The classes that have a percent change from test 2 to test 3 greater than 1.8% contain a total of 120 students.

Item 12

Jack and Chloe, working together at constant rates, complete a job in 6 hours. Working individually, Chloe completes the same job three times as fast as does Jack.

In the table below, identify the number of hours it takes Jack and Chloe to complete the jobs individually. Make only two selections, one in each column.

	Jack	Chloe	Value Title
(A)	○	○	3 hours
(B)	○	○	6 hours
(C)	○	○	8 hours
(D)	○	○	9 hours
(E)	○	○	18 hours
(F)	○	○	24 hours

QUANTITATIVE
37 Questions

Directions: In this section solve each problem, then indicate the best of the answer choices given.

Numbers: All numbers used are real numbers.

Figures: Figures that accompany problems in this section are intended to provide information useful in solving the problems. Figures on problem solving questions are drawn as accurately as possible EXCEPT when it is stated in a specific problem that its figure is not drawn to scale. All figures lie in a plane unless otherwise indicated. Figures on Data Sufficiency questions are not necessarily drawn to scale, but will conform to the information given in the question.

Data Sufficiency: All Data Sufficiency problems consist of two statements, labeled (1) and (2), in which certain data are given. You must use the data given in the statements, plus your knowledge of mathematics and everyday facts (such as the number of days in July or the meaning of *counterclockwise*) to decide whether the data given in the statements are <u>sufficient</u> for answering the question.

---

1. $\dfrac{(6^2)(2^4)(5^3)}{120^2}$

   (A)   3
   (B)   5
   (C)   15
   (D)   25
   (E)   30

2. If $-1 < p < 0$, which of the following expressions has the GREATEST value?

   (A) $p^2 - 0.30$

   (B) $p^2 - 0.32$

   (C) $p^3 - 0.301$

   (D) $p^3 - 0.322$

   (E) $p^4 - 0.313$

3. Integer x is equal to the product of all even numbers from 2 to 60, inclusive. If y is the smallest prime number that is also a factor of $x - 1$, then which of the following expressions must be true?

   (A) $0 < y < 4$
   (B) $4 < y < 10$
   (C) $10 < y < 20$
   (D) $20 < y < 30$
   (E) $y > 30$

4. The wholesale cost of a particular brand of black ink is $2,000 per dekaliter. If the ink is sold in printer cartridges containing 40 milliliters of ink each, then what is the wholesale cost of the ink in a single cartridge? (1 dekaliter $= 10^4$ milliliters)

   (A) $0.08
   (B) $0.20
   (C) $0.80
   (D) $8.00
   (E) $20.00

5. If triangle ABC has sides $AB = 8$ and $BC = 3$, which of the following CANNOT be equal to the perimeter of triangle ABC?

   I. 16
   II. 18
   III. 21

   (A) I only
   (B) II only
   (C) I and II
   (D) II and III
   (E) I, II, and III

6. Is x greater than 30 ?

    (1) x − y is greater than 30

    (2) y is greater than 30

    (A) Statement (1) ALONE is sufficient, but
    statement (2) alone is not sufficient.
    (B) Statement (2) ALONE is sufficient, but
    statement (1) alone is not sufficient.
    (C) BOTH statements TOGETHER are sufficient,
    but NEITHER statement ALONE is sufficient.
    (D) EACH Statement ALONE is sufficient.
    (E) Statements (1) and (2) TOGETHER are NOT
    sufficient to answer the question asked, and
    additional data are needed.

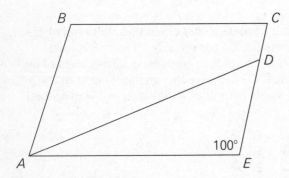

7. In the figure above, if ∠ABC = 110°, and
    ∠AED = 100°, then ∠ADE is how many degrees
    smaller than ∠BCD ?

    (1) ∠DAB = 45°

    (2) ∠ADC + ∠BCD = 205°

    (A) Statement (1) ALONE is sufficient, but
    statement (2) alone is not sufficient.
    (B) Statement (2) ALONE is sufficient, but
    statement (1) alone is not sufficient.
    (C) BOTH statements TOGETHER are sufficient,
    but NEITHER statement ALONE is sufficient.
    (D) EACH Statement ALONE is sufficient.
    (E) Statements (1) and (2) TOGETHER are NOT
    sufficient to answer the question asked, and
    additional data are needed.

8. The line y = 2 contains points J, K, L, and
    M, though not necessarily in that order. The
    coordinates of J are (3, 2), and the distance
    between J and K is 12. If the coordinates of L are
    (−3,2), and the distance between L and M is 10,
    what is the distance between K and M ?

    (1) The x coordinate of M is less than the x
    coordinate of J.

    (2) L is the midpoint between J and K.

    (A) Statement (1) ALONE is sufficient, but
    statement (2) alone is not sufficient.
    (B) Statement (2) ALONE is sufficient, but
    statement (1) alone is not sufficient.
    (C) BOTH statements TOGETHER are sufficient,
    but NEITHER statement ALONE is sufficient.
    (D) EACH Statement ALONE is sufficient.
    (E) Statements (1) and (2) TOGETHER are NOT
    sufficient to answer the question asked, and
    additional data are needed.

9. If p and r are positive integers such that $\frac{p^2}{40} = r$
    and $p \uparrow r$, then which of the following must also
    be an integer?

    I. $\frac{r}{5}$

    II. $\frac{r}{2 \times 5}$

    III. $\frac{r}{3 \times 5}$

    (A) I only
    (B) II only
    (C) I and II
    (D) I and III
    (E) I, II, and III

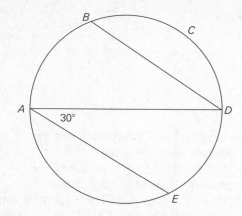

10. In the figure above, lines *AE* and *BD* are parallel, and line *AD* is the diameter of the circle. If the length of arc BCD is equal to 4π, then what is the area of the circle?

(A)   6π
(B)   9π
(C)   12π
(D)   18π
(E)   36π

11. The force of gravity between two objects in space is directly proportional to the product of the masses of the objects and indirectly proportional to the square of the distance between them. If the distance between two objects is doubled, by what percent must the product of the masses increase if the force of gravity is to remain the same?

(A)   50%
(B)   100%
(C)   200%
(D)   300%
(E)   400%

12. If *m* and *n* are positive numbers, and $m^5 = 200 - n^5$, what is the greatest possible value of *n* ?

(A)   Between 1 and 2
(B)   Between 2 and 3
(C)   Between 3 and 4
(D)   Between 4 and 5
(E)   Between 5 and 6

13. The number 152 is equal to the sum of the cubes of two integers. What is the product of those integers?

(A)   8
(B)   15
(C)   21
(D)   27
(E)   39

14. If $5^{n-3} + 5^n = (2)(7)(9)(5^{11})$, what is the value of 2*n* ?

(A)   3
(B   6
(C)   8
(D)   14
(E)   28

15. If *x* and *y* are positive integers, what is the result when the units digit of (5*x* – 3)6 + *y* is divided by 10 ?

(1) *y* = 4

(2) *x* = 5

(A)   Statement (1) ALONE is sufficient, but statement (2) alone is not sufficient.
(B)   Statement (2) ALONE is sufficient, but statement (1) alone is not sufficient.
(C)   BOTH statements TOGETHER are sufficient, but NEITHER statement ALONE is sufficient.
(D)   EACH Statement ALONE is sufficient.
(E)   Statements (1) and (2) TOGETHER are NOT sufficient to answer the question asked, and additional data are needed.

Math

16. On Thursday, the temperature on Mount Washington reached a high of –252 Kelvin. If the formula $K = \left(\dfrac{5}{9} \left(F - 32 \right) \right) - 273.15$ shows the relationship between the Kelvin temperature scale and degrees Fahrenheit, which of the following is closest to the temperature high on Mount Washington in degrees Fahrenheit?

(A) 4°
(B) 44°
(C) 56°
(D) 71°
(E) 85°

17. In the x-y coordinate plane, does the point (3,4) lie on line t ?

   (1) The line $5y - 45 = -x$ is perpendicular to line t.

   (2) The line with the equation $y = \dfrac{3}{4}x - 11$ intersects line t when $y = -11$.

(A) Statement (1) ALONE is sufficient, but statement (2) alone is not sufficient.
(B) Statement (2) ALONE is sufficient, but statement (1) alone is not sufficient.
(C) BOTH statements TOGETHER are sufficient, but NEITHER statement ALONE is sufficient.
(D) EACH Statement ALONE is sufficient.
(E) Statements (1) and (2) TOGETHER are NOT sufficient to answer the question asked, and additional data are needed.

18. Is $x - y > -10$?

   (1) $5x + 2y > -10$

   (2) $2y + x > -10$

(A) Statement (1) ALONE is sufficient, but statement (2) alone is not sufficient.
(B) Statement (2) ALONE is sufficient, but statement (1) alone is not sufficient.
(C) BOTH statements TOGETHER are sufficient, but NEITHER statement ALONE is sufficient.
(D) EACH Statement ALONE is sufficient.
(E) Statements (1) and (2) TOGETHER are NOT sufficient to answer the question asked, and additional data are needed.

19. On Monday, Rhonda made an average of 12 phone calls per hour for the first 6 calls she made, and then an average of 6 phone calls per hour for the remaining 6 calls she made. What was the average number of phone calls per hour that Rhonda made for the entire day?

(A) 7.5
(B) 8.0
(C) 9.5
(D) 10.0
(E) 10.5

20. If $P = 9^{\frac{1}{2}} - 9^{\frac{1}{3}} - 9^{\frac{1}{4}}$, then P is

(A) Less than 0
(B) Equal to 0
(C) Between 0 and 2
(D) Between 2 and 3
(E) Greater than 3

21. Five offices have an average of 8 people per office, and a median of 7 people per office, and none of the offices are vacant. What is the maximum number of people who can be in the largest office?

(A) 23
(B) 24
(C) 25
(D) 26
(E) 27

22. A certain company sells tea in loose leaf and bagged form, and in five flavors: Darjeeling, Earl Grey, chamomile, peppermint, and orange pekoe. The company packages the tea in boxes that contain either 8 ounces of tea of the same flavor and the same form, or 8 ounces of tea of 4 different flavors and the same form. If the order in which the flavors are packed does not matter, how many different types of packages are possible?

   (A) 12
   (B) 15
   (C) 20
   (D) 25
   (E) 30

23. Karen sold her house at a loss of 25 percent of the price that she originally paid for the house, and then bought another house at a price of 30 percent less than the price she originally paid for her first house. If she sold the first house for $225,000, what was her net gain, in dollars, for the two transactions?

   (A) $15,000
   (B) $25,000
   (C) $60,000
   (D) $75,000
   (E) $90,000

24. In a certain company, at least 200 people own manual transmission vehicles. If 12 percent of the people who own manual transmission vehicles also own automatic transmission vehicles, do more people own automatic transmission vehicles than own manual transmission vehicles?

   (1) 5 percent of the people who own an automatic transmission vehicle also own a manual transmission vehicle.

   (2) 15 people own both an automatic transmission vehicle and a manual transmission vehicle.

   (A) Statement (1) ALONE is sufficient, but statement (2) alone is not sufficient.
   (B) Statement (2) ALONE is sufficient, but statement (1) alone is not sufficient.
   (C) BOTH statements TOGETHER are sufficient, but NEITHER statement ALONE is sufficient.
   (D) EACH Statement ALONE is sufficient.
   (E) Statements (1) and (2) TOGETHER are NOT sufficient to answer the question asked, and additional data are needed.

25. What is the value of $\frac{x}{2}$?

   (1) x is $\frac{1}{5}$ less than $\frac{9}{10}$

   (2) x is between $\frac{2}{5}$ and $\frac{4}{5}$

   (A) Statement (1) ALONE is sufficient, but statement (2) alone is not sufficient.
   (B) Statement (2) ALONE is sufficient, but statement (1) alone is not sufficient.
   (C) BOTH statements TOGETHER are sufficient, but NEITHER statement ALONE is sufficient.
   (D) EACH Statement ALONE is sufficient.
   (E) Statements (1) and (2) TOGETHER are NOT sufficient to answer the question asked, and additional data are needed.

Math

26. If $|x| > 5$, is $|x - 5| = 5 - x$?

    (1) $-x(x^2) > 0$

    (2) $x^5 < 0$

    (A) Statement (1) ALONE is sufficient, but statement (2) alone is not sufficient.
    (B) Statement (2) ALONE is sufficient, but statement (1) alone is not sufficient.
    (C) BOTH statements TOGETHER are sufficient, but NEITHER statement ALONE is sufficient.
    (D) EACH Statement ALONE is sufficient.
    (E) Statements (1) and (2) TOGETHER are NOT sufficient to answer the question asked, and additional data are needed.

27. Gayle purchased two items, X and Y, which were both on sale. If the percent decrease on the original price of item Y was four times the percent decrease on the original price of item X, what was the original price of item X ?

    (1) The sale price of item X was three times the sale price of item Y.

    (2) The original price of item X was twice the original price of item Y.

    (A) Statement (1) ALONE is sufficient, but statement (2) alone is not sufficient.
    (B) Statement (2) ALONE is sufficient, but statement (1) alone is not sufficient.
    (C) BOTH statements TOGETHER are sufficient, but NEITHER statement ALONE is sufficient.
    (D) EACH Statement ALONE is sufficient.
    (E) Statements (1) and (2) TOGETHER are NOT sufficient to answer the question asked, and additional data are needed.

28. A certain local newspaper has 80 employees. Of the employees, $\frac{3}{5}$ are either journalists or copy editors. How many of the employees are journalists?

    (1) The newspaper employs more than 10 copy editors.

    (2) There are more than 3 times as many journalists at the paper as there are copy editors.

    (A) Statement (1) ALONE is sufficient, but statement (2) alone is not sufficient.
    (B) Statement (2) ALONE is sufficient, but statement (1) alone is not sufficient.
    (C) BOTH statements TOGETHER are sufficient, but NEITHER statement ALONE is sufficient.
    (D) EACH Statement ALONE is sufficient.
    (E) Statements (1) and (2) TOGETHER are NOT sufficient to answer the question asked, and additional data are needed.

29. On a certain farm the ratio of horses to cows is 7:3. If the farm were to sell 15 horses and buy 15 cows, the ratio of horses to cows would then be 13:7. After the transaction, how many more horses than cows would the farm own?

    (A) 30
    (B) 60
    (C) 75
    (D) 90
    (E) 105

30. The students at The Woodlands High School scored an average of n points on a particular standardized test. If the standard deviation among the scores was 12, what would the standard deviation have been if each student at the school had scored 7 points lower than he or she actually scored?

    (A) 5
    (B) 12
    (C) 14
    (D) 19
    (E) 21

31. If m and n are positive integers, what is the value of $m - n$?

    (1) $\quad 3^{2n} = \dfrac{144}{2^m}$

    (2) $\quad 3^m = \dfrac{243}{3^n}$

(A) Statement (1) ALONE is sufficient, but statement (2) alone is not sufficient.
(B) Statement (2) ALONE is sufficient, but statement (1) alone is not sufficient.
(C) BOTH statements TOGETHER are sufficient, but NEITHER statement ALONE is sufficient.
(D) EACH Statement ALONE is sufficient.
(E) Statements (1) and (2) TOGETHER are NOT sufficient to answer the question asked, and additional data are needed.

32. A certain law firm has departments specializing in four different areas: anti-trust law, tax law, real estate law, and civil rights law. If each department is composed only of lawyers who are either partners or associates, then associates make up what percent of the total number of lawyers in the four departments?

    (1) Of the lawyers in the civil rights law and anti-trust law departments, 60 percent are partners.

    (2) Of the lawyers in the tax law and real estate law departments, 70 percent are associates.

(A) Statement (1) ALONE is sufficient, but statement (2) alone is not sufficient.
(B) Statement (2) ALONE is sufficient, but statement (1) alone is not sufficient.
(C) BOTH statements TOGETHER are sufficient, but NEITHER statement ALONE is sufficient.
(D) EACH Statement ALONE is sufficient.
(E) Statements (1) and (2) TOGETHER are NOT sufficient to answer the question asked, and additional data are needed.

33. If Adam is a centimeters tall, Alfredo is b centimeters tall, and David is c centimeters tall, is b equal to the median of a, b, and c?

    (1) Adam and Alfredo are exactly the same height.

    (2) David is 5 centimeters taller than Alfredo.

(A) Statement (1) ALONE is sufficient, but statement (2) alone is not sufficient.
(B) Statement (2) ALONE is sufficient, but statement (1) alone is not sufficient.
(C) BOTH statements TOGETHER are sufficient, but NEITHER statement ALONE is sufficient.
(D) EACH Statement ALONE is sufficient.
(E) Statements (1) and (2) TOGETHER are NOT sufficient to answer the question asked, and additional data are needed.

34. A certain chef is combining two mixtures to create a soup. If she combines a cups of one mixture that contains 5 percent butter with another mixture of b cups that contains 10 percent butter in order to make c cups of soup that contain 8 percent butter, and nothing else is added to the soup, what is the value of a?

    (1) $b = 3$

    (2) $2c - 2a = 6$

(A) Statement (1) ALONE is sufficient, but statement (2) alone is not sufficient.
(B) Statement (2) ALONE is sufficient, but statement (1) alone is not sufficient.
(C) BOTH statements TOGETHER are sufficient, but NEITHER statement ALONE is sufficient.
(D) EACH Statement ALONE is sufficient.
(E) Statements (1) and (2) TOGETHER are NOT sufficient to answer the question asked, and additional data are needed.

35. On the number line, the distance from *B* to *C* is 10. Is *A* closer to *B* or to *C*?

    (1) The distance from *A* to *B* is 7

    (2) $\left| C \right| - \left| A \right| = 3$

(A) Statement (1) ALONE is sufficient, but statement (2) alone is not sufficient.
(B) Statement (2) ALONE is sufficient, but statement (1) alone is not sufficient.
(C) BOTH statements TOGETHER are sufficient, but NEITHER statement ALONE is sufficient.
(D) EACH Statement ALONE is sufficient.
(E) Statements (1) and (2) TOGETHER are NOT sufficient to answer the question asked, and additional data are needed.

36. A shipping company has two departments, one for standard shipping and one for express shipping. If the employees in the standard department each process an average of 8.7 packages per hour, and the employees in the express department each process an average of 12.4 packages per hour, what is the ratio of the number of employees in the standard department to the number of employees in the express department?

    (1) The average number of packages processed per employee in one hour for the two departments combined is 10.3

    (2) There are 40 employees in the standard department

(A) Statement (1) ALONE is sufficient, but statement (2) alone is not sufficient.
(B) Statement (2) ALONE is sufficient, but statement (1) alone is not sufficient.
(C) BOTH statements TOGETHER are sufficient, but NEITHER statement ALONE is sufficient.
(D) EACH Statement ALONE is sufficient.
(E) Statements (1) and (2) TOGETHER are NOT sufficient to answer the question asked, and additional data are needed.

37. Lou recently painted his guest bedroom pale blue. The mixture of paint he used contained $\frac{2}{3}$ gallon of white paint for every 2 gallons of blue paint used. How many gallons of white paint will Lou need in order to paint his living room the same shade of pale blue?

    (1) Lou will need twice as many gallons of paint for the living room as he needed for the bedroom.

    (2) Lou used 4 gallons of white paint for the guest bedroom.

(A) Statement (1) ALONE is sufficient, but statement (2) alone is not sufficient.
(B) Statement (2) ALONE is sufficient, but statement (1) alone is not sufficient.
(C) BOTH statements TOGETHER are sufficient, but NEITHER statement ALONE is sufficient.
(D) EACH Statement ALONE is sufficient.
(E) Statements (1) and (2) TOGETHER are NOT sufficient to answer the question asked, and additional data are needed.

S T O P

END OF QUANTITATIVE SECTION

YOU MAY NOW TAKE A 10-MINUTE BREAK.

VERBAL SECTION—41 QUESTIONS
TIME—75 MINUTES

Directions for Reading Comprehension: Each passage in this group is followed by questions based on its content. After reading a passage, choose the best answer to each question. Answer all questions following a passage on the basis of what is stated or implied in that passage.

Directions for Critical Reasoning: For each question in this section, select the best of the answer choices given.

Directions for Sentence Correction: In each of the following sentences, some part of the sentence or the entire sentence is underlined. Beneath each sentence you will find five ways of phrasing the underlined part. The first of these repeats the original; the other four are different. If you think the original is the best of these answer choices, choose answer A; otherwise, choose one of the others. Select the best version.

This is a test of correctness and effectiveness of expression. In choosing answers, follow the requirements of standard written English; that is, pay attention to grammar, choice of words, and sentence construction. Choose the answer that produces the most effective sentence; this answer should be clear and exact, without awkwardness, ambiguity, redundancy, or grammatical error.

---

1. A brand-building program was so poorly designed and executed by the marketing team that even James Kirkpatrick, the team leader, admitted it was hopelessly flawed.

   (A) A brand-building program was so poorly designed and executed by the marketing team that
   (B) So poorly designed and executed by the marketing team was a brand-building program
   (C) It was so poorly that a brand-building program was designed and executed by the marketing team
   (D) A brand-building program that was so poorly designed and executed by the marketing team
   (E) Designed and executed so poorly by the marketing team was a brand-building program that

2. Policy initiatives to make students feel safe from attacks by peers in school, an aim the Clinton administration took very seriously, has significantly reduced the percentage of students reporting fearing attack in school.

   (A) has significantly reduced the percentage of students reporting fearing
   (B) has been significant in reducing the percentage of students reporting fearing
   (C) has made a significant reduction in the percentage of students reporting fearing
   (D) have significantly reduced the percentage of students that report fearing
   (E) have been significant in yielding a reduction of the percentage of students that are reporting fearing

3. The Alphatown city council is looking to increase revenues. They decide to reduce the sales tax, since lowering the tax will give consumers an incentive to increase purchases.

   Which of the following, if true, is the best argument against the council's plan?

   (A) Voters are strongly in favor of the decrease in the sales tax.
   (B) Betaville lowered taxes and experienced an increase in expenditures.
   (C) The only shopping mall in Alphatown has recently closed.
   (D) The mayor has threatened to veto the tax reduction.
   (E) The city council is up for re-election this year.

4. Unlike a lower-altitude mountain, which may provide technical and logistical challenges for a climber, <u>a Mount Everest climber must be primarily concerned with</u> the health effects of the severe lack of oxygen above 25,000 feet.

   (A) a Mount Everest climber must be primarily concerned with
   (B) in climbing Mount Everest, one must make a primary concern of
   (C) Mount Everest climbers must be primarily concerned with
   (D) for the Mount Everest climber, the primary concern is regarding
   (E) Mount Everest forces a climber to be primarily concerned with

5. <u>Unlike staff meetings and social events that fall outside of regular work hours, there is a resistance among many employees to accept duties that would extend their regular work hours</u>.

   (A) Unlike staff meetings and social events that fall outside of regular work hours, there is a resistance among many employees to accept work that would extend their regular work hours.
   (B) Unlike staff meetings and social events that fall outside of regular work hours, which they are willing to participate in, many employees are resistant to accepting duties that would extend their regular work hours.
   (C) Unlike staff meetings and social events that fall outside of regular work hours, duties that would extend their regular work hours cause a resistance in many employees to accept the extended hours.
   (D) Many employees, happy to participate in staff meetings and social events that fall outside of regular work hours, are resistant to accepting duties that would extend their regular work hours.
   (E) Many employees have a resistance to accept extended working hours resulting from additional duties while happy to participate in staff meetings and social events that fall outside of regular work hours.

One consequence of social living arrangements in animals is a constant competition for scarce resources. Among the social species, the allocation of these resources is often based on a dominance hierarchy. Each animal occupies a place in the hierarchy, which determines access to food, mating opportunities, and general quality of life. In many species, these hierarchies are fairly stable, although not immutable.

Interestingly, position in the dominance hierarchy has physiological consequences for the animal. Studies of baboons living in East Africa have revealed that individuals on the low end of the hierarchy have an increased level of the stress hormone glucocorticoid in their bloodstream. Typically, glucocorticoid is produced in reaction to environmental stressors, and is, along with adrenaline, instrumental in the fight or flight response, which primes the animal to take either aggressive or evasive action in the face of danger.

Prolonged exposure to glucocorticoid can have adverse effects on the immune system of the animal, which raises a puzzle for physiologists. What is the adaptive utility of response that puts the animal at increased risk of pathology? The answer may lie in the individual animal's responsiveness to stress. Studies have shown that not all the baboons at the top of the dominance structure had the lowest level of glucocorticoid, while not all those at the bottom had the highest concentrations. Thus, these differential responses to stressors may help explain the fluidity of the dominance hierarchy. Individuals on the lower end of the scale who are better able to cope with stress may be able to take advantage of the reduced stress handling ability of members above them and move up the chain.

6. The author would most likely agree with which of the following statements about dominance hierarchies?

(A) Dominance hierarchies are present in most animal species.
(B) Individuals at the bottom of the hierarchy are unlikely to reproduce.
(C) An animal's position in the dominance hierarchy is not necessarily fixed.
(D) Animals at the top of the dominance hierarchy are not under any stress.
(E) Dominance hierarchies cause competition for scarce resources.

7. It may be inferred from the passage that a baboon at the top of the dominance hierarchy

(A) will have lower levels of glucocorticoid in its blood than any other baboon in the troupe
(B) will have higher levels of glucocorticoid in its blood than any other baboon in the troupe
(C) will have levels of glucocorticoid in its blood no different from the other members of the troupe
(D) will remain at the top of the hierarchy as long as its blood contains low levels of glucocorticoid
(E) will have levels of glucocorticoid in its blood based on its individual traits as well as its place in the hierarchy

8. The last line of the passage primarily serves to

(A) resolve a conflict introduced earlier in the passage
(B) demonstrate a possible instance of adaptive utility
(C) summarize a key finding from a study
(D) deny alternative explanations of a known fact
(E) introduce a new interpretation of a scenario

9. Rogers Syndrome (RS) is an inflammation of the rotary cuff of the shoulder. Until recently, it was thought that RS was caused by over-rotation of the shoulder joint. Recently, however, tests in mice conducted by a group of researchers revealed a gene that causes RS-like symptoms. The researchers concluded that, therefore, it is likely that RS has a genetic component.

   Which of the following, if true, would cast the most doubt on the researchers contention that it is not solely over-rotation of the shoulder joint that causes RS?

   (A) The RS-like symptoms in mice abate when treated with a particular combination of drugs.
   (B) The mice selected by the researchers have been used in a variety of studies that resulted in meaningful results.
   (C) After the mice developed the RS-like symptoms, the researchers only observed them for three weeks.
   (D) The researchers in question have been studying RS for only two years.
   (E) The symptoms of RS are similar to, if not identical with, the symptoms of one or more other syndromes or conditions.

10. If the proposed lay-offs, intended to cut costs and improve the bottom line, are carried out, the downsizing has been and will continue to outpace industry norms.

    (A) has been and will continue to outpace
    (B) will continue to outpace, as they already did,
    (C) will continue to outpace, as they have already
    (D) have and will continue to outpace
    (E) will continue to outpace

11. Viewers of our morning talk show have often turned on the television and saw frenetic guests ranting on the program, who's opinions range from controversial to absurd.

    (A) saw frenetic guests ranting on the program, who's opinions range
    (B) saw frenetic guests ranting on the program, who's opinions were ranging
    (C) seen frenetic guests ranting on the program, who's opinions have ranged
    (D) saw frenetic guests ranting on the program, with opinions ranging
    (E) seen frenetic guests ranting on the program, with opinions ranging

12. If the hydrangea blooms in late summer, it is a panicled hydrangea. If it is grown for florists, it is a bigleaf hydrangea. This hydrangea is grown for florists and is therefore not panicled.

    The argument above relies on which of the following to reach its conclusion?

    (A) The panicled hydrangea has no features in common with the bigleaf hydrangea.
    (B) If a hydrangea is panicled, it is not bigleaf.
    (C) No bigleaf hydrangea blooms in the late summer.
    (D) All panicled hydrangea blooms in the late summer.
    (E) Of the hydrangeas used by florists, none blooms in the late summer.

13. While large companies in technology-intensive industries can generally quickly recruit to fill any need, many internet startups are learning that the <u>skill required for</u> website development and for search engine optimization and internet marketing are hard to find.

   (A) skill required for
   (B) skills required for
   (C) skills of
   (D) skill relevant to
   (E) skills relevant to

14. Examining the growing use of international social networking sites reveals that young people in different countries are <u>sharing their tastes in music, movies, and fashion more than never before and</u> pop culture fads in one part of the world can become hits in other parts of the world without any local marketing.

   (A) sharing their tastes in music, movies, and fashion more than never before and
   (B) sharing their tastes in music, movies, and fashion more than never before while
   (C) sharing their tastes in music, movies, and fashion more than ever before and that
   (D) sharing more their tastes in music, movies, and fashion than ever before so
   (E) more sharing than ever before their tastes in music, movies, and fashion as

Early attempts by political scientists to understand voting behavior were sociological in origin, focusing on demographic traits such as class, religion, and race. However, in the late 1950s, a new paradigm emerged, one based on theories from the field of economics. In this view, the vote decision was a rational calculation aimed at maximizing the voter's expected utility. According to this theory, a voter considered the likely benefits of a win by one politician or another, subtracted the expected costs of that win, and cast his vote in line with the results of this process.

However, this rational view of political behavior was unsatisfying to many researchers. For one, a major implication of the economic view of voting behavior was extremely low voter turnout. This is because, from a utilitarian standpoint, the costs of voting to any individual far outweigh the benefits. Since one vote has an extremely low probability of affecting the outcome of the vote and the voter will reap the benefits of a particular politician's victory regardless of his actions, the costs of voting, in the form of information gathering and time spent, should be prohibitive. But voter turnout in the United States, despite the grousing of some civic leaders, is quite robust. Furthermore, many studies have shown that a good number of voters fail to vote 'correctly.' That is, they do not choose the candidate that best expresses their interests. These problems have led to a new model of voting behavior.

This new model, termed bounded rationality, or perhaps more accurately, intuitive decision making, holds that voters make use of various cognitive shortcuts, such as party identification and endorsements, to form a snap judgment about politicians. The vote decision then becomes an almost automatic response to these low information cues.

15. All of the following are critiques of the economic model of voting, as presented in the passage, EXCEPT

   (A) some of the models' predictions were not true
   (B) many individuals vote as if they are not maximizing utility
   (C) it is unlikely that a voter can make the utility calculations required
   (D) voters seem to behave as if their vote has a chance of affecting the outcome of an election
   (E) voters appear to act as if the costs of voting are negligible

16. Which of the following best exemplifies the behavior of a voter employing a bounded rationality model of decision making?

   (A) avidly following the presidential campaign
   (B) carefully comparing the platforms of two opposing candidates
   (C) attending a debate between two candidates
   (D) voting for the candidate favored by his union
   (E) deciding that he is too busy to vote and abstains

17. It may be inferred from the passage that the author believes bounded rationality

   (A) typically results in correct voting
   (B) is not a rational decision making process
   (C) best explains the levels of voter turnout in the United States
   (D) will soon become the dominant model of voting behavior
   (E) is not an accurate description of how voters behave

18. The Healthwork Corporation claims that it has reduced its outstanding debt through buying back loans. Of the 24 outstanding loans, Healthwork Corp. has bought back 13. Therefore the company is less indebted than it was before.

    On which of the following propositions is the claim above regarding Healthwork Corp.'s indebtedness dependent?

    (A) The eleven remaining loans do not constitute the bulk of Healthwork Corp.'s outstanding debt.
    (B) The 13 loans that Healthwork had bought back were not held by the original issuers, but rather by third-party purchasers.
    (C) If the loans are fully redeemed, Healthwork Corp.'s financial situation will be secure.
    (D) The buyback has been financed from revenues earned by the company rather than leveraged.
    (E) If Healthwork Corp. does not redeem the loans, it will risk bankruptcy.

19. The naked mole rat is a pest to the farmers of Pellaville. The farmers plan to reduce the rat population by poisoning the stream out of which the mole rats drink.

    Which of the following, if true, is the best support for the scheme of the farmers?

    (A) The poison that will be used in the stream is not toxic to the farmers' livestock.
    (B) The naked mole rat is not susceptible to most conventional poisons.
    (C) The befurred vole, a relative of the naked mole rat, is most effectively controlled with contraception rather than with poison.
    (D) The poison to be used is less expensive than other poisons.
    (E) The poison will be most effective if administered after the harvest.

20. The first choice to be made during a car audio system <u>being installed is if to buy</u> an amplifier to increase the strength of the signal that the speakers will receive.

    (A) being installed is if to buy
    (B) being installed is whether they should be buying
    (C) being installed is whether or not to buy
    (D) installation is if they should buy
    (E) installation is whether they should buy

21. A politician and a civic activist, <u>the first fire department in the United States and arguably the first truly public library in the world were founded by Benjamin Franklin before he held his first position as a public servant</u>.

    (A) the first fire department in the United States and arguably the first truly public library in the world were founded by Benjamin Franklin before he held his first position as a public servant
    (B) Benjamin Franklin founded the first fire department in the United States and arguably the first truly public library in the world before he held his first position as a public servant
    (C) before he held his first position as a public servant, the first fire department in the United States and arguably the first truly public library in the world were founded by Benjamin Franklin
    (D) was Benjamin Franklin who, before he held his first position as a public servant, founded the first fire department in the United States and arguably the first truly public library in the world
    (E) there were founded, before he held his first position as a public servant, the first fire department in the United States and arguably the first truly public library in the world

22. The study concludes that many Americans do not have, <u>or</u> likely to have, enough money put away to retire comfortably.

    (A) or
    (B) or are
    (C) nor
    (D) nor are not
    (E) nor are they

Perhaps the most important goal of any business manager is to articulate a clear business model, one that is predicated on a cause-and-effect theory. This theory should explicate how a business can achieve long term success through the implementation of specific strategies. However, recent research indicates that very few managers are aware of the role of causal models in successful business plans. Thus, while a good number of companies keep track of performance measures, very few of the managers in these businesses attempt to understand the causal mechanisms that produce such measures. Instead of carefully exploring these underlying causal factors, many managers reported that their business decisions were guided by preconceived notions of what is important to customers, shareholders, and employees. Furthermore, managers, despite their lack of understanding of the connections between performance measures and their drivers, often claimed that no investigation was necessary because such links were self-evident.

If business managers more readily adopted cause-and-effect models into their business plans, experimental data indicates that they may be able to increase their businesses performance measures. Managers who were asked to analyze a set of data and then prompted with the causal mechanism underlying it were better able to interpret and exploit the data than managers who received no such prompting. Even when managers were prompted with an invalid causal model, they still were better able to interpret the data than the control group.

23. The primary purpose of the passage is to

   (A) advocate for a particular way of articulating business plans
   (B) assert that understanding causal mechanisms is essential for successful managers
   (C) explain how to create a viable business model for managers to follow
   (D) direct business analysts toward an understudied phenomenon
   (E) criticize the behavior of typical business managers

24. Which of the following assumptions underlies the results of the experiment detailed in the final paragraph?

   (A) The managers in the study were previously unaware of the role of causal mechanisms.
   (B) None of the participants in the study were managers of unsuccessful companies.
   (C) Invalid causal models are just as beneficial to managers as are valid causal models.
   (D) Managers in the experimental group were able to attribute their increased skill at interpreting data to causal mechanisms.
   (E) An increased ability to interpret and exploit data can lead to gains in performance measures.

25. The second paragraph serves to

   (A) provide empirical confirmation of an earlier assertion
   (B) suggest further experimental tests of a hypothesis
   (C) introduce an alternative theory to be explored
   (D) prove a point introduced in the previous paragraph
   (E) demonstrate the superiority of a viewpoint

26. There are more opera houses than there were two decades ago, and charitable contributions are on the rise. Average audiences for opera, however, have been declining for the past twenty years.

Which of the following, if true, best explains the discrepancy above?

(A) In the past twenty years, musical theater audiences have grown.
(B) A change in the tax code has conferred certain advantages on charitable giving.
(C) Construction codes have been revised on a national level to promote the construction of cultural facilities.
(D) There has been an emphasis on unamplified sound in opera.
(E) The number of new works has declined in the past three decades.

27. The detection of infrared signals is crucial for most remote controlled consumer electronic devices, such as televisions or dvd players. Solar radiation can create alterations across the low end of the radiation spectrum, where infrared signals reside. Therefore solar radiation can interfere with the operation of television remotes.

Which of the following, if true, most strengthens the argument above?

(A) After years of experimentation, engineers can measure variances in infrared radiation to a tolerance 100 times greater than those previously mentioned.
(B) More recent generations of remote control devices use radio waves to compensate for any infrared variance.
(C) Remote control devices are not sensitive enough to detect every variance in low-end radiation.
(D) There are times when the alteration of low-end radiation caused by solar flares creates variances in infrared signals that are greater than the tolerances engineered into consumer electronics.
(E) The types of infrared detectors in consumer electronics are sensitive to distortions in the high end of the radiation spectrum.

28. The income inequality among Gublandians is increasing. 90% of the resources are now controlled by 10% of the population. The average salary of a Gublandian, however, is decreasing.

Which of the following can be inferred from the statements above?

(A) The economy of Gublandia is shrinking.
(B) The labor force of Gublandia is experiencing increasing hardship.
(C) Barring any alteration in the trend, more than 90% of Gublandia's resources will be controlled by 10% of the population.
(D) The income inequality of Gublandia will result in civil unrest.
(E) The growth in income inequlity of Gublandia will continue unabated.

29. When the office of the Commissioner of Baseball was created in 1921, <u>he was entrusted with power beyond his predecessor, the National Commission, which was made up of a Commission Chairman and the presidents of the two leagues that were within its jurisdiction</u>.

(A) he was entrusted with power beyond his predecessor, the National Commission, which was made up of a Commission Chairman and the presidents of the two leagues that were within its jurisdiction
(B) he was entrusted with power beyond his predecessor, the National Commission, which was composed of a Commission Chairman and the presidents of the two leagues that it had within its jurisdiction
(C) he was given power beyond his predecessor, the National Commission, which was a Commission Chairman and the presidents of the two leagues that were underneath its jurisdiction
(D) it was entrusted with power beyond its predecessor, the National Commission, which was composed of a Commission Chairman and the presidents of the two leagues that were within its jurisdiction
(E) it was entrusted with power beyond its predecessor, the National Commission, that which was made up of a Commission Chairman and the presidents of the two leagues that were falling under its jurisdiction

30. Any successful business leader has deep personal resources. All people with deep personal resources have undergone trials in their lives. The experience of trials is more prevalent among those who were not born to great wealth and privilege.

    The statements above support which of the following propositions?

    (A) Those who currently lack deep personal resources can never become successful business leaders.
    (B) It is more likely for a person not born to wealth and privilege to become a successful business leader than for one who is born to wealth and privilege.
    (C) The number of business leaders who were born to wealth is smaller than the number of business leaders who were not born to wealth.
    (D) Those who are born to privilege are more likely to be successful than those who were born to wealth.
    (E) An absence of trials in a person's life indicates that that person cannot have deep personal resources.

31. Introduced by a diplomat bringing books back from a trip to Beijing in the early seventeenth century, in Korea Christianity grew indigenously through the seventeenth and eighteenth centuries, as its message grabbed the attention of certain lay people, typically being those with ties to the Silhak School and those interested in a merit-based social structure.

    (A) in Korea Christianity grew indigenously through the seventeenth and eighteenth centuries, as its message grabbed the attention of certain lay people, typically being
    (B) in Korea Christianity had grown indigenously through the seventeenth and eighteenth centuries, as its message grabbed the attention of certain lay people, who typically were
    (C) through the seventeenth and eighteenth centuries in Korea Christianity grew indigenously, as its message grabbed the attention of certain lay people, typically
    (D) Christianity in Korea grew indigenously through the seventeenth and eighteenth centuries, as its message grabbed the attention of certain lay people, typically
    (E) Christianity grew indigenously through the seventeenth and eighteenth centuries in Korea, as its message grabbed the attention of certain lay people, who typically were

32. The evidence of water on the surface of Mars, away from the polar ice caps, obtained by recent photos of the Martian surface is so much stronger than atmospheric data once trumpeted as proof of water on Mars, and so many astronomers are calling it the first proof of Mars having non-polar water.

    (A) once trumpeted as proof of water on Mars, and so
    (B) once trumpeted as proof of water on Mars that
    (C) once trumpeted that it is proof of water on Mars, and so
    (D) that they had once trumpeted as proof of water on Mars, so that
    (E) that they had once trumpeted as proof of water on Mars, and

Among philosophers of science, there is much debate over the role of sense data. For many thinkers, the entire foundation of empirical science can be reduced to perceptions, and therefore experiences. But some philosophers have taken issue with this perspective. One critique involves the means by which we accept a statement as justified.

Unless we allow that scientific statements be accepted on faith alone, a view distasteful to many members of the scientific enterprise, then we must have some way of justifying our propositions. One approach to justification involves deductive justification, in which a proposition is subject to logical argument. But this method fails because it leads to an infinite regress. The statements used to justify a proposition must themselves be justified, and so too those statements, into infinity.

So justification cannot come through the use of argument. Another way to avoid dogmatism in the sciences is justification through perceptual experience. This sort of sense data, according to some philosophers, is immediate knowledge, through which we may justify our mediate knowledge. From this perspective, all knowledge of facts must be reducible to statements about our direct experiences. But this view fails as well to provide justification for scientific statements. This is because science strives for universals and our immediate experience can be nothing more than particular.

33. The primary purpose of the passage is to

(A) present an overview of a scientific controversy
(B) describe a perplexing philosophical issue
(C) solve a problem in the philosophy of science
(D) present two opposing views on the meaning of science
(E) detail a logical paradox inherent in the scientific method

34. The author of the passage would most likely agree that justification through deductive argument could avoid the problem of infinite regress if

(A) some of the deductive arguments are based on sense data
(B) the deductive argument contains no logical inconsistencies
(C) some statements in the argument require no justification
(D) the assumptions used in the argument are themselves justified
(E) the argument relies on a limited number of premises

35. The author of the passage would mostly agree that

(A) there is no way of justifying scientific propositions
(B) deductive justification and perceptual justification are the only types of scientific justification
(C) some combination of deductive and perceptual justification is sufficient to justify scientific knowledge
(D) all scientific knowledge must be universal
(E) without a way of justifying scientific knowledge, science becomes dogmatic

36. Although <u>people in Canada earn money at a similar rate to the United States, their</u> rate of saving is much higher in Canada.

(A) people in Canada earn money at a similar rate to the United States, their
(B) people in Canada and the United States earn money at a similar rate, the
(C) money is earned by people in Canada at a similar rate to the United States's, their
(D) the rate of money earned in Canada and the United States is similar, the
(E) the rate people earn money is similar in Canada and the United States, the

37. <u>A motion filed by the prosecution has been reviewed by a panel of judges, ruling that the evidence cannot be used in the trial because it was</u> collected in a manner inconsistent with the Fourth Amendment's prohibition of unreasonable searches and seizures.

(A) A motion filed by the prosecution has been reviewed by a panel of judges, ruling that the evidence cannot be used in the trial because it was
(B) A motion filed by the prosecution has been reviewed by a panel of judges, and they rule that the evidence cannot be used in the trial because of being
(C) After reviewing a motion filed by the prosecution, a panel of judges rules that the evidence cannot be used in the trial because it was
(D) After reviewing a motion, filed by the prosecution, a panel of judges rules the evidence cannot be used in the trial because of being
(E) After a motion filed by the prosecution was reviewed by a panel of judges, who rule that the evidence cannot be used in the trial because it was

38. The Steamfitters Union is contemplating a strike against Joe's Plumbing. Some union members are concerned that the strike will prompt repercussions from the employer. Union management responded that the workers would be protected, since the media were covering the event.

Which of the following would be most relevant to determining whether the union management's position is correct?

(A) Does the media coverage consist of television as well as print coverage?
(B) Is the management of Joe's Plumbing aware of the media coverage?
(C) How long would the strike last?
(D) Has the management of Joe's Plumbing retaliated against striking workers previously?
(E) Does the union have the financial resources to withstand a prolonged strike?

39. If the demand for energy were to remain the same, in the absence of nuclear power the cost of energy would rise sharply in the United States.

If the statement above is true, which of the following would be the best approach for the amelioration of energy prices in the United States in the absence of nuclear power?

(A) Import more foreign oil.
(B) Drill for other fossil fuels.
(C) Follow a program of strict energy conservation.
(D) Develop wind energy.
(E) Increase government spending on research and development.

40. <u>Dentist</u>: Your products contain high quantities of sugar, which causes cavities. Since there are other sweeteners that you could use which do not cause cavities, it is clear that you intend to destroy children's teeth.

    <u>Candy Manufacturer</u>: But sugar is natural, whereas the other sweeteners are artificial.

    The candy manufacturer's response is flawed because it _____.

    (A) assumes without warrant that intent is in some way related to artificiality
    (B) does not disprove the dentist's contention that sugar causes cavities
    (C) does not question the dentist's description of the quantity of sugar as "high"
    (D) fails to indicate the link between artificiality and cavities
    (E) contradicts the premise of the dentist's argument rather than the conclusion

41. The Pacific Salmon of the Columbia River exists at just 3% of its original population level, largely <u>on account of being killed by a parasite</u> that is transferred from open net cage salmon farms.

    (A) on account of being killed by a parasite
    (B) on account of their being killed by a parasite
    (C) because it is killed by a parasite
    (D) because of being killed by a parasite
    (E) being that they are killed by a parasite

STOP

END OF VERBAL SECTION

Diagnostic
Answers and
Explanations

ANSWER KEY

Integrated Reasoning

Item 1
Question 1-1: False
Question 1-2: True
Question 1-3: True
Question 1-4: False

Item 2
A: C, 50
B: F, 100

Item 3
Sweatshirts: 8
Baseball caps: 4

Item 4
C, 10 to 9

Item 5
A: No
B: No
C: Yes
D: Yes

Item 6
A: No
B: No
C: No
D: Yes

Item 7
Question 7-1: E, 11 to 3
Question 7-2: B, 600%
Question 7-3: D, 100%

Item 8
A: No
B: No
C: Yes
D: No

Item 9
A: Yes
B: No
C: Yes
D: No

Item 10
B, 7

Item 11
Question 11-1: True
Question 11-2: True
Question 11-3: True
Question 11-4: False

Item 12
Jack: F, 24 hours
Chloe: C, 8 hours

Quantitative

1. B
2. A
3. E
4. D
5. A
6. C
7. D
8. C
9. C
10. E
11. D
12. B
13. B
14. E
15. A
16. D
17. C
18. E
19. B
20. A
21. B
22. C
23. A
24. A
25. A
26. D
27. E
28. C
29. D
30. B
31. A
32. E
33. A
34. D
35. E
36. A
37. C

Verbal

1. A
2. D
3. C
4. E
5. D
6. C
7. E
8. B
9. E
10. E
11. E
12. B
13. B
14. C
15. C
16. D
17. B
18. D
19. A
20. E
21. B
22. E
23. A
24. E
25. A
26. D
27. D
28. C
29. D
30. E
31. D
32. B
33. B
34. C
35. E
36. B
37. C
38. B
39. C
40. A
41. C

EXPLANATIONS

Integrated Reasoning

Item 1

1-1:   False

First, look at the reported and fatal medical incidents involving crocodiles. There were 72 reported medical incidents involving crocodiles; of those, 15 were fatal. Accordingly, the percent of fatal medical incidents involving crocodiles is $\frac{15}{72} = 20.83\%$. Thus, approximately 21% of all medical incidents involving crocodiles were fatal.

1-2:   True

First, look at the rank column for residential holdings and identify the top three ranking exotic animals. You will find that the top three ranking animals are turtles, tarantulas, and scorpions. Next, set up an average pie and fill in what you know. There are three animals and the total number of residential holdings for turtles, tarantulas, and scorpions is 325,412 + 300,652 + 285,335 = 911,399. Now, you will find that the average is 303,800. Accordingly, the average residential holding of the top three ranking exotic animals is 303,800.

1-3:   True

First, identify the exotic animal that experienced the greatest percent decrease in total residential holdings from 2010 to 2011. According to the percent change column for residential holdings, the ostrich experienced the greatest percent decrease. Next, identify the animal that experienced the second greatest percent increase in the number of reported medical incidents. According to the percent change column for reported medical incidents, scorpions experienced the greatest increase and ostriches experienced the second greatest increase. Thus, since the ostrich fulfils both conditions of the statement, this statement is supported.

1-4:   False

First, identify the animal ranked fifth based on the total number of medical incidents; the constrictor, which has 22,045 reported medical incidents. Next, look at the percent change column for fatal medical incidents involving constrictors: The percent change in fatal medical incidents is 12.5. Accordingly, this statement is not supported by the chart.

Item 2

Country A: C, 50

To solve this question, use the percent change formula. The percent change is $\frac{difference}{original} \times 100$. To go from 2 million to 3 million, the difference is 1 million and the original is 2 million. So, $percent\ change = \frac{1}{2} \times 100 = 50$.

Country B: F, 100

Once again, use the percent change formula. The percent change is $\frac{difference}{original} \times 100$. To go from 1.5 million to 3 million, the difference is 1.5 million and the original is 1.5 million. So,

$$percent\ change = \frac{1.5}{1.5} \times 100 = 100.$$

Item 3

Sweatshirts, 8; Baseball caps, 4

To solve this question, systematically test out the answer choices. The equation that you need to solve is $22s + 26h = 280$, in which both s and h are integers and s represents the number of sweatshirts and h represents the number of baseball caps. So, start with plugging in 4 for sweatshirts and see if the number of baseball caps is an integer:

$22s + 26h = 280$
$22(4) + 26h = 280$
$h = 7.38$

Since the number of baseball caps is not an integer, Andre could not have bought 4 sweatshirts. Keep trying more sweatshirts one by one until you find an answer that will give you an integer value for baseball caps. 8 sweatshirts will give you 4 baseball caps, as shown in the equation:

$22s + 26h = 280$
$22(8) + 26h = 280$
$h = 4$

Therefore, the correct answer is 8 sweatshirts and 4 baseball caps.

Item 4

C, 10 to 9

The question asks you for the ratio of the current bus revenue for the average week in August to that after the change in fare is implemented, assuming the analysis is correct. First, you need to determine the current revenue. Add the number for each day. The table gives you the numbers in hundreds. However, since you're asked for the ratio, for simplification, you can treat the numbers in the table like the actual numbers. The total for an average week in August is 21 + 20 + 22 + 19 + 23 = 105. If the fare is $2, then the revenue is $2 × 105 = $210. If the analysis is correct, a decrease of the fare by 50 cents, to $1.50, would increase the numbers of bus commuters by 20%. 20% of 105 is $\frac{20}{100} \times 105 = 21$. Therefore, a 20% increase would bring the number of commuters to 105 + 21 = 126. The revenue, then, would be $1.50 × 126 = $189. Therefore, the ratio is 210 to 189, which can be reduced by 3 to get 70 to 63, then reduced again by 7 to get 10 to 9. Therefore, the answer is C.

Item 5

(A)   No

To determine this, you can add the numbers for each day in February to get 12 + 13 + 11 + 10 + 13 = 59. Then, add the numbers for each day in August to get 13 + 15 + 14 + 9 + 11 = 62. Therefore, the number of commuters in October is greater, making the statement false.

(B)   No

Look at the pie chart. According to the pie chart, 40% of commuters were automobile commuters and 30% were bus commuters. This is a ratio of 40 to 30, which reduces to 4 to 3. This is the reverse of the ratio given in the statement. Remember that order matters in a ratio, so the statement is false.

(C)   Yes

Again, go to the pie chart. This tells you that 7% travel by ferry and 18% travel by train. This is a total of 7% + 18% = 25%, which is less than the 30% of commuters who ride the bus. This statement, therefore, is true.

(D)   Yes

To determine this, you need to look at the table. On Mondays, there are 2,100 bus commuters, which is larger than the number for Mondays on any other month listed. On Tuesdays, there are 2,000 bus commuters, which is larger than the number for Tuesdays on any other month listed. On Wednesdays, there are 2,200 bus commuters, which is larger than the number for Wednesdays on any other month listed. On Thursdays, there are 1,900 bus commuters, which is larger than the number for Thursdays on any other month listed. On Fridays, there are 2,300 bus commuters, which is larger than the number for Fridays on any other month listed. Therefore, the statement is true.

Item 6

(A)   No

The analysis indicates that decreasing the bus fare by 50 cents will increase ridership by 20%. However, you don't have enough information to assume that there would be a similar effect, or even that there would be any effect, caused by raising the fare. Therefore, this cannot be inferred.

(B)   No

Based on the table, there are fewer bus commuters in December than in any of the other months indicated. However, you don't have any information about any of the other six months, or about weekend ridership. Therefore, this cannot be inferred from the table.

(C)   No

According to the analysis, decreasing bus fare by fifty cents will increase the number of bus commuters by 20%. The analysis also indicates that this increase will result from automobile commuters becoming bus commuters. This would appear to indicate that the percent decrease in automobile commuters would be equal to 20%. To find the percent change, you need to calculate $\frac{difference}{original} \times 100$. The decrease in automobile commuters would be equal to the increase in bus commuters, but since the original number of bus commuters is less than the original number of automobile commuters, the percent change in the bus commuters is greater than the percent change in the number of automobile commuters. Therefore, the percent decrease of automobile commuters is less than 20%, so this is not a valid inference.

(D)   Yes

Based on the table, there are 2,100 + 2,000 + 2,200 + 1,900 + 2,300 = 10,500 bus commuters Monday through Friday during the average week in August. Based on the pie chart, you know that during the average weekday in August, 30% of commuters in August are bus commuters. Therefore, you can translate and set up $\frac{30}{100} \times C = 10,500$. Solve for C to get 35,000. Therefore, this statement can be inferred.

Item 7

7-1:   E, 11 to 3

According to the graph, the U.S. population in 2000 was a little bit more than 275 million, and the U.S. population in 1900 was a little over 75 million. Since the question asks what the ratio is "closest to," these numbers are good enough to approximate. 275 to 75 can be reduced by 5 to get 55 to 15, which can be reduced by 5 again to get 11 to 3. Alternatively, you could reduce 275 to 75 by 25 to get this same ratio.

7-2:   B, 600%

The question asks what percent the U.S. population in 1950 is of the U.S. population in 1850. To get this you need to calculate $\frac{population\ 1950}{population\ 1850} \times 100$. Since the U.S. population in 1950 was higher, you want something that is greater than 100%. Eliminate 85% and 15%. Since the sentence says "approximate" and also since the remaining answer choices are not close to each other, you can estimate the values. According to the chart, the population in 1950 was about 150 million and the population in 1850 was about 25 million. Therefore, you need to calculate $\frac{150}{25} \times 100 = 6 \times 100 = 600\%$.

7-3:   D, 100%

To get percent increase, you need to use the formula $\frac{difference}{original} \times 100$. The population in 1900 was about 75 million, and the population in 1950 was about 150 million. The difference between the two figures is 75 million. Therefore, the percent increase is $\frac{75}{75} \times 100 = 100\%$.

Item 8

(A)   No

The chief operating officer's argument is based on a causal argument pattern, because it presumes that the hard drive crash was caused by *industrial espionage* by a competitor who *discovered* the location of the company's secret recipe, and not from some other cause, or by mere coincidence. Also, keep in mind that on any Assumption question, you can use the Negation Test to confirm that an answer choice is correct before you choose it.

In this case, the argument ignores the fact that the computer crash could have been caused by something other than *industrial espionage*, and might be related to the fact that the secret recipe has been stored on that computer *for the last 10 years*. Therefore, you want statements that match that assumption: that it was *industrial espionage*, and not some other factor, that caused the computer crash.

The statement that this is the *first time the company has been the victim of industrial espionage* is not an assumption on which the argument depends; it is irrelevant to the argument, which is concerned with whether this particular computer crash was caused by industrial espionage.

(B)   No

The way the company kept the *number of ounces of ingredients X and Y secret* over the years is irrelevant to the argument, which is concerned with whether the computer crash was caused by industrial espionage.

(C)   Yes

The argument does depend on the assumption that the computer in question did not crash *purely due to age*. Because it eliminates a possible cause other than industrial espionage, this statement is an assumption on which the argument depends. If you negate this answer, it reads "The computer that stored the secret recipe did crash purely due to age," which would destroy the conclusion of the argument.

(D)   No

Whether the secret recipe could be discovered through reverse-engineering is irrelevant to the argument, which is concerned with whether the computer crash was caused by industrial espionage.

Item 9

(A)   Yes

In an Inference question, there is no conclusion or assumption to identify; instead, you simply need to summarize the facts or claims stated and look for an answer that is logically proved by one, or a combination, of those facts or claims.

A strongly worded or extreme statement is unlikely to be correct, as it would be difficult for an extreme statement to be logically proven by the passage, and so weak language is preferred in the answer choices for an Inference question.

The claim that a computer crash *does not always result in the loss of all data* is logically proved by the passage, because the first email indicates that the company was able to recover some data through a *partial hard drive recovery*.

(B)   No

The claim that ingredients X and Y are the most important ingredients in the company's secret recipe is not supported by the passage. Although the first email states that recovering the information is very important, that does not mean that those ingredients are the most important parts of the recipe.

(C)   Yes

The claim that the prices of ingredients X and Y are *not directly related to the level of inflation* is logically proved by the passage. The second e-mail indicates that over a four-year period, the price of ingredient X went down, while the price of ingredient Y went up. If the prices of ingredients X and Y were *directly related to the level of inflation*, they would have risen or fallen by a similar percentage over that time.

(D)   No

The claim that if the company cannot recover the complete secret recipe, the company will *likely incur a large financial loss* is not supported by the passage. The passage gives no information about the potential effect of not recovering the complete recipe, beyond saying in the first e-mail that recovering the information is *very important*.

Item 10

B   7

The first e-mail states that the secret recipe has been used for over 50 years; the second e-mail provides information about the cost of the number of ounces of ingredients X and Y from two years ago and from six years ago. Since the recipe has not been changed, the number of ounces of ingredients X and Y has remained the same over the years.

Therefore, two e-mails provide a word problem that can be expressed in the form of two distinct equations in terms of the amounts and costs of ingredients X and Y that are included in a batch. Note that since the problem uses both dollars and cents, it is simpler to convert \$1.20 to 120 cents, which results in the following equations: $6x + 6y = 120$, and $12x + 3y = 123$.

Since you have two distinct linear equations and two variables, there is only one possible solution for each of the two variables.

While you could solve the problem algebraically (by substituting one equation into another, or by stacking and adding the equations), you can instead Plug In The Answers and eliminate algebra from the problem entirely. Use the numbers given as answer choices and plug each one into one of the equations as the number of ounces of ingredient X, and solve the equation for the number of ounces of ingredient Y. Then plug the same value into the other equation for x. If you come up with the same value for y in each case, you have found the answer.

Start with the middle answer choice: 10 ounces, and plug it in for x in the first equation: $6(10) + 6y = 120$, which simplifies to $60 + 6y = 120$, $6y = 60$, and $y = 10$ ounces. Now plug the answer choice (10) into the second equation for x: $12(10) + 3y = 123$, which simplifies to $120 + 3y = 123$, $3y = 3$, and $y = 1$ ounce. Since the result for y was different for the two equations, 10 ounces is not the correct value of x.

Since plugging in the value of 10 ounces for x resulted in an amount for y in the second equation that was too low, try plugging in a smaller value for x: 7 ounces. Plugging in 7 ounces for x into the first equation results in $6(7) + 6y = 120$, which simplifies to $42 + 6y = 120$, $6y = 78$, and $y = 13$.

Now plug 7 into the second equation for x, which results in $12(7) + 3y = 123$, which simplifies to $84 + 3y = 123$, $3y = 39$, and $y = 13$. Because plugging in 7 ounces for x in both equations resulted in the same value of y, 7 ounces is the correct response for x and no further testing of the answer choices is necessary.

Item 11

11-1:   True

Sort the table by number of students first to find the median. Then sort by average on test 1 and see if it is the same class.

11-2:   True

This question asks for the smallest percent increase, so look at the data to see which scores changed the least from test 1 to test 2. The only 2 sets of test scores that look close are History and Biology, but the average Biology score decreased from test 1 to test 2, so the smallest increase was by the students in History class, and the statement is true.

11-3:   True

The table gives you the number of students in each class and the average score for each of those classes. To find the total points scored, multiply the number of students by the average score.
Chemistry = $16 \times 78.5 = 1,256$
History = $14 \times 89.4 = 1,251.6$
Therefore, in Test 2, the total number of points scored by Chemistry students is higher than the total number of points scored by History students, so the statement is true.

11-4:   False

To find the total number of students in the classes with a percent change greater than 1.8%, start by sorting the table based on percent change. The classes that have a percent change greater than 1.8% are English, Calculus, Geography, and Chemistry. The total number of students in these classes is 58.

Item 12

Jack, F, 24 hours; Chloe, C, 8 hours

On work questions, it's easier to start with the individual rates and solve for the combined rate than it is to do it the other way around. Since the question asks for the individual rates, you should Plug In The Answers. Start in the middle. Say that Jack takes 9 hours to complete the job. The question tells you that Chloe completes the job three times as fast as Jack, so she completes the job in 3 hours. However, since it takes both of them together 6 hours to complete the job, Chloe can't take less than 6 hours to complete the job. Try something larger. Eliminate 9 hours for Jack. Since you want them to work more slowly, eliminate 3 hours, 6 hours, and 8 hours as well. You have two choices remaining. Try 18 hours. If Jack takes 18 hours to complete the job, then Chloe takes 6 hours to complete the job. Plug In for the size of the job. Say they are painting a house with 18 rooms. Jack's rate is 1 room per hour and Chloe's rate is 3 rooms per hour, so their combined rate is 4 rooms per hour. Therefore, the time it will take them working together is $\frac{18}{4} = \frac{9}{2} = 4.5$ hours. This is still too small, so eliminate 18 hours and also 12 hours for Jack. The only choice left is 24, so Jack completes the job in 24 hours. Since Chloe completes the job three times as fast, she completes the job in 8 hours.

Quantitative

1. **B** Start by rewriting (6^2) in the numerator as $(2^2)(3^2)$. Now there are only prime numbers in the numerator. Next, find the prime factors of 120. $120 = (2^3)(3)(5)$. Now you can rewrite the whole expression as $\frac{(2^2)(3^2)(2^4)(5^3)}{((2^3)(3)(5))^2}$, or $\frac{(2^2)(3^2)(2^4)(5^3)}{((2^6)(3^2)(5^2))}$. Now you can start canceling out terms.

   All but one 5 in the numerator are canceled out, so you are left with just 5. The answer is (B).

2. **A** Plug In for p. If $p = -\frac{1}{2}$, then $p^2 = \frac{1}{4}$. In (A) and (B), the values of p are the same, but in (B) you have to subtract 0.32, which is slightly bigger than 0.30, so (A) has a slightly greater value. Eliminate (B). $p^3 = -\frac{1}{8}$. Subtracting 0.301 will only make the overall value smaller, so the value in (C) is smaller than the value of (A). Eliminate (C). Choice (D) also includes p^3, and is therefore also negative, so you can eliminate (D). $p^4 = \frac{1}{16}$, which is smaller than $\frac{1}{4}$. The value subtracted from (E) is also slightly larger than the value subtracted from (A), so the expression in (E) is smaller than the expression in (A). The answer is (A).

3. **E** Integer x is equal to $2 \times 4 \times 6 \dots \times 60$. Alternatively, you can also say that x is equal to $(2 \times 1)(2 \times 2)$ $(2 \times 3) \dots (2 \times 30)$. Thus, it is true that all prime numbers less than 30 are factors of x. If you subtract only 1 from x, the resulting number will not be a multiple of any of the prime factors of x. It must therefore be true that the smallest prime number that is a factor of $x - 1$ must be greater than 30. The answer is (E).

4. **D** The question indicates that 1 dekaliter is equal to 10,000 milliliters, which means that 1 milliliter equals 0.0001 dekaliters. The first step is to convert 40 milliliters into dekaliters. $40 \times 0.0001 = 0.004$, so you have 0.004 dekaliters of ink. Now you can set up a proportion to solve for the wholesale cost of 0.004 dekaliters of ink. Set up the proportion so that you have the relationship you know (1 dekaliter to 2,000 dollars) on one side of the equation, and the relationship you do not know (0.004 dekaliters to x dollars). You should now have the following equation: $\frac{1dl}{\$2000} = \frac{0.004dl}{\$x}$. Cross multiply to find that $x = 8$. The answer is (D).

5. **A** Use the third side rule for triangles. According to the third side rule, the third side must be less than the sum of the other two sides, so side *AC* must be less than *AB* + *BC*. That means that *AC* must be less than 11. The rule also states that the third side must be greater than the difference of the other two sides, so side *AC* must be greater than *AB* – *BC*. That means *AC* is greater than 5. Thus, it must be true that 5 < *AC* < 11. Plug 5 and 11 in for side *AC* to get the total boundary for the perimeter. The resulting inequality is 16 < perimeter of *ABC* < 22. Of the options listed in the choices, only 16 is not a possible value for the perimeter of *ABC*, so the answer is (A).

6. **C** Plug In for *x* and *y* in statement (1). If *x* = 35 and *y* = 2, then *x* – *y* = 33. This produces a yes. If *x* = 10 and *y* = –21, then *x* – *y* = 31. This produces a no. Statement (1) is not sufficient. Eliminate (A) and (D). Statement (2) only indicates a value for *y*, not *x*, so statement (2) is not sufficient. Eliminate (B). Combine both statements to check (C). If *x* – *y* > 30 and *y* is greater than 30, then *x* must be greater than *y* in order for statement (1) to be true, so *x* must be greater than 30. This yields a yes response, so both statements together are sufficient. The answer is (C).

7. **D** Statement (1) indicates that angle *DAB* is equal to 45 degrees. Plug In for angle *ADC*. If angle *ADC* is equal to 120 degrees, then angle *ADE* must be equal to 60 degrees, because angle *ADE* + angle *ADC* = 180 degrees. The angles in quadrilateral *ABCD* must add up to 360 degrees, so the remaining angle, *BCD*, must be equal to 85 degrees. The difference between angle *BCD* and angle *ADE* is equal to 85 – 60 = 25. Angle *ADE* is 25 degrees smaller than angle *BCD*. Plug In again to confirm that the information in Statement (1) is sufficient. If *ADC* is equal to 170 degrees, then angle *ADE* is equal to 10 degrees, and angle *BCD* is equal to 35 degrees. 35 – 10 = 25, so angle *ADE* is 25 degrees smaller than angle *BCD*. Statement (1) is sufficient, so you can eliminate (B), (C), and (E). Now examine statement (2). If the sum of angles *ADC* and *BCD* is 205, then, because quadrilateral *ABCD* must contain 360 degrees, angle *DAB* must be equal to 45 degrees. Statement (1) indicated that angle *DAB* was equal to 45 degrees, and statement (1) was sufficient, so statement (2) must also be sufficient. The answer is (D).

8. **C** Draw the line *y* = 2. If the coordinates of *J* are (3,2), and the distance between *J* and *K* is 12, then the coordinates of *K* must be either (–9,2) or (15,2). If the coordinates of *L* are (–3,2), and the distance between *L* and *M* is 10, then the coordinates of *M* must be either (7,2) or (–13,2). Statement (1) indicates that the *x* coordinate of *M* is less than the *x* coordinate of *J*, so the coordinates of *M* must be (–13,2). However, the coordinates of *K* could still be either (–9,2) or (15,2), so you do not have enough information to determine the distance between *K* and *M*. Statement (1) is insufficient. Eliminate (A) and (D). Statement (2) indicates that *L* is the midpoint between *J* and *K*. If statement (2) is true, then the coordinates of *K* must be (–9,2). However, you do not have enough information to determine the coordinates of *M*, so statement (2) is insufficient. Eliminate (B). Combine the two statements to see if they are sufficient when used together. According to statement (1), the coordinates of *M* must be (–13,2), and according to statement (2), the coordinates of *K* must be (–9,2), so the distance between the two points must be 4. Both statements together are sufficient, so the answer is (C).

9. **C** First, rearrange the equation so that you have $p^2 = r(40)$. Now Plug In for p. If $p = 20$, then $r = 10$. $\frac{10}{5} = 2$, so Statement I is an integer and you can't eliminate anything. For Statement II, $\frac{10}{2 \times 5} = 1$, so this too produces an integer. For Statement III, $\frac{10}{3 \times 5} = \frac{2}{3}$. This is not an integer, so eliminate (D) and (E). Plug In again to confirm that both I and II always result in integers. If $r = 90$, then $p = 60$. $\frac{90}{5} = 18$, so Statement I still works. $\frac{90}{10} = 9$, so Statement II also still works. The answer is (C).

10. **E** Because lines AE and BD are parallel, then angle EAD must be equal to angle ADB, so the measure of angle ADB must be 30 degrees. The measure of an inscribed angle is always equal to half of the measure of the accompanying minor arc, so the measure of minor arc ADB must be 60 degrees. The minor arc $ABCD$ is equal to 180 degrees, because it covers half of the circle, so if ADB uses 60 of those degrees, then 120 degrees remain for arc BCD. If the measure of arc BCD is 120 degrees out of the 360 degrees in the circle, then because $\frac{120}{360} = \frac{1}{3}$, BCD must be equal to one third of the total circle. The question also indicates that BCD is equal to 4π, so the total circumference of the circle must be $3(4\pi)$, or 12π. Circumference $= \pi d$, so the diameter is 12, and the radius is 6. The formula for the area of a circle is πr^2, so the area of the circle equals $6^2\pi$, or 36π. The answer is (E).

11. **D** Plug In for the masses of the two objects. If the mass of the first object is 3, and the mass of the second object is 4, and the distance between the two objects is 2, then the force of gravity is equal to $\frac{3 \times 4}{2^2}$, or $\frac{12}{4} = 3$. If the distance is doubled, then the distance is 4. If the force remains the same, then you can write this as the equation $\frac{x}{4^2} = 3$. Multiply both sides by 16 to get $x = 48$, so the new product is 48. The formula for percent change is $\frac{difference}{original} \times 100$, so the percent increase is equal to $\frac{48-12}{12} \times 100$, or $\frac{36}{12} \times 100 = 300\%$. The answer is (D).

12. **B** Rewrite the equation as $m^5 + n^5 = 200$. If you need n to be as large as possible, then m must be as small as possible. Since m is a positive number, make $m = 1$, then $n^5 = 199$. Plug In numbers from the choices, starting with (C). If $n = 5$, then $5^2 = 25$, so $5^3 = 125$, and $5^4 = 625$. Without even solving for 5^5 you can see that 5 is going to be too big. Eliminate (C), (D), and (E). If $n = 3$, then $n^5 = 243$. 243 is too big, so the greatest value of n must be less than 3. If $n = 2$, then $n^5 = 32$. That is less than 199, so you are in the range. The answer is (B).

13. **B** Because cubes get very large very fast, you know that the two numbers have to be relatively small. Find the cubes of the first few positive numbers. $1^3 = 1$, $2^3 = 8$, $3^3 = 27$, $4^3 = 64$, and $5^3 = 125$. $125 + 27 = 152$, so the two numbers must be 3 and 5. The product of 3 and 5 is equal to 15, so the answer is (B).

14. **E** Try to make the left side of the equation look more like the right side of the equation. First, factor 5^{n-3} out of the equation, so that you have $5^{n-3}(1 + 5^3) = (2)(7)(9)(5^{11})$. Now simplify the numbers inside the parenthesis on the left side of the equation, and multiply the numbers on the right side of the equation, so that you now have $5^{n-3}(126) = 126(5^{11})$. Divide both sides of the equation by 126 to get $5^{n-3} = 5^{11}$. It must be true that $n - 3 = 11$, so $n = 14$, and $2n = 28$. The answer is (E).

15.   A   If $y = 4$, then you can rewrite the equation so that you have $(5x - 3)6 + 4$. Plug In for x to see if statement (1) is sufficient. If $x = 1$, then you have $(5(1) - 3)6 + 4 = 16$, so the units digit is 6 and the result when the units digit is divided by 10 is equal to $\frac{6}{10}$, or $\frac{3}{5}$. Plug In again for x to see if you get the same result. If $x = 2$, then you have $(5(2) - 3)6 + 4 = 46$. The units digit is once again 6, so the result will be the same. In fact, the result will be the same for all values of x. You can confirm this by finding the pattern of units digits for multiples of 6, as follows: $1 \times 6 = 6$, $2 \times 6 = 12$, $3 \times 6 = 18$, $4 \times 6 = 24$, $5 \times 6 = 30$, $6 \times 6 = 36$, $7 \times 6 = 42$, $8 \times 6 = 48$, and so forth. As you can see, the units digits follow a repeating pattern of 6, 2, 8, 4, 0, 6, 2, 8, 4, 0…. The cycle repeats every five multiples. Thus, in the expression $(5x - 3)6 + 4$, you will always be 3 short of a full cycle, so the units digit of $(5x - 3)6$ will always be 2. If you add 4 to that value, you will always end up with a units digit of 6. Statement (1) is sufficient, so you can eliminate (B), (C), and (E). Now examine statement (2) to see if it is sufficient. If $x = 5$, then the expression becomes $(5(5) - 3)6 + y = 22(6) + y$, or $132 + y$. If $y = 5$, then you have $132 + 5 = 137$, and the units digit is 7, so the result when the units digit is divided by 10 is $\frac{7}{10}$. If $y = 3$, then you have $132 + 3 = 135$ and the units digit is 5, so the result when the units digit is divided by 10 is $\frac{5}{10}$ or $\frac{1}{2}$. Statement (2) is insufficient, so the answer is (A).

16.   D   If the temperature high in Kelvin was –252, then you can rewrite the equation so that you have $-252 = \left(\frac{5}{9}(F - 32)\right) - 273.15$. Now you can solve for F to find degrees Fahrenheit. Add 273.15 to both sides so that you have $21.15 = \frac{5}{9}(F - 32)$. Now you can ballpark to find the answer. 21.15 is approximately 21, and $\frac{5}{9}$ is approximately $\frac{1}{2}$, so the whole equation is approximately $21 = \frac{1}{2}(F - 32)$. Multiply both sides by 2 to get $42 = F - 32$, so F is approximately 74°. The only answer that is close to 74° is 71°, so the answer is (D).

17.   C   Rearrange the equation in statement (1) so that it is in $y = mx + b$ format. Add 45 to both sides of the equation so that you have $5y = -x + 45$. Now divide both sides by 5 to get y by itself, so that you have $y = -\frac{1}{5}x + 9$. If the line $y = -\frac{1}{5}x + 9$ is perpendicular to line t, then line t must have a slope of 5. Thus, the equation for line t must be of the form $y = 5x + b$. To see if this is sufficient, Plug In 3 for x and 4 for y in this equation. This yields $4 = 5(3) + b$. If $b = -11$, this yields a "yes" answer. However, if b is equal to any other number, this yields a "no," so statement (1) is insufficient. Eliminate (A) and (D). Statement (2) indicates that line t intersects the line $y = \frac{3}{4}x - 11$ when $y = -11$ or, in other words, when $x = 0$, $y = -11$. This means that the y intercept for line $y = \frac{3}{4}x - 11$ is –11. If line

t intersects this line at point $(0,-11)$, then the y intercept for line t is also equal to $(0,-11)$. However, knowing the y intercept does not give you any information about the slope of line t, so statement (2) is insufficient. Eliminate (B). Combine the two statements to see if they are sufficient when used together. According to statement (1) you know that line t is of the form $y = 5x + b$. According to statement (2) you know that the y intercept is equal to -11, so $b = -11$, so the whole equation is $y = 5x - 11$. Statements (1) and (2) together are sufficient, so the answer is (C).

18. **E** Plug In for x and y in statement (1). If $x = 2$, and $y = 3$, then statement (1) is equal to $5(2) + 2(3) > -10$, which is true. This means that $x - y$ is equal to $2 - 3 = -1$. Because -1 is greater than -10, this produces a yes response. If $x = -2$, and $y = 10$, then statement (1) becomes $5(-2) + 2(10) > -10$, which is also true. This means that $x - y$ now equals $-2 - 10 = -12$. This produces a no response, so statement (1) is insufficient. Eliminate (A) and (D). Plug In for statement (2). Both sets of values plugged in for statement (1) also work for statement (2), so statement (2) is also insufficient. Eliminate (B). If you combine both statements, it is still possible for x to equal either 2 or -2, and for y to equal either 3 or 10. Thus, $x - y$ can still equal either -1 or -12, so statements (1) and (2) together are insufficient. The answer is (E).

19. **B** If Rhonda made 12 phone calls per hour for the first 6 calls she made, then it took her 0.5 hours to make her first 6 phone calls. If she made an average of 6 phone calls per hour for the remaining 6 phone calls she made, then it took her 1 hour to make the remaining 6 phone calls. Add up the times to find out how long it took Rhonda to make all 12 phone calls: $0.5 + 1 = 1.5$, so it took her 1.5 hours to make 12 phone calls. $\dfrac{12}{1.5} = 8$, so Rhonda made an average of 8 phone calls per hour. The answer is (B).

20. **A** $9^{\frac{1}{2}} = \sqrt{9}$, or 3. $9^{\frac{1}{3}} = \sqrt[3]{9}$, which is between 2 and 3. $9^{\frac{1}{4}} = \sqrt[4]{9}$, which is between 1 and 2. Now you can ballpark to find the approximate value of P, by writing $3 - 2^{+} - 1^{+} =$ slightly less than 0. The answer is (A).

21. **B** Draw an average pie to find the total number of people in all of the offices. If the average is 8, and the number of offices is 5, then the total number of people is $8 \times 5 = 40$. If the median is 7, then because 5 is an odd number you also know that one of the offices must have 7 people in it. Plug In the answers, starting with (C), to find the maximum number of people who can be in one office. If there are 25 people in one office, and one of the offices has 7 people in it, then those two offices contain 32 of the 40 people. That means that the other three offices must contain a total of 8 people. If the two smallest offices each contain only 1 person, then the third office would contain only 6 people, so the median would no longer be 7. Eliminate (C), (D), and (E) and try a smaller number. If the number of people in the largest office is equal to 24, then you know that the sum of two of the people in two of the offices is $24 + 7 = 31$. That means that the other two offices must contain a total of 9 people. If the two smallest offices contain 1 person each, then the remaining office must contain 7 people. The list of the number of people in each office is now 1, 1, 7, 7, 24, so the median is still 7. The answer is (B).

22. **C** Begin by figuring out how many different ways you can package the tea in boxes that contain 8 ounces of tea, all of the same flavor. There are five flavors, each flavor can come in either loose leaf or bagged form, so 5 flavors × 2 forms = 10 different ways to package the tea in boxes that contain only one flavor each. Now find the number of different ways to package 4 different flavors of the same form per box. In this case, you must choose 4 of 5 possible flavors, and order does not matter, so the formula is $\frac{5 \times 4 \times 3 \times 2}{4 \times 3 \times 2 \times 1} = 5$ different ways to combine the 4 flavors. Each combination can come in either loose leaf or bagged form, so you have 2 different forms × 5 different combinations = 10 total possible ways to combine the 4 flavors in either bagged or loose-leaf form. Thus, the total number of combinations is 10 + 10 = 20 total combinations. The answer is (C).

23. **A** If Karen sold her first house for $225,000 and at a loss of 25 percent, then 75 percent of the original price equals $225,000. $\frac{75}{100} x = 225,000$, so x, or the price she originally paid, equals $300,000. Thus, Karen lost 75,000 on the sale of her first house. If she bought a second house for a price of 30 percent less than $300,000, then the second house cost $210,000, so she gained $90,000. $90,000 - $75,000 = $15,000, so the answer is (A).

24. **A** According to statement (1), 5 percent of the people who own an automatic transmission vehicle also own a manual transmission vehicle. The question also indicates that 12 percent of the people who own a manual transmission vehicle also own an automatic transmission vehicle. Both figures relate to the total number who own both, so that means that 5 percent of the automatic transmission owners = 12 percent of the manual transmission owners. The overlap in ownership makes up a smaller percent of those who own automatic transmission vehicles, so there must be more people who own automatic transmission vehicles. Statement (1) is sufficient, so you can eliminate (B), (C), and (E). Statement (2) indicates that 15 people own both an automatic transmission vehicle and a manual transmission vehicle, so you know that 12 percent of the people who own a manual transmission is equal to 15 people. $\frac{12}{100} x = 15$, so x = 125. Thus, there are 125 people who own a manual transmission vehicle. However, you have no further information to allow you to calculate the number of people who own automatic transmission vehicles, so statement (2) is insufficient. The answer is (A).

25. **A** Statement (1) allows you to find the value of x, so you can answer the question. (If x is $\frac{1}{5}$ less

than $\frac{9}{10}$, then $\frac{9}{10} - \frac{1}{5} = x$. $\frac{1}{5} = \frac{2}{10}$, so x equals $\frac{9}{10} - \frac{2}{10} = \frac{7}{10}$. If x equals $\frac{7}{10}$, then $\frac{x}{2} = \frac{\frac{7}{10}}{2}$, or

$\frac{7}{20}$.) Statement (1) is sufficient, so eliminate (B), (C), and (E). According to statement (2), x is be-

tween $\frac{2}{5}$ and $\frac{4}{5}$. That means that one possible value for x is $\frac{3}{5}$, but another possible value is $\frac{7}{10}$.

Statement (2) is insufficient, so the answer is (A).

26. **D** If $|x| > 5$, then either $x > 5$, or $x < -5$. If $x > 5$, then $|x - 5| \neq 5 - x$. You can confirm this by plug-
ging in a positive number greater than 5 for x. If $x = 6$, then the equation becomes $|6 - 5| = 5 - 6$, or
$1 = -1$. This is not true, positive values of x within the accepted range will yield a no answer. If
$x < -5$, then $|x - 5| = 5 - x$. You can confirm this by plugging in a negative number less than -5 for
x. If $x = -6$, then the equation becomes $|-6 - 5| = 5 - (-6)$, or $11 = 11$. This is true, so if $x < -5$ then
the answer is yes. Statement (1) indicates that $-x(x^2) > 0$. Because x^2 will always be positive, statement (1) is really indicating that $-x$ times a positive is greater than 0. That means that $-x$ must be
positive, so x must be negative. Statement (1) yields only a yes answer, so statement (1) is sufficient.
Eliminate (B), (C), and (E). Statement (2) indicates that $x^5 < 0$. A positive number raised to any
power will only be positive, but a negative number raised to an odd power will always be negative,
so according to statement (2), x must be negative. This yields only a yes answer, so statement (2) is
also sufficient. The answer is (D).

27. **E** Statement (1) indicates that the sale price of item X was three times the sale price of item Y. Plug In
for the sale prices of the items. If the sale price of item X was $36, then the sale price of item Y was
$12. If item X was discounted 10 percent, then $0.90(\textit{original cost of X}) = \$36$, so the original price
of item X was $40. Since the sale price of item Y was $12, the discount on item Y was 40 percent,
$0.60(\textit{original cost of Y}) = \$12$, so then the original cost of item Y was $20. Plug In again to see if
you can get different numbers. If the sale price of item X was $18, then the sale price of item Y was
$6. If item X was discounted 10 percent, then $0.90(\textit{original cost of Y}) = \$18$, so the original cost of
item X was $20. Since the sale price of item Y was $6, and the discount on item Y was 40 percent,
$0.60(\textit{original price of Y}) = \$6$, so the original cost of item Y was $10. These numbers give you two
different values for the original price of X, so statement (1) is insufficient. Eliminate (A) and (D).
Statement (2) indicates that the original cost of item X was twice the original price of item Y. In
the sets of numbers used above, when the original cost of item X was $40, the original cost of item
Y was $20, and when the original price of item X was $20, then the original price of item Y was $10.

Both values also work for statement (2), so statement (2) is insufficient. Eliminate (B). If both sets of numbers work for both statements, then the two statements together are also insufficient, so the answer is (E).

28. **C** The first piece of information you are given is that of the 80 employees, $\frac{3}{5}$ are either journalists or copy editors. $(80)\left(\frac{3}{5}\right) = 48$, so there are 48 employees who are either copy editors or journalists. Statement (1) only indicates that there are more than 10 copy editors, but does not give you enough information to know either exactly how many copy editors there are, or how many journalists there are. Statement (1) is insufficient, so eliminate (A) and (D). Statement (2) indicates that there are more than 3 times as many journalists at the paper as there are copy editors. The phrase "more than" indicates that there could be 4 times as many journalists, or 5 times as many journalists, or 3.5 times as many journalists as copy editors. Thus, Statement (2) is also insufficient and the remaining answers are (C) and (E). Now, combine both statements. Combined, the question and statements say that there are 48 journalists and copy editors, at least 10 copy editors, and the number of journalists is more than 3 times the number of copy editors. This can all be rewritten as $j + c = 48$, $c > 10$, and $j > 3c$. So, if j was exactly 3 times c ($j = 3c$), then the values could be easily replaced to reveal that $j + c = 48$, $4c = 48$, and $c = 12$. However, since statement 2 says that the value of j is more than 3 times c, c cannot be 12. The value of c is therefore 11, because it also has to be greater than 10 according to Statement (1). So, if there are 11 copy editors, there are 37 journalists, and since 37 is more than 3 times 11, the statements are both satisfied and an answer has been found. The correct answer is (C).

29. **D** Plug In the Answers, starting with (C). In the final ratio of 13:7, the difference in the ratios is 6. If the actual difference between the number of horses and the number of cows were 75, then the difference would have been multiplied by 12.5, so to get the actual number of horses and cows, you would have to multiply the entire ratio by 12.5. Thus, after the transaction there would be 162.5 horses and 87.5 cows. You cannot have fractional cows, so (C) is not a viable option. Additionally, that would mean that there would have been 177.5 horses and 62.5 cows on the farm before the transaction. This is not a 7:3 ratio. You need a bigger number, so try (D). If there were 90 more horses than cows on the farm after the transaction, and the ratio of horses to cows was 13:7, then the difference would have been multiplied by 15, so you would have to multiply the entire ratio by 15. Thus, after the transaction there would be 195 horses and 105 cows, so before the transaction there would have been 210 horses and 90 cows. 210:90 is equal to a 7:3 ratio, so the answer is (D).

30. **B** Because the difference between each score would remain the same if each student scored 7 points below his or her actual score, the standard distribution would also remain the same. For instance, if the scores for five students were 76, 88, 100, 112, and 124 points respectively, then if each student scored 7 points lower on the test, the scores would be 69, 81, 93, 105, and 117 respectively. Changing all of the scores by the same amount will not alter the standard distribution. The answer is (B).

31. **A** Multiply both sides of the expression in statement (1) by 2^m to get $3^{2n} \times 2^m = 144$. Create a factor tree to find the prime factors of 144. $144 = 2 \times 2 \times 2 \times 2 \times 3 \times 3$, or $2^4 \times 3^2$, so $m = 4$, $2n = 2$, and $n = 1$. Thus, $m - n = 4 - 1 = 3$. Statement (1) is sufficient, so you can eliminate (B), (C), and (E). Multiply both sides of statement (2) by 3^n to get $3^m \times 3^n = 243$. $3^5 = 243$, so $m + n = 5$. However, you have no further information about the individual values of m and n, so you cannot state the value of $m - n$. Statement (2) is insufficient, so the answer is (A).

32. **E** According to statement (1), 60 percent of the lawyers in the civil rights and anti-trust law departments are partners, so the remaining 40 percent of the lawyers in those departments are associates. However, you have no information regarding the number of associates in the tax and real estate law departments, so statement (1) is insufficient. Eliminate (A) and (D). According to statement (2), 70 percent of the lawyers in the tax and real estate law departments are associates, but you have no information regarding the number of associates in the other two departments. Statement (2) is insufficient, so eliminate (B). Combine the two statements to see if they are sufficient when used together. If 40 percent of the lawyers in the civil rights and anti-trust law departments are associates, and 70 percent of the lawyers in the tax and real estate law departments are associates, you still do not have any information regarding the number of total lawyers in each department. If there are 10 people each in the civil rights and anti-trust departments, and 100 people each in the tax and real estate law departments, the percentage of associates out of the total will be very different than if there were 100 people in each of the four departments. Statements (1) and (2) together are insufficient, so the answer is (E).

33. **A** If Adam and Alfredo are exactly the same height, then David is either the tallest of the three or the shortest of the three, but he cannot be in the middle. Thus, Alfredo's height must be equal to the median height. Statement (1) is sufficient, so eliminate (B), (C), and (E). Statement (2) indicates that David is 5 centimeters taller than Alfredo is. However, you have no further information regarding Adam's height. For instance, if Alfredo is 170 centimeters tall, then David would be 175 centimeters tall. However, Adam could be 168 centimeters tall, in which case b, or Alfredo's height, would be the median, so this yields a yes answer. However, Adam could be 180 meters tall instead, in which case David's height, or c, would be the median. Statement (2) is insufficient, so the answer is (A).

34. **D** According to the question, you know that $a + b = c$, and because 5 percent of a added to 10 percent of b is equal to 8 percent of c, you can also write the equation $0.05a + 0.10b = 0.08c$. Statement (1) indicates that $b = 3$, so you can now replace $0.10b$ in the equation with $0.10(3)$, so that you have $0.05a + 0.30 = 0.08c$. Because c is also equal to $a + b$, you can also write $0.05a + 0.30 = 0.08(a + b)$, or $0.05a + 0.30 = 0.08a + 0.08(3)$. Simplify to get $0.06 = 0.03a$, or $a = 2$. Statement (1) is sufficient, so eliminate (B), (C), and (E). According to statement (2), $2c - 2a = 6$. Divide the entire equation by 2 to get $c - a = 3$. You already know that $a + b = c$, or $c - a = b$, so b must be 3. Knowing the value of b is sufficient, as indicated above, so statement (2) is also sufficient. The answer is (D).

35. **E** Plug In values for A, B, and C. Let $B = 0$, and $C = 10$. If the distance from A to B is 7, then A can equal either 7 or –7, so the distance between A and C is either 3 or 17. Statement (1) is insufficient, so eliminate (A) and (D). Plug In again for statement (2). If $C = 10$ and $B = 0$, then A must equal either 7 or –7, so the distance between C and A is either 3 or 17, and the distance

between B and A is 7. Statement (2) is insufficient, so eliminate (B). If you combine both statements, it is still possible that $B = 0$, $C = 10$, and A is equal to either 7 or –7, so statements (1) and (2) together are insufficient. The answer is (E).

36.   A   Create an average pie. The question indicates that employees in the standard department each process an average of 8.7 packages per hour. If you label the number of employees in the standard department x, and the average is 8.7, then the total is $8.7x$. Now create a second average pie. The average number of packages shipped per employee in one hour in the express department is 12.4. If you label the number of employees in the express department y, then the total is $12.4y$. According to statement (1), the average number of packages shipped per hour for employees in both departments is 10.3. The number of employees in the two departments combined is equal to $x + y$, so you can write the total of both averages as $10.3(x + y)$, or $10.3x + 10.3y$. However, the total of both averages can also be written as $8.7x + 12.4y$, so it must be true that $10.3x + 10.3y = 8.7x + 12.4y$. Simplify the equation to get $1.6x = 2.1y$. Divide both sides by 1.6 to get $x = \dfrac{2.1y}{1.6}$, and then divide both sides by 2.1 to get $\dfrac{x}{y} = \dfrac{2.1}{1.6}$, or the ratio of employees in the standard department to employees in the express department. Statement (1) is sufficient, so eliminate (B), (C), and (E). Statement (2) indicates that there are 40 people in the standard department, so the total number of packages shipped per hour is equal to $40 \times 8.7 = 348$. If the number of employees in the express department is equal to y, then the total number of packages processed per hour in the express department is equal to $12.4y$. Thus, the total number of packages processed in both departments is equal to $348 + 12.4y$. However, in order to find the ratio, you must be able to write the relationship between the number of employees in the standard department to the number of employees in the express department as a fraction. Statement (2) does not provide you with enough information to write this relationship as a fraction, so statement (2) is insufficient. The answer is (A).

37.   C   Statement (1) indicates that Lou will need twice as many gallons of paint for the living room as he needed for the bedroom, but you have no information regarding how many gallons of paint were used for the bedroom, so statement (1) is insufficient. Eliminate (A) and (D). Statement (2) indicates that Lou used 4 gallons of paint for the bedroom, but does not give you any further information about the relationship between the number of gallons used for the bedroom and the number of gallons used for the living room, so statement (2) is insufficient. Eliminate (B). Combine the two statements to see if they are sufficient when used together. If Lou used 4 gallons of

paint for the bedroom, and he will need twice as many gallons of paint for the living room, then

he will need 8 gallons of paint in total for the living room. Set up a ratio box. If the ratio is $\frac{2}{3}$ gal-

lon of white paint to 2 gallons of blue paint, then the sum of the numbers in the ratio is $\frac{2}{3} + \frac{2}{1}$, or

$\frac{2}{3} + \frac{6}{3} = \frac{8}{3}$. In order to get to the actual total of 8, you must multiply $\frac{8}{3}$ by 3, so 3 is the multiplier.

$\frac{2}{3} \times 3 = 2$, so Lou will need a total of 2 gallons of white paint for the living room. Statements (1)

and (2) together are sufficient, so the answer is (C).

Verbal

1. **A** The idiom being tested here is *so A that B*. Choice (B) omits *that* and is unnecessarily awkward. A pronoun should never precede its antecedent, which does happen in (C). In other words, *it* must come after *a brand-building program*. Choice (D) yields a sentence fragment. Choice (E) omits the subject of the sentence until its twelfth word, which makes it awkward. The original sentence is clear in meaning and correct in its use of the idiom *so A that B*. Choice (A) is the correct answer.

2. **D** The subject of the sentence, *policy initiatives*, is plural, so the verb must be too. Therefore *has* should be *have*, which eliminates (A), (B), and (C). While (E) is awkward and unnecessarily wordy, (D) uses the correct verb form and is concise and clear.

3. **C** The plan is to increase revenues by raising the sales tax; the premise is that lowering the tax will give consumers an incentive to increase purchasing. The argument assumes that purchases will rise more than the total dollar value of the tax previously collected. Choice (A) would seem to be an argument in favor of the plan, although it's not directly relevant to the conclusion; eliminate it. Choice (B) deals with expenditures, while the argument is only concerned with revenues; eliminate it. For (C), if the public has fewer places to spend money, the likelihood of it spending more money is reduced. Keep this for now. Choice (D) might seem to undermine the plan, but a threat is not the same as a veto; eliminate it. Although (E) might be a reason to suspect the council's motives, it is not directly relevant to the argument; eliminate it. The correct answer is (C).

4. **E** The sentence incorrectly contrasts *a lower-altitude mountain* with *an Everest climber*. The proper comparison must be parallel, that is, compare a mountain to a mountain or a climber to a climber. Choice (B) compares *a lower-altitude mountain* to *in climbing Everest*, which is still not parallel, and the second half of this answer is awkward. Choice (C) makes the same mistake as the original sentence. Choice (D) also compares a mountain with a climber, and the use of *for* is unnecessary. Choice (E) correctly contrasts *a lower-altitude mountain* to *Mount Everest* and is the correct choice.

5. **D** The original sentence says that staff meetings and social events are unlike resistance among employees, but the contrast should be between staff meetings and social events and duties that extend work hours. The additional clause in (B) is unnecessary, also it is unclear what "they" refers to because the pronoun *they* precedes its antecedent *many employees*. Choice (C) gets the contrast right (meetings and events to duties), but it does so by becoming convoluted and awkward (whose regular work hours?). Choice (E) also achieves a proper contrast (this time employees to employees),

but it is unnecessarily awkward. *Many employees resist accepting...* is as clear and in the active voice. Choice (D) gets the contrast right (employee's happiness to participate versus their resistance) and the sentence reads smoothly and clearly. Choice (D) is the correct answer.

6. **C** The answer to this question can be found in the line, *In many species, these hierarchies are fairly stable, although not immutable.* This matches (C). Choice (A) is incorrect because the passage only discusses social species, not most animals. Choice (B) is incorrect because while the passage states that place in the hierarchy determines access to *mating opportunities,* it gives no indication of the likelihood of a specific animal reproducing. Choice (D) is contradicted by the passage, which states that some animals at the top of the hierarchy have high amounts of glucocorticoid in their blood. Choice (E) is incorrect because the passage simply states that *allocation of scarce resources is often based on a dominance hierarchy.* This doesn't mean that a dominance hierarchy causes competition, however. The correct answer is (C).

7. **E** According to the third paragraph, *The answer may lie in individual animal's responsiveness to stress. Studies have shown that not all the baboons at the top of the dominance structure had the lowest level of glucocorticoid, while not all those at the bottom had the highest concentrations.* Thus, there is an individual component to glucocorticoid levels in addition to the socially induced levels. Choices (A) and (B) are not necessarily true, because the passage indicates a baboon at the top may have higher or lower levels. Choice (C) is not supported by the passage. Choice (D) goes too far outside the scope of the passage, as the author does not discuss this. The correct answer is (E).

8. **B** Earlier in the paragraph, the author asked what the adaptive utility of the stress response is. The last few lines then explain what a solution to the puzzle might be. Thus, the final lines must be a description of how stress levels might be useful—by allowing fluidity in the hierarchy. Choice (A) is incorrect because the last line does not resolve anything; it is only a possibility. Choice (C) doesn't work because the last line is speculative. The final line suggests a possibility, but it does not deny anything, so (D) is incorrect. And (E) doesn't work because there is no previous interpretation offered. The correct answer is (B).

9. **E** The conclusion is that RS likely has a genetic component; the evidence offered is the presence in mice of a gene that creates RS-like symptoms. To weaken the argument you need to undermine the assumption that the symptoms in the mice have the same cause as RS in humans. The length of time the mice are observed, or that the researchers have been studying RS, is irrelevant, so eliminate (C) and (D). Whether the symptoms are treatable is also irrelevant—eliminate (A). Choice (B) would actually strengthen the conclusion, so eliminate it. But if the symptoms in the mice could be something other than RS, that would hurt the argument. The correct answer is (E).

10. **E** The original sentence is awkward because the first clause is conditional—dealing with what will happen *if,* but *has been* is past, and something that has happened in the past cannot be affected by something that may or may not happen. Additionally, *has been* and *outpace* are incompatible verb tenses: you wouldn't say *has been to outpace* so don't say *has been...to outpace.* Regarding (B), (C), and (D), the use of *continue* makes the use of two different verb tenses to show the trend in two time periods (here continuing from the present, and the past) unnecessary and awkward. If something continues to happen, it is implied that it has been happening in the past and is happening through the present. Choice (E) corrects this mistake and keeps the sentence as simple as possible. It contains both the idea of having outpaced in the past and of continuing to outpace in the present. Choice (E) is the correct answer.

11. **E** The original sentence has two mistakes: *have...turned on* and *saw* are different verb tenses, and *who's* is a contraction for "who is," which doesn't make sense in the sentence. Instead of *saw* the verb tense should be "have seen" to match *have...turned on*. In this case *have* is implied by its earlier use, so *seen* alone is correct, as in (C) and (E). In (C), the use of *who's* is incorrect. Choice (E) corrects the reference problem, reads smoothly, and uses the correct form of the verb "to see." It is the correct answer.

12. **B** The conclusion is that the hydrangea is not panicled; the evidence offered is that it is grown for florists, and therefore must be a bigleaf hydrangea. The assumption of the argument is that a bigleaf hydrangea cannot be a panicled hydrangea. Although (A) would be a good answer to a strengthen question, it's more than the argument requires here (they both might have leaves, after all)—eliminate it. Choice (C) says that no bigleaf blooms in the summer. Although you know that blooming in the summer means that a hydrangea is panicled, you could still have a panicled hydrangea that did not bloom in the summer, so eliminate (C). You don't know anything about when the hydrangea in question blooms, so (D) cannot be the assumption. Similarly, (E) talks about hydrangeas used by florists rather than those grown by florists, so eliminate it. This leaves (B), which seems backwards. But if a panicled hydrangea cannot be a bigleaf, then a bigleaf hydrangea cannot be panicled. You know the hydrangea in question must be bigleaf; (B) would tell you it cannot be panicled. The correct answer is (B).

13. **B** In the original sentence *the skill* is singular, but the verb *are* is plural, so (A) is incorrect. The correct answer must end with *for* in order to make *for website development* parallel with *for search engine optimization and internet marketing*. Choice (C) does not yield parallel structures, so it is incorrect. Choice (D) has the same subject-verb agreement problem as the original sentence, and both (D) and (E) fail the parallel construction test. In (B), there is subject-verb agreement in *skills...are hard to find*, and *for website development* and *for search engine optimization and internet marketing* are parallel. Choice (B) is the correct choice.

14. **C** The idiom is *more than ever before*; the use of never is incorrect. Also, the two things that examining the growing use of international social networking sites reveals must be presented with parallel grammatical structures. In other words, *that young people...* must be matched with "*that pop culture fads....* The original sentence makes both of these mistakes. Choice (B) doesn't resolve the problem with the idiom, and "while" doesn't make the grammar parallel (*that young people* vs. *while pop culture* doesn't work). In (D), *sharing more their...* is awkward and the absence of *that* at the end of the underlined section means the two revelations will not be parallel. Choice (E) is a jumbled mess of words, and *as young people* is not parallel to *that pop culture*. Choice (C) gets the idiom right (*more than ever before*) and uses *that* so that the two revelations are presented with parallel grammar structures.

15. **C** The second paragraph presents a critique of the economic model of voting behavior. It states that one of the implications of the model is *low voter turnout*, but this isn't true. This matches (A). The paragraph also states that many voters fail to vote correctly and do not choose the candidate that meets their interests, which matches (B). Choice (C) is not mentioned, so hold on to it. Choices (D) and (E) are both mentioned in the line *Since one vote has an extremely low probability of affecting the outcome of the vote and the voter will reap the benefits of a particular politician's victory*

regardless of his actions, the costs of voting, in the form of information gathering and time spent, should be prohibitive. Because voters do vote, it shows that they discount the costs of voting or think their vote matters, or both. The correct answer is (C).

16. **D** According to the passage, bounded rationality involves using *low information* shortcuts. Avidly following the presidential campaign involves processing a lot of information, so (A) is wrong. Similarly, a careful comparison of platforms, as in (B), is a high information act. Choice (C) is also incorrect because attending a debate will result in a good deal of information about the candidates. Choice (E) does not deal with information, but costs, so it is more of an example of the economic model. Choice (D) works because the voter is relying on an endorsement, which is a low information cue according to the passage. The correct answer is (D).

17. **B** In the final paragraph, the author states that bounded rationality is *more accurately* termed *intuitive decision making.* Since intuition and rationality are two different things, (B) is best supported. Choice (A) is not mentioned. The author does not say that bounded rationality *best* explains voter turnout, so (C) is incorrect. No prediction is made about the success of bounded rationality, so (D) should be eliminated. The author does not pass judgment on the bounded rationality model, so (E) can be eliminated. The correct answer is (B).

18. **D** The conclusion that Healthwork is less indebted is predicated on the premise that it has bought back 13 of 24 loans. The assumption is that 13 of 24 actually equals less debt. Who holds the loans and the risk of bankruptcy are irrelevant to the argument; eliminate (A), (B), and (E). Choice (C) is stronger than the argument requires, and also the security of Healthwork is not the issue; eliminate (C). Choice (D) tells you that Healthwork did not borrow to accomplish the buyback, so they really do have less debt. The correct answer is (D).

19. **A** The plan is to control the rats with poison. The two main assumptions for any plan are that the plan will work and that the plan will not create any additional problems. Choice (A) eliminates a potential problem of the plan, poisoning livestock, so keep it. Choice (B) would therefore seem to undermine the argument; eliminate it. The most effective means of controlling the befurred vole is out of the scope of the argument, so eliminate (C). The price of the poison is irrelevant and the timing of it is irrelevant; eliminate (D) and (E). The correct answer is (A).

20. **E** *During...being installed* is awkward. *During* indicates that a process is occurring, which obviates the need to use the verb *being. During...installation* is more concise and contains the same meaning. That eliminates (A), (B), and (C). When there are two possibilities, *whether* is preferred to *if.* Choice (E) is the only choice that uses *installation* and *whether,* so it is the correct answer.

21. **B** *A politician and a civic activist* are meant to modify *Benjamin Franklin,* but as the original sentence is written, they modify the fire department and library. Choice (C) doesn't correct this error, in fact it moves *Benjamin Franklin* even further from the modifiers (*politician* and *civic activist*). Choices (D) and (E) are both grammatically incorrect; both are also very awkward, and (E), like (A) and (C), is in the passive voice. Choice (B) brings the modified (*Benjamin Franklin*) next to the modifiers, reads clearly and simply, and is in the active voice (*Benjamin Franklin founded* instead of *were founded by Benjamin Franklin*). Choice (B) is the correct answer.

22.　E　The study says two things: that many Americans do not have enough money, and that many Americans are not likely to have enough money. Choice (E) is the only answer that produces a sentence that clearly expresses this meaning. For (A) and (C), the lack of an additional verb makes it unclear that the sentence has transitioned from the present to a projection about the future and makes the sentence grammatically incorrect. Choice (B) produces a second clause that suggests that Americans *are* likely to have enough, which is a contrast to the first clause and would therefore require a conjunction that shows contrast, like *but* or *however*. Choice (D) is extremely awkward, makes the meaning of the second part of the sentence unclear, and makes the sentence grammatically incorrect. The use of *nor* in (E) guides the reader through the sentence, implying that the sentence will continue to be about lack. It is simple, concise, and clear and is therefore the correct answer.

23.　A　In this passage, the author states that the most important goal of a manager is to articulate a business plan, one based on a *cause-and-effect* theory. The author goes on to state that many managers do not do this. The second half of the passage indicates that if managers were to do this, they may be able to increase their performance measures. This makes (A) the correct answer. Choice (B) is close, but is too extreme. The passage doesn't say that it is *essential* to success to understand causal mechanisms. Choice (C) is not the right answer; the passage doesn't explain how to create a model, just what kind of model is desirable. Choice (D) is not supported by the passage at all. Choice (E) is part of the passage, but is not the primary purpose. The passage deals predominantly with cause-and-effect theories, not just criticism. The correct answer is (A).

24.　E　Answering this question requires an understanding of the argument made in the last paragraph. The author concludes that managers *may be able to increase their businesses performance measures* by using causal mechanisms. The premise is that managers prompted with a causal mechanism were *better able to interpret and exploit the data*. Thus, the missing assumption is that a better ability to interpret and exploit data leads to increased performance measures. This is what (E) says. Whether or not the managers were aware of causal mechanisms, as in (A), is irrelevant to the argument. Nor is the type of company the managers are drawn from, as (B) states. Choice (C) is not a necessary part of the argument; the argument simply states that both types provide a benefit, not that the benefits are equal. It doesn't matter whether the managers could correctly attribute their increased skills; the only point is that they showed the ability. Thus (D) is incorrect. The correct answer is (E).

25.　A　The first paragraph asserts that cause-and-effect theories are important to successful business plans. The second paragraph presents an empirical example that gives confirmation of this view, as (A) states. No further tests are suggested, so (B) is not supported. The passage does not introduce an alternative theory, making (C) incorrect. Choice (D) is tempting, but the word *prove* is too strong; the experiment lends confirmation to the theory, but does not prove it. Choice (E) is also too strong. The second paragraph lends support to a viewpoint, but doesn't demonstrate its superiority. The correct answer is (A).

26.　D　The contradiction here is that although there are more opera houses, and more giving, average audiences are down. There must be a cause for smaller audiences. Musical theater is unrelated to this argument, so eliminate (A). The incentives of the tax and construction codes may explain half of the paradox, but not the decline in average audiences, so eliminate (B) and (C). There is nothing in the argument to indicate that the new works are relevant; eliminate (E). That leaves (D): unamplified sound might require smaller halls, and therefore smaller audiences, even though there are more halls overall. The correct answer is (D).

27. **D** The argument concludes that solar radiation can interfere with TV remotes, since solar radiation can create alterations in the low end of the radiation spectrum, and infrared radiation is a low-end radiation. The argument assumes that the alteration will interfere with the operation of the TV remote. The measurement of the variation, as well as the distortions in the high end of the spectrum, are irrelevant; eliminate (A) and (E). The fact that some remotes use radio signals to compensate for distortion does not actually prove that the distortion affects the remotes; eliminate (B). Choice (C) would seem to weaken the argument, if anything; eliminate it. Choice (D) links the alteration to the remotes' operation. The correct answer is (D).

28. **C** Look for the answer that must be true, based on the statements given. Although income inequality is increasing, there is no evidence of hardship or civil unrest, so eliminate (B) and (D). Although average wages are falling it goes too far to say that the economy is shrinking; eliminate (A). Although you know that the income inequality is increasing, you do not know that it will continue to do so; eliminate (E). Choice (C) is consistent with the information given. The correct answer is (C).

29. **D** The fatal flaws in the original sentence are the improper pronouns, *he* and *his*. *He* and *his* refer to *the office of the Commissioner of Baseball*, which is an office, not a man. Therefore *it* and *its* should be used, and (A), (B), and (C) can be eliminated. Choice (E) is unnecessarily wordy in several places; *that were falling under its jurisdiction* is especially awkward. Choice (D) uses the correct pronouns and is clear. It is the correct choice.

30. **E** Look for the answer that must be true, based on the statements given. Simply because someone currently lacks personal resources does not mean they can never develop them; eliminate (A). The argument does not deal with the likelihood someone will be a success; eliminate (B) and (D). You don't know anything about the numbers of successful business leaders of wealthy or non-wealthy backgrounds; eliminate (C). This leaves (E): if all people with deep personal resources have undergone trials, then if you have not undergone trials you do not have deep personal resources. The correct answer is (E).

31. **D** In the original sentence, *typically being those* is awkward—the verb is unnecessary and the present continuous tense is strange in a statement that is explicitly about people that lived hundreds of years ago. Also, *in Korea* separates *Christianity* from the clause in the beginning of the sentence that aims to modify it. In (B), the switch from the past tense in the first clause (*introduced*) to the past perfect tense in the second (*had grown*) suggests that Christianity's growth occurred before its introduction. Choice (C) removes the awkward *typically being those*, but *Christianity* is further removed from its modifier (the clause about its introduction), making the sentence even more clumsy. In (E), the sentence doesn't state where Christianity has been introduced—where the sentence takes place—until over halfway through the sentence, making the sentence difficult to understand. Also *who typically were* could be reduced to *typically* without any loss of meaning. Choice (D) puts the subject directly after its modifying phrase, and it clarifies the location immediately after that. *Typically those* is also better than *typically being those* or *who typically were those*. Choice (D) is the correct answer.

32. **B** The proper idiom is *so much X that Y.* In the original sentence, *and so* doesn't fit the idiom, nor is it a proper conjunction. *And* links two common clauses; *so* links a cause to an effect. There is no reason to use the two together. Choice (C) has that problem, and it also has an awkward construction in *trumpeted that it is.* Choices (D) and (E) use the pronoun *they* before its antecedent *many astronomers.* A pronoun should never precede its antecedent. Choice (B) gets the idiom right and avoids the use of the *they* before *many astronomers.* It is the correct answer.

33. **B** The passage begins by introducing a *debate* over the role of sense data in the scientific field. The rest of the passage shows the shortcomings inherent in two views of justification in the sciences. Choice (B) is the best match for the passage. Choice (A) is incorrect because the controversy is not in the scientific community, but in the philosophic community. Choice (C) is incorrect because the problem is not solved. Choice (D) is not right because the issue is not about the *meaning of science.* Choice (E) is incorrect because the passage is not about the scientific method, but science in general. The correct answer is (B).

34. **C** The passage describes the problem of infinite regress as one in which *The statements used to justify a proposition must themselves be justified, and so too those statements, into infinity.* This problem could be avoided if some of the statements in the chain do not need to be justified, as (C) states. Choice (A) confuses the two forms of justification. Choice (B) doesn't matter because the point is that, even if the argument is sound, more arguments must be used to justify the argument. Choice (D) won't help because even if the initial argument is sound, the passage states that more arguments are needed to justify the first argument. The number of statements is not the issue, as (E) indicates. The correct answer is (C).

35. **E** To answer this question, use Process of Elimination on the choices. Choice (A) should be eliminated because it goes too far. The author considers two forms of justification and rejects them, but that does not mean there are not other, valid forms of justification. Choice (B) is incorrect because the author does not indicate that those are the only two methods of justification. The author never states that a combination of the methods is workable, so (C) is wrong. Choice (D) is not correct because the author states that science *strives for the universal.* That is not the same as saying that all scientific knowledge must be universal. Choice (E) is supported in the second paragraph, *Unless we allow that scientific statements be accepted on faith alone…then we must have some way of justifying our propositions.* Thus, without justification, science becomes dogmatic. The correct answer is (E).

36. **B** In the original sentence, people in Canada are compared to the country the United States. People should be compared with people, countries with countries, but not people with countries. Both *the rate of saving,* and *their rate of saving,* are correct: one refers to the nation's saving rate, the other to individuals' savings rate, both of which are acceptable. In (C), it is unclear what the United States possesses; apostrophe-s should not be used here. For (D), *the rate of money earned…* is incorrect, it should read, *the rate at which money is earned….* Similarly, in (E), *the rate people earn money* should be *the rate at which people earn money.* Choice (B) is clear and direct, and it is the correct choice.

37. **C** In the original statement *ruling* is not a proper verb construction. In (B), the pronoun *they* is inconsistent with its antecedent *a panel of judges*; *it* would be correct. *Because of being* is also unnecessarily awkward—*because it was* is simpler and better. The use of *after* in (D) makes the transition from past tense (*was reviewed*) to the present tense (*rules*) clearer; however, it contains the awkward phrase *because of being.* Choice (E) results in a sentence fragment. Choice (C) uses

after so the reader can anticipate the coming switch in tenses; the verb *rules* is correct for the singular subject *a panel of judges*; and it uses the simple, clear phrase *because it was*. Choice (C) is the correct answer.

38. **B**   The Union management's position is that the workers will be protected since the media are there. They are assuming that the management will change their actions based on the presence of the media. The composition of the media coverage is irrelevant, so cross off (A). Choice (B) directly addresses the issue of media, so keep it. The length of the strike and the financial resources of the union are irrelevant to that point, so eliminate (C) and (E). Whether the management has retaliated against previous strikes might be of interest to the workers, but it doesn't affect the management's argument so eliminate (D). The correct answer is (B).

39. **C**   The key is to stay within the boundaries of the statements. The argument states that if demand stays the same, and nuclear power vanishes, then prices go up. The only variable that is relevant is demand; eliminate (A), (B), (D), and (E) because they do not address demand. Only (C) addresses demand, so the correct answer is (C).

40. **A**   The key thing for identifying the reasoning questions is to match the answer to what the speaker is doing. The Candy Manufacturer states that sugar is natural, not artificial; the assumption is that this makes sugar somehow preferable to artificial sweeteners. But even so, the Manufacturer has not addressed the main point of the dentist, which is that the Manufacturer *intends* to harm children's teeth. For this reason the main flaw of the Candy Manufacturer's argument is that it does not connect his point about artificiality to the Dentist's argument about intention. Choice (A) does this. You can eliminate (B), (C), and (D) because they do not deal with intention. Choice (E) you can eliminate because the Manufacturer does not deal with the premise of the Dentist's argument. The correct answer is (A).

41. **C**   *On account of* is awkward, and *being killed by* is in the passive voice. Choice (B) still has some of the awkwardness of the original sentence, and it also mistakenly uses the plural *their being* (the subject of the sentence, *the pacific salmon*, is singular). Choice (D) is unnecessarily awkward and passive, and (E) is extremely awkward and incorrectly uses the plural pronoun, *they*. Choice (C) uses the correct singular pronoun *it*. It is also simple and direct: *because* is the best way to introduce a clause that demonstrates a causal relationship. Choice (C) is the correct answer.

Integrated
Reasoning

MEET THE INTEGRATED REASONING SECTION

The Integrated Reasoning section is 30 minutes long and takes the place of one of the GMAT essays. You'll see it as the second section of your test. Officially, there are only 12 questions, which sounds pretty great. However, most of those questions have multiple parts. So, for example, a Table Analysis question—one of the new question types we'll discuss—usually has four statements that you need to evaluate. So, your answer to the question really consists of four separate responses. For the entire section, you'll actually need to select approximately 30 different responses.

Integrated Reasoning Is Not Adaptive

Unlike the Quantitative and Verbal sections, the Integrated Reasoning section is not adaptive. So, you won't see harder questions if you keep answering questions correctly. That's good news because it means that you'll more easily be able to focus your attention on the current question rather than worrying whether you got the previous question right!

Test writers refer to non-adaptive sections as linear. Pacing for a linear section is different from the pacing that we reviewed for the adaptive Quantitative and Verbal sections. For Integrated Reasoning, pacing is motivated by two general principles.

Pacing Guidelines
1. Work the easier questions first. As you'll see, many Integrated Reasoning questions call for more than one response per question.

2. Don't get stubborn. With so many questions to answer in only 30 minutes, the Integrated Reasoning section can seem very fast paced. Spending too much time on one question means that you may not get to see all of the questions. Sometimes it's best to guess and move on.

Integrated Reasoning Scores

The Integrated Reasoning section is scored on a scale from 1 to 8 in one point increments. While GMAC has not released too many details about how they calculate this score, there are two key facts to keep in mind:

- **Scoring is all or nothing.** Most Integrated Reasoning questions include multiple parts. To get credit for the question, you must select the correct response for each part. For example, Table Analysis questions generally include three statements that you must evaluate. If you select the wrong response for even one of these statements, you get no credit for the entire question.

- **There are experimental questions.** GMAC has stated that the Integrated Reasoning section contains experimental questions that do not count toward your score. They have not, however, stated how many experimental questions there are in the section. It's likely that somewhere between two to four of the questions are experimental, so if you find a question particularly difficult or time-consuming, don't be afraid to move on, as it might not even count.

To score the section, GMAC first calculates a raw score. You get one point for each non-experimental question that you get completely correct. Then, your raw score is converted to an Integrated Reasoning scaled score from 1 to 8.

There's a Calculator

There's an onscreen calculator available for the Integrated Reasoning section. The calculator is not available, however, for the Quantitative section. For the Quantitative section, you still need to perform any necessary calculations by hand.

The calculator for the Integrated Reasoning section is relatively basic. There are buttons to perform the four standard operations: addition, subtraction, multiplication, and division. In addition, buttons to take a square root, find a percent, and take a reciprocal round out the available functions. There are also buttons to store and recall a value in the calculator's memory.

To use the calculator, you'll need to open it by clicking on the "calculator" button in the upper left corner of your screen. The calculator will generally open in the middle of your screen, but you can move it around so that you can see the text of the problem or the numbers on any charts or graphs that are part of the question. The calculator is available for all Integrated Reasoning questions. You can enter a number into the calculator either by clicking on the onscreen number buttons or by typing the number using the keyboard.

Here's what the calculator looks like:

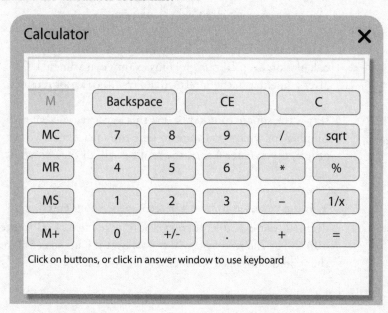

For the most part, the keys on the onscreen calculator work like you might expect. However, a few keys may not work as expected. Oddly enough, that's particularly true if you are used to using a more sophisticated calculator. So, here are few tips about using some of the calculator keys:

MC   MC is the memory clear key. Use this key to wipe out any values that you have stored in the calculator's memory.

MR   MR is the memory recall key. Use this key to return any value that you have stored in the memory to the calculation area. For example, if you want to divide the number currently on your screen by the number in the memory, you would enter the key sequence / MR =.

MS   MS is the memory store key. Use this key to store the number currently on the screen in the calculator's memory.

M+   M+ is the memory addition key. Use this key to add the current onscreen number to the number in the calculator's memory. For example, if 2 is stored in the calculator's memory and 3 is on screen, then clicking M+ will result in 5 being stored in the calculator's memory.

Backspace   Backspace is used to clear the last digit entered. Use this key to correct mistakes when entering numbers without clearing the entire number. For example, if you entered 23 but meant to enter 25, click backspace then enter 5.

CE   CE is the clear entry button. Use this button to correct a mistake when entering a longer calculation without starting over. For example, suppose you entered 2*3+5 but you meant to enter 2*3+9. If you click on CE right after you enter 5, your screen will show 6, the result of 2*3, and you can now enter +9= to finish your intended calculation.

C   C is the clear key. Use this key when you want to start a calculation over. In our previous example, if you click C after you enter 5, the intermediate result, 6, is not retained.

sqrt   sqrt is the square root key. Click this key after you enter the number for which you want to take the square root. For example, if you enter 4 sqrt, the result 2 will display on your screen.

%   % is the key used to take a percentage without entering a decimal. For example, if you want to take 20% of 400, enter 400*20%. The result 80 will now show on your screen. Note that you do not need to enter = after you click %.

Calculator Practice Tip

When you practice for the Integrated Reasoning section, use a calculator similar to the calculator provided by GMAC. If you are doing online practice, use the onscreen calculator. If you are working problems from this book, use a basic calculator rather than that fancy calculator that you might still have from your high school or college math classes.

1/x is used to take a reciprocal. Click this key after you enter the number for which you want to take the reciprocal. For example, the keystrokes 2 followed by 1/x produces the result 0.5 on your screen. Again, note that you do not need to enter = after you click 1/x.

Be sure that you thoroughly understand the way the keys for the onscreen calculator work so as to avoid errors and wasted time when you take your GMAT.

THE QUESTION TYPES

There are four question types in the Integrated Reasoning section. These question types are mostly used to test the same type of content that is tested in the Quantitative section. So, expect to calculate percents and averages. You'll also be asked to make a lot of inferences based on the data presented in the various charts, graphs, and tables that accompany the questions. So, the format of these questions may take some getting used to but the content will probably seem familiar.

Let's take a more detailed look at each of the question types.

Table Analysis

TABLE ANALYSIS

Table Analysis questions present data in a table. If you've ever seen a spreadsheet—and really, who hasn't?—you'll feel right at home. Most tables will have 5 to 10 columns and anywhere from 6 to 25 rows. You'll be able to sort the data in the table by each column heading. The sort function is fairly basic, however. If you're used to how you can sort first by a column such as state and then a column such as city to produce an alphabetical list of cities by state, you can't do that sort of sorting for these questions. You can only sort by one column at a time.

Here's what a table analysis question looks like:

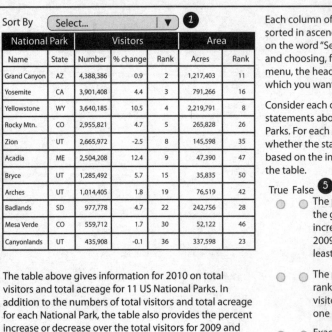

Sort By Select... ▼ ①

| National Park | | Visitors | | | Area | |
Name	State	Number	% change	Rank	Acres	Rank
Grand Canyon	AZ	4,388,386	0.9	2	1,217,403	11
Yosemite	CA	3,901,408	4.4	3	791,266	16
Yellowstone	WY	3,640,185	10.5	4	2,219,791	8
Rocky Mtn.	CO	2,955,821	4.7	5	265,828	26
Zion	UT	2,665,972	-2.5	8	145,598	35
Acadia	ME	2,504,208	12.4	9	47,390	47
Bryce	UT	1,285,492	5.7	15	35,835	50
Arches	UT	1,014,405	1.8	19	76,519	42
Badlands	SD	977,778	4.7	22	242,756	28
Mesa Verde	CO	559,712	1.7	30	52,122	46
Canyonlands	UT	435,908	-0.1	36	337,598	23

Each column of the table can be ② sorted in ascending order by clicking on the word "Select" above the table and choosing, from the drop-down menu, the heading of the column on which you want the table to be sorted.

Consider each of the following ③ statements about these National Parks. For each statement indicate whether the statement is true or false, based on the information provided in the table.

True False ⑤

○ ○ The park that experienced the greatest percent increase in visitors from 2009 to 2010 also had the least total acreage.

○ ○ The park with the median rank by the number of visitors is larger than only one other park by acreage.

○ ○ Exactly 20% of the parks with ranks less than 40 by acreage and showing positive growth in visitors were in Utah (UT).

○ ○ The total number of visitors at Arches in 2009 was less than 1,000,000.

The table above gives information for 2010 on total visitors and total acreage for 11 US National Parks. In addition to the numbers of total visitors and total acreage for each National Park, the table also provides the percent increase or decrease over the total visitors for 2009 and the rank of the National Park for total visitors and total acreage in 2010. ④

One thing you won't see on your screen when you take the Integrated Reasoning section are the circled numbers. We've added those so we can talk about different parts of a Table Analysis question. Here's what each circled number represents:

① This is the Sort By drop-down box. When opened, you'll see all the different ways that you can sort the data in the table. For this table, for example, the possibilities are National Park Name, National Park State, Visitors Number, Visitors % change, Visitors Rank, Area Acreage, and Area Rank. You can always sort by every column.

② These are the standard directions for a Table Analysis question. These directions are the same for every Table Analysis question. So, once you've read these directions once, you don't really need to bother reading them again.

③ These lines are additional directions. These directions are slightly tailored to the question. However, they'll always tell you to base your answers on the information in the table. These directions will also always tell you which type of choice you are making for each statement: true/false, yes/no, agree/disagree, etc. Again, you can probably get by without reading these most of the time.

④ These lines explain the table. Mostly, this information will recap the column headings from the table. Occasionally, you can learn some additional information by reading this explanatory text. For example, the explanatory text for this table states that the Visitors Number column is for 2010 and that % change column shows the change from 2009 to 2010.

⑤ These statements are the questions. Typically, there are four statements and you need to evaluate and select an answer for each. If you try to move to the next question without selecting a response for one or more statements, a pop-up window will open informing you that you have not selected an answer for all statements. You cannot leave any part of the question blank.

If you read through the statements, you may have noticed that the questions asked you to do things such as calculate a percentage or find a median. That's typical for Table Analysis questions. You've probably also realized just how helpful the sorting function can be in answering some questions.

TABLE ANALYSIS DRILLS

Item 1:

Student Scores at XYZ College

Kind of Business	Estimate		Actual								
	Jan-June 2010 Est	Rank	Jan	Feb	March	April	May	June	6 Month Total	% Change 2009	% of Estimated Sales
Motor vehicle & parts dealers	402,357	1	61,592	58,779	54,655	60,005	61,547	69,397	365,412	−1.5	90.82%
Food services & drinking places	370,880	2	42,311	49,887	45,332	48,776	58,672	53,221	298,199	1	80.40%
Food & beverage stores	342,564	3	51,650	52,346	52,122	55,432	54,332	52,266	318,148	0.2	92.87%
General merchandise stores	310,755	4	51,148	48,366	51,777	49,588	46,166	53,108	300,153	0.1	96.59%
Gasoline stations	254,678	5	34,970	38,999	35,798	32,667	37,596	39,880	219,910	−2.5	86.35%
Health & personal care stores	226,629	6	25,699	34,577	32,987	38,791	30,912	19,776	182,742	−6.3	80.63%
Non-store retailers	180,765	7	35,604	33,980	39,887	34,576	33,761	35,972	213,780	3.7	118.26%
Building materials & supplies	175,664	8	22,986	19,887	18,330	19,877	17,776	15,998	114,854	−4.3	65.38%
Clothing & clothing accessories	175,638	9	21,345	17,498	14,665	23,457	21,789	28,229	126,983	0.2	72.30%
Electronics & appliance stores	77,892	10	7,658	7,652	8,235	7,399	7,685	8,692	47,321	−0.3	60.75%
Furniture & home furn. stores	72,434	11	9,987	9,076	9,087	10,998	10,332	11,002	60,482	0.3	83.50%
Miscellaneous store retailers	60,998	12	6,592	8,196	9,934	9,922	9,065	9,732	53,441	1.1	87.61%
Hobby, book, & music	49,877	13	7,793	8,072	8,973	9,982	9,057	10,227	54,104	4.9	108.47%

The table above shows estimated and realized monthly and total sales in millions of dollars for the first six months of 2010. These 13 categories were chosen because they comprise the largest publicly-held non-financial companies worldwide. Percent change from the same period in 2009 is given. Actual sales as a percent of estimated sales are also calculated.

Each column of the table can be sorted in ascending order by clicking on the word "Select" above the table and choosing, from the drop-down menu, the heading of the column on which you want the table to be sorted.

Consider each of the following statements about the information on the previous page. For each statement indicate whether the statement is true or false, based on the information provided in the table.

	True	False	
Question 1-1	○	○	The category experiencing the smallest percent change in sales from 2009 has the sales estimate closest to 100% of actual sales for 2010.
Question 1-2	○	○	The category with the median rank based on estimated sales for 2010 is the same as the category with the median 6-month sales total based on actual sales for 2010.
Question 1-3	○	○	The total number of actual sales for Building materials & supplies during the same period in 2009 was approximately $120,000.
Question 1-4	○	○	For all categories in which there was a decrease in sales from 2009 to 2010, there was greater than a 10% difference between actual and estimated sales.

Item 2:

Patient	Dose of Medication A (mg)	Dose of Medication B (mg)	Dose of Medication C (mg)	Age	Sex
AD	3.5	4.1	2.4	13	F
CA	3.2	2.1	0.2	34	M
DE	2.8	3.4	0	65	F
DS	1.2	0	1.3	11	M
ED	1.8	2.3	0	24	F
EG	1.9	2.4	2.5	43	M
FA	2.3	1.2	2.3	58	F
GE	2.3	4.1	2.3	35	M
SE	2.8	3.7	3.2	63	M

The table above provides information on a sample of participants in a medical trial. Each patient is identified by a two-letter code. For each patient, the table lists the patient's dose of three medications – A, B, and C – in milligrams (mg), the patient's age, and the patient's sex – Male (M) or Female (F). The "total dose" is defined as the sum of the patient's doses for medications A, B, and C.

Each column of the table can be sorted in ascending order by clicking on the word "Select" above the table and choosing, from the drop-down menu, the heading of the column on which you want the table to be sorted.

Alternate Sort 1: *Age*

Patient	Dose of Medication A (mg)	Dose of Medication B (mg)	Dose of Medication C (mg)	Age	Sex
DS	1.2	0	1.3	11	M
AD	3.5	4.1	2.4	13	F
ED	1.8	2.3	0	24	F
CA	3.2	2.1	0.2	34	M
GE	2.3	4.1	2.3	35	M
EG	1.9	2.4	2.5	43	M
FA	2.3	1.2	2.3	58	F
SE	2.8	3.7	3.2	63	M
DE	2.8	3.4	0	65	F

Alternate Sort 2: *Dose of Medication B*

Patient	Dose of Medication A (mg)	Dose of Medication B (mg)	Dose of Medication C (mg)	Age	Sex
DS	1.2	0	1.3	11	M
ED	1.8	2.3	0	24	F
EG	1.9	2.4	2.5	43	M
FA	2.3	1.2	2.3	58	F
GE	2.3	4.1	2.3	35	M
DE	2.8	3.4	0	65	F
SE	2.8	3.7	3.2	63	M
CA	3.2	2.1	0.2	34	F
AD	3.5	4.1	2.4	13	M

Consider each of the following questions about the medical trial. For each statement indicate whether the question has an answer with a value between 40% and 60%, exclusively.

	Yes	No	
Question 2-1	○	○	The percent of males in the sample who are older than the average (arithmetic mean) age for males in the sample.
Question 2-2	○	○	The total dose of the female with the greatest dose of Medication A given as a percent of the total dose of the male with the greatest dose of Medication A.
Question 2-3	○	○	The percent of the median-aged patient's total dose that Medication B comprises.
Question 2-4	○	○	The percent by which the median female age is greater than the median male age.

Item 3:

EMR		Installations			Adverse Events			
Vendor	Location	Number	% Change	Rank	Total	% Change	Preventable	Fatal
Meditech	MA	1,212	10.4	1	10,452	12.4	8,412	28
Cerner	MO	606	8.6	2	10,312	16.2	8,624	18
McKesson	GA	573	15.4	3	10,002	5.4	9,142	21
Epic	WI	413	7.3	4	9,896	16.3	8,546	42
Siemens	PA	397	−1.2	5	11,453	17.5	10,412	83
CPSI	AL	392	0.4	6	8,432	1.2	8,132	25
HMS	TN	347	3.2	7	7,421	4.4	7,003	31
Self-Developed	—	273	18.4	8	8,321	0.02	6,895	17
Healthland	MN	223	−2.4	9	5,612	-2.1	4,590	45
Allscripts	GA	185	−6.1	10	5,212	-5.3	4,784	27

The table above gives information for 2011 on vendors, installations, and associated usability ratings for 10 types of Enterprise Electronic Medical Record (EMR) systems. In addition to total installations and the number of adverse events, the table also gives the percent change in the total installations and adverse events from 2010 to 2011 and the rank of the EMR for total installations. The table also includes the number of the adverse events that were preventable and the number that were fatal.

Each column of the table can be sorted in ascending order by clicking on the word "Select" above the table and choosing, from the drop-down menu, the heading of the column on which you want the table to be sorted.

Alternate Sort 1: *Installations - % Change*

EMR		Installations			Adverse Events			
Vendor	Location	Number	% Change	Rank	Total	% Change	Preventable	Fatal
Allscripts	GA	185	-6.1	10	5,212	−5.3	4,784	27
Healthland	MN	223	−2.4	9	5,612	−2.1	4,590	45
Siemens	PA	397	−1.2	5	11,453	17.5	10,412	83
CPSI	AL	392	0.4	6	8,432	1.2	8,132	25
HMS	TN	347	3.2	7	7,421	4.4	7,003	31
Epic	WI	413	7.3	4	9,896	16.3	8,546	42
Cerner	MO	606	8.6	2	10,312	16.2	8,624	18
Meditech	MA	1,212	10.4	1	10,452	12.4	8,412	28
McKesson	GA	573	15.4	3	10,002	5.4	9,142	21
Self-Developed	—	273	18.4	8	8,321	0.02	6,895	17

Alternate Sort 2: *Adverse Events - Total*

EMR		Installations			Adverse Events			
Vendor	Location	Number	% Change	Rank	Total	% Change	Preventable	Fatal
Allscripts	GA	185	−6.1	10	5,212	−5.3	4,784	27
Healthland	MN	223	−2.4	9	5,612	−2.1	4,590	45
HMS	TN	347	3.2	7	7,421	4.4	7,003	31
Self-Developed	—	273	18.4	8	8,321	0.02	6,895	17
CPSI	AL	392	0.4	6	8,432	1.2	8,132	25
Epic	WI	413	7.3	4	9,896	16.3	8,546	42
McKesson	GA	573	15.4	3	10,002	5.4	9,142	21
Cerner	MO	606	8.6	2	10,312	16.2	8,624	18
Meditech	MA	1,212	10.4	1	10,452	12.4	8,412	28
Siemens	PA	397	−1.2	5	11,453	17.5	10,412	83

Consider each of the following statements about EMRs. For each statement indicate whether the statement is supported based on the information provided in the table.

	Yes	No	
Question 3-1	○	○	In 2011, The EMR Vendor having the second greatest number of installations had both the third greatest number of adverse events and the lowest number of fatal adverse events.
Question 3-2	○	○	In 2010, there were approximately 197 installations of the Allscripts EMR.
Question 3-3	○	○	The ratio of preventable adverse events to fatal adverse events, for the EMR that experienced the second greatest percent decrease in total installations from 2010 to 2011, is 102:1.
Question 3-4	○	○	The EMR that ranks ninth in total installations has reduced the total number of adverse events since 2010, but still ranks second in terms of the number of fatal adverse events.

Item 4:

Country	# of Pan-Global Games (Judge)	Average Score (Judge)	Highest Score Given	Lowest Score Given	# of Pan-Global Games (Competitor)	Average Score (Competitor)
Albania	1	6.7	9.2	5.4	1	8.6
Estonia	2	8.4	9	6.9	3	7.7
Finland	3	6.2	8.9	4.2	2	8.5
Germany	3	8.2	9.4	7.6	2	8.3
Japan	1	7.3	9.7	6.4	3	8.8
Norway	2	7.9	8.4	5.2	4	6.5
Russia	5	6.8	9.6	5.4	3	7
South Korea	3	7.9	9.3	6.3	2	8.3
United States	4	8.1	9.2	7.1	2	7.1

The table above provides information on a group of judges at the 2012 Pan-Global Games. The table lists the country each judge represents, the number of Pan-Global Games each had participated in as a judge, the average (arithmetic mean) score given as a judge, highest score given as a judge, lowest score given as a judge, the number of Pan-Global Games each had participated in as a competitor, and the average (arithmetic mean) score received as a competitor. The scores are given on a scale from 1 – 10 in increments of one-tenth of a point.

Each column of the table can be sorted in ascending order by clicking on the word "Select" above the table and choosing, from the drop-down menu, the heading of the column on which you want the table to be sorted.

Alternate Sort 1: *Number of Pan-Global Games (Judge)*

Country	# of Pan-Global Games (Judge)	Average Score (Judge)	Highest Score Given	Lowest Score Given	# of Pan-Global Games (Competitor)	Average Score (Competitor)
Albania	1	6.7	9.2	5.4	1	8.6
Japan	1	7.3	9.7	6.4	3	8.8
Estonia	2	8.4	9	6.9	3	7.7
Norway	2	7.9	8.4	5.2	4	6.5
Finland	3	6.2	8.9	4.2	2	8.5
Germany	3	8.2	9.4	7.6	2	8.3
South Korea	3	7.9	9.3	6.3	2	8.3
United States	4	8.1	9.2	7.1	2	7.1
Russia	5	6.8	9.6	5.4	3	7

Alternate Sorts 2: *Number of Pan-Global Games (Competitor)*

Country	# of Pan-Global Games (Judge)	Average Score (Judge)	Highest Score Given	Lowest Score Given	# of Pan-Global Games (Competitor)	Average Score (Competitor)
Albania	1	6.7	9.2	5.4	1	8.6
Finland	3	6.2	8.9	4.2	2	8.5
Germany	3	8.2	9.4	7.6	2	8.3
South Korea	3	7.9	9.3	6.3	2	8.3
United States	4	8.1	9.2	7.1	2	7.1
Japan	1	7.3	9.7	6.4	3	8.8
Estonia	2	8.4	9	6.9	3	7.7
Russia	5	6.8	9.6	5.4	3	7
Norway	2	7.9	8.4	5.2	4	6.5

Consider each of the following statements about the Pan-Global Games judges' scores. For each statement indicate whether the statement is supported based on the information provided in the table.

	Yes	No	
Question 4-1	○	○	On average, the lowest score given by judges who had judged in 3 Pan-Global Games was higher than that given by judges who had competed in 3 Pan-Global Games.
Question 4-2	○	○	The judge with the greatest absolute difference between the highest score given and lowest score given also had the greatest percent difference between the lowest score given and highest score given.
Question 4-3	○	○	The average (arithmetic mean) number of Pan-Global Games that judges participated in as judges was higher than the average number of Pan-Global Games that judges participated in as competitors.
Question 4-4	○	○	The probability that a given judge competed in more Pan-Global Games than she judged is the same as the probability that a judge gave a higher average score as a judge than she received as a competitor.

Check your answers on page 95.

Table Analysis
Answers and
Explanations

ANSWER KEY

Table Analysis

Item 1
Question 1-1: True
Question 1-2: False
Question 1-3: True
Question 1-4: False

Item 2
Question 2-1: No
Question 2-2: No
Question 2-3: Yes
Question 2-4: No

Item 3
Question 3-1: No
Question 3-2: Yes
Question 3-3: Yes
Question 3-4: Yes

Item 4
Question 4-1: No
Question 4-2: Yes
Question 4-3: Yes
Question 4-4: Yes

EXPLANATIONS:

Item 1:

1-1.   True
The category experiencing the smallest percent change from 2009 to 2010 was General Merchandise Stores, with a 0.1 percent change. Realize that the smallest percent change is the number closest to 0. A negative percent change wouldn't necessarily be a smaller change. The estimate for this category was also closest to actual sales. The estimate was 96.59% of actual sales, which is closer to 100% than any other estimate.

1-2.   False
The category with the median rank based on estimated sales for 2010 is the one ranked 7th out of 13, which is Non-store retailers. However, when you sort the column with the actual 6-month total sales, this category comes in 6th, so these ranks are not the same.

1-3.   True
Use your calculator to figure out the sales figure for 2009 for Building materials & supplies. The percent change is -4.3, so that means that the 2010 sales figure is 95.7% (100 - 4.3) of the 2009 sales figure. You ask yourself: 114,854 is 95.7% of what number? Translated into algebra: $114,854 = 0.957x$. Divide both sides by 0.957:

$$\frac{114,854}{0.957} = x \qquad x = 120,014.63$$

So the 2009 figure was about $120,000, which makes this statement true.

1-4.   False
If you do a sort on the % Change 2009 column, you see that the sales categories for which there was a decline from 2009 to 2010 were: Health & personal care stores, Building materials and supplies, Gasoline stations, Motor vehicle & parts dealers, and Electronics and appliance stores. Most of them are more than 10% off the actual sales figure, but the actual sales figures for Motor vehicles and parts dealers were 90.82% of the estimated sales. That is less than 10% difference between the actual and estimated sales, so this statement is false.

Item 2:

2-1.   No
Divide the sum of the patients' ages by the number of patients:
$$\frac{34+11+43+35+63}{5} = 37.2$$
Of the five male patients, two, EG and SE, are older than the average. Since $\frac{2}{5}$ is 40%, the answer is not between 40% and 60%, exclusively, and the answer is No.

2-2.   No
Start by sorting the table by Dose of Medication A (mg). CA and AD are the Male and Female with greatest doses, respectively. CA's total dose is 3.2 + 2.1 + 0.2 = 5.5. AD's total dose is 3.5 + 4.1 + 2.4 = 10. To find what percent of 5.5 is 10, divide 10 by 5.5 and multiply by 100 to get approximately 181%; the answer is No.

2-3. Yes

Start by finding the patient with the median age. To do this, sort the table by Age. Since there are 9 patients, the median will be the fifth patient, GE, whose total dose is 2.3 + 4.1 + 2.3 = 8.7. Since 4.1 / 8.7 is about 0.47, Medication B makes up about 47% of the total dose; the answer is Yes.

2-4. No

Start by sorting the table by Sex. The median female Age is the average of 24 and 58, which is $\frac{24+58}{2} = 41$. The median male age is 35. To find the percent increase from 35 to 41, use the formula:

Percent Increase $= \frac{\text{difference}}{\text{original}} \times 100$ which is $\frac{41-35}{35} \times 100 \approx 17\%$. The answer is No.

Item 3:

3-1. No

First, find the EMR Vendor having the second greatest number of installations; Cerner is the Vendor having the second greatest number of installations in 2011. Next, identify the EMR Vendor having the third greatest total number of adverse events. Siemens experienced the greatest number of adverse events (11,453), Meditech experienced the second greatest number of adverse events (10,452), and Cerner experienced the third greatest number of adverse events (10,312). Finally, locate the EMR Vendor that experienced the lowest number of fatal adverse events. Self-developed EMRs experienced the lowest number, 17, of fatal adverse events. Therefore, since the EMR Vendor having the second greatest number of installations does not have both the third greatest number of adverse events and the lowest number of fatal adverse events, this statement is incorrect.

3-2. Yes

First, you need to find the number of installations of the Allscripts EMR and the percent change from 2010 to 2011. In 2011, there were 185 installations of the Allscripts EMR which represents a -6.1% change from 2010. Therefore, 185 represents 93.9% as many installations as in 2010. This gives the equation $185 = 0.939x$. Divide both sides by 0.939, and $x = 197$. Thus, in 2010, there were approximately 197 installations of the Allscripts EMR.

3-3. Yes

First, identify the EMR that experienced the second greatest percent decrease in total installations from 2010 to 2011. According to the percent change column for installations, Healthland experienced the second greatest percent decrease. Next, identify the number of preventable and fatal adverse events for the Healthland EMR. Healthland experienced 4,590 preventable adverse events and 45 fatal adverse events. Therefore, the ratio of preventable adverse events to fatal adverse events is $\frac{4,590}{45} = \frac{102}{1}$.

3-4.   Yes

First, identify the EMR that ranks ninth in terms of total installations; according to the chart, Healthland ranks ninth in this category. Next, determine whether the Healthland EMR has reduced the total number of adverse events since 2010. When you consult the percent change column adjacent to the total adverse events for the Healthland EMR, you will find that the Healthland EMR has reduced the number of adverse events by 2.1%. Finally, determine the EMR that ranks second in terms of the number of fatal adverse events. Siemens experienced the greatest number of fatal adverse events and Healthland experienced the second greatest number of fatal adverse events. Accordingly, this statement is correct.

Item 4:

4-1.   No

This question asks about the judges who had Judged in 3 Pan-Global Games, so sort the table by # of Pan-Global Games (Judge) and note the Lowest Score Given for Finland, Germany, and South Korea. To find the average, divide the total by the number of judges: $\frac{4.2+7.6+6.3}{3}=\frac{18.1}{3}\approx 6.03$. Now sort the table by # of Pan-Global Games (Competitor) and note the Lowest Score Given for Japan, Estonia, and Russia. The average is $\frac{6.4+6.9+5.4}{3}=\frac{18.7}{3}\approx 6.23$, which is greater than 6.03; therefore the statement is incorrect and the answer is No.

4-2.   Yes

Start by finding the differences between Highest Score Given and Lowest Score Given. It is useful to Ballpark here. Albania: 4, Estonia: 2, Finland: 5, Germany: 2, Japan: 3, Norway: 3, Russia: 4, South Korea: 3, and the United States: 2. Thus the country with the greatest difference is Finland (the exact difference is 8.9 − 4.2 = 4.7). Now to find the percent difference from Lowest Score Given to Highest Score Given, use the formula:

$$Percent\ Change = \frac{Highest - Lowest}{Lowest} \times 100.$$

Again, Ballparking is useful here.

Albania: $\frac{4}{5}$, Estonia: $\frac{2}{7}$, Finland: $\frac{5}{4}$, Germany: $\frac{2}{8}$, Japan: $\frac{2}{6}$, Norway: $\frac{3}{5}$, Russia: $\frac{3}{6}$, South Korea: $\frac{3}{6}$, and the United States: $\frac{2}{7}$.

Finland also has the greatest percent change (the exact percent change is $\frac{8.9-4.2}{4.2}\times 100 = \frac{4.7}{4.2}\times 100 = 111.9\%$). Therefore the answer is Yes.

4-3.   Yes

To find the average number of Pan-Global Games as a judge, add up the values in # of Pan-Global Games (Judge) and divide by the number of judges: $\frac{1+2+3+3+1+2+5+3+4}{9}=\frac{24}{9}$. Now do the same for # of Pan-Global Games (Competitor): $\frac{1+3+2+2+3+4+3+2+2}{9}=\frac{22}{9}$ which is less than $\frac{24}{9}$. Therefore the answer is Yes.

4-4.   Yes

The probability that a judge

participated in more Pan-Global Games

as a competitor than as a judge is

$\dfrac{\text{\# of judges who competed more than judged}}{\text{total \# of judges}}$.

Those judges are *Estonia*, *Japan*, and *Norway*.

Thus the probability is $\dfrac{3}{9} = \dfrac{1}{3}$. The probability

that a judge gave a higher average score as a

judge than they received as a competitor is

$\dfrac{\text{\# of judges whose score as judge} > \text{score as competitor}}{\text{total \# of judges}}$.

Those judges are *Estonia*, *Norway*, and *United

States*. Thus the probability is also $\dfrac{3}{9} = \dfrac{1}{3}$.

Therefore the answer is Yes.

Graphics
Interpretation

GRAPHICS INTERPRETATION

Now, let's take a look at the Graphics Interpretation question. For this question type, you are given one chart, graph, or image and asked to answer three questions based on that information. The questions are statements that include one drop-down box. You select your answer from the drop-down box to complete the statement.

Here's an example of a Graphics Interpretation question:

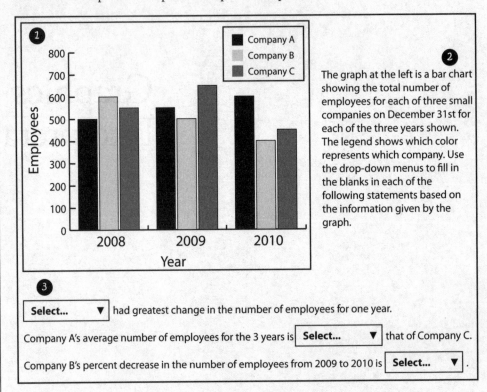

The graph at the left is a bar chart showing the total number of employees for each of three small companies on December 31st for each of the three years shown. The legend shows which color represents which company. Use the drop-down menus to fill in the blanks in each of the following statements based on the information given by the graph.

| Select... ▼ | had greatest change in the number of employees for one year.

Company A's average number of employees for the 3 years is | Select... ▼ | that of Company C.

Company B's percent decrease in the number of employees from 2009 to 2010 is | Select... ▼ | .

As with the Table Analysis questions, we've added the circled numbers so we can point out the different things that you'll see on your screen for a Graphics Interpretation question. Here's what each circled number represents:

① The chart, graph, or image is always in the upper left of the screen. As shown here, the chart will take up a good deal of the screen. It will certainly be large enough that you can clearly extract information from it. You can expect to see a variety of different types of charts or graphs including scatter plots, bar charts, line graphs, and circle (or pie) charts. For the most part, you'll see fairly standard types of graphs, however. Be sure to check out any labels on the axes as well as any sort of included legend.

② These lines are an explanation of the graph or chart. Mostly, you'll be told what the chart represents as well as what individual lines, bars, or sectors may represent. Sometimes, you'll be given some additional information such as when measurements were made. For example, here you are told that the bars show the numbers of employees for each firm on December 31st of the year in question. This information is typically extraneous to answering the questions. The explanatory information always ends with the same line about selecting your answers from the drop-down menu.

③ These are the questions. Graphics Interpretation questions typically include three statements. Each statement is typically a single sentence with one drop-down menu. Each drop-down menu typically includes three to five answer choices. Choose the answer choice that makes the statement true.

Graphics Interpretation questions mostly ask you to find relationships and trends for the data. You can also be asked to calculate percentage increases or decreases, averages, and medians.

GRAPHICS INTERPRETATION DRILLS

Item 1:

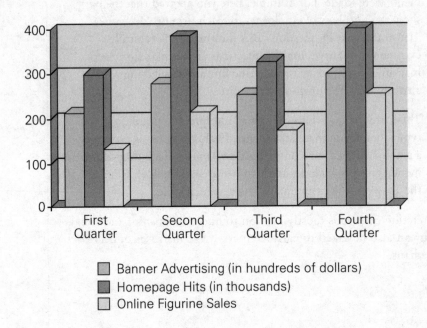

The graph above is a bar chart representing various data for TinyToys Company over the last fiscal year: Banner Advertising, Homepage Hits, and Online Figurine Sales. Use the drop-down menus to fill in the blanks in each of the following statements based on the information given by the graph.

Question 1-1:

There were _____ more homepage hits in the 4th quarter than in the 1st quarter.

      (A)   100
      (B)   400
      (C)   100,000
      (D)   700,000

Question 1-2:

The quarter that had the lowest ratio of Online Figurine Sales to Banner Advertising was the _____.

      (A)   First Quarter
      (B)   Second Quarter
      (C)   Third Quarter
      (D)   Fourth Quarter

Question 1-3:

If graphed, the slope of the line representing the overall trend in Homepage Hits would be

      (A)   positive
      (B)   negative
      (C)   zero
      (D)   undefined

Item 2:

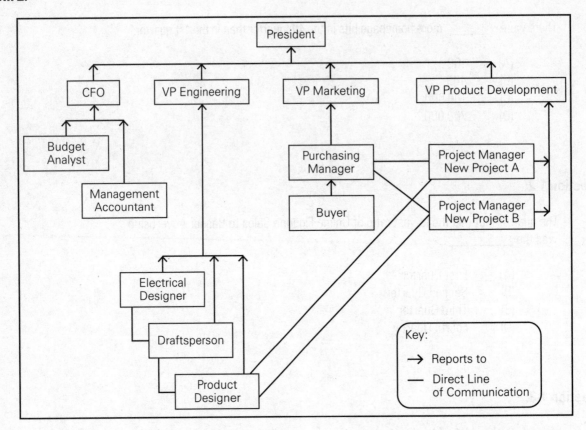

The organizational flow chart shown above shows the reporting structure of an electronics company. Any employee who reports directly to the president is at salary Level A. Employees who report to Level A employees are at salary Level B. Employees who report to Level B employees are at salary Level C. Use the drop-down menus to fill in the blanks in each of the following statements based on the information given by the graph.

Question 2-1:

A buyer is at salary Level _____.

    (A)   A
    (B)   B
    (C)   C

Question 2-2:

A draftsperson reports directly to _____.

    (A)   the electrical designer
    (B)   the product designer
    (C)   a project manager
    (D)   the VP of engineering
    (E)   the president

Question 2-3:

The management accountant's salary ranking is on the same level as the _____.

    (A)   product manager for new product A
    (B)   VP of product development
    (C)   buyer

Item 3:

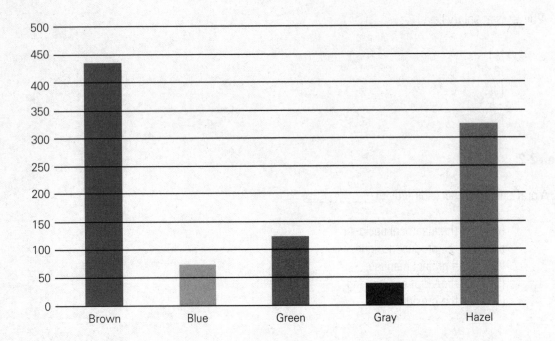

The graph above is a bar chart with six measurements, each representing a certain eye color, based on 1,000 observations made in February of 2012. Use the drop-down menus to fill in the blanks in each of the following statements based on the information given by the graph.

Question 3-1:

Individuals with gray eyes comprise approximately _____ of the individuals.

    (A)   1%
    (B)   4%
    (C)   5%
    (D)   40%
    (E)   95%

Question 3-2:

If a study of 1,000 individuals conducted in February of 1912 found that 90 individuals had blue eyes, the number of individuals having blue eyes has _____ since February of 1912.

    (A)   increased by 15%
    (B)   decreased by 15%
    (C)   decreased by 16.67%
    (D)   increased by 20%
    (E)   decreased by 20%

Question 3-3:

The difference between the most and least common eye color is approximately _____.

    (A)   150
    (B)   275
    (C)   350
    (D)   400

Item 4:

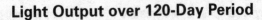

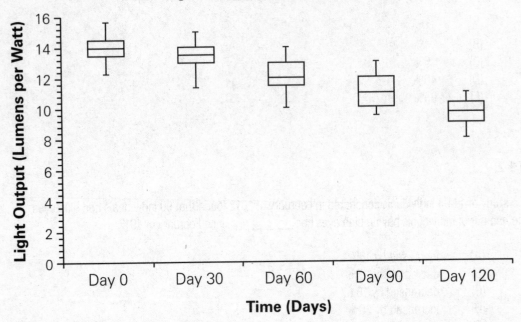

The graph above is a box plot with five measurements, each representing the average light output (in lumens per watt) of 25 60-Watt incandescent light bulbs, measured over a 120-day period. Each box represents the middle 50%, also known as the interquartile range, and the lines extending vertically upwards or downwards represent the top 25% and bottom 25%, respectively. The solid line inside the box represents the median light output for each measurement. Use the drop-down menus to fill in the blanks in each of the following statements based on the information given by the graph.

Question 4-1:

Light output ranges from _____ lumens per watt between Day 30 and Day 120.

    (A)   15 to 8

    (B)   14 to 9.5

    (C)   13.5 to 9.75

Question 4-2:

The greatest interquartile range occurs on _____.

    (A)   Day 0

    (B)   Day 30

    (C)   Day 60

    (D)   Day 90

    (E)   Day 120

Question 4-3:

Light output and time have _____ relationship.

    (A)   a direct

    (B)   an inverse

    (C)   no

Item 5:

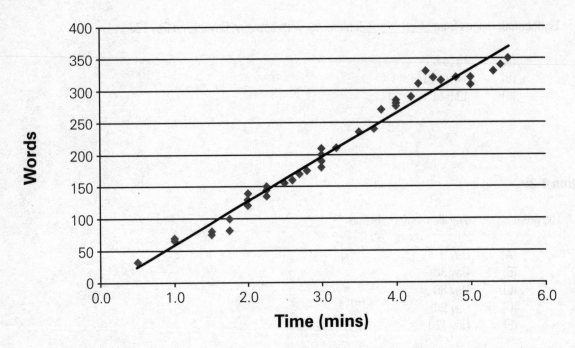

The graph above is a scatter plot with 40 points, each representing the number of words typed in a given time period. The amount of time each individual spent typing is given in minutes. The solid line is the regression line. Use the drop-down menus to fill in the blanks in each of the following statements based on the information given by the graph.

Question 5-1:

The slope of the regression line is _____ the slope of a line that would pass through points (0,0) and (4, 200).

        (A)   greater than
        (B)   less than
        (C)   equal to

Question 5-2:

Based on the line of regression, an individual who types for 5.5 minutes should expect to type approximately _____ words than an individual who types for 3 minutes.

        (A)   50% fewer
        (B)   50% more
        (C)   100% fewer
        (D)   100% more
        (E)   120% more

Question 5-3:

Time and the number of words typed have _____ relationship.

        (A)   a direct
        (B)   an inverse
        (C)   no

Item 6:

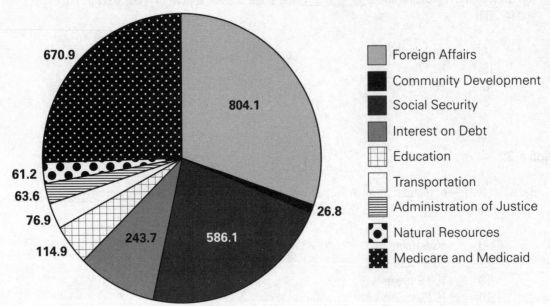

The graph above is a circle graph with 9 sectors, each representing an area in which the U.S. government spent money (in millions of dollars) during the 2006 fiscal year. Use the drop-down menus to fill in the blanks in each of the following statements based on the information given by the graph.

Question 6-1:

If Medicare and Medicaid spending in 2005 were $824,400,000, spending in this sector approximately _____ from 2005 to 2006.

- (A)   increased by 22.88%
- (B)   decreased by 22.88%
- (C)   increased by 18.62%
- (D)   decreased by 18.62%
- (E)   experienced no change

Question 6-2:

The sectors of _____ comprise approximately 25% of the total amount spent by the U.S. Government in 2006.

- (A)   Social Security and Interest on Debt
- (B)   Medicare & Medicaid and Community Development
- (C)   Interest on Debt, Education, Administration of Justice, and Transportation
- (D)   Social Security and Education
- (E)   Social Security and Transportation

Question 6-3:

The total amount of money that the U.S. government spent on the four lowest ranking sectors is _____ than the average amount of money that the U.S. government spent on the two highest-ranking sectors.

- (A)   509 million dollars less
- (B)   509 million dollars more
- (C)   680.4 million dollars less
- (D)   1,246.5 million dollars less
- (E)   1,246.5 million dollars more

Item 7:

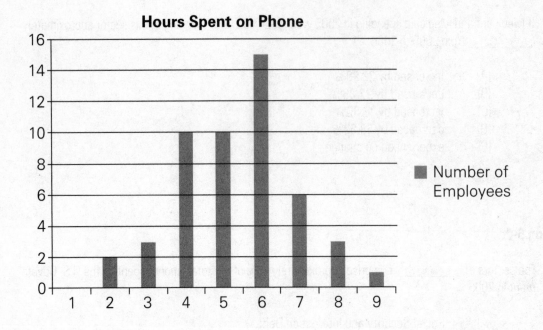

Hours Spent on Phone

The table above shows the number of hours spent on the phone by the 50 employees on a certain day at the call center for RPT Corporation. Use the drop-down menus to fill in the blanks in each of the following statements based on the information given by the graph.

Question 7-1:

The median number of hours spent on the phone by the employees at RPT Corporation is _____.

       (A)   4
       (B)   4.5
       (C)   5
       (D)   5.5
       (E)   6

Question 7-2:

The ratio of the number of employees who spent greater than 5 hours on the phone to those who spent less than 4 hours on the phone is _____.

       (A)   1 : 1
       (B)   3 : 1
       (C)   5 : 1
       (D)   7 : 1
       (E)   7 : 3

Question 7-3:

If the employees who spent 2 hours on the phone increased their total hours spent on the phone by 50%, then the total hours spent on the phone by these employees would be _____.

       (A)   2
       (B)   4
       (C)   6
       (D)   8

Check your answers on page 119.

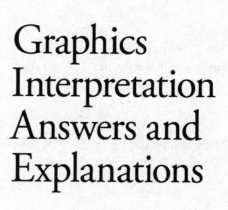

Graphics
Interpretation
Answers and
Explanations

ANSWER KEY

Graphics Interpretation

Item 1
Question 1-1: C, 100,000
Question 1-2: A, First Quarter
Question 1-3: A, Positive

Item 2
Question 2-1: C, Level C
Question 2-2: D, The VP of Engineering
Question 2-3: A, Product manager for new Product A

Item 3
Question 3-1: B, 4%
Question 3-2: C, Decreased by 16.67%
Question 3-3: D, 400

Item 4
Question 4-1: A, 15 to 8
Question 4-2: D, Day 90
Question 4-3: B, an inverse

Item 5
Question 5-1: A, Greater than
Question 5-2: D, 100% more words
Question 5-3: A, a direct

Item 6
Question 6-1: D, Medicare and Medicaid spending
decreased by 18.62%
Question 6-2: E, Social Security and Transportation
Question 6-3: A, 509 million dollars less

Item 7
Question 7-1: D, 5.5
Question 7-2: C, 5 : 1
Question 7-3: C, 6

EXPLANATIONS

Item 1:

1-1. C, 100,000

The question asks you how many more Homepage Hits there were in the 4th quarter compared to the 1st quarter. According to the legend, Homepage Hits are represented in thousands. For the 4th quarter, the bar reflecting Homepage Hits reaches the 400 mark; while for the 1st quarter the bar reflecting Homepage Hits reaches the 300 mark. Since Homepage Hits are represented in thousands, the difference is actually 100 thousand, or 100,000.

1-2. A, First Quarter

The question asks which quarter reflects the lowest ratio of Online Figurine Sales to Banner Advertising, which can be expressed as the relationship $\frac{\text{Online Figurine Sales}}{\text{Banner Advertising}}$. So, for the First Quarter, the ratio would be approximately $\frac{130}{210}$ or 0.62. For the Second Quarter, the ratio would be approximately $\frac{210}{275}$ or 0.76. For the Third Quarter, the ratio would be approximately $\frac{170}{250}$ or 0.68. For the Fourth Quarter, the ratio would be approximately $\frac{250}{295}$ or 0.84. Thus, the correct answer is the First Quarter.

1-3. A, Positive

This question asks about the slope of the line that, if graphed, would represent the overall trend in Homepage Hits. The overall trend in Homepage Hits is upward, even though there is a dip in the third quarter. Because the general trend for Homepage Hits is upwards, the slope of the line would be Positive. The correct answer is (A).

Item 2:

2-1. C, Level C

The chart indicates that the buyer reports to the purchasing manager, who in turn reports to the VP of marketing, who in turn reports to the president. So a map of this would look like this:

buyer ➔ purchasing manager ➔ VP marketing ➔ president

The VP of marketing is a Level A employee because he/she reports directly to the president. The purchasing manager is a Level B employee because he/she reports to a Level A employee (marketing VP). The buyer must be a Level C employee because he/she reports to a Level B employee (purchasing manager).

2-2. D, The VP of engineering

Use the key to see how you can tell who reports directly to whom. Since the arrow goes from the draftsperson's box to the line under the VP of engineering's box, the draftsperson reports directly to the VP of engineering. The lines connecting from the draftsperson's box to the electrical designer and the product designer indicate a direct line of communication, not a reporting relationship.

2-3. A, Product manager for new Product A
The management accountant is two levels under the president, so he/she is a Level B employee. The product manager for new product A is also two levels under the president, so the management accountant and the product manager have the same salary ranking. The VP of product development is a Level A employee, so this is not the same as the management accountant's salary ranking (B). The buyer is three levels under the president, so he/she is a Level C employee, which is not the same as the management accountant's ranking.

Item 3:

3-1. B, 4%
First, you need to identify the number of individuals with gray eyes; the bar for gray shows 40 individuals having gray. Since you were previously told that the study was based on 1,000 observations, you need to find what percent of 1,000 is 40. Translate from English to math: *What percent of 1,000 is 40* is the same as $\frac{x}{100} \times 1,000 = 40$, $10x = 40$, and $x = 4$. Thus, individuals with gray eyes comprise 4% of the individuals.

3-2. C, Decreased by 16.67%
First, write down the formula for percent change: $percent\ change = \frac{difference}{original} \times 100$. Next, find the number of individuals with blue eyes in February 2012 and February 1912. The chart indicates that 75 individuals had blue eyes in February 2012 and the question states that 90 individuals had blue eyes in February 1912. Accordingly, the difference between February 1912

and February 2012 is 90 − 75 = 15. Now, when you plug in the information to the percent change formula, you will find that $percent\ change = \frac{15}{90} \times 100 = 16.67\%$. Thus, if an identical study conducted in February of 1912 found that 90 individuals had blue eyes, the number of individuals having blue eyes has decreased by 16.67% since February 1912.

3-3. D, 400
The most common eye color is Brown, at approximately 430. The least common is Gray, at approximately 40. The difference between the two is 430 − 40 = 390, which is closest to 400.

Item 4:

4-1. A, 15 to 8
In order to find the range of light output between Day 30 and Day 120, you need to identify the greatest light output on Day 30 and the lowest light output on Day 120. On Day 30, the maximum light output was 15 lumens per watt. On Day 120, the minimum light output was 8 lumens per watt. Accordingly, light output ranges from 15 to 8 lumens per watt between Day 30 and Day 120.

4-2. D, Day 90
First, you want to find interquartile range, as defined in the chart explanation, for each observation. On Day 0, the middle 50% range is 14.5 -13.5 = 1. On Day 30, the middle 50% range is 14 -13 = 1. On Day 60, the middle 50% range is 13 -11.5 = 1.5. On Day 90, the middle 50% range is 12 - 10 = 2. On Day 120, the middle 50% range is 10.5 - 9 = 1.5. Therefore, the greatest range in the middle 50% occurs at Day 90.

4-3.   B, an inverse

In order to answer this question, you need to identify the trend for Light Output and Time. In this graph, as time increases, the light output decreases. Therefore, light output and time have an inverse relationship.

Item 5:

5-1.   A, Greater than

First, you want to find the slope of the regression line. Utilizing points of the graph, you can estimate the slope is $\frac{y_2 - y_1}{x_2 - x_1} = \frac{350 - 70}{5.5 - 1} = \frac{280}{4.5} \approx 62.2$. Next, you want to find the slope of the line crossing through points (0,0) and (4,200). Utilizing, the same formula, you can estimate the slope of the line crossing through points (0,0) and (4,200) to be $\frac{y_2 - y_1}{x_2 - x_1} = \frac{200 - 0}{4 - 0} = \frac{200}{4} = 50$. Accordingly, since 62.2 > 50, the slope of the regression line is greater than the slope of the line crossing through points (0,0) and (4,200).

5-2.   D, 100% more words

First, write down the percent change formula: $\frac{difference}{original} \times 100$. Next, using the regression line, find the number of words typed by an individual who types for 3 minutes; an individual who types for 3 minutes will type approximately 190 words. Next, according to the line of regression, an individual who types for 5.5 minutes will type approximately 375 words. Finally, plug the appropriate information into the percent change formula.

When you do, you will find that the percent change equals $\frac{185}{190} \times 100 \approx 97\%$. Therefore, based on the regression line, an individual who types for 5.5 minutes should expect to type 100% more words than an individual who types for 3 minutes.

5-3.   A, a direct

First, identify what is happening with both typing time and the number of words typed. According to the regression line, as the amount of time spent typing increases, the number of words typed increases. Therefore, time and the number of words typed have a direct relationship.

Item 6:

6-1.   D, decreased by 18.62%

Since this question asks about percent change, you want to write down the necessary formula: $percent\ change = \frac{difference}{original} \times 100$. Next, since the question asks about the percent change from 2005 to 2006, you need to find the amount the U.S. Government spent on Medicare and Medicaid in 2006. According to the circle graph, the U.S. Government spent 670.9 million dollars on Medicare and Medicaid in 2006. Thus, the difference in spending from 2005 to 2006 is 824.4 – 670.9 = 153.5. Next, fill in the information in the percent change formula to find that $percent\ change = \frac{153.5}{824.4} \times 100 = 18.62$. Since more was spent in 2005 than in 2006, you can conclude that Medicare and Medicaid spending decreased by 18.62%.

6-2.   E, Social Security and Transportation

First, you need to calculate the total amount of money spent by the U.S. Government in 2006. When you total the money spent in each sector, you will find that 26.8 + 61.2 + 63.6 + 76.9 + 114.9 + 243.7 + 586.1 + 670.9 + 804.1 = 2,648.2. Next, check each answer choice and see how much the stated sectors comprise of the total amount spent. A total of 829.8 was spent on Social Security and Interest on Debt; $\frac{829.8}{2648.2} \times 100 = 31.33\%$ of the total amount spent in 2006. A total of 697.7 was spent on Medicare and Medicaid and Community and Regional Development; $\frac{697.7}{2648.2} \times 100 = 26.35\%$ of the total amount spent in 2006. A total of 499.1 was spent on Interest on Debt, Education and Technology, Administration of Justice and General Government, and Transportation; $\frac{499.1}{2648.2} \times 100 = 18.85\%$ of the total amount spent in 2006. A total of 701.0 was spent on Social Security and Education and Technology; $\frac{701}{2648.2} \times 100 = 26.47\%$ of the total amount spent in 2006. A total of 663.0 was spent on Social Security and Transportation; $\frac{663}{2648.2} \times 100 = 25.04\%$ of the total amount spent in 2006. Accordingly, the sectors that comprise approximately 25% of the total amount spent by the U.S. Government in 2006 are Social Security and Transportation.

6-3.   A, 509 million dollars less

First, identify the four lowest ranking sectors: Community and Regional Development, Natural Resources and the Environment, Administration of Justice and General Government, and Transportation. Next, calculate the total amount spent on these four sectors: 26.8 + 61.2 + 63.6 + 76.9 = 228.5. Next, in order to find the average amount of money that the U.S. government spent on the two highest-ranking sectors, set up an average pie and find the two highest-ranking sectors. You will find that 1,475.0 was spent on Defense and Foreign Affairs and Medicare and Medicaid. Accordingly, the average amount spent on these two sectors was $\frac{1,475}{2} = 737.5$. Finally, find the difference between the total amount of money that the US government spent on the four lowest ranking sectors (228.5) and the average amount of money that the U.S. government spent on the two highest-ranking sectors (737.5) is 737.5 − 228.5 = 509.0. Thus, the U.S. government spent 509.0 less on the four lowest ranking sectors than the average of the two highest-ranking sectors.

Item 7:

7-1.   **D, 5.5**
To find the median you can either write out all of the data points for the number of hours spent and start eliminating numbers from each side, or, since you know that there are 50 employees at the call center, you can just find the 25th and 26th data points and average them. The 25th person spent 5 hours on the phone and the 26th person spent 6 hours on the phone. The median is therefore 5.5.

7-2.   **C, 5 : 1**
From the chart, the number of people who spent more than 5 hours on the phone is 25, and the number of people who spent less than 4 hours on the phone is 5. The ratio is therefore 25:5, or 5:1.

7-3.   **C, 6**
From the chart, you can see that there are 2 employees who spent 2 hours on the phone. So, the total hours spent by these employees is 4 hours. If you increase that by 50 percent, then you will get 6 total hours.

Two-Part Analysis

TWO-PART ANALYSIS

Next up is the Two-Part Analysis question. In many ways, the Two-Part Analysis question is most similar to a standard math question. You'll typically be presented with a word problem that essentially has two variables in it. You'll need to pick an answer for each variable that makes some condition in the problem true.

Here's an example of a Two-Part Analysis question:

Two families buy new refrigerators using installment plans. Family A makes an initial payment of $750. Family B makes an initial payment of $1200. Both families make five additional payments to pay off the balance. Both families pay the same amount for their refrigerators including all taxes, fees and finance charges. **1**

In the table below, identify a monthly payment, in dollars, for Family A and a monthly payment, in dollars, for Family B that are consistent with the installment plan described above. Make only one selection in each column. **2**

Family A	Family B	Monthly payment (in dollars)
○	○	50
○	○	80
○	○	120 **3**
○	○	160
○	○	250
○	○	300

As you might have surmised, we have once again added the circled numbers so we can describe the different parts of the question. Here's what each circled number represents:

1   This first block of text is the actual problem. Here, you'll find the description of the two variables in the problem. You'll also find the condition that needs to be made true. As with any word problem, make sure that you read the information carefully. For these problems, you'll also want to make sure that you are clear about which information goes with the first variable and which information goes with the second.

2   This part of the problem tells you how to pick your answers. Mostly this part will tell you to pick a value for column A and a value for column B based on the conditions of the problem. This part is mostly boilerplate text that is slightly varied from problem to problem.

③ These are the answer choices. Two-Part Analysis questions generally have six answer choices. You choose only one answer choice for each column. It is possible that the same number is the answer for both columns. So, if that's what your calculations indicate, go ahead and choose the same number for both columns.

Most Two-Part Analysis questions can be solved using math that is no more sophisticated than simple arithmetic. There is one exception to that, however. While most Two-Part Analysis questions are math problems, you may see one that looks like a Critical Reasoning question. For these, you'll be given an argument and you'll need to do something like pick one answer that strengthens and one answer that weakens the argument.

TWO-PART ANALYSIS DRILLS

Item 1:

The quotient $\dfrac{a}{b}$ is a multiple of 7.

In the table below, choose the value of a and the value of b that are consistent with the statement above. Make only one selection in each column.

	a	b	Value
(A)	○	○	12
(B)	○	○	28
(C)	○	○	52
(D)	○	○	88
(E)	○	○	168
(F)	○	○	175

Item 2:

The International Association of Musical Artist Rights (IAMAR) argues that because many artists strive to earn a living from composing and/or performing new musical works, the current regulations constricting the use of file-sharing on the Internet are insufficient to ensure that a musician is justly compensated for his artistic pursuits. IAMAR wants to prevent fans from accessing free music in any format. However, the widespread distribution of MP3 files over the web has encouraged a "broader awareness" of lower-profile musicians. This may translate into more interest and an increased demand for their live concert appearances.

In the table below, identify the single sentence that would most strengthen and the single sentence that would most weaken IAMAR's position on the impact of file-sharing over the internet on the earnings potential of musical artists.

	Strengthen	Weaken	Value Title
(A)	○	○	No industries other than the music industry have requested stronger controls over file-sharing.
(B)	○	○	Music fans are more likely to buy a musician's album in any format or attend a live concert if they can first sample the musician's work for free.
(C)	○	○	Stronger regulations for music file-sharing do not prevent independent artists from directly emailing electronic media to a fan base.
(D)	○	○	File-sharing of recorded books is nationally regulated and monitored by federal agencies.
(E)	○	○	Music fans who download free samples of a musician's work are less likely to buy albums by that musician or go to that musician's live concert.

Item 3:

x and y are odd two-digit integers. The digits of x have a sum of 3 and the digits of y have a product of 4.

In the table below, select a possible value for x and for y. Make only one selection in each column.

	x	y	Value
(A)	○	○	12
(B)	○	○	13
(C)	○	○	21
(D)	○	○	22
(E)	○	○	30
(F)	○	○	41

Item 4:

At Arlen University, there are a total of 120 Science majors. There are twice as many physics majors as chemistry majors and 30 students who major in both physics and chemistry. Arlen University offers majors in no other sciences.

In the table below, select the number of students who major in physics and the number of students who major in chemistry.

	Physics	Chemistry	Students
(A)	○	○	20
(B)	○	○	35
(C)	○	○	40
(D)	○	○	50
(E)	○	○	70
(F)	○	○	100

Item 5:

Over the last five years, ratings for music radio stations have decreased significantly. Radio executives believe that the availability of digital music has caused a decrease in the number of people who listen to music on the radio. In order to increase radio ratings, executives have changed the format of many radio stations around the country from music to talk.

In the table below, select one sentence to strengthen and one sentence to weaken the argument above.

	Strengthen	Weaken	Value Title
(A)	○	○	There are many experienced radio personalities available for jobs as talk radio hosts.
(B)	○	○	During this same time period, the number of tickets sold for music concerts has increased.
(C)	○	○	Talk programming is also available in a digital form.
(D)	○	○	The cost of producing a talk radio show is less than the cost of producing a music radio show.
(E)	○	○	The overall decrease in radio ratings is less than that in music radio ratings.

Item 6:

Lisa bought 2 $500 CDs, each at a different interest rate. The interest on both CDs was compounded annually and the interest rate on CD A was two percentage points percent less than the interest rate on CD B. When Lisa sold both CDs after 1 year, she received $1,060.

In the table below, identify the interest rate of each CD that will be necessary for Lisa to receive $1,060 back after 1 year. Make only one selection in each column.

	CD A	CD B	Interest Rate
(A)	○	○	3%
(B)	○	○	4%
(C)	○	○	5%
(D)	○	○	6%
(E)	○	○	7%
(F)	○	○	8%

Item 7:

Margaret has $7.20 to spend on candy bars and jawbreakers. She can buy either 6 candy bars and 16 jawbreakers or 12 candy bars and 8 jawbreakers.

In the table below, choose the exact price of a candy bar and the exact price of a jawbreaker that are consistent with the amounts Margaret can buy. Make only one selection in each column.

	Candy Bar	Jawbreaker	Price
(A)	○	○	20 cents
(B)	○	○	25 cents
(C)	○	○	30 cents
(D)	○	○	40 cents
(E)	○	○	45 cents
(F)	○	○	50 cents

Check your answers on page 135.

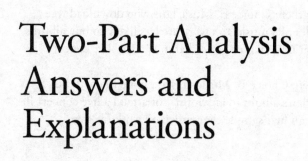

Two-Part Analysis
Answers and
Explanations

ANSWER KEY

Two-Part Analysis

Item 1
Value of A: Choice E, 168
Value of B: Choice A, 12

Item 2
Strengthen: Choice E, Music fans who download free samples of a musician's work are less likely to buy albums by that musician or go to that musicians' live concert.

Weaken: Choice B, Music fans are more likely to buy a musician's album in any format or attend a live concert if they can first sample the musician's work for free.

Item 3
Value for x: Choice C, 21
Value for y: Choice F, 41

Item 4
Major in Physics: Choice F, 100
Major in Chemistry: Choice D, 50

Item 5
Strengthen: Choice E, The overall decrease in radio ratings is less than that in music radio ratings

Weaken: Choice C, Talk programming is also available in a digital form.

Item 6
Interest rate on CD A: Choice C, 5%
Interest rate on CD B: Choice E, 7%

Item 7
Price of Candy Bar: Choice D, 40 cents
Price of Jawbreaker: Choice C, 30 cents

EXPLANATIONS

Item 1:

1-1.   Value of A: Choice E, 168
Value of B: Choice A, 12
The problem asks for values of *a* and *b* such that when *a* is divided by *b*, the result is a multiple of 7. You could approach this problem by simply dividing each answer choice by the other answer choices and testing the result to see if it is divisible by 7, but there is a much more efficient way.

When a problem discusses multiples, factors, or whether one number is divisible by another, the best approach to start is generally to find the prime factors of the numbers involved.

In this case, if the quotient of *a* and *b* is a multiple of 7, then 7 must be one of the prime factors of *a*. And for the quotient to be a multiple of 7, the prime factors of *b* must also be prime factors of *a*, so that the numbers divide evenly.

Start by checking each of the answer choices to see if 7 is a factor; once you find one, try dividing it by the other answer choices and see if the result is divisible by 7.

The first answer choice, 12, has the prime factors 3, 2, and 2. Since 7 is not one of its prime factors, 12 is not a possible answer choice for *a*.

The second answer choice, 28, has the prime factors 7, 2, and 2, so 28 is a possible solution for *a*. However, 28 is not evenly divisible by 12, so 28 is not a possible answer choice for *a*.

The third answer choice, 88, has the prime factors 11, 2, 2, and 2. Since 7 is not one of its prime factors, 88 is not a possible answer choice for *a*. Similarly, the fourth answer choice, 52, has the prime factors 13, 2, and 2, so 52 is not a possible answer choice for *a*.

The fifth answer choice, 168, has the prime factors 7, 3, 2, 2, and 2, so 168 is a possible solution for *a*. The first answer choice, 12, has the factors 3, 2, and 2, which are also factors of 168. The result when 168 is divided by 12 is 14 (the product of the remaining factors, 7 and 2), which is a multiple of 7.

Therefore, 168 is the correct response for *a*, 12 is the correct response for *b*, and no further testing of the answer choices is necessary.

Item 2:

2-1.   Strengthen: Choice E, Music fans who download free samples of a musician's work are less likely to buy albums by that musician or go to that musicians' live concert.

Weaken: Choice B, Music fans are more likely to buy a musician's album in any format or attend a live concert if they can first sample the musician's work for free.

The conclusion of the IAMAR's argument is that musical artists are earning less money because fans can download the artists' music for free. IAMAR is assuming that the fans would spend money to hear that artist if they could not get free music downloads.

Choice (A) brings other industries into the argument. What other industries do is outside the scope of this argument. Other industries' failure to ask for the same protection does not strengthen or weaken the IAMAR argument.

Choice (B) directly attacks this assumption. It says fans are actually *more likely* to buy music or go to concerts if they can listen to a free music sample. That means that IAMAR's suggestion to ban fans' access to free music has the potential to reduce the earnings potential for musicians.

Choice (C) doesn't strongly strengthen or weaken IAMAR's argument since it is not directly linked to the likelihood of whether a fan will buy an album or a concert ticket.

Choice (D) is about another industry, so, in the same way that (A) is irrelevant, (D) is irrelevant to IAMAR's argument. It is outside the scope of the argument.

Choice (E) strongly strengthens IAMAR's argument because it reinforces IAMAR's assumption. It directly links the free downloading to a reduction of income for musicians, which is the cornerstone of IAMAR's argument.

Item 3:

3-1.   Value for x: Choice C, 21
The digits of x have to have a sum of 3. Based on this fact, the only possible values of x are 12, 21, and 30. However, the first sentence tells you that x is odd. Therefore, the only possible value is 21.

Value for y: Choice F, 41
The digits of y have to have a sum of 4. Based on this fact, the only possible values of y are 14, 22, and 41. However, the first sentence tells you that y is odd. Therefore, the only possible value is 41.

Item 4:

4-1.   Major in Physics: Choice F, 100
Major in Chemistry: Choice D, 50

The question gives you two groups and uses the word "both". When this is the case, use the group formula, which is

$$T = G_1 + G_2 + N - B$$

You know that there are 120 science majors, so this is your total. You know that 30 students major in both physics and chemistry. Arlen University offers majors in no other science, so $N = 0$. Since there are twice as many physics majors as there are chemistry majors. Set $G_1 = 2C$ and $G_2 = C$. Now, substitute these into the group formula to get

$120 = 2C + C + 0 - 30$
$120 = 3C - 30$
$150 = 3C$
$50 = C$

This tells you that there are 50 Chemistry majors. Since there are twice as many physics majors as chemistry majors, there are 100 physics majors.

Item 5:

5-1. **Strengthen:** Choice E, The overall decrease in radio ratings is less than that in music radio ratings.

Weaken: Choice C, Talk programming is also available in a digital form.

In an argument question, you want to determine the conclusion, premise, and any assumptions. In this argument, the conclusion is that switching from music radio format to talk radio format will increase ratings. The premise is that because of digital music formats, there is less need to listen to music on the radio. The author assumes that, for talk radio, there is either no problem or less of a problem than there is for music radio. Go through the answers.

Choice (A) tells you that there are many experienced talk radio personalities available. However, whether the personalities are available is irrelevant to whether this format will increase ratings. Eliminate this option.

Choice (B) indicates interest in music, but still doesn't indicate interest in music radio, so this is also irrelevant. Eliminate this as well.

Answer choice (C) says that talk radio programming is also available in digital formats. If this is the case, there may be fewer people who listen to talk radio as well. This weakens the argument.

Choice (D) describes the cost, and while this may be relevant to the overall business model, the argument specifically refers to ratings, so this is irrelevant.

Finally, (E) says that the overall decrease in radio ratings is less than that of music radio ratings. This would suggest that other formats do better than music formats, which strengthens the argument. Therefore, only the third option can weaken and only the fifth option can strengthen.

Item 6:

6-1. Interest rate on CD A: Choice C, 5%
Interest rate on CD B: Choice E, 7%

The question asks you for the rate of CD A and CD B. Since you know that rate A has to be 2% less than rate B, test out some combination of rate A and rate B and see what interest is earned. Start in the middle with some easy numbers, so if CD A is 4%, then CB B is 6%. Calculate the interest earned:
Value of A: 500 × 1.04 = 520
Value of B: 500 × 1.06 = 530
The total amount earned would then be $1,050. Since Lisa needs to earn more, the interest rates need to be higher. So try 5% and 7%:
Amount earned on A: 500 × 1.05 = 525
Amount earned on B: 500 × 1.07 = 535
The total amount earned is now $1,060, which matches the information given and is therefore the correct answer.

Item 7:

7-1.   Price of Candy Bar: Choice D, 40 cents
Price of Jawbreaker: Choice C, 30 cents

The word problem can be expressed in the form of two distinct equations in terms of the combined costs of candy bars and jawbreakers. Note that since the problem uses both dollars and cents, it simplifies the problem to convert $7.20 to 720 cents, which results in the following equations: $6c + 16j = 720$, and $12c + 8j = 720$. Since you have two distinct linear equations and two variables, there is only one possible solution for each of the two variables.

While you could solve the problem algebraically (by substituting one equation into another, or by finding a way to stack and add the equations), you can instead Plug In The Answers and eliminate algebra from the problem entirely. Use the numbers given as answer choices and plug each one into one of the equations as the price of a candy bar, and solve the equation for the price of a jawbreaker, looking to see whether the exact result is also an answer choice and stopping when you find an answer choice that works. Start with the first answer choice: 20 cents, and substitute it for the price of a candy bar in the first equation: $6(20) + 16j = 720$, which simplifies to $120 + 16j = 720$, $16j = 600$, and $j = 37.5$ cents. Since 37.5 cents is not an available response, 20 cents is not the correct price for a candy bar.

Plugging in the second answer choice (25 cents) for the price of a candy bar results in a rough number approximately equal to 35 cents, so 25 cents is not the correct price for a candy bar. The third choice (30 cents) results in a price of 33.75 cents for a jawbreaker, but again, since 33.75 cents is not an available answer choice, 30 cents is not the correct price for a candy bar.

Plugging in the fourth choice (40 cents) for the price of a candy bar gives $6(40) + 16j = 720$, which simplifies to $240 + 16j = 720$, $16j = 480$, and when solved, $j = 30$ cents. Since 30 cents is also an available response, 40 cents is the correct price of a candy bar and 30 cents is the correct price of a jawbreaker, and no further testing of the answer choices is necessary.

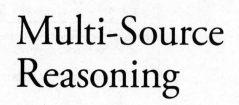

Multi-Source Reasoning

MULTI-SOURCE REASONING

Finally, we come to the Multi-Source Reasoning question. Multi-Source Reasoning questions present information on tabs. The information can be text, charts, graphs, or a combination. In other words, GMAC can put almost anything on the tabs! The layout looks a little bit like Reading Comprehension because the tabbed information is on the left side of your screen while the right side shows the questions.

Here's an example of a Multi-Source Reasoning question:

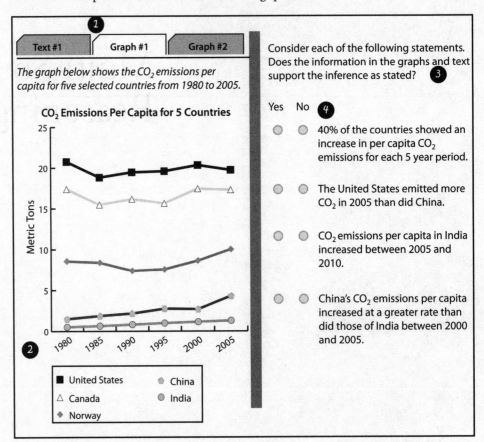

Like we've done for the other three new question types, we've added circled numbers to indicate the different parts of the question. Here's what each circled number represents:

 The tabs appear across the top left of the screen. Some questions have two tabs and some, as in this example, have three. The tabs typically give you some sort of indication about what's on the tab. The currently selected tab is white while the unselected tabs are grey. GMAC can put almost anything on each tab including graphs, tables, charts, text, or some combination. It's a good idea to take a few seconds and get your bearings before attempting the questions. Make sure you know what is on each tab and how the information on one tab relates to information on the other tab or tabs.

② The information for each tab appears on the left of the screen. In this case, the information is a graph. When you see a chart or graph, be sure to check out the axes. You'll also want to look for a legend or other information to help explain the information shown by the graph or chart. For tables, check out the column headings so as to better understand the table. Finally, don't neglect to read any supplied headings for the chart, graph, or table. Sometimes, that's all you need for the chart to make sense.

③ These are the basic instructions for how to respond to the statements. These instructions help to explain how you need to evaluate each statement. Here, for example, you need to determine whether the statements are valid inferences. In other cases, you may be asked to evaluate the statements for a different choice such as true or false.

④ These are the actual questions. You need to pick a response for each statement. If you fail to respond to one or more statements, you won't be able to advance to the next question in the section. In other words, these statements work just like the statements for the Table Analysis question type.

Multi-Source Reasoning questions usually come in sets. Each set typically consists of three separate questions. Two of those questions are typically in the statement style as shown in the example above. It's also possible to get a standard multiple-choice question as part of the set. For a standard multiple-choice question, there are five answer choices and you select one response.

You may need information from more than one tab to respond to a statement or multiple-choice question. Don't forget to think about the information on the other tabs while evaluating the statements. That's why it's important to take a few moments and get familiar with what's on each tab before starting work on the questions.

MULTI-SOURCE REASONING DRILLS

Data for Items 1, 2, and 3

| Memo | Bar Graph |

To: Beecham Air, In Flight Food & Drink Manager
From: Arthur Beecham Jr., CEO, Beecham Air
Subject: Beverage expenses
Date: April 24, 2012

The airline business has drastically changed in recent decades. While the number of passengers continues to increase, passengers have demonstrated an unwillingness to pay more for airline tickets.

In the past 15 years, Beecham Air's annual in-flight complimentary beverage expenses have nearly doubled. In order to avoid raising the price of an airline ticket without losing customers, we need to act now to control our costs. It is clear from recent reports that the price of coffee has skyrocketed, and thus we should switch to a less expensive brand of coffee.

| Memo | Bar Graph |

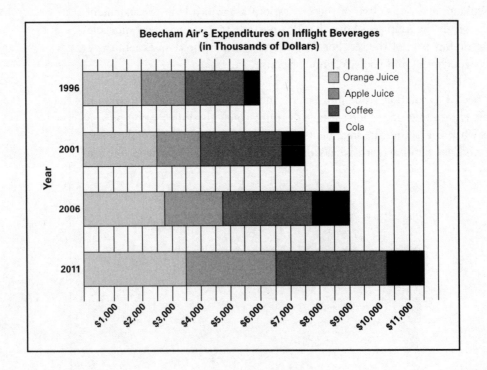

Item 1

Beecham Air's average (arithmetic mean) expenditure on Apple Juice for the four years given was approximately which of the following?

    (A) $1,750
    (B) $2,000
    (C) $400,000
    (D) $1,750,000
    (E) $2,000,000

Item 2

For each of the following statements, determine whether it would, if true, weaken or strengthen the CEO's argument.

	Strengthen	Weaken	
(A)	○	○	The brand of coffee served in-flight plays no role in a passenger's decision of which airline to fly.
(B)	○	○	Coffee has increased from 25% of all beverages served in-flight in 1996 to 50% in 2011.
(C)	○	○	Airline supplier contracts often impose sizeable penalties for changing the brand of goods to be provided.
(D)	○	○	Switching the brand of coffee served is unlikely to result in passengers increasing consumption of a more costly complimentary beverage.

Item 3

Beecham Air's median annual expenditure on Cola is approximately what percent of its median annual expenditure on Coffee for the years given in the table?

    (A)   26%
    (B)   35%
    (C)   47%
    (D)   113%
    (E)   288%

Data for Items 4, 5, and 6

| Finance Email | Registrar Email | Resource Administrator Email |

The following emails circulated through various divisions of Eastern University, a traditional four-year college.

From: Office of the Vice President of Finance, Eastern University
To: Registrar
cc: Resource Administrator, Office of Student Services

Please have your office prepare a summary of the current student enrollment for our upcoming Fall 2011 semester. The financial shortfall from the drop in enrollment last spring necessitates some tightening of the purse strings; how much of that tightening will be seen in a reduction in student services will depend upon the data, which we will use to project the revenues for Spring 2012. Although we are also considering an increase in individual student service fees, any funds from these additional student service fees would not be collected until the next billing cycle at the commencement of the Spring semester. Therefore, in the meantime, cost-saving measures must be explored to help close this current financial gap.

| Finance Email | Registrar Email | Resource Administrator Email |

From: Registrar's Office
To: Office of the Vice President, Finance
Subj: August Report on the 2011 - 2012 Student Registration

Although our registration for the 2011 Spring semester has dropped over 10% from the previous fall, this fall's undergraduate registration appears to be consistent with the numbers from Fall 2010, and indeed even surpasses last year's totals slightly. A total of 17,201 students are currently registered: new freshmen account for 35%, while sophomores, juniors, and seniors combined account for 65%. It is worth noting that of the current registration total, transfers from other universities account for 1%.

| Finance Email | Registrar Email | Resource Administrator Email |

From: Resource Administrator, Office of Student Services
To: Office of the Vice President, Finance

Regarding your concerns about the current budget shortfall, I have been evaluating which student services could most easily be contracted or reduced. I strongly recommend against cutting services, as a department or position once removed from the books requires work to re-create. Hopefully this is a temporary situation that we can redress by reducing the work-week instead of eliminating positions or services entirely.

For example, two areas that could most easily stand a reduction in hours are the Computer Lab and the Writing Lab. The Computer Lab currently employs one supervising technician and her five student assistants and operates Monday through Saturday, ten hours per day, with two 5-hour shifts per day. The Computer Lab could probably reduce hours by 20% to 33%. The Writing Lab operates 5 days per week, 8 hours per day, with four writing tutors. Since the Writing Lab is mostly deserted during late morning and early afternoon classes, it need not be open continuously, but only during those times of highest use.

I understand that measures like these will not redress the entire shortfall, but I'd like to schedule a time to talk more about how we can cut costs while preserving essential student services.

Item 4

In the Computer Lab, the supervising technician must assign exactly one student assistant per five-hour shift, for Monday and Tuesday. If a student can work only one shift per day, how many possible schedules of workers could the supervisor create for the two days?

(A)   20
(B)   25
(C)   120
(D)   320
(E)   400

Item 5

In the list below, choose whether each statement would weaken the Vice President's assertion that "cost-saving measures must be explored to help close this current financial gap."

	Yes	No	
(A)	○	○	The costs of student services per student exceed any revenues that might be realized from additional student fees.
(B)	○	○	There is no way to substantially increase revenues through increasing students' daily costs for food, materials, and books.
(C)	○	○	Cutting student services will likely induce students to transfer to other universities.
(D)	○	○	The donations from Eastern University's alumni organization were smaller than usual last Spring.

Item 6

Consider each of the following statements about Eastern University. Does the information in the three emails support the statement below?

	Yes	No	
(A)	○	○	Most of the currently enrolled students are freshmen.
(B)	○	○	Revenues from next Spring's student service fees will not be sufficient to address the financial shortfall.
(C)	○	○	The number of students who transferred in to the university this semester is one-tenth the number of students who left the university last year.
(D)	○	○	Current enrollment represents more than a ten percent increase from the previous Spring semester.

Data for Items 7, 8, and 9

Announcement | Line Graph

We are happy to announce that, beginning in 2011, we will overhaul our compensation system for our sales staff. Our company previously paid each of its five salespeople the same annual salary with a constant raise each year. However, we don't believe this system rewarded our most proficient salespeople. Therefore, we have decided to give each salesperson a base salary of $20,000 plus a commission of 10% on the total value of the sales on which he or she was the primary salesperson. Furthermore, in order to ensure no bias in distribution of sales, our phone system will reroute each prospective buyer's call from our calling center to the extension of a random salesperson. It is our belief that this will best encourage our sales staff to continue to help grow this great company and push it further into the future.

Announcement | Line Graph

The graph below is a linear function of the salary of a sales associate in the company under the original pay system from 2001-2010.

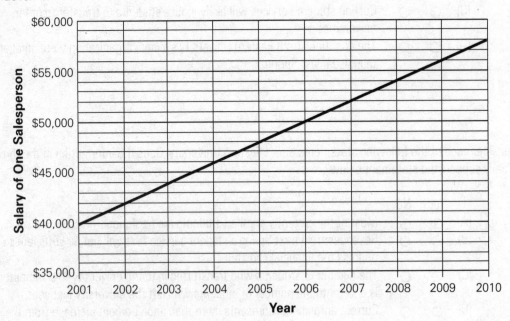

Item 7

In 2006, a particular sales person had $200,000 in sales. Had the new pay system been in place at that time, her total earnings would have been what percent less than her actual salary for the year 2006?

(A)   10%
(B)   15%
(C)   20%
(D)   27%
(E)   80%

Item 8

Consider each of the following statements. Based on the line graph, if x represents the year and y represents the salary of one salesperson, are the following statements true or false?

True   False

(A) ○ ○ Each year, there was a 5% increase in salary for each salesperson.
(B) ○ ○ A salesman who worked from 2001 to 2010, inclusive, earned a total salary of $490,000.
(C) ○ ○ If the original system were to continue into the year 2012, a salesperson's salary would have been $60,000.
(D) ○ ○ The equation of this line is $y = 2{,}000x - 3{,}962{,}000$

Item 9

If three prospective buyers call into the call center at separate times, what is the probability that a particular sales person would receive at least one of these calls?

(A) $\dfrac{1}{125}$

(B) $\dfrac{61}{125}$

(C) $\dfrac{64}{125}$

(D) $\dfrac{3}{5}$

(E) $\dfrac{124}{125}$

Check your answers on page 151.

Multi-Source
Reasoning Answers
and Explanations

ANSWER KEY

Multi-Source Reasoning Drills

Item 1
E, $2,000,000

Item 2
(A): Strengthen
(B): Weaken
(C): Weaken
(D): Strengthen

Item 3
B, 35%

Item 4
E, 400

Item 5
(A): No
(B): No
(C): Yes
(D): No

Item 6
(A): No
(B): No
(C): No
(D): Yes

Item 7
C, 20 %

Item 8
(A): False
(B): True
(C): False
(D): True

Item 9
B, $\frac{61}{125}$

EXPLANATIONS

Item 1:

(E) $2,000,000

To find the average, divide the total expenditures on Apple Juice for each of the four years by the number of years:

$$\frac{1,500+1,500+2,000+3,000}{4} = \$2,000.$$

However, since the totals are written *in thousands of dollars*, the average is $2,000,000.

The answer is choice (E).

Item 2:

Strengthen, Weaken, Strengthen, Weaken

(A) Strengthen
One possible objection to the CEO's plan would be that switching coffee brands would drive away customers. Statement 1 eliminates a possible objection, which strengthens the argument.

(B) Weaken
In 1996, coffee expenditures were $1,500 out of $6,000, which is 25%. In 2011, coffee expenditures were $3,750 out of $11,500, which is about 33%. This means that in 1996, coffee expenditures were proportional to coffee consumption, but that by 2011, coffee consumption was disproportionately higher than expenditures. This means that either the price of coffee has gone down or that the price of the other beverages has increased. Either way, this undermines the CEO's claim that the price of coffee is skyrocketing. Note that it's OK to use the shorthand for numbers like 150,000 and 600,000, because the percentage is still the same. Don't convert unless the question asks you to, or the answer choices are converted.

(C) Weaken
If this is true, then once the penalty is taken into consideration, the CEO's plan could end up costing Beecham Air more money than if it had kept the current coffee brand.

(D) Strengthen
A possible objection to the CEO's plan is that if people stop drinking coffee, they might start drinking something else that is even more expensive, which would actually result in even higher expenditures than currently. This statement states that such a switch is unlikely and thus strengthens the argument.

Item 3:

(B) 35%

To solve this question find the medians of the annual expenditures on Coffee and Cola. The annual expenditures for Coffee are about $2,000, $2,750, $3,000, and $3,750. To find the median, average the two middle numbers, $2,750 and $3,000 to get a median of $2,875. The annual expenditures for Cola are about $500, $750, $1,250, and $1,250, with a median of about $1,000. Now set up an equation: $1,000 is what percent of $2,875, $1,000 = \frac{x}{100} 2,875$. Solve for x to get $1,000 is 34.78% of $2,875, which makes choice (B) the correct answer.

Item 4:

(E) 400

The question asks how many different schedules the technician can create. Since, for example "A, B, C, D" is one schedule and "D, C, B, A" is a separate schedule, then order is important to this question. You must calculate the number of spots available for each shift assignment: Monday morning, Monday afternoon, Tuesday morning, Tuesday afternoon. For Monday morning, there are 5 possible workers available, since this is the first shift of the week. For Tuesday afternoon, however, there are only 4 workers available, as whoever worked Monday morning may not work the next consecutive shift. Likewise, there are 5 workers available for Tuesday morning, and 4 workers available for Tuesday afternoon, as any worker is eligible…except the worker who was staffed for the immediately preceding shift. So to calculate the total number of distinct schedules that the technician could create, multiply all the possibilities: $5 \times 4 \times 5 \times 4 = 400$.

Item 5:

No, No, Yes, No

The point or conclusion of the vice president's argument is "Therefore, in the meantime, cost-saving measures must be explored to help close this current financial gap." The fact or premise behind this conclusion is: the university will not have access to any funds from increased fees in the meantime. So the Vice President must believe that implementing the cost-saving measures is the only solution will mitigate the shortfall, that there is no other solution that would mitigate the shortfall, and that this solution will work without any problems.

Your task is to hurt the argument by providing additional evidence that will undermine the Vice President's assumptions.

(A) No

If the costs of student services per student exceed any revenues that might be realized from additional student fees, this might actually support the Vice President's argument, since the Vice President's plan is to reduce the costs to address the budget shortfall. This statement would seem to indicate that reducing the student services costs is the way to address the financial problems.

(B) No

Again, this statement would support the Vice President's argument. If there is no way to substantially increase revenues through increasing students' daily costs for food, materials, and books, then that suggests there is no way to raise the needed finances; thus the only solution is to save money by instituting cost-saving measures.

(C) Yes

If this statement is true, and cutting student services induces students to transfer, then any expected future revenue from those students would be lost. This would weaken the Vice President's assertion that cost cutting measures would help the financial gap. In this case, cutting out the services would worsen the financial situation.

(D) No

This answer does not weaken the Vice President's argument; it merely explains the possible cause of the budget shortfall. This statement is about events in the past and does not address the Vice President's proposed future actions.

Item 6:

No, No, No, Yes

(A) No

Although information on Tab 2 states that freshmen account for 35%, sophomores, juniors, and seniors combined account for 65%, it is not clear that freshmen represent the largest group. Sophomores could be 40% of the student population, for example, leaving 25% for juniors and freshmen combined.

(B) No

There is no information on whether the Spring's fees will be sufficient, just when they will be available. The information on Tab 1 specifies that the additional student service fees could not be realized until next Spring, because the new billing cycle does not start until then. There is no indication of whether those fees would be sufficient once collected.

(C) No

Although the Information on Tab 2 makes it clear that 1% of the current enrollment (Fall 2011) represents transfer students, and that last Spring's enrollment dropped 10% from the previous semester (Fall 2010), Tab 3 makes it clear that the totals from Fall 2010 and Fall 2011 are not equal: "and indeed even surpasses last year's totals slightly." Since the percentages are based on different totals, you cannot simply conclude that 1% of Fall 2011 total is equivalent to one-tenth of 10% of the Fall 2010 total.

(D) Yes

The Information on Tab 2 states that the current enrollment of 17,201 "surpasses last year's totals slightly." Suppose that the enrollment of Fall 2010 had been 17,200. Given a 10% decrease as reported on Tab 2, the enrollment for Spring 2011 would have been 17,200 – 1,720 or 15,480. So the percent increase from Spring 2011 to the current enrollment would be

$$\frac{17,201 - 15,480}{15,480} = \frac{1,721}{15,480} \approx 0.11, \text{ which}$$

is larger than 10%.

Item 7:

(C) 20%

The question asks what percent less a sales person's salary would have been in 2006 had the new system been in place and the salesperson had $200,000 in sales. To get this, you need to find $\frac{difference}{original} \times 100$. According to the line graph, a person's salary in 2006 was $50,000. Now, you need to determine how much a person would have made had the new system been in place at that time. The base salary is $20,000. The sales person also gets 10% of the $200,000 in sales. 10% of $200,000 is $20,000. This means that the sales person got $40,000 in total. The difference between the two is $10,000. Since the question says percent less than the larger number is the original. Therefore, you need to calculate $\frac{\$10,000}{\$50,000} \times 100 = \frac{1}{5} \times 100 = 20$. Therefore, it is 20% less.

Item 8:

False, True, False, True

(A) False

The percent change is $\frac{difference}{original} \times 100$. Since the graph is a linear function, the difference for each year is constant. However, the original will change each year. Therefore, percent increase cannot be the same number each year. Although the percent increase from 2001 to 2002 is 5%, the percent is less each of the successive years. Therefore, the statement is false. For instance, from 2006 to 2007, the salary increased by $2,000, from $50,000 to $52,000, an increase of 4%.

(B) True

Rather than adding up every single year, use the sum of an arithmetic sequence formula: $s_n = \frac{n}{2}(a_1 + a_n)$. The salary for the first year is $40,000, and the salary for the last year, 2010, is $58,000. There are a total of 10 years, so $n = 10$, and the formula becomes $s_{10} = \frac{10}{2}(40,000 + 58,000) = 5(98,000) = \$490,000$, and the statement is true.

(C) False

Since the graph is of a linear function, y increases by a constant amount each year. Since the salary in 2001 was $40,000 and the salary in 2002 was $42,000, the annual increase is $2,000. Since a salesperson's salary in 2010 is $58,000, then a salesperson's salary in 2011 would have been $60,000 and a salesperson's salary in 2012 would have been $62,000 under the old system. Therefore, the statement is false.

(D) True

Since x represents the year and the starting point is 2001, the number of years that have passed since 2001 is represented by $x - 2001$. The salary of a salesperson increases by $2,000 per year. Therefore, the increase in salary since 2001 is represented by $2,000(x - 2001)$. Since the salary in 2001 is $40,000, then the equation is $y = 2,000(x - 2001) + 40,000 = 2,000x - 4,002,000 + 40,000 = 2,000x - 3,962,000$. Therefore, the statement is true.

Item 9:

(B) $\dfrac{61}{125}$

The question asks for the probability that at least one of three calls goes to a particular sales person. The announcement tab tells you that there are five sales people. This means that each call that comes in has a $\frac{1}{5}$ probability of going to a particular sales person. The question says "at least one" call. Anytime a probability question uses the term "at least one," subtract the probability of no calls going to a particular sales person from 1: $1 -$ Probability of not receiving any of the three calls $= 1 - \frac{4}{5} \times \frac{4}{5} \times \frac{4}{5} = 1 - \frac{64}{125} = \frac{61}{125}$.

Quantitative

QUANTITATIVE

The math section of the GMAT follows the essay section and the Integrated Reasoning section. You have 75 minutes to answer 37 questions. There are two question types: Problem Solving and Data Sufficiency. You will receive a separate math score that ranges from 0 to 60. The mean math score is 35.

Although the math section tests basic math skills, very few people get a perfect score. One reason is the time restriction. If you had unlimited time it would be much easier to get a stellar score. Another reason is that the test writers design tricks and traps to make the questions harder.

The good news is that The Princeton Review has strategies that will help you work more quickly and avoid traps. Learn these strategies and use them on the test to maximize your score. First, learn some general math strategies and then learn some strategies that are specific to the two question types.

Trap Answers

One way to improve your math score is to train yourself to look for trap answers. Trap answers are any answers you can come up with too easily on a hard question. These include numbers in the answers that also appear in the question or answer choices that are an easy manipulation of the numbers in the problem.

Hard questions have hard answers, so if you can get to an answer too easily on a hard question, you know it's a trap and you should eliminate it. Here's an example.

1. A rectangular wooden crate has inside dimensions 3 meters by 4 meters by 12 meters. What is the length, in meters, of the longest, straight, inflexible rod of negligible diameter that can be placed completely within the crate?

   (A) 12
   (B) 12.6
   (C) 13
   (D) 19
   (E) 24

You're looking for the diagonal of the crate. There's a formula to find the diagonal of the box, which you will learn in the geometry chapter, but for now just look for trap answers. Choice (A) is a trap because it is the longest side of the box. Since the question asks for the longest rod that can be placed within the box, and the diagonal length within the box is greater than the length of one of the sides, this is incorrect. Choice (D) is a trap because it is the sum of the numbers in the problem (3 + 4 + 12). Choice (E) is a trap because it is the largest answer choice. When a question asks for the largest or longest thing, the largest answer choice is usually a trap, and when a question asks for the smallest or shortest thing, the smallest number is often a trap. Even if you weren't sure how to do this problem, you could eliminate three trap answers and guess from the remaining two.

Ballparking

Ballparking is another strategy that can help you eliminate answers and work more quickly. Although the math section involves some calculation, the test writers' primary goal is to test whether you understand the concepts well enough to set up the problems. This means you don't always have to find the exact answer. Often, you can use approximation to find the answer that's in the right "ballpark."

2.   Four containers of flour are on a table: The first contains $\frac{1}{3}$ of a pound, the second contains $\frac{1}{6}$ of a pound, the third contains $\frac{1}{9}$ of a pound, and the fourth contains $\frac{1}{18}$ of a pound. If each container can hold one pound of flour, how many additional pounds of flour are required to fill all four containers?

   (A) $\frac{2}{9}$

   (B) $\frac{2}{3}$

   (C) $\frac{11}{9}$

   (D) $\frac{25}{9}$

   (E) $\frac{10}{3}$

You need to fill up each of the containers. The first one needs $\frac{2}{3}$, the second one needs $\frac{5}{6}$, the third one needs $\frac{8}{9}$, and the fourth one needs $\frac{17}{18}$. Now, you could add up all four fractions, but that would be time-consuming and tedious. Instead, ballpark. $\frac{5}{6}$, $\frac{8}{9}$, and $\frac{17}{18}$ are all pretty close to 1. If you call each of them 1 and then add $\frac{2}{3}$, the total needed to fill up all four containers is $3\frac{2}{3}$. You rounded up, so you should look for a number a little less than that. Choices (A) and (B) don't even equal one, so get rid of them. Choice (C) is a little bit more than 1 and (D) is less than 3. Only (E) is "in the ballpark."

You can ballpark on all types of questions (including geometry) whenever the answer choices are fairly far apart. Even when you don't feel comfortable enough to ballpark away all of the wrong answers, Ballparking can help you avoid obviously wrong answers.

Here are some strategies you can use on the Problem Solving questions.

Algebra Versus Arithmetic

Answer this question.

3. Max has a 10-dollar bill. He goes into a candy store and buys 3 pieces of candy that cost 50 cents each. How much change, in dollars, does Max receive?

    (A) $9.50
    (B) $8.50
    (C) $7.00
    (D) $1.50
    (E) $0.50

The correct answer is $8.50, (B). Easy, right?

Now try this question. Try to answer it as quickly as you did the first one.

4. Max has x dollars. He goes into a candy store and buys y pieces of candy that cost z cents each. How much change, in dollars, does Max receive?

    (A) $x - yz$

    (B) $yz - x$

    (C) $\dfrac{x - yz}{100}$

    (D) $100x - yz$

    (E) $x - \dfrac{yx}{100}$

The second question is a little harder. Did you pick (A)? If you did, you're not alone, but the correct answer is (E). Max has *dollars* but the cost of the candy is in *cents*, so you have to convert the cents to dollars.

You didn't have to think about the conversion in the first problem because you were working with numbers; you were doing arithmetic, whereas in the second problem you were doing algebra. It's much easier to work with numbers than it is with variables, isn't it? No matter how good you are at algebra, you're better at arithmetic. Wouldn't it be great if you could turn algebra problems into arithmetic problems? Well, guess what? You can!

Plugging In

Plugging In is a strategy that changes algebra problems into arithmetic problems. It will help you do problems more quickly, more easily and more accurately. It will even help you solve problems you didn't know how to do algebraically. Here's how it works.

Step 1: Assign a number to each variable in the problem.

Step 2: Work the problem step-by-step using the numbers you chose. You should end up with a numerical answer (with no variables left over) that answers the question in the problem. Circle the answer. This is your target.

Step 3: Plug the number(s) you assigned to the variable(s) into the answer choices. Choose the answer choice that matches your target. Be sure to check all five answer choices.

Example

5. The Amazing soft drink company interviewed c consumers for a market-research study. The study found that $\frac{2}{5}$ of consumers preferred Zing cola to Diet Zing cola. Of those who preferred Diet Zing, $\frac{1}{6}$ preferred Caffeine Free Diet Zing. How many consumers, in terms of c, did <u>not</u> prefer Caffeine Free Diet Zing?

(A) $\dfrac{c}{11}$

(B) $\dfrac{c}{10}$

(C) $\dfrac{7c}{15}$

(D) $\dfrac{9c}{10}$

(E) $\dfrac{10c}{11}$

Plug In 30 for c. Write "$c = 30$" on your scratch paper. $\frac{2}{5} \times 30 = 12$, so 12 consumers preferred Zing and the remaining 18 preferred diet. $\frac{1}{6} \times 18 = 3$, so 3 consumers preferred Caffeine Free Diet Zing. That means $30 - 3$, or 27 consumers did <u>not</u> prefer Caffeine Free Diet Zing. That's your target answer. Circle it on your scratch paper. Your work should look something like this:

$$C = 30$$

$$
\begin{array}{rl}
30 & \text{consumers} \\
- \;\; 12 & \text{prefer Zing} \\
\hline
18 & \text{prefer diet} \\
- \;\;\; 3 & \text{prefer caffeine free diet} \\
\hline
15 &
\end{array}
$$

$$30 - 3 = 27$$

Now Plug In your c, which is 30, into each of the answer choices, looking for 27.

Choice (A) is $\frac{30}{11}$; that's not 27, so eliminate it. Choice (B) is $\frac{30}{10}$ which equals 3. That's not 27; eliminate it. Choice (C) is $\frac{7(30)}{15}$ which equals 14. Eliminate it. Choice (D) is $\frac{9(30)}{10}$ which equals 27. That works, but you have to check all of them. Choice E is $\frac{10(30)}{11}$ which does not equal 27. The correct answer is (D).

It's that simple. When you Plug In, always check all the answer choices just in case more than one works. If that happens, simply Plug In again with different numbers. You only have to check the ones that worked. The ones you crossed off the first time are gone forever. You can generally avoid having to Plug In twice by picking good numbers. Follow these guidelines.

Avoid numbers that can make several answer choices match your target.

- Do not use 0 or 1.

- Do not use numbers that appear in the question or in the answer choices.

- Do not use the same number for more than one variable.

Choose numbers to make the calculations easy:

- If there are fractions in the question, choose a number that's a common multiple of the denominators. (Multiplying the denominators together is an easy way to find a good number.)

- If a question involves different units, use a multiple or a factor of the conversion number.

- If a question involves percents, use 100 or a multiple of 100.

Of course, in order to Plug In you must be able to recognize Plug In problems.

The ID

Plug In whenever you see

- Variables in the answer choices
- The expression, "in terms of"

The question above had both cues, but you only need to see one or the other.

Sometimes, you can Plug In even if there aren't variables in the answers or if you don't see the expression "in terms of." These problems are called **Hidden Plug Ins**.

HIDDEN PLUG INS

In a Hidden Plug In question, the variable is invisible. The question will ask for a fraction or percent of an unknown total, or there will be a missing piece of information you need in order to solve the problem. Take a look at the example on the following page.

6. Maggie pays $\frac{1}{8}$ of her monthly income for food, $\frac{1}{8}$ for utilities, $\frac{1}{8}$ for student loans, and $\frac{4}{5}$ of the remainder for rent. If at the end of each month Maggie puts $\frac{1}{2}$ of her remaining income into a CD account, what portion of Maggie's monthly income does she put into the account?

(A) $\frac{1}{8}$

(B) $\frac{1}{10}$

(C) $\frac{7}{80}$

(D) $\frac{1}{16}$

(E) $\frac{1}{20}$

What is the missing piece of information you need to solve this problem? It's Maggie's monthly income. If you know her income, you can figure out everything else. Plug In $80 for her monthly income. She spends $\frac{1}{8}$, or $10 on food, which leaves her $70. She spends another $10 on utilities which leaves her $60. She spends another $10 on student loans which leaves $50. She spends $\frac{4}{5}$ of the remainder, $40, on rent, which now leaves her with $10. At the end of the month, she puts half of her remaining income ($\frac{1}{2}$ of $10 = $5) into a CD account. So she puts $\frac{5}{80}$ into the account, which reduces to $\frac{1}{16}$. The correct answer is (D).

Wow, that's much easier than algebra. So how do you recognize a Hidden Plug In?

The ID
Plug In whenever

- There is a missing piece of information needed to solve the problem
- The question asks for a fraction or percent of an unknown total

PLUGGING IN THE ANSWERS

There is one more type of Plugging In you can do on the GMAT. It's called Plugging In the Answers, or PITA for short. You're still changing algebra to arithmetic, but this time you're working with the answer choices.

When there are numbers in the answer choices (which is the case on all PITA questions), the numbers in the answers always go from lowest to highest or highest to lowest. You start with the answer in the middle, because if it doesn't work, you can often tell which direction to go. Follow these steps.

Step 1: Identify what the question is asking.

Step 2: Plug In the middle answer choice. Work the problem step-by-step and see if everything matches.

Step 3: Eliminate answers that don't work. Keep plugging in answers until you find one that works.

Example

7. Julie is twice as old as her brother Paolo, who is five times as old as their dog Winnie. In 10 years, Julia will be four times as old as Winnie will be then. How old is Paolo?

    (A) 25
    (B) 27
    (C) 30
    (D) 33
    (E) 35

The question asks for Paolo's age, so that's what the answer choices represent. Start with (C) and say that Paolo is 30. Now go back to the beginning of the problem. If Paolo is 30, then Julia is twice that, or 60. The problem says that Paolo is five times as old as the dog, Winnie, which means that Winnie is 6.

Now, how will you know if this is the right answer choice? The problem says that in 10 years, Julia will be 4 times as old as Winnie. In 10 years, Julia will be 70 and Winnie will be 16. Julia is not 4 times as old as Winnie, so cross off answer (C).

You need Julia's age and Winnie's age to be closer together, so try smaller numbers. (If you needed them to be farther apart, you'd try larger numbers.) Go to (B). Choice (B) says that Paolo's age is 27. You may remember that to get Winnie's age, you divided Paolo's age by 5. 27 isn't divisible by 5, so eliminate this choice. There are no fractional ages on the GMAT.

Try (A). If Paolo is 25 then Julia is 50. Paolo is 5 times as old as Winnie, so Winnie is 5. In 10 years, Julia will be 60 and Winnie will be 15. 60 is four times 15, so the correct answer is (A).

When you PITA, make a table to keep track of your work. It should look something like this.

	Paolo	Julia	Winnie	J + 10	W + 10
A)	25	50	5	60	15
B)	27				
C)	30	60	6	70	16
D)	33				
E)	35				

One good thing about PITA is that when you get to an answer that works, you can stop. Because there can only be one correct answer to a question, you don't have to check all the answer choices.

Another good thing about PITA is that you can start working a problem even if you don't understand what it says. You're working backwards so you can figure out the problem as you go along. That way you don't waste time reading and re-reading the problem.

So how do you know when you can Plug In The Answers?

The ID
PITA whenever

- The question asks for a specific amount, such as "How many," "How much," or "What is x"?

AND

- There are no variables in the answer choices

Now that you have learned the basic strategies for the Problem Solving questions, here is some basic strategy for Data Sufficiency questions.

DATA SUFFICIENCY

Data Sufficiency is a special question type that does not appear on any other test besides the GMAT. Lucky you! A lot of people are intimidated by these questions because of their unfamiliar format. However, once you learn how to do these problems, you will find they are not hard to do. In fact, some people end up liking them even more than the Problem Solving questions.

For each Data Sufficiency question, you are given a question and two statements, labeled (1) and (2), which provide certain data. Your job is to figure out which of the statements, if any, are sufficient to answer the question. The important thing to remember is that you don't actually have to answer the questions; you just have to know if you have enough information to answer them. You will be asked to choose from the following answer choices:

(A) Statement (1) ALONE is sufficient, but statement (2) ALONE is not sufficient.
(B) Statement (2) ALONE is sufficient, but statement (1) ALONE is not sufficient.
(C) BOTH statements TOGETHER are sufficient, but NEITHER statement ALONE is sufficient.
(D) EACH statement ALONE is sufficient.
(E) Statements (1) and (2) TOGETHER are NOT sufficient to answer the question asked, and additional data are needed.

Here's a graphic that shows what the answer choices really mean.

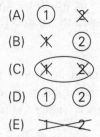

Pick (A) if the first statement is sufficient, but the second one is not. Pick (B) if the second statement is sufficient, but the first one is not, and so on. Think of (C) as **combine**. Choice (C) means you have to combine the two statements; they don't work individually, but they do work when you put them together. With practice, you won't even have to think consciously about what the answer choices mean; they will be ingrained in your memory.

AD/BCE

Data Sufficiency questions are all about Process of Elimination. Based on whether the first statement is sufficient to answer the question, you will narrow your choices down to either **AD** or **BCE**. Then you will go to the second statement, and keep eliminating until you get down to one answer choice.

Try one.

What is the value of x ?

(1) If x is subtracted from 60, the result is 20.

(2) If x is divided by z, the result is 20.

(A) Statement (1) ALONE is sufficient, but statement (2) ALONE is not sufficient.
(B) Statement (2) ALONE is sufficient, but statement (1) ALONE is not sufficient.
(C) BOTH statements TOGETHER are sufficient, but NEITHER statement ALONE is sufficient.
(D) EACH statement ALONE is sufficient.
(E) Statements (1) and (2) TOGETHER are NOT sufficient to answer the question asked, and additional data are needed.

Look only at the first statement. Can you tell what the value of x is from this statement? Yes. If you look at the graphic from the previous page, you will notice that (A) and (D) are the only choices in which the first statement is sufficient. Thus, at this point, your choices are down to (A) and (D). Write "AD" on your scratch paper.

Now, use your finger to cover statement (1) and look only at statement (2). Does statement (2) provide enough information to tell the value of x? No. Cross off "D" and circle "A" on your scratch paper. Choice (A) is correct.

If the second statement **had** provided enough information to answer the question then the answer would have been (D).

Try another.

If $x + y + z = 180$, what is the value of x ?

(1) $y = 75$

(2) $y + z = 141$

(A)   Statement (1) ALONE is sufficient, but statement (2)
ALONE is not sufficient.
(B)   Statement (2) ALONE is sufficient, but statement (1)
ALONE is not sufficient.
(C)   BOTH statements TOGETHER are sufficient, but NEITHER
statement ALONE is sufficient.
(D)   EACH statement ALONE is sufficient.
(E)   Statements (1) and (2) TOGETHER are NOT sufficient
to answer the question asked, and additional data are
needed.

The first statement is not sufficient to tell the value of x, so write "BCE" on your scratch paper. If you look at the graphic from page 167, you will notice that (B), (C), and (E) are the only choices in which the first statement is not sufficient. Now cover the first statement with your finger. Does the second statement provide enough information to find the value of x? Yes. Circle "B" on your scratch paper. If you look at the graphic, you will see that (B) is the choice in which the second statement works, but the first one doesn't.

Try one more.

If $x + y = 3$, what is the value of xy ?

(1) x and y are integers.

(2) x and y are positive.

(A)   Statement (1) ALONE is sufficient, but statement (2)
ALONE is not sufficient.
(B)   Statement (2) ALONE is sufficient, but statement (1)
ALONE is not sufficient.
(C)   BOTH statements TOGETHER are sufficient, but NEITHER
statement ALONE is sufficient.
(D)   EACH statement ALONE is sufficient.
(E)   Statements (1) and (2) TOGETHER are NOT sufficient
to answer the question asked, and additional data are
needed.

The first statement is not sufficient to tell the value of xy, because x and y could be 1 and 2 or 0 and 3. Write "BCE" on your scratch paper. Now look only at statement (2). The second statement is not sufficient to tell the value of xy, because x and y could be 1 and 2 or any decimal combination, such as 2.5 and .5. Cross off "B."

Remember, (C) means combine. If you look at the two statements together, can you then tell the value of xy? Yes. If x and y are positive integers then the only two values that work are 1 and 2, which means that xy has to be 2. By combining, you can tell that the correct answer is (C).

If combining the two statements **had not** been sufficient to determine the value of xy, you would have crossed off "C" and circled "E".

AD/BCE is the basic approach you will use on all Data Sufficiency questions.

A NOTE ABOUT GEOMETRY

The geometry you will see on the GMAT is fairly simple. There are no proofs, no statements of theorems and there is no trigonometry. That doesn't mean that GMAT geometry problems are always easy. As they do on the rest of the exam, the test writers create some very tricky questions that involve geometry. However, if you learn the basic rules and formulas and know them backwards and forwards, you will be able handle the geometry problems you encounter.

Can You Trust the Diagram?

In problem-solving questions, the diagrams are drawn to scale, meaning that you can trust what they look like on the screen. In data sufficiency questions, however, the diagrams are misleading, inaccurate, and designed to confuse you. You may need to redraw the diagram in a different way using the information given in the question or the statements as your guide. Even on problem solving questions, you will nearly always need to transcribe geometry figures to your scratch paper in order to solve the questions. Be careful when you do this, and double-check your diagram.

- Problem solving: You can trust what you see. Figures are drawn to scale unless a problem states otherwise.

- Data sufficiency: Be wary of what you see. Figures are not necessarily drawn to scale, and they may be drawn inaccurately in order to confuse you.

- Make sure you have correctly transcribed the diagram before you begin solving a problem. If no diagram is provided, draw one yourself.

Arithmetic

ARITHMETIC

The math portion of the GMAT tests nothing but "basic" skills, which sounds good until you realize that this is exactly how the test writers hope to get you—by testing you on terms and concepts that you haven't dealt with since high school. And you don't get to use a calculator on the GMAT.

Math Terminology

In order to beat the test writers at their own game, you need to make sure you understand several core concepts and terms. Many questions on the GMAT are unanswerable unless you know what these terms mean. Here is a list of common terms you must know backwards and forwards:

Term	Definition	Examples
Integer	A whole number that does not contain decimals, fractions, or radicals (Integers can be negative, positive, or 0.)	-500, 0, 1, 28
Positive	Greater than 0	0.5, 25, $\dfrac{5}{3}$
Negative	Less than 0	-72.3, $-\dfrac{7}{4}$, -2
Even	An integer that is divisible by 2	-40, 0, 2
Odd	An integer that is not divisible by 2	-41, 1, 3
Sum	The result of addition	The sum of 3 and 4 is 7.
Difference	The result of subtraction	The difference of 7 and 2 is 5.
Product	The result of multiplication	The product of 2 and 7 is 14.
Divisor	The number you are dividing by	$8 \div 2 = 4$ (2 is the divisor.)
Dividend	The number you are dividing into	$8 \div 2 = 4$ (8 is the dividend.)
Quotient	The result of division	$8 \div 2 = 4$ (4 is the quotient.)
Prime	A number that is divisible only by itself and 1 (Negative numbers, 0, and 1 are NOT prime.)	2, 3, 5, 7, 11
Consecutive	In order, not necessarily ascending	-1, 0, 1 or 10, 9, 8
Digits	0–9; the numbers on the phone pad	0, 1, 2, 3, 4, 5, 6, 7, 8, 9

Term	Definition	Examples
Distinct	Different	2 and 3 are distinct; 4 and 4 are not distinct
Absolute Value	The distance from 0 on a number line (The absolute value is always positive)	$\lvert 4 \rvert = 4$; $\lvert -4 \rvert = 4$
Factorial	The factorial of an integer n is the successive product of n times all the positive integers smaller than n.	$4! = 4 \times 3 \times 2 \times 1$

Positive/Negative and Even/Odd

You will save yourself a lot of time on the test if you also know the rules of positive/negative and even/odd. You can always figure out these rules by trying out numbers, but if you know them by heart, you will be able to work problems more quickly.

Negative × or ÷ Negative = Positive
Positive × or ÷ Positive = Positive
Negative × or ÷ Positive = Negative
Even × Even = Even
Even × Odd = Even
Odd × Odd = Odd
Even ± Even = Even
Odd ± Odd = Even
Odd ± Even = Odd

Note that there are no even/odd rules for division. Division often produces fractions, which are neither even nor odd.

Properties of Zero

Zero has some special properties that are important to remember:

- 0 is an integer.
- 0 is an even number.
- 0 is neither positive nor negative.
- 0 times anything is equal to 0.
- 0 divided by anything is equal to 0.
- Anything divided by 0 is undefined. Division by 0 is impossible.

Order of Operations

When you're answering test questions, you must know in what order to perform calculations. The standard acronym for this is **PEMDAS**, which you can also remember with the sentence: Please Excuse My Dear Aunt Sally.

More properly it looks like this.

P|E|MD|AS

P stands for *parentheses*. Solve expressions in parentheses first.
E stands for *exponents*. Solve expressions with exponents next.
M stands for *multiplication*, and **D** stands for *division*.
Do all the multiplication and division together in the same step, going from left to right.
A stands for *addition*, and **S** stands for *subtraction*.
Do all the addition and subtraction together in the same step, going from left to right.

TERMINOLOGY DRILL

1. For which of the following values of a is $\dfrac{a}{3}$ prime?

   (A) 3
   (B) 4
   (C) 5
   (D) 6
   (E) 7

2. If $\dfrac{90}{k}$ is an integer, is k an integer?

   (1) $k > 1$

   (2) k is a multiple of a prime number

   (A) Statement (1) ALONE is sufficient, but statement (2) alone is not sufficient.
   (B) Statement (2) ALONE is sufficient, but statement (1) alone is not sufficient.
   (C) BOTH statements TOGETHER are sufficient, but NEITHER statement ALONE is sufficient.
   (D) EACH statement ALONE is sufficient.
   (E) Statements (1) and (2) TOGETHER are NOT sufficient to answer the question asked, and additional data are needed.

3. How many different positive prime factors does integer x have?

   (1) $\dfrac{x}{12} = 3$

   (2) $\dfrac{x}{36}$ is an integer

   (A) Statement (1) ALONE is sufficient, but statement (2) alone is not sufficient.
   (B) Statement (2) ALONE is sufficient, but statement (1) alone is not sufficient.
   (C) BOTH statements TOGETHER are sufficient, but NEITHER statement ALONE is sufficient.
   (D) EACH statement ALONE is sufficient.
   (E) Statements (1) and (2) TOGETHER are NOT sufficient to answer the question asked, and additional data are needed.

4. If a is an even integer, b is an integer and 2 is not a factor of $a + b$, which of the following could be the value of b ?

   (A) 0
   (B) 2
   (C) 4
   (D) 10
   (E) 15

5. Are positive numbers a and b integers?

   (1) $\dfrac{a}{b}$ is an integer.

   (2) ab is an integer.

   (A) Statement (1) ALONE is sufficient, but statement (2) alone is not sufficient.
   (B) Statement (2) ALONE is sufficient, but statement (1) alone is not sufficient.
   (C) BOTH statements TOGETHER are sufficient, but NEITHER statement ALONE is sufficient.
   (D) EACH statement ALONE is sufficient.
   (E) Statements (1) and (2) TOGETHER are NOT sufficient to answer the question asked, and additional data are needed.

6. How many multiples of 3 are there between 9 and 99, inclusive?

   (A) 30
   (B) 31
   (C) 32
   (D) 33
   (E) 34

7. What is the range of Set S ?

    (1) The median of Set S is 12.

    (2) The lowest term in Set S is the smallest prime number and the largest term in Set S is equal to the square of the first term multiplied by 7.

(A) Statement (1) ALONE is sufficient, but statement (2) alone is not sufficient.
(B) Statement (2) ALONE is sufficient, but statement (1) alone is not sufficient.
(C) BOTH statements TOGETHER are sufficient, but NEITHER statement ALONE is sufficient.
(D) EACH statement ALONE is sufficient.
(E) Statements (1) and (2) TOGETHER are NOT sufficient to answer the question asked, and additional data are needed.

8. If a is an integer and $b = 5a + 3$, which of the following can be a divisor of b ?

(A) 5
(B) 10
(C) 13
(D) 17
(E) 25

9. If $|r| \neq 1$, is integer r even?

    (1) r is not positive.

    (2) $2r > -5$.

(A) Statement (1) ALONE is sufficient, but statement (2) alone is not sufficient.
(B) Statement (2) ALONE is sufficient, but statement (1) alone is not sufficient.
(C) BOTH statements TOGETHER are sufficient, but NEITHER statement ALONE is sufficient.
(D) EACH statement ALONE is sufficient.
(E) Statements (1) and (2) TOGETHER are NOT sufficient to answer the question asked, and additional data are needed.

10. If x and y are integers and $x^2 - y^2$ is odd, which of the following must be odd?

(A) x
(B) y
(C) x^2
(D) $x^2 + 1$
(E) $x + y$

11. Integer d is the product of the integers a, b, and c and $1 < a < b < c$. If the remainder when 233 is divided by d is 79, what is the value of $a + c$?

(A) 7
(B) 9
(C) 13
(D) 14
(E) 18

12. If a, b, c, and d are distinct even integers and a is prime, is the four digit number $abcd$ divisible by 8 ?

    (1) The two digit number ba is a multiple of 21, and 40 is a factor of the two digit number dc.

    (2) 10 is a divisor of the two digit number bc, and the product of a and d is a perfect square.

(A) Statement (1) ALONE is sufficient, but statement (2) alone is not sufficient.
(B) Statement (2) ALONE is sufficient, but statement (1) alone is not sufficient.
(C) BOTH statements TOGETHER are sufficient, but NEITHER statement ALONE is sufficient.
(D) EACH statement ALONE is sufficient.
(E) Statements (1) and (2) TOGETHER are NOT sufficient to answer the question asked, and additional data are needed.

13. When m is divided by 5, the quotient is 2 and the remainder is b. When n is divided by 7, the quotient is 2 and the remainder is also b. If $mn = 221$, what is the value of b ?

(A) 2
(B) 3
(C) 4
(D) 13
(E) 27

14. C is the finite sequence $C_1 = 0$, $C_2 = \dfrac{1}{2}$, $C_3 = \dfrac{2}{3}$,...., determined by the equation $C_f = \dfrac{f-1}{f}$

where f is a positive integer. D is a similar finite

sequence determined by the equation $D_g = \dfrac{g}{g+1}$

where g is a positive integer. Is the sum of all

the values in C equal to the sum of all the values

in D ?

(1) $g \neq f$

(2) The difference between the median of C and the median of D is $\dfrac{3}{43}$.

(A) Statement (1) ALONE is sufficient, but statement (2) alone is not sufficient.
(B) Statement (2) ALONE is sufficient, but statement (1) alone is not sufficient.
(C) BOTH statements TOGETHER are sufficient, but NEITHER statement ALONE is sufficient.
(D) EACH statement ALONE is sufficient.
(E) Statements (1) and (2) TOGETHER are NOT sufficient to answer the question asked, and additional data are needed.

15. Which of the following is a multiple of $4! + 6$?

(A) $2! + 3$
(B) $4! + 12$
(C) $5! + 6$
(D) $5! + 30$
(E) $8! + 12$

16. S is a set of non-zero integers. Is the sum of all the numbers in S even?

(1) The sum of all the odd numbers is even.

(2) The sum of all the positive numbers is odd.

(A) Statement (1) ALONE is sufficient, but statement (2) alone is not sufficient.
(B) Statement (2) ALONE is sufficient, but statement (1) alone is not sufficient.
(C) BOTH statements TOGETHER are sufficient, but NEITHER statement ALONE is sufficient.
(D) EACH statement ALONE is sufficient.
(E) Statements (1) and (2) TOGETHER are NOT sufficient to answer the question asked, and additional data are needed.

Check your answers on page 205.

FRACTIONS

Fractions are one way of expressing part-to-whole s. On the GMAT you will be required to add, subtract, multiply and divide fractions.

Here's a quick review of the basic properties of fractions.

- A fraction describes a $\frac{part}{whole}$ relationship.
- The top of the fraction is called the **numerator** and the bottom is called the **denominator**. For example, in the fraction $\frac{5}{7}$, 5 is the numerator and 7 is the denominator.
- The fraction bar (the line between the numerator and the denominator) is equivalent to division. For example, $\frac{10}{5}$ means 10 ÷ 5, or 2.
- When the numerator is greater than the denominator—and they're both positive—you have a fraction greater than 1, also called an **improper fraction**. For example, $\frac{5}{2}$ is greater than 1. If you did the division, you would get $2\frac{1}{2}$. This is called a **mixed number**.
- The **reciprocal** (also called the inverse) of a fraction is that fraction flipped over. The reciprocal of $\frac{5}{7}$ is $\frac{7}{5}$.

Adding Fractions

If fractions have the same denominator, you can simply add or subtract the numerators and put the sum over the denominator.

Example

$$\frac{3}{11} + \frac{5}{11} = \frac{8}{11}$$

If fractions don't have the same denominator, you have to do a little more work. Try the bowtie method. Here's how it works.

Let's say you are adding $\frac{3}{2}$ and $\frac{5}{6}$. First, multiply diagonally up (opposing denominators and numerators).

$$\overset{\displaystyle 18 \quad 10}{\frac{3}{2}\diagdown\!\!\!\!\diagup\frac{5}{6}}$$

Next, add (or subtract if you are subtracting fractions) across the top.

$$\frac{3}{2} \diagdown \hspace{-0.8em} \times \hspace{-0.8em} \diagup \frac{5}{6} = \frac{\overset{18 + 10}{28}}{\rule{0.8em}{0.4pt}}$$

Finally, multiply across the bottom.

$$\frac{3}{2} \diagdown \hspace{-0.8em} \times \hspace{-0.8em} \diagup \frac{5}{6} = \frac{\overset{18 + 10}{28}}{12}$$

To reduce a fraction, divide the top and bottom by the same number. In the example above you can divide the top and bottom by 4 so that $\frac{28}{12}$ becomes $\frac{7}{3}$.

Handy as the bowtie is, when you need to add or subtract a series of fractions it may be easier to find the lowest common denominator. To do this, decide what number could serve as a common denominator for all of your fractions, then decide what number you need to multiply each denominator by in order to convert it to the common denominator.

For example, this problem

$$\frac{2}{3} + \frac{5}{9} + \frac{4}{27}$$

would become

$$\frac{18}{27} + \frac{15}{27} + \frac{4}{27} = \frac{37}{27}$$

Multiplying Fractions

To multiply fractions, simply multiply straight across the top and the bottom.

$$\frac{13}{6} \times \frac{20}{1} = \frac{260}{6} = \frac{130}{3}$$

If possible, try to reduce before you multiply. When multiplying fractions, you can divide either numerator or denominator by the same number to reduce. (You CANNOT do this with addition and subtraction problems, only with multiplication.) Look at the previous problem again.

$$\overset{10}{\underset{3}{\frac{13}{6}}} \times \frac{20}{1} = \frac{130}{3}$$

Dividing Fractions

To divide fractions, simply multiply by the reciprocal of the second fraction. Remember this adage: "Don't ask why, just flip it over and multiply."

$$\frac{3}{4} \div \frac{5}{7} = \frac{3}{4} \times \frac{7}{5} = \frac{21}{20}$$

FRACTIONS DRILL

1. Each of the following could be a value of $\dfrac{2}{10-x}$ EXCEPT

   (A) $\dfrac{1}{10}$

   (B) $\dfrac{1}{5}$

   (C) 0

   (D) 2

   (E) 10

2. If Marvin saves $\dfrac{x}{10}$ of his income each month for savings, what is x ?

   (1) Marvin saves 10% of his income.

   (2) Marvin's income is $2,500 a month.

   (A) Statement (1) ALONE is sufficient, but statement (2) alone is not sufficient.
   (B) Statement (2) ALONE is sufficient, but statement (1) alone is not sufficient.
   (C) BOTH statements TOGETHER are sufficient, but NEITHER statement ALONE is sufficient.
   (D) EACH statement ALONE is sufficient.
   (E) Statements (1) and (2) TOGETHER are NOT sufficient to answer the question asked, and additional data are needed, and additional data are needed.

3. $1 - \left[\left(\dfrac{1}{2} \div \dfrac{5}{8} \right) \div \dfrac{1}{3} \right] + \dfrac{7}{5} =$

   (A) $-\dfrac{4}{5}$

   (B) 0

   (C) $\dfrac{32}{15}$

   (D) $\dfrac{12}{5}$

   (E) $\dfrac{19}{5}$

4. Which of the following does NOT equal 2 ?

   (A) $\dfrac{1}{4}(2+2+2+2)$

   (B) $\dfrac{1}{2}+\dfrac{1}{2}+\dfrac{1}{2}+\dfrac{1}{2}$

   (C) $\dfrac{1}{2}+\dfrac{2}{4}+\dfrac{3}{6}+\dfrac{4}{8}$

   (D) $\dfrac{1}{2}(1+1+1+1)$

   (E) $\dfrac{1}{2}+\dfrac{2}{3}+\dfrac{3}{4}+\dfrac{4}{5}$

5. What is the value of $\dfrac{x}{3} + \dfrac{y}{6}$?

    (1) $\dfrac{x}{y} = \dfrac{2}{3}$

    (2) $\dfrac{y - x}{9} = \dfrac{1}{3}$

(A) Statement (1) ALONE is sufficient, but statement (2) alone is not sufficient.
(B) Statement (2) ALONE is sufficient, but statement (1) alone is not sufficient.
(C) BOTH statements TOGETHER are sufficient, but NEITHER statement ALONE is sufficient.
(D) EACH statement ALONE is sufficient.
(E) Statements (1) and (2) TOGETHER are NOT sufficient to answer the question asked, and additional data are needed.

6. At a dinner party, $\dfrac{2}{3}$ of the diners ordered salad, and $\dfrac{1}{4}$ of those who ordered salad also ordered soup. What fraction of diners at the party did not order both salad and soup?

(A) $\dfrac{1}{6}$

(B) $\dfrac{1}{4}$

(C) $\dfrac{1}{3}$

(D) $\dfrac{3}{4}$

(E) $\dfrac{5}{6}$

7. If $ab \neq 0$ in the equation $V = \dfrac{\dfrac{3}{a}}{\dfrac{4}{b} + \dfrac{7}{8c}}$, what is V?

    (1) $a = 8$ and $c = 12$

    (2) $b = 3a$ and $c = \dfrac{b}{2}$

(A) Statement (1) ALONE is sufficient, but statement (2) alone is not sufficient.
(B) Statement (2) ALONE is sufficient, but statement (1) alone is not sufficient.
(C) BOTH statements TOGETHER are sufficient, but NEITHER statement ALONE is sufficient.
(D) EACH statement ALONE is sufficient.
(E) Statements (1) and (2) TOGETHER are NOT sufficient to answer the question asked, and additional data are needed.

8. If q and r are positive integers and $qr = 64$, what is q?

    (1) $\dfrac{r}{8}$ is an integer.

    (2) $\dfrac{q}{4}$ is an integer.

(A) Statement (1) ALONE is sufficient, but statement (2) alone is not sufficient.
(B) Statement (2) ALONE is sufficient, but statement (1) alone is not sufficient.
(C) BOTH statements TOGETHER are sufficient, but NEITHER statement ALONE is sufficient.
(D) EACH statement ALONE is sufficient.
(E) Statements (1) and (2) TOGETHER are NOT sufficient to answer the question asked, and additional data are needed.

Check your answers on page 205.

DECIMALS

Like fractions, decimals are a way to express part-to-whole relationships. Fractions and decimals are interchangeable. Any fraction can be written as a decimal and vice versa. That means you can do your calculations in the format with which you're most comfortable.

Converting Decimals to Fractions

To convert a decimal into a fraction, place the decimal over 1, move the decimal points the same number of places on the top and bottom until you have whole numbers on both the top and bottom, and then reduce.

Example

$$.25 = \frac{.25}{1.00} = \frac{25}{100} = \frac{1}{4}$$

Converting Fractions to Decimals

To convert a fraction into a decimal, divide the bottom into the top.

$$\frac{1}{4} = 4\overline{)1.00}^{\,.25} = 0.25$$

On the GMAT, you will need to be able to add, subtract, multiply and divide decimals.

Adding and Subtracting Decimals

To add or subtract decimals, simply line up the decimal points and add or subtract as you normally would. You can add zeros onto the end of a decimal without changing the value. For example, 3.25 – 3.025 becomes

$$
\begin{array}{r}
3.250 \\
-\ 3.025 \\
\hline
0.225
\end{array}
$$

Multiplying Decimals

To multiply decimals, ignore the decimals at first, and multiply the numbers as if they were plain integers. Then count the total number of decimal places that were in your original numbers and put the decimals back into your final product, moving from right to left.

For example, multiply 4.3 by 2.5: ignore the decimals and multiply to get 1,075. Now count the decimal places. 4.3 and 2.5 each have one decimal place for a total of 2 decimal places. Put the decimals back into the final product to get 10.75.

Dividing Decimals

To divide decimals, change the decimal into a whole number by moving the decimal point in both your numerator and denominator the same number of places to the right. The number with the most decimal places determines how many places you move the decimal. Then divide as you normally would.

For example $\dfrac{.004}{.02}$ becomes $\dfrac{4}{20} = \dfrac{1}{5}$

Place Value

It's useful to understand place value when dealing with decimals on the GMAT. Each place contains a digit, which is a whole number from 0 to 9. Here are the place values for the number 6,493.783.

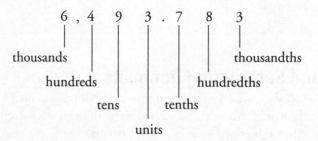

DECIMALS DRILL

1. What number is .03 of z ?

   (1) 0.0008 is 0.02 of z.

   (2) 0.01 of z is 0.0004.

(A) Statement (1) ALONE is sufficient, but statement (2) alone is not sufficient.
(B) Statement (2) ALONE is sufficient, but statement (1) alone is not sufficient.
(C) BOTH statements TOGETHER are sufficient, but NEITHER statement ALONE is sufficient.
(D) EACH statement ALONE is sufficient.
(E) Statements (1) and (2) TOGETHER are NOT sufficient to answer the question asked, and additional data are needed.

2. $\dfrac{5.055}{2.022} =$

(A) 2.025
(B) 2.05
(C) 2.499
(D) 2.5
(E) 2.525

3. When $\dfrac{3}{22}$ is written in decimal form, which of the following is the 19th digit to the right of the decimal point?

(A) 2
(B) 3
(C) 4
(D) 5
(E) 6

4. If $b = 0.cdef$ where c, d, e, and f represent nonzero digits, what is b ?

   (1) $1{,}000 \times b$ is divisible by 4,938.

   (2) $c > d > e > f$ and $f = 6$.

(A) Statement (1) ALONE is sufficient, but statement (2) alone is not sufficient.
(B) Statement (2) ALONE is sufficient, but statement (1) alone is not sufficient.
(C) BOTH statements TOGETHER are sufficient, but NEITHER statement ALONE is sufficient.
(D) EACH statement ALONE is sufficient.
(E) Statements (1) and (2) TOGETHER are NOT sufficient to answer the question asked, and additional data are needed.

5. If k and l are positive and l is a single digit, what is the value of k ?

   (1) $\dfrac{1}{3} - 0.01 = 0.3l$ rounded to the nearest hundredth digit.

   (2) $k = 3.927l$

(A) Statement (1) ALONE is sufficient, but statement (2) alone is not sufficient.
(B) Statement (2) ALONE is sufficient, but statement (1) alone is not sufficient.
(C) BOTH statements TOGETHER are sufficient, but NEITHER statement ALONE is sufficient.
(D) EACH statement ALONE is sufficient.
(E) Statements (1) and (2) TOGETHER are NOT sufficient to answer the question asked, and additional data are needed.

6. When $\dfrac{x}{32}$ is expressed in decimal form, it is a terminating decimal. Which of the following could be a value of x ?

    I. 3
    II. 5
    III. 8

(A) I only
(B) II only
(C) I and II
(D) III only
(E) I, II, and III

7. X and Y are single digits in the decimal 7.381XY9. What is X ?

    (1) When the decimal is rounded to the nearest ten thousandth, the result is 7.3814.

    (2) When the decimal is rounded to the nearest thousandth, the result is 7.381.

(A) Statement (1) ALONE is sufficient, but statement (2) alone is not sufficient.
(B) Statement (2) ALONE is sufficient, but statement (1) alone is not sufficient.
(C) BOTH statements TOGETHER are sufficient, but NEITHER statement ALONE is sufficient.
(D) EACH statement ALONE is sufficient.
(E) Statements (1) and (2) TOGETHER are NOT sufficient to answer the question asked, and additional data are needed.

8. $\dfrac{8{,}103}{x}$ is a non-terminating decimal. Which of the following could be a value of x ?

(A) 2
(B) 5
(C) 9
(D) 12
(E) 15

Check your answers on page 205.

PERCENTS

Like fractions and decimals, percents are one more way to express part-to-whole relationships. Percents can be converted easily into decimals and fractions, and vice versa.

Conversion

"Percent" literally means *per cent*—per 100. When you see the word "percent" think "over one hundred." Any percent can be expressed as a fraction by putting it over 100, then reducing the fraction (if necessary).

Example

$$25\% = \frac{25}{100} = \frac{1}{4}$$

To convert a fraction into a percent, you have to know that $\frac{part}{whole} = \frac{x}{100}$, where x is the percent. To convert $\frac{3}{5}$ into a percent, set up a proportion and solve for x.

$$\frac{3}{5} = \frac{x}{100}$$
$$5x = 300$$
$$x = 60$$

Thus, $\frac{3}{5}$ is the same as $\frac{60}{100}$, or 60%.

Another way to convert a fraction into a percent is to convert the fraction into a decimal (by dividing bottom into top) and then convert the decimal into a percent.

To convert a decimal into a percent, move the decimal point two spaces to the right and add a percent sign.

$$.6 = 60\% = \frac{3}{5} \qquad 3.5 = 350\% = \frac{350}{100} \qquad .002 = .2\% = \frac{.2}{100}$$

To convert a percent into a decimal, drop the percent sign and move the decimal point two spaces to the left.

$$25\% = .25 = \frac{25}{100} \qquad .1\% = .001 = \frac{.1}{100} \qquad 200\% = 2.0 = \frac{200}{100}$$

Percent Translation

The test writers like to phrase percent problems on the GMAT as long word problems. Use this table to translate a percent word problem into a mathematical equation.

English	Mathematical translation
percent	$\overline{100}$
of	$\times$ (times)
what	$x, y,$ or z (a variable)
is, are, were,	$=$

Thus,

20 is what percent of 125 ?

becomes

$$20 = \frac{x}{100} \times 125$$

PERCENTS DRILL

1. Matthew's van contained 10 gallons of gasoline before he stopped at a gas station, where he added an additional 6 gallons to the tank. If the fuel tank is still 4 gallons short of capacity, what percent of the total capacity did the van's tank originally contain prior to stopping at the gas station?

   (A) 20%
   (B) 40%
   (C) 50%
   (D) 60%
   (E) 80%

2. If Dre's salary last year was $50,000, what is his salary this year?

   (1) Dre's salary this year increased by 20% compared to last year's salary.

   (2) If Dre had earned an additional $10,000 in salary this year, his salary would have increased by 40% compared to last year.

   (A) Statement (1) ALONE is sufficient, but statement (2) alone is not sufficient.
   (B) Statement (2) ALONE is sufficient, but statement (1) alone is not sufficient.
   (C) BOTH statements TOGETHER are sufficient, but NEITHER statement ALONE is sufficient.
   (D) EACH statement ALONE is sufficient.
   (E) Statements (1) and (2) TOGETHER are NOT sufficient to answer the question asked, and additional data are needed.

3. Laura makes a weekly salary of $200 as a courier, plus 15 percent of the number of miles that she drives after her first 50 miles, which are unpaid. If she made $350 last week, how many total miles did she drive last week?

   (A)   550
   (B)   950
   (C) 1,000
   (D) 1,050
   (E) 2,000

4. In a five year period starting in 2002 at MegaCorp, each year p% of total revenues were profit. If revenues in 2002 were $80 million, what is p ?

   (1) Profits doubled each year at MegaCorp during the five year period.

   (2) Profits in 2005 were $56 million more than profits in 2002.

   (A) Statement (1) ALONE is sufficient, but statement (2) alone is not sufficient.
   (B) Statement (2) ALONE is sufficient, but statement (1) alone is not sufficient.
   (C) BOTH statements TOGETHER are sufficient, but NEITHER statement ALONE is sufficient.
   (D) EACH statement ALONE is sufficient.
   (E) Statements (1) and (2) TOGETHER are NOT sufficient to answer the question asked, and additional data are needed.

5. WINK, Inc. recently conducted a survey and found that 180,000 of its customers live in rural areas. If the number of its customers who live in urban areas is 200 percent greater than the number of customers who live in rural areas, how many of WINK, Inc.'s customers live in urban areas?

   (A) 200,000
   (B) 216,000
   (C) 360,000
   (D) 480,000
   (E) 540,000

6. Monique, Shannon, and Rosemary go fishing. What percentage of the fish caught were caught by Shannon?

    (1) Monique caught three times as many fish as Rosemary, who caught half as many fish as Shannon.

    (2) Shannon caught 10 fish.

(A) Statement (1) ALONE is sufficient, but statement (2) alone is not sufficient.
(B) Statement (2) ALONE is sufficient, but statement (1) alone is not sufficient.
(C) BOTH statements TOGETHER are sufficient, but NEITHER statement ALONE is sufficient.
(D) EACH statement ALONE is sufficient.
(E) Statements (1) and (2) TOGETHER are NOT sufficient to answer the question asked, and additional data are needed.

7. Bob is booking an airline flight, and the airline is running a special. Bob can choose either to receive 15,000 air miles immediately, or to receive 7,000 air miles, plus 20 percent of the miles that he flies over the next six months. How many miles must Bob fly in the next six months in order to receive equal miles from either option?

(A) 11,000
(B) 15,000
(C) 22,000
(D) 40,000
(E) 80,000

8. Salad dressing A is made up of 30 percent vinegar and 70 percent oil, and salad dressing B contains 10 percent vinegar and 90 percent oil. If the two dressings are combined to produce a salad dressing that is 15 percent vinegar, dressing A comprises what percent of the new dressing?

(A) 15%
(B) 20%
(C) 25%
(D) 40%
(E) 55%

9. If x, y, and z are positive and y% of x is greater than 100, is x% of z less than 10 ?

    (1) z% of y is 10.

    (2) z is less than 10% of y.

(A) Statement (1) ALONE is sufficient, but statement (2) alone is not sufficient.
(B) Statement (2) ALONE is sufficient, but statement (1) alone is not sufficient.
(C) BOTH statements TOGETHER are sufficient, but NEITHER statement ALONE is sufficient.
(D) EACH statement ALONE is sufficient.
(E) Statements (1) and (2) TOGETHER are NOT sufficient to answer the question asked, and additional data are needed.

10. At Anjelina Winery, the vintner wants to blend this year's New Sherry with last year's Old Sherry to create next year's Future Sherry. The vintner decides to use a hogshead with a total capacity of 240 liters that is partially full of Old Sherry. If the hogshead is filled up to full capacity with New Sherry, and Future Sherry will have 17% alcohol by volume (or a.b.v.), what is the a.b.v. of New Sherry?

    (1) There will be 40% more New Sherry than Old Sherry in the filled hogshead, and the Old Sherry is 1.72% higher in a.b.v. than the New Sherry.

    (2) 100 liters of Old Sherry is in the hogshead, at 18% a.b.v.

(A) Statement (1) ALONE is sufficient, but statement (2) alone is not sufficient.
(B) Statement (2) ALONE is sufficient, but statement (1) alone is not sufficient.
(C) BOTH statements TOGETHER are sufficient, but NEITHER statement ALONE is sufficient.
(D) EACH statement ALONE is sufficient.
(E) Statements (1) and (2) TOGETHER are NOT sufficient to answer the question asked, and additional data are needed.

Check your answers on page 205.

PERCENT CHANGE

Some questions on the GMAT ask you to calculate the **percent increase** or the **percent decrease** from one number to another. To calculate percent change, use this formula

$$\% \text{ Change} = \frac{difference}{original} \times 100$$

The *difference* is what you get when you subtract the smaller number from the larger number. The *original* is the starting number.

If the problem says *increase* or *greater,* then the original number is the **smaller** number.

If the problem says *decrease* or *less,* then the original number is the **larger** number.

If the problem says *greater than* or *less than*, whatever comes after the word *than* is the original number.

Try this problem.

> J. J.'s music collection contains 600 CDs. Caleb's music collection contains 500 CDs. Caleb's music collection is what percent smaller than J.J.'s?

J. J.'s (collection) comes after the word *than,* so 600, the number of CDs in J.J.'s collection, is the original amount.

$$\% \text{ Change} = \frac{600 - 500}{600} = \frac{100}{600} = \frac{1}{6} = 16.67\%$$

PERCENT CHANGE DRILL

1. A company's earnings increased by 15% last quarter. If the company's earnings continue to increase at the same rate this quarter, by what percent will the earnings have increased from the beginning of last quarter to the end of this quarter?

   (A) 15%
   (B) 22.5%
   (C) 30%
   (D) 32.25%
   (E) 37.5%

2. Burbuja Inc. analyzes home values in the Miami area, where there has been a six-month freeze on new construction. Its clients would like to know whether the percent change in the average price of condominiums in Miami over the previous six-month period exceeded the known change in home values in Boca Raton during the same period.

   (1) Average condominium listings in Miami fell from $800,000 to $650,000 over the previous six months.

   (2) Six months ago, Miami condos sold for an average of $520/sq ft., while today, they sell for an average of $482/sq ft.

   (A) Statement (1) ALONE is sufficient, but statement (2) alone is not sufficient.
   (B) Statement (2) ALONE is sufficient, but statement (1) alone is not sufficient.
   (C) BOTH statements TOGETHER are sufficient, but NEITHER statement ALONE is sufficient.
   (D) EACH statement ALONE is sufficient.
   (E) Statements (1) and (2) TOGETHER are NOT sufficient to answer the question asked, and additional data are needed.

3. The average of three distinct positive integers x, y, and z is 64. If a new number d is added, will the percent increase exceed 13% ?

   (1) d is twice the value of one of the original numbers.

   (2) d is half the value of the largest of the original numbers.

   (A) Statement (1) ALONE is sufficient, but statement (2) alone is not sufficient.
   (B) Statement (2) ALONE is sufficient, but statement (1) alone is not sufficient.
   (C) BOTH statements TOGETHER are sufficient, but NEITHER statement ALONE is sufficient.
   (D) EACH statement ALONE is sufficient.
   (E) Statements (1) and (2) TOGETHER are NOT sufficient to answer the question asked, and additional data are needed.

4. Lori's Laminate has set an annual goal of cutting head count at its Texas factory by 7% yearly, while maintaining or increasing laminate tile production. Did Lori's Laminate achieve this goal from 2006-2007 ?

   (1) For 2006, the Texas factory employed 100 workers and produced 1,110,000 tiles.

   (2) For 2007, Lori's Laminate employed 85 workers and produced 1,540,000 tiles.

   (A) Statement (1) ALONE is sufficient, but statement (2) alone is not sufficient.
   (B) Statement (2) ALONE is sufficient, but statement (1) alone is not sufficient.
   (C) BOTH statements TOGETHER are sufficient, but NEITHER statement ALONE is sufficient.
   (D) EACH statement ALONE is sufficient.
   (E) Statements (1) and (2) TOGETHER are NOT sufficient to answer the question asked, and additional data are needed.

Check your answers on page 205.

FACTORS

Factors are frequently tested on the GMAT. A factor is a positive integer that divides evenly into another positive integer. For example, 6 is a factor of 18 because 6 divides evenly into 18 three times. 18 ÷ 6 = 3. This also means that 3 is a factor of 18 because 3 divides evenly into 18 six times. Thus, 3 and 6 are both factors of 18.

To find all the factors of a number, start with 1 and the number itself. Move up in pairs until the numbers converge.

Here are all the factors of 60. (On the GMAT, you should only concern yourself with positive factors.)

> 1 and 60
> 2 and 30
> 3 and 20
> 4 and 15
> 5 and 12
> 6 and 10

That's it. Notice that the pairs have gotten closer together. There are no factors between 6 and 10, so you know you've found them all.

Prime Factors

A prime factor is a factor that is also a prime number. To find the prime factors of a number, use the factor tree and keep breaking the numbers into factors until you have only prime numbers.

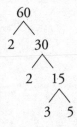

Thus, the prime factors of 60 are 2, 2, 3, and 5.

Rules of Divisibility

To help you find factors and make other GMAT computations easier, you should memorize the rules of divisibility. Knowing these rules will save you precious time on the test.

A number is divisible by	Rule	Example
2	It's even (i.e., its last digit is even)	1,576✓
3	Its digits add up to a multiple of 3	8,532 8 + 5 + 3 + 2 = 18✓
4	Its last two digits are divisible by 4	121,532 32 ÷ 4 = 8✓
5	Its last digit is 5 or 0	568,745✓ 320✓
6	Apply the rules of 2 and 3	55,740 It's even and 5 + 5 + 7 + 4 + 0 = 21✓✓
9	Its digits add up to a multiple of 9	235,692 2 + 3 + 5 + 6 + 9 + 2 = 27✓
10	Its last digit is zero	11,130✓
12	Apply the rules of 3 and 4	3,552 3 + 5 + 5 + 2 = 15 and 52 ÷ 4 = 13✓✓

FACTORS DRILL

1. Is positive integer x divisible by 7 ?

    (1) The sum of the prime factors of x is 12.

    (2) The sum of the distinct prime factors of x is 12.

(A) Statement (1) ALONE is sufficient, but statement (2) alone is not sufficient.
(B) Statement (2) ALONE is sufficient, but statement (1) alone is not sufficient.
(C) BOTH statements TOGETHER are sufficient, but NEITHER statement ALONE is sufficient.
(D) EACH statement ALONE is sufficient.
(E) Statements (1) and (2) TOGETHER are NOT sufficient to answer the question asked, and additional data are needed.

2. If x and y are positive integers such that x is a factor of 10 and y is a factor of 12, all of the following could be the value of xy EXCEPT

(A) 1
(B) 4
(C) 15
(D) 36
(E) 40

3. How many distinct prime factors does 14! have?

(A) 2
(B) 5
(C) 6
(D) 7
(E) 9

4. If x is the product of all the integers between the integers a and b, non-inclusive, is 5 a factor of x ?

    (1) $b - a = 7$

    (2) $b = 9$

(A) Statement (1) ALONE is sufficient, but statement (2) alone is not sufficient.
(B) Statement (2) ALONE is sufficient, but statement (1) alone is not sufficient.
(C) BOTH statements TOGETHER are sufficient, but NEITHER statement ALONE is sufficient.
(D) EACH statement ALONE is sufficient.
(E) Statements (1) and (2) TOGETHER are NOT sufficient to answer the question asked, and additional data are needed.

5. If the positive integers a and b are distinct factors of 9, then the smallest possible value for ab is

(A) 1
(B) 3
(C) 9
(D) 81
(E) 162

6. If x is even, and $90 \leq x \leq 100$, what is the value of x ?

    (1) x and $\dfrac{x}{2}$ have the same distinct prime factors.

    (2) $\dfrac{x}{2}$ has two prime factors.

(A) Statement (1) ALONE is sufficient, but statement (2) alone is not sufficient.
(B) Statement (2) ALONE is sufficient, but statement (1) alone is not sufficient.
(C) BOTH statements TOGETHER are sufficient, but NEITHER statement ALONE is sufficient.
(D) EACH statement ALONE is sufficient.
(E) Statements (1) and (2) TOGETHER are NOT sufficient to answer the question asked, and additional data are needed.

7. If integer x has at least three distinct prime factors, then which of the following could be an integer?

(A) $\dfrac{3}{x}$

(B) $\dfrac{15}{x}$

(C) $\dfrac{24}{x}$

(D) $\dfrac{35}{x}$

(E) $\dfrac{42}{x}$

8. The product of distinct integers a, b, and c is 1,001. If a, b, and c are each greater than 1, what is the smallest value any one of the integers can have?

(A) 3
(B) 7
(C) 11
(D) 13
(E) 77

9. If a, b, c, d, and e are 5 consecutive positive integers, and $a < b < c < d < e$, does c have 4 as a factor?

(1) a is even.

(2) The products bcd and cde both have 4 as a factor.

(A) Statement (1) ALONE is sufficient, but statement (2) alone is not sufficient.
(B) Statement (2) ALONE is sufficient, but statement (1) alone is not sufficient.
(C) BOTH statements TOGETHER are sufficient, but NEITHER statement ALONE is sufficient.
(D) EACH statement ALONE is sufficient.
(E) Statements (1) and (2) TOGETHER are NOT sufficient to answer the question asked, and additional data are needed.

10. If m and n are both positive integers, and $m > n$, is 6 a factor of the product mn ?

(1) $m + n = 188$

(2) m is 150% of n

(A) Statement (1) ALONE is sufficient, but statement (2) alone is not sufficient.
(B) Statement (2) ALONE is sufficient, but statement (1) alone is not sufficient.
(C) BOTH statements TOGETHER are sufficient, but NEITHER statement ALONE is sufficient.
(D) EACH statement ALONE is sufficient.
(E) Statements (1) and (2) TOGETHER are NOT sufficient to answer the question asked, and additional data are needed.

Check your answers on page 205.

MULTIPLES

A multiple is the product of one positive integer and any other positive integer. For example, the multiples of 12 are 12, 24, 36, 48, 60 and on and on, because $12 \times 1 = 12$, $12 \times 2 = 24$, $12 \times 3 = 36$ and so on. Basically, you start with the number itself and then count up by that number.

To put it another way, a multiple is a number that is divisible by a factor. Because 6 is a factor of 18, 18 is a multiple of 6.

The smallest multiple of any number is always the number itself. While you can list all the factors of a number, you can't list all the multiples, because they go on forever. To keep you from mixing up multiples and factors, remember this adage.

Multiples are many. Factors are few.

MULTIPLES DRILL

1. If *n* is a three-digit number, is *n* a multiple of 3 ?

   (1) The units digit of *n* is 3.

   (2) The sum of the tens and hundreds digits is 8.

   (A) Statement (1) ALONE is sufficient, but statement (2) alone is not sufficient.
   (B) Statement (2) ALONE is sufficient, but statement (1) alone is not sufficient.
   (C) BOTH statements TOGETHER are sufficient, but NEITHER statement ALONE is sufficient.
   (D) EACH statement ALONE is sufficient.
   (E) Statements (1) and (2) TOGETHER are NOT sufficient to answer the question asked, and additional data are needed.

2. If *r* and *s* are positive integers, and if *r* is a multiple of 3 and *s* is a multiple of 6, then *rs* must be a multiple of which of the following?

   (A) 9
   (B) 12
   (C) 24
   (D) 36
   (E) 54

3. If *m* and *k* are even integers, which of the following must be a multiple of *m* ?

   I. $\dfrac{5k}{4}m$

   II. $3km$

   III. $\dfrac{7k}{2}m$

   (A) I only
   (B) II only
   (C) III only
   (D) I and III only
   (E) II and III only

4. If positive integer *x* is a multiple of all of the single-digit prime numbers, then *x* must be a multiple of all of the following EXCEPT

   (A) 30
   (B) 42
   (C) 66
   (D) 105
   (E) 210

5. If *a*, *b*, and *c* are consecutive positive integers, and *a* < *b* < *c* , is *abc* a multiple of 15 ?

   (1) *b* – 4 is a multiple of 5.

   (2) The units digit of the product of *a* and *c* is 0.

   (A) Statement (1) ALONE is sufficient, but statement (2) alone is not sufficient.
   (B) Statement (2) ALONE is sufficient, but statement (1) alone is not sufficient.
   (C) BOTH statements TOGETHER are sufficient, but NEITHER statement ALONE is sufficient.
   (D) EACH statement ALONE is sufficient.
   (E) Statements (1) and (2) TOGETHER are NOT sufficient to answer the question asked, and additional data are needed.

Check your answers on page 205.

RATIOS

Earlier you learned about fractions, decimals, and percents, which express part-to-whole relationships. Now it's time to discuss ratios, which express **part-to-part** relationships.

A ratio is like a recipe. It tells you the relative amounts of each ingredient in your final concoction. Consider a recipe for punch that calls for 2 parts grape juice and 3 parts orange juice. The relationship, or ratio, of grape juice to orange juice is 2:3. That relationship remains constant no matter how much punch you make.

Ratios can be written in several ways. All of the following express the ratio of grape juice to orange juice in the punch recipe above.

- The ratio of grape juice to orange juice is 2 to 3.

- The ratio of grape juice to orange juice is 2:3.

- The ratio of grape juice to orange juice is $\frac{2}{3}$

Even though ratios can be expressed in fraction form as in the last example above, ratios are not fractions. In the punch recipe the 2 parts grape juice and 3 parts orange juice add up to 5 total parts. Thus, the **fraction** of grape juice in the mixture is $\frac{2}{5}$ and the **fraction** of orange juice in the mixture is $\frac{3}{5}$, but the **ratio** of grape juice to orange juice remains $\frac{2}{3}$.

The important thing to remember about ratios is that they don't tell you actual amounts. Knowing that the ratio of grape juice to orange juice is 2:3 doesn't tell you the actual amounts of grape juice and orange juice. It simply tells you that whether you make a pitcher or a large vat of the punch, if the recipe is followed, dividing the amount of grape juice by the amount of orange juice will always give you $\frac{2}{3}$.

> A ratio tells you only the relative amounts of each quantity. It does not, by itself, tell you the actual amounts.

Ratio Box

If you're given a ratio and want to determine actual amounts, you need more information. The **ratio box** is a very helpful tool you can use when you are given a ratio and one actual amount. Here's an example.

1. In a club with 35 members, the ratio of men to women is 2 to 3. How many men belong to the club?

Set up a ratio box to keep track of the information. Start by putting the ratio numbers from the problem into the top row of the box, and then add across to get your *ratio total*. The problem provides one actual amount, 35 members. Put that number in the bottom right hand corner of the box. It is your *actual total*. Now you need to figure out the multiplier. What do you have to divide 35 by to get to 5? Seven. So, 7 is the multiplier. Enter it in the middle row all the way across, and then multiply down to get the remaining actual amounts. Thus, the actual number of men is $2 \times 7 = 14$.

	Men	Women	Total
Ratio	2 +	3 =	5
	×	×	×
Multiply by	7 =	7 =	7
	=	=	=
Actual Number	14 +	21 =	35

Proportions

Some problems look like ratio problems but are actually proportion problems. **Proportions** set two ratios equal to one another in a fixed relationship. For example, the relationship between hours and minutes is reflected by this proportion:

$$\frac{1 \text{ hour}}{60 \text{ minutes}} = \frac{3 \text{ hours}}{180 \text{ minutes}}$$

The key to doing a proportion problem is to set one ratio equal to another, making sure to keep your units in the same place. In the example above, hours and hours are on top and minutes and minutes are on the bottom.

Example

2.   On a certain map, the ratio of inches to miles is 4:500. How many miles does 1 inch represent on the map?

Although the problem uses the word *ratio*, you can solve this problem with a proportion. 4 inches represent 500 miles, so 1 inch represents x miles. Your proportion should look like this.

$$\frac{4 \text{ inches}}{500 \text{ miles}} = \frac{1 \text{ inch}}{x \text{ miles}}$$

Now just solve by cross multiplying and you find that 1 inch represents 125 miles.

RATIOS DRILL

1. If *a* and *b* are positive integers such that the ratio of *a* to *b* is 5 to 3, which of the following could be the remainder when *a* is divided by *b* ?

   (A)   3
   (B)   5
   (C)   6
   (D)   9
   (E)   15

2. A music store sells used and new CDs, at *x* dollars per used CD and *y* dollars per new CD. If Adrian and Betty each made a purchase at the store, what is the value of *x* ?

   (1)   Adrian paid $33.75 for 1 used CD and 1 new CD.

   (2)   Betty paid $24 for 3 used CDs.

   (A)   Statement (1) ALONE is sufficient, but statement (2) alone is not sufficient.
   (B)   Statement (2) ALONE is sufficient, but statement (1) alone is not sufficient.
   (C)   BOTH statements TOGETHER are sufficient, but NEITHER statement ALONE is sufficient.
   (D)   EACH statement ALONE is sufficient.
   (E)   Statements (1) and (2) TOGETHER are NOT sufficient to answer the question asked, and additional data are needed.

3. For all numbers *x* and *y*, the ratio *x* to *y* is equivalent to which ratio?

   (A)   *x* to 2*y*

   (B)   2*x* to 2*y*

   (C)   *x* + 3 to *y* + 3

   (D)   *xy* to *xy*

   (E)   3*x* to $\dfrac{x}{3}$

4. A math professor maintains the same ratio of the number of students who pass to the number who fail every semester. The numbers of students who passed the last four semesters, and the total numbers for each, are as follows: 76 out of 80, 57 out of 60, 38 out of 40, and 95 out of 100. If the professor currently has 120 students, how many students are expected to fail this semester?

   (A)   6
   (B)   7
   (C)   8
   (D)   112
   (E)   114

5. The ratio of *x* to *y* is less than 1. What is the ratio of *x* to *y* ?

   (1) $\dfrac{3}{5}x = 9$.

   (2)   If one of the values is doubled, the new ratio is $\dfrac{3}{2}$.

   (A)   Statement (1) ALONE is sufficient, but statement (2) alone is not sufficient.
   (B)   Statement (2) ALONE is sufficient, but statement (1) alone is not sufficient.
   (C)   BOTH statements TOGETHER are sufficient, but NEITHER statement ALONE is sufficient.
   (D)   EACH statement ALONE is sufficient.
   (E)   Statements (1) and (2) TOGETHER are NOT sufficient to answer the question asked, and additional data are needed.

6. In one division of a large electronics company, the ratio of the number of managers to the number of business analysts is 3 to 7. If the division were to hire 3 new analysts, the ratio of managers to analysts would be 3 to 8. How many managers are there in the division?

   (A)   3
   (B)   8
   (C)   9
   (D)   21
   (E)   30

7. A certain IT department of fewer than 15 people hires coders and systems administrators. Coders are paid $55,000 per year on average, while systems administrators are paid an average yearly salary of $45,000. What is the ratio of coders to systems administrators?

    (1) If two of the coders were made systems administrators instead, the yearly payroll for the IT department would be $535,000.

    (2) If systems administrators' salaries were reduced by one-third, and coders' salaries were increased to $58,000, the department would save $57,000 in yearly payroll.

(A) Statement (1) ALONE is sufficient, but statement (2) alone is not sufficient.
(B) Statement (2) ALONE is sufficient, but statement (1) alone is not sufficient.
(C) BOTH statements TOGETHER are sufficient, but NEITHER statement ALONE is sufficient.
(D) EACH statement ALONE is sufficient.
(E) Statements (1) and (2) TOGETHER are NOT sufficient to answer the question asked, and additional data are needed.

8. The ratio, in ounces, of coffee to cream to sugar in one diner's beverage is 8:2:1. Another diner wants to double the ratio of coffee to sugar but maintain the ratio of coffee to cream. If the new drink will fill a 42-ounce thermos, how many ounces of cream are needed?

(A) 1
(B) 2
(C) 4
(D) 8
(E) 32

9. The ratio of SUVs to passenger cars sold at a particular automobile dealership has been declining from 2003 to 2007, while total sales have remained constant. The total number of vehicles sold in 2007 was divisible by 10. In 2007, were more cars sold than SUVs?

    (1) If in 2007 as many SUVs had been sold as cars were sold in 2003, there would have been a 36% increase in total vehicle sales.

    (2) In 2003, twice as many SUVs were sold as cars.

(A) Statement (1) ALONE is sufficient, but statement (2) alone is not sufficient.
(B) Statement (2) ALONE is sufficient, but statement (1) alone is not sufficient.
(C) BOTH statements TOGETHER are sufficient, but NEITHER statement ALONE is sufficient.
(D) EACH statement ALONE is sufficient.
(E) Statements (1) and (2) TOGETHER are NOT sufficient to answer the question asked, and additional data are needed.

10. The afternoon after a party, Traci prepares a cleaning solution of x liters of water and y liters of bleach. The bleach comes in half-liter containers. How many such containers will Traci require for her cleaning solution?

    (1) Traci will need a total of 25 liters of solution altogether.

    (2) To halve the concentration of bleach in her solution, Traci would need to add $2.4y$ liters of water, and reduce the number of liters of bleach by 1.

(A) Statement (1) ALONE is sufficient, but statement (2) alone is not sufficient.
(B) Statement (2) ALONE is sufficient, but statement (1) alone is not sufficient.
(C) BOTH statements TOGETHER are sufficient, but NEITHER statement ALONE is sufficient.
(D) EACH statement ALONE is sufficient.
(E) Statements (1) and (2) TOGETHER are NOT sufficient to answer the question asked, and additional data are needed.

Check your answers on page 205.

Arithmetic
Answers and
Explanations

ANSWER KEY

Terminology

1. D
2. B
3. A
4. E
5. E
6. B
7. B
8. C
9. C
10. E
11. C
12. D
13. B
14. E
15. D
16. A

Fractions

1. C
2. A
3. B
4. E
5. C
6. E
7. B
8. E

Decimals

1. D
2. D
3. E
4. B
5. C
6. E
7. E
8. C

Percents

1. C
2. D
3. D
4. C
5. E
6. A
7. D
8. C
9. E
10. D

Percent Change

1. D
2. D
3. B
4. E

Factors

1. B
2. D
3. C
4. A
5. B
6. C
7. E
8. B
9. C
10. B

Multiples

1. C
2. A
3. E
4. C
5. D

Ratios

1. C
2. B
3. B
4. A
5. B
6. C
7. D
8. D
9. A
10. C

EXPLANATIONS

Terminology

1. **D**   Plug In each of the answer choices to find the one that makes the result of the expression prime. For (A), the result is 1. While this answer may fool a lot of people, 1 is not a prime number. For (B), (C), and (E), the results are not integers. For (D), the result is 2, which is a prime number. The answer is (D).

2. **B**   Statement (1) is not sufficient. If $k = 2$, then the condition in the question is satisfied and k is an integer. If $k = 1.5$, then the condition in the question is still satisfied but k is not an integer. Eliminate (A) and (D). Statement (2) says that k is a multiple of a prime number, so k equals the product of two integers and must therefore be an integer. This is sufficient. Thus, since only statement (2) is sufficient alone, the answer is (B).

3. **A**   Statement (1) states that $\dfrac{x}{12} = 3$. Multiply both sides by 12 to get $x = 36$. Because the prime factorization of 36 is $2 \times 2 \times 3 \times 3$, this is sufficient to answer the question. Eliminate (B), (C), and (E). Statement (2) states that $\dfrac{x}{36}$ is an integer, so x has at least the prime factors of 36. Because it might also have more, this is not sufficient. Thus, since statement (1) is sufficient alone, the answer is (A).

4. **E**   If 2 is not a factor of $a + b$, then $a + b$ is odd. Because a is even, the only way to make the sum odd is to make b odd. The numbers in (A), (B), (C), and (D) are all even. The answer is (E).

5. **E**   Statement (1) states that the quotient of the two numbers is an integer, but this does not imply that the two numbers are integers. This information only implies that a is a multiple of b, so it is not sufficient. Eliminate (A) and (D). Statement (2) states that the product of the two numbers is an integer, but this does not imply that the two numbers are integers. For example, if $ab = 15$, then one possible solution is $a = 3$ and $b = 5$, but another is $a = 2$ and $b = 7.5$, so this is not sufficient. Eliminate (B). Taking both statements (1) and (2) together does not give enough information to determine whether a and b are integers. If $a = 4$ and $b = 0.5$, then both statements are satisfied. However, the statements are still satisfied if $a = 4$ and $b = 2$. Thus, since both statements together are still not sufficient, the answer is (E).

6. **B**   Since every third number in the range is divisible by 3, there are $\dfrac{99 - 9}{3} + 1 = 31$ multiples of 3 in the range. Note that simply calculating $\dfrac{99 - 9}{3} = 30$, (A), counts 12 as the first multiple in the range. However, 9 also needs to be counted because the question uses the word "inclusive." So, add 1. The answer is (B).

7. **B**   To solve for the range, it is necessary to know the smallest and largest terms in Set S. Statement (1) provides the middle term, which by itself does not provide either the smallest or the largest term. Eliminate (A) and (D). Statement (2) tells you that the lowest term is 2, and the largest term is 28. The answer is (B).

8. **C**   Note that $5a$ is divisible by 5 but that 3 is not. Therefore, $5a + 3$ cannot be divisible by 5 or any multiple of 5. That eliminates (A), (B), and (E). Try Plugging In a few values for a. If $a = 1$, then $b = 8$. However, none of the answers is a divisor of 8. If $a = 2$, then $b = 13$, which is divisible by 13. The answer is (C).

9. **C**   Plug In numbers for statement (1); try 0 for r, which answers the question "yes," then try to get a "no" answer, which happens if r is -3. Since statement (1) is not sufficient, eliminate (A) and (D). In statement (2), Plugging In numbers for r such as -2 gives you a "yes" answer, and Plugging In numbers such as 3 gives you a "no." Eliminate (B). With both statements combined, if r is a non-positive integer and cannot be negative 1, and $2r > -5$, then r has to be 0 or -2, both of which are even. The answer is (C).

10. **E**   Try to find counterexamples for each answer choice. For (A) and (C), if $x = 4$ then y could equal 3. Since x does not have to be odd, (A) and (C) can be eliminated. For (B), if $y = 4$, then x could equal 5. Since y does not have to be odd, (B) can be eliminated. For (D), if $x = 5$, then $x^2 + 1 = 26$ and y could equal 3. Eliminate (D). So, (E) must be correct. Moreover, note that $x^2 - y^2 = (x + y)(x - y)$ which means that both $(x + y)$ and $(x - y)$ must be odd. The answer is (E).

11. **C**   If the remainder when 233 is divided by d is 79, then $233 - 79 = 154$ is divisible by d. The factors of 154 are 1, 2, 7, 11, 14, 22, 77, and 154. Because 154 is the only factor on the list that is greater than 79, only 154 can produce the necessary remainder. So, $d = 154$. The only way to factor 154 into the product of 3 distinct integers is $154 = 2 \times 7 \times 11$. So, $a = 2$, $b = 7$, $c = 11$ and $a + c = 13$. The answer is (C).

12. **D**   The question tells you the possible values for the variables are 0, 2, 4, 6, or 8; the only prime even number is 2, so $a = 2$. Statement (1) tells you ba is either 21, 42, 63 or 84; since you already know a is 2, then b must be 4. The statement also tells you dc is either 40 or 80, and because you just figured out that b is 4, d must be 8 and c is 0. The four digit number $abcd$ is therefore 2,408, which gives an answer to the Yes/No question (in this case, "yes"). Eliminate (B), (C), and (E). In statement (2), if 10 is a divisor of bc, and you know from the question already that a is 2, then bc is 40, 60, or 80; and since a is 2, the only perfect square you can create with a and d is 16, so d is 8 (the number 4 is another perfect square, but the question says a and d are distinct, so they can't both be 2). So the number $abcd$ is either 2,408 or 2,608, and with a little bit of arithmetic you can determine that both possible values are divisible by 8, so statement (2) provides another "yes" answer to the Yes/No question. The answer is (D).

13. **B**   Plug In The Answers. Since the remainder cannot be larger than the divisor, (D) and (E) can be eliminated. Since (B) is the middle value of the remaining answers, start there. If $b = 3$, then $m = (5 \times 2) + 3 = 13$ and $n = (7 \times 2) + 3 = 17$. Because $mn = 13 \times 17 = 221$, $b = 3$. The answer is (B).

14. **E** This is a tricky and complicated Yes/No question, so it's important to note for this problem that you don't have to compute the sum of both sequences if you can more simply and quickly compare the two groups of numbers and see if you can detect a pattern. In statement (1), Plug In a small number for f, such as 3, and see the three values in C as the question has it: $0, \frac{1}{2}, \frac{2}{3}$. Plug In a larger number for g, such as 10; the values in D would be $\frac{1}{2}, \frac{2}{3}, \frac{3}{4}, \ldots \frac{10}{11}$. The sum of the values in D will be much larger than the sum of the three values in C, giving an answer of "no" to this Yes/No question. Now try to get a "yes" answer; note how similar the values in the two sequences are, except for the fact C begins at 0, so try making f one more than g, such as $f = 3$ and $g = 2$. C will still contain $0, \frac{1}{2}$, and $\frac{2}{3}$, while D will contain $\frac{1}{2}$ and $\frac{2}{3}$. The sums of the two sequences will be identical here, giving a "yes" answer. Since statement (1) is not sufficient, eliminate (A) and (D). Statement (2) can lead to the trap answer (B) if you're not careful. A difference is always given as a positive value, so you can't assume the median of C is bigger than the median of D. If f is 6 and g is 5, the median of the values in C is $\frac{17}{24}$ while the median in D is $\frac{3}{4}$, giving a difference of $\frac{1}{24}$ and answering the question "yes" since the sums of the two sequences would be identical. But you can also Plug In 7 for f and 4 for g to achieve the same difference yet a different outcome: the median of C would now be $\frac{3}{4}$ and the median of D would be $\frac{17}{24}$, still giving a difference of $\frac{1}{24}$; now the sum of values in C will be larger than the sum in D, yielding an answer of "no." Since Statement (2) is not sufficient, eliminate (B). When you combine the statements, you can Plug In the same values you used for statement (2), with the same results. Combined, the statements are still not sufficient, so the answer is (E).

15. **D** A multiple of $4! + 6$ can be factored into $4! + 6$ and an integer. So, one way to determine a multiple is to divide the answer choices by $4! + 6$. For (D), $\frac{5! + 30}{4! + 6} = \frac{5(4! + 6)}{4! + 6} = 5$. Be careful of (E): $4! \times 2 \neq 8!$ The answer is (D).

16. **A** The sum of all the numbers in S is the sum of all the odd numbers plus the sum of all the even numbers. Statement (1) tells you that the sum of all odd numbers is even. You know that the sum of all the even numbers has to be even. The sum of two even numbers is even, so the sum of all the numbers in S is even. Statement (1) is sufficient, so eliminate (B), (C), and (E). Statement (2) says that the sum of all the positive numbers is odd. You know the sum of all the negative even numbers must be even, but you don't know what the sum of the negative odd numbers is. If the negative odd numbers sum to an even number, then the sum of all negative numbers will be even. The sum of all numbers is the sum of the positives plus the sum of the negatives, which in this case would be odd plus even, giving you an odd total for all the numbers. But if the negative odd numbers sum to an odd number, the sum of all negatives would be odd, and the total would be odd plus odd, which is even. So Statement (2) is insufficient.

Fractions

1. **C**   Two divided by a number will never equal 0. Alternatively, you can try to set $\dfrac{2}{10-x}$ equal to each answer choice. The answer is (C).

2. **A**   A fraction is equivalent to part over whole, and a percentage is another way of giving a fraction. Statement (1) gives you a percentage: $\dfrac{10}{100}$, which can be reduced to $\dfrac{1}{10}$. So $x = 1$. Statement (1) is sufficient, so eliminate (B), (C), and (E). Statement (2) is not sufficient. It only provides income without saying how much goes into savings. The answer is (A).

3. **B**   Apply the order of operations. First, work inside parentheses to get $1-\left[\left(\dfrac{1}{2}\div\dfrac{5}{8}\right)\div\dfrac{1}{3}\right]+\dfrac{7}{5}=1-\left[\dfrac{4}{5}\div\dfrac{1}{3}\right]+\dfrac{7}{5}$. Again work inside parentheses to get $1-\left[\dfrac{4}{5}\div\dfrac{1}{3}\right]+\dfrac{7}{5}=1-\left[\dfrac{12}{5}\right]+\dfrac{7}{5}$. Next, add and subtract in order of the problem, finding a common denominator if necessary. This gives $1-\dfrac{12}{5}+\dfrac{7}{5}=\dfrac{5}{5}-\dfrac{12}{5}+\dfrac{7}{5}=-\dfrac{7}{5}+\dfrac{7}{5}=0$. The answer is (B).

4. **E**   Simplify each answer choice using the order of operations. Choice (A) equals $\dfrac{1}{4}(2+2+2+2)=\dfrac{1}{4}(8)=2$. Choice (B) equals $\dfrac{1}{2}+\dfrac{1}{2}+\dfrac{1}{2}+\dfrac{1}{2}=\dfrac{4}{2}=2$. Choice (C) equals $\dfrac{1}{2}+\dfrac{2}{4}+\dfrac{3}{6}+\dfrac{4}{8}=\dfrac{12}{24}+\dfrac{12}{24}+\dfrac{12}{24}+\dfrac{12}{24}=\dfrac{48}{24}=2$. Choice (D) equals $\dfrac{1}{2}(1+1+1+1)=\dfrac{1}{2}(4)=2$. That leaves (E), $\dfrac{1}{2}+\dfrac{2}{3}+\dfrac{3}{4}+\dfrac{4}{5}=\dfrac{30}{60}+\dfrac{40}{60}+\dfrac{45}{60}+\dfrac{48}{60}=\dfrac{163}{60}\ne 2$. The answer is (E).

5. **C**   You can Plug In for statement (1) and find different values of x and y to fit the equation, such as 2 and 3 or 4 and 6, that will yield different values for the question. Statement (1) is not sufficient, so eliminate (A) and (D). The equation in statement (2) can be cross-multiplied to give $3y-3x=9$, and then dividing both sides by 3 gives you $y-x=3$, which by itself is not enough. Eliminate (B). Combining both statements together yields simultaneous equations with two variables, two equations. These can be solved for both x and y (but don't actually do the work), so the answer is (C).

6. **E**   If $\dfrac{2}{3}$ ordered salad and, of those, $\dfrac{1}{4}$ ordered soup, then the fraction of diners who ordered both is $\dfrac{1}{4}\times\dfrac{2}{3}=\dfrac{2}{12}=\dfrac{1}{6}$. The fraction of diners who did not order both is $1-\dfrac{1}{6}=\dfrac{5}{6}$. The answer is (E).

7. **B**   The equation for V contains 3 variables, so the information provided seems to be set up for the trap answer choice (C). Statement (1) by itself does not solve for V since there is no value for b. Eliminate (A) and (D). In statement (2), if you solve for a in terms of b ($\dfrac{b}{3}=a$) and substitute $\dfrac{b}{3}$ for a

and substitute $\dfrac{b}{2}$ for c, you get $V = \dfrac{\dfrac{3}{b}}{\dfrac{4}{b} + \dfrac{7}{4b}}$. Simplifying this equation, you get the numerator to

be $\dfrac{9}{b}$ and the denominator to be $\dfrac{23}{4b}$. Dividing by a fraction is equivalent to multiplying by its

reciprocal, so you end up with $V = \dfrac{36b}{23b}$, or $\dfrac{36}{23}$. Statement (2) is actually sufficient alone, so the

answer is (B).

8. **E** The possible pairs of factors for q and r according to the question are 1 and 64, 2 and 32, 4 and 16, and 8 and 8. Statement (1) tells you that r can be 8, 16, 32 or 64, and q could be 1, 2, 4 or 8. That isn't sufficient, so eliminate (A) and (D). Statement (2) tells you q can be 4, 8, 16, 32, or 64, and r can be 16, 8, 4, 2, or 1. That isn't sufficient, so eliminate (B). Both statements combined allow two possible pairs of factors: 4 and 16, or 8 and 8. The trap answer here is (C) if you assume the two variables are distinct, which the question never states. The statements combined are still not sufficient, so the answer is (E).

Decimals

1. **D** If you can solve for z, you can answer the question. Translate statement (1) to get $0.0008 = 0.02 \times z$ and you can solve for z. Eliminate (B), (C), and (E). Translate statement (2) to get $0.01 \times z = 0.0004$ and again you can solve for z. Since both statements (1) and (2) are sufficient on their own, the correct answer is (D).

2. **D** Factor 1.011 out of the numerator and denominator to get $\dfrac{5.055}{2.022} = \dfrac{5 \times 1.011}{2 \times 1.011} = \dfrac{5}{2} = 2.5$. The correct answer is (D).

3. **E** The decimal form of $\dfrac{3}{22}$ is $0.13\overline{63636}$, so every even place to the right of the decimal point is 3, and every odd place, after the first digit, is 6. The correct answer is (E).

4. **B** Statement (1) tells you that the number is divisible by 4,938, which leaves two possibilities: 4,938 or 9,876, so there are two possible values for b. Statement (1) is not sufficient, so eliminate (A) and (D). In statement (2) you get the inequality $c > d > e > 6$, which tells you that $e = 7$, $d = 8$, and $c = 9$, and $b = 0.9876$. Since statement (2) is sufficient, the correct answer is (B).

5. **C** Statement (1) is not sufficient. From statement (1), you can find that $l = 2$, but there is no information regarding k. Eliminate (A) and (D). Statement (2) gives k as a decimal with a variable in it, so you cannot find k from that alone. Eliminate (B). Combine both statements together and you have a value for l and can find the value for k. The correct answer is (C).

6. **E** The only prime factor of 32 is 2, and any number divided by 2 will yield a terminating decimal. So any value of x will generate a terminating decimal. The correct answer is (E).

7. **E** Statement (1) is not sufficient. From statement (1), you can find two possible values for X. X is 3 if Y is 5, 6, 7, 8, or 9, and X is 4 if Y is 1, 2, 3, or 4. Eliminate (A) and (D). Statement (2) is not sufficient. From statement (2), there are 4 possible values for X: 1, 2, 3, or 4. Eliminate (B). Combine both statements together and X can still be 1, 2, 3, or 4. Since the statements together are also not sufficient, the correct answer is (E).

8. **C** Examine the answer choices. Any number divided by 2 will yield halves, which are terminating decimals. Eliminate (A). Any number divided by 5 will yield fifths, which are terminating decimals. Eliminate (B). Choices (C), (D), and (E) all have a prime factor of 3. $\frac{8,103}{3} = 2,701$, so $\frac{8,103}{12} = \frac{2,701}{4}$ and $\frac{8,103}{15} = \frac{2,701}{5}$, both of which are equivalent to terminating decimals. Only 2,701 divided by 3 will result in a non-terminating decimal, since thirds are non-terminating decimals and 2,701 is not divisible by 3. The correct answer is (C).

Percents

1. **C** The total capacity equals $10 + 6 + 4 = 20$ gallons. The van originally had 10 gallons, and $\frac{10}{20} = 50\%$. The answer is (C).

2. **D** For any percent change question, there are three pieces: the percent change, the difference between the two values, and the original amount. The question gives you one piece of information (Dre's salary last year). Statement (1) gives you a second piece of information (the percent change), allowing you to solve for the difference, and hence this year's salary. Eliminate (B), (C), and (E). If you set up the percent change formula for statement (2) and let x equal the actual difference between Dre's salary this year and last year, you can set up the percent change formula to be $40\% = \frac{x + \$10,000}{\$50,000}$, which would allow you to solve for x (which turns out to be \$10,000) and add it to last year's salary to solve the question. Statement (2) is also sufficient, so the answer is (D).

3. **D** Plug In The Answers, beginning with (C). If Laura drove 1,000 miles, then she earned 15% of 950 miles, which is \$142.50, plus her salary of \$200. That gives her a total of \$342.50, which is too small. Eliminate (A), (B), and (C). Try (D). If Laura drove 1,050 miles, then she earned 15% of 1,000 miles, which is \$150, plus her salary of \$200. That gives her a total of \$350.00, which is what you are looking for, so the answer is (D). Alternatively, subtract Laura's weekly salary from her total earnings to get $\$350 - \$200 = \$150$. Then \$150 equals 15 percent of her paid miles, so $150 = \frac{15}{100}m$, and the number of paid miles, m, equals 1,000. Add the 50 unpaid miles to get $1,000 + 50 = 1,050$. The answer is (D).

4.   C   Statement (1) says profits doubled each year, but without knowing what relation profits and revenues have, that's not enough to solve the question. Eliminate (A) and (D). Statement (2) gives a dollar amount increase in a four year period, but again without providing any information about revenues during any of the five years, it's not enough to solve the question. Eliminate (B). Using both statements together, you can see that if x is the dollar amount of profits in 2002, then according to statement (1) in 2003 it would be $2x$, in 2004 it would be $4x$, and in 2005 it would be $8x$. The difference, in terms of x, between 2005 and 2002 is $7x$. You can use the information in statement (2), the difference in profit in dollars, to get the equation $7x = \$56$ million, and determine that $x = \$8$ million. You can now divide the profit in 2002 by the revenue in 2002 to solve for p. The answer is (C).

5.   E   The number of customers who live in urban areas is 200 percent greater than the number of customers who live in rural areas. 180,000 live in rural areas, so you need to find 200 percent of 180,000, which is $2 \times 180,000$, or 360,000. However, this is how much *greater* the number of rural customers is than the number of urban customers. In order to find the total number of urban customers, add the original 180,000 to 360,000 to find the total. $180,000 + 360,000 = 540,000$, so there are 540,000 customers living in urban areas and the answer is (E).

6.   A   Percentages can be solved using real numbers, or ratios, or fractions, or proportions. In statement (1), there is a proportion between the three parts, which is enough. You can also Plug In and say Shannon caught 10 fish, then Rosemary would catch 5 fish and Monique would catch 15 fish, allowing you to solve for a percentage. If you Plug In a second number for Shannon's fish, say 100 fish, then Rosemary catches 50 fish and Monique catches 150 fish. Both sets of numbers give an identical percentage value for Shannon's catch. Statement (2) gives only one real number, but without knowing anything about the total number of fish caught you don't know what percentage Shannon's catch is. The answer is (A).

7.   D   Plug In the Answers, starting with (C). If Bob flies 22,000 miles over the next six months, then with the second deal he would receive 4,400 miles, plus the original 7,000 miles, so the total would be 11,400 miles. This number is too small to match the 15,000 miles of the first deal, so eliminate (C) and try (D). If Bob flies 40,000 miles over the next six months, then with the second deal he would receive 8,000 miles, plus the original 7,000 miles. The total is 15,000, so the answer is (D). Alternatively, you can solve this algebraically. With the second deal, Bob would receive 7,000 miles. That leaves 8,000 more miles he would have to earn through flying to equal the 15,000 miles offered in the first deal. Set up the equation $\dfrac{20}{100}x = 8,000$, in which x represents the number of miles Bob will have to fly in order to have the 20% equal 8,000 miles. Solve for x and you will get 40,000. The answer is (D).

8. **C** Suppose that there were 100 ounces of salad dressing A and 100 ounces of salad dressing B. Based on the percentages stated in the problem, there would be 30 ounces of vinegar in dressing A and 10 ounces in dressing B. Now, assume that you are going to make 100 ounces of the combined dressing. In that case, the new dressing has 15 ounces of vinegar—some of which came from dressing A and the rest of which came from dressing B. That allows the following equation to be written:

$$\frac{x}{100}(30) + \left(\frac{100-x}{100}\right)(10) = 15$$

This equation shows that x % of the vinegar in the new dressing came from the 30 ounces in dressing A while the remaining percentage of the vinegar comes from the 10 ounces in dressing B. Now, solve the equation for x:

$$30x + (100 - x)10 = 1,500$$
$$30x + 100 - 10x = 1,500$$
$$20x = 500$$
$$x = 25$$

The answer is (C).

9. **E** Plugging In is a good option for this yes/no data sufficiency question. First, however, it is worthwhile to simplify some of the information provided. Translate the relationship provided in the question stem into the inequality $(\frac{y}{100})x > 100$ and simplify that to get $xy > 100$ by multiplying both sides by 100. Next, translate the actual question to obtain the inequality $(\frac{x}{100})z < 10$. Again, simplify to find that the question is asking "is $xz < 1000$"? Now, it's time to tackle the statements. Once again, it's best to translate and simplify before picking numbers to evaluate. The first statement translates to the equation $(\frac{z}{100})y = 10$, which simplifies to $yz = 1000$. You need to pick numbers for x, y and z and remember to satisfy both the statement and the condition in the question stem. If $y = 1000$, $z = 1$ and $x = 11$, both the statement and the condition in the question stem are satisfied and the answer to the question is "yes" because $(11)(1) < 1000$. But, if $y = 1$, $z = 1000$ and $x = 10,001$, the answer to the question is "no." So, write down BCE. The second statement translates to $z < 0.1y$. If $y = 11,000$, $z = 1,000$ and $x = 1$, both the statement and the condition in the question stem are satisfied and the answer to the question is "no" because $(1)(1000) = 1000$. If $y = 100$, $z = 9$ and $x = 101$, the answer to the question is "yes" so cross off B. When the statements are combined, you can again make $y = 1000$, $z = 1$ and $x = 11$ to get an answer of "yes" to the question. However, if $y = 101$, $z = \frac{1000}{101}$, and $x = 1010$, the answer to the question is "no." The answer is (E).

10. **D** There are two equations in the question: First, the hogshead holds 240 liters and it is filled with New and Old Sherry, so let x equal the number of liters of New Sherry and y equal the number of liters of Old Sherry, and you get $x + y = 240$. You can also set up an equation to see how the amounts of alcohol in the two sherries will combine, if you let $a\%$ be the a.b.v. of New Sherry and $b\%$ be the a.b.v. of Old Sherry, then you come up with $x\,(a\%) + y\,(b\%) = 240$ liters (17%). The question is asking for the a.b.v. of New Sherry, so you want to solve for a. Now consider the first part of statement (1): if there is 40% more New than Old Sherry, then $x = 1.4y$, and you can substitute that into the first equation and get $1.4y + y = 240$ and solve for y. The second part of statement (1) tells you that $b\% = a\% + 1.72\%$, which you can put into the second equation and get $1.4y\,(a\%) + y\,(a\% + 1.72\%) = 240$ liters (17%). If you can solve for y, then you can solve for a and answer the question. Since statement (1) is sufficient, eliminate (B), (C), and (E). In statement (2), set up the first equation as $x + 100 = 240$, and after solving for x set up the second equation as $140(a\%) + 100(18\%) = 240(17\%)$. You can solve for a now to answer the question. Since statement (2) is also sufficient, the answer is (D).

Percent Change

1. **D** Call the company's earnings E. Last quarter, the company earned $E + \dfrac{15}{100}E = \dfrac{115}{100}E$. This quarter, the company earns $\dfrac{115}{100}E + \dfrac{15}{100}\left(\dfrac{115}{100}E\right) = \dfrac{115}{100}\left(\dfrac{115}{100}E\right) = \dfrac{13{,}225}{10{,}000}E$, or 132.25%. Therefore, the increase in earnings is 32.25%. The answer is (D).

2. **D** The problem states that the percent change of home values in Boca Raton is known. So, if the percent change in the average price of condominiums in Miami is known or determinable, then the comparison can be made successfully. If statement (1) is granted, then the percent change in the average price of Miami condos can be determined; eliminate (B), (C), and (E). If statement (2) is granted, then the percent change in the average price per square foot can be determined, and since the square footage is fixed, this is effectively the percent change in average housing price. Either of the statements will provide enough information to make the determination, so the answer is (D).

3. **B** The problem states that x, y, and z are positive integers with an average of 64, but it does not provide any information about what those numbers might be. If they were 63, 64, and 65, then doubling the value of one of them would cause a very large percent change in the average value; if they were 1, 2, and 189, then doubling the value of the smaller numbers would actually cause the average to drop. Thus, statement (1) is not sufficient to answer the question. Eliminate (A) and (D). However, statement (2) is sufficient, because even in the most extreme case, the largest of the original numbers cannot be more than 189. Adding half this value, 94.5, to the set and finding the new average would make a percent change of about 12%, which is less than 13%. The answer is (B).

4. **E** To determine whether Lori's Laminate has achieved this goal, one would have to know the head count and production figures for the Texas factory for both 2006 and 2007. Figures for either year alone will not be sufficient. Statement (1) gives these figures for 2006. That's not sufficient, so eliminate (A) and (D). Statement (2) gives the 2007 figures for the company as a whole. Since the question asks about the Texas factory only, this is not relevant. Eliminate (B). Combine statements (1) and (2). It may look like you have before and after figures for both headcount and tile production, but remember, statement (2) is about the entire company, not just the Texas factory. Thus, there is not sufficient data to solve the problem, even with both statements taken together. The answer is (E).

Factors

1. **B** For statement (1), think of all the ways you can add prime numbers to get 12. 5 + 7 = 12, so x could equal 35, because the prime factors of 35 are 5 and 7. In that case, x is divisible by 7 and you get a "yes." But 12 also equals 5 + 5 + 2, so x could also be 50, because the prime factors of 50 are 5, 5, and 2. 50 is not divisible by 7, so there you get a "no" answer. Statement (1) is not sufficient, so eliminate (A) and (D). Statement (2) tells you that the sum of the DISTINCT prime factors of x sum to 12. x could still be 35, because the distinct prime factors of 35 are 5 and 7. That gives you a "yes" answer. And x could be 42, because the distinct prime factors of 42 are 2, 3, and 7, which sum to 12. That also gives you a "yes" answer. No other set of distinct prime numbers will sum to 12, so statement (2) tells you that x must be divisible by 7. The answer is (B).

2. **D** If x is a factor of 10, x could equal 1, 2, 5, and 10. If y is a factor of 12, y could equal 1, 2, 3, 4, 6, and 12. Choice (A) is the result of multiplying 1 and 1. Choice (B) is the result of multiplying 1 and 4 or 2 and 2. Choice (C) is the result of multiplying 5 and 3. Choice (E) is the result of multiplying 10 and 4. The answer is (D).

3. **C** 14! equals $14 \times 13 \times 12 \times 11 \times 10 \times 9 \times 8 \times 7 \times 6 \times 5 \times 4 \times 3 \times 2 \times 1$. Its distinct prime factors are the prime numbers from 1 to 14, which are 2, 3, 5, 7, 11, and 13. The answer is (C).

4. **A** Plug In. For statement (1), let $a = 1$ and $b = 8$. Then $x = 2 \times 3 \times 4 \times 5 \times 6 \times 7$, which has 5 as a factor. Plug In again: If $a = 15$ and $b = 22$, then $x = 16 \times 17 \times 18 \times 19 \times 20 \times 21$, which also has 5 as a factor ($20 = 4 \times 5$). If statement (1) is true, then x will always be the product of six consecutive numbers. Any five consecutive numbers has exactly one multiple of 5, so x will always have at least one multiple of 5 as a factor. Statement (1) is sufficient, so eliminate (B), (C), and (E). Statement (2) tells you that $b = 9$. Plug In 7 for a, making $x = 8$, which does not have 5 as a factor. Now plug 4 in for a, which makes $x = 5 \times 6 \times 7 \times 8$. Here x does have 5 as a factor, so statement (2) is insufficient. The answer is (A).

5. **B** The distinct factors of 9 are 1, 3, and 9. The smallest product of any two of these is $1 \times 3 = 3$. The answer is (B).

6. **C** Plug In. From the question, x can be 90, 92, 94, 96, 98, or 100. For statement (1), list the distinct prime factors for each value of x and $\dfrac{x}{2}$. The distinct prime factors of both 92 and $\dfrac{92}{2} = 46$ are 2 and 23. So x could be 92. But the distinct prime factors for both 100 and 50 are 2 and 5, so statement (1) is not sufficient because x could be 92 or 100. Eliminate (A) and (D). Statement (2) says $\dfrac{x}{2}$ has two prime factors. So x could be 92, because the prime factors of 46 are 2 and 23. But x could also be 98, because the prime factors of $\dfrac{98}{2} = 49$ are 7 and 7. Statement (2) is not sufficient, so eliminate (B). Combine the statements. Only 92 makes both statements true, so x must be 92. The answer is (C).

7. **E** For a number divided by x to be an integer, that number must share the factors of x. Choice (A) has only one prime factor, 3. Choice (B) has only two prime factors, 3 and 5. Choice (C) has only two distinct prime factors, 2 and 3. Choice (D) has only two prime factors, 5 and 7. Choice (E) has three prime factors, 2, 3, and 7. The answer is (E).

8. **B** The prime factorization of 1,001 is $7 \times 11 \times 13$, so each integer a, b, and c must equal one of these values. The smallest value any of the integers can have, then, is 7. The answer is (B).

9. **C** Plug In. Statement (1) tells you a must be even. So let a, b, c, d, and e be 2, 3, 4, 5, and 6. Here, c is 4, so the answer to the question is "yes." But if a is 4, then c is 6, which does not have 4 as a factor. This would make the answer "no," so statement (1) is insufficient. Eliminate (A) and (D). Statement (2) tells you bcd and cde both have 4 as a factor. This is true if you Plug In 2, 3, 4, 5, and 6 again, which gives the answer "yes." But a could also be 1, because bcd would be $2 \times 3 \times 4$ and cde would be $3 \times 4 \times 5$, both of which have 4 as a factor. Here, c is 3, which means the answer to the question is "no." Eliminate (B). Combining the statements tells you that a is even, which means c and e are also even, and b and d are both odd. Statement (2) tells you bcd has 4 as a factor. Since b and d are odd, c must have 4 as a factor. The information combined is sufficient. The answer is (C).

10. **B** Plug In. If $m + n = 188$, m could be 1 and n could be 187. The product would be 187, which is odd, so the answer to the question would be "no." But if m were 2, n would be 186. The product would have 6 as a factor, because 186 is divisible by 2 and 3. In this case, the answer to the question would be "yes," so statement (1) is insufficient. Eliminate (A) and (D). Statement (2) tells you that m is 150% of n, which means that $m = 1.5n = n + .5n = n + \dfrac{n}{2}$. Since m and n are both integers, $\dfrac{n}{2}$ must be an integer. Another way to write statement (2) is $m = \dfrac{3n}{2}$, or $\dfrac{m}{3} = \dfrac{n}{2}$. You know $\dfrac{n}{2}$ is an integer, so $\dfrac{m}{3}$ is also an integer. This means m must be a multiple of 3 and n a multiple of 2. Therefore mn is a multiple of both 3 and 2, which means it is a multiple of 6. So the answer to the question must be "yes." The answer is (B).

Multiples

1. **C**   Plug In for n. Statement (1) tells you the units digit of n is 3. So n could be 103 or 123. You know 103 is not divisible by 3 because the digits sum to 4, which is not a multiple of 3. But the sum of the digits of 123 is 6, which is a multiple of 3. Statement (1) is not sufficient, so eliminate (A) and (D). If statement (2) is true, then n could be 710, which is not a multiple of 3, or n could be 261, which is a multiple of 3. Eliminate (B). When you combine the two statements, you know that the sum of the digits is $8 + 3 = 11$, which is not divisible by 3, so you know n is not a multiple of 3. The correct answer is (C).

2. **A**   The product rs must be a multiple of $3 \times 6 = 18$ and any of its factors, which are 1, 2, 3, 6, 9, and 18. The correct answer is (A).

3. **E**   Plug In. Let $k = 2$ and $m = 2$. For I, then, you get 5, which is not a multiple of 2. Eliminate (A) and (D). Using those same numbers for II, you get 12, which is a multiple of 2. In fact, since m is an integer, then any integer times m is a multiple of m. So, $3km$ is a multiple of m and II will always be true. Eliminate (C). Using your numbers for III, you get 14, which is divisible by 2. And because k is even, k is a multiple of 2, so $\dfrac{7k}{2}$ will always be an integer. So, $\dfrac{7k}{2}m$ is a multiple of m. The correct answer is (E).

4. **C**   If x is a multiple of all single-digit prime numbers, then x must also be a multiple of their product, $2 \times 3 \times 5 \times 7 = 210$, and all of its factors, which are 1, 2, 3, 5, 7, 10, 14, 15, 21, 30, 42, 70, 105, and 210. The correct answer is (C).

5. **D**   Plug In. Statement (1) tells you that $b - 4$ is a multiple of 5, so let a, b, and c be 8, 9, and 10, respectively. Then $abc = 720$, which is a multiple of 15. In fact, if $b - 4$ is a multiple of 5, then c must also be a multiple of 5, because every fifth number is a multiple of 5. So abc must be a multiple of 5. Because a, b, and c are three consecutive numbers, one of them must be a multiple of 3. So abc must be a multiple of 3, and Statement (1) told you that abc is a multiple of 5. If a number is a multiple of both 5 and 3, then it is a multiple of 15. Statement (1) is sufficient, so eliminate (B), (C), and (E). Statement (2) tells you that the units digit of ac is 0, which means it is a multiple of 10, and thus also a multiple of 5. You already know that abc must be a multiple of 3, and if ac is a multiple of 5, then abc is a multiple of 5. So abc must be a multiple of 15, and Statement (2) is also sufficient. The correct answer is (D).

Ratios

1. **C**   If the ratio of a to b is 5 to 3, a could equal 5 when b equals 3, or a could equal 10 when b equals 6, or a could equal 15 when b equals 9, and so on. When a is divided by b in any case, the remainder is going to be an even number. The only even number in the answer choices is 6. The answer is (C).

2. **B** Statement (1) is not sufficient to determine the price of a single used CD, since it is not possible to separate the contribution of the used and new CDs to Adrian's total. Eliminate (A) and (D). Statement (2) is sufficient, because Betty bought only used CDs; if she bought 3 used CDs at x dollars each, then her total must be $3x$, so x can be found. The answer is (B).

3. **B** Multiplying both values in a ratio by the same number yields an equivalent ratio. So, the ratio of x to y is equal to the ratio of $2x$ to $2y$. The answer is (B).

4. **A** The ratio of the number of students who pass to the number who fail remains the same every semester, so use the numbers for one semester to determine the ratio. If 76 out of 80 students passed, then 4 students failed. The ratio of the number who pass to the number who fail is 76 to 4, or 19 to 1. So for every 20 students, 19 students pass and 1 student fails. Apply this to the current semester: Let s be the number of students who fail. Then $\dfrac{s}{120} = \dfrac{1}{20}$ and s equals 6. The answer is (A).

5. **B** The first statement provides information about the value of x, but not the value of y, so it is insufficient to determine their ratio. Eliminate (A) and (D). Statement (2) seems ambiguous, but in order for a ratio less than 1 to become greater than 1, the smaller value must be the one that is doubled. Thus, statement (2) says $\dfrac{2x}{y} = \dfrac{3}{2}$, which can be solved for $\dfrac{x}{y}$ to determine their ratio, $\dfrac{3}{4}$. The answer is (B).

6. **C** Let m be the number of managers and a be the number of analysts. Then the current ratio is $\dfrac{m}{a} = \dfrac{3}{7}$. If 3 more analysts were hired, then the new ratio would be 3 to 8, so $\dfrac{m}{a+3} = \dfrac{3}{8}$. Solve the first equation for a to get $3a = 7m$, or $a = \dfrac{7m}{3}$. Rearrange the second equation to get $3(a + 3) = 8m$. Substitute $\dfrac{7m}{3}$ for a to get $3(\dfrac{7m}{3} + 3) = 8m$, or $7m + 9 = 8m$. Combine like terms to get $m = 9$. Alternatively, try Plugging In the Answer Choices. The answer is (C).

7. **D** The first statement can be set up as an equation such that x is the number of coders and y is the number of systems administrators (under the hypothetical shift in roles). Then, $55x + 45y = 535$, which may be solved for x and y, and can then be adjusted to find the original number of coders and systems administrators. Statement 1 is sufficient to provide a ratio. Eliminate (B), (C), and (E). Statement 2 can also be set up as a system of equations with a single possible solution with fewer than 15 people total (6 coders and 5 systems administrators). Either statement is sufficient by itself. The answer is (D).

8. **D** To double the ratio of coffee to sugar, double the coffee value in the original ratio. If the original coffee to sugar ratio is 8:1, the doubled ratio will be 16:1. To maintain the ratio of coffee to cream, it is necessary to change the original ratio of 8:2 to 16:4 so that the coffee value is the same in both of the new ratios and the two new ratios can be combined. The new ratio of coffee to cream to sugar is then 16:4:1. Let $16x$ be the number of ounces of coffee, $4x$ be the number of ounces of cream, and x be the number of ounces of sugar. Then $16x + 4x + x = 42$, or $21x = 42$. Divide both

sides by 21 to get $x = 2$. Then the number of ounces of cream is $4x = (4)(2) = 8$. Alternatively, try Plugging In the Answer Choices. The answer is (D).

9.   **A**   Statement (1) invites complex calculations to determine the respective values of SUVs and cars, but ultimately, the only significant fact is that the number of cars sold in 2003 exceeded the number of SUVs sold in 2007. Since more cars were sold in 2007 than in 2003, and more cars were sold in 2003 than SUVs in 2007, more cars must have been sold than SUVs in 2007, making statement (1) sufficient on its own. Eliminate (B), (C), and (E). Statement (2) does not tell you anything about the situation in 2007, so it is not sufficient by itself. The answer is (A).

10.   **C**   Statement (1) by itself does not provide any information about the ratio of the ingredients, so it is not sufficient. Eliminate (A) and (D). Statement (2) can be used to set up an equation with two variables, x and y, but it is not possible to solve a single equation with two variables for either of the variables in isolation. Eliminate (B). Taking the two statements together, you can represent x in statement (2) in terms of y, allowing you to solve for the original value of y. The answer is (C).

Algebra

EQUATIONS AND INEQUALITIES

Although you can often avoid algebra on the GMAT by using Plugging In and PITA, you will still need to know how to manipulate equations. When working with equations, the goal is often to solve for a variable, but sometimes you simply need to shift terms around.

To solve a linear equation (one without exponents) you need to get all the variables on one side and all the numbers on the other. When manipulating equations, remember the following fundamental rule:

> Whatever you do to one side of an equation, you must do to the other side.

Example

1. If $\dfrac{x}{2} + 7 = 21$, then $x =$

The fraction in this equation is awkward so clear it by multiplying everything by 2.

$$2\left(\frac{x}{2} + 7\right) = (21)2$$

That gives you

$$x + 14 = 42$$

To isolate the variable, subtract 14 from both sides of the equation which gives you

$$x = 28$$

Cross Multiplication

Whenever you have an equal sign between two fractions, you can solve by cross multiplying. Thus,

$$\frac{3}{2y} = \frac{2}{5}$$

becomes

$$4y = 15 \text{ and } y = \frac{15}{4}$$

Note that you can only cross multiply when you have an equal sign between two fractions. You cannot cross multiply across an addition, subtraction or multiplication sign.

Inequalities

Manipulating inequalities is the same as manipulating equalities with one exception

> Whenever you multiply or divide an inequality by a negative number, you have to flip the direction of the inequality sign.

Try solving this inequality for x

$$-2x - 9 < 11$$

Add 9 to both sides to get

$$-2x < 20$$

Now divide both sides by -2. Don't forget to flip the sign. Thus,

$$x > -10$$

Simultaneous Equations

Some GMAT problems involve sets of equations with more than one variable. These are known as simultaneous equations. To solve multiple equations, stack them and either add or subtract so that you end up with the value you are being asked to find.

Example

2. If $2x + 3y = 14$ and $x - 3y = 4$, what is the value of y ?

If you stack the equations and add them, the quantity $3y$ drops out of the sum:

$$
\begin{array}{r}
2x + 3y = 14 \\
\underline{x - 3y = 4} \\
3x = 18 \\
x = 6
\end{array}
$$

Now plug $x = 6$ into either equation to get $y = \dfrac{2}{3}$.

In order to solve simultaneous equations, you must have the same number of equations as you have variables, i.e., two equations, two variables, three equations, three variables, and so on.

EQUATIONS AND INEQUALITIES DRILL

1. If x and y are integers, and $1 < x < 7$ and $-3 < y < 4$, what is one possible value of $\dfrac{x}{y}$?

    (A) $-\dfrac{1}{3}$

    (B) $-\dfrac{2}{5}$

    (C) 1

    (D) $\dfrac{7}{4}$

    (E) 7

2. A chocolate shop sells only two kinds of chocolate bars, one for $3 and one for $7. If the shop had 30 customers yesterday, and each customer bought exactly one chocolate bar, how many of the $7 bars were sold yesterday?

    (1) The shop made the same amount of money on the $3 bars and on the $7 bars yesterday.

    (2) The shop made over $100 on the chocolate bars yesterday.

    (A) Statement (1) ALONE is sufficient, but statement (2) alone is not sufficient.
    (B) Statement (2) ALONE is sufficient, but statement (1) alone is not sufficient.
    (C) BOTH statements TOGETHER are sufficient, but NEITHER statement ALONE is sufficient.
    (D) EACH statement ALONE is sufficient.
    (E) Statements (1) and (2) TOGETHER are NOT sufficient to answer the question asked, and additional data are needed.

3. If $3a + 2b = 21$, what is the value of b ?

    (1) b is a positive integer.

    (2) $3a = 5b$

    (A) Statement (1) ALONE is sufficient, but statement (2) alone is not sufficient.
    (B) Statement (2) ALONE is sufficient, but statement (1) alone is not sufficient.
    (C) BOTH statements TOGETHER are sufficient, but NEITHER statement ALONE is sufficient.
    (D) EACH statement ALONE is sufficient.
    (E) Statements (1) and (2) TOGETHER are NOT sufficient to answer the question asked, and additional data are needed.

4. Is $x > 0$?

    (1) $6^x > 1$

    (2) $5x^2 - 45 = 0$

    (A) Statement (1) ALONE is sufficient, but statement (2) alone is not sufficient.
    (B) Statement (2) ALONE is sufficient, but statement (1) alone is not sufficient.
    (C) BOTH statements TOGETHER are sufficient, but NEITHER statement ALONE is sufficient.
    (D) EACH statement ALONE is sufficient.
    (E) Statements (1) and (2) TOGETHER are NOT sufficient to answer the question asked, and additional data are needed.

5. What is the value of $8x^2 - 6x + 3$?

 (1) $(x - 1)(x + 3) = 0$

 (2) $x - 1 = 0$

 (A) Statement (1) ALONE is sufficient, but statement (2) alone is not sufficient.
 (B) Statement (2) ALONE is sufficient, but statement (1) alone is not sufficient.
 (C) BOTH statements TOGETHER are sufficient, but NEITHER statement ALONE is sufficient.
 (D) EACH statement ALONE is sufficient.
 (E) Statements (1) and (2) TOGETHER are NOT sufficient to answer the question asked, and additional data are needed.

6. If $\dfrac{2}{5} + \dfrac{24}{n} = 2 + \dfrac{8}{n}$, what is the value of n ?

 (A) 0

 (B) $\dfrac{4}{5}$

 (C) 5

 (D) 8

 (E) 10

7. What is the value of $2x + 2y$?

 (1) $4x + 4y = 32$

 (2) $x = 8 - y$

 (A) Statement (1) ALONE is sufficient, but statement (2) alone is not sufficient.
 (B) Statement (2) ALONE is sufficient, but statement (1) alone is not sufficient.
 (C) BOTH statements TOGETHER are sufficient, but NEITHER statement ALONE is sufficient.
 (D) EACH statement ALONE is sufficient.
 (E) Statements (1) and (2) TOGETHER are NOT sufficient to answer the question asked, and additional data are needed.

8. The cost of paper per month in Julie's office is represented by the equation $\dfrac{4}{3}(p + 68) = c$, in which p represents the number of packages of paper purchased, and c represents the cost in dollars. If the cost c of paper for the month of August was \$356, how many packages did Julie's office purchase that month?

 (A) 68
 (B) 199
 (C) 267
 (D) 335
 (E) 406

9. Is $a > b$?

 (1) $\dfrac{a}{b} = 0$

 (2) $b + 2 < -5$

 (A) Statement (1) ALONE is sufficient, but statement (2) alone is not sufficient.
 (B) Statement (2) ALONE is sufficient, but statement (1) alone is not sufficient.
 (C) BOTH statements TOGETHER are sufficient, but NEITHER statement ALONE is sufficient.
 (D) EACH statement ALONE is sufficient.
 (E) Statements (1) and (2) TOGETHER are NOT sufficient to answer the question asked, and additional data are needed.

10. If $2x(3x - 1) = 0$, and $(x - \frac{1}{3})(5x - 6) = 0$, what is the value of x ?

   (A) 3

   (B) $\dfrac{6}{5}$

   (C) $\dfrac{1}{3}$

   (D) 0

   (E) $-\dfrac{1}{3}$

11. If $r > s + t$, is r positive?

   (1) $s > t$

   (2) $\dfrac{r}{s + t} > 1$

   (A) Statement (1) ALONE is sufficient, but statement (2) alone is not sufficient.
   (B) Statement (2) ALONE is sufficient, but statement (1) alone is not sufficient.
   (C) BOTH statements TOGETHER are sufficient, but NEITHER statement ALONE is sufficient.
   (D) EACH statement ALONE is sufficient.
   (E) Statements (1) and (2) TOGETHER are NOT sufficient to answer the question asked, and additional data are needed.

12. WINK, Inc., has two sales divisions, division A and division B. Yesterday, each member of division A made $\frac{2}{3}$ as many phone calls as each member of division B. If division B has $\frac{1}{4}$ as many members as division A, what fraction of all the phone calls made yesterday were placed by members of division B?

   (A) $\dfrac{1}{12}$

   (B) $\dfrac{3}{25}$

   (C) $\dfrac{1}{6}$

   (D) $\dfrac{3}{11}$

   (E) $\dfrac{3}{8}$

13. Hanks Manufacturing recently conducted a survey of its employees. The results showed that of the n people who work at the company, $\frac{1}{3}$ drink decaffeinated coffee, and the remainder drink regular coffee. Of those who do not drink decaf, $\frac{2}{5}$ add cream to their coffee. Which of the expressions below accurately represents the number of employees who do not drink regular coffee with cream?

   (A) $\dfrac{2n}{3}$

   (B) $\dfrac{n}{8}$

   (C) $\dfrac{4n}{15}$

   (D) $\dfrac{11n}{15}$

   (E) $\dfrac{13n}{15}$

14. At Webster Publishing, $\frac{1}{10}$ of the employees work in the accounting department, — work in sales, $\frac{1}{3}$ work in production, and the remaining 20 work in shipping. How many employees does Webster Publishing have?

(A) 40
(B) 120
(C) 150
(D) 300
(E) 600

15. If $a > 0$, is $b < 0$?

(1) $\frac{a}{b} > -6$

(2) $a + b > -2$

(A) Statement (1) ALONE is sufficient, but statement (2) alone is not sufficient.
(B) Statement (2) ALONE is sufficient, but statement (1) alone is not sufficient.
(C) BOTH statements TOGETHER are sufficient, but NEITHER statement ALONE is sufficient.
(D) EACH statement ALONE is sufficient.
(E) Statements (1) and (2) TOGETHER are NOT sufficient to answer the question asked, and additional data are needed.

Check your answers on page 281.

QUADRATICS

Unlike the simple linear equations you saw in the previous chapter, quadratic equations have exponents. On the GMAT, the key to working with quadratic equations is converting them to their other form by **foiling** or **factoring**.

FOIL

FOIL stands for First, Outside, Inside, Last, and it's the method used to multiply two algebraic terms. Here's an example.

$$(x - 5)(x + 8) =$$

First: $(x - 5)(x + 8) = x^2$

Outsides: $(x - 5)(x + 8) = x^2 + 8x$

Insides: $(x - 5)(x + 8) = x^2 + 8x - 5x$

Lasts: $(x - 5)(x + 8) = x^2 + 8x - 5x - 40$

Combine the middle terms, and your final answer is $x^2 + 3x - 40$.

Factor

If you already have the quadratic equation, reverse the FOIL process to find the factors. Follow these steps to factor $x^2 + 4x - 12$.

First, set up the parentheses.

$$x^2 + 4x - 12 = (\quad)(\quad)$$

Now find the first parts. To get x^2, the F in FOIL must have been x multiplied by x.

$$x^2 + 4x - 12 = (x \quad)(x \quad)$$

Now put in the signs. If the last sign in the quadratic is positive, then both parentheses have the same sign as the first sign in the quadratic. In other words, if the quadratic is $x^2 - 5x + 6$, then both parentheses will have minus signs. If the quadratic is $x^2 + 5x + 6$, then both parentheses will have plus signs.

If the last sign in the quadratic is negative, then one parenthesis will have a plus sign and the other will have a minus sign. Because the second sign in the example quadratic has a minus sign, your parentheses will look like this.

$$x^2 + 4x - 12 = (x + \quad)(x - \quad)$$

Now find the last parts of the factors. The middle term of the original quadratic must equal the sum of the factors of the last term of the original quadratic. Therefore, you need two factors of 12 that will add up to 4. The factors of 12 are (1, 12), (2, 6) and (3, 4). Only 2 and 6 will work and only if you place them as below.

$$x^2 + 4x - 12 = (x + 6)(x - 2)$$

You can always double check to make sure you factored correctly by adding the product of the two inner terms (in this case, $6x$) to the product of the two outer terms ($-2x$). The sum should equal the middle term of your original quadratic. $6x + -2x = 4x$, so you know you factored correctly.

Finding Roots

The **roots** of a quadratic equation are the solutions of the equation; they are values of x that make the equation true. If a quadratic is set equal to 0, you can factor it, and solve for x to find the roots.

Find the roots of this quadratic.

$$x^2 - 8x = -15$$

First subtract 15 from both sides so that the equation is set equal to 0.

$$x^2 - 8x + 15 = 0$$

Now, factor the quadratic.

$$x^2 - 8x + 15 = 0 = (x - 5)(x - 3)$$

Now set each term equal to 0 and solve.

$$\text{If } (x - 5) = 0, \text{ then } x = 5$$

$$\text{If } (x - 3) = 0, \text{ then } x = 3$$

Common Quadratics

There are certain quadratics that the test writers love to test repeatedly. You will save yourself a lot of time on the test if you memorize them.

$$(x + y)^2 = x^2 + 2xy + y^2$$

$$(x - y)^2 = x^2 - 2xy + y^2$$

$$(x + y)(x - y) = x^2 - y^2$$

QUADRATICS DRILL

1. $\left(\dfrac{1}{\sqrt{11}} + \dfrac{1}{\sqrt{11}}\right)^2 =$

   (A) $\dfrac{1}{121}$

   (B) $\dfrac{1}{44}$

   (C) $\dfrac{4}{11}$

   (D) $\dfrac{1}{22}$

   (E) $\dfrac{4}{\sqrt{11}}$

2. If $x^2 + bx + 26 = 8$, what is the value of b ?

   (1) $(x + 9)$ is one of the factors of $x^2 + bx + 26 = 8$.

   (2) -2 is one of the roots of $x^2 + bx + 26 = 8$.

   (A) Statement (1) ALONE is sufficient, but statement (2) ALONE is not sufficient.
   (B) Statement (2) ALONE is sufficient, but statement (1) ALONE is not sufficient.
   (C) BOTH statements TOGETHER are sufficient, but NEITHER statement ALONE is sufficient.
   (D) EACH statement ALONE is sufficient.
   (E) Statements (1) and (2) TOGETHER are NOT sufficient to answer the question asked, and additional data are needed.

3. $\left(\sqrt{48} - \sqrt{12}\right)^2 =$

   (A) 36
   (B) 12
   (C) 6
   (D) 4
   (E) 2

4. If $x^2 - cx + 20 = 0$, what is the value of x ?

   (1) $c = 12$

   (2) x is prime.

   (A) Statement (1) ALONE is sufficient, but statement (2) ALONE is not sufficient.
   (B) Statement (2) ALONE is sufficient, but statement (1) ALONE is not sufficient.
   (C) BOTH statements TOGETHER are sufficient, but NEITHER statement ALONE is sufficient.
   (D) EACH statement ALONE is sufficient.
   (E) Statements (1) and (2) TOGETHER are NOT sufficient to answer the question asked, and additional data are needed.

5. If $x^2 + 3x - 28 = 0$, what is one possible value of

   $\dfrac{2x - 1}{x^2}$?

   (A) $-\dfrac{9}{16}$

   (B) $\dfrac{1}{7}$

   (C) $\dfrac{13}{49}$

   (D) $\dfrac{15}{49}$

   (E) $\dfrac{7}{16}$

6. What is the value of $x^2 + y^2$?

   (1) $\left(x - y\right)^2 = 4$

   (2) $xy = 15$

   (A) Statement (1) ALONE is sufficient, but statement (2) ALONE is not sufficient.
   (B) Statement (2) ALONE is sufficient, but statement (1) ALONE is not sufficient.
   (C) BOTH statements TOGETHER are sufficient, but NEITHER statement ALONE is sufficient.
   (D) EACH statement ALONE is sufficient.
   (E) Statements (1) and (2) TOGETHER are NOT sufficient to answer the question asked, and additional data are needed.

7. In the equation $x^2 + 4x - c = 30$, 5 is one of the roots of the equation, and c is a constant. What is the value of the other root?

   (A) −9
   (B) −5
   (C) 4
   (D) 9
   (E) 15

8. If $\left(a^2 - b^2\right) = 30$, what is the value of a^2 ?

   (1) $(a + b) = 10$

   (2) $\sqrt{a}$ is not an integer.

   (A) Statement (1) ALONE is sufficient, but statement (2) ALONE is not sufficient.
   (B) Statement (2) ALONE is sufficient, but statement (1) ALONE is not sufficient.
   (C) BOTH statements TOGETHER are sufficient, but NEITHER statement ALONE is sufficient.
   (D) EACH statement ALONE is sufficient.
   (E) Statements (1) and (2) TOGETHER are NOT sufficient to answer the question asked, and additional data are needed.

9. If 3 is one root of an equation, and the second root is a negative even number, which of the following expressions might represent the equation?

   (A) $x^2 - 8x + 15$
   (B) $x^2 - 9x + 18$
   (C) $x^2 - 3x - 10$
   (D) $x^2 + x - 12$
   (E) $x^2 - 3x - 18$

10. Does $x = 3$?

    (1) $x^2 + 4x - 18 = 3$

    (2) $x^2 - 6x + 9 = 0$

    (A) Statement (1) ALONE is sufficient, but statement (2) ALONE is not sufficient.
    (B) Statement (2) ALONE is sufficient, but statement (1) ALONE is not sufficient.
    (C) BOTH statements TOGETHER are sufficient, but NEITHER statement ALONE is sufficient.
    (D) EACH statement ALONE is sufficient.
    (E) Statements (1) and (2) TOGETHER are NOT sufficient to answer the question asked, and additional data are needed.

11. If $\dfrac{r + 15}{r + 3} = r$, what is the value of $r^2 + 2r - 15$?

    (A) −5
    (B) −3
    (C) 0
    (D) 3
    (E) 5

12. If $(m + 2)^2 = 900$, what is one possible value of $m + 10$?

    (A) −32
    (B) −30
    (C) −22
    (D) 28
    (E) 30

13. Is $x^2 - 8x + 15$ equal to 0 ?

    (1) x is not equal to 3

    (2) $x - 5$ is not equal to 0

(A) Statement (1) ALONE is sufficient, but statement (2) ALONE is not sufficient.
(B) Statement (2) ALONE is sufficient, but statement (1) ALONE is not sufficient.
(C) BOTH statements TOGETHER are sufficient, but NEITHER statement ALONE is sufficient.
(D) EACH statement ALONE is sufficient.
(E) Statements (1) and (2) TOGETHER are NOT sufficient to answer the question asked, and additional data are needed.

14. What is the value of x ?

    (1) $x^2 + 6x + 5 = 0$

    (2) $x > -10$

(A) Statement (1) ALONE is sufficient, but statement (2) ALONE is not sufficient.
(B) Statement (2) ALONE is sufficient, but statement (1) ALONE is not sufficient.
(C) BOTH statements TOGETHER are sufficient, but NEITHER statement ALONE is sufficient.
(D) EACH statement ALONE is sufficient.
(E) Statements (1) and (2) TOGETHER are NOT sufficient to answer the question asked, and additional data are needed.

15. $\dfrac{(\sqrt{5} + 2)(\sqrt{5} - 2)}{(\sqrt{10} + 2)(\sqrt{10} - 2)} =$

(A) $\dfrac{1}{6}$

(B) $\dfrac{1}{5}$

(C) $\dfrac{1}{2}$

(D) $\dfrac{\sqrt{10}}{10}$

(E) $\dfrac{\sqrt{5}}{2}$

Check your answers on page 281.

PLUGGING IN

You learned about Plugging In in the math introduction on page 161. Remember, Plugging In will help you do problems more easily, more quickly and more accurately. Here is a review of the steps.

> Step 1: Assign a number to each variable in the problem.
>
> Step 2: Work the problem step-by-step using the numbers you chose. You should end up with a numerical answer (with no variables left over) that answers the question in the problem. Circle the answer. This is your target.
>
> Step 3: Plug the number(s) you assigned to the variable(s) into the answer choices. Choose the answer choice that matches your target. Be sure to check all five answer choices.

Avoid numbers that can make several answer choices match your target.

- Do not use 0 or 1.
- Do not use numbers that appear in the question or in the answer choices.
- Do not use the same number for more than one variable.

Choose numbers to make the calculations easy.

- If there are fractions in the question, choose a number that's a common multiple of the denominators. (Multiplying the denominators together is an easy way to find a good number.)
- If a question involves different units, use a multiple or a factor of the conversion number.
- If a question involves percents, use 100 or a multiple of 100.

The following problems are designed to help you hone your Plugging In skills.

PLUGGING IN DRILL

1. A filing cabinet has d drawers. Each drawer contains h hanging folders, and each hanging folder holds 20 manila folders. How many manila folders are contained in 3 cabinets?

   (A) $\dfrac{30d}{h}$

   (B) $30dh$

   (C) $\dfrac{60}{dh}$

   (D) $60dh$

   (E) $\dfrac{60d}{h}$

2. Jim and Michael both completed work for extra credit in a course. Which one raised his overall grade by the greatest number of points?

   (1) Jim raised his grade by 10 percent.

   (2) Michael raised his grade by 6 percent.

   (A) Statement (1) ALONE is sufficient, but statement (2) ALONE is not sufficient.
   (B) Statement (2) ALONE is sufficient, but statement (1) ALONE is not sufficient.
   (C) BOTH statements TOGETHER are sufficient, but NEITHER statement ALONE is sufficient.
   (D) EACH statement ALONE is sufficient.
   (E) Statements (1) and (2) TOGETHER are NOT sufficient to answer the question asked, and additional data are needed.

3. How many hours does it take Mordecai to run w miles if he runs at a rate of z miles per hour?

   (A) $\dfrac{w}{60z}$

   (B) $\dfrac{60z}{w}$

   (C) $\dfrac{w}{z}$

   (D) wz

   (E) $\dfrac{z}{w}$

4. What is the value of $2\left(\dfrac{x}{3} - \dfrac{y}{3}\right)$?

   (1) $x - y = 5$

   (2) $x + y = 11$

   (A) Statement (1) ALONE is sufficient, but statement (2) ALONE is not sufficient.
   (B) Statement (2) ALONE is sufficient, but statement (1) ALONE is not sufficient.
   (C) BOTH statements TOGETHER are sufficient, but NEITHER statement ALONE is sufficient.
   (D) EACH statement ALONE is sufficient.
   (E) Statements (1) and (2) TOGETHER are NOT sufficient to answer the question asked, and additional data are needed.

5. If x and y are positive integers, is xy an odd integer?

    (1) $\dfrac{x}{3}$ is an even integer.

    (2) $x + y$ is an even integer.

(A) Statement (1) ALONE is sufficient, but statement (2) ALONE is not sufficient.
(B) Statement (2) ALONE is sufficient, but statement (1) ALONE is not sufficient.
(C) BOTH statements TOGETHER are sufficient, but NEITHER statement ALONE is sufficient.
(D) EACH statement ALONE is sufficient.
(E) Statements (1) and (2) TOGETHER are NOT sufficient to answer the question asked, and additional data are needed.

6. Miriam sells homemade jewelry. If she sells $\dfrac{3}{5}$ as many necklaces in May as she does in April, and $\dfrac{1}{6}$ as many necklaces in June as she does in May, then the number of necklaces she sold in April was how many times the average (arithmetic mean) number of necklaces she sold in May and June?

    (A) $\dfrac{7}{20}$

    (B) $\dfrac{10}{7}$

    (C) $\dfrac{5}{3}$

    (D) $\dfrac{20}{7}$

    (E) 10

7. Is $\dfrac{1}{m} < \dfrac{1}{n}$?

    (1) $m - n = 3$

    (2) $3n = m + 2$

(A) Statement (1) ALONE is sufficient, but statement (2) ALONE is not sufficient.
(B) Statement (2) ALONE is sufficient, but statement (1) ALONE is not sufficient.
(C) BOTH statements TOGETHER are sufficient, but NEITHER statement ALONE is sufficient.
(D) EACH statement ALONE is sufficient.
(E) Statements (1) and (2) TOGETHER are NOT sufficient to answer the question asked, and additional data are needed.

8. Noah bought 30 horses at a total cost of g dollars. He later sold each of the horses at 25 percent above the original cost per horse. If all the horses originally cost the same price, then, in terms of g, for what dollar amount did each horse sell?

    (A) $\dfrac{30}{g}$

    (B) $\dfrac{g}{30}$

    (C) $\dfrac{4g}{120}$

    (D) $\dfrac{75}{g}$

    (E) $\dfrac{g}{24}$

9. If x is an integer, is x positive?

   (1) $7 - x$ is a positive integer

   (2) $\dfrac{x}{y^4}$ is a positive integer

   (A) Statement (1) ALONE is sufficient, but statement (2) ALONE is not sufficient.
   (B) Statement (2) ALONE is sufficient, but statement (1) ALONE is not sufficient.
   (C) BOTH statements TOGETHER are sufficient, but NEITHER statement ALONE is sufficient.
   (D) EACH statement ALONE is sufficient.
   (E) Statements (1) and (2) TOGETHER are NOT sufficient to answer the question asked, and additional data are needed.

10. If r, s, and t are integers, is $r + s = \sqrt{t}$?

    (1) $r < -s$

    (2) $\left(r + s\right)^2 = t$

    (A) Statement (1) ALONE is sufficient, but statement (2) ALONE is not sufficient.
    (B) Statement (2) ALONE is sufficient, but statement (1) ALONE is not sufficient.
    (C) BOTH statements TOGETHER are sufficient, but NEITHER statement ALONE is sufficient.
    (D) EACH statement ALONE is sufficient.
    (E) Statements (1) and (2) TOGETHER are NOT sufficient to answer the question asked, and additional data are needed.

11. A candle maker made p pillar candles and t taper candles during the 2nd week of July. If the number of pillar candles made was 7 greater than the number of taper candles made, this relationship is expressed by which of the following?

    (A) $p = t + 7$
    (B) $p = t - 7$
    (C) $p > t - 7$
    (D) $p > t + 7$
    (E) $p > 7t$

12. If $\dfrac{p}{q} > 5$, is $q < 2$?

    (1) $q > 1$

    (2) $-2p > -20$

    (A) Statement (1) ALONE is sufficient, but statement (2) ALONE is not sufficient.
    (B) Statement (2) ALONE is sufficient, but statement (1) ALONE is not sufficient.
    (C) BOTH statements TOGETHER are sufficient, but NEITHER statement ALONE is sufficient.
    (D) EACH statement ALONE is sufficient.
    (E) Statements (1) and (2) TOGETHER are NOT sufficient to answer the question asked, and additional data are needed.

13. At Liz's Bakery $\dfrac{2}{7}$ of the cupcakes sold during August had chocolate frosting and $\dfrac{1}{4}$ of the other cupcakes sold had sprinkles. If s cupcakes with sprinkles were sold in August, then, in terms of s, how many cupcakes with chocolate frosting were sold?

    (A) $\dfrac{5s}{8}$

    (B) $\dfrac{s}{25}$

    (C) $\dfrac{8s}{5}$

    (D) $\dfrac{25}{s}$

    (E) $\dfrac{28s}{5}$

14. If x and y are distinct points on a number line, and integer z is located between x and y, how many different values of z are possible?

    (1) The distance between x and y is 6.

    (2) xy is not an integer.

    (A) Statement (1) ALONE is sufficient, but statement (2) ALONE is not sufficient.
    (B) Statement (2) ALONE is sufficient, but statement (1) ALONE is not sufficient.
    (C) BOTH statements TOGETHER are sufficient, but NEITHER statement ALONE is sufficient.
    (D) EACH statement ALONE is sufficient.
    (E) Statements (1) and (2) TOGETHER are NOT sufficient to answer the question asked, and additional data are needed.

15. At a baseball game, each player on the red team hit $\frac{2}{3}$ as many balls as each player on the blue team did. If the red team has $\frac{5}{6}$ as many players as the blue team, then approximately what percent of all the balls hit at the game were hit by the blue team?

    (A) 25%

    (B) 56%

    (C) 64%

    (D) $66\frac{2}{3}$%

    (E) 83%

16. Issen is trying to select an assistant from a pool of a applicants. If $\frac{1}{5}$ of them really want to be actors, and of those $\frac{2}{3}$ really want to be directors, then, in terms of a, how many of the applicants do not want to be both actors and directors?

    (A) $\frac{2}{15}a$

    (B) $\frac{a}{5}$

    (C) $\frac{a}{3}$

    (D) $\frac{7}{8}a$

    (E) $\frac{13}{15}a$

17. If x and y are integers, and $\frac{x}{y}$ is an odd integer, what is the value of x ?

    (1) $xy = 36$

    (2) y is an even integer.

    (A) Statement (1) ALONE is sufficient, but statement (2) ALONE is not sufficient.
    (B) Statement (2) ALONE is sufficient, but statement (1) ALONE is not sufficient.
    (C) BOTH statements TOGETHER are sufficient, but NEITHER statement ALONE is sufficient.
    (D) EACH statement ALONE is sufficient.
    (E) Statements (1) and (2) TOGETHER are NOT sufficient to answer the question asked, and additional data are needed.

18. At the opening night performance of a new play, 5 percent of the theater patrons are late and are seated immediately, but 30 percent of the patrons who are late are not seated until the end of the first act. Approximately what percent of the theater patrons that evening are late?

(A) 5%
(B) 7%
(C) 35%
(D) 70%
(E) 80%

19. If p and q are integers and neither p nor q is equal to 0, is $\dfrac{p}{q} > \dfrac{q}{p}$?

(1) $p^2 > q^2$

(2) $p^3 > q^3$

(A) Statement (1) ALONE is sufficient, but statement (2) ALONE is not sufficient.
(B) Statement (2) ALONE is sufficient, but statement (1) ALONE is not sufficient.
(C) BOTH statements TOGETHER are sufficient, but NEITHER statement ALONE is sufficient.
(D) EACH statement ALONE is sufficient.
(E) Statements (1) and (2) TOGETHER are NOT sufficient to answer the question asked, and additional data are needed.

20. Are negative integers s and t both less than r ?

(1) $s < r + t$

(2) $\dfrac{s}{r} < t$

(A) Statement (1) ALONE is sufficient, but statement (2) ALONE is not sufficient.
(B) Statement (2) ALONE is sufficient, but statement (1) ALONE is not sufficient.
(C) BOTH statements TOGETHER are sufficient, but NEITHER statement ALONE is sufficient.
(D) EACH statement ALONE is sufficient.
(E) Statements (1) and (2) TOGETHER are NOT sufficient to answer the question asked, and additional data are needed.

21. Rebecca wants to climb a mountain, but she has to return to her camp at the base of the mountain in r hours. If she climbs up at w miles per hour and climbs down at z miles per hour, how far can she climb up so that she spends a total of r hours for the round trip?

(A) $\dfrac{w + z + r}{wz}$

(B) $\dfrac{rwz}{w + z}$

(C) $\dfrac{wr}{z}$

(D) $\dfrac{z + r}{w} - \dfrac{r}{z}$

(E) $\dfrac{r + w}{wz}$

22. The amount of money Michael makes in a year is represented by m. The amount of money Gary makes in a year is represented by g. If Michael's yearly salary is p percent of Gary's yearly salary, then, in terms of p, Gary's yearly salary is what percent of Michael's yearly salary?

(A) $\dfrac{10}{p}$

(B) $\dfrac{p}{100}$

(C) $100p$

(D) $\dfrac{10{,}000}{p}$

(E) p

23. If x and y are positive integers, and x is prime, is y even?

   (1) xy is even.

   (2) (x − 2)(y − 1) is odd.

(A) Statement (1) ALONE is sufficient, but statement (2) ALONE is not sufficient.
(B) Statement (2) ALONE is sufficient, but statement (1) ALONE is not sufficient.
(C) BOTH statements TOGETHER are sufficient, but NEITHER statement ALONE is sufficient.
(D) EACH statement ALONE is sufficient.
(E) Statements (1) and (2) TOGETHER are NOT sufficient to answer the question asked, and additional data are needed.

24. The productivity P at a certain manufacturing plant can be measured with the formula $P = .05abc^3$ where a is the number of workers, b is the temperature of the room and c is the speed of the assembly line. If a is decreased by 40 percent, b is increased by 100 percent, and c is decreased by 60 percent, by approximately what percent will the productivity at the plant change?

(A) 92% decrease
(B) 81% decrease
(C)   5% decrease
(D) 12% increase
(E) 92% increase

Check your answers on page 281.

PITA

You learned about PITA in the math introduction on page 165. Remember, PITA will help you do problems more easily, more quickly and more accurately. Here is a review of the steps.

> Step 1: Identify what the question is asking.
>
> Step 2: Plug In the middle answer choice. Work the problem step-by-step and see if everything matches.
>
> Step 3: Eliminate answers that don't work. Keep Plugging In answers until you find one that works.

The following problems are designed to help you hone your PITA skills.

PITA DRILL

1. In the three weeks between November 14, 2003, and December 5, 2003, the number of viewers of a particular television program decreased by 13 percent. The number of viewers on November 14, 2003, was 30 million. How many viewers, to the nearest million, viewed the program on December 5, 2003 ?

(A) 29
(B) 28
(C) 27
(D) 26
(E) 25

2. At the Meinhart Modeling agency, there are 6 more women with blonde hair than there are with brown hair. If there are 30 women at the agency, and they all have either blonde or brown hair, how many women at the agency have brown hair?

(A) 10
(B) 11
(C) 12
(D) 13
(E) 14

3. Zelda has a 20 inch piece of red rope licorice that she must share with her younger brother Randy. If she divides the licorice so that her piece is 8 inches longer than Randy's piece, how long, in inches, is Randy's piece?

(A) 17
(B) 14
(C) 11
(D) 8
(E) 6

4. Lila is baking a batch of chocolate chip cookies and a batch of oatmeal raisin cookies to take to the office potluck. The total number of cookies in both batches is 100. If three times the number of chocolate chip cookies she baked is 20 more than the number of oatmeal cookies she baked, how many chocolate chip cookies did she bake?

(A) 30
(B) 40
(C) 50
(D) 60
(E) 70

5. A DVD rental costs d dollars to rent for 2 days and $2.25 for each additional day. Carl rents a DVD for 5 days and it costs $10.25. What is the value of d ?

(A) $1.60
(B) $2.05
(C) $3.25
(D) $3.50
(E) $4.00

6. At a certain restaurant, all tips are added together to be split among the employees at the end of a shift. The 4 waiters divide $\frac{2}{3}$ of the money equally among themselves, the manager receives $\frac{1}{4}$, and the busboy receives the remainder. If 1 waiter and the busboy together receive $30, how much money was earned in tips for the entire shift?

(A) $90
(B) $96
(C) $108
(D) $120
(E) $180

7. Abigail and Bernard earned a total of $90 for painting a room. If Abigail worked for 1 hour and 30 minutes, Bernard worked for 45 minutes, and they split their earnings in proportion to the amount of time each spent working, then how much did Bernard receive?

(A) $25.50
(B) $30.00
(C) $32.50
(D) $45.00
(E) $60.00

8. A certain vase contains 17 roses and 8 daffodils. How many roses must be removed from the vase so that 40 percent of the flowers will be daffodils?

(A) 5
(B) 8
(C) 10
(D) 13
(E) 15

9. 40 percent of the singers in the community chorus can sight-read. Among those who *cannot* sight-read, 17 have taken music theory and 25 have not. How many singers are in the chorus?

(A) 50
(B) 70
(C) 90
(D) 110
(E) 130

10. If Jasmine were three times as old as she is, she would be 20 years younger than Blake. If Blake is 40 years older than Jasmine, how old is Blake?

(A) 70
(B) 60
(C) 50
(D) 40
(E) 30

11. In a particular police precinct, an officer can take the sergeant's exam when the officer's age plus years of employment with the force total at least 50. In what year could a male officer hired in 1992 on his 28th birthday first be eligible to take the sergeant's exam?

(A) 2006
(B) 2005
(C) 2004
(D) 2003
(E) 2002

12. Kim's Cafe has 20 waiters, 30 percent of whom are men. If 8 new waiters will be hired, and all of the present waiters remain, how many of the additional waiters must be women in order to decrease the percent of male waiters to 25 percent?

(A) 1
(B) 5
(C) 7
(D) 10
(E) 17

13. If Jeff tips more than 15 percent on a meal, and the tip is more than $4 dollars, what is the least possible cost of the meal before tip, rounded to the nearest dollar?

(A) $26
(B) $27
(C) $30
(D) $32
(E) $60

14. At a particular zoo, $\frac{2}{5}$ of all the animals are mammals, and $\frac{2}{3}$ of the mammals are allowed to interact directly with the public. If 24 mammals are allowed to interact directly with the public, how many animals in this zoo are NOT mammals?

(A) 36
(B) 48
(C) 54
(D) 60
(E) 72

15. Reservoir A contains 450 million gallons of water more than does Reservoir B. If 100 million gallons of water were drained from Reservoir A into Reservoir B, then Reservoir A would contain twice as much water as would Reservoir B. How many million gallons of water does Reservoir A currently contain?

(A) 500
(B) 600
(C) 700
(D) 800
(E) 900

16. The New Age Entertainment Company produces x mood rings at a cost, in cents, of $80x + 9,000$. These x mood rings can be sold for a price, in cents, of $260x$. What is the least value of x for which the New Age Entertainment Company does not lose money?

(A) 107
(B) 82
(C) 63
(D) 51
(E) 50

17. If n is positive, $\frac{n}{m} = 4$, and $mn = 9$, then $m =$

(A) $\frac{1}{6}$

(B) $\frac{2}{3}$

(C) $\frac{3}{2}$

(D) 6

(E) $\frac{27}{2}$

18. A sports league encourages collaboration by awarding 3 points for each goal scored without assistance and 5 points for each goal scored with assistance. A total of 48 points were scored by a team in a single game. Which of the following CANNOT be the number of goals scored without assistance by this team in this game?

(A) 1
(B) 6
(C) 11
(D) 12
(E) 16

19. If $\dfrac{(x + 2)(x - 5)}{(x - 3)(x + 4)} = 1$, then $x =$

(A) -2

(B) $-\dfrac{1}{2}$

(C) 1

(D) $\dfrac{1}{2}$

(E) 2

20. Benji is booking an airline flight, and the airline is running a special. Benji can choose either to receive 15,000 air miles immediately, or to receive 7,000 air miles, plus 20 percent of the miles that he flies over the next six months. How many miles must Benji fly in order to receive equal miles from either option?

(A) 11,000
(B) 15,000
(C) 22,000
(D) 40,000
(E) 80,000

21. If $4x^2 + 24x + 27 = 0$, then $|x + 3| =$

(A) $\dfrac{1}{2}$

(B) $\dfrac{3}{2}$

(C) $\dfrac{5}{2}$

(D) 3

(E) $\dfrac{7}{2}$

22. At his weekly poker game, Ron bought $200 worth of chips in $5 and $10 denominations. By the end of the evening, Ron had lost all but 12 of his chips. If the number of $10 chips Ron had left was two more or two less than the number of $5 chips he had left, what is the minimum possible value of the chips that Ron lost?

(A) $140
(B) $105
(C) $95
(D) $85
(E) $80

23. Of the 43 players on the Furse Finance softball team, 15 have uniforms and 8 have uniforms and can play on Saturdays. If the number of players who can play on Saturdays is twice the number of players who neither have uniforms nor can play on Saturdays, then how many of the players can play on Saturdays?

(A) 5
(B) 6
(C) 11
(D) 12
(E) 24

24. At Hotel Isabella, the ratio of paying guests to non-paying guests is 56 to 3. If 12 more paying guests were to check into the hotel, the ratio of paying guests to non-paying guests would be 59 to 3. How many total guests does Hotel Isabella have?

(A) 212
(B) 224
(C) 236
(D) 248
(E) 260

Check your answers on page 281.

MUST BE TRUE

When you learned about Plugging In, you learned there are certain numbers that are not good to Plug In because they yield more than one right answer. If that happens, you have to Plug In a second or even a third time. However, sometimes you might have to Plug In more than once even if you haven't plugged in "bad numbers." That happens if the problem says "must be true."

As always, if you Plug In numbers and more than one answer choice works, Plug In again with different numbers until you get it down to one answer choice. The answers you crossed off the first time are gone forever; you only have to Plug In again on the answers that worked the first time. When you Plug In the second time, try using weird numbers.

Weird numbers include

- Zero
- One
- Negatives
- Extremes
- Fractions

You can remember them by using the acronym **ZONEF**. **Extremes** are very large or small numbers. They can also be "different" numbers. For example, if you plugged in negative numbers the first time, try positive numbers the second time. If you tried odd, then try even, etc. Using weird numbers will help you narrow your choices more quickly.

Must Be True on I/II/III Questions

I/II/III questions are all about POE. If the question asks "which of the following **can be** true" and you determine that one of the statements is not true, you can eliminate all the answer choices that have that statement. If you determine that one of the statements is true, you can eliminate all the answer choices that don't have that statement.

Must be true means you probably will have to Plug In more than once. That means if a I/II/III question asks "which of the following **must be** true" you can only eliminate answers if you determine that one of the statements is not true. If you determine that one of the statements is true, you have to Plug In again to make sure it's always true no matter what. You keep Plugging In until you narrow your choices down to one.

Example

1. If x, y, and z are nonzero integers and $x > yz$, which of the following must be true?

    I. $\dfrac{x}{y} > z$

    II. $\dfrac{x}{z} > y$

    III. $\dfrac{x}{yz} > 1$

    ○ None of the above
    ○ I only
    ○ III only
    ○ I and II only
    ○ I, II, and III

Since there are variables, plug in. Start by picking some nice, normal numbers for x, y, and z. Make sure that your numbers satisfy $x > yz$, the condition in the problem. For example, $x = 8$, $y = 2$ and $z = 3$ work because $8 > (2)(3)$.

Now, check each of the roman numerals using these numbers. For these numbers, I, II, and III are all true. But, don't choose an answer yet!

Remember that you should always plug in at least twice when the problem uses the words "must be." The second time you Plug In, you want to try to make the numbers as different as possible. For example, what if $x = 8$, $y = -2$ and $z = 3$? Note that these numbers still satisfy the inequality in the problem. Roman numeral I is now false, so eliminate any answers that contain I. That eliminates (B), (D), and (E). Since the only choices left are "None of the above" and "III only," you don't need to worry about checking roman numeral II. There must be numbers that make roman numeral II false. Move on to checking roman numeral III, which is also false for these numbers. Eliminate (C). The correct answer is (A).

MUST BE TRUE DRILL

1. If x is a positive integer and is a multiple of both 3 and 11, then x must also be a multiple of which of the following?

    I. 14
    II. 33
    III. 66

    (A) I only
    (B) II only
    (C) I and II
    (D) II and III
    (E) None of the above

2. If $w > 0$, which of the following must be equal to 0 ?

    I. w^0

    II. $\sqrt{w}$

    III. $\dfrac{1}{w} + -\dfrac{1}{w}$

    (A) I, II, and III
    (B) II and III only
    (C) I and II only
    (D) III only
    (E) I only

3. If $x = -0.5$, which of the following must be true?

    I. $x < x^2$
    II. $x^3 < x$
    III. $x^3 < x^2$

    (A) I only
    (B) I and III
    (C) II and III
    (D) I, II, and III
    (E) None of the above

4. If positive integer r is divisible by both 6 and 8, then r must also be divisible by which of the following?

    I. 48
    II. 15
    III. 96

    (A) None
    (B) I only
    (C) II only
    (D) I and III
    (E) I, II, and II

5. If both x and y are positive integers, and 8 is a factor of x, and 9 is a factor of y, which of the following must be a factor of xy ?

    I. 12
    II. 16
    III. 24

    (A) I only
    (B) II only
    (C) I and II
    (D) I and III
    (E) I, II, and III

6. If $2r - 3s = 0$ and $s < 2$, which of the following must be true?

    (A) $r = 3$
    (B) $r > 3$
    (C) $r < 2$
    (D) $r > -3$
    (E) $r < 3$

7. If p and r are distinct, odd integers, and $p < r$, then which of the following must be true?

    I. $p + r$ is even

    II. pr is positive

    III. $\dfrac{p}{r} < 1$

(A) I only
(B) II only
(C) I and II
(D) II and III
(E) I, II, and III

8. Olivia has twice as many marbles as Josh and Josh has 3 fewer marbles than Hugo. If Olivia, Josh and Hugo all receive 4 more marbles, which of the following must be true?

    I. Olivia has more marbles than Hugo.
    II. Olivia has twice as many marbles as Josh.
    III. Josh has 3 fewer marbles than Hugo.

(A) I only
(B) III only
(C) I and III
(D) II and III
(E) I, II, and III

9. If $0 < x < y < 1$, then which of the following must be true?

    I. $x^{-2} > y^2$
    II. $xy > 1$
    III. $x^2 < y^3$

(A) I only
(B) II only
(C) I and III
(D) II and III
(E) None of the above

10. If $0 < p < 1$, which of the following must be true?

    I. $p^4 - p^5 < p^2 - p^3$
    II. $p^5 < p^3$
    III. $p^4 + p^5 < p^3 + p^2$

(A) I, II, and III
(B) I and II only
(C) II only
(D) I only
(E) None

11. If $5x + 3y = 0$, and $x < 3$, then which of the following must be true?

(A) $y < -5$
(B) $y = -5$
(C) $y > -5$
(D) $y > 3$
(E) $y > 5$

12. The crew of the Voelke Mountain Observatory records the outdoor temperature rounded to the nearest whole degree for x days. If the temperature increases by exactly 1 degree per day, and the sum of all of the temperatures is 0, then which of the following must be true?

    I. x represents an even number of days.
    II. x represents an odd number of days.
    III. The average temperature for the x days is 0.

(A) I only
(B) II only
(C) I and III
(D) II and III
(E) None of the above

$$a, b, c, d, e$$

13. A series of numbers in which the difference between any two successive members of the sequence is a constant is called an arithmetic sequence. Which of the following must also be an arithmetic sequence if the series above is an arithmetic sequence?

    I. $(a - 2), (b - 2), (c - 2), (d - 2), (e - 2)$

    II. $3a, 3b, 3c, 3d, 3e$

    III. $\sqrt{a}, \sqrt{b}, \sqrt{c}, \sqrt{d}, \sqrt{e}$

(A) I only
(B) II only
(C) I and II only
(D) II and III only
(E) I, II, and III

14. Tom is preparing for a race, and each day he runs one mile farther than he did on the previous day. If he runs w miles one day, x miles the next day, y miles the day after that, and on the next and final day he runs z miles, and w, x, y and z are all integers, then which of the following must be true?

    I. $z - w = 3$

    II. $wxyz$ is an even number.

    III. $\dfrac{w + x + y + z}{4}$ is an integer.

(A) I only
(B) II only
(C) I and II
(D) I and III
(E) I, II, and III

15. If $0 < 1 - \dfrac{f}{g} < 1$, and $g > 0$, which of the following must be true?

    I. $f^2 + g^2 > 1$

    II. $f > 0$

    III. $\dfrac{f}{g} < 1$

(A) I only
(B) III only
(C) I and III only
(D) II and III only
(E) I, II, and III

16. If a is a multiple of 15 and b is a multiple of 22, then which of the following must be a factor of ab?

(A) 4
(B) 6
(C) 12
(D) 20
(E) 25

17. If $\dfrac{1}{z} < z < 0$, then which of the following must be true?

(A) $1 < z^2$

(B) $z^2 < z$

(C) $-1 < z^3 < 0$

(D) $\dfrac{1}{z} > -1$

(E) $z^3 < z$

18. If x and y are prime numbers such that $x < 3 < y < 11$, which of the following must also be prime?

(A) $x^2 + y^2$
(B) $x + y$
(C) xy
(D) $5xy$
(E) $y^2 - x^2$

19. If $a < b < c < 0 < d$, then which of the following expressions must be negative?

(A) $c + d$
(B) abd
(C) $b - c$
(D) $d - a$
(E) $bc - d$

20. If $-1 < p < 1$ and $p \neq 0$, then which of the following must be true?

(A) $p^7 < p^5$
(B) $p^6 + p^8 < p^2 + p^4$
(C) $p^3 = (-p)^3$
(D) $(-p)^3 < p^3$
(E) $p^4 < p^6$

21. If x is a negative odd integer and y is a positive even integer, then which of the following must be true?

(A) xy is a negative odd integer.

(B) $\dfrac{x}{y}$ is a negative even integer.

(C) $x - y$ is a negative odd integer.

(D) $x + y$ is a negative odd integer.

(E) $y - x$ is a positive even integer.

22. If s is a multiple of 12, then $s + 15$ must be a multiple of

(A) 3
(B) 9
(C) 12
(D) 15
(E) 27

23. If x, y, and z are positive integers such that $x < y < z$, then which of the following must be true?

(A) $x + y > z$
(B) $x + 2 = y + 1 = z$
(C) $xy > z$
(D) $-x > -y$
(E) $z - y > x$

24. If $a - b$ is a multiple of 5, then which of the following must also be a multiple of 5 ?

(A) $\dfrac{a - b}{5}$

(B) $a^2 - b^2$

(C) $a + b$

(D) ab

(E) $5a - b$

Check your answers on page 281.

YES/NO DATA SUFFICIENCY

Yes/No data sufficiency questions are questions to which the answer is "yes" or "no." They start with words such as "Is," "Has," "Do," "Does," or "Are." These questions can be tricky because it's easy to get confused about whether you are answering the question "yes" or "no" or whether you are answering whether you have enough information "yes" or "no."

The important thing to remember is that, as with all data sufficiency questions, the actual answer to the question doesn't matter; the only thing that matters is whether you have enough information to answer the question.

Example

1.   Does $x = 10$?

(1)   Ten percent of x is 1.

(2)   One-fifth of x is an even prime number.

(A)   Statement (1) ALONE is sufficient, but statement (2) alone is not sufficient.
(B)   Statement (2) ALONE is sufficient, but statement (1) alone is not sufficient.
(C)   BOTH statements TOGETHER are sufficient, but NEITHER statement ALONE is sufficient.
(D)   EACH statement ALONE is sufficient.
(E)   Statements (1) and (2) TOGETHER are NOT sufficient to answer the question asked, and additional data are needed.

If you translate the first statement you get an equation that can be solved to find the value of x. That means you have enough information to answer whether $x = 10$ or not. The actual answer to the question "Does $x = 10$?" doesn't matter. Write "AD" on your scratch paper.

Because there is only one even prime number, 2, the second statement also can be solved to find the value of x. That means you have enough information to answer the question. Again, the actual answer to the question doesn't matter. Thus, the correct answer is (D).

As on all data sufficiency questions, if on a Yes/No data sufficiency question there are algebraic expressions in the statements that can be simplified, simplify them before proceeding. If there are algebraic expressions in the statements that cannot be simplified, Plug In.

Plugging In on Yes/No Data Sufficiency

- Start by rewriting the question as an either/or question. For example, prime vs. not prime, integer vs. non-integer, positive vs. negative, odd vs. even, etc. This tells you what types of numbers you will Plug In.
- For each statement, try to Plug In numbers that fit both sides of the either/or statement. For example, if it's odd vs. even, try to Plug In an odd number that would work with the statement, and then try to Plug In an even number that would work with the statement. **You must Plug In numbers that work <u>with</u> the statement.** (The statement is law.)
- If numbers for only ONE side of the either/or statement work (for example, only odd numbers work), the statement is sufficient.
- If numbers for BOTH sides of the either/or statement work (for example, both odd and even numbers work), the statement is not sufficient.
- When you combine, you must plug the same numbers into both statements.

Example

2. Is x an odd integer?

    (1) $2x + 3$ is an odd integer.

    (2) $x + 11$ is an even integer.

    (A) Statement (1) ALONE is sufficient, but statement (2) alone is not sufficient.
    (B) Statement (2) ALONE is sufficient, but statement (1) alone is not sufficient.
    (C) BOTH statements TOGETHER are sufficient, but NEITHER statement ALONE is sufficient.
    (D) EACH statement ALONE is sufficient.
    (E) Statements (1) and (2) TOGETHER are NOT sufficient to answer the question asked, and additional data are needed.

The question is whether x is odd or even. Look at the first statement and start with odd. Is it possible to Plug In an odd number that would work with the first statement? Yes. Three, for example, makes the first statement true. Is it possible to Plug In an even number that would work with the first statement? Yes. Two, or any other even number, would make the first statement true. Because both odd and even numbers work with the first statement, you can't tell whether x is odd or even. Therefore, statement (1) is insufficient. Write "BCE" on your noteboard.

Look at the second statement. Is it possible to Plug In an odd number that would work with the second statement? Sure. Three would work. Is it possible to Plug In an even number that would work with the second statement? No. Even plus odd is always odd, so no even number will work with the second statement. Because only odd numbers will work with the second statement, you know that x is odd. So statement (2) is sufficient. The correct answer is (B).

Try one more.

3.   Is x a positive number?

(1) $x + 6 > 2$

(2) $x^2 > 25$

(A)   Statement (1) ALONE is sufficient, but statement (2) alone is not sufficient.
(B)   Statement (2) ALONE is sufficient, but statement (1) alone is not sufficient.
(C)   BOTH statements TOGETHER are sufficient, but NEITHER statement ALONE is sufficient.
(D)   EACH statement ALONE is sufficient.
(E)   Statements (1) and (2) TOGETHER are NOT sufficient to answer the question asked, and additional data are needed.

The question is whether x is positive or negative. Any positive number will work with the first statement. It is also possible to Plug In a negative number, –2, for example, that will work with the first statement. Both a positive and a negative number work with the first statement, so statement (1) is insufficient. Write "BCE" on your scratch paper.

For the second statement you could Plug In both a positive number and a negative number, 6 and –6 for example. Therefore, because x could be either positive or negative, statement (2) is insufficient. Eliminate (B).

When you combine, the same number must work with both statements. Is there a positive number that could work with both statements? Sure. Six works with both statements. Is there a negative number that works with both statements? No. For the second statement, the least negative number possible is –6. Any number that is less negative (–5, –4, –3, and so on) won't work. However, –6 or any number that is more negative than –6 won't work with statement (1). Only a positive number will work with both statements. Therefore, by combining you can tell that x is positive and the correct answer is (C).

YES/NO DATA SUFFICIENCY DRILL

1. Is x less than $\dfrac{1}{3}$?

   (1) x is less than 0.35

   (2) x is equal to 0.29

   (A) Statement (1) ALONE is sufficient, but statement (2) alone is not sufficient.
   (B) Statement (2) ALONE is sufficient, but statement (1) alone is not sufficient.
   (C) BOTH statements TOGETHER are sufficient, but NEITHER statement ALONE is sufficient.
   (D) EACH statement ALONE is sufficient.
   (E) Statements (1) and (2) TOGETHER are NOT sufficient to answer the question asked, and additional data are needed.

2. If m and n are positive integers, is $m - n$ a multiple of 5 ?

   (1) $m - n$ is a multiple of 10.

   (2) n is a multiple of 5

   (A) Statement (1) ALONE is sufficient, but statement (2) alone is not sufficient.
   (B) Statement (2) ALONE is sufficient, but statement (1) alone is not sufficient.
   (C) BOTH statements TOGETHER are sufficient, but NEITHER statement ALONE is sufficient.
   (D) EACH statement ALONE is sufficient.
   (E) Statements (1) and (2) TOGETHER are NOT sufficient to answer the question asked, and additional data are needed.

3. If p and r are positive integers, is $\dfrac{p}{r} < 3$?

   (1) $3 \le p \le 6$ and $1 \le r \le 3$

   (2) $pr = 4$

   (A) Statement (1) ALONE is sufficient, but statement (2) alone is not sufficient.
   (B) Statement (2) ALONE is sufficient, but statement (1) alone is not sufficient.
   (C) BOTH statements TOGETHER are sufficient, but NEITHER statement ALONE is sufficient.
   (D) EACH statement ALONE is sufficient.
   (E) Statements (1) and (2) TOGETHER are NOT sufficient to answer the question asked, and additional data are needed.

4. Is line j parallel to line k ?

   (1) The slope of j is $\dfrac{1}{3}$.

   (2) The equation of line k is $x - 3y = 6$.

   (A) Statement (1) ALONE is sufficient, but statement (2) alone is not sufficient.
   (B) Statement (2) ALONE is sufficient, but statement (1) alone is not sufficient.
   (C) BOTH statements TOGETHER are sufficient, but NEITHER statement ALONE is sufficient.
   (D) EACH statement ALONE is sufficient.
   (E) Statements (1) and (2) TOGETHER are NOT sufficient to answer the question asked, and additional data are needed.

5. Is integer x prime?

    (1) $x^2 - 3$ is an even integer.

    (2) $x + 2$ is an odd integer.

(A) Statement (1) ALONE is sufficient, but statement (2) alone is not sufficient.
(B) Statement (2) ALONE is sufficient, but statement (1) alone is not sufficient.
(C) BOTH statements TOGETHER are sufficient, but NEITHER statement ALONE is sufficient.
(D) EACH statement ALONE is sufficient.
(E) Statements (1) and (2) TOGETHER are NOT sufficient to answer the question asked, and additional data are needed.

6. Did Madeline run for more than 24 miles?

    (1) Madeline ran for a total of 3 hours.

    (2) Madeline's average speed for the first mile was 8 miles per hour.

(A) Statement (1) ALONE is sufficient, but statement (2) alone is not sufficient.
(B) Statement (2) ALONE is sufficient, but statement (1) alone is not sufficient.
(C) BOTH statements TOGETHER are sufficient, but NEITHER statement ALONE is sufficient.
(D) EACH statement ALONE is sufficient.
(E) Statements (1) and (2) TOGETHER are NOT sufficient to answer the question asked, and additional data are needed.

7. Is x^2 a multiple of 8 ?

    (1) x is a multiple of 4.

    (2) x is a multiple of 2.

(A) Statement (1) ALONE is sufficient, but statement (2) alone is not sufficient.
(B) Statement (2) ALONE is sufficient, but statement (1) alone is not sufficient.
(C) BOTH statements TOGETHER are sufficient, but NEITHER statement ALONE is sufficient.
(D) EACH statement ALONE is sufficient.
(E) Statements (1) and (2) TOGETHER are NOT sufficient to answer the question asked, and additional data are needed.

8. Is $\dfrac{x}{y} > 8$?

    (1) $x^2 < 16$ and $y < \dfrac{1}{2}$

    (2) $x > 16$ and $1 < 2y < 4$

(A) Statement (1) ALONE is sufficient, but statement (2) alone is not sufficient.
(B) Statement (2) ALONE is sufficient, but statement (1) alone is not sufficient.
(C) BOTH statements TOGETHER are sufficient, but NEITHER statement ALONE is sufficient.
(D) EACH statement ALONE is sufficient.
(E) Statements (1) and (2) TOGETHER are NOT sufficient to answer the question asked, and additional data are needed.

9. Does $x = \sqrt{25}$?

    (1) $x^2 - 3x - 10 = 0$

    (2) $x^2 = 25$

(A) Statement (1) ALONE is sufficient, but statement (2) alone is not sufficient.
(B) Statement (2) ALONE is sufficient, but statement (1) alone is not sufficient.
(C) BOTH statements TOGETHER are sufficient, but NEITHER statement ALONE is sufficient.
(D) EACH statement ALONE is sufficient.
(E) Statements (1) and (2) TOGETHER are NOT sufficient to answer the question asked, and additional data are needed.

10. Is $\sqrt{n}$ less than n ?

    (1) $n^2 < n$

    (2) $0 < n^3 < 1$

(A) Statement (1) ALONE is sufficient, but statement (2) alone is not sufficient.
(B) Statement (2) ALONE is sufficient, but statement (1) alone is not sufficient.
(C) BOTH statements TOGETHER are sufficient, but NEITHER statement ALONE is sufficient.
(D) EACH statement ALONE is sufficient.
(E) Statements (1) and (2) TOGETHER are NOT sufficient to answer the question asked, and additional data are needed.

11. Is $p < r$?

    (1) $2p = r + 6$

    (2) $p = 3 - r$

(A) Statement (1) ALONE is sufficient, but statement (2) alone is not sufficient.
(B) Statement (2) ALONE is sufficient, but statement (1) alone is not sufficient.
(C) BOTH statements TOGETHER are sufficient, but NEITHER statement ALONE is sufficient.
(D) EACH statement ALONE is sufficient.
(E) Statements (1) and (2) TOGETHER are NOT sufficient to answer the question asked, and additional data are needed.

12. If p, q, and r are negative integers, is $p > q > r$?

    (1) $pq < pr$

    (2) $pr < qr$

(A) Statement (1) ALONE is sufficient, but statement (2) alone is not sufficient.
(B) Statement (2) ALONE is sufficient, but statement (1) alone is not sufficient.
(C) BOTH statements TOGETHER are sufficient, but NEITHER statement ALONE is sufficient.
(D) EACH statement ALONE is sufficient.
(E) Statements (1) and (2) TOGETHER are NOT sufficient to answer the question asked, and additional data are needed.

13. If b, c, d, and e are positive integers, does $d = 20$?

   (1) $b = c - e$

   (2) $\dfrac{b + c + d + e}{4} = 10$

   (A) Statement (1) ALONE is sufficient, but statement (2) alone is not sufficient.
   (B) Statement (2) ALONE is sufficient, but statement (1) alone is not sufficient.
   (C) BOTH statements TOGETHER are sufficient, but NEITHER statement ALONE is sufficient.
   (D) EACH statement ALONE is sufficient.
   (E) Statements (1) and (2) TOGETHER are NOT sufficient to answer the question asked, and additional data are needed.

14. If a, b, and c are positive integers, is $\dfrac{a}{b} = 8$?

   (1) $c(a - 8b) = 0$

   (2) $48b = 6a$

   (A) Statement (1) ALONE is sufficient, but statement (2) alone is not sufficient.
   (B) Statement (2) ALONE is sufficient, but statement (1) alone is not sufficient.
   (C) BOTH statements TOGETHER are sufficient, but NEITHER statement ALONE is sufficient.
   (D) EACH statement ALONE is sufficient.
   (E) Statements (1) and (2) TOGETHER are NOT sufficient to answer the question asked, and additional data are needed.

15. Does $x = y$?

   (1) $\dfrac{x}{y} < 0$

   (2) $\dfrac{x - y}{2} < -2$

   (A) Statement (1) ALONE is sufficient, but statement (2) alone is not sufficient.
   (B) Statement (2) ALONE is sufficient, but statement (1) alone is not sufficient.
   (C) BOTH statements TOGETHER are sufficient, but NEITHER statement ALONE is sufficient.
   (D) EACH statement ALONE is sufficient.
   (E) Statements (1) and (2) TOGETHER are NOT sufficient to answer the question asked, and additional data are needed.

16. Does $z(5x - y) = 12$?

   (1) $5xz = 12 + yz$

   (2) $xz = 4.2$ and $yz = 9$

   (A) Statement (1) ALONE is sufficient, but statement (2) alone is not sufficient.
   (B) Statement (2) ALONE is sufficient, but statement (1) alone is not sufficient.
   (C) BOTH statements TOGETHER are sufficient, but NEITHER statement ALONE is sufficient.
   (D) EACH statement ALONE is sufficient.
   (E) Statements (1) and (2) TOGETHER are NOT sufficient to answer the question asked, and additional data are needed.

17. Is $m > 0$?

   (1) $\dfrac{m^2}{-3} < 0$

   (2) $(-m)(-5) > 0$

(A) Statement (1) ALONE is sufficient, but statement (2) alone is not sufficient.
(B) Statement (2) ALONE is sufficient, but statement (1) alone is not sufficient.
(C) BOTH statements TOGETHER are sufficient, but NEITHER statement ALONE is sufficient.
(D) EACH statement ALONE is sufficient.
(E) Statements (1) and (2) TOGETHER are NOT sufficient to answer the question asked, and additional data are needed.

18. If $\sqrt{x}$ is an integer, is a an even integer?

   (1) $a = x^2$

   (2) $\sqrt{x}$ is an even integer

(A) Statement (1) ALONE is sufficient, but statement (2) alone is not sufficient.
(B) Statement (2) ALONE is sufficient, but statement (1) alone is not sufficient.
(C) BOTH statements TOGETHER are sufficient, but NEITHER statement ALONE is sufficient.
(D) EACH statement ALONE is sufficient.
(E) Statements (1) and (2) TOGETHER are NOT sufficient to answer the question asked, and additional data are needed.

19. Is $\dfrac{81}{3^{y-2}} < 9$?

   (1) $y < 5$

   (2) $3^y < 27$

(A) Statement (1) ALONE is sufficient, but statement (2) alone is not sufficient.
(B) Statement (2) ALONE is sufficient, but statement (1) alone is not sufficient.
(C) BOTH statements TOGETHER are sufficient, but NEITHER statement ALONE is sufficient.
(D) EACH statement ALONE is sufficient.
(E) Statements (1) and (2) TOGETHER are NOT sufficient to answer the question asked, and additional data are needed.

20. Points A and B lie on a circle with center O in the coordinate plane. Is the area of the circle greater than 25π?

   (1) The distance from A to B is equal to 10.

   (2) $\overline{AB}$ does not go through point O.

(A) Statement (1) ALONE is sufficient, but statement (2) alone is not sufficient.
(B) Statement (2) ALONE is sufficient, but statement (1) alone is not sufficient.
(C) BOTH statements TOGETHER are sufficient, but NEITHER statement ALONE is sufficient.
(D) EACH statement ALONE is sufficient.
(E) Statements (1) and (2) TOGETHER are NOT sufficient to answer the question asked, and additional data are needed.

21. Is m less than n ?

(1) $\dfrac{m}{n} = 3$

(2) $m^2 - n^2 > 0$

(A) Statement (1) ALONE is sufficient, but statement (2) alone is not sufficient.
(B) Statement (2) ALONE is sufficient, but statement (1) alone is not sufficient.
(C) BOTH statements TOGETHER are sufficient, but NEITHER statement ALONE is sufficient.
(D) EACH statement ALONE is sufficient.
(E) Statements (1) and (2) TOGETHER are NOT sufficient to answer the question asked, and additional data are needed.

22. If x and y are even integers, is $\dfrac{x}{y}$ an integer?

(1) $x > y$

(2) y is a prime number

(A) Statement (1) ALONE is sufficient, but statement (2) alone is not sufficient.
(B) Statement (2) ALONE is sufficient, but statement (1) alone is not sufficient.
(C) BOTH statements TOGETHER are sufficient, but NEITHER statement ALONE is sufficient.
(D) EACH statement ALONE is sufficient.
(E) Statements (1) and (2) TOGETHER are NOT sufficient to answer the question asked, and additional data are needed.

23. If x is an integer, is x even?

(1) x is equal to the difference between two consecutive prime numbers

(2) x is greater than 1

(A) Statement (1) ALONE is sufficient, but statement (2) alone is not sufficient.
(B) Statement (2) ALONE is sufficient, but statement (1) alone is not sufficient.
(C) BOTH statements TOGETHER are sufficient, but NEITHER statement ALONE is sufficient.
(D) EACH statement ALONE is sufficient.
(E) Statements (1) and (2) TOGETHER are NOT sufficient to answer the question asked, and additional data are needed.

24. John must select a marble from a bag containing red, green, and blue marbles. If there are 20 marbles or fewer in the bag, is the probability that he will select a red marble greater than $\dfrac{1}{4}$?

(1) There are twice as many blue marbles as there are green marbles

(2) There is a $\dfrac{3}{5}$ probability that the marble chosen will not be blue

(A) Statement (1) ALONE is sufficient, but statement (2) alone is not sufficient.
(B) Statement (2) ALONE is sufficient, but statement (1) alone is not sufficient.
(C) BOTH statements TOGETHER are sufficient, but NEITHER statement ALONE is sufficient.
(D) EACH statement ALONE is sufficient.
(E) Statements (1) and (2) TOGETHER are NOT sufficient to answer the question asked, and additional data are needed.

25. Is $2^{-x} > 0.25$?

   (1) $2^{-(x-2)} < 0.5$

   (2) $\dfrac{2}{3}x > 1$

(A) Statement (1) ALONE is sufficient, but statement (2) alone is not sufficient.
(B) Statement (2) ALONE is sufficient, but statement (1) alone is not sufficient.
(C) BOTH statements TOGETHER are sufficient, but NEITHER statement ALONE is sufficient.
(D) EACH statement ALONE is sufficient.
(E) Statements (1) and (2) TOGETHER are NOT sufficient to answer the question asked, and additional data are needed.

Check your answers on page 281.

For additional practice problems, log on to your online Student Tools to download some Mixed Drills.

FUNCTIONS

You may have a vague memory of functions from high school. You were given an expression like this

$$f(x) = x^2 + 3x + 5$$

and asked to find a specific value for the function $f(2)$, for example. You would then substitute 2 in for x in the original equation in order to find the solution.

$$f(2) = 2^2 + 3(2) + 5 = 15$$

You will see functions on the GMAT, but the test writers often use weird symbols or words to freak you out and make you think it's some weird math you've never learned. There is no weird math you've never learned on the GMAT; so, if you see a weird symbol or word, simply follow the directions.

Example

1. If $x \# y = xy^2$, then what is the value of $3 \# 4$?

The weird symbol, #, means follow the directions. Simply substitute 3 for x and 4 for y to get

$$3 \# 4 = 3(4^2) = 48$$

FUNCTIONS DRILL

1. Scientists studying a new strain of bacteria under lab conditions calculate the growth of the batch using the formula $500 + 2^x$, in which x represents the number of hours that the strain has been under observation. The population is calculated and documented once per hour on the hour over a number of days. Which of the following CANNOT represent a documented bacterial population after a given number of hours?

   (A)   504
   (B)   524
   (C)   628
   (D)   756
   (E)   1,012

2. $b@a = a - b$. What is the value of $x@2$?

   (1) $2@x = 2$

   (2) $y@x = 2@2$

   (A) Statement (1) ALONE is sufficient, but statement (2) ALONE is not sufficient.
   (B) Statement (2) ALONE is sufficient, but statement (1) ALONE is not sufficient.
   (C) BOTH statements TOGETHER are sufficient, but NEITHER statement ALONE is sufficient.
   (D) EACH statement ALONE is sufficient.
   (E) Statements (1) and (2) TOGETHER are NOT sufficient to answer the question asked, and additional data are needed.

3. If the function ♣ is defined as $p \clubsuit q = \dfrac{p + q}{p^2 - q^2}$ for all numbers except $p^2 - q^2 = 0$, and if $h \clubsuit j = 1$, then what is the value of h in terms of j ?

   (A) $-j$

   (B) $\dfrac{1}{j}$

   (C) $j - 1$

   (D) $j + 1$

   (E) j^2

4. $\#m = ((m!)!)$. If m is a positive integer, what is the value of m ?

   (1) $2! = (m - 1)!$

   (2) $\#m$ is six times the value of 5!

   (A) Statement (1) ALONE is sufficient, but statement (2) ALONE is not sufficient.
   (B) Statement (2) ALONE is sufficient, but statement (1) ALONE is not sufficient.
   (C) BOTH statements TOGETHER are sufficient, but NEITHER statement ALONE is sufficient.
   (D) EACH statement ALONE is sufficient.
   (E) Statements (1) and (2) TOGETHER are NOT sufficient to answer the question asked, and additional data are needed.

5. The function ◙ is defined by $a \, ◙ \, b = (\sqrt{a} + \sqrt{b})^2$ for all positive integers a and b. What is the value of $(3 \, ◙ \, 48) \, ◙ \, 3$?

   (A)   51
   (B)   54
   (C)   75
   (D)   93
   (E)   108

6. For all x, $\S x$ is defined as $\S x = x^2 + x$. What is the value of $\S y$?

    (1) $\S y = 3((\S 10) + 30)$

    (2) $\S y = \S(\S(4))$

(A) Statement (1) ALONE is sufficient, but statement (2) ALONE is not sufficient.
(B) Statement (2) ALONE is sufficient, but statement (1) ALONE is not sufficient.
(C) BOTH statements TOGETHER are sufficient, but NEITHER statement ALONE is sufficient.
(D) EACH statement ALONE is sufficient.
(E) Statements (1) and (2) TOGETHER are NOT sufficient to answer the question asked, and additional data are needed.

7. If $p \,\diamond\, r = p\left(\dfrac{p}{2r} - r\right) - \dfrac{24}{pr}$, and both r and $p \neq 0$, what is the value of $(-6) \,\diamond\, 2$?

(A) −23
(B) −19
(C) −12
(D) 19
(E) 23

8. An Elbow Composite is the difference between the product of a number's distinct prime factors and the sum of its distinct prime factors. If p and q are even integers, is the Elbow Composite of p greater than the Elbow Composite of q ?

    (1) $p > q$

    (2) $p = 2q$

(A) Statement (1) ALONE is sufficient, but statement (2) ALONE is not sufficient.
(B) Statement (2) ALONE is sufficient, but statement (1) ALONE is not sufficient.
(C) BOTH statements TOGETHER are sufficient, but NEITHER statement ALONE is sufficient.
(D) EACH statement ALONE is sufficient.
(E) Statements (1) and (2) TOGETHER are NOT sufficient to answer the question asked, and additional data are needed.

9. If $a \,\varphi\, b = -2\left(a^2 b - \dfrac{18}{ab}\right) + 27$, for all integers a and b such that $a \neq 0$ and $b \neq 0$, then what is the value of $(-2 \,\varphi\, 3) \,\varphi\, 2$?

(A) −299
(B) −296
(C) −15
(D) −3
(E) 9

10. The function $w \& v$ is defined as an alpha if the difference between w and v is positive and a beta if the difference between w and v is negative. If w and v are positive integers, is $w \& v$ an alpha?

    (1) $2w + 3v = 19$
         $w - v = 7$

    (2) $w^2 - v^2 = 63$

(A) Statement (1) ALONE is sufficient, but statement (2) ALONE is not sufficient.
(B) Statement (2) ALONE is sufficient, but statement (1) ALONE is not sufficient.
(C) BOTH statements TOGETHER are sufficient, but NEITHER statement ALONE is sufficient.
(D) EACH statement ALONE is sufficient.
(E) Statements (1) and (2) TOGETHER are NOT sufficient to answer the question asked, and additional data are needed.

Check your answers on page 281.

ROOTS

Roots are the flip side of exponents. For example, $\sqrt{9}$ indicates that some number times itself equals nine. Because $3^2 = 9$, $\sqrt{9} = 3$.

A square root is defined as the positive root only. Thus, although $x^2 = 16$ means that $x = \pm 4$, $x = \sqrt{16}$ means that $x = 4$.

Combining Roots

You can **add** and **subtract** roots when the numbers under the radical signs are the same. For example you can do this

$$4\sqrt{3} + 7\sqrt{3} = 11\sqrt{3}$$

but you cannot do this

$$4\sqrt{3} + 5\sqrt{7} = ?$$

To **multiply** and **divide** square roots, simply put everything under the same radical sign.

$$\sqrt{12} \times \sqrt{3} = \sqrt{36} = 6 \qquad \frac{\sqrt{75}}{\sqrt{3}} = \sqrt{\frac{75}{3}} = \sqrt{25} = 5$$

Factoring Square Roots

Because you can combine square roots with multiplication, you can also split them apart by factoring. Look for a perfect square and pull it out from your original number.

$$\sqrt{75} = \sqrt{25 \times 3} = \sqrt{25} \times \sqrt{3} = 5\sqrt{3} \qquad \sqrt{48} = \sqrt{16 \times 3} = \sqrt{16} \times \sqrt{3} = 4\sqrt{3}$$

Rationalizing Square Roots

Sometimes you end up with a fraction that has a radical in the denominator, such as $\dfrac{10}{\sqrt{2}}$. There's nothing wrong with this if you're going to do something with the fraction, for example, multiply it, add to it, or compare it to something else. However, the fraction is not considered fully reduced. In order to reduce it, you need a little trick called rationalizing the denominator.

Rationalize the denominator by multiplying the numerator and denominator by the root. Because you're multiplying the fraction by 1, you won't change the value. Here's an example.

$$\frac{10}{\sqrt{2}} = \frac{10}{\sqrt{2}} \times \frac{\sqrt{2}}{\sqrt{2}} = \frac{10\sqrt{2}}{2} = 5\sqrt{2}$$

Remember, you don't need to rationalize the denominator unless the fraction is your final answer. You will often get rid of the radical in the denominator by completing the calculations necessary to finish the problem.

There's one more thing you should remember about roots. When you take the square root of a number between 0 and 1 it gets **larger**.

$$\sqrt{\frac{1}{4}} = \frac{\sqrt{1}}{\sqrt{4}} = \frac{1}{2}$$

ROOTS DRILL

1. $\sqrt{50 + 25} =$

   (A) 5
   (B) $5\sqrt{2}$
   (C) $5\sqrt{3}$
   (D) $10\sqrt{5}$
   (E) $25\sqrt{2}$

2. What is the value of x ?

   (1) $x^2 = 625$

   (2) $x^{\frac{1}{2}} = 5$

   (A) Statement (1) ALONE is sufficient, but statement (2) alone is not sufficient.
   (B) Statement (2) ALONE is sufficient, but statement (1) alone is not sufficient.
   (C) BOTH statements TOGETHER are sufficient, but NEITHER statement ALONE is sufficient.
   (D) EACH statement ALONE is sufficient.
   (E) Statements (1) and (2) TOGETHER are NOT sufficient to answer the question asked, and additional data are needed.

3. $\sqrt{(25)(22) - (30)(5)} =$

   (A) 4
   (B) $5\sqrt{5}$
   (C) 20
   (D) $25\sqrt{5}$
   (E) 400

4. Which of the following is closest in value to

   $\sqrt{\dfrac{23.09 - 5.13}{0.96 + 1.21}}$?

   (A) 2
   (B) 3
   (C) 7
   (D) 9
   (E) 18

5. Is a greater than 1 ?

   (1) $a^2 > a^3$

   (2) $a^{\frac{1}{3}} > a$

   (A) Statement (1) ALONE is sufficient, but statement (2) alone is not sufficient.
   (B) Statement (2) ALONE is sufficient, but statement (1) alone is not sufficient.
   (C) BOTH statements TOGETHER are sufficient, but NEITHER statement ALONE is sufficient.
   (D) EACH statement ALONE is sufficient.
   (E) Statements (1) and (2) TOGETHER are NOT sufficient to answer the question asked, and additional data are needed.

6. If $\sqrt{\dfrac{p + q}{2}} = p$, what is q in terms of p ?

   (A) $p\sqrt{2}$
   (B) $p\sqrt{p}$
   (C) $p^2 - 2$
   (D) $2p^2$
   (E) $2p^2 - p$

7. If b and c are positive numbers, does $\sqrt{b} \times \sqrt{c} = b$?

    (1) $b = c$

    (2) $5b + 2c = 7$
       $91 - 65b = 26c$

    (A) Statement (1) ALONE is sufficient, but statement (2) alone is not sufficient.
    (B) Statement (2) ALONE is sufficient, but statement (1) alone is not sufficient.
    (C) BOTH statements TOGETHER are sufficient, but NEITHER statement ALONE is sufficient.
    (D) EACH statement ALONE is sufficient.
    (E) Statements (1) and (2) TOGETHER are NOT sufficient to answer the question asked, and additional data are needed.

8. If $\sqrt{3x} - 2 = \sqrt{4x + 3}$, what is the value of $x^2 - 50x$?

    (A) −1
    (B) 0
    (C) 5
    (D) 16
    (E) 48

9. Does the product of k and l equal 1 ?

    (1) $k^{\frac{1}{2}} = l^{\left(-\frac{1}{2}\right)}$

    (2) k divided by l is an integer.

    (A) Statement (1) ALONE is sufficient, but statement (2) alone is not sufficient.
    (B) Statement (2) ALONE is sufficient, but statement (1) alone is not sufficient.
    (C) BOTH statements TOGETHER are sufficient, but NEITHER statement ALONE is sufficient.
    (D) EACH statement ALONE is sufficient.
    (E) Statements (1) and (2) TOGETHER are NOT sufficient to answer the question asked, and additional data are needed.

10. If $p = \sqrt{\left(\dfrac{16}{25}\right)}$, what is the value of $5\sqrt{p}$?

    (A) $\dfrac{2}{3}$

    (B) $\dfrac{4}{5}$

    (C) 2

    (D) $\sqrt{5}$

    (E) $2\sqrt{5}$

11. What is $\sqrt[3]{m} \sqrt{} \sqrt[3]{n}$?

    (1) n is equal to 50% of m.

    (2) the square of n is equal to twice m.

(A) Statement (1) ALONE is sufficient, but statement (2) alone is not sufficient.
(B) Statement (2) ALONE is sufficient, but statement (1) alone is not sufficient.
(C) BOTH statements TOGETHER are sufficient, but NEITHER statement ALONE is sufficient.
(D) EACH statement ALONE is sufficient.
(E) Statements (1) and (2) TOGETHER are NOT sufficient to answer the question asked, and additional data are needed.

12. $\left(\sqrt{2}\right)\left(\sqrt[3]{4}\right)\left(\sqrt{8}\right) =$

(A) $2^{\frac{1}{2}}$

(B) $2^{\frac{5}{2}}$

(C) $2^{\frac{8}{3}}$

(D) 2^4

(E) 2^5

13. Is the product of p and q a non-positive number?

    (1) $p = q^2$

    (2) $\sqrt[3]{pq}$ does not equal 0

(A) Statement (1) ALONE is sufficient, but statement (2) alone is not sufficient.
(B) Statement (2) ALONE is sufficient, but statement (1) alone is not sufficient.
(C) BOTH statements TOGETHER are sufficient, but NEITHER statement ALONE is sufficient.
(D) EACH statement ALONE is sufficient.
(E) Statements (1) and (2) TOGETHER are NOT sufficient to answer the question asked, and additional data are needed.

14. $\dfrac{\left(\sqrt{7}\right)\left(\sqrt{5}\right)\left(\sqrt{2}\right)}{\sqrt[3]{70}}$

(A) $\dfrac{1}{70}$

(B) $70^{-\frac{1}{2}}$

(C) $70^{\frac{1}{6}}$

(D) $70^{\frac{1}{3}}$

(E) 70

15. Is z a non-negative number ?

    (1) $y^2 = x$
        $4x = yz$
        $z = 4y$

    (2) $\sqrt{x} = y$

(A) Statement (1) ALONE is sufficient, but statement (2) alone is not sufficient.
(B) Statement (2) ALONE is sufficient, but statement (1) alone is not sufficient.
(C) BOTH statements TOGETHER are sufficient, but NEITHER statement ALONE is sufficient.
(D) EACH statement ALONE is sufficient.
(E) Statements (1) and (2) TOGETHER are NOT sufficient to answer the question asked, and additional data are needed.

Check your answers on page 281.

EXPONENTS

Exponents are shorthand notation for repeated multiplication. Instead of writing $3 \times 3 \times 3 \times 3$, write 3^4.

There are three basic rules to remember about exponents.

1. When **multiplying** terms with the same base, **add** the exponents:

    $$x^4 \cdot x^3 = x^7 \qquad 6^3 \cdot 6^2 = 6^5$$

2. When **dividing** terms with the same base, **subtract** the exponents.

    $$\frac{x^8}{x^5} = x^3 \qquad \frac{\left(\sqrt{3}\right)^7}{\left(\sqrt{3}\right)^3} = \left(\sqrt{3}\right)^4 = 9$$

3. When raising a power to another **power,** **multiply** the exponents.

    $$(x^3)^2 = x^6 \qquad (6^4)^3 = 6^{12}$$

Together, these rules give you the acronym **MADSPM.** What happens if you forget one of the rules? **When in doubt, expand it out.** For example, $(x^3)^2$ can be rewritten as

$$(x \cdot x \cdot x) \cdot (x \cdot x \cdot x) = x^6$$

Special Exponent Rules

There are some special rules for exponents that you need to be familiar with.

*   Any number raised to the first power is itself. ($5^1 = 5$)
*   1 raised to any power is 1. ($1^{37} = 1$)
*   0 raised to any power is 0. ($0^{23} = 0$)*
*   Any number raised to the 0 power is 1. ($15^0 = 1$)*
*   Any negative number raised to an **even** power is **positive.**
*   Any negative number raised to an **odd** power is **negative.**

*0^0 is undefined, but that fact is not tested on the GMAT.

Negative Exponents

A negative sign in an exponent means reciprocal. If you need to work with a negative exponent, put the whole expression under 1 and change the negative exponent to a positive one.

Example

$$\frac{x^6}{x^8} = x^{6-8} = x^{-2} = \frac{1}{x^2}$$

Fractional Exponents

If you see a fractional exponent, remember that the bottom of the fraction is the root, and the top is the exponent.

Example

$$x^{\frac{1}{2}} = \sqrt[2]{x^1} = \sqrt{x} \qquad 8^{\frac{2}{3}} = \sqrt[3]{8^2} = \sqrt[3]{64} = 4$$

Factoring and Canceling Exponents

Because exponents are all about multiplication, you can break an exponent problem into factors that are equivalent to your original number. This is helpful when simplifying expressions that involve exponents.

Example

$$\frac{12^9}{3^6} = \frac{(4 \times 3)^9}{3^6} = \frac{4^9 \times 3^9}{3^6} = 4^9 \times 3^{9-6} = 4^9 \times 3^3 = 27 \times 4^9$$

There is one more rule to remember about exponents. When you raise a fraction between 0 and 1 to a positive power, it gets **smaller**.

Example

$$\left(\frac{1}{2}\right)^2 = \frac{1^2}{2^2} = \frac{1}{4}$$

EXPONENTS DRILL

1. $\dfrac{37^2 - 2(37)}{37} =$

   (A) −1
   (B) 2
   (C) 1
   (D) 35
   (E) 37

2. What is the value of $\dfrac{2a^2}{-4}$ if $a = -2$?

   (A) −2
   (B) −1
   (C) 1
   (D) 2
   (E) 4

3. If n is a positive integer, is $4^n < 1{,}500$?

   (1) $4^{n-1} < 1{,}000$

   (2) $4^{n+2} = 4^n + 240$

   (A) Statement (1) ALONE is sufficient, but
   statement (2) ALONE is not sufficient.
   (B) Statement (2) ALONE is sufficient, but
   statement (1) ALONE is not sufficient.
   (C) BOTH statements TOGETHER are sufficient,
   but NEITHER statement ALONE is sufficient.
   (D) EACH statement ALONE is sufficient.
   (E) Statements (1) and (2) TOGETHER are NOT
   sufficient to answer the question asked, and
   additional data are needed.

4. If x is a positive integer, and $3^x < 81^5$, what is the
   largest possible value of x ?

   (A) 3
   (B) 4
   (C) 19
   (D) 20
   (E) 27

5. If $x \neq 0$, is $x^3 < x$?

   (1) $x < 1$

   (2) $x < -1$

   (A) Statement (1) ALONE is sufficient, but
   statement (2) ALONE is not sufficient.
   (B) Statement (2) ALONE is sufficient, but
   statement (1) ALONE is not sufficient.
   (C) BOTH statements TOGETHER are sufficient,
   but NEITHER statement ALONE is sufficient.
   (D) EACH statement ALONE is sufficient.
   (E) Statements (1) and (2) TOGETHER are NOT
   sufficient to answer the question asked, and
   additional data are needed.

6. Last year, a certain pharmaceutical company
   allocated $\$4.8 \times 10^7$ for research and development.
   This year, the company allocated $72,000,000 for
   research and development. If each year the funds
   are evenly divided among 1.2×10^2 departments,
   how much more will each department receive this
   year than it did last year?

   (A) $\$2.0 \times 10^5$
   (B) $\$2.4 \times 10^5$
   (C) $\$4.0 \times 10^5$
   (D) $\$6.0 \times 10^5$
   (E) $\$2.4 \times 10^7$

7. If $27^{4a-10} \times 3^{4a+2} = 81$, what is the value of a ?

   (A) 1
   (B) 2
   (C) 3
   (D) 4
   (E) 5

8. If $x^k = 1$, what is the value of k ?

   (1) x is negative

   (2) $x > -1$

   (A) Statement (1) ALONE is sufficient, but statement (2) ALONE is not sufficient.
   (B) Statement (2) ALONE is sufficient, but statement (1) ALONE is not sufficient.
   (C) BOTH statements TOGETHER are sufficient, but NEITHER statement ALONE is sufficient.
   (D) EACH statement ALONE is sufficient.
   (E) Statements (1) and (2) TOGETHER are NOT sufficient to answer the question asked, and additional data are needed.

9. Each of the following is equal to x^{12} EXCEPT

   (A) $x^4 \times x^8$

   (B) $\dfrac{x^{16}}{x^4}$

   (C) $(x^3)^4$

   (D) $\dfrac{1}{x^{-12}}$

   (E) $x^6 + x^6$

10. What is the value of w ?

    (1) $w^2 = 18$

    (2) $\dfrac{w^3}{\sqrt{18}}$ is an integer.

    (A) Statement (1) ALONE is sufficient, but statement (2) ALONE is not sufficient.
    (B) Statement (2) ALONE is sufficient, but statement (1) ALONE is not sufficient.
    (C) BOTH statements TOGETHER are sufficient, but NEITHER statement ALONE is sufficient.
    (D) EACH statement ALONE is sufficient.
    (E) Statements (1) and (2) TOGETHER are NOT sufficient to answer the question asked, and additional data are needed.

11. What is the value of $3^y \times 3^{yz}$?

    (1) $yz = 6$

    (2) $y(1 + z) = 8$

    (A) Statement (1) ALONE is sufficient, but statement (2) ALONE is not sufficient.
    (B) Statement (2) ALONE is sufficient, but statement (1) ALONE is not sufficient.
    (C) BOTH statements TOGETHER are sufficient, but NEITHER statement ALONE is sufficient.
    (D) EACH statement ALONE is sufficient.
    (E) Statements (1) and (2) TOGETHER are NOT sufficient to answer the question asked, and additional data are needed.

12. If $\left(5^r\right)^{\frac{1}{8}} = 25$, what is the value of $\sqrt{r}$?

    (A) 2
    (B) 4
    (C) 5
    (D) 8
    (E) 16

13. Is z between -1 and 0 ?

    (1) $z^5 < z$

    (2) z^4 is positive.

(A) Statement (1) ALONE is sufficient, but statement (2) ALONE is not sufficient.
(B) Statement (2) ALONE is sufficient, but statement (1) ALONE is not sufficient.
(C) BOTH statements TOGETHER are sufficient, but NEITHER statement ALONE is sufficient.
(D) EACH statement ALONE is sufficient.
(E) Statements (1) and (2) TOGETHER are NOT sufficient to answer the question asked, and additional data are needed.

14. $(3)^{-4}(27)^{-3}(81)^{-2} =$

(A) $\left(\dfrac{1}{3}\right)^{288}$

(B) $\left(\dfrac{1}{9}\right)^{-21}$

(C) $\left(\dfrac{1}{3}\right)^{21}$

(D) $\left(\dfrac{1}{9}\right)^{9}$

(E) $\left(\dfrac{1}{3}\right)^{9}$

15. What is the value of y^x ?

    (1) $y^{-x} = 4$

    (2) $y = \dfrac{1}{2}$ and $x = \dfrac{1}{y}$

(A) Statement (1) ALONE is sufficient, but statement (2) ALONE is not sufficient.
(B) Statement (2) ALONE is sufficient, but statement (1) ALONE is not sufficient.
(C) BOTH statements TOGETHER are sufficient, but NEITHER statement ALONE is sufficient.
(D) EACH statement ALONE is sufficient.
(E) Statements (1) and (2) TOGETHER are NOT sufficient to answer the question asked, and additional data are needed.

Check your answers on page 281.

INTEREST

GMAT problems may ask you to calculate simple or compound interest. To find **simple interest** simply take a percentage of the principal amount.

Example

1. If Molly puts $500 in a savings account that pays 4 percent simple annual interest, how much money will be in the account after one year?

    (A) $20
    (B) $500
    (C) $504
    (D) $520
    (E) $540

4% of $500 = $20. Add the interest to principal and you have $520 in the account at the end of the year. The correct answer is (D).

Compound interest is slightly more complicated, because you earn interest on your interest. However, you really only end up earning slightly more than you would have earned from simple interest. Compound interest problems are fairly rare on the GMAT, but when they do show up, you can usually calculate the simple interest and pick the answer that is slightly more than that.

Example

2. If Molly puts $500 in a savings account that pays 4 percent annual interest compounded semiannually, how much money will be in the account after one year?

    (A) $5.20
    (B) $504.00
    (C) $520.00
    (D) $520.20
    (E) $540.00

You previously determined that with simple interest there would be $520 in the account at the end of the year. With compound interest there would be slightly more, so the correct answer is (D).

Occasionally you might see a problem that requires you to recognize the correct use of the compound interest formula; however, you will probably never need to use the formula to actually calculate compound interest.

Principal + interest = principal $\times (1+r)^t$

r = interest rate for the compounding period expressed as a decimal

t = number of compounding periods

So, for Molly use $r = 0.02$ because she earns 2 percent per half year. Use $t = 2$ because one year contains two compounding periods. Thus, principal + interest = $500 \times (1 + 0.02)^2 = 520.20$.

For more about algebra problems see *Cracking the GMAT* 2016 Edition.

INTEREST DRILL

1. A certain bank is offering a special promotion for new customers in the month of November. For every dollar in excess of $100 in a customer's savings account, the bank will pay 6 percent interest. If Rebekah has $178.61 in her savings account after the interest is paid, how much did she have in the account before the interest was paid?

   (A) $155.50
   (B) $167.89
   (C) $168.00
   (D) $168.50
   (E) $189.33

2. If one of Jean's credit cards charges more than 2 percent interest each month on any balance, and this month Jean paid more than $17.85 in interest, which of the following could be Jean's balance for this month?

   (A) $357.00
   (B) $357.50
   (C) $892.00
   (D) $892.50
   (E) $893.00

3. A basic savings account pays interest once per year on December 31. If Alan deposits $300 into the account on January 1, 2004, and does not deposit or withdraw any money in the meantime, then to the nearest cent, how much was in the account when he withdrew the money on January 1, 2009?

   (1) The savings account interest rate is 2% per year.

   (2) If Alan had left the money in the account for 2 more years, he would have had, to the nearest cent, $13.12 more.

   (A) Statement (1) ALONE is sufficient, but statement (2) ALONE is not sufficient.
   (B) Statement (2) ALONE is sufficient, but statement (1) ALONE is not sufficient.
   (C) BOTH statements TOGETHER are sufficient, but NEITHER statement ALONE is sufficient.
   (D) EACH statement ALONE is sufficient.
   (E) Statements (1) and (2) TOGETHER are NOT sufficient to answer the question asked, and additional data are needed.

4. Pam is buying a car that costs $12,500. The value of her trade-in vehicle covers 30 percent of the cost of the new car, and her down payment covers 60 percent of the remaining cost. She then takes out a loan to finance the amount not covered by the trade-in and the down payment. If the interest rate on the loan is 6 percent compounded annually, and the loan term is 1 year, how much will Pam pay in interest?

(A) $180
(B) $210
(C) $345
(D) $525
(E) $570

5. A certain bank offers two different savings accounts: MegaSaver and InvestPro. Does MegaSaver offer a greater return over a 5-year period than InvestPro?

(1) MegaSaver has an interest rate of 3% paid quarterly. InvestPro has an interest rate of 4% paid semi-annually.

(2) The MegaSaver account will first pay a return at least 100% greater than the InvestPro account after 17.5 years.

(A) Statement (1) ALONE is sufficient, but statement (2) ALONE is not sufficient.
(B) Statement (2) ALONE is sufficient, but statement (1) ALONE is not sufficient.
(C) BOTH statements TOGETHER are sufficient, but NEITHER statement ALONE is sufficient.
(D) EACH statement ALONE is sufficient.
(E) Statements (1) and (2) TOGETHER are NOT sufficient to answer the question asked, and additional data are needed.

Check your answers on page 281.

Algebra Answers
and Explanations

ANSWER KEY

Equations and Inequalities
1. C
2. A
3. B
4. A
5. B
6. E
7. D
8. B
9. C
10. C
11. B
12. D
13. D
14. B
15. E

Quadratics
1. C
2. D
3. B
4. C
5. E
6. C
7. A
8. A
9. D
10. B
11. C
12. C
13. C
14. E
15. A

Plugging In
1. D
2. E
3. C
4. A
5. A
6. D
7. A
8. E
9. B
10. A
11. A
12. B
13. C
14. C
15. C
16. E
17. E
18. B
19. E
20. B
21. B
22. D
23. B
24. A

PITA
1. D
2. C
3. E
4. A
5. D
6. D
7. B
8. A
9. B
10. C
11. D
12. C

13. B
14. C
15. B
16. E
17. C
18. D
19. D
20. D
21. B
22. B
23. E
24. C

Must Be True
1. B
2. D
3. B
4. A
5. D
6. E
7. A
8. B
9. A
10. A
11. C
12. D
13. C
14. C
15. D
16. B
17. C
18. A
19. C
20. B
21. C
22. A
23. D
24. B

Yes/No Data Sufficiency

1. B
2. A
3. C
4. C
5. E
6. E
7. A
8. B
9. C
10. D
11. C
12. C
13. E
14. D
15. D
16. D
17. B
18. C
19. B
20. C
21. E
22. B
23. C
24. C
25. A

Functions

1. B
2. A
3. D
4. D
5. E
6. D
7. E
8. B
9. C
10. D

Roots

1. C
2. B
3. C
4. B
5. D
6. E
7. A
8. A
9. A
10. E
11. A
12. C
13. E
14. C
15. C

Exponents

1. D
2. A
3. D
4. C
5. B
6. A
7. B
8. C
9. E
10. E
11. B
12. B
13. A
14. C
15. D

Interest

1. E
2. E
3. D
4. B
5. A

EXPLANATIONS

Equations and Inequalities

1. **C** Use the answer choices to find a value that works, starting with (C). Can $\frac{x}{y} = 1$? Yes. Using $x = 2$ and $y = 2$, for instance, gives $\frac{x}{y} = 1$. When you Plug In the answers, you can stop as soon as you find one that works. None of the other answer choices will work. Choice (A) does not work because x cannot equal 1, but rather it must be greater than one. Choice (B) is incorrect because while x can equal 2, y cannot equal –5. Choice (D) does not work because x must be less than 7, not equal to it, and y cannot be equal to 4, but rather must be less than 4. Choice (E) does not work either, because x must be less than 7. Also, in each of the answers, there is no fraction that might reduce to any of these answer choices. For instance, not only is $-\frac{2}{5}$ an impossible result, but $-\frac{4}{10}$ also does not work for the ranges given for x and y.

2. **A** Let x be the number of \$3 bars sold and y be the number of \$7 bars sold. Then $x + y = 30$, the value of the \$3 bars sold is $3x$, and the value of the \$7 bars sold is $7y$. Statement (1) means that $3x = 7y$. Combine this with $x + y = 30$. Solve the first equation for x to get $x = \frac{7y}{3}$. Substitute this into the second equation to get $\frac{7y}{3} + y = 30$, or $\frac{10y}{3} = 30$. Solve for y to get $y = 9$. Therefore, 9 of the \$7 bars were sold yesterday, so this is sufficient. Eliminate (B), (C), and (E). Statement (2) means that $3x + 7y > 100$. Combine this with $x + y = 30$. Since one of these is an inequality, it will not give you a value for y, only a value that is less than y. Since statement (2) is not sufficient, the answer is (A).

3. **B** Statement (1) doesn't give enough information about b to find b. Eliminate (A) and (D). Statement (2) is sufficient because, with manipulation, it allows you to put in $\frac{5}{3}b$ for a and then solve for b.

4. **A** Statement (1) states that $6x$ is greater than 1, so x must be positive. Note that $x^{-y} = \frac{1}{x^y}$, so if x were negative, $6x$ would be a fraction between 0 and 1. This is sufficient. Eliminate (B), (C), and (E). Statement (2) states that $5x^2 - 45 = 0$. Add 45 to both sides of the equation to get $5x^2 = 45$, so $x^2 = 9$ and $x = 3$ or $x = -3$, and this is not sufficient. Thus, because only statement (1) is sufficient alone, the answer is (A).

5. **B** Statement (1) lets you know that either $(x - 1)$ equals 0, or $(x + 3) = 0$. In order to find the value of the expression you need a value for x. This information alone is insufficient, because it gives you 2 different values for x. Eliminate (A) and (D). Statement (2) tells you that $x = 1$, which is sufficient.

6. **E** Plug In the Answers, starting with (C), to find the value that makes the equation true. Choice (C) gives $\frac{2}{5} + \frac{24}{5} = 2 + \frac{8}{5}$, or $\frac{26}{5} = \frac{18}{5}$, which is incorrect. Choice (D) gives $\frac{2}{5} + \frac{24}{8} = 2 + \frac{8}{8}$, or $\frac{136}{40} = 3$, which is also untrue. Plugging In (E), the equation becomes $\frac{2}{5} + \frac{24}{10} = 2 + \frac{8}{10}$, or $\frac{28}{10} = \frac{28}{10}$, so (E) is correct. Neither (A) nor (B) results in a correct equation. An alternative approach is to solve the problem algebraically. First, multiply both sides of the equation by $5n$ to get rid of the fractions. The result is $2n + 120 = 10n + 40$. Solve for n by isolating the variable, so that the equation becomes $8n = 80$, or $n = 10$.

7. **D** Statement (1) states that $4x + 4y = 32$. Divide this equation by 2 to get $2x + 2y = 16$, so this is sufficient. Eliminate (B), (C), and (E). Statement (2) states that $x = 8 - y$. Add y to both sides of this equation to get $x + y = 8$. Multiply by 2 to get $2x + 2y = 16$, so this is also sufficient.

8. **B** To solve for p, first Plug In the value given for c, so that you have $\frac{4}{3}(p + 68) = 356$. Now multiply both sides by 3, so that the equation becomes $4(p + 68) = 1068$. Now divide both sides by 4, so that you now have $(p + 68) = 267$. Subtract 68 from both sides, and the result is $p = 199$. Alternatively, you could solve this problem by Plugging In the answers. Start with (C). The answer should give you an equation that equals 356. Does $\frac{4}{3}(267 + 68) = 356$? No. The result is too large, so try (B) to get a smaller number. Does $\frac{4}{3}(199 + 68) = 356$? Yes.

9. **C** Statement (1) means that $a = 0$. There is no information concerning the value of b, so it cannot be determined if $a > b$, and this is not sufficient. Eliminate (A) and (D). Statement (2) states that $b + 2 < -5$. Subtract 2 from both sides of the equation to get $b < -7$. There is no information concerning the value of a, so it cannot be determined if $a > b$, and this is not sufficient. Eliminate (B). Taking (1) and (2) together, it is known that $a = 0$ and $b < -7$. Therefore, it must be true that $a > b$. Thus, since both statements together are sufficient, the answer is (C).

10. **C** Plug In the Answers, starting with (C), to find the value of x that makes both equations true. If x equals $\frac{1}{3}$, then the first equation can be written as $2\left(\frac{1}{3}\right)\left(3\left(\frac{1}{3}\right)-1\right)=0$, or $\left(\frac{2}{3}\right)(1-1)=0$. This expression is true, so $\frac{1}{3}$ works for the first equation. If you plug $\frac{1}{3}$ into the second equation you have $\left(\frac{1}{3}-\frac{1}{3}\right)(5x-6)=0$, or $(0)(5x-6)$. This is also true, so (C) is the answer. Alternatively, you could solve this question algebraically. In order for $2x(3x-1)$ to equal 0, it must be true that either the part of the equation outside the parentheses equals 0, so $2x$ equals 0, and $x=0$, or it must be true that the part of the equation inside the parentheses equals 0, that is, that $3x-1=0$, and $x=\frac{1}{3}$. Thus the first equation yields two possible values of x, 0 and $\frac{1}{3}$. Solve for x in the second equation to see which value of x works for both equations. If $(x-\frac{1}{3})(5x-6)=0$, then either $x-\frac{1}{3}=0$, so $x=\frac{1}{3}$, or $5x-6=0$, so $x=\frac{6}{5}$. Only $x=\frac{1}{3}$ makes both equations true. Note that $\frac{6}{5}$ and 0 are also answer choices, so (B) and (D) are traps.

11. **B** Statement (1) gives no information about the values of s and t, and therefore gives no information about r, so it is not sufficient. Eliminate (A) and (D). Statement (2) states that $\frac{r}{s+t}>1$, so $s+t$ must be positive. If $r>s+t$ and $s+t<0$, then $\frac{r}{s+t}$ would be less than 1, because the direction of the inequality sign switches when dividing or multiplying by a negative number. Because $r>s+t$, r must also be positive; so this is sufficient. Thus, since only statement (2) is sufficient alone, the answer is (B).

12. **D** Take this question in bite-sized pieces. The first part of the problem tells you that each member of division A made $\frac{2}{3}$ as many phone calls as each member of division B. Plug In for the number of phone calls made by each person in division B. If each member in B made 15 phone calls, then each member in A made 10 phone calls. The next sentence tells you that division B has $\frac{1}{4}$ as many members as division A. Plug In for the number of members in division A. If there are 20 people in division A, then there are 5 members in division B. If each of the 5 members in division B makes 15 phone calls, then a total of 75 phone calls were placed by division B. If there are 20 people in division A, and each of them made 10 phone calls, then the total number of phone calls placed by

division A is 200. 200 + 75 = 275, so the total number of calls placed is 275. The fraction of calls placed by division B can now be expressed as $\dfrac{75}{275}$, which simplifies to $\dfrac{3}{11}$, so the answer is (D).

13. **D** Plug In a value for n. If $n = 30$, then 10 of the employees drink decaf, so the remaining 20 drink regular. Of the employees who drink regular coffee, $\dfrac{2}{5}$ use cream, so 8 people put cream in their coffee. The question asks for the number of employees who do not put cream in their coffee. $30 - 8 = 22$, so 22 people do not put cream in their coffee. When you Plug In 30 for n in the answer choices, one of them should give you the target answer of 22. Choice (A) becomes $\dfrac{2(30)}{3}$, which does not equal 22. Note that $\dfrac{2}{3}$ is also the fraction of employees who drink regular coffee, so (A) is a trap answer. Choice (B) is $\dfrac{30}{8}$, which does not equal 22. Choice (C) is $\dfrac{4(30)}{15}$, which does not equal 22. $\dfrac{4}{15}$ also represents the fraction of employees who do put cream in their coffee, so (C) is a trap answer. Choice (D) is $\dfrac{11(30)}{15}$, which simplifies to 22. Choice (E) is $\dfrac{13(30)}{15}$. This does not equal 22.

14. **B** Plug In the Answers, starting with (C). If the company has 150 employees, then $\dfrac{1}{10}$, or 15 of them, work in accounting, $\dfrac{2}{5}$, or 60 of them, work in sales, and $\dfrac{1}{3}$, or 50 of them, work in production. $15 + 60 + 50 = 125$, which leaves 25 employees for the shipping department, so (C) is too big. Try (B) next. If the company has 120 employees, then 12 of them work in accounting, 48 work in sales, and 40 work in production. $12 + 48 + 40 = 100$, which leaves 20 employees for the shipping department.

15. **E** Statement (1) is not sufficient. The quotient of two positive numbers is positive; given this statement, b could be positive. However, if b is negative, $\dfrac{a}{b}$ will be negative and can still satisfy this statement. Eliminate (A) and (D). Statement (2) is not sufficient. Given this information, b could be a negative number such that the sum of a and b is greater than -2. However, b could also be a positive number, and the sum of a and b will still be greater than -2. Eliminate (B). When statements (1) and (2) are taken together, there is still not enough information to determine whether b is negative. Either scenario, $b < 0$ or $b > 0$, can satisfy both statements. Thus, since both statements together are still not sufficient, the answer is (E).

Quadratics

1. **C** Remember that $\left(\dfrac{1}{\sqrt{11}} + \dfrac{1}{\sqrt{11}}\right)^2$ is equivalent to $\left(\dfrac{1}{\sqrt{11}} + \dfrac{1}{\sqrt{11}}\right)\left(\dfrac{1}{\sqrt{11}} + \dfrac{1}{\sqrt{11}}\right)$. Use FOIL to multiply out the equation. The first two terms give $\left(\dfrac{1}{\sqrt{11}}\right)\left(\dfrac{1}{\sqrt{11}}\right)$, or $\dfrac{1}{11}$. Multiplying the outer terms also results in $\left(\dfrac{1}{\sqrt{11}}\right)\left(\dfrac{1}{\sqrt{11}}\right)$, or $\dfrac{1}{11}$. Multiplying the inner terms results in $\left(\dfrac{1}{\sqrt{11}}\right)\left(\dfrac{1}{\sqrt{11}}\right)$, or $\dfrac{1}{11}$, and finally multiplying out the last terms results again in $\left(\dfrac{1}{\sqrt{11}}\right)\left(\dfrac{1}{\sqrt{11}}\right)$, or $\dfrac{1}{11}$. Add up all the results, and you have $\dfrac{1}{11} + \dfrac{1}{11} + \dfrac{1}{11} + \dfrac{1}{11} = \dfrac{4}{11}$.

2. **D** Statement (1) is sufficient. If $x^2 + bx + 26 = 8$, then $x^2 + bx + 18 = 0$. When you factor the equation, it will take the form $(x\ )(x\ ) = 0$. The two numbers in the parentheses must multiply to 18 and add to b. Fact 1 tells you that $(x + 9)$ is one of the factors, so the other factor must be $(x + 2)$ because $2 \times 9 = 18$. The value of b would then be 11. Eliminate (B), (C), and (E). Statement (2) is also sufficient. Roots of quadratic equations have the opposite sign of the numbers in the parentheses when you factor the equation. Thus if -2 is a root of the equation $x^2 + bx + 18 = 0$, then $(x + 2)$ must be one of the factors. From here you can find the other factor $(x + 9)$ as you did above. Alternatively, since the root is just another name for the solution of a quadratic equation, you could take -2, plug it into the equation for x, and solve for b.

3. **B** First, simplify $\sqrt{48}$ by writing it instead as $\sqrt{4 \times 12}$. Now you can take out the 4 from the root, so that the expression is now $2\sqrt{12}$. You could simplify this further, but now you have the same base under both roots, so that the full equation is $\left(2\sqrt{12} - \sqrt{12}\right)^2$. It is now possible to subtract, so that the equation becomes $\left(\sqrt{12}\right)^2$, which is simply 12.

4. **C** Statement (1) is insufficient. If $c = 12$ that allows you to write $x^2 - 12x + 20 = 0$. Factoring gives you $(x - 2)(x - 10) = 0$. Thus $x = 2$ or $x = 10$. Since there are two possible values for x, you can't answer the question. Eliminate (A) and (D). Statement (2) is insufficient. Knowing that x is prime does not help. There are an infinite number of prime numbers. Eliminate (B). Statements (1) and (2) together are sufficient. Based on statement (1) you know that $x = 2$ or $x = 10$. Statement (2) says that x is prime, which means that the only number that satisfies both facts is 2.

5. **E** Factor the first equation, so that you have $(x - 4)(x + 7)$. That means that x must equal either 4 or -7. Now plug $x = 4$ into the second equation, so that you have $\dfrac{2(4) - 1}{4^2}$. Simplify the equation and the result is $\dfrac{7}{16}$, (E). If you plugged -7 into the equation, you would have $-\dfrac{15}{49}$, which is not an option. Note that (D) is positive $\dfrac{15}{49}$, and is a trap answer.

6. **C** Statement (1) is insufficient. $(x - y)^2 = 4$ can be expanded to $x^2 - 2xy + y^2 = 4$. This, however, is insufficient to find $x^2 + y^2$ since you can't evaluate the middle term $-2xy$. Eliminate (A) and (D). Statement (2) is insufficient. The value of xy by itself cannot give you the value of $x^2 + y^2$. Eliminate (B). Statements (1) and (2) together are sufficient. From statement (1) you know that $x^2 - 2xy + y^2 = 4$. Statement (2) tells you that $xy = 15$. Substituting that into the middle term gives you $x^2 - 30 + y^2 = 4$. Adding 30 to both sides gives you $x^2 + y^2 = 34$.

7. **A** First, solve for c by Plugging In 5 for x in the equation. This gives you $25 + 20 - c = 30$, so c must equal 15. Now you can rewrite the equation as $x^2 + 4x - 15 = 30$. Now Plug In your answer choices, starting with (C) to see which choice makes this equation true. $16 + 16 - 15$ does not equal 30, so (C) is incorrect. Choice (D) gives $81 + 36 - 15$, which still does not equal 30. Because (D) yielded such a big number, try a negative number to get the equation closer to equaling 30. Choice (A) correctly gives $81 - 36 - 15 = 30$. Because this is a Plugging In the Answers question, stop when you find a number that works. An alternative approach to this problem would be to solve for c as above, and then simplify the equation $x^2 + 4x - 15 = 30$ by subtracting 30 from both sides, so that the equation becomes $x^2 + 4x - 45 = 0$. Now factor the equation so that you have $(x - 5)(x + 9)$. Thus the roots of the equation must be 5 and -9. Note that (D) is a trap answer: 9 is the result if you forget that the root is negative.

8. **A** Statement (1) is sufficient. The equation $(a^2 - b^2) = 30$ can be factored into $(a + b)(a - b) = 30$. Fact 1 tells you that $(a + b) = 10$. Thus $(a - b) = 3$. With these two equations (simultaneous equations) you can solve for a and thus a^2. Eliminate (B), (C), and (E). Statement (2) is insufficient. If $\sqrt{a}$ is not an integer, then a is not a perfect square. However, this doesn't allow you to find the value of a or a^2.

9. **D** Factor each of the equations in the answer choices. The answer, when factored, should have positive 3 as one of the roots, and a negative even number as the second root. Choice (A), when factored, becomes $(x - 3)(x - 5)$. The second root is positive 5, so (A) is incorrect. Choice (B), when factored, becomes $(x - 3)(x - 6)$. The second root is positive 6, so (B) is incorrect. Note that (B) is also a trap answer: if you forget that $(x - 6)$ means that $x = 6$, (B) might appear to be a plausible answer. When you factor (C), you have $(x - 5)(x + 2)$. This is incorrect because neither of the roots is a 3. When you factor (D), you have $(x - 3)(x + 4)$, so one of the roots is positive 3, and the other root is negative 4. Choice (D) is the answer. Factoring (E) gives $(x + 3)(x - 6)$, so the roots are negative 3 and positive 6. In this case, both roots have the wrong sign.

10. **B** Statement (1) is insufficient. Subtracting 3 from both sides of the equation gives $x^2 + 4x - 21 = 0$. Factoring that equation produces $(x + 7)(x - 3) = 0$. The roots of that equation are -7 and 3. While x *could* equal 3, you don't know it for certain. Eliminate (A) and (D). Statement (2) is sufficient. $x^2 - 6x + 9 = 0$ will factor into $(x - 3)(x - 3) = 0$. The only value for x that satisfies that equation is $x = 3$. Thus x is definitely equal to 3 and the answer to the question is "yes."

11. **C** Start with the first equation, which is $\dfrac{r+15}{r+3} = r$. Multiply both sides by the denominator $r + 3$ in order to get rid of the fraction. Now the equation is $r + 15 = r(r + 3)$, or $r + 15 = r^2 + 3r$. Now subtract r and 15 from both sides of the equation so that you have $r^2 + 2r - 15 = 0$. The question asks for the value of the equation $r^2 + 2r - 15$, so the answer is 0. Note that if you factored this equation to solve for r, rather than for the value of the whole equation, the result would be $(r + 5)(r - 3)$, which gives values of $r = -5$ and $r = 3$, so (A) and (D) are trap answers.

12. **C** Plug In the Answers, starting with (C), to see which answer choice makes the first equation true. If $m + 10 = -22$, then $m = -32$. Does $(-32 + 2)^2 = 900$? Yes, it does. When you Plug In the Answers, you can stop as soon as you find one that works. None of the other choices yields the correct values for the first equation. Alternatively, you can solve this problem algebraically. If $(m + 2)^2 = 900$, then $m + 2 = \pm 30$. Thus $m = -32$ or $m = 28$. Note that both -32 and 28 are trap answer choices. The problem asks for a possible value of $m + 10$, which must be either -22 or 38. Only -22 is listed as an answer, so the answer is (C).

13. **C** Statement (1) is insufficient. If you factor the quadratic expression $x^2 - 8x + 15$, you get $(x - 3)(x - 5)$. If one of these factors is equal to 0, then so will be $x^2 - 8x + 15$. The two roots of the equation are 3 and 5. Statement (1) tells you that x is not 3, but it could still be 5, so $x^2 - 8x + 15$ might be equal to 0. However, x could be other numbers, in which case $x^2 - 8x + 15$ would not be equal to 0. Eliminate (A) and (D). Statement (2) is insufficient. If $x - 5$ is not equal to 0, that still leaves open the possibility that x is equal to 3 which would make $x^2 - 8x + 15$ equal to 0. But x could be other numbers, in which case $x^2 - 8x + 15$ would not be equal to 0. Eliminate (B). Statements (1) and (2) together are sufficient. Statement (1) tells you that x is not 3. Statement (2) allows you to determine that x is not 5. Since those are the only two numbers that will make $x^2 - 8x + 15$ equal to 0, you know for certain that it will not be 0. The answer to the question then is "no."

14. **E** Statement (1) is insufficient. $x^2 + 6x + 5 = 0$ will factor to $(x + 5)(x + 1) = 0$. Thus, $x = -5$ or $x = -1$. You don't know which, so you can't solve for x. Eliminate (A) and (D). Statement (2) is insufficient. Since x could be any number greater than -10, you can't solve for x. Eliminate (B). Statements (1) and (2) together are insufficient. From statement (1) you know that x is equal to either -5 or -1. Since both of those numbers are greater than -10, statement (2) does not allow you to determine which one is the value of x.

15. **A** First FOIL the upper half of the equation. The result is $(\sqrt{5} \times \sqrt{5}) + (2 \times \sqrt{5}) - (2 \times \sqrt{5}) - (2 \times 2)$, which simplifies to $5 - 4$, or 1. Next FOIL the denominator: $(\sqrt{10} \times \sqrt{10}) + (2 \times \sqrt{10}) - (2 \times \sqrt{10}) - (2 \times 2)$. This simplifies to $10 - 4$, or 6. Thus the simplified fraction is $\dfrac{1}{6}$.

Plugging In

1. **D** There are variables in the answers, so this is a good opportunity to Plug In. Let's say $d = 4$ and $h = 5$. Then each cabinet has 4 drawers and each drawer has 5 hanging folders so that's a total of 20 hanging folders. Each hanging folder has 20 manila folders, so that gives you 400 manila folders in each cabinet. There are 3 cabinets, so your target answer is 1,200. Only (D) yields 1,200 when you plug your numbers into the answer choices, so the correct answer is (D).

2. **E** Statement (1) does not give you any actual values for Jim and gives you no information about Michael's grade increase, so statement (1) is insufficient. Eliminate (A) and (D). Statement (2) does not give you any actual values for Michael and gives you no information about Jim's grade increase, so statement (2) is insufficient. Eliminate (B). Combine the two statements to see if they are sufficient when used together. If Jim had a starting grade of 90 points, and he raised that grade by 10 percent, then his grade would increase by 9 points to 99. If Michael had a starting grade of 50, and he increased that grade by 6 percent, then his grade would increase by 3 points to 53. In this case, Jim would have increased his grade by the greatest number of points. However, if Jim had a starting grade of 50, and he increased it by 10 percent, then his grade would increase by 5 points to 55. If Michael had a starting grade of 94, and he raised his grade by 6 percent, then his grade would increase by 5.64 points to 99.64. In this situation, Michael would have increased his grade by the greatest number of points. Statements (1) and (2) together are insufficient, so the correct answer is (E).

3. **C** There are variables in the answer choices, so this is a good opportunity to Plug In. Let's say $w = 10$ and $z = 2$. It will take Mordecai 5 hours to run 10 miles, so your target is 5. Only (C) yields 5, so the correct answer is (C).

4. **A** Plug In for x and y in statement (1). If $x = 15$, and $y = 10$, then the equation becomes $2\left(\dfrac{15}{3} - \dfrac{10}{3}\right) = \dfrac{10}{3}$. Plug In to the information in statement (1) again to see if you get the same result. If $x = -7$ and $y = -12$, then the equation becomes $2\left(\dfrac{-7}{3} - \dfrac{-12}{3}\right) = \dfrac{10}{3}$. Statement (1) is sufficient, so you can eliminate (B), (C), and (E). Plug In for x and y in statement (2). If $x = 1$ and $y = 10$, then the equation becomes $2\left(\dfrac{1}{3} - \dfrac{10}{3}\right) = -\dfrac{18}{3}$, or -6. Plug In different numbers to ensure that you get the same result every time. If $x = 5$ and $y = 6$, then the equation becomes $2\left(\dfrac{5}{3} - \dfrac{6}{3}\right) = -\dfrac{2}{3}$. Statement (2) is insufficient, so you can eliminate (D).

5.   **A**   Plug In for x according to the information in statement (1). If $x = 6$, then $\frac{x}{3} = 2$. Now Plug In for y. If $y = 3$, then $xy = 18$, so xy is even. This yields a "no" answer. Plug In again, but choose an even number for y this time. If $x = 12$ and $y = 4$, then $xy = 48$, so xy is even. This also yields a "no" answer. In fact, if $\frac{x}{3}$ is an even integer, then x must be even. The product of an even number and another number will always be even, so statement (1) is sufficient. Eliminate (B), (C), and (E). Plug In for x and y in statement (2). If $x = 3$ and $y = 5$, then $x + y = 8$, and $xy = 15$. This yields a "yes" answer. If $x = 2$ and $y = 4$, then $x + y = 6$, and $xy = 8$. This yields a "no" answer, so statement (2) is insufficient.

6.   **D**   You don't know the number of necklaces for any of the months, so this is a good opportunity to Plug In. Let's say the number of necklaces sold in April is 60. Then the number of necklaces sold in May is 36 and the number sold in June is 6. You can use an average pie to figure out that the average number of necklaces sold in May and June is 21. 60 divided by 21 is $\frac{20}{7}$, so the correct answer is (D).

7.   **A**   Plug In for m and n to make statement (1) true. If $m = 5$ and $n = 2$, then you have $\frac{1}{5} < \frac{1}{2}$, so this yields a "yes." Plug In again using different numbers. If $m = -5$ and $n = -8$, then the equation becomes $-\frac{1}{5} < -\frac{1}{8}$. This once again yields a "yes" response. In fact, statement (1) will always yield a "yes" response, because you could rearrange statement (1) by simply adding n to both sides, so that you would then have: $m = n + 3$. This means that m will always be 3 greater than n, so $\frac{1}{m}$ will always be less than $\frac{1}{n}$. Statement (1) is sufficient, so you can eliminate (B), (C), and (E). Plug In for m and n to make statement (2) true. If $n = 1$, then $m = 1$, so the equation in the question becomes $\frac{1}{1} < \frac{1}{1}$, which is not true, so this yields a "no" response. Plug In again using different numbers. If $n = 3$, then $m = 7$, so the equation in the question becomes $\frac{1}{7} < \frac{1}{3}$, which is true, so this yields a "yes" response. Statement (2) is insufficient, so the correct answer is (A).

8.   **E**   The question says "in terms of," so Plug In. Let's say $g = 180$. Then each horse was bought for $6 and sold for $7.50. So your target answer is 7.50. When you plug 180 into the answers, only (E) gives you 7.50, so the correct answer is (E).

9. **B** Plug In for x to make statement (1) true. If $x = 3$, then $7 - x = 4$. In this case x is positive, so the answer is "yes." Plug In again to make statement (1) true. If $x = -3$, then $7 - x = 10$, but in this case x is negative, so this yields a "no." Statement (1) is insufficient, so you can eliminate (A) and (D). Plug In for x and y to make statement (2) true. If $y = -2$, then $y^4 = 16$. If $x = 32$, then $\frac{x}{y^4} = 2$. In this case x is positive, so this yields a "yes" answer. In fact, because y^4 will always be positive, then in order for $\frac{x}{y^4}$ to be positive x must also always be positive. Statement (2) is sufficient, so the correct answer is (B).

10. **A** Plug In for r and s to make statement (1) true. If $r = 3$ and $s = -5$, then statement (1) becomes $3 < -(-5)$. That means that $r + s = -2$. However, any number that is equal to a square root must be positive, so $\sqrt{t}$ cannot be equal to -2. This yields a "no" response. In fact, you can rewrite statement (1) by adding s to both sides, so that you then have $r + s < 0$. This means that $r + s$ will always be equal to a negative number, so $r + s$ can never be equal to $\sqrt{t}$. Statement (1) is sufficient, so you can eliminate (B), (C) and (E). Plug In for r and s to make statement (2) true. If $r = -3$, and $s = -2$, then $(r + s)^2 = 25$, so $t = 25$. However, $-3 + (-2) \neq \sqrt{25}$, so this yields a "no." However, if $r = 3$ and $s = 2$, then $(r + s)^2 = 25$. $3 + 2 = \sqrt{25}$, so this yields a "yes." Statement (2) is insufficient, so the correct answer is (A).

11. **A** There are variables in the answers, so Plug In. Say $t = 2$. The number of pillar candles made is 7 more than the number of taper candles, so that means $p = 9$. When you plug 2 for t and 9 for p into the answer choices, only (A) works.

12. **B** Plug In for p and q to make statement (1) true. If $p = 18$ and $q = 3$, then $\frac{p}{q} = 6$, and because $q > 3$ this yields a "no" response. If $p = 9$ and $q = 1.5$, then $\frac{p}{q} = 6$, and because $q < 2$ this yields a "yes" response. Statement (1) is insufficient, so you can eliminate (A) and (D). Simplify statement (2) by dividing both sides by -2 and flipping the inequality so that you have $p < 10$. Plug In for p and q to make statement (2) true. If $p = 9$ and $q = 1.5$, then $\frac{p}{q} = 6$, and because $q < 2$ this yields a "yes" response. You know that $\frac{10}{2} = 5$, but because $p < 10$, then even if p is at its maximum value q must be less than 2 in order for the expression $\frac{p}{q} > 5$ to be true. Statement (2) is sufficient, so the correct answer is (B).

13. **C** Plug In, but rather than Plugging In for *s*, Plug In for the total number of cupcakes sold. Let's use 28 for that total. That means 8 cupcakes had chocolate frosting, and *of the remaining* 20 cupcakes, 5 cupcakes had sprinkles. Therefore *s* = 5 and your target answer is 8. Only (C) yields 8, so the correct answer is (C).

14. **C** Plug In for *x* and *y* to make statement (1) true. If *x* = 3 and *y* = 9, then *z* can be 4, 5, 6, 7, or 8, so there are 5 different possible values of *z*. Plug In again to make statement (1) true. If *x* = 3.5 and *y* = 9.5, then *z* can be 4, 5, 6, 7, 8, or 9, so there are 6 possible values of *z*. Statement (1) is insufficient, so you can eliminate (A) and (D). Plug In for *x* and *y* to make statement (2) true. If *x* = 2 and *y* = 4.5, then *xy* = 9.5, and *z* can be 3 or 4. Plug In again to make statement (2) true. If *x* = 2.2 and *y* = 3.3, then *xy* = 6.93, and *z* can only be 3. Statement (2) is insufficient, so you can eliminate (B). Combine statements (1) and (2) to see if they are sufficient when used together. If the distance between *x* and *y* is 6, and *xy* is not an integer, then you can Plug In *x* = 3.5 and *y* = 9.5, so there are 6 possible values of *z*. In fact, in order for both statements to be true, then neither *x* nor *y* can be an integer, so if the distance between *x* and *y* is 6, then there must always be 6 possible values of *z*. Statements (1) and (2) together are sufficient, so the correct answer is (C).

15. **C** This is a double Plug In. Let's say there are 6 players on the blue team and each player on the blue team hit 12 balls. That means there are 5 players on the red team and each player on the red team hit 8 balls. Therefore, the blue team hit a total of 72 balls and the red team hit a total of 40 balls for a grand total of 112 balls hit. 72 out of 112 balls is approximately 64%, so the correct answer is (C).

16. **E** Plug In. Let's say *a* = 15. Then 3 applicants want to be actors and, of those, 2 also want to be directors. Therefore, the other 13 don't want to be both actors and directors. That's your target answer. Only (E) yields 13 when 15 is plugged in for *a*, so the correct answer is (E).

17. **E** Plug In for *x* and *y* to make statement (1) true. If *x* = 18 and *y* = 2, then $\frac{x}{y}$ = 9. If *x* = 6 and *y* = 6, then $\frac{x}{y}$ = 1. Statement (1) is insufficient, so write down BCE. Plug In again to make statement (2) true. If *y* = 2 and *x* = 6, then $\frac{x}{y}$ = 3. Or, *y* = 2 and *x* = 10 then $\frac{x}{y}$ = 5. Statement (2) is insufficient, so you can eliminate (B). Combine the two statements to see if they are sufficient when used together. If both statements are combined, it is possible that *x* = 18, *y* = 2 and $\frac{x}{y}$ = 9. Or, *x* = *y* = 6 and $\frac{x}{y}$ = 1. Statement (1) and (2) together are insufficient, so the correct answer is (E).

18. **B** This is a hard question so get rid of trap answers (A) and (C). Now, Plug In, but rather than Plugging In for the total number of theater patrons, Plug In 100 for the number of theater patrons who are late. That means 30 are late and aren't seated until the end of the first act, and the other 70 are late and seated immediately. Because 5 percent of the total patrons are late and seated immediately, you can solve for the total number of patrons, which is 1,400. 100 out of 1,400 or approximately 7% of the total patrons are late, so the correct answer is (B).

19. **E**   Plug In for p and q to make statement (1) true. If $p = 3$ and $q = 2$, then the inequality in statement (1) can now be written as $3^2 > 2^2$, or $9 > 4$. You can now write the inequality $\frac{p}{q} > \frac{q}{p}$ as $\frac{3}{2} > \frac{2}{3}$. This inequality is true, so these values yield a "yes" answer. Plug In for p and q again to make statement (1) true. If $p = -3$ and $q = 2$, then $\frac{p}{q} > \frac{q}{p}$ can now be written as $-\frac{3}{2} > -\frac{2}{3}$. This statement is false, so these values yield a "no" answer. Statement (1) is insufficient, so you can eliminate (A) and (D). Plug In for p and q to make statement (2) true. If $p = 3$ and $q = 2$, then statement (2) becomes $3^2 > 2^2$, or $27 > 8$. You can now write the inequality $\frac{p}{q} > \frac{q}{p}$ as $\frac{3}{2} > \frac{2}{3}$. This inequality is true, so these values yield a "yes" answer. Plug In again using different values that make statement (2) true. If $p = 2$ and $q = -2$, then statement (2) can be written as $2^3 > -2^3$, or $8 > -8$. The inequality $\frac{p}{q} > \frac{q}{p}$ can now be written as $-\frac{2}{2} > -\frac{2}{2}$. This equation is not true, so statement (2) is insufficient. Eliminate (B). Combine the two statements to see if they are sufficient when used together. If $p^2 > q^2$ and $p^3 > q^3$, then you can Plug In $p = 3$ and $q = -2$, so $\frac{p}{q} > \frac{q}{p}$ can be written as $-\frac{3}{2} > -\frac{2}{3}$. This yields a "no" answer. Alternatively, you could Plug In $p = 3$ and $q = 2$, so you could write the inequality as $\frac{3}{2} > \frac{2}{3}$. This yields a "yes" answer, so both statements combined are not sufficient.

20. **B**   Plug In for r, s, and t to make statement (1) true. If $s = -8$, $r = 3$, and $t = -4$, then both s and t are less than r, so this yields a "yes." Plug In again to make statement (1) true. If $s = -9$, $r = -5$, and $t = -3$, then t is greater than r, so this yields a "no." Statement (1) is insufficient, so you can eliminate (A) and (D). Plug In for r, s, and t to make statement (2) true. If $s = -8$, $r = 2$, and $t = -1$, then both s and t are less than r. In this case, you cannot Plug In a negative number for r. This must be true because t is a negative number, and $\frac{s}{r}$ is less than t, so $\frac{s}{r}$ must be negative. You already know that s is negative, so in order for the fraction to remain negative, r must be positive. According to statement (2) both s and t will always be less than r, so statement (2) is sufficient.

21. **B**   This one's a little tricky. Let's begin by Plugging In $w = 2$ and $z = 4$. Now let's Plug In a one-way distance up the mountain of 12 miles. With those numbers it will take Rebecca 6 hours to climb up the mountain and 3 hours to climb down for a total of 9 hours. Thus $r = 9$ and the target is 12. Only (B) yields 12 when you plug your numbers into the answers.

22. **D**   Plug In, starting with Gary's salary. Let's say $g = 200$ and $p = 50$. That makes $m = 100$. 200 is 200% of 100, so your target answer is 200. Only (D) yields 200 when you Plug In 50 for p, so the correct answer is (D).

23. **B** Plug In for x and y to make statement (1) true. If $x = 3$ and $y = 2$, then $xy = 6$. In this case, y is even, so this yields a "yes" answer. Plug In again to make statement (2) true. If $x = 2$ and $y = 3$, then $xy = 6$, but in this case y is odd, so this yields a "no" answer. Statement (1) is insufficient, so you can eliminate (A) and (D). Plug In to make statement (2) true. If $x = 3$ and $y = 4$, then $(x - 2)(y - 1) = 3$. If you Plug In again, x cannot equal 2 because then the equation would be $0(y - 1) = 0$, which is even. The outcome of the equation must be odd, so this does not work. If $x = 5$ and $y = 6$, $(x - 2)(y - 1) = 15$. Because y is even this yields a "yes" answer. In fact, any time you multiply two numbers together to get an odd number the two numbers being multiplied must both be odd, so you know that $y - 1$ must be odd, so y must be even. Statement (2) is sufficient, so the correct answer is (B).

24. **A** Plug In. Let's say $a = 20$, $b = 2$ and $c = 10$. The initial productivity is $(0.05)(20)(2)(10^3) = 20{,}000$. The new numbers are $a = 12$, $b = 4$ and $c = 4$, so the new productivity is $(0.05)(12)(4)(64) = 1{,}536$. The productivity is decreasing, so eliminate (D) and (E). Now apply the percent change formula. The difference between the two amounts is 18,464 and the original is 20,000, so that gives you a decrease of 92.3, so the correct answer is (A).

PITA

1. **D** Plug In the Answers, using the percent change formula, starting with (C). If 27 million people viewed the program in December, then the difference between the two dates is $30 - 27$, or 3 million. Thus, the percent decrease is 10%. Eliminate (C). You want a greater percent decrease, so you need a greater difference between the two months. Try (D). If 26 million people viewed the program in December, then the percent decrease is 4 million divided by 30 million, or $13\frac{1}{3}$%.

2. **C** Plug In the Answers, starting with (C). If 12 women have brown hair, then $6 + 12$, or 18 women have blonde hair. Thus, the total number of women at the agency is $18 + 12 = 30$.

3. **E** Plug In the Answers, starting with (C). If Randy's piece is 11 inches, then Zelda's piece is 19 inches, and the whole piece is $11 + 19$, or 30 inches. That's too long, so get rid of (A), (B), and (C). If Randy's piece is 8 inches, then Zelda's piece is 16 inches, for a total of 24 inches. Eliminate (D). The answer must be (E). If Randy's piece is 6 inches, then Zelda's piece is 14 inches, and the total is 20 inches.

4. **A** Plug In the Answers, starting with (C). If she baked 50 chocolate chip cookies, then $3(50)$ is 20 more than the number of oatmeal cookies she baked, so she baked 130 oatmeal cookies. The total number of cookies is 100, so this is too big. Eliminate (C), (D), and (E). Try (B). If she baked 40 chocolate chip cookies, then $3(40)$ is 20 more than the number of oatmeal cookies she baked, so she baked 100 oatmeal cookies. Still too big. The answer must be (A). If she baked 30 chocolate chip cookies, then $3(30)$ is 20 more than the number of oatmeal cookies she baked, so she baked 70 oatmeal cookies. The total number of cookies she baked is $30 + 70$, which equals 100.

5. **D** First, note that the question is asking for a specific number, the value of d. That tells you that you need to Plug In the Answers. Label the answer choices as the value of d and start by Plugging In (C): $3.25. If Carl spends $3.25 for the first 2 days, he owes money for the next three. According to the problem, the fee per day is $2.25. For three rental days, Carl owes (3)($2.25), which is $6.75. Now, check these values against the information in the problem. The total fee should be $10.25. Is $3.25 + $6.75 equal to $10.25? No, it is equal to $10.00, which is just slightly under the value you want. Choice (C) yielded a value that was too small, so eliminate (A), (B), and (C). Try (D). If Carl spends $3.50 for the first two days and $6.75 for the next three (this value doesn't change). The total of $3.50 + $6.75 is $10.25.

6. **D** The question asks for the total amount of tips, so try Plugging In the Answers. Start with (C): $108. 4 waiters combined receive $\frac{2}{3}$ of $108, or $72. The manager receives $\frac{1}{4}$ of $108, or $27, and the busboy receives the remaining $9. If the 4 waiters received $72, that means that 1 waiter received $18, so 1 waiter and the busboy together receive $27. The question says they received $30, so (C) is slightly too small. Eliminate (A), (B), and (C). Try (D). If the total amount earned in tips was $120, then the 4 waiters combined receive $\frac{2}{3}$ of $120, or $80. The manager receives $\frac{1}{4}$ of $120, or $30, and the busboy receives the remaining $10. If the 4 waiters received $80, that means that 1 waiter received $20, so 1 waiter and the busboy together receive $30.

7. **B** The problem asks how much Bernard was paid. Plug In the Answers. Start with (C): if Bernard received $32.50, then how much did Abigail receive? The problem says that they were paid in proportion to their work, and Abigail worked twice as long as Bernard did, so she gets twice the money. If Bernard gets $32.50, then Abigail gets $65.00. Now, check that against the information in the problem. The total received should be $90.00, but $65.00 + $32.50 is too big. Eliminate (C), (D), and (E). If Bernard received $30.00, as in (B), then Abigail received $60.00, and they received the desired total of $90.00.

8. **A** Plug In the Answers starting with (C). If 10 roses are removed, there will be 8 daffodils out of 15 flowers, which is approximately 53%. Eliminate (C). There need to be slightly more flowers, so you need to remove fewer roses. Try (B). If 8 roses are removed, there will be 8 daffodils out of 17 flowers. That's approximately 47%, so get rid of (B). With (A), there will be 8 daffodils out of 20 flowers, which is 40% daffodils.

9. **B** Plug In the Answers, starting with (C). If there are 90 singers in the chorus, then 36 can sight-read and 54 can't. The number of singers who have taken music theory and the number who haven't should add up to the number of singers who can't sight-read. 42 does not equal 54, so eliminate (C). Now try (B). If there are 70 singers in the chorus, then 28 can sight-read and 42 can't. 42 matches the number of singers who have and have not taken music theory, so the answer is (B).

10.   C   You can Plug In the Answers, but get rid of some answers by Ballparking first. If Blake is 40 years older than Jasmine, he has to be at least 40. Eliminate (E). Try (C). If Blake is 50, then Jasmine is 50 – 40, or 10. If Jasmine were three times as old as she is, she would be 30, which is, in fact, 20 years younger than Blake's current age.

11.   D   Plug In the Answers, starting with (C). If an officer were eligible to take the sergeant's exam in 2004, he would have been on the job for 12 years (2004 – 1992 = 12). Because he started the job at age 28, his age in 2004 is 28 + 12, or 40. His age plus his years on the job total 52, which is fine for him to take the exam. Eliminate (A) and (B). But could he take the exam earlier? Try (D). If he were eligible to take the sergeant's exam in 2003, he would have been on the job for 11 years, and his age in 2003 would be 39. His age plus his years on the job total 50, so the answer is (D).

12.   C   Plug In the Answers, starting with (C). There are currently 6 male waiters (30% of 20). If 7 of the new waiters are women, then 1 of the new waiters is a man. The number of male waiters is now 7 out of a total of 28 waiters, which is 25%.

13.   B   Plug In the Answers, starting with (C). If the total cost of the meal were $30, then a 15 percent tip would be $4.50. This is greater than $4, so eliminate (D) and (E). Now check (B) to see if it is possible to get an acceptable smaller value for the price of the meal. 15 percent of $27 is $4.05. Choice (B) works, so eliminate (C). Try (A). 15 percent of $26 is $3.90, which is too small. Eliminate (A). Alternatively, you could solve this problem algebraically. Set up the equation $\frac{15}{100}x = 4$, in which x represents the total cost of the meal. Now multiply both sides of the equation by x so that you have $15x = 400$, or $x = \frac{400}{15}$, which is approximately 26.6. The tip was slightly more than $4, so the cost of the meal is slightly more than 26.6.

14.   C   This problem is a bit tricky because at first it looks like a hidden Plug In. The question does not tell you the number of animals in the zoo and gives you a bunch of fractions. But in fact, this is a Plug In the Answers problem, because the question asks for the total number of non-mammals in the zoo and the answer choices are real numbers, not fractions or percents. Start by Plugging In (C), 54, for the number of non-mammals. Now, use the information in the problem to find the number of mammals. According to the problem, 24 mammals are allowed to interact with the public, and this is $\frac{2}{3}$ of all the mammals. Thus, there must be 36 total mammals in the zoo (because 24 is $\frac{2}{3}$ of 36). If there are 36 mammals and 54 non mammals, then there are 90 animals

in the zoo. Now, check this number against the information in the problem. The problem says that $\frac{2}{5}$ of all the animals are mammals and 36 is $\frac{2}{5}$ of 90.

15. **B** This algebra problem has numbers in the answers, so solve it by Plugging In the Answers. Start with (C): if Reservoir A contains 700 million gallons of water, then Reservoir B has 450 million gallons less, or 250 million gallons. When 100 million gallons are drained from Reservoir A to Reservoir B, then the reservoirs will hold 600 million and 350 million gallons of water, respectively. That's not the relationship you're looking for—Reservoir A should have twice as much water as Reservoir B—so eliminate (C). Try (B): if Reservoir A contains 600 million gallons of water, then Reservoir B has 450 million gallons less, or 150 million gallons. When 100 million gallons are drained from Reservoir A to Reservoir B, then the reservoirs will hold, respectively, 500 million and 250 million gallons of water. That's the relationship you're looking for—Reservoir A has twice as much water as Reservoir B—so the answer is (B).

16. **E** The problem asks for the least value of x. Plug In the Answers. The question asks for the least value, so start with the smallest value given and work your way up. Start with (E). If x equals 50, then the cost is 80(50) + 9,000, which is 13,000. The money made from sale of the rings is 260(50), or 13,000. No money is made or lost at this price. The problem says the company must not lose money (which is not the same as making money), so the answer is (E).

17. **C** This is another question on which you can avoid algebra by simply Plugging In the Answers. The question asks for the value of m, so see which of the choices works in the problem. Start with (C), which is $\frac{3}{2}$. The problem states that $mn = 9$, so that means $\frac{3}{2}n = 9$. Solve for n, you get 6. Now you just have to make sure that $\frac{n}{m} = 4$. It does, because $\frac{6}{\frac{3}{2}} = 6 \times \frac{2}{3}$, which is 4.

18. **D** Plug In the Answers to see which value cannot work. If 1 goal for 3 points is scored, then the team scored 45 points on unassisted goals (because the team had 48 points and 1 goal was worth 3 points, that leaves 48 – 3 = 45). To score 45 points, the team would need 9 assisted goals (9 goals at 5 points each gives you 9 × 5 = 45), so (A) can be the number of goals. Eliminate it. If 6 goals for 3 points are scored, then there are 18 points scored on unassisted goals and 30 points remain to be accounted for. 30 points can be achieved by 6 goals scored with assistance, so (B) can be the number of goals. Eliminate it. If 11 goals for 3 points are scored, there are 33 points scored and 15 left over, so that equals 3 goals scored without assistance. Choice (C) can be the number of goals. Eliminate it. If 12 goals for 3 points are scored, then 36 points have been scored and there are 12 points remaining. This is not divisible by 5, so (D) does not work.

19. **D** Plug In the Answers to see which one works. Start with (C), which is 1. That makes the top of the fraction $(3)(-4)$ and the bottom $(-2)(5)$. This doesn't equal 1. Try (D). The top of the fraction becomes $(2.5)(-4.5)$ and the bottom becomes $(-2.5)(4.5)$. This does equal 1, so the answer is (D).

20. **D** Plug In the Answers, starting with (C). If Benji purchases 22,000 miles, then he receives 4,400 miles plus the original 7,000 miles, so the total is 11,400 miles. This number is too small, so go to (D). If Benji purchases 40,000 miles, then he will receive 8,000 miles, plus the original 7,000 miles. The total is 15,000, so the answer is (D).

21. **B** This one is a little more difficult to Plug In the Answers on, but it can still be done. The answers represent the value of $|x + 3|$, so work backward. For example, if you Plug In (B), you can solve for x to get $x = -\frac{3}{2}$. If you plug this back into the original equation, it works. Alternatively, you could solve this problem algebraically. Factoring the quadratic polynomial, the equation becomes $(2x + 9)(2x + 3) = 0$, so $x = -\frac{9}{2}$ or $-\frac{3}{2}$. In either case, the value of $|x + 3|$ is $\frac{3}{2}$, so the answer is (B).

22. **B** Ron only had two kinds of chips, $5 and $10, and ended the game with only 12 chips total. Because Ron had either two more or two fewer $10 chips than $5 chips, he had either seven $10 chips and five $5 chips, or five $10 chips and seven $5 chips. So, Ron ended the game with either $7(\$10) + 5(\$5) = \$95$ in chips, or $5(\$10) + 7(\$5) = \$85$ in chips. The question asks for the minimum possible value of chips that Ron lost. The minimum possible value of chips lost would result in the greatest value of chips remaining. The greatest possible value of chips remaining for Ron is $95, and since he started with $200, the minimum possible value of chips that Ron lost is $200 – $95 = $105. The correct answer is (B).

23. **E** The number of players who can play on Saturdays needs to be an even number, so eliminate (A) and (C). Plug In the Answers, but first use the numbers you have with the group formula (T = Group 1 + Group 2 – Both + Neither). 43 = 15 + Saturday – 8 + Neither. Simplify that to 36 = Saturday + Neither. Neither = 36 – Saturday. Now Plug In the Answers with (D). If 12 players can play on Saturdays, then the number of players who can neither play on Saturdays nor have uniforms is 36 – 12, or 24. The number of players who can play on Saturdays is supposed to be twice the number of players in the neither category, not the other way around; eliminate (D). Try (E). If 24 players can play on Saturdays then the number of players who can neither play on Saturdays nor have uniforms is 36 – 24 or 12. The number who can play on Saturdays is, in fact, twice the number of players in the neither category, so the answer is (E).

24. **C** Use a ratio box and Plug In the Answers, starting with (C). If there are 236 guests in the hotel, then our multiplier is 4, which means there are 224 paying guests and 12 non-paying guests. If 12 more paying guests check in, the number of paying guests is now 236. Because the number of non-paying guests is still 12, the ratio of paying to non-paying is 236 to 12, which reduces to 59 to 3.

Must Be True

1. **B** Plug In a number for x that satisfies the conditions of the problem. If $x = 66$, then II and III work, but I does not. Eliminate (A) and (C). In order to decide between (B) and (D), Plug In again. If $x = 33$, the conditions of the problem are still satisfied. 33 is a factor of 66, but is not a multiple of 66. Eliminate (D). The answer is (B). Alternatively, you can solve this by using the properties of numbers. Both 3 and 11 are prime numbers, so any number that is a factor of both must also be divisible by (3)(11), or 33.

2. **D** This is a must be true question, so you may have to Plug In more than once. If $w = 2$, Statement I is not true because $2^0 = 1$. In fact, anything to the zero power equals 1. Get rid of all the answers that have I in them, so eliminate (A), (C), and (E). That leaves (B) and (D). Both have III in them, so there's no need to check III. For Statement II, $\sqrt{2}$ does not equal 0, so eliminate (B).

3. **B** If $x = -0.5$, then $x < x^2$ can be written as $-0.5 < 0.25$, which is true. Eliminate (C) and (E). The expression $x^3 < x$ can now be written as $-0.125 < -0.5$. This is false, so eliminate (D). The expression $x^3 < x^2$ becomes $-0.125 < 0.25$. This is true, so the answer is (B).

4. **A** This is a "must be" question, so Plug In. If $r = 48$, statement I is true, but you have to Plug In again to make sure it's always true. Statement II is not true so eliminate (C) and (E). Statement III is not true, so eliminate (D). At this point your choices are "I only" and "None." Is there a number you can Plug In that is divisible by both 6 and 8, but not divisible by 48? Yes. 24. Thus, you can eliminate (B) and the answer is (A).

5. **D** Plug In for x and y. If $x = 8$, and $y = 9$, then $xy = 72$. 12 is a factor of 72, so keep (A), (C), (D), and (E) for now. 16 is not a factor of 72, so eliminate (B), (C), and (E). 24 is a factor of 72, so keep (D). Plug In again to confirm that both 12 and 24 work for all possible values of xy. If $x = 16$, and $y = 18$, then $xy = 288$. Both 12 and 24 are factors of 288, so (D) is the answer. Alternatively, you can use the properties of numbers to solve this problem. If x is a multiple of 8, and y is a multiple of 9, then xy must be a multiple of 72 and any of its factors.

6. **E** This is a must be true question, so Plug In. First, though, solve the given equation for r because all the answer choices refer to r. That gives you $r = \frac{3}{2}s$. Now Plug In for s. If $s = 1$, then $r = \frac{3}{2}$. Eliminate (A) and (B). Plug In again: if $s = -2$, then $r = -3$; eliminate (D). Plug In again: if $s = \frac{3}{2}$, then $r = \frac{9}{4} = 2\frac{1}{4}$. Eliminate (C).

7. **A** Plug In values for p and r. If $p = -5$, and $r = -3$, then $p + r$ is -8. Because -8 is even, I works for now. Try II with those numbers: $(-5) \times (-3) = 15$, and 15 is positive, so II works for now. Try III with those numbers: $\dfrac{-5}{-3} = \dfrac{5}{3}$, which is greater than 1, so eliminate (D) and (E). Now try another set of values for r and p. If $p = -3$, and $r = 5$, then $p + r = 2$, so I still works. $(-3) \times 5 = -15$. Because the result is a negative number, you can eliminate (B) and (C). The only choice left, and therefore the answer, is (A).

8. **B** This is a must be true question so you may need to Plug In more than once. Say that Olivia has 10 marbles. That means Josh has 5 and Hugo has 8. If they each get 4 more marbles, Olivia will have 14, Josh will have 9 and Hugo will have 12. Looking at statement I, Olivia does have more marbles than Hugo. For statement II, Olivia does not have twice as many marbles as Josh, so cross off answers that include II. Eliminate (D) and (E). For statement III Josh does have 3 fewer marbles than Hugo. Now Plug In with smaller numbers. If Olivia has 2 marbles, Josh has 1 and Hugo has 4. If they each get 4 more marbles, then Olivia has 6, Josh has 5 and Hugo has 8. Statement I is no longer true. Eliminate (A) and (C). That leaves III only, so the answer is (B).

9. **A** Plug In for x and y. Let $x = \dfrac{1}{3}$ and $y = \dfrac{1}{2}$. Now the expression $x^{-2} > y^2$ becomes $\left(\dfrac{1}{3}\right)^{-2} > \left(\dfrac{1}{2}\right)^2$, which simplifies to $9 > \dfrac{1}{4}$. That is a true statement, so I works for now. Try II with those numbers: $xy > 1$ is now $\left(\dfrac{1}{3}\right) \times \left(\dfrac{1}{2}\right) > 1$. $\left(\dfrac{1}{3}\right) \times \left(\dfrac{1}{2}\right) = \dfrac{1}{6}$, and $\dfrac{1}{6}$ is not greater than 1, so eliminate (B) and (D). Try III with those numbers: $x^2 < y^3$ now becomes $\left(\dfrac{1}{3}\right)^2 < \left(\dfrac{1}{2}\right)^3$, or $\dfrac{1}{9} < \dfrac{1}{8}$. This is a true statement, so III works for now. Plug In again to see if both I and III are true in all circumstances. Let $x = \dfrac{1}{5}$ and $y = \dfrac{1}{4}$. Now $x^{-2} > y^2$ becomes $\left(\dfrac{1}{5}\right)^{-2} > \left(\dfrac{1}{4}\right)^2$. This simplifies to $25 > \dfrac{1}{16}$. This is true. For III, the expression $x^2 < y^3$ becomes $\left(\dfrac{1}{5}\right)^2 < \left(\dfrac{1}{4}\right)^3$, or $\dfrac{1}{25} < \dfrac{1}{64}$. This expression is not true, so eliminate (D).

10. **A** Plug In. The inequality in the question stem means that p is a fraction, so Plug In $\frac{1}{2}$ for p. Before you Plug In for statement I, simplify it. If you factor p^4 out of the left side and p^2 out of the right side and then cancel, you get $p^4 < p^2$. Now Plug In $p = \frac{1}{2}$ and you get $\frac{1}{16} < \frac{1}{4}$. This is true, so don't eliminate anything. For statement II, you get $\frac{1}{32} < \frac{1}{8}$, which is also true, so don't eliminate anything. If you simplify statement III by factoring p^4 out of the left side and p^2 out of the right side and canceling, you again get $p^4 < p^2$. Don't eliminate anything. If you Plug In again with another fraction, all three statements will work. When a fraction is raised to a positive power greater than 1, the result is a number that is smaller than the original fraction. Thus, all three statements will always work and the answer is (A).

11. **C** Plug In values that fit both the equation and the inequality in order to eliminate answer choices. If $x = -3$, then $y = 5$. Eliminate (A), (B), and (E). If $x = 1$, then $y = -\frac{5}{3}$. This eliminates (D), leaving only (C). Alternatively, you can solve this problem algebraically. The first equation indicates that $5x + 3y = 0$. Rewrite the equation in terms of x by first subtracting $3y$ from both sides, so that you have $5x = -3y$. Now divide both sides by 5, so that the equation is now $x = -\frac{3}{5}y$. Now you can replace x with $-\frac{3}{5}y$ in the inequality $x < 3$, so that it becomes $-\frac{3}{5}y < 3$. Now solve for y by first multiplying both sides by 5, so that you have $-3y < 15$. Next divide both sides by -3, and don't forget to flip the sign in the inequality so that you now have $y > -5$.

12. **D** Plug In an even number for x. Let $x = 4$. The question says that each day was 1 degree warmer than the previous one, so you need 4 consecutive integers. If the daily temperatures were -2, -1, 0, and 1, the sum is -2, not 0. Notice, however, that the three numbers, -1, 0, and 1 effectively cancel each other out, so that the sum is 0. This suggests that odd numbers may work, whereas even ones may not. Because the information in I is not true, eliminate (A) and (C). Now try an odd number for x. If $x = 5$, then you can use -2, -1, 0, 1, and 2 for your consecutive numbers. Each number is canceled out by its opposite, so the sum is 0. The information in II does work, so eliminate (E). The average of these numbers is 0, so III works also. The answer is (D).

13. **C** Start by plugging in something simple for the original sequence: 2, 3, 4, 5, 6. For statement I the sequence will be 0, 1, 2, 3, 4. This is an arithmetic sequence, so you can't cross off any answer choices yet. For statement II the sequence will be 6, 9, 12, 15, 18. This is also an arithmetic sequence so you can't cross off any answer choices. For statement III you get $\sqrt{2}$, $\sqrt{3}$, 2, $\sqrt{5}$, $\sqrt{6}$. You know that $\sqrt{2} \approx 1.4$ and $\sqrt{3} \approx 1.7$ so the difference between the first three terms in statement

III is 1, .4, .3. The sequence in statement III is not an arithmetic sequence so get rid of all the answers that contain III. That eliminates (D) and (E.) Plug In again for statements I and II. Try 0, 1, 2, 3, 4 this time. The sequence for statement I is now –2, –1, 0, 1, 2. This is an arithmetic sequence. In fact, anytime you add or subtract a constant (in this case, subtracting 2) from an arithmetic sequence, you will still have an arithmetic sequence, so statement I will always be true. Eliminate (B). Using 0, 1, 2, 3, 4 for statement II gives you 0, 3, 6, 9, 12 which is also an arithmetic sequence.

14. **C** Plug In for w, x, y, and z. Let $w = 3$, $x = 4$, $y = 5$, and $z = 6$. That means that $z - w$ is equal to 6 – 3, or 3. Additionally, the numbers are consecutive, so the difference between z and w will always be 3, so I will always be true. Eliminate (B). According to II, $wxyz$ is an even number. $3 \times 4 \times 5 \times 6 = 360$, which is an even number. There are four consecutive numbers, so you will always have two odd numbers multiplied by two even numbers, so the result will always be even and II is also true. Eliminate (A) and (D). Finally, III indicates that $\dfrac{w + x + y + z}{4}$ is an integer. $\dfrac{3 + 4 + 5 + 6}{4} = \dfrac{18}{4}$, which is not an integer, so this is not true. Eliminate (E).

15. **D** This is a must be true question so you may need to Plug In more than once. If $f = 2$ and $g = 3$, all three statements work so you don't get to cross off anything. Try some weird numbers to see if you can disprove any of the statements. When you are dealing with fractions, it is often a good idea to Plug In fractions. Make $f = \dfrac{1}{2}$ and $g = \dfrac{2}{3}$. For statement I then, you get $\dfrac{1}{4} + \dfrac{4}{9} = \dfrac{25}{36}$, which is less than 1. Eliminate (A), (C), and (E). The remaining choices both have III in them so there's no need to check III. For statement II, you get $\dfrac{1}{2} > 0$, which is true. You cannot Plug In a negative value for f, since $g > 0$, so statement II will always be true.

16. **B** Solve for the prime factors of the given values for $a = 15$ and $b = 22$. The prime factors of 15 are 3×5 and the prime factors for 22 are 2×11, so $ab = 2 \times 3 \times 5 \times 11$. To answer this question, break the answer choices down to their prime factors. $4 = 2 \times 2$, but there is only one 2 in the prime factors of ab, so that cannot be the correct answer. $6 = 2 \times 3$, and there are both a 2 and a 3 in the prime factors of ab, so that could be the answer. $12 = 2 \times 2 \times 3$, but again there is only one 2 in the prime factors of ab, so eliminate (C). $20 = 2 \times 2 \times 5$, so eliminate (D) because there is only one 2 in the prime factors of ab. $25 = 5 \times 5$, so (E) also cannot be correct because there is only one 5 in the prime factors of ab. The correct answer is (B).

17. **C** The algebra for this question is cumbersome, so Plug In a value for z. First off, z is negative since it's less than 0. Say $z = -2$. Then the inequality is $-\dfrac{1}{2} < -2$, which is not true. Try making z a fraction. If $z = -\dfrac{1}{2}$, then the inequality is $-2 < -\dfrac{1}{2} < 0$, which is correct, so that is a possible

value for z. Now, check the answer choices. Choice (A) is incorrect because $\left(-\dfrac{1}{2}\right)^2 = \dfrac{1}{4}$, which is not greater than 1. Choice (B) is not correct because z^2 is positive and z is negative. Choice (C) works because $\left(-\dfrac{1}{2}\right)^3 = -\dfrac{1}{8}$, which is greater than –1 but less than 0. Choice (D) is not correct because $\dfrac{1}{-\dfrac{1}{2}} = -2$, which is less than –1. Choice (E) is not correct because $-\dfrac{1}{8} > -\dfrac{1}{2}$. The correct answer is (C).

18.   **A**   Pick numbers for x and y. x has to be prime but also less than 3: the only option is $x = 2$. Keep in mind that 1 is not prime because it only has one factor; 2 is prime because it has exactly two factors. Now consider the options for y. The only prime numbers between 3 and 11 are 5 and 7. Try $y = 5$. Choice (A) is 4 + 25 = 29, which is prime, so keep it. Choice (B) is 7, which is prime, so keep it. Choice (C) is 10, which is not prime, so eliminate it. Choice (D) is 50, which is not prime, so eliminate it. Choice (E) is 25 – 4 = 21, which is not prime, so eliminate it. Now check (A) and (B) with $y = 7$. Choice (A) is 4 + 49 = 53, which is prime. Choice (B) is 9, which is not prime, so the correct answer is (A).

19.   **C**   Try Plugging In numbers. Say $a = -4$, $b = -3$, $c = -2$, and $d = 5$. Choice (A) is 3, so eliminate it. Choice (B) is 60, so eliminate it. Choice (C) is –1, so keep it. Choice (D) is 9, so eliminate it. Choice (E) is 1, so eliminate it. The correct answer is (C).

20.   **B**   Plugging In numbers is possible here, but considering how great the exponents are, it may be better to reason the answer choices out instead. Notice that p must be either a positive or negative fraction. Consider if p is a positive fraction such as $\dfrac{1}{2}$. The basic principle to keep in mind is that a fraction decreases when raised to a power. So choice (A) works because the greater power is going to be a lesser number. Choice (B) also works because the powers on the left are both lesser than the powers on the right for a positive fraction. Choice (C) is not correct because a negative number to an odd power is negative, so the right side of the equation is negative and the left is positive. Eliminate it. Choice (D) is true with $\dfrac{1}{2}$ because the left side is negative and the right is positive. Choice (E), while true for a positive whole number, isn't true for a fraction because fractions decrease when put to powers. Eliminate it. Choices (A), (B), and (D) are left. Now consider what would happen in those answer choices with a negative fraction for p such as $p = -\dfrac{1}{2}$. This can be confusing, so it may be helpful to change the powers to similar numbers, so for (A), consider p^3 versus p^1.

$\left(-\dfrac{1}{2}\right)^3 = -\dfrac{1}{8}$, which is greater than $-\dfrac{1}{2}$. This disproves choice (A). Check choice (B). Notice the powers are all even, so they will all be positive. This has the same result as the positive fraction, so it still works. Check choice (D). In this case the left side is positive and the right is negative, so it doesn't work. The correct answer is (B).

21. **C** Try Plugging In numbers for x and y: say $x = -3$ and $y = 6$. Choice (A) is -18, which is not odd, so eliminate it. Choice (B) is not an integer, so eliminate it. Choice (C) is -9, which is a negative odd integer, so keep it. Choice (D) is 3, which is positive, so eliminate it. Choice (E) is 9, which is odd, so eliminate it. The correct answer is (C).

22. **A** Plug In a number for s, such as $s = 12$. In this case, $s + 15 = 27$. 37 is a multiple of 3, 9, and 27, but not a multiple of 12 or 15, so eliminate (C) and (D). Now try another number, such as $s = 24$. Then $s + 15 = 39$. 39 is still a multiple of 3 but not of 9 or 27, so eliminate (B) and (E). The correct answer is (A).

23. **D** Pick numbers for x, y, and z, such as $x = 2$, $y = 3$, and $z = 4$. Choice (A) is $5 > 4$, which is true, so keep it. Choice (B) is $4 = 4 = 4$, which is true, so keep it. Choice (C) is $6 > 4$, which is true, so keep it. Choice (D) is $-2 > -3$, which is true, so keep it. Choice (E) is $1 > 2$, which is not true, so eliminate it. Now try different numbers. While the value of the numbers must be least to greatest, they don't need to be consecutive. Try picking numbers that are more spread out, like $x = 2$, $y = 4$, and $z = 10$. In this case, (A) is $6 > 10$, which is not true, so eliminate it. Choice (B) is $4 = 5 = 11$, which is not true, so eliminate it. Choice (C) is $8 > 10$, which is not true, so eliminate it. Choice (D) is $-2 > -4$, which is true. The correct answer is (D).

24. **B** Pick numbers for a and b. The difference is a multiple of 5, so try $a = 12$ and $b = 7$ because $12 - 7 = 5$. Now check the answer choices. Choice (A) is $\dfrac{5}{5} = 1$, which is not a multiple of 5, so eliminate it. Choice (B) is $144 - 49 = 95$, which is a multiple of 5, so keep it. Choice (C) is $12 + 7 = 19$, which is not a multiple of 5, so eliminate it. Choice (D) is 84, which is not a multiple of 5, so eliminate it. Choice (E) is $60 - 7 = 53$, which is not a multiple of 5, so eliminate it. The correct answer is (B).

Yes/No Data Sufficiency

1. **B** Statement (1) indicates that x is less than 0.35. However, the question asks whether x is less than $\frac{1}{3}$. In order to compare the two numbers, first write $\frac{1}{3}$ in decimal format. $\frac{1}{3} = 0.3\overline{3}$. Thus, for statement (1), x could be 0.34, which would produce a "no" answer, or it could be equal to 0.32, which would produce a "yes" answer. Eliminate (A) and (D). According to statement (2), x is equal to 0.29, which is less than $0.3\overline{3}$, so the answer to the question is "yes," which makes (B) the correct answer.

2. **A** Plug In for statement (1). If $m = 15$ and $n = 5$, then $m - n = 10$. 10 is a multiple of 5, so this produces a "yes" for statement (1). Any set of acceptable numbers you Plug In for statement (1) will yield a multiple of 10 as a result, and any multiple of 10 is divisible by 5, so statement (1) is sufficient. Eliminate (B), (C), and (E). Statement (2) only states that n is a multiple of 5, but does not provide any information about m. If $m = 12$ and $n = 5$, then $m - n = 7$, but if $m = 10$ and $n = 5$, then $m - n = 5$. Statement (2) is not sufficient.

3. **C** Plug In for statement (1). If $p = 3$ and $r = 2$, the result is a "yes" answer. If $p = 6$ and $r = 1$, then the result is a "no" answer. Eliminate (A) and (D). Plug In for statement (2). If $p = 4$ and $r = 1$, the result is a "no" answer. If $p = 2$ and $r = 2$, the result is a "yes" answer. Eliminate (B). Combine the two statements to test (C). According to statement (1), p can equal 3, 4, 5, or 6, and r can equal 1, 2, or 3. In order to satisfy the conditions of statement (2), the product of p and r must equal 4. The only two numbers from the lists in statement (1) that fit this condition are $p = 4$ and $r = 1$. This produces a "no" answer to the question, so the answer is (C).

4. **C** Statement (1) does not provide any information about the slope of line k, so statement (1) is insufficient. Eliminate (A) and (D). Statement (2) provides only information about line k. If you know that the equation of k is $x - 3y = 6$, then you can solve for y to get the slope of the line. First subtract x from both sides, so that you have $-3y = -x + 6$. Next, divide both sides by -3 to get $y = \frac{1}{3}x + 6$. Thus the slope of line k is equal to $\frac{1}{3}$. However, no information is included regarding the slope of line j, so statement (2) is insufficient. Eliminate (B). Now try both statements together. Statement (1) indicates that the slope of line j is $\frac{1}{3}$, and statement (2) indicates that the slope of line k is $\frac{1}{3}$. The two lines have the same slope, so they are parallel. Both statements together are sufficient. So the answer is (C).

5. **E** Plug In for x in statement (1). If $x = 5$, then $x^2 - 3 = 22$, and the answer to the question is "yes." If $x = 9$, then $x^2 - 3 = 78$, and the answer is "no." Thus, statement (1) is insufficient. Eliminate (A) and (D). Plug In again for statement (2). If $x = 5$, then this produces a "yes" answer. If $x = 9$, then this produces a "no" answer. Statement (2) is insufficient. Eliminate (B). Now try both statements

together. If $x^2 - 3$ is an even number and $x + 2$ is an odd number, then both 5 and 9 are still acceptable values of x. Both statements together are insufficient; the answer is (E).

6. E Statement (1) provides information regarding the time it took Madeline to run the race, but does not tell you anything regarding either the rate or the distance. Statement (1) is insufficient, so eliminate (A) and (D). Statement (2) provides you with the average speed for the first mile only, but does not provide any information for any subsequent miles, so it is possible that Madeline ran any number of miles after that. Statement (2) is insufficient, so eliminate (B). Combine the two statements to see whether it is possible to answer the question. Statements (1) and (2) combined indicate that Madeline ran for a total of 3 hours, and that she ran at a rate of 8 miles per hour for the first mile. Plug In for her rate for the final two hours. If she ran at a speed of 10 miles per hour for the last two hours, then she would have run a total of 28 miles, and the answer to the question is "yes." Alternatively, if she ran at a rate of 5 miles per hour for the last two hours, then she would have run a total of 18 miles. This produces a "no" answer, so both statements together are insufficient. So the answer is (E).

7. A Plug In for x in statement (1). If $x = 4$, then $x^2 = 16$. 16 is a multiple of 8, so this produces a "yes" answer. Plug In again for x. If $x = 12$, then $x^2 = 144$. 144 is a multiple of 8, so this also produces a "yes" answer. In fact any value of x that is a multiple of 4 when squared will be a multiple of 16, and thus also a multiple of 8. Statement (1) is sufficient, so eliminate (B), (C), and (E). Plug In for x in statement (2). If $x = 2$, then $x^2 = 4$. 4 is not a multiple of 8, so this produces a "no" answer. Plug In again for x. If $x = 4$, then $x^2 = 16$. 16 is a multiple of 8, so this produces a "yes" answer. Statement (2) is insufficient, so eliminate (D).

8. B Simplify the first part of statement (1). If $x^2 < 16$, then $-4 < x < 4$. Now Plug In values for x and y in statement (1). If $x = -3$ and $y = -\frac{1}{3}$, then $\frac{x}{y} = 9$. This produces a "yes" answer to the question. If $x = -3$ and $y = \frac{1}{3}$, then $\frac{x}{y} = -9$. This produces a "no" answer, so statement (1) is insufficient. Eliminate (A) and (D). Simplify the second part of statement (2). If $1 < 2y < 4$, then you can divide the equation by 2 to get $\frac{1}{2} < y < 2$. If $x > 16$, and $\frac{1}{2} < y < 2$, then it must be true that $\frac{x}{y} > \frac{16}{2}$, or 8. It is not possible to Plug In either a greater value or a negative value for y in order to get a smaller result, nor is it possible to Plug In a smaller value for x, so statement (2) is sufficient.

9. C The question asks whether $x = \sqrt{25}$, or in other words, does $x = 5$? Factor the equation in statement (1) to solve for x, so that you have $(x - 5)(x + 2)$. This means that $x = 5$ or $x = -2$. Statement (1) is insufficient, so eliminate (A) and (D). Statement (2) indicates that $x^2 = 5$, so $x = 5$ or $x = -5$. Statement (2) is insufficient, so eliminate (B). Combine the two statements to see whether they are sufficient when used together. According to statement (1), $x = 5$ or $x = -2$, and according to statement (2), $x = 5$ or $x = -5$, so the only value that works for both statements is $x = 5$. This produces a "yes" answer to the question, so statements (1) and (2) together are sufficient.

10. **D** Plug In for n in statement (1). If $n = \frac{1}{4}$, then $n^2 = \frac{1}{16}$ and $\sqrt{n} = \frac{1}{2}$. $\frac{1}{2}$ is greater than $\frac{1}{4}$, so this produces a "no" answer to the question. Any number that fits statement (1) will also be a positive fraction less than one, and the square root of a fraction is always bigger than the fraction itself, so statement (1) is sufficient. Eliminate (B), (C), and (E). Plug In for statement (2). If $n = \frac{1}{4}$, then $n^3 = \frac{1}{64}$ and $\sqrt{n} = \frac{1}{2}$. Any value of n that fits statement (2) will also be a positive fraction less than 1, so the square root of n will always be greater than n. Statement (2) is sufficient, so the answer is (D).

11. **C** Plug In for p and r in statement (1). If $r = -2$, then $p = 2$. This produces a "no" answer to the question. If $r = 8$, then $p = 7$, and this produces a "yes" answer. Statement (1) is insufficient. Eliminate (A) and (D). Plug In for p and r in statement (2). If $r = -3$, then $p = 6$, and this produces a "no" answer. If $r = 4$ then $p = -1$, and this produces a "yes" answer. Statement (2) is insufficient, so you can eliminate (B). Now combine the two statements to see whether they are sufficient when used together. You now have two equations with the same two variables, so you can solve for each of them (The first step is to rearrange the equations so that you can stack and add or subtract them. Statement (1) becomes $2p - r = 6$, and statement (2) becomes $p + r = 3$. If you add the two equations, you have $3p = 9$, so $p = 3$. Plug 3 back into the first equation in place of p, and you have $6 - r = 6$, so $r = 0$). Statements (1) and (2) together are sufficient, so the answer is (C).

12. **C** Plug In for p, q, and r in statement (1). If $p = -2$, $q = -3$ and $r = -4$, then you have $(-2)(-3) < (-2)(-4)$ or $6 < 8$. Since $(-2) > (-3) > (-4)$, the answer to the question is "yes." If $p = -5$, $q = -3$ and $r = -4$, then you have $(-5)(-3) < (-5)(-4)$, or $15 < 20$. Now answer the question. Does $(-5) > (-3) > (-4)$? No. So statement (1) is insufficient. Note that it is impossible to Plug In values of q that are less than the assigned values of r. However, you do not have any information concerning the value of p. Eliminate (A) and (D). Plug In for statement (2). If $p = -2$, $q = -3$, and $r = -4$, then you have $(-2)(-4) < (-3)(-4)$, or $8 < 12$. Since $(-2) > (-3) > (-4)$, the answer to the question is "yes." Plug In again. If $p = -3$, $q = -4$ and $r = -2$, then you have $(-3)(-2) < (-4)(-2)$, or $6 < 8$. This statement produces a "no" answer, so statement (2) is insufficient. Eliminate (B). Note that if statement (2) is true, p must be greater than q, but you have no information regarding the value of r. Combine the two statements to see whether they are sufficient when used together. According to the information provided in statement (1), q must be greater than r, and according to statement (2), p must be greater than q. Thus, you can write $p > q > r$. The two statements together are sufficient, so the answer is (C).

13. **E** Statement (1) provides no information about d at all, so it is insufficient. Eliminate (A) and (D). Simplify the equation in statement (2) by multiplying both sides by 4, so that you have $b + c + d + e = 40$. You still don't know whether $d = 20$. Statement (2) is insufficient, so eliminate (B). Combine the two statements to see whether they are sufficient when used together. Plug In. If $c = 10$, and $e = 2$, then $b = 8$. Thus $8 + 10 + 2 + d = 40$, so $d = 20$. This produces a "yes" answer. Plug In again to see whether this works in all cases. If $c = 20$ and $e = 5$, then $b = 15$, then $20 + 5 + 15 + d = 40$, so $d = 0$. This produces a "no" answer, so both statements together are insufficient.

14. **D** If $c(a - 8b) = 0$, and c is a positive integer, then c does not equal 0. So in order for this to be true, $a - 8b = 0$. Add $8b$ to both sides to get $a = 8b$. Now divide both sides by b and you have $\dfrac{a}{b} = 8$. Statement (1) is sufficient, so eliminate (B), (C), and (E). Examine statement (2) to see whether it is sufficient. If $48b = 6a$, then if you divide both sides by 6, the result is $8b = a$, or $\dfrac{a}{b} = 8$. Statement (2) is sufficient, so the answer is (D).

15. **D** If statement (1) is true, then there is no way to Plug In equal values for x and y. Since $\dfrac{x}{y}$ is negative, one value must always be positive and the other negative. Statement (1) is sufficient, so eliminate (B), (C), and (E). Simplify statement (2) by multiplying both sides by 2, so that you have $x - y < -4$. In order for x and y to be equal, the difference between the two numbers would have to be 0, so this yields a "no" answer. Statement (2) is sufficient, so the answer is (D).

16. **D** The first step is to put all of the variables on the same side of the equation in statement (1). Subtract yz from both sides so that you have $5xz - yz = 12$. Factor out z on the left hand side of the equation and you have $z(5x - y) = 12$. This produces a "yes" answer, so statement (1) is sufficient. Eliminate (B), (C), and (E). Statement (2) provides values for xz and yz. Distribute the z in the original equation so that this information will be more useful. The question now becomes, does $5xz - yz = 12$? Substitute the values in statement (2) for xz and yz, so that you have $5(4.2) - 9 = 12$. This produces a "yes" answer, so statement (2) is sufficient.

17. **B** Plug In for m in statement (1). If $m = 2$, then $\dfrac{m^2}{-3} = -\dfrac{4}{3}$, which is less than 0. This produces a "yes" answer to the question. If $m = -2$, then $\dfrac{m^2}{-3}$ still equals $-\dfrac{4}{3}$, but this produces a "no" answer. Statement (1) is insufficient, so eliminate (A) and (D). Plug In for statement (2). If $m = 2$, then $(-m)(-5) = (-2)(-5) = 10$, which is greater than 0. This produces a "yes" answer. You cannot Plug In a negative number for m, or $(-m)(-5)$ becomes negative, which contradicts statement (2). So m must be greater than 0 and statement (2) is sufficient.

18. **C** Plug In for a and x in statement (1). If $\sqrt{x} = 3$, then $x = 9$, and $x^2 = 81$, so $a = 81$. This produces a "no" answer to the question. If $\sqrt{x} = 2$, then $x = 4$, and $x^2 = 16$, so $a = 16$. This produces a "yes" answer to the question, so statement (1) is insufficient. Eliminate (A) and (D). Statement (2) gives you no information about the value of a, so statement (2) is insufficient. Eliminate (B). Combine the two statements to see whether they are sufficient when used together. According to statement (1), a is either even or odd depending upon whether $\sqrt{x}$ is even or odd. According to statement (2), $\sqrt{x}$ is even, so a must also be even.

19. **B** In order for $\dfrac{81}{3^{y-2}}$ to be less than 9, it must be true that 3^{y-2} is greater than 9, because $\dfrac{81}{9} = 9$. 9 is equal to 3^2, so 3^{y-2} must be greater than 3^2. Thus y must be greater than 4. Statement (1) only indicates that y is less than 5. The question does not specify that y must be an integer, so if y could equal either 4.5 or 3, statement (1) is insufficient. Eliminate (A) and (D). Statement (2) indicates that $3^y < 27$, so y must be less than 3. Since $y < 3$, the answer to the question will always be "no." Statement (2) is sufficient, so the answer is (B).

20. **C** The question asks whether the area of the circle is greater than 25π. In order for the area to be greater than 25π, the radius must be greater than 5, so the diameter must be greater than 10. Statement (1) tells you that the distance from A to B is equal to 10, but does not provide any information as to whether $\overline{AB}$ is equal to the diameter of the circle. If $\overline{AB}$ is the diameter, then the radius of the circle is equal to 5, and the area is equal to, not greater than, 25π. However, if $\overline{AB}$ is not equal to the diameter of the circle, then the diameter is greater than 10, because the diameter is always the longest line that can be drawn through a circle. If the diameter is greater than 10, then the radius is greater than 5, and the area of the circle is greater than 25π. Statement (1) is insufficient, so eliminate (A) and (D). Statement (2) only indicates that $\overline{AB}$ does not go through point O, which means only that $\overline{AB}$ is not equal to the diameter of the circle. However, this statement provides no information concerning the length of $\overline{AB}$, so statement (2) is insufficient. Eliminate (B). Combine the two statements to see whether they are sufficient when used together. If $\overline{AB}$ is equal to 10, and $\overline{AB}$ is not the diameter, then the diameter is greater than 10, so the radius is greater than 5 and the area is greater than 25π. Statements (1) and (2) when used together are sufficient, so the answer is (C).

21. **E** Plug In for m and n in statement (1). If $m = 9$ and $n = 3$, then $\dfrac{m}{n} = 3$. This produces a "no" answer to the question. However, if $m = -9$ and $n = -3$, then $\dfrac{m}{n}$ is still equal to 3, the answer to the question is "yes." Statement (1) is insufficient, so eliminate (A) and (D). Plug In for statement (2). If $m = 9$ and $n = 3$, then $m^2 - n^3 = 81 - 9$, or 72, which is greater than 0. This produces a "no" answer. However, if $m = -9$ and $n = -3$, then $m^2 - n^2$ is still equal to 72, but the answer is "yes." Statement (2) is insufficient, so eliminate (B). For both statements, $m = 9$ and $n = 3$ worked, as did $m = -9$ and $n = -3$, so both statements together are insufficient.

22. **B** Plug In for x and y in statement (1). If $x = 6$ and $y = 4$, then $\dfrac{x}{y}$ is not an integer, so this produces a "no" answer. If $x = 8$ and $y = 4$, then $\dfrac{x}{y} = 2$, so this produces a "yes" answer. Statement (1) is insufficient, so eliminate (A) and (D). Statement (2) indicates that y is prime, and 2 is the only even number that is also prime, so y must equal 2. The question states that x is an even number, and any even number when divided by 2 produces an integer, so statement (2) is sufficient.

23. **C** Plug In for the two consecutive prime numbers in statement (1). If the two numbers are 3 and 5, then $x = 2$, so this produces a "yes" answer. If the two numbers are 2 and 3, then $x = 1$, so this produces a "no" answer. Statement (1) is insufficient, so eliminate (A) and (D). Statement (2) only indicates that x is greater than 1, so x could be even or odd. Statement (2) is insufficient, so eliminate (B). Combine the two statements to see whether they are sufficient when used together. If x is equal to the difference between two consecutive prime numbers, and it is also greater than 1, then the two numbers cannot be 2 and 3. The difference between any two consecutive primes greater than 2 and 3 will always be even, because an odd number minus an odd number will always equal an even number. Statements (1) and (2) together are sufficient.

24. **C** Plug In for the number of red, green and blue marbles in statement (1). If there are 12 blue marbles, then there are 6 green marbles and at most 4 red marbles. That means that the greatest possibility of pulling out a red marble is $\dfrac{4}{20}$ or $\dfrac{1}{5}$. This yields a "no" answer. If there are 8 blue marbles, then there are 4 green marbles, and at most 8 red marbles. If there are 20 marbles total in the bag, this yields a probability of $\dfrac{8}{20}$ or $\dfrac{2}{5}$ that John will select a red marble. This produces a "yes" answer. Statement (1) is insufficient, so eliminate (A) and (D). According to statement (2) there is a $\dfrac{3}{5}$ probability that the marble will not be blue. That means that there is a $\dfrac{2}{5}$ probability that it will be blue, and a $\dfrac{3}{5}$ probability that it will be either red or green. However, there is no way to solve specifically for the probability that a red marble will be selected, so statement (2) is insufficient. Combine the two statements to see whether they are sufficient when used together. $\dfrac{2}{5}$ of the marbles are blue, and there are twice as many blue marbles as green marbles, so the probability that John will draw a green marble is half the probability that he will draw a blue marble, so he has a $\dfrac{1}{5}$ probability of drawing a green marble. Thus, he has a $\dfrac{3}{5}$ probability of drawing a blue or a green marble, and the probability that he will choose a red marble will be $\dfrac{2}{5}$. That answers the question with a "yes," so statements (1) and (2) together are sufficient.

25. **A** Put the numbers in the question in fractional form so that they are easier to work with. $2^{-x} = \dfrac{1}{2^x}$ and $0.25 = \dfrac{1}{4}$, or $\dfrac{1}{2^2}$. Thus, a "yes" response means that $x < 2$, and a "no" response means that $x \geq 2$. Put the numbers in statement (1) in fractional form as well. $2^{-(x-2)} = \dfrac{1}{2^{x-2}}$, and $0.5 = \dfrac{1}{2}$, so if $\dfrac{1}{2^{x-2}} < \dfrac{1}{2}$, then $x - 2 > 1$, and $x > 3$. This produces a "no" response, so statement (1) is sufficient. Eliminate (B), (C), and (E). Statement (2) indicates that $\dfrac{2}{3}x > 1$, so, by solving for x, you can see only that $x > \dfrac{3}{2}$. It is not clear that $x \geq 2$, or that $x < 2$, so statement (2) is insufficient.

Functions

1. **B** All bacteria strains will have at least a population of 500, because the equation is $500 + 2^x$, so if you subtract 500 from a population that is valid, the remainder should be a power of 2. Check each of the answer choices. Choice (A): $504 - 500 = 4$. $2^2 = 4$, so 504 is a valid population. Eliminate (A). Choice (B): $524 - 500 = 24$. Because 24 is not a power of 2, this is not a valid population, so (B) is the answer.

2. **A** Statement (1) means that $x - 2 = 2$, which means that $x = 4$, and this is sufficient. Eliminate (B), (C), and (E). Statement (2) states that $y@x = 2@2$, which means that $y@x = 2 - 2 = 0$, which means that $y = x$, but since it does not state what the value of x is, it is not sufficient.

3. **D** First, write the equation in terms of h and j. The new equation is $\dfrac{h+j}{h^2 - j^2} = 1$. Factor the denominator, so that you have $\dfrac{h+j}{(h+j)(h-j)} = 1$. Now cancel the $h + j$ on both the top and bottom, so that you have $\dfrac{1}{h-j} = 1$. Now multiply both sides of the equation by $(h - j)$. The result is $1 = h - j$. Now solve for h by adding j to both sides. The result is $h = j + 1$.

4. **D** Statement (1) means that $2 = (m - 1)$, which means that $m = 3$. Statement (1) is sufficient, so eliminate (B), (C), and (E). Statement (2) means that $((m!)!) = 6(5!)$, which means that $(m!)! = 6(5!) = 6!$, and that $m! = 6$. This is sufficient. Knowing that factorials get very large very quickly, you can actually write out the options: $1! = 1$, $2! = (2)(1) = 2$, $3! = (3)(2)(1) = 6$. Therefore $m = 3$. Since statements (1) and (2) are both sufficient, the answer is (D).

5. **E** Start with the numbers in parentheses. $3 \; \blacksquare \; 48 = (\sqrt{3} + \sqrt{48})^2$, or $(\sqrt{3} + 4\sqrt{3})^2$. Add the like terms to get $(5\sqrt{2})^2$. Now square the expression to get 75. Because $(3 \; \blacksquare \; 48) = 75$, you can now use this new value to find $(3 \; \blacksquare \; 48) \; \blacksquare \; 3$, or $75 \; \blacksquare \; 3$. Plug these numbers into the formula so that you have $(\sqrt{75} + \sqrt{3})^2$. Simplify this expression to get $(5\sqrt{3} + \sqrt{3})^2$. Add the like terms to get $(6\sqrt{3})^2$. Now square the expression to get 108.

6. **D** Statement (1) states that $f(y) = 3((10^2 + 10) + 30)$, and thus $f(y) = 3((110)+30) = 3(140) = 420$. This is sufficient. Eliminate (B), (C), and (E). Statement (2) states that $f(y) = f(f(4))$, which is also sufficient because $f(y) = f(4^2+4) = f(20) = 20^2 + 20 = 420$. Since statements (1) and (2) are both sufficient alone, the answer is (D).

7. **E** Plug In -6 for p and 2 for r in the formula. The result is $-6\left(\dfrac{-6}{2(2)} - 2\right) - \left(\dfrac{24}{(2)(-6)}\right)$. Simplify the equation inside the first set of parentheses, so that you have $\left(\dfrac{-6}{4} - 2\right)$, or $\left(\dfrac{-6}{4} - \dfrac{8}{4}\right) = -\dfrac{14}{4}$. Now you have $-6\left(\dfrac{-14}{4}\right) - \left(\dfrac{24}{-12}\right)$, or $\dfrac{84}{4} - (-2)$, which can be rewritten as $\dfrac{84}{4} + \dfrac{8}{4} = \dfrac{92}{4} = 23$.

8. **B** Statement (1) states that p is greater than q, which is insufficient. If p were equal to 4 and q equal to 2, then their Elbow Composites would be $(2) - (2) = 0$ and $(2) - (2) = 0$, respectively, and thus the two would be equal. This provides a "no" answer to the question. However, if p were equal to 10 and q equal to 4, then their Elbow Composites would be $(5)(2) - (5 + 2) = 3$ and $(2) - (2) = 0$, respectively, and thus the Elbow Composite of p is greater and the answer to the question is "yes." Since statement (1) is not sufficient, eliminate (A) and (D). Statement (2) states that p is twice q, which means that p is a multiple of q, which is sufficient. For example, remember that if p were equal to 4 and q equal to 2, then their Elbow Composites would be equal and the answer is "no." If p were equal to 20 and q equal to 10, then their Elbow Composites would be $(5)(2) - (5 + 2) = 3$ and $(5)(2) - (5 + 2) = 3$, respectively, and thus they would also be equal. Indeed, since p is a multiple of q and both p and q are even, then they will always have the same prime factors, and thus their Elbow Composites must be equal in all cases. Since statement (1) is not sufficient and statement (2) is, then the answer is (B).

9. **C** Start with $-2 \venus 3$. Plug In -2 for a and 3 for b in the formula. Now you have $-2\left((-2)^2 \times 3 - \dfrac{18}{(-2) \times 3}\right) + 27$. First, simplify the equation inside the parentheses, so that you have $-2(12 - (-3)) + 27$, or $-2(15) + 27 = -3$. Notice that -3 is (D). However, the question is only partially completed, so (D) is a trap answer. The question asks for $(2 \venus 3) \venus 2$. You now know that $(2 \venus 3) = -3$, so you are now looking for $-3 \venus 2$. Plug -3 in for a and 2 in for b in the equation. The resulting equation is $-2\left((-3)^2 \times 2 - \dfrac{18}{(-3) \times 2}\right) + 27$. Again, start by simplifying the equation inside the parentheses. You now have $-2(18 - (-3)) + 27$, or $-2(21) + 27 = -15$.

10. **D** Statement (1) provides two equations, which together are sufficient. Setting up a system of equations provides:

$$2w + 3v = 19$$
$$w - v = 7$$

If the second equation is multiplied by 2, the result is:

$$2w + 3v = 19$$
$$- (2w - 2v = 14)$$
$$5v = 5$$
$$v = 1$$

Thus, since $y = 1$, $x = 8$, and their difference is positive. Eliminate (B), (C), and (E). Statement (2) provides $w^2 - v^2 = 63$, which is a difference of squares. Factoring out the equation provides that $(w + v)(w - v) = 63$. Now, since w and v must be positive integers, $(w + v)$ and $(w - v)$ must also be integers. The factors of 63 are 1 and 63, 3 and 21, and 7 and 9. Since w and v are both positive, their sum will be greater than their difference regardless of their values. Thus, you can try the pairs of factors. If $(w + v) = 63$ and $(w - v) = 1$, then $2w = 64$, and thus $w = 32$ and $v = 31$. However, if $(w + v) = 21$ and $(w - v) = 3$, then $2w = 24$, and thus $w = 12$ and $v = 9$. Finally, if $(w + v) = 9$ and $(w - v) = 7$, then $2w = 16$, and $w = 8$ and $v = 1$. Thus, since in all three cases the difference between w and v is positive, w&v must be an alpha. Since statements (1) and (2) are each sufficient alone, the answer is (D).

Roots

1. **C** Simplify under the root. $\sqrt{50 + 25} = \sqrt{75}$, which can also be written as $\sqrt{25 \times 3}$. Because $25 = 5^2$, you can remove a 5 from beneath the root, so that you now have $5\sqrt{3}$. The answer is (C).

2. **B** Statement (1) states that x squared equals 625, which means that x could equal either 25 or –25; statement (1) therefore is insufficient. Eliminate (A) and (D). Statement (2) states that the square root of x is equal to 5, which means that x equals 25; statement (2) therefore is sufficient. Thus, since statement (1) is not sufficient and statement (2) is sufficient, the answer is (B).

3. **C** Reorder the information under the root, so that you can find the greatest common factor. $\sqrt{(25)(22) - (30)(5)} = \sqrt{(25)(22) - (2)(3)(5)(5)}$. Now you can make the second part of the equation more like the first part by rewriting the equation again so that you have $\sqrt{(25)(22) - (6)(25)}$. Next, factor out the 25, so that you have $\sqrt{25(22 - 6)}$. $25 = 5^2$, so you can remove a 5 from under the root. The equation is now $5\sqrt{22 - 6}$, or $5\sqrt{16}$, which can be simplified to $5 \times 4 = 20$.

4. **B**   First, round each number in the equation to the nearest whole number. 23.09 is approximately 23, and 5.13 is approximately 5, so 23.09 − 5.13 is approximately 18. 0.96 + 1.21 is about 2, so you can rewrite the equation as $\sqrt{\dfrac{18}{2}}$, or $\sqrt{9}$, so the result is approximately 3.

5. **D**   Statement (1) states that a^2 is greater than a^3, which means that a must be less than 1. For example, if a were equal to 2, then 2^2 would equal 4 and 2^3 would equal 8, thus not satisfying statement (1). On the other hand, if a were equal to $\dfrac{1}{2}$, then a^2 would be $\dfrac{1}{4}$, which is greater than a^3, which is equal to $\dfrac{1}{8}$, which does satisfy statement (1). Therefore, since numbers greater than 1 do not satisfy statement 1, but numbers smaller than 1 do, statement (1) is sufficient to answer the question of whether a is greater than 1. Eliminate (B), (C), and (E). Statement (2) states that the third root of a is greater than a, which also means that a must be less than 1. For example, if a were equal to $\dfrac{1}{8}$, then $a^{\frac{1}{3}}$ would equal $\dfrac{1}{2}$, which is greater than a, thus satisfying statement (1) and showing that a is not greater than 1. However, numbers greater than or equal to 1 do not satisfy statement 1. For example, if a were equal to 8, then $a^{\frac{1}{3}}$ would equal 2, which is not greater than a; in fact, statement (2) will never be satisfied by any number greater than 1. Thus, statement (2) is sufficient. Both statements (1) and (2) are sufficient, so the answer is (D).

6. **E**   Plug In for the value of the entire expression. If $\sqrt{\dfrac{p+q}{2}} = 3$, then $p = 3$, and $\dfrac{p+q}{2} = 9$. That means that $p + q = 18$, so if $p = 3$, then $q = 15$. When you Plug In $p = 3$, one of the answer choices should give you the target of $q = 15$. $3\sqrt{2}$ is not equal to 15, so eliminate (A). $3\sqrt{3}$ is also not equal to 15, so (B) is incorrect. $3^2 - 2 = 7$, so eliminate (C). $2(3)^2 = 18$, so (D) is not the answer. $2(3)^2 - 3 = 15$, so (E) is correct. Alternatively, you could solve this problem algebraically. First, square both sides of the equation so that you have $\dfrac{p+q}{2} = p^2$. Next, multiply both sides by 2, so that the equation is now $p + q = 2p^2$. Then subtract p from both sides, so that the result is $q = 2p^2 - p$.

7. **A**   Statement (1) states that b is equal to c, which means that $\sqrt{b} = \sqrt{c}$, and thus $\sqrt{b}$ may be substituted for $\sqrt{c}$ thus showing that since $\sqrt{b} \times \sqrt{b} = b$, then it must be true that $\sqrt{b} \times \sqrt{c} = b$, which means that statement (1) is sufficient. Eliminate (B), (C), and (E). Statement (2) provides two equations, which is normally sufficient to find the values of two variables. However, here these two equations are identical. If $91 - 65b = 26c$ is ordered the same way as the first equation, then it becomes $65b + 26c = 91$, which is merely the first equation multiplied by 13. Thus statement (2) does not provide sufficient information to determine if b is equal to c and thus whether $\sqrt{b} \times \sqrt{c} = b$. Therefore, since statement (1) is sufficient, but statement (2) is not, the answer is (A).

8. **A** First, remove the radicals by squaring both sides: $(\sqrt{3x} - 2)(\sqrt{3x} - 2) = (\sqrt{4x + 3})(\sqrt{4x + 3})$, or $3x - 4\sqrt{3x} + 4 = 4x + 3$. Next, subtract $3x$ from both sides so that you have $-4\sqrt{3x} + 4 = x + 3$. Now subtract 4 from both sides to get the radical by itself on the left side of the equation. The result is $-4\sqrt{3x} = x - 1$. Square both sides again to remove the remaining radical so that you have $(16)(3x) = (x - 1)^2$, or $48x = (x - 1)(x - 1)$. Multiply out the right side of the equation so that it becomes $48x = x^2 - 2x + 1$. Now set the equation equal to zero by subtracting $48x$ from both sides of the equation. The result is $x^2 - 50x + 1 = 0$. The question asks you to find the value of $x^2 - 50x$, so subtract 1 from both sides of the equation to get $x^2 - 50x = -1$.

9. **A** Statement (1) states that the square root of k is equal to the reciprocal of the square root of l, which means that the product of k and l is equal to 1. For example, if k were equal to 9, then $9^{\frac{1}{2}} = l^{-\frac{1}{2}}$, and $\sqrt{9} = \frac{1}{\sqrt{l}}$, and $\sqrt{l} = \frac{1}{\sqrt{9}}$, and $\sqrt{l} = \frac{1}{3}$, and finally, that $l = \frac{1}{9}$. This means that k and l are reciprocals and thus that their product is equal to 1. In fact, this must always be so, as the only difference between $k^{\frac{1}{2}}$ and $l^{-\frac{1}{2}}$ is the negative exponent, which means that l must be a reciprocal of k. Thus, statement (1) is sufficient. Eliminate (B), (C), and (E). Statement (2) states that k is a multiple of l; which is not enough information to answer the question. For example, using the same numbers chosen for statement (1), 9 divided by $\frac{1}{9}$ equals 81, which is an integer, and thus the product of k and l could equal 1. However, if one were to use different numbers, say 6 and 2, while 6 divided by 2 equals 3, which is an integer, the product of 6 and 2 is 12, not 1. Since given statement (2), the answer to the question could be either yes or no, the information is not sufficient. Statement (1) is sufficient and statement (2) is not, and the answer is (A).

10. **E** Work the problem in steps. If $p = \sqrt{\left(\frac{16}{25}\right)}$, then $p = \frac{4}{5}$, and $\sqrt{p} = \sqrt{\frac{4}{5}}$. Separate the radicals on the top and bottom of the fraction in order to simplify: $\frac{\sqrt{4}}{\sqrt{5}} = \frac{2}{\sqrt{5}}$. Now multiply the fraction by $\frac{\sqrt{5}}{\sqrt{5}}$ in order to remove the radical from the denominator $\frac{2}{\sqrt{5}} \times \frac{\sqrt{5}}{\sqrt{5}} = \frac{2\sqrt{5}}{5} = \sqrt{p}$. The question asks for $5\sqrt{p}$, so multiply the entire fraction by 5, so that you have $\frac{5 \times 2\sqrt{5}}{5}$, or $2\sqrt{5}$.

11. **A** Statement (1) states that n is equal to 50% of m, which means that $m = 2n$. This information by itself is sufficient as it tells you that $\sqrt[3]{2n} \div \sqrt[3]{n} = \sqrt[3]{\frac{2n}{n}} = \sqrt[3]{2}$. Eliminate (B), (C), and (E). Statement (2) states that $n^2 = 2m$, which is insufficient to answer the question as $m = \frac{n^2}{2}$ and thus $\sqrt[3]{\frac{n^2}{2}} \div \sqrt[3]{n} = \sqrt[3]{\frac{\frac{n^2}{2}}{n}} = \sqrt[3]{\frac{n^2}{2n}} = \sqrt[3]{\frac{n}{2}}$. Therefore, since you cannot determine a value for n, you cannot determine the answer to the question. Therefore, statement (1) is sufficient and statement (2) is not, and the answer is (A).

12. **C** First, combine $\sqrt{2}$ and $\sqrt{8}$ under the same root, so that the expression is now $(\sqrt{2 \times 8})(\sqrt[3]{4})$, or $(\sqrt{16})(\sqrt[3]{4}) = 4(\sqrt[3]{4})$. The answer choices are written in powers of 2, so rewrite the expression in powers of 2. $4(\sqrt[3]{4}) = (2)^2(\sqrt[3]{(2)^2})$. Next, write the root in terms of a fractional exponent, so that you have $(2)^2(2)^{\frac{2}{3}}$. Finally, add the exponents so that you have $2^{\frac{8}{3}}$. The answer is (C).

13. **E** Statement (1) states that p is equal to the square of q, which is not sufficient to answer the question, since q could be positive or negative. For example, if p were equal to 9, q could equal either 3 or –3, and thus pq could equal either 27 or –27. Thus, statement (1) is not sufficient. Eliminate (A) and (D). Statement (2) states that the third root of pq is a non-zero number, which is not sufficient, as it only means that neither p nor q can be 0; p could be positive and q negative, p negative and q positive, or both p and q could be either positive or negative. Since statement (2) is not sufficient, eliminate (B). When both statements are considered together, as a square, p must be non-negative and $\sqrt[3]{pq} = \sqrt[3]{q^2 q} = \sqrt[3]{q^3} = q$, thus q must not equal 0. Thus while p must be non-negative, q can either be positive or negative. Therefore, it cannot be determined whether their product is non-positive. Since statements (1) and (2) are insufficient alone, and insufficient when combined, the answer is (E).

14. **C** First, combine the numbers in the numerator under the same root, so that you have $\frac{\sqrt{7 \times 5 \times 2}}{\sqrt[3]{70}} = \frac{\sqrt{70}}{\sqrt[3]{70}}$. This is also equal to $\frac{70^{\frac{1}{2}}}{70^{\frac{1}{3}}}$. Next, subtract the exponents in order to simplify the expression. The result is $70^{\frac{1}{6}}$, so the answer is (C).

15. **C** Statement (1) provides three variables and three equations, which would appear to be enough, but is not. The first equation states that y squared equals x. This means that y could be either positive or negative and that x must be positive. Combining this with the second equation shows that $4(y^2) = yz$, and thus $4y = z$, which is the same as the third equation. Thus, statement (1) is not sufficient. Eliminate (A) and (D). Statement (2) states that the square root of x is equal to y. This means that both x and y must be non-negative, but says nothing about z. Statement (2) is not sufficient. Eliminate (B). Combining statements (1) and (2) tells you that in the third equation, $z = 4y$, if y is non-negative, then z must also be non-negative. Since statements (1) and (2) are both insufficient on their own, but sufficient when combined, the answer is (C).

Exponents

1. **D** Find the greatest common factor in the numerator. 37 is the greatest common factor, so you can rewrite the equation as follows: $\dfrac{37(37-2)}{37}$. Divide both the numerator and denominator by 37, so that the result is simply $37 - 2 = 35$. The answer is (D).

2. **A** Plug -2 into the equation in place of a. The equation now becomes $\dfrac{2(-2)^2}{-4}$, or $\dfrac{2(4)}{-4}$, which simplifies to $\dfrac{8}{-4}$, or -2.

3. **D** Statement (1) is sufficient. The first several powers of 4 are as follows: $4^1 = 4$, $4^2 = 16$, $4^3 = 64$, $4^4 = 256$, $4^5 = 1024$. The next power of 4 will be more than 4,000, so for 4^n to be less than 1,500, n must be less than or equal to 5. So the yes/no issue is whether you can tell for certain that n is greater than 5, or less than or equal to 5. Because 4^{n-1} is less than 1,000, $n - 1$ must be less than or equal to 4. Thus n must be less than or equal to 5, which answers the question. Eliminate (B), (C), and (E). Statement (2) is sufficient. This fact tells you that the value of 4^{n+2} exceeds the value of 4^n by 240. Looking back at the powers of 4 listed for statement (1), the only powers for which this will be true are 4^4 and 4^2. $256 - 16 = 240$. Thus $n = 2$, which answers the question.

4. **C** The left side of the inequality is written in powers of 3, so rewrite the right side of the inequality so that it is also in powers of 3. $81 = 3^4$, so you can write the inequality as $3^x < (3^4)^5$. Now multiply the exponents on the right side of the inequality and you have $3^x < 3^{20}$, so the largest possible value of x is 19.

5. **B** Statement (1) is insufficient. If x is a positive fraction, then you get a smaller number when exponents are applied to it. For example, if $x = \dfrac{1}{3}$, then $x^3 = \dfrac{1}{27}$, which is smaller, and the answer to the question is yes. But if x is a negative fraction and is raised to an odd exponent, the result will still be negative and now larger than x. For example, if $x = -\dfrac{1}{3}$, then $x^3 = -\dfrac{1}{27}$, which is larger, and the answer to the question is no. Since you can get both yes and no answers, statement (1) is insufficient and you should eliminate (A) and (D). Statement (2) is sufficient. When odd exponents

are applied to numbers less than –1, the results will still be negative, and will be smaller than what you began with. For example, if $x = -3$, then $x^3 = -27$, which is smaller. There are no exceptions to this rule, so the answer to the question is definitely "yes."

6. **A** The first number in the problem is in scientific notation, so write the second number in scientific notation also. $\$72,000,000 = \$7.2 \times 10^7$. You need to know how much more the company spent on research and development this year than it did last year, so subtract $\$4.8 \times 10^7$ from $\$7.2 \times 10^7$. The difference is $\$2.4 \times 10^7$, so in order to find out how much more each department received this year than it did last year, divide $\$2.4 \times 10^7$ by $\$1.2 \times 10^2$. $\dfrac{\$2.4 \times 10^7}{\$1.2 \times 10^2} = \$2.0 \times 10^5$, so the answer is (A).

7. **B** $27 = 3^3$, so you can rewrite 27^{4a-10} as $\left(3^3\right)^{4a-10}$. Now multiply the exponents, so that you have 3^{12a-30}. Now the whole equation is $3^{12a-30} \times 3^{4a+2} = 81$. Note that both numbers on the left side of the equation have the same base, so you can add the exponents to get $3^{16a-28} = 81$. However, $81 = 3^4$, so you can also write $3^{16a-28} = 3^4$, which means that $16a - 28 = 4$, or $16a = 32$. Thus $a = 2$. Alternatively, you can Plug In The Answers for a.

8. **C** Statement (1) is insufficient. There are three possible ways for x^k to be equal to 1: $x = 1$; $k = 0$; or $x = -1$ and k is an even exponent. Only one of these possibilities ($k = 0$) gives an exact value of k. Statement (1) says that x is negative. That still leaves multiple possibilities for k, however. For example, x could be any negative number and k could be 0. But x could be –1 and k could be 2 or 4 or any even exponent. Since statement (1) is insufficient, eliminate (A) and (D). Statement (2) is insufficient. If x is greater than –1, that still leaves multiple possibilities for k. For example, x could be any positive number and k could be 0. Or x could be 1 and k could any number. Eliminate (B). Statements (1) and (2) together are sufficient. If x is negative and x is also greater than –1, then x cannot be either –1 or 1. Thus the only way for x^k to equal 1 is for k to be equal to 0.

9. **E** Simplify each of the answer choices to find the one that is not equal to x^{12}. Choice (A) is $x^4 \times x^8$. Here you are multiplying the variables, so add the exponents in order to simplify. The result is x^{12}, so eliminate (A). In order to simplify $\dfrac{x^{16}}{x^4}$, subtract the exponents. The result is x^{12}, so eliminate (B). In the expression $(x^3)^4$ the exponent in the parentheses is being raised to a power, so multiply the exponents in order to simplify the expression. The result is x^{12}, so eliminate (C). For (D), flip the fraction $\dfrac{1}{x^{-12}}$ in order to get rid of the negative exponent. The result is again x^{12}, so eliminate (D). $x^6 + x^6$ can only be simplified to $2x^6$, which is not equal to x^{12}.

10. **E** Statement (1) is insufficient. If $w^2 = 18$, then there are two possible values for w: $\sqrt{18}$ or $-\sqrt{18}$. Eliminate (A) and (D). Statement (2) is insufficient. If $\dfrac{w^3}{\sqrt{18}}$ is an integer, then w^2 divides evenly by $\sqrt{18}$. But there are many possibilities here. For example, w^2 could equal $5\sqrt{18}$ or $8\sqrt{18}$ or $22\sqrt{18}$ and so on. Taking the cube root of any of these examples would give the value of w, but they would all be different. Eliminate (B). Statements (1) and (2) together are also insufficient. From statement (1) you know that $w = \sqrt{18}$ or $-\sqrt{18}$. Statement (2) tells you that $\dfrac{w^3}{\sqrt{18}}$ is an integer, but that will be true for both $\sqrt{18}$ and $-\sqrt{18}$. $\sqrt{18}^3 = \sqrt{18} \times \sqrt{18} \times \sqrt{18} = 3\sqrt{18}$, which is divisible by $\sqrt{18}$. $\left(-\sqrt{18}\right)^3 = -\sqrt{18} \times -\sqrt{18} \times -\sqrt{18} = 3 \times -\sqrt{18} = -3\sqrt{18}$, which is divisible by $\sqrt{18}$. Thus, even with both facts, the value of w cannot be determined.

11. **B** Statement (1) is insufficient. Exponent rules tell you that when multiplying with a common base, add the exponents. Thus $3^y \times 3^{yz} = 3^{y+yz}$. To find the value of 3^{y+yz} you need to know the value of $y + yz$. Statement (1) only gives the value of yz. There are multiple values of y and z that can multiply to 6, so you can't solve for y, and therefore can't solve for $y + yz$. Since statement (1) is insufficient, eliminate (A) and (D). Statement (2) is sufficient. As explained for statement (1), you need to know the value of $y + yz$ to answer the question. By the distributive rule, $y(1 + z) = y + yz$, so $y + yz = 8$. Thus $3^y \times 3^{yz} = 3^8$.

12. **B** First, simplify the left side of the equation by multiplying the exponents, so that you have $5^{\frac{r}{8}} = 25$. 25 is also equal to 5^2, so you can now write $5^{\frac{r}{8}} = 5^2$. Thus, $\dfrac{r}{8} = 2$, so $r = 16$. The question asks for $\sqrt{r}$, and $\sqrt{16} = 4$, so the answer is (B).

13. **A** Statement (1) is sufficient. When an odd exponent such as 5 is applied to any number between –1 and 0, the result is a *larger* number. For example, if $z = -\dfrac{1}{2}$, then $z^5 = -\dfrac{1}{32}$, which is larger. Since that violates statement (1), z cannot be between –1 and 0. Eliminate (B), (C), and (E). Statement (2) is insufficient. Since raising any number (except 0) to an even exponent produces a positive result, this doesn't tell you whether z is between –1 and 0. It could be, but it doesn't have to be.

14. **C** Both 27 and 81 are powers of 3, so rewrite the expression in terms of 3, so that you have $(3)^{-4} (3^3)^{-3} (3^4)^{-2}$. Next, distribute the exponents, so that you have $(3)^{-4} (3)^{-9} (3)^{-6}$, or $(3)^{-21}$. In order to remove a negative exponent, you need to flip the fraction, so $(3)^{-21} = \left(\dfrac{1}{3}\right)^{21}$.

15. **D** Statement (1) is sufficient. A negative exponent indicates the reciprocal of the positive exponent. So $y^{-x} = \dfrac{1}{y^x}$. If $\dfrac{1}{y^x} = 4$ then $y^x = \dfrac{1}{4}$. Since statement (1) is sufficient, eliminate (B), (C), and (E). Statement (2) is sufficient. Given values for both x and y, the value of y^x can be found. $y = \dfrac{1}{2}$ and $x = \dfrac{1}{y}$ then $x = \dfrac{1}{\frac{1}{2}} = 2$. Thus $y^x = \left(\dfrac{1}{2}\right)^2 = \dfrac{1}{4}$.

Interest

1. **E** Plug In The Answers, starting with (C). If Rebekah had $168.00 in her account before the interest was added, then after the interest she would have ($168.00)(1.06) = $178.08. The actual amount she had in her account after interest was $178.61, so you need a slightly bigger number. Plug In (D). If Rebekah had $168.50 in her account, then after interest she would have ($168.50)(1.06) = $178.61.

2. **E** Plug In The Answers, starting with (C). If the total balance were $892.00, then 2 percent interest would be $17.84. This is less than $17.85, so eliminate (A), (B), and (C). Now check (D) to see if it is possible to get an acceptable smaller value for the total balance. 2% of $892.50 is $17.85. However, the question indicates that Jean paid *more* than $17.85 in interest, so (D) is too small. The correct answer must be (E). Alternatively, you could solve this problem algebraically. Set up the equation $\dfrac{2}{100}x = 17.85$, in which x represents the total balance. Now multiply both sides of the equation by 100 so that you have $2x = 1{,}785$ or $x = \dfrac{1785}{2}$, which is $892.50. The interest paid was slightly more than $17.85, so the balance must be slightly more than $892.50.

3. **D** Statement (1) provides the interest rate paid and thus is sufficient. To calculate interest, you can use the formula: $End = $Start(1+ i)n$ where i is the interest rate and n is the number of periods, in this case years. Here, since statement (1) gives the starting amount, the interest rate, and the number of periods, you can fill in the equation $300(1.02)4 = $324.73 and therefore it is sufficient to answer the question. Eliminate (B), (C), and (E). Statement (2) states the difference between the two amounts and is also sufficient. Here, you know that $300(1+ i)6 – $300(1+ i)4 = $13.12. Since there is only one variable in the equation, it can be solved and is sufficient. (Don't waste time actually solving it!) Since statements (1) and (2) are each sufficient alone to answer the question, the correct answer is (D).

4. **B**   The initial cost of the car was $12,500, and the value of Pam's trade-in covered 30 percent of the $12,500 miles. $12,500 \times 0.30 = 3,750$, so her trade-in covers $3,750 of the total cost, and $8,750 remain. Pam's down payment then covers 60 percent of the $8,750 remaining dollars. $8,750 \times 0.60 = 5,250$ so her down payment was $5,250. $8,750 - \$5,250 = 3,500$, so the loan is for $3,500. If the interest rate on the loan is 6 percent compounded annually, then Pam will pay $3,500 \times 0.06 = \$210$.

5. **A**   Statement (1) states that the MegaSaver account will pay 3% four times a year and InvestPro will pay 4% twice a year, which is sufficient. Here, you can use the equation $\$End = \$Start(1 + i)n$ and fill in the facts from statement (1) to find that MegaSaver will return $\$Start(1.03)(5)(4) = \$Start(1.81)$ and InvestPro will return $\$Start(1.04)(5)(2) = \$Start(1.48)$, thus regardless of the starting investment, MegaSaver will have a higher return than InvestPro. Eliminate (B), (C), and (E). Statement (2) states that MegaSaver will have at least double the return of InvestPro after 17.5 years, which is not sufficient. Since statement (2) states neither the respective interest rates of each account, nor how often the interest is paid, it is not sufficient.

Statistics

AVERAGES

Average is also called *arithmetic mean*, or *mean*. Regardless of how it is described, average is defined by the equation

$$\text{Average} = \frac{\text{Total}}{\text{Number of Things}}$$

The average pie is a really handy tool that will help you do average problems easily and quickly. Every time you see the word average (or arithmetic mean or mean), draw the pie.

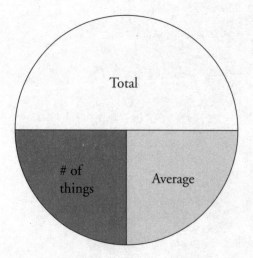

Here's how it works. You divide across the horizontal line and you multiply across the vertical line. Thus, if you want to find the average, you divide the total by the number of things. If you want to find the number of things, you divide the total by the average. If you want to find the total, you multiply the number of things by the average.

Any time you have two pieces of the pie you can always find the third.

Try a problem.

1. The average (arithmetic mean) weight of three people is 160 pounds. If one of these people weighs 200 pounds, what is the average weight, in pounds, of the two remaining people?

    (A) $73\frac{1}{3}$

    (B) 140

    (C) 160

    (D) 240

    (E) 480

The problem says *average* so draw a pie and fill in the pieces you have. The average is 160 and the number of things is 3, so multiply those together to get the total, 480. Cross off (E); it's a trap. The question asks for the *average* of the remaining two people, so draw another pie. You know the number of things is 2, so you need the total weight of those two to find their average. The total of all three people is 480, so if you subtract the total of the person who weighs 200, you get the total weight of the remaining two, which is 280. Thus, the average is 280 divided by 2, or 140. The correct answer is (B).

The average pie is great because it helps you organize information and it gives you a way to approach the problem. If you are looking at a hard problem and you're not sure how to do it, then when you see the word average (or arithmetic mean or mean) you can draw a pie and start plugging in the pieces. That way you can start the problem even if you don't know how to finish it. This keeps your pencil moving and your mind working so you don't waste valuable time.

AVERAGE DRILL

1. A local auto shop employs 7 workers. The shop pays a salary of $19,000 to each of four of the employees, a salary of $15,000 to each of two of the employees and a salary of $12,000 to one of the employees. The average salary of the seven employees is closest to

   (A) 16,250
   (B) 16,500
   (C) 16,900
   (D) 17,200
   (E) 17,500

2. A set of numbers has a sum of 465. What is its average (arithmetic mean)?

   (1) There are six numbers in the set.

   (2) The largest number in the set is 122, and the smallest is 14.

   (A) Statement (1) ALONE is sufficient, but statement (2) ALONE is not sufficient.
   (B) Statement (2) ALONE is sufficient, but statement (1) ALONE is not sufficient.
   (C) BOTH statements TOGETHER are sufficient, but NEITHER statement ALONE is sufficient.
   (D) EACH statement ALONE is sufficient.
   (E) Statements (1) and (2) TOGETHER are NOT sufficient to answer the question asked, and additional data are needed.

3. A set of 5 distinct numbers has the values $\{3, n, n + 3, 2n, p\}$, with an average (arithmetic mean) value of 8. What is the value of n ?

   (1) The largest number in the set is 14.

   (2) $4n + p = 34$

   (A) Statement (1) ALONE is sufficient, but statement (2) ALONE is not sufficient.
   (B) Statement (2) ALONE is sufficient, but statement (1) ALONE is not sufficient.
   (C) BOTH statements TOGETHER are sufficient, but NEITHER statement ALONE is sufficient.
   (D) EACH statement ALONE is sufficient.
   (E) Statements (1) and (2) TOGETHER are NOT sufficient to answer the question asked, and additional data are needed.

4. The average of x numbers is y and the average of r numbers is s. Which of the following represents the average of all $x + r$ numbers?

   (A) $\dfrac{(y+s)}{2}$

   (B) $\dfrac{(x+r)}{(y+s)}$

   (C) $\dfrac{(x+y+r+s)}{4}$

   (D) $\dfrac{(xy+rs)}{(x+r)}$

   (E) $\dfrac{(xs+yr)}{(x+r)}$

5. The average (arithmetic mean) of 5, 25, and 45 is 10 more than the average of 15, 10 and

   (A) 20
   (B) 30
   (C) 40
   (D) 50
   (E) 60

6. A particular dentists' office subscribes to *Days*, *Entertainment Hourly*, and *North American Flyfishing Review*. It pays a total of $118.05 yearly for these subscriptions. What is the average annual savings off the newsstand price?

    (1) Each of these magazines releases new issues weekly.

    (2) The cover price for *Days* is twice that of *Entertainment Hourly*, which is half that of *North American Flyfishing Review*, which costs $16 per issue.

(A) Statement (1) ALONE is sufficient, but statement (2) ALONE is not sufficient.
(B) Statement (2) ALONE is sufficient, but statement (1) ALONE is not sufficient.
(C) BOTH statements TOGETHER are sufficient, but NEITHER statement ALONE is sufficient.
(D) EACH statement ALONE is sufficient.
(E) Statements (1) and (2) TOGETHER are NOT sufficient to answer the question asked, and additional data are needed.

7. A particular IT department employs 8 people at an average (arithmetic mean) salary of $80,000 yearly. The company pays yearly bonuses equal to 15% of the employee's annual salary. Does the maximum individual bonus payment due to an employee in the IT department exceed $10,000 ?

    (1) The average salary of the five lowest-paid and one highest-paid IT employees is $93,600.

    (2) IT employee salaries run from 65% to 135% of the average departmental salary.

(A) Statement (1) ALONE is sufficient, but statement (2) ALONE is not sufficient.
(B) Statement (2) ALONE is sufficient, but statement (1) ALONE is not sufficient.
(C) BOTH statements TOGETHER are sufficient, but NEITHER statement ALONE is sufficient.
(D) EACH statement ALONE is sufficient.
(E) Statements (1) and (2) TOGETHER are NOT sufficient to answer the question asked, and additional data are needed.

8. In a certain company, the senior employees have an average of 16 years of work experience and the junior employees have an average of 4 years of work experience. If the average number of years of experience for all the senior and junior members is 7 years, then what is the ratio of senior members to junior members at the company?

(A) 1:4
(B) 1:3
(C) 1:2
(D) 4:1
(E) It cannot be determined from the information given

9. Josiah walked at the rate of 2 miles per hour for the first 2 miles of his hike. For the next 2 miles, he walked at a rate of 4 miles per hour. What was his average speed, in miles per hour, for the entire trip?

(A) 4

(B) $\dfrac{11}{3}$

(C) $\dfrac{10}{3}$

(D) 3

(E) $\dfrac{8}{3}$

10. At Vicki's Vending, the 24 sales staff are paid at three different commission rates, 8 representatives in each category. The top rate is three percentage points greater than the middle rate, which is three points above the lowest rate. The top third of sales staff represent 50% of the total sales, the middle third represent 30% of sales, and the bottom third represent the remaining 20%. Within each tier, sales staff sell at equal overall rates. Overall sales receipts are $48,000,000 per year. What is the middle commission rate?

   (1) The top half of the sales staff was paid an average commission of $320,000.

   (2) The bottom half of the sales staff was paid an average commission of $116,000.

(A) Statement (1) ALONE is sufficient, but statement (2) ALONE is not sufficient.
(B) Statement (2) ALONE is sufficient, but statement (1) ALONE is not sufficient.
(C) BOTH statements TOGETHER are sufficient, but NEITHER statement ALONE is sufficient.
(D) EACH statement ALONE is sufficient.
(E) Statements (1) and (2) TOGETHER are NOT sufficient to answer the question asked, and additional data are needed.

11. In a certain sequence with terms $X_1, X_2, X_3, \ldots X_n$ the sum of the n terms is 1,458. If the average of the n terms is 6, what is n ?

(A) 241
(B) 242
(C) 243
(D) 245
(E) 246

12. Atlantic Holdings LLC has six subsidiary companies with combined total yearly sales of $23,100,000. By how much do the sales at the top-selling company exceed the average sales per company?

   (1) The average sales at the lower five companies is 87.79% of the total average sales at all of Atlantic Holdings' subsidiaries.

   (2) The average sales at the highest five companies is $\dfrac{12}{11}$ of the total average sales at all of Atlantic Holdings' subsidiaries.

(A) Statement (1) ALONE is sufficient, but statement (2) ALONE is not sufficient.
(B) Statement (2) ALONE is sufficient, but statement (1) ALONE is not sufficient.
(C) BOTH statements TOGETHER are sufficient, but NEITHER statement ALONE is sufficient.
(D) EACH statement ALONE is sufficient.
(E) Statements (1) and (2) TOGETHER are NOT sufficient to answer the question asked, and additional data are needed.

13. During the season, a hockey team scores 262 goals. Its top two scorers averaged 40 goals each, while its next three highest scorers averaged 24 goals. If ten other players on the roster scored goals, what is the average number of goals scored by these remaining players?

(A)   8
(B)   9
(C) 10
(D) 11
(E) 12

14. A set of nonnegative integers consists of $\{x, x + 7, 2x, y, y + 5\}$. The numbers of this set have four distinct values. What is its average (arithmetic mean)?

(1) $x \neq 5$

(2) $4y + 12 = 6(y + 2)$

(A) Statement (1) ALONE is sufficient, but statement (2) ALONE is not sufficient.
(B) Statement (2) ALONE is sufficient, but statement (1) ALONE is not sufficient.
(C) BOTH statements TOGETHER are sufficient, but NEITHER statement ALONE is sufficient.
(D) EACH statement ALONE is sufficient.
(E) Statements (1) and (2) TOGETHER are NOT sufficient to answer the question asked, and additional data are needed.

15. A certain website received 500 visits per day over a 14 day period. If during this period, the average number of visitors for the first 8 days was 650, what was the average number of visitors per day for the remaining 6 days?

(A) 300
(B) 350
(C) 400
(D) 450
(E) 500

Check your answers on page 373.

MEDIAN

Median is the middle number in a set of consecutive numbers. If the set has an even number of numbers, the median is the average of the middle two numbers.

If you forget the definition of median, just remember that the median is that thing in the **middle** of the road you're not supposed to drive over.

Example

1.   What is the median of {2, 25, 10, 6, 13, 50, 6}?

Start by putting the numbers in consecutive order. That gives you 2, 6, 6, 10, 13, 25, 50. There is an odd number of numbers so the median is the number in the middle, 10. If the number 50 were taken out of the set, there would be an even number of numbers so the new median would be $\frac{6+10}{2} = 8$.

MEDIAN DRILL

1. The table below shows the number of compact discs sold at a particular store during a certain period. If the top row represents the number of discs sold per day and the bottom row represents the number of days on which that number of sales occurred, then what was the median number of compact discs sold during the period?

Amount/day	45	51	60	41	32
# of days	8	6	5	7	4

(A) 41
(B) 43
(C) 45
(D) 48
(E) 51

2. What is the median of set A ?

   (1) Set A contains 3 integers.

   (2) The mean and mode of set A are both equal to 4.

(A) Statement (1) ALONE is sufficient, but statement (2) ALONE is not sufficient.
(B) Statement (2) ALONE is sufficient, but statement (1) ALONE is not sufficient.
(C) BOTH statements TOGETHER are sufficient, but NEITHER statement ALONE is sufficient.
(D) EACH statement ALONE is sufficient.
(E) Statements (1) and (2) TOGETHER are NOT sufficient to answer the question asked, and additional data are needed.

13, 15, 17, 19, x, 14, 16, 18, 20

3. If x is an integer between 11 and 21, inclusive, then the median of the list of numbers above must be

(A) either 15 or 16
(B) either 16 or 17
(C) either 17 or 18
(D) 16.5
(E) x

4. The distances jumped in feet by a certain athlete were recorded as 9, 7, 12, 14, 10, and 17. What is the median of these distances?

(A) 9.0
(B) 10.0
(C) 10.5
(D) 11.0
(E) 12.0

Check your answers on page 373.

MODE

The *Mode* is the most frequently occurring number in a set of numbers.

To remember the definition, remember that *mode* sounds like "most." The mode is the number that appears the most.

Let's look at a simple example.

1. What is the mode of {2, 25, 10, 6, 13, 50, 6}?

Look for the number that appears the most. Only 6 occurs more than once, so 6 is the mode.

MODE DRILL

1. Consider the following:

   {The single-digit prime integers}
   {The prime factorization of 84}

   If a set of numbers is constructed using the above elements, what is the mode of the set?

   (A) 1
   (B) 2
   (C) 3
   (D) 5
   (E) 7

2. Set A is $\{x, 2x + y, 2y, y + z, x + z\}$. If $x, y,$ and z are positive integers, then what is the value of the mode of set A ?

   (1) x is equal to one half of y and twice z.

   (2) The median of set A is equal to 125.

   (A) Statement (1) ALONE is sufficient, but statement (2) ALONE is not sufficient.
   (B) Statement (2) ALONE is sufficient, but statement (1) ALONE is not sufficient.
   (C) BOTH statements TOGETHER are sufficient, but NEITHER statement ALONE is sufficient.
   (D) EACH statement ALONE is sufficient.
   (E) Statements (1) and (2) TOGETHER are NOT sufficient to answer the question asked, and additional data are needed.

3.   8, 10, 14, 14, 15, 17, 17, 17, 18, 20

   If in the list of numbers above, m is the mode, n is the median, and o is the average, which of the following statements is true?

   (A) $m < n < o$
   (B) $m = n = o$
   (C) $o > m > n$
   (D) $m > n > o$
   (E) $o < m < n$

4. In a set of A consecutive integers, which of the following CANNOT be true?

       I. The median is equal to the mean.
      II. The mean equals zero.
      III. The median is equal to the mode.

   (A) I only
   (B) I and II only
   (C) II only
   (D) II and III only
   (E) III only

5. Set X is composed of the total daily rainfall for a 5-day period. Is the mode of set X greater than the median?

   (1) The mean and median of set X is equal to 5.

   (2) If the median were removed from set X, the mean and mode would remain unchanged, but the median would decrease.

   (A) Statement (1) ALONE is sufficient, but statement (2) ALONE is not sufficient.
   (B) Statement (2) ALONE is sufficient, but statement (1) ALONE is not sufficient.
   (C) BOTH statements TOGETHER are sufficient, but NEITHER statement ALONE is sufficient.
   (D) EACH statement ALONE is sufficient.
   (E) Statements (1) and (2) TOGETHER are NOT sufficient to answer the question asked, and additional data are needed.

   Check your answers on page 373.

RANGE

The *Range* is the difference between the highest and lowest numbers in a set of numbers.

Example

1. What is the range of {2, 25, 10, 6, 13, 50, 6}?

Start by putting the numbers in consecutive order. That gives you 2, 6, 6, 10, 13, 25, 50. Now subtract the lowest number from the highest: 50 − 2 = 48, so the range is 48.

RANGE DRILL

1. Set A: {6, 9, 14, x)

   If x represents the sum of the other three numbers in Set A, what is the range of Set A ?

   (A) 58
   (B) 29
   (C) 23
   (D) 14
   (E) 8

2. Set B consists of all prime numbers less than 40. What is the range of Set B ?

   (A) 34
   (B) 35
   (C) 36
   (D) 37
   (E) 38

3. Set C consists of all numbers that, when squared, produce one of the following numbers: 49, 16, or 9. What is the range of Set C ?

   (A) 0
   (B) 4
   (C) 14
   (D) 40
   (E) 49

4. Is the range of positive integers 8, 6, 7, 5, m and n greater than 7 ?

   (1) m > 2n

   (2) m > n > 5

   (A) Statement (1) ALONE is sufficient, but statement (2) ALONE is not sufficient.
   (B) Statement (2) ALONE is sufficient, but statement (1) ALONE is not sufficient.
   (C) BOTH statements TOGETHER are sufficient, but NEITHER statement ALONE is sufficient.
   (D) EACH statement ALONE is sufficient.
   (E) Statements (1) and (2) TOGETHER are NOT sufficient to answer the question asked, and additional data are needed.

5. P is a set of four numbers a, b, c and d. Is the range of the numbers in set P greater than 3 ?

   (1) d is the least number in set P.

   (2) a − d > 3

   (A) Statement (1) ALONE is sufficient, but statement (2) ALONE is not sufficient.
   (B) Statement (2) ALONE is sufficient, but statement (1) ALONE is not sufficient.
   (C) BOTH statements TOGETHER are sufficient, but NEITHER statement ALONE is sufficient.
   (D) EACH statement ALONE is sufficient.
   (E) Statements (1) and (2) TOGETHER are NOT sufficient to answer the question asked, and additional data are needed.

Check your answers on page 373.

STANDARD DEVIATION

Standard deviation is a statistical term like mean, median, range and mode. If you see a problem that uses the terms *normal distribution* or *standard deviation*, think about the bell curve.

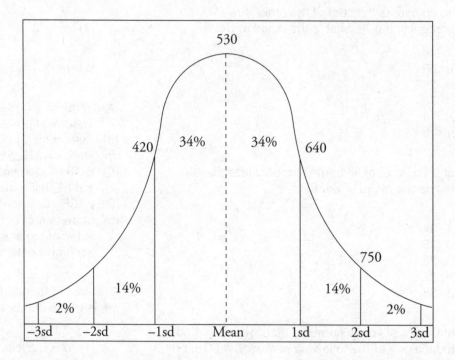

Any set of values that has a *normal distribution* can be plotted along this bell curve. Here are the key parts of the curve.

- The **mean** is indicated by the line down the center of the curve. In questions involving standard deviation, the mean will either be given to you or it will be easy to figure out.

- The **standard deviation** is a statistically derived specified distance from the mean. In the figure above, the standard deviations are represented by the solid lines. GMAT problems give you the standard deviation for a set of data. You will probably never have to calculate it.

- The **percentages** indicated in the picture represent the portion of the data that falls between each line. These percentages are valid for **any** question involving normal distribution. You must memorize them: 34:14:2. The percentages correspond to the 1st, 2nd, and 3rd standard deviations on each side of the mean.

- **Variance** is the measure of the spread of numbers in relation to the mean. It's easiest to think about variance in visual terms. The variance is low if all the numbers in a set are close to the mean. When you graph the set, the points cluster near the mean and create a high, narrow curve. On the other hand, the curve for a set with a larger variance looks lower and flatter because there are more values far away from the mean. Variance is not frequently tested on the GMAT. You won't need to calculate the variance of a data set, but you might be asked about the concept.

Working with standard deviation on the GMAT is mostly a matter of drawing the curve and filling in the information. Take the case of an exam scored on a scale of 200 to 800.

If the mean on an exam is 530 and the standard deviation is 110, what percent of the test takers score between 420 and 750 ?

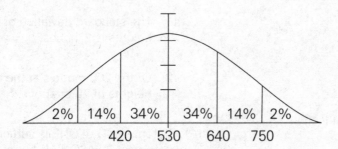

Start by drawing the curve and labeling what you know. The mean is 530; it goes at the top. The standard deviation is 110, so add 110 to 530 to get the first *sd* on the right. Then add 110 to 640 to get the second *sd*. Now go to the left side. Subtract 110 from 530 to get the first *sd* on the left, which is 420. There is no need to calculate the second *sd* on the left because the question only asks about scores between 420 and 750. Add the percentages between 420 and 750 and you get 34% + 34% + 14% = 82%.

As long as you understand how to draw the chart and you memorize the percentages that correspond to each standard deviation, standard deviation problems should be very manageable.

STANDARD DEVIATION DRILL

1. Which of the following correctly lists the data sets below from greatest standard deviation to least?

   I.   101, 101, 101, 101, 101
   II. 20, 40, 60, 100, 120
   III. –25, –24, –24, –24, –23

   (A) I, II, III
   (B) II, I, III
   (C) II, III, I
   (D) III, II, I
   (E) I, III, II

2. In a certain normal distribution, what is the standard deviation?

   (1) The arithmetic mean and the data point one standard deviation greater than the mean are 4.7 and 6.3, respectively.

   (2) The range of the data is 8.

   (A) Statement (1) ALONE is sufficient, but statement (2) ALONE is not sufficient.
   (B) Statement (2) ALONE is sufficient, but statement (1) ALONE is not sufficient.
   (C) BOTH statements TOGETHER are sufficient, but NEITHER statement ALONE is sufficient.
   (D) EACH statement ALONE is sufficient.
   (E) Statements (1) and (2) TOGETHER are NOT sufficient to answer the question asked, and additional data are needed.

3. Thirty children acquired a total of 2,700 baseball cards. If 16% had fewer than 70 baseball cards and the number of cards per child has a normal distribution, what percent of the children had greater than 130 baseball cards?

   (A) 2
   (B) 4
   (C) 14
   (D) 34
   (E) 68

4. The heights of the models at the *XYZ* modeling agency have a normal distribution. If the average height of the models is 72 inches and the bottom 16% of the models will be cut from the agency, what is the height at or below which models will be cut?

   (1) The standard deviation of the models' heights is 2 inches.

   (2) Of the 200 models at the agency, 4 have heights of 76 or above.

   (A) Statement (1) ALONE is sufficient, but statement (2) ALONE is not sufficient.
   (B) Statement (2) ALONE is sufficient, but statement (1) ALONE is not sufficient.
   (C) BOTH statements TOGETHER are sufficient, but NEITHER statement ALONE is sufficient.
   (D) EACH statement ALONE is sufficient.
   (E) Statements (1) and (2) TOGETHER are NOT sufficient to answer the question asked, and additional data are needed.

5. There are 50 students in Mrs. Harrison's honors English class. All students receiving a grade of 84 or higher on the final exam will be recommended for advancement to AP English. How many of Mrs. Harrison's students will be recommended for advancement?

   (1) 34 of the students got between 62 and 84 on the final exam.

   (2) The average score on the final exam was 73.

   (A) Statement (1) ALONE is sufficient, but statement (2) ALONE is not sufficient.
   (B) Statement (2) ALONE is sufficient, but statement (1) ALONE is not sufficient.
   (C) BOTH statements TOGETHER are sufficient, but NEITHER statement ALONE is sufficient.
   (D) EACH statement ALONE is sufficient.
   (E) Statements (1) and (2) TOGETHER are NOT sufficient to answer the question asked, and additional data are needed.

6. After collecting a set of data, a researcher computed the mean, the median, and the standard deviation. However, the researcher realized that a measurement error caused all of the values in the set to be off by 3. After adding 3 to each of the values in the set, the researcher found that

(A) only the mean changed
(B) only the median changed
(C) the mean, median and standard deviation changed
(D) only the standard deviation changed
(E) only the mean and the median changed

7. If set S consists of an odd number of even integers that have a normal distribution, what is the standard deviation of set S ?

(1) The mean of set S is 4.

(2) The median of set S is 4.

(A) Statement (1) ALONE is sufficient, but statement (2) ALONE is not sufficient.
(B) Statement (2) ALONE is sufficient, but statement (1) ALONE is not sufficient.
(C) BOTH statements TOGETHER are sufficient, but NEITHER statement ALONE is sufficient.
(D) EACH statement ALONE is sufficient.
(E) Statements (1) and (2) TOGETHER are NOT sufficient to answer the question asked, and additional data are needed.

8. A meteorologist keeps track of temperatures at the North Pole. Over a seven day period, the meteorologist records temperatures of –19, –15, –15, –12, –10, –9, and –7 degrees. Which of the following must be true of the data collected by the meteorologist?

(A) The mean is greater than the median
(B) The mode is greater than the median
(C) The mean is greater than the standard deviation
(D) The standard deviation is greater than the mean
(E) The mode, median, and mean are greater than the standard deviation

9. Is the standard deviation of the set of
temperatures t_1, t_2, t_3, t_4, ..., t_{20} less than 4 ?

    (1) For each temperature, the difference
        between the mean and that temperature
        is 5.

    (2) The variance for the set of temperatures
        is 25.

(A) Statement (1) ALONE is sufficient, but
    statement (2) ALONE is not sufficient.
(B) Statement (2) ALONE is sufficient, but
    statement (1) ALONE is not sufficient.
(C) BOTH statements TOGETHER are sufficient,
    but NEITHER statement ALONE is sufficient.
(D) EACH statement ALONE is sufficient.
(E) Statements (1) and (2) TOGETHER are NOT
    sufficient to answer the question asked, and
    additional data are needed.

Check your answers on page 373.

RATE

Rate problems are very similar to average problems because they often ask about average speed or distance traveled. Other problems ask about how fast someone works or how long it takes to complete a task.

Regardless of the problem, rate is defined as

$$\text{Rate} = \frac{\text{Distance}}{\text{Time}} \quad \text{or} \quad \text{Rate} = \frac{\text{Amount of Work}}{\text{Time}}$$

Like average problems, rate problems are easy to do if you use a pie.

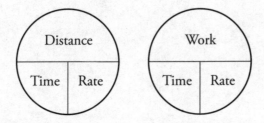

Just as with averages, whenever you have 2 pieces of the pie, you can find the third.

There are a couple of other things you need to remember about rate problems.

- Whenever people travel toward or away from each other **add their rates.**
- Whenever people (or things) work together **add their rates.**
- If you have a work problem in which the task is not defined, define the task by **Plugging In.**

Try a problem.

1. Rob and David live 200 miles apart. Deciding to have a picnic, they both start driving at 9:00 a.m., traveling in a straight line towards each other. Rob drives at a steady speed of 50 miles per hour, and David drives at a steady speed of 30 miles per hour. What is the time when they meet for their picnic?

    (A) 11:30 a.m.
    (B) 1:00 p.m.
    (C) 1:30 p.m.
    (D) 2:00 p.m.
    (E) 3:40 p.m.

Start by drawing a pie. You are given the distance so put 200 miles in the top of the pie. Rob and David are driving towards each other, so add their rates to get a combined rate of 80 mph. 200 divided by 80 is 2.5, so it will take them 2½ hours to meet. That means they meet at 11:30 a.m. and the correct answer is (A).

Try another one.

2. Joan can do an entire job in 12 hours. Ken can do an entire job in 6 hours. If Joan and Ken work together for 3 hours, how many hours will it take Ken to finish the rest of the job by himself?

(A) 1

(B) $1\dfrac{1}{2}$

(C) $4\dfrac{1}{2}$

(D) 6

(E) 9

Joan and Ken are doing a job, but you don't know what the job is. Say the job is making widgets. If you plug in a number that's divisible by both 6 and 12 for the number of widgets in the job, you can calculate each person's rate.

Plug In 24 widgets for the job. Now draw a pie for Joan. She can do 24 widgets in 12 hours so her rate is 2 widgets per hour. Draw a pie for Ken. He can do 24 widgets in 6 hours, so his rate is 4 widgets per hour. When people work together, add their rates. Joan and Ken's combined rate is 6 widgets per hour. Put the combined rate into another pie. The problem says they work together for 3 hours. 6 × 3 =18 so they complete 18 widgets. Now Joan leaves and Ken has to finish. You need another pie. 24 – 18 = 6, so Ken has 6 widgets left to finish. Put 6 in the top of the pie. When he works by himself, Ken's rate is 4 widgets per hour. 6 divided by 4 is 1.5, so the correct answer is (B).

RATE DRILL

1. How many pumpkins did Silas pick on Tuesday?

    (1) On Tuesday Silas picked pumpkins for 6 hours.

    (2) Silas can pick 200 pumpkins in 12 hours.

    (A) Statement (1) ALONE is sufficient, but statement (2) alone is not sufficient.
    (B) Statement (2) ALONE is sufficient, but statement (1) alone is not sufficient.
    (C) BOTH statements TOGETHER are sufficient, but NEITHER statement ALONE is sufficient.
    (D) EACH statement ALONE is sufficient.
    (E) Statements (1) and (2) TOGETHER are NOT sufficient to answer the question asked, and additional data are needed.

2. The term hypersonic is used to define a speed that is 5 times the speed of sound. The threshold value for an object that is traveling at hypersonic speed is approximately 1.05 miles per second. This approximate speed is how many miles an hour?

    (A)   63
    (B)   82
    (C)   3,780
    (D)   18,900
    (E)   228,300

3. What was Alex's income from her employment last week?

    (1) Last week, Alex worked for 35 hours.

    (2) Alex's income two weeks ago was $700.

    (A) Statement (1) ALONE is sufficient, but statement (2) alone is not sufficient.
    (B) Statement (2) ALONE is sufficient, but statement (1) alone is not sufficient.
    (C) BOTH statements TOGETHER are sufficient, but NEITHER statement ALONE is sufficient.
    (D) EACH statement ALONE is sufficient.
    (E) Statements (1) and (2) TOGETHER are NOT sufficient to answer the question asked, and additional data are needed.

4. How many hours does it take for Calvin to pick a apples if he picks apples at a rate of b apples per hour?

    (A) $\dfrac{a}{b}$

    (B) $\dfrac{b}{a}$

    (C) ab

    (D) $\dfrac{60b}{a}$

    (E) $\dfrac{a}{60b}$

5. Monica and Thomas each work on an automobile assembly line tightening screws at different rates. Is Thomas's rate faster than Monica's?

    (1) Thomas can tighten 5 screws per minute. Monica can tighten 400 screws per hour.

    (2) If Thomas's rate were increased by 50 percent, it would be 12.5% higher than Monica's rate.

(A) Statement (1) ALONE is sufficient, but statement (2) alone is not sufficient.
(B) Statement (2) ALONE is sufficient, but statement (1) alone is not sufficient.
(C) BOTH statements TOGETHER are sufficient, but NEITHER statement ALONE is sufficient.
(D) EACH statement ALONE is sufficient.
(E) Statements (1) and (2) TOGETHER are NOT sufficient to answer the question asked, and additional data are needed.

6. If it takes a machine 12 minutes to produce z zippers, how many minutes will it take the machine to produce y zippers at the same rate?

(A) $\dfrac{12y}{z}$

(B) $\dfrac{12z}{y}$

(C) $\dfrac{y}{12z}$

(D) $\dfrac{12}{yz}$

(E) $\dfrac{yz}{12}$

7. Train X departs Rockburg for Williamsland at 1:00 p.m. and train Y departs Williamsland for Rockburg at 2:00 p.m. If Rockburg and Williamsland are 200 miles apart, how much faster is train X than train Y ?

    (1) Train X arrives at Williamsland at 5:00 p.m.

    (2) Train X and train Y pass each other at 3:30 p.m.

(A) Statement (1) ALONE is sufficient, but statement (2) alone is not sufficient.
(B) Statement (2) ALONE is sufficient, but statement (1) alone is not sufficient.
(C) BOTH statements TOGETHER are sufficient, but NEITHER statement ALONE is sufficient.
(D) EACH statement ALONE is sufficient.
(E) Statements (1) and (2) TOGETHER are NOT sufficient to answer the question asked, and additional data are needed.

8. Working together on a political campaign, Janet and Tameka have been asked to address envelopes that will go out to potential contributors. Janet can address 320 letters in 4 hours. Tameka can address 300 letters in 6 hours. If Janet and Tameka work together, each at her own constant rate, and without taking a break, how many hours will it take them to address 390 letters?

(A) 2.8
(B) 3.0
(C) 3.9
(D) 6.0
(E) 7.8

9. Frida and Diego are working together to paint a mural. How long will it take them to finish?

   (1) Diego's rate is three-fourths of Frida's rate.

   (2) Working alone, Diego can finish in 24 hours and Frida can finish in 18 hours.

(A) Statement (1) ALONE is sufficient, but statement (2) alone is not sufficient.
(B) Statement (2) ALONE is sufficient, but statement (1) alone is not sufficient.
(C) BOTH statements TOGETHER are sufficient, but NEITHER statement ALONE is sufficient.
(D) EACH statement ALONE is sufficient.
(E) Statements (1) and (2) TOGETHER are NOT sufficient to answer the question asked, and additional data are needed.

10. Sasha is shopping for an espresso machine. In order to make her decision, she decides to use the formula $Y = \dfrac{C}{S}$ to determine which machine is the best bargain; Sasha will purchase the machine with the lower value for Y. If C represents the cost of the machine and S represents the number of shots of espresso the machine can make per minute, then which machine will Sasha purchase?

   (1) Machines A and B cost $300 and $250, respectively.

   (2) Machine A produces fewer shots per minute than machine B.

(A) Statement (1) ALONE is sufficient, but statement (2) alone is not sufficient.
(B) Statement (2) ALONE is sufficient, but statement (1) alone is not sufficient.
(C) BOTH statements TOGETHER are sufficient, but NEITHER statement ALONE is sufficient.
(D) EACH statement ALONE is sufficient.
(E) Statements (1) and (2) TOGETHER are NOT sufficient to answer the question asked, and additional data are needed.

11. It takes Lynda 5 hours to paint a certain room. It takes Alex 4 hours to paint the same room. How many hours would it take Lynda and Alex working together at their respective rates to paint the room together?

(A) $\dfrac{9}{20}$

(B) $2\dfrac{2}{9}$

(C) $2\dfrac{1}{2}$

(D) $4\dfrac{1}{2}$

(E) 9

12. Sam and Kathy are each working on a job for different lengths of time at different rates. Does Sam complete more than 50% of the job?

   (1) If Sam worked alone for 1.5 hours, then Sam would complete the same percentage of the job that Kathy would complete working alone for 2 hours.

   (2) Kathy worked alone for the first two hours, and then Sam and Kathy worked together until the job was finished.

(A) Statement (1) ALONE is sufficient, but statement (2) alone is not sufficient.
(B) Statement (2) ALONE is sufficient, but statement (1) alone is not sufficient.
(C) BOTH statements TOGETHER are sufficient, but NEITHER statement ALONE is sufficient.
(D) EACH statement ALONE is sufficient.
(E) Statements (1) and (2) TOGETHER are NOT sufficient to answer the question asked, and additional data are needed.

13. 8 identical machines can produce 360 aluminum cans per hour. If all of the machines work at the same constant rate, how many cans could 5 such machines produce in 3 hours?

(A) 675
(B) 750
(C) 1,800
(D) 5,900
(E) 7,500

14. To see a fireworks display on the 4th of July, Sydney drives from his home to a local park. He drives at a rate of m miles per hour to the park. On his return trip he drives at a rate of n miles per hour. How far away from his home is the park if he spends a total of z hours in the car, making no stops along the way?

(A) $\dfrac{n+z}{m} - \dfrac{z}{n}$

(B) $\dfrac{m+n+z}{mn}$

(C) $\dfrac{mnz}{m+n}$

(D) $\dfrac{m+z}{mn}$

(E) $\dfrac{mz}{n}$

15. Clint sells tea for two different prices. Customers can purchase loose-leaf tea by the ounce or in 2.24 gram tea bags. Are tea bags more expensive per ounce than loose-leaf tea?
(1 ounce = 28 grams).

(1) 100 tea bags and 8 ounces of loose-leaf tea cost a total of $21.00.

(2) 5 tea bags cost the same as 0.2 ounces of loose-leaf tea.

(A) Statement (1) ALONE is sufficient, but statement (2) alone is not sufficient.
(B) Statement (2) ALONE is sufficient, but statement (1) alone is not sufficient.
(C) BOTH statements TOGETHER are sufficient, but NEITHER statement ALONE is sufficient.
(D) EACH statement ALONE is sufficient.
(E) Statements (1) and (2) TOGETHER are NOT sufficient to answer the question asked, and additional data are needed.

16. Ryan and Phil are building a brick house. Ryan can lay bricks two times faster than Phil can. If they worked together, how long would it take them to build the house?

(1) Working alone, Ryan can complete the job in 36 hours.

(2) Phil can lay 25 bricks per hour.

(A) Statement (1) ALONE is sufficient, but statement (2) alone is not sufficient.
(B) Statement (2) ALONE is sufficient, but statement (1) alone is not sufficient.
(C) BOTH statements TOGETHER are sufficient, but NEITHER statement ALONE is sufficient.
(D) EACH statement ALONE is sufficient.
(E) Statements (1) and (2) TOGETHER are NOT sufficient to answer the question asked, and additional data are needed.

17. One machine, running at a constant rate, can complete a certain job order in 11 hours. A second machine, running at a constant rate can complete the same job order in 8 hours. If both machines are used, approximately how many hours will it take to complete the job order?

(A) 0.18
(B) 0.22
(C) 2.25
(D) 4.63
(E) 5.6

18. Lex took a yellow cab to the airport. A yellow cab charges a flat fee of $2.50 and $0.20 for each quarter of a mile. A checkered cab charges $1.00 per minute regardless of distance driven. Was the yellow cab less expensive than a checkered cab would have been?

(1) Lex's trip took 30 minutes.

(2) The cab drove at an average speed of 24 miles per hour.

(A) Statement (1) ALONE is sufficient, but statement (2) alone is not sufficient.
(B) Statement (2) ALONE is sufficient, but statement (1) alone is not sufficient.
(C) BOTH statements TOGETHER are sufficient, but NEITHER statement ALONE is sufficient.
(D) EACH statement ALONE is sufficient.
(E) Statements (1) and (2) TOGETHER are NOT sufficient to answer the question asked, and additional data are needed.

19. It will take Sarah and Sadie working together, each at her own constant rate, 4 hours to pave a driveway. If Sarah did the job by herself it would take her 6 hours to complete the job. If Sadie were to do the job by herself it would take her x hours to do the job. What is the value of x ?

(A) 12
(B) 9
(C) 7
(D) 5
(E) $3\frac{1}{2}$

Check your answers on page 373.

FACTORIALS

When you see a factorial such as 21!, the **factorial symbol** (!) means you need to multiply the integer by all the positive integers that are less than it.

Example

$$8! = 8 \times 7 \times 6 \times 5 \times 4 \times 3 \times 2 \times 1$$

$$n! = (n) \times (n - 1) \times (n - 2) \times \ldots \times 1$$

The test writers will often throw factorials into questions to try to make the questions look harder than they really are. Most factorial problems can be solved by either reducing or breaking the question down into smaller parts.

Example

1.   What is the value of $\dfrac{6!}{3!}$?

You can't just divide and say that the answer is 2!. You probably don't want to compute 6! and then divide it by the value of 3! either. That would take too long, even though in this case the numbers are not that large. Instead, write out the problem and look for ways to simplify.

$$\frac{6 \times 5 \times 4 \times 3 \times 2 \times 1}{3 \times 2 \times 1}$$

3, 2 and 1 cancel out on top and bottom, leaving just 6 × 5 × 4, which equals 120.

There's one more helpful thing to remember when dealing with factorials.

> 0! = 1! = 1
> 0! and 1! are the only odd factorials because all other factorials have 2 as a factor.

FACTORIALS DRILL

1. For which of the following values of x is the equation $\dfrac{x!}{(x+2)!} = \dfrac{x}{(x+1)!}$ true?

   (A) 3
   (B) 4
   (C) 5
   (D) 6
   (E) 7

2. If integer y is less than positive integer x, and $x! = xy$, what is the greatest possible value of y ?

   (A) 0
   (B) 1
   (C) 2
   (D) 3
   (E) 6

3. If x and y are both positive integers, is $y!$ a factor of $x!$?

   (1) $x > y$

   (2) $23x - 10y = 150$
       $2.5y = 5.5x - 35$

   (A) Statement (1) ALONE is sufficient, but statement (2) alone is not sufficient.
   (B) Statement (2) ALONE is sufficient, but statement (1) alone is not sufficient.
   (C) BOTH statements TOGETHER are sufficient, but NEITHER statement ALONE is sufficient.
   (D) EACH statement ALONE is sufficient.
   (E) Statements (1) and (2) TOGETHER are NOT sufficient to answer the question asked, and additional data are needed.

4. If x, y, and z are positive integers, and $\dfrac{x! + x}{z} = y$, then what is the value of z ?

   (1) x is a factor of y.

   (2) $z < x$

   (A) Statement (1) ALONE is sufficient, but statement (2) alone is not sufficient.
   (B) Statement (2) ALONE is sufficient, but statement (1) alone is not sufficient.
   (C) BOTH statements TOGETHER are sufficient, but NEITHER statement ALONE is sufficient.
   (D) EACH statement ALONE is sufficient.
   (E) Statements (1) and (2) TOGETHER are NOT sufficient to answer the question asked, and additional data are needed.

5. If a and b are positive integers, is the value of $a! - b!$ greater than the product of a and b ?

   (1) b is an even prime number.

   (2) $b^a = a^b$

   (A) Statement (1) ALONE is sufficient, but statement (2) alone is not sufficient.
   (B) Statement (2) ALONE is sufficient, but statement (1) alone is not sufficient.
   (C) BOTH statements TOGETHER are sufficient, but NEITHER statement ALONE is sufficient.
   (D) EACH statement ALONE is sufficient.
   (E) Statements (1) and (2) TOGETHER are NOT sufficient to answer the question asked, and additional data are needed.

> Check your answers on page 373.

PROBABILITY

Probability is the likelihood that something will happen. If something can absolutely never happen, its probability is 0. If something absolutely will happen, its probability is 1 (or 100%). All other probabilities are between 0 and 1 and are defined as

$$\text{probability} = \frac{\text{number of outcomes you want}}{\text{number of total possible outcomes}}$$

Although probability is defined as a fraction, it can be expressed as a fraction, a decimal, or a percent.

Multiple Events

To find the probability of multiple events, **multiply** the individual probabilities if you're trying to find the probability of one thing **and** another thing happening, and **add** the individual probabilities if you're trying to find the probability of one thing **or** another thing happening.

In other words:

$$\text{Probability } (A \textbf{ and } B) = \text{Probability } (A) \times \text{Probability } (B)$$

$$\text{Probability } (A \textbf{ or } B) = \text{Probability } (A) + \text{Probability } (B)$$

When calculating the probability of multiple events, assume that each event has occurred.

Example

1.   Griffin has a bag of marbles that contains only 6 black marbles and 4 red marbles. If he removes three marbles at random without replacing any of the marbles, what is the probability that all three marbles selected will be red?

(A) $\dfrac{2}{5}$

(B) $\dfrac{1}{6}$

(C) $\dfrac{3}{25}$

(D) $\dfrac{8}{125}$

(E) $\dfrac{1}{30}$

There are 4 red marbles and 10 total marbles, so the probability that the first marble will be red is $\frac{4}{10}$. Assume that Griffin has successfully removed one red marble when he goes to remove the second; therefore, the probability that the second marble is red is $\frac{3}{9}$. Then, assuming that he successfully removed the first two marbles, the probability that the third marble is red is $\frac{2}{8}$. The probability that the first **and** the second **and** the third marble are red is found by **multiplying**. Thus, the probability that all three marbles are red is $\frac{4}{10} \times \frac{3}{9} \times \frac{2}{8} = \frac{1}{30}$. The answer is (E).

Not or At Least

In some cases it may be easier to find the probability that something happened by finding the probability that it did NOT happen, and subtracting from 1. You can usually recognize these problems when you see the words "not" or "at least."

Probability (event happens) + Probability (event does NOT happen) = 1

2.   Kevin flips a coin four times. What is the probability that he gets heads on at least one of the four flips?

(A) $\frac{1}{16}$

(B) $\frac{1}{4}$

(C) $\frac{3}{4}$

(D) $\frac{13}{36}$

(E) $\frac{15}{16}$

Rather than figure out all the ways Kevin could get at least one head and add those individual probabilities together, it will be easier to figure out the number of ways Kevin **won't** get at least one head, and subtract that from one. The words "at least" confirm that this is the right approach.

The only way Kevin won't get heads on at least one of the flips is if he gets all tails. The probability that Kevin gets all tails is

$$\frac{1}{2} \times \frac{1}{2} \times \frac{1}{2} \times \frac{1}{2} = \frac{1}{16}$$

Eliminate (A); it's a trap. Every other scenario will have at least one head, so the probability that Kevin gets heads on at least one of the four flips is

$$\frac{16}{16} - \frac{1}{16} = \frac{15}{16}$$

The correct answer is (E).

PROBABILITY DRILL

1. Bob has a 10-sided die whose sides are labeled with the first 10 positive odd integers. What is the probability that the product of two rolls will equal 15 ?

(A) $\dfrac{1}{100}$

(B) $\dfrac{1}{50}$

(C) $\dfrac{1}{25}$

(D) $\dfrac{3}{20}$

(E) $\dfrac{1}{5}$

2. Jack has a jar full of quarters, nickels, and dimes. He picks n coins, totaling 45 cents. What is the value of n ?

(1) The probability of randomly picking a nickel from the n coins is 50%.

(2) The probability of randomly picking a dime from the n coins is 50%.

(A) Statement (1) ALONE is sufficient, but statement (2) alone is not sufficient.
(B) Statement (2) ALONE is sufficient, but statement (1) alone is not sufficient.
(C) BOTH statements TOGETHER are sufficient, but NEITHER statement ALONE is sufficient.
(D) EACH statement ALONE is sufficient.
(E) Statements (1) and (2) TOGETHER are NOT sufficient to answer the question asked, and additional data are needed.

3. If n is a positive integer, what is the probability that a randomly selected factor of n will be even?

(1) n is even.

(2) $\dfrac{n}{2}$ is odd.

(A) Statement (1) ALONE is sufficient, but statement (2) alone is not sufficient.
(B) Statement (2) ALONE is sufficient, but statement (1) alone is not sufficient.
(C) BOTH statements TOGETHER are sufficient, but NEITHER statement ALONE is sufficient.
(D) EACH statement ALONE is sufficient.
(E) Statements (1) and (2) TOGETHER are NOT sufficient to answer the question asked, and additional data are needed.

4. The integers 1 through n are each written on a slip of paper and placed into a hat. If $2 \leq n \leq 10$, what is the probability that a slip randomly chosen from the hat will have an odd number on it?

(1) n is prime.

(2) n is even.

(A) Statement (1) ALONE is sufficient, but statement (2) alone is not sufficient.
(B) Statement (2) ALONE is sufficient, but statement (1) alone is not sufficient.
(C) BOTH statements TOGETHER are sufficient, but NEITHER statement ALONE is sufficient.
(D) EACH statement ALONE is sufficient.
(E) Statements (1) and (2) TOGETHER are NOT sufficient to answer the question asked, and additional data are needed.

5. Diana is going on a school trip along with her two brothers, Bruce and Clark. The students are to be randomly assigned into 3 groups, with each group leaving at a different time. What is the probability that Diana leaves at the same time as at least one of her brothers?

(A) $\dfrac{1}{27}$

(B) $\dfrac{4}{27}$

(C) $\dfrac{5}{27}$

(D) $\dfrac{4}{9}$

(E) $\dfrac{5}{9}$

6. Shinie is drying a load of laundry that includes her socks. The load has 2 identical red socks, 4 identical black socks, and 6 identical white socks. What is the fewest number of socks she must pull out of the dryer to have at least a 50% chance of pulling out at least one red sock?

(A) 1
(B) 2
(C) 3
(D) 4
(E) 10

7. If the 6 letters in the word NEEDED are randomly rearranged, what is the probability that the resulting string of letters will not be in alphabetical order?

(A) $\dfrac{1}{720}$

(B) $\dfrac{1}{120}$

(C) $\dfrac{1}{60}$

(D) $\dfrac{59}{60}$

(E) $\dfrac{719}{720}$

8. Sets R and S each contain three distinct positive integers. If integer r is randomly selected from R, and integer s is randomly selected from S, what is the probability that $rs = r$?

(1) The probability that $rs = s$ is $\dfrac{1}{3}$.

(2) The probability that $r + s = 2$ is $\dfrac{1}{9}$.

(A) Statement (1) ALONE is sufficient, but statement (2) alone is not sufficient.
(B) Statement (2) ALONE is sufficient, but statement (1) alone is not sufficient.
(C) BOTH statements TOGETHER are sufficient, but NEITHER statement ALONE is sufficient.
(D) EACH statement ALONE is sufficient.
(E) Statements (1) and (2) TOGETHER are NOT sufficient to answer the question asked, and additional data are needed.

9. James and Colleen are playing basketball. The probability of James missing a shot is x, and the probability of Colleen not making a shot is y. If they each take 2 shots, what is the probability that they both make at least 1 shot apiece?

(A) $1 - (x^2 y^2)$
(B) $(1 - x^2)(1 - y^2)$
(C) $(1 - (1 - x)^2)(1 - (1 - y)^2)$
(D) $(1 - (1 - x)^2)(1 - y^2)$
(E) $(1 - (1 - y)^2)(1 - x^2)$

10. Alan is a bartender, and someone has removed all the labels from the bottles. Some bottles contain an alcoholic liquor, and the rest contain alcohol-free mixers. If Alan randomly selects three bottles and mixes a drink, what is p, the probability that the drink will contain no alcohol?

    (1) There are twice as many bottles of liquor as there are of mixers.

    (2) $\dfrac{1}{80} < p < \dfrac{1}{50}$

(A) Statement (1) ALONE is sufficient, but statement (2) alone is not sufficient.
(B) Statement (2) ALONE is sufficient, but statement (1) alone is not sufficient.
(C) BOTH statements TOGETHER are sufficient, but NEITHER statement ALONE is sufficient.
(D) EACH statement ALONE is sufficient.
(E) Statements (1) and (2) TOGETHER are NOT sufficient to answer the question asked, and additional data are needed.

$$S = \{4, 4, 6, 9, 11\}$$
$$T = \{9, 11, 11, 12, 13\}$$

11. Two integers will be randomly selected from the lists above, one integer from list S and one integer from list T. What is the probability that the difference between the two integers is less than 4 ?

(A) $\dfrac{1}{5}$

(B) $\dfrac{2}{5}$

(C) $\dfrac{11}{25}$

(D) $\dfrac{9}{20}$

(E) $\dfrac{1}{2}$

12. A committee of 6 people is to be formed by randomly selecting from a group of 10, consisting of 5 women and 5 men. What is the probability that the committee will have more women than men?

(A) $\dfrac{1}{42}$

(B) $\dfrac{11}{42}$

(C) $\dfrac{22}{42}$

(D) $\dfrac{4}{9}$

(E) $\dfrac{5}{9}$

13. A bag contains only black, green, and silver marbles. If there are 21 marbles in the bag, what is the probability of randomly selecting a silver marble?

    (1) There are more black marbles than green marbles.

    (2) When two marbles are randomly chosen from the bag one at a time, and the first marble is placed back in the bag before the second marble is chosen, the probability that both marbles are silver is the same as the probability that the first marble is black and the second marble is green.

(A) Statement (1) ALONE is sufficient, but statement (2) alone is not sufficient.
(B) Statement (2) ALONE is sufficient, but statement (1) alone is not sufficient.
(C) BOTH statements TOGETHER are sufficient, but NEITHER statement ALONE is sufficient.
(D) EACH statement ALONE is sufficient.
(E) Statements (1) and (2) TOGETHER are NOT sufficient to answer the question asked, and additional data are needed.

14. Jane has a 6-sided die, and each face is labeled with a random positive integer. If Jane rolls her die three times, what is the probability that both the sum and the product of her rolls are odd?

    (1) If Jane rolls twice, the probability that the sum of her rolls is even equals $\frac{26}{36}$.

    (2) If Jane rolls twice, the probability that the product of her rolls is even equals $\frac{11}{36}$.

(A) Statement (1) ALONE is sufficient, but statement (2) alone is not sufficient.
(B) Statement (2) ALONE is sufficient, but statement (1) alone is not sufficient.
(C) BOTH statements TOGETHER are sufficient, but NEITHER statement ALONE is sufficient.
(D) EACH statement ALONE is sufficient.
(E) Statements (1) and (2) TOGETHER are NOT sufficient to answer the question asked, and additional data are needed.

15. There is a set of beads, and each bead is painted either red or blue. The beads are split, with each bead being cut in half. Then they are merged, such that all the halves are randomly reassembled back into the same number of beads that there were to begin with. This results in r red beads, b blue beads, and p beads that are half red and half blue. Before the split and merge, were there more red beads than blue beads?

    (1) After the split and merge, the probability of picking a bead that is only red is less than the probability of picking a bead that is at least half-blue.

    (2) After the split and merge, the probability of picking a bead that is only blue is greater than the probability of picking a bead that is at least half-red.

(A) Statement (1) ALONE is sufficient, but statement (2) alone is not sufficient.
(B) Statement (2) ALONE is sufficient, but statement (1) alone is not sufficient.
(C) BOTH statements TOGETHER are sufficient, but NEITHER statement ALONE is sufficient.
(D) EACH statement ALONE is sufficient.
(E) Statements (1) and (2) TOGETHER are NOT sufficient to answer the question asked, and additional data are needed.

Check your answers on page 373.

PERMUTATIONS

Some problems on the GMAT deal with calculating the number of ways to arrange or order a group of objects. It is possible to arrange objects from different sources or from the same source.

Different Sources

If the things you are arranging are from different sources, simply multiply the number of choices for each item. Here's an example.

1. Each night before he goes to bed, Jordan likes to pick out an outfit to wear the next day. He has 12 different shirts, 10 different pairs of jeans, and 8 pairs of sneakers. If an outfit consists of 1 shirt, 1 pair of jeans, and 1 pair of sneakers, how many different outfits does Jordan have?

    (A) 30
    (B) 90
    (C) 240
    (D) 480
    (E) 960

Jordan has 12 different shirts, 10 different pairs of jeans, and 8 pairs of sneakers, so he can make a total of $12 \times 10 \times 8$, or 960 different outfits. The correct answer is (E).

Same Source

Some problems involve choosing objects from the same source. If the order of those objects matters, the problem is a **permutation**. Permutation problems work a lot like different-source problems. You multiply the number of possible choices for the first item by the number of choices left for the second item, and so forth. The size of the source group gets smaller as you go. Here's an example.

2. Five people are running in a race. The first one to finish wins a gold medal, the second wins a silver medal, and the third wins a bronze medal. How many different arrangements of medal winners, in order from first to third, are possible?

    (A)   5
    (B)   10
    (C)   60
    (D) 120
    (E) 125

In this problem order matters, because if the race places like this.

Joe	1st
Sue	2nd
Sam	3rd

That's a different outcome than if the race places like this.

Sue	1st
Sam	2nd
Joe	3rd

Each ordering of the top three places is a different outcome, so the order is important.

When the gold medal is awarded there are 5 possible runners who could win it. Once the gold has been awarded, there are 4 runners available to win the silver. Once the gold and silver have been awarded, there are 3 runners available to win the bronze. The total number of arrangements of medal winners is $5 \times 4 \times 3 = 60$ The correct answer is (C).

If you are arranging items from the same source and order matters, count down and multiply.

The Formula

The formula to calculate a permutation is

$$\text{Number of arrangements (permutations)} = \frac{n!}{(n-r)!}$$

where n is the number of objects in the source and r is the number of objects selected.

The formula has to be adjusted for harder problems, so you may find it easier and simpler to use the count down method.

COMBINATIONS

Combination problems ask you to calculate the number of distinct groups that can be formed from a collection of objects. As with most permutation problems, you are pulling the items from the same source; however, with combinations, order **doesn't** matter. Here's an example.

3. Five people are running in a race. The first three to finish win gift certificates. How many different groups of people could win the gift certificate?

    (A)   5
    (B)   10
    (C)   60
    (D) 120
    (E) 125

This problem is very similar to the race problem you saw in the permutations chapter, but in this race order doesn't matter. The first three people to finish all get the same gift certificate, so it doesn't matter whether the race places Joe, Sue and Sam, or Sam, Sue and Joe. In fact, the second outcome is a duplicate of the first, because regardless of the order, the group of people is still Joe, Sue and Sam.

The first part of a combination problem is the same as a permutation problem. When the first gift certificate is awarded there are 5 possible runners who could win it. Once the first gift certificate has been awarded, there are 4 runners available to win the second gift certificate, and so on.

Now because order doesn't matter, you need to get rid of the duplicate outcomes. You do this by dividing by the number of ways to arrange the items chosen. An easy way to do this is to simply divide by the factorial of the number of spots you have. Here you have three spots (there are 3 runners in the race), so divide by 3!. Thus, the number of different groups of people who could win the gift certificates is

$$\frac{5 \times 4 \times 3}{3 \times 2 \times 1} = 10$$

The correct answer is (B).

If you are arranging items from the same source and order doesn't matter, count down and divide.

Combining Concepts

Some questions combine the same source and different sources in the same problem, so before continuing, make sure you're solid on the concepts from the Permutation section. For these, calculate everything for one source and then multiply the different sources together. Here's an example.

4. Kris is purchasing gear to ride his bike this winter. He wants to buy 2 pairs of gloves, 1 parka, 2 hats, and 3 pairs of boots. If the catalog from which he will order offers 5 types of gloves, 3 different parkas, 4 hats, and 6 pairs of boots, how many different orders could he place?

(A)   360
(B)   720
(C)   3,600
(D)   7,200
(E)   36,000

This problem has different sources because Kris is purchasing a parka, gloves, hats and boots, but it's also a same source problem because Kris is buying more than one kind of glove, more than one kind of hat and more than one kind of boot. No problem. Simply lay out all your spots on your scratch paper: 2 spots for gloves, 1 spot for a parka, 2 spots for hats and 3 spots for gloves.

Start with gloves. When he goes to pick his first pair of gloves, Kris has 5 gloves from which to choose. Once he has chosen the first pair, he now has 4 gloves from which to choose for the second pair. The order of the gloves doesn't matter. Because order doesn't matter, divide by 2!.

Kris is picking one parka and he has 3 to choose from. He's only picking one item, so just divide by 1.

Now continue this process for the hats and boots. Your scratch paper should look something like this.

$$\frac{5 \times 4}{2 \times 1} \times \frac{3}{1} \times \frac{4 \times 3}{2 \times 1} \times \frac{6 \times 5 \times 4}{3 \times 2 \times 1} = 3,600$$

The correct answer is (C). For problems that combine same source with different sources, calculate the possibilities for each item, and then multiply the possibilities together.

The Formula

The formula to calculate a combination is

$$\text{Number of different groups (combinations)} = \frac{n!}{r!(n-r)!}$$

where n is the number of objects in the source and r is the number of objects selected.

The formula has to be adjusted for harder problems, so you may find it easier and simpler to use the count down and divide method.

PERMUTATIONS AND COMBINATIONS DRILL

1. Gretchen is having a cheese tasting, and is going to offer each guest one cheddar, one brie, one bleu, and one mozzarella. If she has three types of cheddar, three types of brie, four types of bleu, and six types of mozzarella, how many different combinations of cheese are available to her guests?

   (A)   54
   (B)   72
   (C) 108
   (D) 216
   (E) 432

2. A certain acting troupe is putting on a play that has four female roles and three male roles. If the troupe consists of ten actors, with an equal number of men and women, how many ways can the roles be assigned to the troupe, assuming each actor can only play one part?

   (A) 604,800
   (B)   50,400
   (C)   7,200
   (D)   180
   (E)   50

3. A car collector plans to take 4 of his cars to an auto show. How many cars does the collector have to choose from?

   (1) The number of possible groups of cars he can bring is greater than 50.

   (2) The number of possible groups of cars he can bring is less than 125.

   (A) Statement (1) ALONE is sufficient, but statement (2) ALONE is not sufficient.
   (B) Statement (2) ALONE is sufficient, but statement (1) ALONE is not sufficient.
   (C) BOTH statements TOGETHER are sufficient, but NEITHER statement ALONE is sufficient.
   (D) EACH statement ALONE is sufficient.
   (E) Statements (1) and (2) TOGETHER are NOT sufficient to answer the question asked, and additional data are needed.

4. Uduak is getting married, and wants her bridesmaids to line up for a picture with her. There are six bridesmaids, including one maid of honor. If Uduak is to be in the middle, and her maid of honor is to stand next to her, how many possible arrangements are there?

   (A) 5,040
   (B) 2,520
   (C)   720
   (D)   240
   (E)   120

5. Marilyn is going to order a pizza with several toppings. Is the number of 4-topping pizzas she can order equal to the number of 3-topping pizzas she can order?

   (1) There are 8 toppings to choose from.

   (2) There are at least 6 toppings to choose from.

   (A) Statement (1) ALONE is sufficient, but statement (2) ALONE is not sufficient.
   (B) Statement (2) ALONE is sufficient, but statement (1) ALONE is not sufficient.
   (C) BOTH statements TOGETHER are sufficient, but NEITHER statement ALONE is sufficient.
   (D) EACH statement ALONE is sufficient.
   (E) Statements (1) and (2) TOGETHER are NOT sufficient to answer the question asked, and additional data are needed.

6. Sean is making a playlist of five songs. He has 5 duets and 4 solos to choose from. If Sean alternates duets and solos, how many arrangements of songs are there?

   (A) 15,120
   (B)   1,200
   (C)   720
   (D)   480
   (E)   160

7. Six kids will be lined up from left to right. Boys may not be at either end (the first and last spot). In how many ways can the kids be lined up?

   (1) There are 4 girls.

   (2) There are 12 different ways to fill the first and last spot.

(A) Statement (1) ALONE is sufficient, but statement (2) ALONE is not sufficient.
(B) Statement (2) ALONE is sufficient, but statement (1) ALONE is not sufficient.
(C) BOTH statements TOGETHER are sufficient, but NEITHER statement ALONE is sufficient.
(D) EACH statement ALONE is sufficient.
(E) Statements (1) and (2) TOGETHER are NOT sufficient to answer the question asked, and additional data are needed.

8. A committee of 5 will be made up from a group of 11. Six women and five men are available. Restrictions will be placed on the committee's composition so that not all possible combinations of men and women will be permitted. In how many ways can the committee be formed?

   (1) The number of men on the committee divided by the number of women on the committee is equal to 4, $\frac{2}{3}$, or 0.

   (2) The committee has an odd number of women.

(A) Statement (1) ALONE is sufficient, but statement (2) ALONE is not sufficient.
(B) Statement (2) ALONE is sufficient, but statement (1) ALONE is not sufficient.
(C) BOTH statements TOGETHER are sufficient, but NEITHER statement ALONE is sufficient.
(D) EACH statement ALONE is sufficient.
(E) Statements (1) and (2) TOGETHER are NOT sufficient to answer the question asked, and additional data are needed.

9. A conference is to have eight presentations over the course of one day, consisting of three long presentations, and five short presentations. If the conference organizer doesn't want consecutive long presentations, and the conference is to start with a short presentation, how many schedules of presentations are possible?

(A) 120
(B) 720
(C) 2,880
(D) 5,760
(E) 11,520

10. A museum just received a new shipment of paintings to go with its current collection of five paintings. Including these new paintings, how many ways can the museum arrange their entire collection of paintings, from left to right, in a new exhibit?

   (1) Including the new shipment, the museum has seven paintings in their collection.

   (2) The museum only plans to arrange five paintings in the new exhibit.

(A) Statement (1) ALONE is sufficient, but statement (2) ALONE is not sufficient.
(B) Statement (2) ALONE is sufficient, but statement (1) ALONE is not sufficient.
(C) BOTH statements TOGETHER are sufficient, but NEITHER statement ALONE is sufficient.
(D) EACH statement ALONE is sufficient.
(E) Statements (1) and (2) TOGETHER are NOT sufficient to answer the question asked, and additional data are needed.

11. Every night, Jon and his brothers randomly determine the schedule in which they will get to use the shower in the morning. How many distinct schedules are possible?

    (1) The probability that Jon will be first or last is 40%.

    (2) There are 48 ways Jon could be first or last.

(A) Statement (1) ALONE is sufficient, but statement (2) ALONE is not sufficient.
(B) Statement (2) ALONE is sufficient, but statement (1) ALONE is not sufficient.
(C) BOTH statements TOGETHER are sufficient, but NEITHER statement ALONE is sufficient.
(D) EACH statement ALONE is sufficient.
(E) Statements (1) and (2) TOGETHER are NOT sufficient to answer the question asked, and additional data are needed.

12. A meal consists of one appetizer, one entrée, and one dessert. How many entrees are on the menu?

    (1) There are 4 appetizers on the menu.

    (2) The number of total possible meals is 80.

(A) Statement (1) ALONE is sufficient, but statement (2) ALONE is not sufficient.
(B) Statement (2) ALONE is sufficient, but statement (1) ALONE is not sufficient.
(C) BOTH statements TOGETHER are sufficient, but NEITHER statement ALONE is sufficient.
(D) EACH statement ALONE is sufficient.
(E) Statements (1) and (2) TOGETHER are NOT sufficient to answer the question asked, and additional data are needed.

13. Chris and Val are at dinner with three friends. If the table is round and has exactly five seats, how many ways can the group sit such that Chris and Val are not sitting together?

(A) 30
(B) 60
(C) 90
(D) 120
(E) 720

14. Alfred is renting three movies for the weekend. How many groups of movies can he rent?

    (1) Alfred never rents more than 4 movies at a time.

    (2) The store has 10 movies available for rental.

(A) Statement (1) ALONE is sufficient, but statement (2) ALONE is not sufficient.
(B) Statement (2) ALONE is sufficient, but statement (1) ALONE is not sufficient.
(C) BOTH statements TOGETHER are sufficient, but NEITHER statement ALONE is sufficient.
(D) EACH statement ALONE is sufficient.
(E) Statements (1) and (2) TOGETHER are NOT sufficient to answer the question asked, and additional data are needed.

15. Herb bought a different present for each of his four grandchildren, but he forgot to label the gifts after wrapping them. If Herb randomly gives each grandchild a present, what is the probability that at least one grandchild gets the correct gift?

(A) $\dfrac{23}{24}$

(B) $\dfrac{7}{8}$

(C) $\dfrac{5}{8}$

(D) $\dfrac{4}{8}$

(E) $\dfrac{3}{8}$

16. Britt is selecting books to take with him on vacation. The categories he will select from are biographies, comic books, and novels. How many combinations of books can he bring?

   (1) Britt has 4 biographies to choose from and 3 comic books.

   (2) Britt has 7 novels to choose from.

   (A) Statement (1) ALONE is sufficient, but statement (2) ALONE is not sufficient.
   (B) Statement (2) ALONE is sufficient, but statement (1) ALONE is not sufficient.
   (C) BOTH statements TOGETHER are sufficient, but NEITHER statement ALONE is sufficient.
   (D) EACH statement ALONE is sufficient.
   (E) Statements (1) and (2) TOGETHER are NOT sufficient to answer the question asked, and additional data are needed.

17. Fifteen runners from four different countries are competing in a tournament. Each country holds a qualifying heat to determine who its fastest runner is. These four runners then run a final race for first, second and third place. If no country has more than one more runner than any other country, how many arrangements of prize-winners are there?

   (A)   24
   (B)   384
   (C)   455
   (D) 1,248
   (E) 2,730

18. Some models are in a competition. The winner will receive $100 and the runner-up will receive $50. How many models are in the competition?

   (1) 4 of the models will advance to the final round, and 2 of the finalists will win the prizes.

   (2) There are 90 different ways to rank the winners, in order, first and second.

   (A) Statement (1) ALONE is sufficient, but statement (2) ALONE is not sufficient.
   (B) Statement (2) ALONE is sufficient, but statement (1) ALONE is not sufficient.
   (C) BOTH statements TOGETHER are sufficient, but NEITHER statement ALONE is sufficient.
   (D) EACH statement ALONE is sufficient.
   (E) Statements (1) and (2) TOGETHER are NOT sufficient to answer the question asked, and additional data are needed.

19. Hank is making a salad, which is going to have two types of lettuce, three types of vegetables, and one type of dressing. If he can choose from five types of lettuce, seven types of vegetables, and four types of dressing, how many salads can Hank make?

   (A)   28
   (B)   140
   (C)   280
   (D) 1,400
   (E) 2,800

20. Five people are set to give speeches at a convention. One will speak in the Enterprise Room, two will speak in the Excelsior Room, and the rest will speak in the Voyager Room. How many different ways are there to assign the speakers to rooms?

   (A)   15
   (B)   30
   (C)   60
   (D)   90
   (E)   120

21. A pirate will select 4 prisoners to walk the plank. Is the number of plank-walking groups equal to a prime number?

    (1) There are fewer than 6 prisoners on board.

    (2) The number of prisoners on board is a prime number.

(A) Statement (1) ALONE is sufficient, but statement (2) ALONE is not sufficient.
(B) Statement (2) ALONE is sufficient, but statement (1) ALONE is not sufficient.
(C) BOTH statements TOGETHER are sufficient, but NEITHER statement ALONE is sufficient.
(D) EACH statement ALONE is sufficient.
(E) Statements (1) and (2) TOGETHER are NOT sufficient to answer the question asked, and additional data are needed.

22. If there are n groups of size x that can be formed from y distinct objects, how many groups of size x, in terms of n, x, and y, can be formed from $y + 1$ distinct objects?

(A) $n - y$

(B) $\dfrac{y + 1}{y - x + 1}$

(C) $\dfrac{ny + y}{x}$

(D) $\dfrac{n(y + 1)}{x + 1}$

(E) $\dfrac{yn + n}{y - x + 1}$

23. Ben and Shari have invited three other couples to their apartment for a game of charades. Everyone is to be split into two equal teams, but each team must consist of either two couples or no couples. How many different pairs of teams are possible?

(A) 11
(B) 14
(C) 22
(D) 35
(E) 70

24. Mary is starting a band, which is to consist of a bassist, a drummer, two guitarists, and a keyboardist, Mary will play either the bass or the drums, but not both. She has 1 bassist, 3 drummers, 5 guitarists, and 2 keyboardists interested in joining the band, each of whom plays only one instrument. How many different bands can Mary form?

(A) 30
(B) 60
(C) 80
(D) 120
(E) 160

25. Brian is having a birthday party at Rowdy Rick's Ranch'n Rides Rodeo for his friends from school. If he can invite exactly five of his classmates, how many groups of classmates can Brian invite?

    (1) Twelve of Brian's classmates will not be invited.

    (2) If the number of classmates Brian can invite were to increase by 20%, the number of groups Brian could invite would be k times greater, where k equals $\dfrac{1}{9}$ of the total number of people in Brian's class.

(A) Statement (1) ALONE is sufficient, but statement (2) ALONE is not sufficient.
(B) Statement (2) ALONE is sufficient, but statement (1) ALONE is not sufficient.
(C) BOTH statements TOGETHER are sufficient, but NEITHER statement ALONE is sufficient.
(D) EACH statement ALONE is sufficient.
(E) Statements (1) and (2) TOGETHER are NOT sufficient to answer the question asked, and additional data are needed.

Check your answers on page 373.

GROUPS

Some GMAT problems involve different groups of people or things. For these problems use the Group Equation or the Group Grid.

Group Equation

Do you remember Venn diagrams from high school? If you don't, it's no problem. The group equation is an easy way to deal with these problems and it's much more intuitive.

$$\text{Total} = \text{Group 1} + \text{Group 2} + \text{Neither} - \text{Both}$$

Anyone who is in both groups is double counted: once in the first group and once in the second. That's why you subtract out anyone who's in both. You add anyone who is in neither group because they haven't been counted. When you see the words **both** and/or **neither** in a problem, you know you can use the group equation.

Example

1. A country club has 230 members, 60 of whom play tennis. If 130 members play golf, and 40 members play both golf and tennis, how many members play neither golf nor tennis?

    (A)   10
    (B)   40
    (C)   60
    (D)   80
    (E)   100

Simply plug the numbers into the formula. There are 230 members **total**, 60 **who play tennis**, 130 **who golf**, and 40 who play **both**. Now you can solve for the number who play neither.

$$230 = 60 + 130 + N - 40$$
$$230 = 150 + N$$
$$80 = N$$

The correct answer is (D).

Group Grid

Other group problems have two sets of groups with either/or characteristics. For these problems it's helpful to set up a grid. Look at an example.

2. A manufacturing company employs 125 people. Each employee is either a blue-collar employee or a white-collar employee. 67 of the employees are female, and 75 of the employees are blue-collar. If there is a total of 35 male white-collar employees, then the number of female white-collar employees is

    (A) 15
    (B) 23
    (C) 52
    (D) 50
    (E) 58

There are two sets of groups with either/or characteristics (male/female and blue-collar/white collar), so set up a grid and fill in the information provided in the problem. Circle what you're looking for so you don't fill in parts of the grid you don't need.

Although the group grid looks a bit like a ratio box, the grid is all addition and subtraction. You know that there are 50 white-collar employees (because 125 workers – 75 blue-collar workers = 50). Then subtract across the top row to get the female white collar workers: 50 – 35 = 15. The correct answer is (A).

	male	female	total
white-collar	35	15	50
blue-collar			75
total		67	125

For more about statistics problems, see *Cracking the GMAT*.

GROUPS DRILL

1. Of the 56 automobiles for sale on a used car lot, 24 have sunroofs, 39 have leather interiors, and 12 have neither. How many automobiles have both sunroofs and leather interiors?

   (A) 15
   (B) 19
   (C) 24
   (D) 27
   (E) 29

2. At the Santos L. Halpern High School, seniors must pass both a math test and a verbal test in order to graduate. If the number of students who passed both tests is twice as many as the number of students who failed both, what percent of students failed exactly one test?

   (1) 10% of the students failed both tests.

   (2) 40% of the students failed the verbal test.

   (A) Statement (1) ALONE is sufficient, but statement (2) alone is not sufficient.
   (B) Statement (2) ALONE is sufficient, but statement (1) alone is not sufficient.
   (C) BOTH statements TOGETHER are sufficient, but NEITHER statement ALONE is sufficient.
   (D) EACH statement ALONE is sufficient.
   (E) Statements (1) and (2) TOGETHER are NOT sufficient to answer the question asked, and additional data are needed.

3. Farmington Inc. employs two types of employees: salespeople and information technology technicians. The employees can choose between two types of cellular phones: smart phones or flip phones. If 30 percent of all employees choose flip phones, an equal number of salespeople and technicians choose smart phones, a total of 50 salespeople choose flip phones and 70 choose smart phones, how many information technology technicians choose flip phones?

   (A)   5
   (B) 10
   (C) 30
   (D) 40
   (E) 80

4. Smithtown High School is holding a lottery to raise money. The tickets are assigned numbers from 1 to 200. Tickets with numbers divisible by 2 win t-shirts, tickets with numbers divisible by 3 win gift-certificates, and tickets with numbers divisible by 7 win movie passes. How many tickets win none of the prizes?

   (A)   6
   (B)   52
   (C)   58
   (D) 142
   (E) 194

5. In a certain state, every county is represented by two senators. Last week, a bill to lower taxes was brought to the floor. Every senator voted either yes or no on the bill, and the bill needs more yes votes than no votes to pass. Did the bill pass?

   (1) 90% of the senators up for re-election this year voted yes.

   (2) 90% of the no votes came from senators not up for re-election this year.

   (A) Statement (1) ALONE is sufficient, but statement (2) alone is not sufficient.
   (B) Statement (2) ALONE is sufficient, but statement (1) alone is not sufficient.
   (C) BOTH statements TOGETHER are sufficient, but NEITHER statement ALONE is sufficient.
   (D) EACH statement ALONE is sufficient.
   (E) Statements (1) and (2) TOGETHER are NOT sufficient to answer the question asked, and additional data are needed.

6. A certain history test has 100 questions, and every question is either multiple choice or free-response. If exactly 30% of the multiple choice questions are about the Stone Age, how many of the free-response questions are about the Stone Age?

    (1) Exactly 8 of the free-response questions are not about the Stone Age.

    (2) Exactly half of the questions are about the Stone Age.

(A) Statement (1) ALONE is sufficient, but statement (2) alone is not sufficient.
(B) Statement (2) ALONE is sufficient, but statement (1) alone is not sufficient.
(C) BOTH statements TOGETHER are sufficient, but NEITHER statement ALONE is sufficient.
(D) EACH statement ALONE is sufficient.
(E) Statements (1) and (2) TOGETHER are NOT sufficient to answer the question asked, and additional data are needed.

7. Every citizen in Bellaville owns at least one kind of television among flat panel, projection, and plasma televisions. If there are a total of 1,000 citizens in Bellaville, and 52 percent of the citizens own exactly two of the three kinds of televisions and 22 percent own all three kinds of televisions, then how many citizens own only one kind of television?

(A) 26
(B) 30
(C) 260
(D) 485
(E) 740

8. Every student at Preston School of Business must take a foreign language. 75 students take French and 48 students take Spanish. If half as many students take both French and Spanish as take Spanish, and 10 percent of all students take neither French nor Spanish, how many students attend Preston School of Business?

(A) 11
(B) 24
(C) 99
(D) 110
(E) 123

9. At Pete's Halloween party this year, everyone had to dress either as a ninja or as a pirate. If there are 18 people dressed as pirates, how many people are at the party?

    (1) There are three times as many women dressed as pirates as there are men dressed as ninjas.

    (2) There are three times as many men dressed as pirates as there are women dressed as ninjas.

(A) Statement (1) ALONE is sufficient, but statement (2) alone is not sufficient.
(B) Statement (2) ALONE is sufficient, but statement (1) alone is not sufficient.
(C) BOTH statements TOGETHER are sufficient, but NEITHER statement ALONE is sufficient.
(D) EACH statement ALONE is sufficient.
(E) Statements (1) and (2) TOGETHER are NOT sufficient to answer the question asked, and additional data are needed.

10. A group of students is traveling to a conference 400 miles away. Students travel either by car or by plane. Two-thirds of students are not presenting papers at the conference. If there are a total of 36 students attending the conference, four students who traveled by car are presenting papers, and one-fourth of the students travel by plane, then how many students who traveled by plane are not presenting papers?

   (A) 0
   (B) 1
   (C) 8
   (D) 12
   (E) 23

11. In a certain sample, 65% of dogs were less than 3 years old and 40% of dogs greater than 3 years old were over 40 pounds. If there were 300 dogs in the sample, how many of the dogs were greater than 3 years old and under 40 pounds?

   A) 42
   B) 63
   C) 52
   D) 78
   E) 117

12. Chance just took his daughter's soccer team to Al's Pizza Buffet to celebrate another tie game. A sixth of the team had exactly one slice each, a sixth of the team had exactly two slices each, a sixth of the team had exactly 3 slices each, and the rest of the team each had at least 4 slices each. If a whole pizza is 6 slices, did any of the players eat a whole pizza alone?

   (1) There are 12 players on the team.

   (2) The players ate an average of 3 slices per person.

   (A) Statement (1) ALONE is sufficient, but statement (2) alone is not sufficient.
   (B) Statement (2) ALONE is sufficient, but statement (1) alone is not sufficient.
   (C) BOTH statements TOGETHER are sufficient, but NEITHER statement ALONE is sufficient.
   (D) EACH statement ALONE is sufficient.
   (E) Statements (1) and (2) TOGETHER are NOT sufficient to answer the question asked, and additional data are needed.

Check your answers on page 373.

Statistics Answers
and Explanations

ANSWER KEY

Averages

1. C
2. A
3. E
4. D
5. A
6. C
7. B
8. B
9. E
10. D
11. C
12. A
13. D
14. C
15. A

Median

1. C
2. C
3. B
4. D

Mode

1. B
2. C
3. D
4. E
5. B

Range

1. C
2. B
3. C
4. C
5. B

Standard Deviation

1. C
2. A
3. A
4. D
5. A
6. E
7. C
8. D
9. D

Rate

1. C
2. C
3. E
4. A
5. D
6. A
7. C
8. B
9. B
10. C
11. B
12. E
13. A
14. C
15. B
16. A
17. D
18. C
19. A

Factorials

1. B
2. C
3. D
4. C
5. E

Probability

1. C
2. B
3. B
4. B
5. E
6. D
7. D
8. B
9. B
10. C
11. B
12. B
13. E
14. B
15. B

Permutations and Combinations

1. D
2. C
3. C
4. D
5. A
6. B
7. D
8. D
9. C
10. C
11. D
12. E
13. B
14. B
15. C
16. C
17. D
18. B
19. D
20. B
21. C
22. E
23. A
24. C
25. D

Groups

1. B
2. A
3. B
4. C
5. E
6. C
7. C
8. D
9. C
10. B
11. B
12. B

EXPLANATIONS

Averages

1. **C** In order to calculate the average, find the total of the items and divide that by the number of items. Make sure to use the average pie to organize your information. You have four employees with a salary of $19,000. To ballpark, drop the thousands. So for these four, there is a total of 4×19, or 76. To this, add 2×15, or 30, for the total of the next two employees. That gives a total of 106. Finally, add 12 for the last worker. Thus, the grand total is 118. Now, divide this by the number of employees, which is 7. 118/7 is about 16.8.

2. **A** If you know the sum of the numbers in the set and the total number of numbers in the set, you can determine the average. The problem statement gives the sum, and Statement (1) gives the number of items, so statement (1) is sufficient. Eliminate (B), (C), and (E). The values of individual numbers are irrelevant, and knowing the value extremes does not matter if the number of items is unknown, so Statement (2) is insufficient by itself.

3. **E** Statement (1) is not sufficient to determine the individual value of n. Within the bounds of the question, granting (1) as true, n could be 5 or 7. Eliminate (A) and (D). Statement (2) seems insightful, but it is actually a restatement of information given in the problem stem: if the average of 5 numbers is 8, then their sum must be 40, and $3 + n + (n + 3) + 2n + p = 40$ simplifies to Statement (2). The statements, taken alone or together, are not sufficient to determine the requested information.

4. **D** Because this problem involves variables, Plug In. Let $x = 2$, $y = 3$, $r = 4$, and $s = 5$. If 2 numbers average 3, then the total must be 6, and if 4 numbers average 5, the total must be 20. To figure out the average of all 6 numbers, now divide the total of 26 by 6. You are left with 4 and 1/3 as your target. The only answer that matches this target is (D).

5. **A** To solve this problem, first calculate the average of 5, 25, and 45. There are three items here and they have a sum of 75. The average, then, is 75 divided by 3, or 25. According to the problem, 25 is 10 more than the average of 15, 40, and one other number. At this point, you have two choices. You can plug the answers into the problem and see which one works. For example, if you plug (C) into the problem, it reads, "25 is 10 more than the average of 15, 40, and 40." Is this true? The average of 15, 10, and 40 is 65 divided by 3, which is a little more than 20. 25 is not 10 more than 20. Thus, you need a smaller number. Choice (A) works because the average of 15, 10, and 20 is 45. The average of these three numbers is 15. 25 is in fact 10 more than 15, so it works. Or, you can translate the problem to read: $25 = 10 +$ the average of three numbers. Subtracting 10 from each side, you can see that 15 must be the average of the three numbers. If three numbers have an average of 15, they must have a sum of 45. Subtracting 15 and 10 from 45 leaves 20.

6. **C**   Statement (1) tells you nothing about the numeric value of the newsstand prices, so it is insufficient by itself. Eliminate (A) and (D). Statement (2) gives the newsstand price, but without knowing how many issues are released yearly, this is not sufficient information to determine the yearly savings. Eliminate (B). Taken together, the two statements provide both a newsstand price and a number of issues received, which is enough to calculate the total newsstand price of the three magazines. Since you have the total subscription price for the three magazines, the total savings must be (newsstand - subscription); as you are looking for the average savings, the distribution of savings does not matter when the total savings and number of magazines are both known.

7. **B**   Statement (1) provides information that constrains the salary distribution, but does not determine it, so it is not sufficient on its own. Eliminate (A) and (D). Statement (2) sets a strict upper bound on the possible salary range, which determines the size of bonuses payable. Knowing the highest IT department salary, it is possible to calculate the maximum bonus liability, so Statement (2) is sufficient on its own.

8. **B**   This is a difficult average question, but it is possible to get through if you keep track of the different pieces of information. First, the problem says that the senior employees have an average of 16 years experience. You don't know how many senior employees there are, so call the number s. That means that the total number of years of experience for the senior employees is $16s$. Second, you know that the junior members have an average of 4 years of work experience. Since you don't know how many junior employees there are, call that number j. As above, you can figure that the total number of years worked by the junior employees is $4j$. Third, you know that the average work experience for the senior and junior members combined is 7. You don't know the number of junior and senior employees, but you can express it as $s + j$. Thus, the total number of years worked for all the employees is $7(s + j)$, or $7s + 7j$. Now, put everything together. The total number of years worked by the senior employees plus the total number of years worked by the junior employees should equal $7s + 7j$ (the value you just found for all the employees combined). That means that $16s + 4j = 7s + 7j$. By subtracting $7s$ and $4j$ from each side, you can simplify this to $9s = 3j$. From here, you can get $s{:}j$ by dividing the left side of the equation by j and the right side by 9. That leaves you with the ratio of s to j as 3:9, or 1:3. Alternatively, you can Plug In The Answers until you find one that works.

9. **E**   In order to calculate the average speed for the entire trip, you need both the total distance traveled and the total time spent. You know that Josiah's trip was 4 miles long, so that is the total distance. So you need to find the total time. For the first 2 miles, Josiah's rate was 2 miles per hour, which means he spent 1 hour walking. For the second 2 miles, his rate was 4 miles per hour, which means it took him a half hour to complete the trip. Thus, his total time was 1.5 hours. Now that you have the total distance and the total time, find the average rate by dividing. 4 divided by 1.5 is 8/3.

10. **D** The question requires you to determine the three sales commission rates. Enough information is given about each of the three sales categories to determine the total dollar value of sales among top performers, middle performers, and bottom performers. Let x represent the top-performers' commission and y the middle-performers' commission. Given the average for the top half of sales staff, you can find their total commissions paid, which must be equal to $24{,}000{,}000x + 7{,}200{,}000y$, with $x = y + .03$; this system of simultaneous equations can be solved for x. Thus Statement (1) is sufficient. Eliminate (B), (C), and (E). A similar process applies with Statement (2) and the bottom half of performers, so either statement is sufficient to find the requested information.

11. **C** This problem tests a familiar concept in an unfamiliar way. You know that the sum of the n terms is 1,458. That means the average of the terms is $1{,}458/n$. You also know that the average of the n terms is 6. Thus, $6 = 1{,}458/n$ and $n = 243$.

12. **A** From Statement (1), the total sales of the lower 5 companies can be determined, which means the exact value of sales at the top-selling company may be determined, which is sufficient to answer the given question. Eliminate (B), (C), and (E). Statement (2) is not sufficient to determine the distribution of sales in the top five companies, so it cannot be used to determine the total sales at the top-selling company, and is thus insufficient to answer the question.

13. **D** The total number of goals scored is 262. You need the average number of goals scored by the 10 remaining players. Since you have the number of items, you need the total number of goals scored by these ten players. To find that value, you can subtract the number of goals scored by the top five scorers. The top two scorers averaged 40 goals each, meaning that between the two of them, they scored 80 goals. The next three scorers averaged 24 goals each, for a total of 72 goals. Thus, the top five scorers accounted for 152 goals. That leaves 110 goals scored by the remaining 10 players. Dividing 110 by 10 gives 11.

14. **C** In order to know the average of a set, you must know the sum of the set and the number of members in the set. The stem indicates there are 5 elements in this set. Statement (1) is not in itself adequate to identify any of the numbers, nor their sum. Eliminate (A) and (D). Statement (2) is not sufficient by itself, as it provides no data about the value of x. Eliminate (B). However, Statement (2) does work out to $4y + 12 = 6y + 12$, or $4y = 6y$. That can only be true if $y = 0$. Knowing this, the set consists of $\{x, x + 7, 2x, 0, 5\}$, which includes four distinct values. x cannot be 0, because the resulting set $\{0, 7, 0, 0, 5\}$ would have fewer than four distinct numbers. Because x is a positive integer other than 5, the values $\{0, 5\}$ are unique in the set, so $\{x, x + 7, 2x\}$ must have one repeated value. With a positive x, the only way that is possible is if $2x = x + 7$, which solves for $x = 7$, and gives the sum of the set as 40, average value of 8.

15. **A** The website received a total of 7,000 visitors; 500 visits per day for 14 days. The total number of visitors in the first 8 days was 650×8, or 5,200. That leaves 1,800 for the remaining 6 days. 1,800 divided by 6 days is 300 per day.

Median

1. **C** This is a good question to test your understanding of the concept of median. The median is the middle number in a list of numbers, found after putting the numbers in order from least to greatest. For this question, you could simply write out all the numbers in the set and find the middle number. However, a little strategy will save you some work. First, note that there are 30 days in the period (found by adding up the numbers in the second row). If there is an even number of numbers in a set, the median is the average of the two middle numbers, in this case the average of the 15th and 16th number. Thus, you don't need to figure out what the entire list looks like, just what the 15th and 16th numbers are. The first 4 numbers are each 32, and then there are 7 numbers with a value of 41. That gives you the first 11 numbers in the set. The next 8 numbers are all 45. Thus, the 15th and 16th numbers in the list must be 45.

2. **C** Statement (1) states that there are 3 integers in set A. However, this is not sufficient to determine the median as it says nothing about the numbers contained in set A. Eliminate (A) and (D). Statement (2) states that the average of set A and the most frequently appearing number in set A are each equal to 4, which is insufficient to answer the question. For example, if set A were {-4, 4, 4, 5, 6, 7, 8} then the mean and mode would both be equal to 4, and the median would equal 5. However if set A were {4, 4, 4} then the mean, median, and mode would all equal 4. Eliminate (B). Combined however, then set A must be {4, 4, 4} as $\frac{4 + 4 + x}{3} = 4$ then $4 + 4 + x = 12$, thus x must equal 4. Since statements (1) and (2) are insufficient alone, and they are sufficient together, the answer is (C).

3. **B** The list contains an odd number of numbers, meaning that the median will be a member of the set (which is enough information to eliminate (D)). Leaving x aside for a moment, if you place the values in order you get: 13, 14, 15, 16, 17, 18, 19, 20. Now think about where x fits into this list. If x is 11, 12, 13, 14, 15, or 16, the median will be 16 (because all of these numbers will be added to the list to the left of 16). But if x is 17, 18, 19, 20, or 21, then the median will be 17 (because any of these numbers would be placed to the right of 17.

4. **D** To find the median of a list of numbers that has an even number of elements, find the average of the two middle numbers. First, list the values from least to greatest, yielding 7, 9, 10, 12, 14, 17. Next, take the two middle values, 10 and 12, and find their average. The average of 10 and 12 is 11. The answer is (D).

Mode

1. **B** First, list out the numbers. The single digit primes are: 2, 3, 5, and 7. To prime factorize 84, break it down into prime numbers: $2 \times 2 \times 3 \times 7$. The set composed of these numbers is thus: 2, 2, 2, 3, 3, 5, 7, 7. The number that appears the most, or the mode, is 2.

2. **C** Statement (1) gives two equations: $2x = y$ and $x = 2z$, which is insufficient. Combining these equations provides that $2x = y = 4z$, which means that set A is {0.5y, 2y, 2y, 1.25y, 0.75y}. Thus while you know that the mode of set A is $2y$, you do not know the value of the mode. Eliminate (A) and (D). Statement (2) states that the middle number of set A is 125. However, you do not know what the middle number is based upon statement (2) alone. Eliminate (B). Combined, statement (1) tells you that, in order, set A is {0.5y, 0.75y, 1.25y, 2y, 2y} because you know that x, y, and z are positive integers, and statement (2) tells you that $1.25y = 125$, and thus that $y = 100$, which is enough information to find the values of the other members of set A and the mode. Since statements (1) and (2) are insufficient alone, but are sufficient together, the answer is (C).

3. **D** You need to find the mean, median, and mode of the list of numbers. The mode is the easiest to find; it is the number that appears most, which in this case is 17. Thus, $m = 17$. The median is the middle value. Since there are ten numbers in the set, the median is the average of the 5th and 6th values. In this case, the median is the average of 15 and 17, or 16. So $n = 16$. Finally, you need the average. There are ten numbers and their sum is 150, so the average is 15.

4. **E** This problem may be easier to handle if you Plug In a set of consecutive integers, such as 1, 2, 3. In this simple case, you can see that the median and the mean are equal. Eliminate (A) and (B) because statement I can be true. Statement II is a bit of a trap, but you can get a mean of 0 if the set of consecutive integers is, for example, –1, 0, 1. That eliminates (C) and (D). Choice (E) cannot be true because in a set of consecutive integers, no number appears more than once. Thus, there is no mode.

5. **B** Statement (1) tells you that the sum of the members of set X is equal to 25 and that the middle number of set X is 5, which is not sufficient to answer the question. For example, set X could be {2, 2, 5, 7, 9} in which case the mode is less than the median or set X could be {1, 3, 5, 8, 8} in which case the mode is greater than the median. Eliminate (A) and (D). Statement (2) states that if the median were removed from set X, the mean and mode would stay the same, but the median would change, which is sufficient to answer the question. For example, if set X had a mode less than the median, such as {2, 2, 5, 7, 9} which has a mode of 2, median of 5, and mean of 5, then removing the median would produce: {2, 2, 7, 9} which has a mode of 2, a median of 4.5, and a mean of 5; the mode and mean remained unchanged but the median decreased. However, if the mode were greater than the median, such as {1, 3, 5, 8, 8}, which has a mode of 8, median of 5, and mean of 5, then removing the median would produce {1, 3, 8, 8}, which has a mode of 8, median of 5.5, and mean of 5; the mode and mean remained unchanged, but the median increased, which means that the mode must be less than the mean. Since statement (1) is insufficient but statement (2) is sufficient, the answer is (B).

Range

1. **C** $6 + 9 + 14 = 29$, so $x = 29$. Thus Set A is $\{6, 9, 14, 29\}$. The range is simply the high value minus the low value, so $29 - 6 = 23$.

2. **B**   Range is the high value minus the low value. The smallest prime number is 2, and the largest prime number less than 40 is 37. So the range will be $37 - 2 = 35$.

3. **C**   The numbers that square to 49 are -7 and 7. The numbers that square to 16 are -4 and 4. The numbers that square to 9 are -3 and 3. Thus Set C contains $\{-7, -4, -3, 3, 4, 7\}$. Range is the high value minus the low value so $7 - (-7) = 14$.

4. **C**   This is a range question, but it's also yes-no data sufficiency, so Plug In. For statement (1), if you make $n = 2$, and $m = 5$, the range of the set is 6, which is less than 7. However, if you make $n = 2$ and $m = 10$, the range of the set is 8, which is greater than 7. This statement is not sufficient. Eliminate (A) and (D). For Statement (2), if you make $n = 6$ and $m = 7$, the range of the set is 3, which is less than 7. However, if you make $n = 6$ and $m = 20$, the range of the set is 15, which is greater than 7. This statement is not sufficient. Eliminate (B). If you combine the two statements and make $n = 6$ and $m = 13$, the range is 8, which is greater than 7. If you make $n = 6$ and $m = 20$, the range is 15, which is still greater than 7. Because 6 is the minimum value of n (and that makes 13 the minimum value of m), the range will always be 8 or greater. Combining is sufficient.

5. **B**   Statement (1) tells you that d is the smallest number, but it doesn't tell you its value or the value of the largest number. The first statement is insufficient. Eliminate (A) and (D). For Statement (2), since this is a yes-no data sufficiency question, Plug In some numbers. If a, b, c and d are 1, 2, 3 and 5, respectively, the range of the set is 4, which is greater than 3. If a, b, c and d are 1, 7, 9 and 5, respectively, the range of the set is 8, which is also greater than 3. If the difference between two numbers of the set is greater than 3, then the range must also be greater than 3. This statement is sufficient, and the correct answer is (B).

Standard Deviation

1. **C**   On the GMAT, you probably won't ever need to calculate standard deviation, but you will have to have an understanding of the concept. Standard deviation is a measure of the variation in a data set; basically, how far the data points, on average, deviate from the mean of the set. Thus, a data set that has all the same numbers in it, as in I, has no standard deviation because there is no variation. Data set III has a small amount of variation. Note that the fact that the values in set III are negative has no bearing on the standard deviation; standard deviations are never negative. Set II has the greatest variation in its values and thus will have the largest standard deviation. Thus, the correct order from greatest to least is II, III, I.

2. **A** Statement (1) is sufficient. If the data point one standard deviation greater than the mean is 6.3 and the mean is 4.7, the standard deviation is 6.3 – 4.7, or 1.6. Eliminate (B), (C), and (E). Statement (2) is not sufficient. The range does nothing to tell you the standard deviation.

3. **A** The use of the word "normal distribution" should clue you in to the fact that this is a standard deviation problem. To work with standard deviations, you first need to calculate the average number of baseball cards per child. Take 2,700 and divide by 30 to yield an average of 90 cards. Now, the bottom 16% of the children had fewer than 70, which represents all data one standard deviation to the left of the mean. This tells you your standard deviation is equal to 20. To calculate how many children had greater than 130 baseball cards, you must move two standard deviations to the right and this tells you that the top 2% of children had greater than 130 baseball cards.

4. **D** In order to answer this question, you need to know the standard deviation. Thus, statement (1) obviously works. If the standard deviation is 2, then models that are 70 inches or shorter will be cut. Eliminate (B), (C), and (E). Statement (2) does not look particularly helpful, but if you look more closely at statement (2) you can see that it is telling you that $\frac{4}{200}$, or 2%, of the models have heights of 76 inches or above. That means that the second standard deviation is 76. To get from the mean of 72 to the second standard deviation of 76, you have to add 2 two times. That means that the standard deviation is 2. Statement (2) actually tells you the same thing as statement (1).

5. **A** To find the number of students who will be recommended for advancement, you need the average score and the standard deviation. Statement (1) does not give this to you directly, but it tells you that $\frac{34}{50}$, or 68%, of the students got between 62 and 84 on the final exam. That means that 16% got below 62 and 16% got above 84. 16% of 50 is 8, so 8 students will be recommended for advancement. Eliminate (B), (C), and (E). By itself, statement (2) does nothing to tell you how many students will be recommended for advancement, so the answer is (A).

6. **E** Both the median and the mean of a set would be affected by changing the values of the numbers in the set. For example, if the set of numbers was 2, 4, 6 and you added 3 to each value, the new set would be 5, 7, 9. Clearly, the mean and the median would be different. The standard deviation, however, would remain the same. That's because the standard deviation measures the average distance from the mean. Since all values were changed by a constant, the average distance from the mean will not change.

7. **C** Statement (1) is not sufficient because it tells you the mean, but nothing about the other numbers in the set. You could Plug In two sets of numbers for the set and get two different standard deviations. Eliminate (A) and (D). Statement (2) is also insufficient. Again, you could Plug In two sets of numbers to get two different standard deviations. Eliminate (B). Combining the two statements tells you that the numbers in set S are consecutive, because in a consecutive set of numbers, the mean equals the median. If the numbers are consecutive, even integers and the mean is 4, you know that the standard deviation is 2.

8. **D**   This is a trick question of sorts. As long as you know the basics of standard deviation, the answer is fairly apparent. The standard deviation is the measure of the average distance from the mean of the members of a set of numbers. Thus, it must always be non-negative. But the mean, median, and mode of a set of numbers can be negative. In this case, since all of the numbers in the set are negative, the mean, median, and mode will be negative. But the standard deviation will still be positive.

9. **D**   Statement (1) is sufficient. If the difference between the mean and each temperature is 5, then the standard deviation is 5. Eliminate (B), (C), and (E). For statement (2), you need to know that standard deviation is the square root of the variance of a set of data. Thus, if the variance is 25, the standard deviation is 5.

Rate

1. **C**   Statement (1) states the time Silas spent picking pumpkins, but does not state the rate, therefore it is not sufficient. Eliminate (A) and (D). Statement (2) states Silas's rate but does not state how long he worked, therefore it is insufficient. Eliminate (B). Combining statements (1) and (2), you know how long Silas worked and his rate, therefore you have enough information, thus the answer is (C).

2. **C**   There are 60 seconds in a minute and 60 minutes to an hour. $1.05 \times 60 \times 60 = 3{,}780$ miles per hour.

3. **E**   Statement (1) states that the time that Alex worked but not her hourly rate, thus it is insufficient. Eliminate (A) and (D). Statement (2) states Alex's income from the previous week, but does not state whether the income stayed the same, and thus statement (2) is insufficient. Eliminate (B). Statement (2) does not establish what Alex's hourly rate is and statement (1) does not state that her total income stayed the same, and thus the two statements combined are insufficient. Since statements (1) and (2) alone and combined are insufficient to answer the question, the answer is (E).

4. **A**   Plug In numbers for the variables. Say that Calvin picks 2 apples per hour. So, $b = 2$. Then say that $a = 10$. So, if he is picking apples at the rate of 2 per hour then in 10 hours he picks 10/2 or 5 per hour. 5 is the target. Plug $b = 2$ and $a = 10$ into the answer choices. The only one that equals the target of 5 is (A).

5. **D** Statement (1) reveals that Thomas's rate is 300 screws per hour and Monica's rate is 400 screws per hour, and thus is sufficient to answer the question. Eliminate (B), (C), and (E). Statement (2) states that 1.5 times Thomas's rate would be equal to 1.125 times Monica's rate. This means that $1.5T = 1.125M$, and thus that $\dfrac{T}{M} = \dfrac{1.125}{1.5}$, which means that Thomas's rate is lower than Monica's and thus statement (2) is sufficient. Therefore, since statements (1) and (2) are both sufficient, the answer is (D).

6. **A** Plug In numbers. Say that $z = 2$ and $y = 4$. If it takes the machine 12 minutes to produce 2 zippers, then it will take 24 minutes to produce 4 zippers. So, 24 is the target. Plug $z = 2$ and $y = 4$ into the answers. The only one that equals the target of 24 is (A).

7. **C** Statement (1) states that train X reached Williamsland at 5 p.m., which means that it traveled 200 miles in 4 hours, and thus had a rate of 50 mph. However, this tells you nothing about train Y and thus is insufficient. Eliminate (A) and (D). Statement (2) states that trains X and Y pass each other at 3:30 p.m., or 2.5 hours into X's trip and 1.5 hours into Y's trip. This means that you can construct the equation: (2.5 hours)(X's rate) + (1.5 hours)(Y's rate) = 200 miles. However, this still gives you two variables and only one equation, and thus it is insufficient. Eliminate (B). Now combine. Statement (1) states that X's rate is 50 miles per hour. Adding this to the equation from statement (2) gives you: (2.5 hours)(50 mph) + (1.5 hours)(Y's rate) = 200 miles; and thus: (125 miles) + (1.5 hours)(Y's rate) = 200 miles; and thus: (1.5 hours)(Y's rate) = 75 miles; and finally that Y's rate is also 50 mph, which is sufficient to answer the question. Therefore, since statements (1) and (2) alone were insufficient, but together are sufficient, the answer is (C).

8. **B** Remember the rate formula: Work = Rate × Time. Plugging In Janet's numbers, you get 320 = $r \times 4$. Janet's rate is 80 envelopes per hour. Plugging In Tameka's rates, you get 300 = $r \times 6$. Tameka's rate = 50 envelopes per hour. Working together, Tameka and Janet can address 80 + 50 = 130 envelopes per hour. So, again applying the rate formula: 390 = 130 × t. Solving for the combined time, you get $t = 3$.

9. **B** Statement (1) states that Diego's rate is $\dfrac{3}{4}$ of Frida's rate. However, without knowing either of their times, this is not sufficient. Eliminate (A) and (D). Statement (2) states Diego's and Frida's times respectively to finish the mural. Thus Diego can finish $\dfrac{1}{24}$ of the mural in one hour and Frida, $\dfrac{1}{18}$ in one hour. Combining these two rates, you get $\dfrac{1}{24} + \dfrac{1}{18} = \dfrac{3}{72} + \dfrac{4}{72} = \dfrac{7}{72}$, and thus you know that combined they can finish $\dfrac{7}{72}$ of the mural per hour. Thus you can find that $1\,mural = (\dfrac{7\,murals}{72\,hours})(\dfrac{72}{7}\,hours)$, and can therefore answer the question of how long it will take them to finish. Since statement (1) is insufficient and statement (2) is sufficient to answer the question, the answer is (B)

10. **C** Statement (1) states the cost of machines A and B, but not their S values and thus is insufficient. Eliminate (A) and (D). Statement (2) provides that machine A's S value is lower than machine B's S value but does not provide the price of either and thus is also insufficient. Eliminate (B). Combined you know that A: $Y = \dfrac{\$300}{S_1}$ and B: $Y = \dfrac{\$250}{S_2}$ and that $S_1 < S_2$, which means that statement (2) is sufficient. For example, if machine A makes 1 shot per minute ("spm") and machine B makes 2 spm, then you would get A: $Y = \dfrac{\$300}{1spm} = 300$ and B: $Y = \dfrac{\$250}{2spm} = 125$, and thus Sasha will buy machine B. In fact, since the numerator for machine B is lower than that for A, as long as the denominator for B is not bigger than the denominator for A, Sasha will always choose B. Since statements (1) and (2) are not sufficient by themselves and together are sufficient to answer the question, the answer is (C).

11. **B** The rate formula states that work = rate × time. Plug In a number for the total amount of work. If it takes 20 brush strokes to paint a room, then Lynda's rate will be 4 per hour. Alex's rate will be 5 per hour. Their combined rate will then be 9 per hour. Working together, their time will be $\dfrac{20}{9}$ or $2\dfrac{2}{9}$.

12. **E** Statement (1) states that Kathy's hourly rate is $\dfrac{3}{4}$ of Sam's hourly rate. This means that Sam's rate is higher than Kathy's rate, but does not establish for how long each worked and thus is insufficient. Eliminate (A) and (D). Statement (2) states that Kathy worked for two hours longer than Sam, but does not establish how long each worked in total or what their rates were. Eliminate (B). Combined, statement (1) only gives the ratio of Sam's to Kathy's rate, not the rates themselves and statement (2) only gives the difference between the times, not the times themselves. Thus, since statements (1) and (2) alone are insufficient and together are still insufficient to answer the question, the answer is (E).

13. **A** Set up the following proportion: 8 machines/360 cans = 5 machines/x cans, where x cans will equal the number of cans 5 machines can produce in one hour. Cross multiply and you get $8x = 360(5)$. $8x = 1,800$. $x = 225$. Multiply that by 3 hours to get 675.

14. **C** Plug In. Make the park 12 miles away from his house. So, 12 is the target. Say that $m = 3$ and $n = 4$. The distance formula is Distance = Rate × Time. Plugging In the values that you have chosen into the distance formula gives you the following: On the trip to the park $12 = 3 \times t$. Solving for t, it takes Sydney 4 hours to get to the park. On the way back from the park, $12 = 4 \times t$. Solving for t, it takes Sydney 3 hours to get home from the park. z = the total hours which = 3 + 4, or 7.

Now that you have all of the numbers, Plug Into the answers. The only one that equals the target of 12 is (C).

15. **B** Statement (1) states the combined cost of given quantities of tea bags and loose-leaf tea, but does not give the individual costs and thus is not sufficient. Eliminate (A) and (D). However, it is helpful to do some conversions between ounces and grams: $100\,tea\,bags\left(\dfrac{2.24\,grams}{1\,tea\,bag}\right)=224\,grams$ and $224\,grams\times\left(\dfrac{1\,oz}{28\,grams}\right)=8\,oz$. Therefore, statement 1 states that 8 ounces of tea bags and 8 ounces of loose-leaf together cost $21, but not the individual prices. Statement (2) states that 5 tea bags cost the same as 0.2 ounces of loose-leaf tea. This allows you to determine which costs more per ounce. Remembering that each tea bag weighs 2.24 grams, at that rate, 5 tea bags weigh 11.2 grams, and thus $11.2\,grams\times\left(\dfrac{1\,oz}{28\,grams}\right)=\dfrac{11.2}{28}\,oz=0.4\,oz$. Therefore if 0.20 oz of loose-leaf cost the same as 0.4 ounces of tea bags, then loose-leaf costs twice as much per ounce. Since statement (1) is insufficient and statement (2) is sufficient to answer the question, the answer is (B).

16. **A** Statement (1) states that Ryan can complete the job in 36 hours, this means that Phil can complete the job in 72 hours, because Ryan works twice as fast as Phil. Even though this does not tell you what their actual rates are, you can still find out that their combined rate is $\dfrac{1}{36}+\dfrac{1}{72}=\dfrac{2}{72}+\dfrac{1}{72}=\dfrac{3}{72}=\dfrac{1\,job}{24\,hours}$, which is sufficient. Eliminate (B), (C), and (E). Statement (2) states that Phil's rate is 25 bricks/hour, which means that Ryan's rate is 50 bricks/hour. Working together, Ryan and Phil have a combined rate of 75 bricks/hour. However, you still do not know the size of the job, and thus statement (2) is insufficient. Since statement (1) is sufficient and statement (2) is not, the answer is (A).

17. **D** The rate formula states that work = rate × time. Plug In a number for the job. Say the machines are making 88 widgets. The first machine's rate then is 8 widgets per hour. The second machine's rate is 11 widgets per hour. Working together, they have a rate of 11 + 8 = 19 widgets per hour. At that rate, they can complete the job of 88 widgets in 4.63 hours. The answer is (D). Alternatively, you can work this with fractions. In this case the machines are completing one job so $w = 1$. The rate for the first machine can be then calculated as $1 = r \times 11$. The rate $=\dfrac{1}{11}$. For the second machine

the rate can be calculated as $1 = r \times 8$. The rate $= \dfrac{1}{8}$. The combined rate for the two machines $=$ $\dfrac{1}{8} + \dfrac{1}{11} = \dfrac{19}{88}$ per hour. Plugging the combined rate into the rate formula gives you $1 = \dfrac{19}{88} \times t$. $t = 4.63$ hours.

18. **C** Statement (1) states the time the trip took. This means that the checkered cab would have cost $30. However, this says nothing about how much the yellow cab cost. Eliminate (A) and (D). Statement (2) tells you the rate at which the cab traveled, but does not state either the distance traveled or the time the trip took. Taken together, the trip took 30 minutes, which means that the trip was 12 miles long. This means that the yellow cab cost $2.50 + 12 \, miles\left(\dfrac{\$0.20}{1/4 \, mile}\right) = \$2.50 + \$9.60 = \$12.10$. This means that the yellow cab was less expensive than the checkered cab, which cost $30.00. Since statements (1) and (2) alone were insufficient, and together are sufficient, the answer is (C).

19. **A** The rate formula states that work = rate × time. Plug In a number for the total amount of work. If it takes 24 bricks to pave the driveway, then Sarah's rate is 4 per hour. Plug In The Answers for Sadie's time. Start with (C). If it takes Sadie 7 hours by herself, then her rate is $\dfrac{7}{24}$ per hour. That's not going to work out evenly. Try (A). If Sadie's time is 12 hours for the 24 bricks, then her rate is 2 per hour. Together, their rate is 6 per hour. They can do 24 bricks in 4 hours, as the question states. So, the answer is (A). Alternatively, you can work this question with fractions. In one hour Sarah completes $\dfrac{1}{6}$ of the job, while Sadie completes $\dfrac{1}{x}$ of the job. Working together Sarah and Sadie can complete $\dfrac{1}{4}$ of the job in one hour. Therefore, $\dfrac{1}{6} + \dfrac{1}{x} = \dfrac{1}{4}$. Solve for x and you get $x = 12$ hours.

Factorials

1. **B**   Plug In The Answers, starting with (C). When $x = 5$, the equation becomes $\dfrac{5!}{7!} = \dfrac{5}{6!}$. You can rewrite this as $\dfrac{5 \times 4 \times 3 \times 2 \times 1}{7 \times 6 \times 5 \times 4 \times 3 \times 2 \times 1} = \dfrac{5}{6 \times 5 \times 4 \times 3 \times 2 \times 1}$. After reducing, you are left with $\dfrac{1}{42} = \dfrac{1}{144}$, which is incorrect. Eliminate (C). Plugging In (B) gives you $\dfrac{4!}{6!} = \dfrac{4}{5!}$. Cancel and simplify to $\dfrac{1}{5 \times 6} = \dfrac{1}{5 \times 3 \times 2 \times 1}$, which both equal $\dfrac{1}{30}$.

2. **C**   Plug In The Answers, starting with (E), the greatest value listed. If $y = 6$, the equation becomes $x! = 6x$, which can only be true if x is 4. But 6 is not less than 4 and the question says $y < x$, so eliminate (E). Try (D). When $y = 3$, the equation becomes $x! = 3x$. There are no integer values for x that make this true, so eliminate (D) and try (C). If $y = 2$, then $x! = 2x$, which makes $x = 3$. Here y is less than x, so (C) can be correct and is the greatest possible value that can be correct. Therefore, the answer is (C).

3. **D**   Statement (1) states that x is greater than y, which means that $y!$ is a factor of $x!$. For example if, $x = 4$ and $y = 3$, then $x! = (4)(3)(2)(1)$ and $y! = (3)(2)(1)$, which means that $x!$ has at least the same factors as $y!$. Statement (1) is sufficient to answer the question. Eliminate (B), (C), and (E). Statement (2) provides you with two equations involving x and y, so you can solve for each. If you rearrange the information in Statement (2), you find that $23x - 10y = 150$ and that $-5.5x + 2.5y = -35$. If you multiply the second equation by 4, you get $-22x + 10y = -140$. Now, if you set up simultaneous equations, you get

$$
\begin{array}{rcl}
23x - 10y &=& 150 \\
-22x + 10y &=& 140 \\
\hline
x &=& 10
\end{array}
$$

  Substituting 10 for x in the first equation gives you $230 - 10y = 150$, which means that $y = 8$. Since Statements (1) and (2) are both sufficient to answer the question, the correct answer is (D).

4. **C**   Plug In 3 for x, and the equation becomes $\dfrac{3! + 3}{z} = \dfrac{9}{z} = y$. Statement (1) tells you 3 must be a factor of y, and you know from the problem that z and y are integers. You could then Plug In 1 or 3 for z, and get 9 or 3 for y, respectively. Both these values of y have $x = 3$ as a factor, so since you cannot find one definitive value for z, statement (1) is not sufficient. Eliminate (A) and (D). Statement (2) tells you that $z < x$, so you can Plug In $x = 3$ and $z = 1$ to give $y = 9$. This is the only value for z that works when $x = 3$, because z must be less than 3, and $z = 2$ doesn't make y an integer. But when you Plug In $x = 4$, you can Plug In 1 or 2 for z, and both make y an integer. Since you cannot find one definitive value for z, statement (2) is not sufficient, so eliminate (B). When you combine the information, you can use the numbers you already plugged in to see that when $z = 1$, both

statements are true. Here more Plugging In would be messy, and so it is useful to rearrange the equation. Factor an x out from the numerator and move it to the other side, leaving $\dfrac{(x-1)!+1}{z} = \dfrac{y}{x}$. You know x is a factor of y, so the right hand side of the equation must be an integer. You also know that because z is less than x, z must be a factor of $(x-1)!$, and that $\dfrac{(x-1)!}{z}$ is an integer. So $\dfrac{(x-1)!}{z} + \dfrac{1}{z} = \dfrac{y}{x}$, and the only thing you can add to an integer to get another integer is an integer. So $\dfrac{1}{z}$ must be an integer, and because z is an integer itself, z must be equal to 1.

5. E   Statement (1) states that $b = 2$ since 2 is the only even prime number, which is insufficient. For example, a could equal 1, in which case $a! = 1$ and $b! = (2)(1) = 2$, and $1 - 2 < (1)(2)$. However, if $a = 3$, then $a! = (3)(2)(1) = 6$ and $b! = (2)(1) = 2$, and $6 - 6 = (3)(2)$. Statement (2) states that b raised to the a power equals a raised to the b power, which is insufficient. For example, if $a = 3$, and $b^3 = 3^b$, then b must equal 3 also and $3! - 3! = 0$, which is less than $(3)(3)$. However, if $a = 4$ and $b = 2$, then $4^2 = 16 = 2^4$, which means that $a! = (4)(3)(2)(1) = 24$ and $b! = (2)(1) = 2$, and $24 - 2 > (4)(2)$. Taken together, you know from statement 1 that b must equal 2. However, as a and b could both equal 2, in which case $2! - 2! < (2)(2)$ or a could equal 4 and b equal 2, in which case $4! - 2! > (4)(2)$, it is still insufficient. Thus, since statements (1) and (2) are insufficient alone, and insufficient together, the correct answer is (E).

Probability

1. ·C   There are four ways Bob can roll two numbers whose product equals 15. He can roll a 3 and then a 5, a 5 and then a 3, a 1 and then a 15, or a 15 and then a 1. Each way will have the same probability. For example, there is 1 way out of 10 to roll a 5, and 1 way out of 10 to roll a 3, so there is a $\dfrac{1}{10} \times \dfrac{1}{10} = \dfrac{1}{100}$ probability Bob rolls a 5 and then a 3. So there is a $\dfrac{1}{100} + \dfrac{1}{100} + \dfrac{1}{100} + \dfrac{1}{100} = \dfrac{4}{100}$ probability of Bob rolling one of the 4 ways to get a product of 15. Simplify to get $\dfrac{1}{25}$.

2. B   Write out the different ways to have quarters, nickels, and dimes add up to 45 cents (There are 8 ways). Statement (1) tells you that half the n coins are nickels. That means Jack could have 1 quarter, 1 dime, and 2 nickels, or 3 dimes and 3 nickels. This is insufficient to determine n, so eliminate (A) and (D). Statement (2) tells you half of the n coins are dimes, and this means Jack must have 3 dimes and 3 nickels, so $n = 6$.

3. B   Plug In. If n is 6, the factors of n are 6, 3, 2, and 1, and the probability that a randomly selected factor will be even is $\dfrac{1}{2}$. If n is 4, the factors are 1, 2, and 4. In this case the probability that a randomly selected factor is even is $\dfrac{2}{3}$. Different answers means that statement (1) is insufficient, so eliminate

(A) and (D). For statement (2), Plug In values for n where $\frac{n}{2}$ is odd. n could be 10, whose factors are 10, 5, 2, and 1, half of which are odd. You also know half the factors of 6 are even. If $\frac{n}{2}$ is odd, $\frac{n}{2}$ has no even factors. To get the factors of n, take each factor of $\frac{n}{2}$, and multiply it by 2. These will all be even numbers, and with the factors of $\frac{n}{2}$, make up the factors of n. Since each odd factor corresponds to a distinct even one, half of the factors of n are even. Statement (2) is sufficient.

4. **B** Plug In. If n is 2, then there are two slips, with 1 and 2 on them, respectively, and the probability of picking an odd number is $\frac{1}{2}$. But if n is 3, then there are 3 slips, with 1, 2 and 3. Here the probability of picking an odd number is $\frac{2}{3}$. Two different answers means that statement (1) is not sufficient, so eliminate (A) and (D). Plug In for statement (2) as well. n could be 2, 4, 6, 8, or 10. In each case, half the slips will have odd numbers and half will have even. So the probability of picking an odd number must be $\frac{1}{2}$. Statement (2) is sufficient.

5. **E** The words *at least one* hint that you should calculate the probability of Diana leaving without either of her brothers, and then subtract this from 1. Diana leaves at some time with a probability of 1, and there are 2 ways out of 3 that each of her brothers could leave at a different time than Diana. The probability that neither of her brothers leave at the same time as Diana is $1 \times \frac{2}{3} \times \frac{2}{3} = \frac{4}{9}$, so the probability that at least one of her brothers leaves at the same time as Diana is $1 - \frac{4}{9} = \frac{5}{9}$.

6. **D** Plug In the Answers, starting with (C). You want the probability that *at least one* sock is red to be 50% or more. This means that the probability of pulling no red socks would be less that 50%, and this is your target answer. There are 12 socks, 10 of which are not red. So if Shinie pulls 3 socks, the probability of getting no reds is $\frac{10}{12} \times \frac{9}{11} \times \frac{8}{10} = \frac{6}{11}$. This is more than 50%, so she has less than a 50% chance of getting at least one red. Eliminate (C). She needs to pull more socks to increase her chance of getting one, so eliminate (A) and (B), and Plug In (D). The probability of pulling no reds on 4 tries is $\frac{10}{12} \times \frac{9}{11} \times \frac{8}{10} \times \frac{7}{9} = \frac{14}{33}$. This is less than 50%, so there is more than a 50% chance that Shinie pulls at least one red sock on 4 tries.

7. **D**   The word NEEDED arranged alphabetically is DDEEEN. If you determine the probability of arranging the letters in this order, you can subtract it from 1 to determine the probability of not getting an alphabetical ordering. The probability of getting a D in the first position is $\frac{2}{6}$. You used one D and now have one fewer letter, so the probability of picking a D second is $\frac{1}{5}$. The probability of picking an E for the third spot is $\frac{3}{4}$. Continuing like this, the probability for the entire alphabetical ordering would be $\frac{2}{6} \times \frac{1}{5} \times \frac{3}{4} \times \frac{2}{3} \times \frac{1}{2} \times \frac{1}{1} = \frac{1}{60}$. So the probability of *not* arranging the letters in alphabetical order is $1 - \frac{1}{60} = \frac{59}{60}$, and the answer is (D).

8. **B**   Because r and s are both positive integers, the only way $rs = r$ is if s is 1. So the probability that $rs = r$ is equal to the probability that s is 1. Plug In for R and S. If $R = \{1,2,3\}$ and $S = \{1,2,4\}$, then there are 9 possible ways to pick r and s, 3 of which make $rs = s$. This makes Statement (1) true, because the probability that $rs = s$ is $\frac{3}{9} = \frac{1}{3}$. The probability that s is 1 is $\frac{1}{3}$. However, if $R = \{1,2,3\}$ and $S = \{2,3,4\}$, the probability that $rs = s$ is still $\frac{1}{3}$, but there is a 0 probability that s is equal to 1. Statement (1) is not sufficient, so eliminate (A) and (D). Statement (2) tells you that there is a non-zero probability that $r + s = 2$. Because r and s are both positive integers, the only way this can happen is if both r and s are 1. This means there is a $\frac{1}{3}$ chance 1 is selected from S.

9. **B**   There are variables in the choices, so Plug In. Let $x = \frac{1}{4}$ and $y = \frac{1}{3}$. Do the rest one step at a time. To determine the probability that James hits *at least one* shot, you first find the probability that he hits no shots, and subtract that from 1. The probability that he misses both shots is $\frac{1}{4} \times \frac{1}{4} = \frac{1}{16}$, so he has a $1 - \frac{1}{16} = \frac{15}{16}$ chance of hitting at least one shot. When you do the same thing for Colleen, you find that she has a $\frac{8}{9}$ chance of hitting at least one shot. Thus, the probability of James AND Colleen both hitting at least one shot is $\frac{15}{16} \times \frac{8}{9} = \frac{5}{6}$. This is your target answer. Plug the values you used for x and y into the answer choices to see which one gives you the target answer. Only (B) yields $\frac{5}{6}$.

10. **C** Statement (1) tells you that there are twice as many bottles of liquor as there are of mixers. So there could be 2 bottles of mixers and 4 bottles of liquor, in which case there is a 0% chance that a selection of 3 bottles will contain no alcohol. Or there could be 3 bottles of mixers and 6 bottles of liquor, in which case it is possible to mix an alcohol-free drink. Since the probability is either 0 or not 0, statement (1) is not sufficient, eliminate (A) and (D). Statement (2) gives you a range for p. So again, Plug In. If there are 3 bottles of mixers and 5 bottles of liquor, making 8 total bottles, then the probability of picking three bottles with no alcohol is $\frac{3}{8} \times \frac{2}{7} \times \frac{1}{6} = \frac{1}{56}$, which is in the range. But if there are 4 bottles of mixers and 8 bottles of liquor, the probability of mixing a non-alcoholic drink is $\frac{4}{12} \times \frac{3}{11} \times \frac{2}{10} = \frac{1}{55}$, which is also in the range for p. Since you can get 2 different values for p, statement (2) is not sufficient; eliminate (B). When the information is combined, there have to be at least 3 bottles of mixers, because there cannot be a 0 probability that the drink contains no alcohol. Dealing with statement (1) first, there could be 3 mixers and 6 liquors, 4 mixers and 8 liquors, 5 mixers and 10 liquors, etc. If there are 3 mixers and 6 liquors, then the probability of mixing a drink with no alcohol is $\frac{3}{9} \times \frac{2}{8} \times \frac{1}{7} = \frac{1}{84}$, which is lower than the range from Statement (2). You know that 4 bottles of mixers and 8 bottles of liquor give a 1 in 55 chance of mixing an alcohol-free drink, which is in the range. 5 mixers and 10 liquors give a probability of $\frac{5}{15} \times \frac{4}{14} \times \frac{3}{13} = \frac{2}{91}$, which is too big. Increasing the bottles will only increase the probability that the drink will be useless, so the only possible number of bottles is 12. Both statements together are sufficient.

11. **B** This is a probability question, so first determine the total number of possible outcomes. There are 5 integers in each list, so the number of possible outcomes is $5 \times 5 = 25$. Now, count how many of the possible integer pairs have a difference of less than 4. There are 10 integer pairs that have a difference of less than 4 (6 and 9, 9 and 9, 9 and 11, 9 and 11, 9 and 12, 11 and 9, 11 and 11, 11 and 11, 11 and 12, and 11 and 13). Therefore, the probability is $\frac{10}{25} = \frac{2}{5}$ and the correct answer is (B).

12. **B** The probability that the committee will have more women than men $= \frac{\text{\# of committees with more women than men}}{\text{\# of total possible committees}}$. The number of total possible committees is how many ways you can choose 6 people from 10, where order does not matter. So the number of total possible committees is $\frac{10 \times 9 \times 8 \times 7 \times 6 \times 5}{6 \times 5 \times 4 \times 3 \times 2 \times 1} = 210$. If there are more women than men on the committee, then there is either 1 man and 5 women, or 2 men and 4 women. The number of ways to pick 1 man from 5 is 5, and the number of ways to pick 5 women from 5 is 1. So there are $1 \times 5 = 5$ ways to have 1 man and 5 women. The number of ways to pick 2 men from 5 is $\frac{5 \times 4}{2 \times 1} = 10$,

and the number of ways to pick 4 women from 5 is $\frac{5 \times 4 \times 3 \times 2}{4 \times 3 \times 2 \times 1} = 5$. So there are $10 \times 5 = 50$ ways to have 2 men and 4 women, which means there are $50 + 5 = 55$ ways to have more women than men. Divide 55 by 210 to get the probability.

13. **E** Statement (1) is insufficient because you don't know how many silver marbles there are. Eliminate (A) and (D). Statement (2) tells you that pulling two silver marbles with replacement is the same as pulling a black and then a green marble with replacement. This would be true if there were an equal number of each color marble in the bag. If there are 7 of each color, there are 21 total marbles, and the probability of pulling a silver marble twice, with replacement, is $\frac{7}{21} \times \frac{7}{21} = \frac{49}{442}$. The probability of pulling a black and then green with replacement would be the same thing. So there could be 7 silver marbles. Plug In different numbers. If there are 6 silver marbles, 3 green marbles, and 12 black marbles, the probability of pulling two silvers with replacement would be $\frac{6}{21} \times \frac{6}{21} = \frac{36}{441}$, and the probability of pulling a black and then a green, with replacement, would be $\frac{12}{21} \times \frac{3}{21} = \frac{36}{441}$. So there could be 7 silver marbles, or 6 silver marbles. Two different answers means that statement (2) alone is not sufficient; eliminate (B). If you combine the information, there can't be 7 of each color anymore, but there still could be 6, 3, and 12 silver, green, and black marbles respectively. Check for other values that work. If there are 4 silver, 1 green, and 16 black marbles, the probabilities in question are equal. Two possible values for the number of silver marbles means that the statements combined are not sufficient.

14. **B** The only way for the sum and product of the three rolls to be odd is for Jane to roll three odd numbers, so you only need the probability of rolling an odd number. Fact 1 tells you the probability of two rolls adding to an even number. This can happen by rolling either two odd numbers or two even numbers. You can plug in values for the number of odds and evens on the die. If there are 5 odd numbers and 1 even number, the probability of rolling two odd numbers is $\frac{5}{36} \times \frac{5}{36} = \frac{25}{36}$. The probability of rolling two evens is $\frac{1}{36} \times \frac{1}{36} = \frac{1}{36}$. The probability of rolling two odds or two evens is the sum of the probabilities of each, or $\frac{26}{36}$. However, this would also be true if there were 1 odd number and 5 even numbers, so Fact 1 does not tell you the probability of rolling an

odd number. Eliminate (A) and (D). Fact 2 tells you that the probability that the product of the two rolls being even equals $\frac{11}{36}$. Because the product of two rolls has to be either even or odd, the probability that the product is odd equals $1 - \frac{11}{36} = \frac{25}{36}$. The only way for the product to be odd is for Jane to roll two odd numbers. You can plug in values for the number of odd numbers on the die. If there are 5 odd numbers on the die, then the probability of rolling two odd numbers is $\frac{5}{36} \times \frac{5}{36} = \frac{25}{36}$, which you know to be true. No other number of odd numbers on the die gives you this value. So Fact 2 tells you the probability of rolling an odd number. Fact 2 is sufficient alone, and the answer is (B).

15. **B** Plug In. Statement (1) tells you that after the split and merge, the probability of picking an all-blue bead is less than the probability of picking a bead that is at least half red. Start with 6 red beads and 4 blue beads. After splitting, you have 12 red halves and 8 blue halves. After merging them randomly, suppose you only get 4 beads that are half red and half blue. You used 4 of your red halves and 4 of your blue halves, so the other 8 red halves must have formed all-red beads. The other 4 blue halves formed 2 all-blue beads. So r, b, and p, are 4, 2, and 4, respectively. Here the probability of picking an all-red bead is $\frac{4}{10}$. The probability of picking a bead that is at least half blue is the probability of picking a half-red, half-blue bead plus the probability of picking an all-blue bead. Since $\frac{4}{10} < \frac{4}{10} + \frac{2}{10}$, statement (1) is true, and it is possible there were more red beads to begin with. But you could have also started with 4 red beads and 6 blue beads, and let r, b, and p be 2, 4, and 4 respectively. Here, the probability of picking an all-red bead is $\frac{2}{10}$, which is less than the probability of picking a bead that is at least half-blue($\frac{4}{10} + \frac{4}{10}$). So Statement (1) is again true, but there were fewer red beads to begin with. Two different answers means statement (1) is not sufficient. Eliminate (A) and (D). Statement (2) tells you that after the split and merge, the probability of picking an all-blue bead is more than the probability of picking a bead that is at least half-red. The split and merge decreased the number of all-blue and the number of all-red beads equally. So if there is a higher fraction of all blue-beads after the split and merge, there must have been more before the split and merge. Statement (2) tells you that there were not more red beads than blue beads to begin with, so it is sufficient.

Permutations and Combinations

1. **D** Gretchen is choosing one cheese from each of four groups, so there are $3 \times 3 \times 4 \times 6 = 216$ groups.

2. **C** There are two groups: male roles and female roles. There are 5 men, so there are $5 \times 4 \times 3 = 60$ ways to assign the three male roles. Similarly, there are $5 \times 4 \times 3 \times 2 = 120$ ways to assign the four female roles. These events are independent, so there are $60 \times 120 = 7,200$ ways to assign all the roles.

3. **C** Order is not relevant to the collector's selection, so this is a combination problem. Statement (1) is insufficient because there is more than one number of cars to choose from that will produce more than 50 combinations. For example, if the collector has 9 cars then the number of possibilities is $9 \times 8 \times 7 \times 6 / 4 \times 3 \times 2 \times 1 = 126$. But if the collector has 10 cars the number of possibilities is $10 \times 9 \times 8 \times 7 / 4 \times 3 \times 2 \times 1 = 210$. Eliminate (A) and (D). Statement (2) is insufficient because there is more than one number of cars that will produce fewer than 125 combinations. For example, 8 cars will produce $8 \times 7 \times 6 \times 5 / 4 \times 3 \times 2 \times 1 = 70$ combinations. But 7 cars will produce $7 \times 6 \times 5 \times 4 / 4 \times 3 \times 2 \times 1 = 35$ combinations. Eliminate (B). Statements (1) and (2) together are sufficient. There is only one number of cars that produces a number of combinations between 50 and 125—8 cars, which produces 70 combinations.

4. **D** Suppose the maid of honor stands to Uduak's left. Then the third and fourth positions are fixed. There are 5 people left to fill the first position, 4 to fill the second, 3 to fill the fifth, and so on. So there are $5 \times 4 \times 3 \times 2 \times 1 = 120$ ways to line everyone up if the maid of honor is on Uduak's left. If the maid of honor is on Uduak's right, the same thing applies, so the total number of arrangements is $120 + 120 = 240$.

5. **A** Statement (1) is sufficient. As long as you know the number of available toppings you can find the number of 3-topping pizzas and 4-topping pizzas. (They would be $8 \times 7 \times 6 / 3 \times 2 \times 1 = 56$ and $8 \times 7 \times 6 \times 5 / 4 \times 3 \times 2 \times 1 = 70$ respectively.) Eliminate (B), (C), and (E). Statement (2) is insufficient. For 6 toppings, the number of 3-topping pizzas ($6 \times 5 \times 4 / 3 \times 2 \times 1 = 30$) is greater than the number of 4-topping pizzas ($6 \times 5 \times 4 \times 3 / 4 \times 3 \times 2 \times 1 = 15$). But for 7 toppings, the number of 3-topping pizzas ($7 \times 6 \times 5 / 3 \times 2 \times 1 = 35$) is equal to the number of 4-topping pizzas ($7 \times 6 \times 5 \times 4 / 4 \times 3 \times 2 \times 1 = 35$). Different results mean the yes/no question cannot be definitively answered.

6. **B** Sean can either have a duet or a solo first. If he has a solo first, solos will be the first, third, and fifth tracks, while duets will be the second and fourth tracks. There are $4 \times 3 \times 2 = 24$ ways to assign the three solo positions, and $5 \times 4 = 20$ ways to assign the two duet positions. So there are $24 \times 20 = 480$ playlists that start with a solo. If a duet is first, there will be three duets, and two solos. There are $5 \times 4 \times 3 = 60$ ways to assign the duets, and $4 \times 3 = 12$ to assign the solos, so the number of playlists with a duet first is $12 \times 60 = 720$. The total is $720 + 480 = 1,200$, so the answer is (B).

7. **D** Statement (1) is sufficient. If there are 4 girls, then there must be 2 boys. Since boys cannot be first or last, you must have girls in those spots. There are 4 possibilities for the first spot, and (once one of the girls has been assigned) 3 possibilities for the last spot. The remaining 2 boys and 2 girls can be arranged into the middle four spots in any way. The final multiplication problem would be $4 \times 4 \times 3 \times 2 \times 1 \times 3$. Eliminate (B), (C), and (E). Statement (2) is sufficient. Since there are no restrictions on the middle 4 slots, there will be $4 \times 3 \times 2 \times 1 = 24$ ways of arranging them. Multiplying that by 12 gives the total possibilities.

8. **D** Statement (1) is sufficient. The number of men divided by the number of women is 4, $\frac{2}{3}$, or 0. The only way to get 4 is to have 4 men and 1 woman($\frac{4}{1} = 4$). The only way to get $\frac{2}{3}$ is to have 2 men and 3 women. The only way to get 0 is to have 0 men and 5 women($\frac{0}{5} = 0$). For each of these options the number of possibilities can be calculated. For example, 2 men and 3 women would be calculated as follows: $\frac{5 \times 4}{2 \times 1} \times \frac{6 \times 5 \times 4}{3 \times 2 \times 1} = 200$. The others can be done in a similar way. Statement (2) is also sufficient. If the committee has an odd number of women, that could mean 1, 3, or 5 women. Thus the committee would either have 1 woman and 4 men, 3 women and 2 men, or 5 women and 0 men. These are the same three options that Statement (1) produced and they can be calculated in the same way.

9. **C** Let S represent a short presentation, and L represent a long presentation. The schedule must start with a short presentation, and every long presentation must be followed by at least one short presentation. So the schedule must be SLSLSLS, along with one more short presentation inserted somewhere. There are four ways to do this; SSLSLSLS, SLSSLSLS, SLSLSSLS, and SLSLSLSS. For each of these there are $5 \times 4 \times 3 \times 2 \times 1 = 120$ arrangements of the short presentations, and $3 \times 2 \times 1 = 6$ arrangements of the long presentations, giving $120 \times 6 = 720$ possible schedules for each ordering. So there are $4 \times 720 = 2,880$ total possible schedules. The answer is (C).

10. **C** First, evaluate the information in the question. The museum has five paintings in their current collection and receives a new shipment of paintings. Now, evaluate the statements to determine if, given the information, it is possible to answer the question of how many ways the museum can arrange the entire collection of paintings, including the new shipment. Statement 1 indicates that, with the new shipment, the museum has seven paintings in their collection. However, this does not give any information about how many paintings are to be arranged for the new exhibit, so eliminate (A) and (D). Now, evaluate Statement 2. The museum only plans to arrange five paintings in the new exhibit. While this seems like enough information considering the museum's current collection is five paintings, this does not give any information about how many new paintings were received in the shipment, so eliminate (B). Now, evaluate both statements together. Statement 1 gives the total number of paintings in the collection including the new shipment and Statement 2 expresses how many paintings they plan to arrange in the new exhibit. There is now enough information to answer the question, so select (C).

11. **D** Choice (C) is a trap. Statement (1) tells you that there is a 40% or $\frac{2}{5}$ chance of Jon going first or last, so $\frac{2}{5}$ equals the probability Jon goes first plus the probability he goes last. The probability of Jon going first is 1 out of however many brothers Jon has plus himself. The probability of going last is the same, so Statement (1) tells you that the probability of Jon going first is $\frac{1}{5}$. This means Jon has 4 brothers, so you can then determine how many arrangements there are. Eliminate (B), (C), and (E). Statement (2) tells you there are 48 ways Jon could be first or last, so there are 24 ways Jon could be first. Try some values for the number of brothers Jon has. If Jon has 3 brothers, then when Jon goes first, there are $3 \times 2 \times 1 = 6$ ways his brothers could go after him. If Jon has 4 brothers, there are 24 ways, and if he has 5 brothers, there are 120 ways. So Statement (2) tells you Jon has 4 brothers, which is sufficient.

12. **E** Statement (1) is insufficient. It says nothing about the number of entrees. Eliminate (A) and (D). Statement (2) is insufficient. You know that the number of appetizers, number of entrees, and number of desserts multiply to 80, but that doesn't allow you to find the number of entrees. Eliminate (B). Statements (1) and (2) together are insufficient. With 4 appetizers and 80 total meals, you know that 80/4 = 20 is the product of the number of entrees and the number of desserts. However, knowing that desserts × entrees = 20 is not enough information to find the number of entrees.

13. **B** This is a permutation problem with a restriction, so you should first determine what the answer would be without the restriction. There are $5 \times 4 \times 3 \times 2 \times 1 = 120$ ways for 5 people to sit in five chairs. But some of these will have Chris and Val sitting together, so eliminate (D) and (E). Find the number of ways for them to sit together and subtract it from 120. There are 5 places Val can sit, and for each one, Chris can sit on either side of her, so there are 10 places they can sit together. For each of these ways, the other 3 people can arrange themselves in the three remaining seats in $3 \times 2 \times 1 = 6$ ways. So there are $10 \times 6 = 60$ out of 120 ways that Chris and Val can sit together, and $120 - 60 = 60$ ways in which they don't.

14. **B** Statement (1) is insufficient. Without knowing how many movies are available, you can't find the number of groups. This information tells you nothing about the number of movies. Eliminate (A) and (D). Statement (2) is sufficient. If 10 movies are available, then the number of combinations would be $10 \times 9 \times 8 / 3 \times 2 \times 1 = 120$.

15. **C** In order to calculate the probability that at least one grandchild gets the right gift, first calculate the probability that no grandchild gets the right gift, and then subtract that from 1. There are $4 \times 3 \times 2 \times 1 = 24$ total possible ways for Herb to randomly dole out the gifts. The fastest way to work this problem is to write out all 24 ways, and identify how many of them correspond to no grandchild getting the correct gift. Call the four grandchildren W, X, Y, and Z, and call the four gifts 1, 2, 3, and 4. W's gift should be gift 1, X's gift should be gift 2, and so on. So writing WXYZ means W got gift 1, X got gift 2, Y got gift 3, and Z got gift 4. WXYZ corresponds to each

grandchild getting the correct gift. WXZY corresponds to W and X getting the correct gifts, but Z and Y getting the wrong ones. There are 9 ways for no grandchild to get the correct gift, so the probability of this is $\frac{9}{24} = \frac{3}{8}$. The probability of at least 1 child getting the right gift is $1 - \frac{3}{8} = \frac{5}{8}$.

16. **C** Statement (1) is insufficient. Without knowing the number of novels available, the total combinations cannot be found. Eliminate (A) and (D). Statement (2) is insufficient. Without knowing the number of biographies and comic books available, the total combinations cannot be found. Eliminate (B). Statements (1) and (2) together are sufficient. With 4 biographies, 3 comic books, and 7 novels available to choose from, there are $4 \times 3 \times 7 = 84$ different ways to pick the numbers of each type of book to bring. For each of these 84, the number of ways to do it can be calculated. For example, one of the 84 possibilities is 2 biographies, 2 comic books, and 4 novels. The number of ways to do this is $\frac{4 \times 3}{2 \times 1} \times \frac{3 \times 2}{2 \times 1} \times \frac{7 \times 6 \times 5 \times 4}{4 \times 3 \times 2 \times 1} = 630$. The other 83 possibilities can be calculated in a similar manner.

17. **D** The last statement tells you that three of the countries have 4 runners, and one country has 3 runners. Call the four-runner countries A, B, and C, and call the three-runner country X. Each country has one runner in the final, so 3 of the 4 countries will have a prize-winning runner. Suppose that the three countries that win prizes are A, B and C. There are $4 \times 4 \times 4 = 64$ possible groups of three runners from these three countries, and each group of three can be arranged $3 \times 2 \times 1 = 6$ ways, so there are $64 \times 6 = 384$ arrangements of prize-winners from A, B and C. But you could also have a prize-winner from X, so 384 is too small. Eliminate (A). Suppose the prize-winners came from countries A, B, and X. There are $4 \times 4 \times 3 = 48$ groups that can be formed from the runners of these countries, and each group can be arranged 6 ways, so there are $48 \times 6 = 288$ arrangements of winners from countries A, B, and X. There would be the same number of arrangements if the winners were from either A, C, and X or B, C, and X. So the total number of arrangements is $384 + 288 + 288 + 288 = 1248$.

18. **B** Statement (1) is insufficient. This tells you there are at least 4 models, but there could be more who don't advance to the final round. Eliminate (A) and (D). Statement (2) is sufficient. Since the prizes are different, the order of the finalists matters, making this a permutation. If there are 90 ways to rank the winners, that can only be calculated as a permutation of 10×9. Thus there are 10 models in the competition.

19. **D** First, Hank has to select two types of lettuce from five, and there are $\frac{5 \times 4}{2 \times 1} = 10$ ways to do this. Next, Hank has $\frac{7 \times 6 \times 5}{3 \times 2 \times 1} = 35$ ways to pick three types of vegetables from seven. Finally, there are 4 ways Hank can pick one dressing from four. So there are $10 \times 35 \times 4 = 1400$ salads Hank can make.

20. **B** There are 5 ways to assign one person to the first room. There are $\dfrac{4 \times 3}{2 \times 1} = 6$ ways to assign two of the remaining four people to the second room. The last two people can be assigned to the last room in $\dfrac{2 \times 1}{2 \times 1} = 1$ way. So there are $5 \times 6 \times 1 = 30$ ways to assign the speakers, and the answer is (B).

21. **C** Statement (1) is insufficient. There are at least 4 prisoners since 4 walk the plank. Because there are fewer than 6, the number must be 5 or 4. If there are 5 prisoners then the number of possibilities is $\dfrac{5 \times 4 \times 3 \times 2}{4 \times 3 \times 2 \times 1} = 5$, a prime number. However, if there are 4 prisoners then the number of possibilities is $\dfrac{4 \times 3 \times 2 \times 1}{4 \times 3 \times 2 \times 1} = 1$, which is not a prime number. Both prime and non-prime numbers work, thus the yes/no question cannot be definitively answered. Eliminate (A) and (D). Statement (2) is insufficient. If the number of prisoners on the boat is a prime number such as 5, then the possibilities (as previously calculated in Statement (1)) are 5, a prime number. But if the number of prisoners is a prime number such as 7, then the number of possibilities is $\dfrac{7 \times 6 \times 5 \times 4}{4 \times 3 \times 2 \times 1} = 35$, which is not a prime number. Both prime and non-prime numbers work, thus the yes/no question cannot be definitively answered. Eliminate (B). Statements (1) and (2) together are sufficient. Statement (1) tells you that there must be either 4 or 5 prisoners on the boat. Statement (2) tells you the number of prisoners must be prime. Thus the only number that satisfies both statements is 5. 5 prisoners yields 5 possibilities. With both statements, the yes/no question can be answered definitively.

22. **E** Plug In. If y is 4 and x is 3, then the number of groups of size three that can be formed from four distinct objects is $n = \dfrac{4 \times 3 \times 2}{3 \times 2 \times 1} = 4$. If one object is added, then there are $\dfrac{5 \times 4 \times 3}{3 \times 2 \times 1} = 10$ groups of size three that can be formed from five distinct objects. 10 is your target answer, so plug 3, 4, and 4 in for x, y, and n in each of the answer choices, and identify the one that gives you 10.

23. **A** First count how many pairs of teams you can make if each team has no couples. A team with no couples has one person from each couple on it. There are two ways to pick a person from the first couple, two ways to pick one person from the second couple, etc. So there are $2 \times 2 \times 2 \times 2 = 16$ ways to build a team of four with no couples on it. If the couples are Aa, Bb, Cc, and Dd, then one

of the 16 teams is ABCD, making the other team abcd. However, you could also pick the teams in the other order, with abcd first and ABCD second. Because you don't care about the order the teams are picked in, divide 16 by 2 to get the 8 different pairs of teams with no couple on the same team. Next, count how many teams have exactly two couples. There are $\left(\dfrac{4 \times 3}{2 \times 1}\right)\left(\dfrac{2 \times 1}{2 \times 1}\right) = 6$ ways to assign two couples from four to the first team and the remaining two couples to the second team. Again, divide by two because order of the teams does not matter. So there are 8 ways to have teams with no couples, and 3 ways to have teams with two couples each, so having either of these is $8 + 3 = 11$.

24. **C** Mary can play either the bass or the drums. In each case, Mary is picking from 4 sources, and order does not matter. If Mary plays the bass, she picks 1 person (herself) to play bass, 1 person from 3 to play drums, 2 people from 5 to play guitar, and 1 person from 2 to play keyboard. So the number of bands in which Mary plays bass is $\left(\dfrac{1}{1}\right)\left(\dfrac{3}{1}\right)\left(\dfrac{5 \times 4}{2 \times 1}\right)\left(\dfrac{2}{1}\right) = 60$. If Mary plays drums, she picks 1 person from 1 to play bass, 1 person to play drums (herself), 2 people from 5 to play guitar, and 1 person from 2 to play keyboard. So there are $\left(\dfrac{1}{1}\right)\left(\dfrac{1}{1}\right)\left(\dfrac{5 \times 4}{2 \times 1}\right)\left(\dfrac{2}{1}\right) = 20$ bands in which Mary drums. So the total number of bands is $20 + 60 = 80$, and the answer is (C).

25. **D** Statement (1) tells you that 12 people will not be invited. Since 5 people are being invited, there must be $5 + 12 = 17$ people in Brian's class, other than himself. If you know how many people are in the class, you can determine how many groups of 5 can be picked (but don't actually do it!) Statement (1) is sufficient, so eliminate (B), (C), and (E). Statement (2) is long, so take it one step at a time. Brian can invite 5 people, and 20% of 5 is 1. So if the number of people Brian can invite goes up by 20%, he could invite $5 + 1 = 6$ people. Now Plug In for the number of people in Brian's class, picking a number that works well with the fractions you see in the problem. Taking $\dfrac{1}{9}$ of 18 would be easy, so start with 18 total people in Brian's class. This 18 includes Brian, so he has 17 classmates

from whom he can invite 5. There are $\dfrac{17 \times 16 \times 15 \times 14 \times 13}{5 \times 4 \times 3 \times 2 \times 1} = 6{,}188$ ways he can select 5 from 17.

If the number he can invite goes up to 6, there are then $\dfrac{17 \times 16 \times 15 \times 14 \times 13 \times 12}{6 \times 5 \times 4 \times 3 \times 2 \times 1} = 12{,}376$ groups

he could invite. 12,376 is twice 6,188, so $k = 2$. 2 is $\dfrac{1}{9}$ of 18, so 18 works. No other value for the

number of people in Brian's class will work for Statement (2). So Statement (2) is sufficient. Eliminate (A).

Groups

1. **B**   To solve this question, use the group equation: Total = Group 1 + Group 2 − Both + Neither. Here, the total is 56, Group 1 is cars with sunroofs, which is 24, Group 2 is cars with leather interiors, which is 39, and Neither is 12. To solve for Both, set up the equation, 56 = 24 + 39 − Both + 12. Solving the equation gives you Both = 19.

2. **A**   Statement (1) tells you 10% failed both tests, which means 20% passed both. That is a total of 30%, which means the remaining 70% passed one test and failed one test. Eliminate (B), (C), and (E). Statement (2) says 40% of the students failed the verbal test, so 60% passed the verbal test. You don't know anything about the Math test, so this is insufficient.

3. **B**   To solve this question, set up a group grid with the information that you know.

	Smart	Flip Phone	Total
Sales	70	50	
IT			
Total			

Now you can find that the total number of salespeople is 120. And, since there are an equal number of salespeople and technicians that choose smart phones, you know that 70 technicians choose smart phones, and thus that a total of 140 employees choose smart phones. Now, since you know that 30 percent of employees choose flip phones, then 70 percent choose smart phones, and thus 70 percent of the total number of employees is 140. You can set up 70% (Total) = 140 and find out that the total is 200. Now you can fill in everything else.

	Smart	Flip Phone	Total
Sales	70	50	120
IT	70	**10**	**80**
Total	140	**60**	200

Be careful—there are some trap answers. Choice (C) is the percentage of all employees who choose flip phones. Choice (D) is the percentage of all employees who are technicians. Choice (E) is the total number of technicians.

4. **C** To solve this very difficult question, you need to calculate the number of tickets that win at least one prize and subtract it from the total number of tickets sold, and then divide that number by the total number of tickets. In order to find the number of tickets that win at least one prize, find the X union Y union Z, or $X \cup Y \cup Z$, where X is the set of tickets that win t-shirts, Y, the set of tickets that win gift-certificates, and Z, the set tickets that win movie passes.

First, remember that $X + Y + Z = (X \cup Y \cup Z) + (X \cap Y) + (X \cap Z) + (Y \cap Z) - (X \cap Y \cap Z)$. Next, find the sum of X, Y, and Z to get the total number of prizes awarded. The number of tickets that win t-shirts, X, is 200/2, or 100, because half of the numbers are divisible by 2. The number of tickets that win gift-certificates, Y, is 200/3 = 66.6667, or 66 because that is the integer value of the quotient (in other words, round down to find out how many multiples of 3 are under 200). The number of tickets that win movie passes, Z, is 200/7, or 28, because that is the result of rounding down. Thus, $X + Y + Z = 194$. Then find the intersection of X and Y, or $X \cap Y$, (the total who win either t-shirts or gift-certificates), $Y \cap Z$ (the total who win either gift-certificates or movie passes), and $X \cap Z$.

The set of tickets that are BOTH X and Y is $X \cap Y$. This set is both multiples of 2 and 3, thus multiples of 6. Therefore $X \cap Y$ is 200/6 or 33. Now find $Y \cap Z$, which is the tickets that are multiples of 3 and 7, thus multiples of 21. Thus $Y \cap Z = 200/21$, which is 9. Now find $X \cap Z$, which is the tickets that are multiples of 2 and 7, thus multiples of 14. Thus $X \cap Z = 200/14$, which is 14. Finally, find $X \cap Y \cap Z$, which is the tickets that are multiples of 2, 3, and 7, thus multiples of 42. Thus $X \cap Y \cap Z = 200/42$, which is 4.

Putting everything together, you get $194 = (X \cup Y \cup Z) + 33 + 9 + 14 - 4$. Thus $X \cup Y \cup Z = 142$. Therefore, since $200 - 142 = 58$, 58 tickets win no prizes.

5. **E** Statement (1) tells you how the senators up for re-election voted, 90% yes and 10% no. But without knowing what fraction of senators are up for re-election, you don't know how many votes they represent. Eliminate (A) and (D). For statement (2), without knowing the fraction of senators not up for re-election voted, you can't know how many no votes are represented by the 90%. Eliminate (B). Combine both statements. Statement (1) tells you 90% of the senators up for re-election voted yes, which means the other 10% of the senators up for re-election voted no. From statement (2) you

can infer that 10% of the no votes came from senators up for re-election. Since the number of no votes by senators up for re-election is constant, then the number of no votes must equal the number of senators up for re-election. If 80% of the senators are up for re-election, the bill succeeds. If 30% of the senators are up for re-election the bill fails. The information is not sufficient.

6. **C** Statement (1) tells you 8 free-response questions are not about the Stone Age. There could be 2 free-response questions about the Stone Age, which means there would be 10 free-response questions, and 90 multiple choice questions. Or there could be 11 free-response questions about the Stone Age, making 19 total free-response and 81 total multiple choice. Two different answers means statement (1) is not sufficient. Eliminate (A) and (D). Statement (2) tells you that there are 50 questions about the Stone Age, and 50 that are not. But you don't know how many of those are free-response, so statement (2) is not sufficient. Eliminate (B). Combined, you know there are 50 total questions not about the Stone Age, and 8 of those are free-response. This means there are 42 multiple choice questions not about the Stone Age. 30% of all multiple choice questions are about the Stone Age, so 70% of the multiple choice questions are not about the Stone Age. 42 equals 70% of the total multiple choice questions, so there must be 60 multiple choice questions. This means there are 40 free-response questions, 8 of which are not about the Stone Age. So the other 32 free-response questions must be about the Stone Age.

7. **C** To answer this question, you can slightly modify the group equation: Total = Group 1 + Group 2 − Both + Neither. In this case, Group 1 would be people who own exactly 2 kinds, Group 2 would be people who own all three kinds, and Neither would be people who owned only one kind. You can exclude "Both" in this case because it doesn't apply (you can't "both" own exactly 2 and exactly 3 kinds of televisions). 52% of 1000, is 520 and 22% of 1000 is 220. Applying these numbers to the equation, you get: 1000 = 520 + 220 + Neither. This gives you Neither = 260. Watch out for trap answers—(A) is the answer you would get if you only solved for the percentage and (E) is the sum of those who own either 2 or 3 kinds of televisions.

8. **D** To solve this question, use the group equation: Total = Group 1 + Group 2 − Both + Neither. Here, Group 1 will be French and Group 2 will be Spanish. The number of students that take both is one half of the total number of students who take Spanish, or 24 students. So fill in the equation: Total = 75 + 48 − 24 + 0.1(Total). Simplify this to 0.9 = 99. So the total = 110. Watch out for trap answers. Choice (A) is the number of students who took neither French nor Spanish. Choice (B) is the number of students who took both French and Spanish. Choices (C) and (E) are partial answers.

9. **C** Statement (1) only tells you a ratio between female pirates and male ninjas. You don't know anything about male pirates or female ninjas. Eliminate (A) and (D). In a similar manner, statement (2) fails to give you enough information, so eliminate (B). But when you put the information together, you know there are three times as many female pirates as male ninjas, and three times as many male pirates as female ninjas. So let there be 3 male ninjas. Statement (1) tells you that there must then be 9 female pirates. The question says there are 18 total pirates, so there must be 9 male pirates. Statement (2) tells you that there are then 3 female ninjas. So there are 24 people at the party.

10. **B** To solve this question, set a group grid with the information that you know.

	Presenting	Not Presenting	Total
Car	4		
Plane			
Total			36

Now, since two-thirds of the students are not presenting, and two-thirds of 36 is 24, you know that 24 students are not presenting. Since one-fourth of students travel by plane, you know that 9 students travel by plane. Now you can fill in everything else.

	Presenting	Not Presenting	Total
Car	4	23	27
Plane	8	1	9
Total	12	24	36

Watch for trap answers. Choice (C) is the number of students who travel by plane who ARE presenting. Choice (D) is the total number of students who are presenting. Choice (E) is the number of students who travel by car who are not presenting. The answer is (B).

11. **B** There were 300 dogs in the sample, so begin working with the problem one step at a time. 65% of the dogs were less than 3 years old, which means that 35% of the dogs were greater than 3 years old. 35% of 300 is 105 dogs greater than 3 years old. If 40% of the dogs greater than 3 years old were over 40 pounds, than 60% of those dogs were under 40 pounds. So, 60% of 105 is 63 dogs over 3 years old and under 40 pounds. The correct answer is (B).

12. **B** If there are 12 players on the team, then 2 players had 1 slice each, 2 players had 2 slices each, 2 players had 3 slices, and 6 players had at least 4 slices. So that means that the team had at least $(2 \times 1) + (2 \times 2) + (2 \times 3) + (6 \times 4) = 36$ slices of pizza. This is not enough information to determine if anyone had 6 slices or more. Eliminate (A) and (D). Statement (2) tells you that $S = 3P$, where S is the number of slices eaten by all the players, and P is the number of players. If a sixth of the players had

exactly one slice, then the number of slices eaten by players who had only one slice is $1 \times \dfrac{P}{6}$. The number of slices eaten by players who had exactly two slices is $2 \times \dfrac{P}{6}$, and the number of slices eaten by players who had 3 is $3 \times \dfrac{P}{6}$. That means the other half of the team had at least 4 slices. The least number this half could have eaten is $\left(4 \times \dfrac{P}{2} \right)$. So the lowest number of slices the team could have had is $\dfrac{P}{6} + \dfrac{2P}{6} + \dfrac{3P}{6} + \dfrac{4P}{2} = P + 2P = 3P$. Statement (2) tells you that the team only ate $3P$ slices, so you know they ate the least possible amount, and no one could have had more than 4 slices.

Geometry

LINES AND ANGLES

When working with lines and angles, there are several basic rules you need to know.

A line is determined by two points.

There are 180° in a line and 360° in a circle.

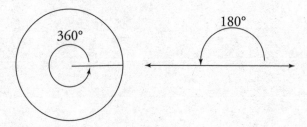

Vertical Angles

When two straight lines intersect, the angles opposite each other are equal.

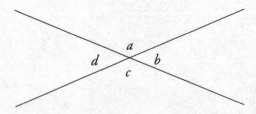

Thus, $\angle a = \angle c$ and $\angle d = \angle b$.

Perpendicular Lines

An angle that measures 90° is a **right angle**. Two lines that meet at a right angle are **perpendicular**, indicated by the ⊥ symbol.

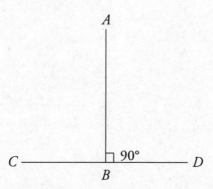

In a figure, the right angle sign (which looks like a little box in the corner) indicates that two lines are perpendicular. In this case, line $CD \perp$ line AB.

Parallel Lines

If two lines in a plane never intersect, they are **parallel**. The symbol for parallel is $\parallel$.

When a third line crosses two parallel lines, two kinds of angles are formed: big angles and little angles.

- All big angles are equal and all small angles are equal. I.e., big equals big and little equals little.
- Any big angle plus any little angle equals 180°.

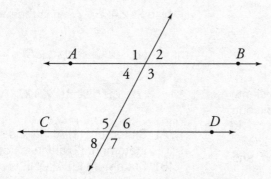

Thus, in the figure above, $\angle$ 1, 3, 5 and 7 are big angles and they are all equal, and $\angle$ 2, 4, 6 and 8 are small angles and they are all equal.

LINES AND ANGLES DRILL

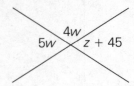

1. In the figure shown, what is the value of z ?

   (A) 10
   (B) 20
   (C) 55
   (D) 80
   (E) 100

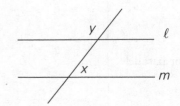

2. In the figure above, $\ell \parallel m$. What is the value of x ?

   (1) $x = 3y$

   (2) $y = 180 - x$

   (A) Statement (1) ALONE is sufficient, but
       statement (2) alone is not sufficient.
   (B) Statement (2) ALONE is sufficient, but
       statement (1) alone is not sufficient.
   (C) BOTH statements TOGETHER are sufficient,
       but NEITHER statement ALONE is sufficient.
   (D) EACH statement ALONE is sufficient.
   (E) Statements (1) and (2) TOGETHER are NOT
       sufficient to answer the question asked, and
       additional data are needed.

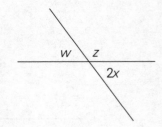

3. In the figure above, if $\dfrac{z}{w+z} = \dfrac{2}{5}$, then $3x + 40 =$

   (A) 54
   (B) 72
   (C) 108
   (D) 162
   (E) 202

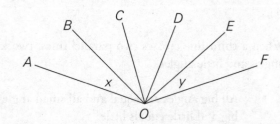

4. In the figure above, $x = 20$, $y = 30$, and $\overline{OC}$
   bisects $\angle AOF$. What is the measure of $\angle BOE$?

   (1) $\overline{OD}$ bisects $\angle BOF$

   (2) $\overline{OE}$ bisects $\angle FOC$

   (A) Statement (1) ALONE is sufficient, but
       statement (2) alone is not sufficient.
   (B) Statement (2) ALONE is sufficient, but
       statement (1) alone is not sufficient.
   (C) BOTH statements TOGETHER are sufficient,
       but NEITHER statement ALONE is sufficient.
   (D) EACH statement ALONE is sufficient.
   (E) Statements (1) and (2) TOGETHER are NOT
       sufficient to answer the question asked, and
       additional data are needed.

Check your answers on page 449.

TRIANGLES

A triangle is a three-sided figure with three corresponding angles. Each corner of the triangle is called a **vertex** (**vertices** is the plural). The **perimeter** of a triangle (or of any figure) is the sum of the lengths of its sides.

Angles of a Triangle

There are some important rules you need to know about the angles of a triangle.

In any triangle

- There are 180°.
- The longest side is opposite the largest angle.
- The shortest side is opposite the smallest angle.
- Equal sides are opposite equal angles.

An **equilateral triangle** is a triangle with three equal sides and three equal angles. The measure of each angle is 60°. **Isosceles triangles** have two equal sides, and the two angles opposite those sides are also equal.

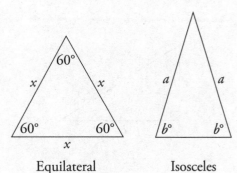

Equilateral   Isosceles

Area of a Triangle

The formula for the area of a triangle is

$$\text{Area of a triangle} = \frac{1}{2} \times \text{base} \times \text{height} = \frac{1}{2}\,bh$$

Although any side of a triangle can serve as the base, you usually use the one on the bottom for convenience. The key is that regardless of which side you use as the base, *the height of a triangle must be perpendicular to its base.*

The Third Side of a Triangle Rule

This rule is not tested frequently, but when it is, it's usually the key to solving the problem.

> The length of any side of a triangle must be less than the sum of the other two sides and greater than the difference between the other two sides.

Right Triangles

A right triangle is a triangle with one right angle (90º). The side opposite the right angle is called the **hypotenuse** and it is the longest side. The other two sides are called the **legs**. If you know two of the sides of a right triangle, you can always find the third with the Pythagorean theorem: $a^2 + b^2 = c^2$.

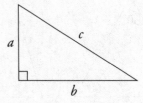

Special Right Triangles

You will save yourself a lot of time on the test if you memorize the **Pythagorean triples**. These are common versions of right triangles that the test writers use frequently. They are the 3:4:5 triangle, the 6:8:10 triangle and the 5:12:13 triangle. Notice that 6:8:10 is a multiple of 3:4:5. Other multiples of the triangles work too.

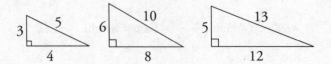

The triples work the same way that the Pythagorean theorem does: if you know two of the sides of the triangle, you can always find the third. Thus, if you have a right triangle and you know that the hypotenuse is 13 and one of the legs is 5, you automatically know the other leg is 12.

There are two other special right triangles you must know.

- The 45º:45º:90º right triangle, also known as the isosceles right triangle.
- The 30º:60º:90º right triangle.

For these triangles you must memorize the relationships among the sides. For example, you must know that in a 45:45:90 triangle, the legs are always equal to *a*, and the hypotenuse is always equal to $a\sqrt{2}$. Thus, if you have a 45:45:90 triangle with legs that are each 3, the hypotenuse will be $3\sqrt{2}$.

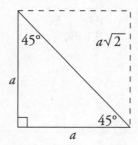

Splitting a square on the diagonal results in two 45:45:90 triangles.

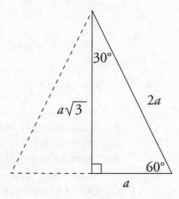

Splitting an equilateral triangle in half creates two 30:60:90 triangles. Again, you must know the relationship among the sides. The short leg is *a*, the long leg is $a\sqrt{3}$ and the hypotenuse is 2*a*. Thus, if you have a 30:60:90 in which the side across from 30º is 4, then you automatically know that the side across from 60º is $4\sqrt{3}$ and that the hypotenuse is 8. It is also helpful to know the approximate values of $\sqrt{2}$ and $\sqrt{3}$ in case you need to estimate answers.

$$\sqrt{2} \approx 1.4 \qquad\qquad \sqrt{3} \approx 1.7$$

TRIANGLES DRILL

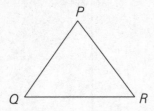

1. If PQ = PR, what is the area of triangle PQR ?

   (1) Angle PQR = 60

   (2) QR = 10

   (A) Statement (1) ALONE is sufficient, but
        statement (2) alone is not sufficient.
   (B) Statement (2) ALONE is sufficient, but
        statement (1) alone is not sufficient.
   (C) BOTH statements TOGETHER are sufficient,
        but NEITHER statement ALONE is sufficient.
   (D) EACH statement ALONE is sufficient.
   (E) Statements (1) and (2) TOGETHER are NOT
        sufficient to answer the question asked, and
        additional data are needed.

2. If a triangle has sides with lengths 4 and 10,
   respectively, which of the following could be the
   length of the third side?

       I.   6
       II. 12
       III. 14

   (A) I only
   (B) II only
   (C) I and II only
   (D) I and III only
   (E) I, II and III

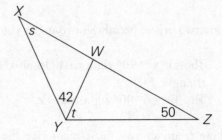

3. In the figure above, what is s in terms of t ?

   (A) t – 88
   (B) t + 88
   (C) 88 – t
   (D) t – 50
   (E) 50 – t

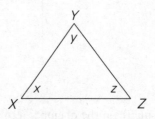

4. Is XY > YZ ?

   (1) 50 < x < 60

   (2) 60 < y < 70

   (A) Statement (1) ALONE is sufficient, but
        statement (2) alone is not sufficient.
   (B) Statement (2) ALONE is sufficient, but
        statement (1) alone is not sufficient.
   (C) BOTH statements TOGETHER are sufficient,
        but NEITHER statement ALONE is sufficient.
   (D) EACH statement ALONE is sufficient.
   (E) Statements (1) and (2) TOGETHER are NOT
        sufficient to answer the question asked, and
        additional data are needed.

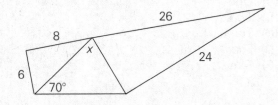

5. In the figure above, what is the value of x ?

(A) 40
(B) 50
(C) 60
(D) 70
(E) 80

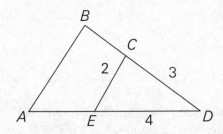

6. In the figure above, AB is parallel to EC. What is the perimeter of quadrilateral ABCE ?

(1) AE = 2

(2) AB = 3

(A) Statement (1) ALONE is sufficient, but statement (2) alone is not sufficient.
(B) Statement (2) ALONE is sufficient, but statement (1) alone is not sufficient.
(C) BOTH statements TOGETHER are sufficient, but NEITHER statement ALONE is sufficient.
(D) EACH statement ALONE is sufficient.
(E) Statements (1) and (2) TOGETHER are NOT sufficient to answer the question asked, and additional data are needed.

7. Triangle ABC has lengths of AB = 2 and BC = 5. What is the length of AC ?

(1) The length of AC is an odd integer.

(2) Triangle ABC is isosceles.

(A) Statement (1) ALONE is sufficient, but statement (2) alone is not sufficient.
(B) Statement (2) ALONE is sufficient, but statement (1) alone is not sufficient.
(C) BOTH statements TOGETHER are sufficient, but NEITHER statement ALONE is sufficient.
(D) EACH statement ALONE is sufficient.
(E) Statements (1) and (2) TOGETHER are NOT sufficient to answer the question asked, and additional data are needed.

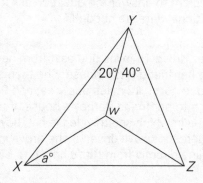

8. In triangle XYZ above, XW=WY=WZ. What is the value of 2a ?

(A) 20
(B) 30
(C) 40
(D) 60
(E) 80

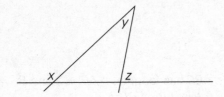

9. In the figure above, what is the measure of angle *y* ?

(1) $x + z = 195$

(2) $x - z = 45$

(A) Statement (1) ALONE is sufficient, but statement (2) alone is not sufficient.
(B) Statement (2) ALONE is sufficient, but statement (1) alone is not sufficient.
(C) BOTH statements TOGETHER are sufficient, but NEITHER statement ALONE is sufficient.
(D) EACH statement ALONE is sufficient.
(E) Statements (1) and (2) TOGETHER are NOT sufficient to answer the question asked, and additional data are needed.

10. Mercedes drove 15 miles due east from her house to her friend Rita's house. She then drove 4 miles due north, 12 miles due west and 9 miles due south to her friend Barney's house. If the entire area in which she traveled is flat, how far would Mercedes have driven if she drove in a straight line directly from Rita's house to Barney's house?

(A)   5

(B) 13

(C) 15

(D) $\sqrt{241}$

(E) 17

11. For how many different values of *p* is there a triangle with sides of 3, 9 and *p*, if *p* is an integer between 3 and 9 ?

(A) One
(B) Two
(C) Three
(D) Four
(E) Five

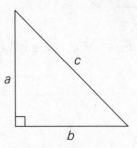

12. In the figure above, does *c* = 5 ?

(1) $a + b = 7$

(2) $b + c = 9$

(A) Statement (1) ALONE is sufficient, but statement (2) alone is not sufficient.
(B) Statement (2) ALONE is sufficient, but statement (1) alone is not sufficient.
(C) BOTH statements TOGETHER are sufficient, but NEITHER statement ALONE is sufficient.
(D) EACH statement ALONE is sufficient.
(E) Statements (1) and (2) TOGETHER are NOT sufficient to answer the question asked, and additional data are needed.

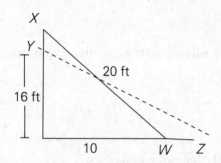

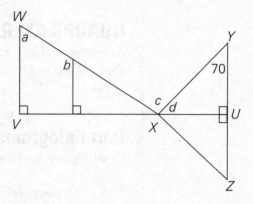

13. A contractor builds a 20-foot slide against a wall so that the base of the slide is 10 feet from the wall, as shown above. If the contractor later decides that the slide is too steep and moves the bottom of the slide from point W to point Z so that the top of the slide is 16 feet from the ground, what is the approximate difference, in feet, between WZ and XY ?

(A) 1
(B) 2
(C) 6
(D) 8
(E) 10

15. What is the value of $b + c$ in the figure above, if $a = 40$?

(A) 130
(B) 160
(C) 180
(D) 200
(E) 250

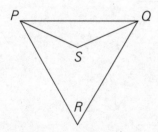

14. In the figure above, $PR = QR$ and $PS = QS$. Angle PSQ is how much greater than angle PRQ ?

(1) Angle $RPS = 20$

(2) Angle $SPQ = 30$

(A) Statement (1) ALONE is sufficient, but statement (2) alone is not sufficient.
(B) Statement (2) ALONE is sufficient, but statement (1) alone is not sufficient.
(C) BOTH statements TOGETHER are sufficient, but NEITHER statement ALONE is sufficient.
(D) EACH statement ALONE is sufficient.
(E) Statements (1) and (2) TOGETHER are NOT sufficient to answer the question asked, and additional data are needed.

Check your answers on page 449.

QUADRILATERALS

A quadrilateral is a four-sided figure. The **rule of 360°** states that the interior angles of any quadrilateral add up to 360°.

Parallelograms

Parallelograms are four-sided figures with the following properties:

- Opposite sides are equal and parallel.
- Opposite angles are equal.
- Adjacent angles add up to 180°.
- Area = bh

As with triangles, when you're calculating the area of a parallelogram, the height must be perpendicular to the base (as shown below).

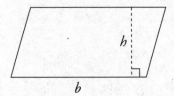

Rectangles

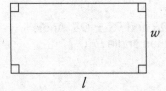

A rectangle is a parallelogram with four right angles. Therefore, it has all the same properties that parallelograms do. In a rectangle, you don't need to use the notation bh to express the idea that the height and base are perpendicular, because the sides of a rectangle are perpendicular by definition.

Thus, the area of a rectangle is usually given as

- Area = lw, where l is the length and w is the width

To find the perimeter of a rectangle (or a parallelogram) you don't need to add up all four sides. Instead, because the sides are equal, you can just add the length and width and double the result.

$$\text{Perimeter} = 2(l + w) \text{ or } 2l + 2w$$

Squares

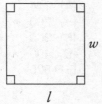

A square is a rectangle with four equal sides. Therefore, it has all the properties of parallelograms and rectangles. Because the length and width are the same, you can just multiply one side by itself to find the area, and because all sides are equal, you can multiply one side by 4 to find the perimeter.

Thus, for squares

$$\text{Area} = s^2$$
$$\text{Perimeter} = 4s$$

QUADRILATERALS DRILL

1. Two rectangular paintings, R and S, have equal areas. Painting R is 2 feet by 6 feet. If painting S has a height of 4 feet, what is the width, in feet, of painting S ?

   (A) $2\frac{3}{4}$
   (B) 3
   (C) 4
   (D) 8
   (E) 12

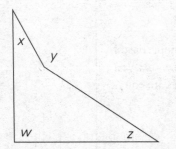

2. In the figure above, what is the measure of angle w ?

   (1) $x + z = 75$

   (2) $y = 135$

   (A) Statement (1) ALONE is sufficient, but statement (2) alone is not sufficient.
   (B) Statement (2) ALONE is sufficient, but statement (1) alone is not sufficient.
   (C) BOTH statements TOGETHER are sufficient, but NEITHER statement ALONE is sufficient.
   (D) EACH statement ALONE is sufficient.
   (E) Statements (1) and (2) TOGETHER are NOT sufficient to answer the question asked, and additional data are needed.

3. A rectangular placemat is solid-colored on one side and striped on the other side. If the mat has dimensions 16 inches by $12\frac{1}{2}$ inches, what is the total area of both sides, in square inches?

   (A) 114
   (B) 200
   (C) 300
   (D) 400
   (E) 526

4. Is the area of parallelogram $ABCD = 24$?

   (1) $AD = 6$

   (2) $AB = 4$

   (A) Statement (1) ALONE is sufficient, but statement (2) alone is not sufficient.
   (B) Statement (2) ALONE is sufficient, but statement (1) alone is not sufficient.
   (C) BOTH statements TOGETHER are sufficient, but NEITHER statement ALONE is sufficient.
   (D) EACH statement ALONE is sufficient.
   (E) Statements (1) and (2) TOGETHER are NOT sufficient to answer the question asked, and additional data are needed.

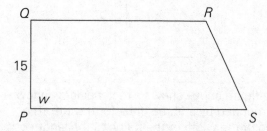

5. In the figure above, QR and PS are parallel, and PQ is perpendicular to PS. What is the length of side PS ?

    (1) QR = 18

    (2) RS = 17

(A) Statement (1) ALONE is sufficient, but statement (2) alone is not sufficient.
(B) Statement (2) ALONE is sufficient, but statement (1) alone is not sufficient.
(C) BOTH statements TOGETHER are sufficient, but NEITHER statement ALONE is sufficient.
(D) EACH statement ALONE is sufficient.
(E) Statements (1) and (2) TOGETHER are NOT sufficient to answer the question asked, and additional data are needed.

6. A certain square is divided into two smaller squares, I and II, and two rectangles, A and B. If the area of square I is greater than the area of square II, and the total area of the figure is 64, what is the area of square I ?

    (1) The area of rectangle A = 12.

    (2) The area of square II = 4.

(A) Statement (1) ALONE is sufficient, but statement (2) alone is not sufficient.
(B) Statement (2) ALONE is sufficient, but statement (1) alone is not sufficient.
(C) BOTH statements TOGETHER are sufficient, but NEITHER statement ALONE is sufficient.
(D) EACH statement ALONE is sufficient.
(E) Statements (1) and (2) TOGETHER are NOT sufficient to answer the question asked, and additional data are needed.

7. A square floor has a diagonal of 30 feet. Which is the closest estimate of the perimeter, in feet, of the floor?

(A) 45
(B) 60
(C) 85
(D) 96
(E) 120

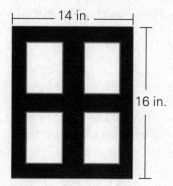

8. A small rectangular tabletop is painted as shown in the figure above. The tabletop has dimensions 14 inches by 16 inches, and the painted strips are 2 inches wide. What fraction of the surface of the tabletop is painted?

(A) $\dfrac{2}{7}$

(B) $\dfrac{5}{14}$

(C) $\dfrac{3}{8}$

(D) $\dfrac{1}{2}$

(E) $\dfrac{9}{14}$

9. Is quadrilateral *ABCD* a square?

   (1) Diagonals *AC* and *BD* bisect each other.

   (2) *AC* and *BD* are perpendicular.

   (A) Statement (1) ALONE is sufficient, but statement (2) alone is not sufficient.
   (B) Statement (2) ALONE is sufficient, but statement (1) alone is not sufficient.
   (C) BOTH statements TOGETHER are sufficient, but NEITHER statement ALONE is sufficient.
   (D) EACH statement ALONE is sufficient.
   (E) Statements (1) and (2) TOGETHER are NOT sufficient to answer the question asked, and additional data are needed.

10. A set of stationary comes with sheets of paper that are twice as long as they are wide. If the perimeter of one sheet of paper is 32 inches, what are the dimensions, in inches, of each sheet of paper?

   (A) 4 by 8

   (B) $\dfrac{10}{3}$ by $\dfrac{22}{3}$

   (C) $\dfrac{16}{3}$ by $\dfrac{32}{3}$

   (D) 6 by 12

   (E) $\dfrac{32}{3}$ by $\dfrac{64}{3}$

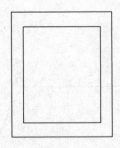

11. The figure above shows a rectangular window surrounded by a frame of uniform width. The ratio of the width of the frame to the length of the frame is 3 to 4. What is the ratio of the width of the window to the length of the window?

   (1) The area of the window is the same as the area of the frame.

   (2) The frame has a width of 1.

   (A) Statement (1) ALONE is sufficient, but statement (2) alone is not sufficient.
   (B) Statement (2) ALONE is sufficient, but statement (1) alone is not sufficient.
   (C) BOTH statements TOGETHER are sufficient, but NEITHER statement ALONE is sufficient.
   (D) EACH statement ALONE is sufficient.
   (E) Statements (1) and (2) TOGETHER are NOT sufficient to answer the question asked, and additional data are needed.

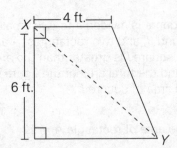

12. The side of a large display case is in the shape of a trapezoid, as shown above. The distance from *X* to *Y* is 10 feet. Albert needs to paint the side of the case. What is the area, in square feet, of the side he needs to paint?

   (A) 24
   (B) 30
   (C) 32
   (D) 36
   (E) 40

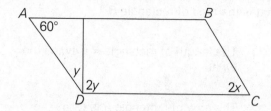

13. *ABCD* is a parallelogram, as shown in the figure above. What is the value of $x + y$?

(A) 30
(B) 40
(C) 60
(D) 70
(E) 120

14. A square and a rectangle have equal areas. What is the length, in inches, of a side of the square?

(1) The rectangle is 40 inches longer and 20 inches narrower than the square.

(2) The rectangle is twice as long and half as wide as the square.

(A) Statement (1) ALONE is sufficient, but statement (2) alone is not sufficient.
(B) Statement (2) ALONE is sufficient, but statement (1) alone is not sufficient.
(C) BOTH statements TOGETHER are sufficient, but NEITHER statement ALONE is sufficient.
(D) EACH statement ALONE is sufficient.
(E) Statements (1) and (2) TOGETHER are NOT sufficient to answer the question asked, and additional data are needed.

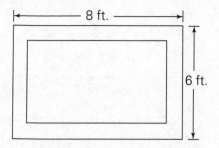

15. A rectangular garden patio is bordered by a thick hedge wall, as shown in the figure above. The patio and the wall have equal areas. The length and width of the patio have the same ratio as do the length and width of the wall. If the wall has outer dimensions 8 feet by 6 feet, what is the length, in feet, of the patio?

(A) $\dfrac{4}{3}$

(B) $\dfrac{4}{\sqrt{2}}$

(C) $4\sqrt{2}$

(D) $6\sqrt{2}$

(E) 10

16. If a rectangular park has length *l*, width *w*, area *a*, and perimeter *p*, which equation describing this park must be true?

(A) $wp - 2w^2 = 2a$
(B) $wl + a = 2p$
(C) $l^2 + w^2 - p = 0$
(D) $wp + w^2 = a$
(E) $2a - 2w^2 - wp = 0$

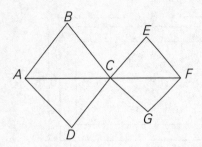

17. In the figure above, line *AF* bisects squares *ABCD* and *CEFG*. What is the perimeter of *CEFG* ?

    (1) The length of *AC* is twice the length of *CF*.

    (2) The length of *CF* is equal to the area of *CEFG*.

    (A) Statement (1) ALONE is sufficient, but statement (2) alone is not sufficient.
    (B) Statement (2) ALONE is sufficient, but statement (1) alone is not sufficient.
    (C) BOTH statements TOGETHER are sufficient, but NEITHER statement ALONE is sufficient.
    (D) EACH statement ALONE is sufficient.
    (E) Statements (1) and (2) TOGETHER are NOT sufficient to answer the question asked, and additional data are needed.

18. A rectangle with integer side lengths has an area of 12. If the diagonal of the rectangle equals 5, then what is the perimeter of the rectangle?

    (A) 10
    (B) 14
    (C) 17
    (D) 24
    (E) 30

19. What is the area of rectangle *R* ?

    (1) The length of rectangle *R* is twice the width.

    (2) The area of rectangle *R* is twice the perimeter.

    (A) Statement (1) ALONE is sufficient, but statement (2) alone is not sufficient.
    (B) Statement (2) ALONE is sufficient, but statement (1) alone is not sufficient.
    (C) BOTH statements TOGETHER are sufficient, but NEITHER statement ALONE is sufficient.
    (D) EACH statement ALONE is sufficient.
    (E) Statements (1) and (2) TOGETHER are NOT sufficient to answer the question asked, and additional data are needed.

20. Two rectangular carpets, carpet *A* and carpet *B*, have equal perimeters. Is the area of carpet *A* greater than the area of carpet *B* ?

    (1) Carpet *A* is 5 feet longer than carpet *B*.

    (2) Carpet *B* is a square.

    (A) Statement (1) ALONE is sufficient, but statement (2) alone is not sufficient.
    (B) Statement (2) ALONE is sufficient, but statement (1) alone is not sufficient.
    (C) BOTH statements TOGETHER are sufficient, but NEITHER statement ALONE is sufficient.
    (D) EACH statement ALONE is sufficient.
    (E) Statements (1) and (2) TOGETHER are NOT sufficient to answer the question asked, and additional data are needed.

Check your answers on page 449.

CIRCLES

Here are some of the basic facts you need to know about circles.

- All circles contain 360°.
- The radius of a circle is the distance from the center to the outer edge.
- The diameter is the longest distance within a circle and passes through the center. The diameter is twice the radius.
- The formula for area of a circle is A = πr^2.
- The formula for circumference (perimeter) of a circle is πd, or $2\pi r$.

Notice that both formulas for circles include the radius. The radius is the key to virtually every circle question. Always find the radius.

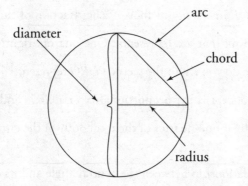

Here are some other facts you should know about circles.

- A chord is a line segment that goes from one point on the circle to another. The diameter is the longest chord in a circle.
- An arc is a fraction of the circumference, a piece of the circle's outer edge.
- A sector is a wedge of a circle. Think of it as a pizza slice.
- A central angle is an angle with the vertex at the center of the circle.

Proportionality of a Circle

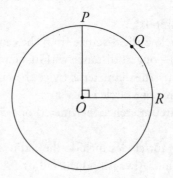

Consider the arc *PQR* in the figure above. What fraction of the circumference of the circle do you think that arc represents? One quarter, right? What fraction of the area of the circle do you think the sector *PQRO* represents? It's the same thing: one-quarter. This concept is the **proportionality of a circle** and it is true because the right angle of 90° is one-quarter of the total 360° of the circle: $\dfrac{90}{360} = \dfrac{1}{4}$.

In any circle, the relationship between the central angle and its corresponding arc and sector can be described as

$$\frac{\text{central angle}}{360°} = \frac{\text{arc}}{\text{circumference}} = \frac{\text{sector}}{\text{area}}$$

Thus, if you have an arc that is $\dfrac{1}{6}$ of the circle, its corresponding central angle must be $\dfrac{1}{6}$ of 360°, or 60°, and its corresponding sector must be $\dfrac{1}{6}$ of the area of the circle.

CIRCLES DRILL

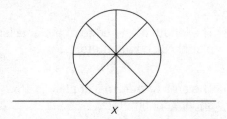

x

1. If a wheel sits on a track as shown above, and the circumference of the wheel is 12π, what is the distance from the center of the wheel to point X ?

    (A)   3
    (B)   6
    (C) 12
    (D) 18
    (E) 36

2. Line m and Circle Q lie in the xy-plane. If Circle Q is centered at the origin and has radius 3, does line m intersect Circle Q ?

    (1) The slope of line m is $\dfrac{1}{20}$.

    (2) The x-intercept of line m is less than –3.

    (A) Statement (1) ALONE is sufficient, but statement (2) alone is not sufficient.
    (B) Statement (2) ALONE is sufficient, but statement (1) alone is not sufficient.
    (C) BOTH statements TOGETHER are sufficient, but NEITHER statement ALONE is sufficient.
    (D) EACH statement ALONE is sufficient.
    (E) Statements (1) and (2) TOGETHER are NOT sufficient to answer the question asked, and additional data are needed.

3. A circular racetrack has a circular fence around it, a green flag at its center, and a radius of 12 meters. A blue flag and a red flag are placed within the vicinity of the racetrack. Does the red flag lie outside the racetrack?

    (1) The distance between the green flag and the blue flag is 12.5 meters.

    (2) The distance between the blue flag and the red flag is 25 meters.

    (A) Statement (1) ALONE is sufficient, but statement (2) alone is not sufficient.
    (B) Statement (2) ALONE is sufficient, but statement (1) alone is not sufficient.
    (C) BOTH statements TOGETHER are sufficient, but NEITHER statement ALONE is sufficient.
    (D) EACH statement ALONE is sufficient.
    (E) Statements (1) and (2) TOGETHER are NOT sufficient to answer the question asked, and additional data are needed.

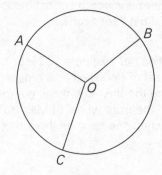

4. If O is the center of the circle above, and sector AOB constitutes $\dfrac{3}{8}$ of the circle and sector BOC constitutes $\dfrac{2}{5}$ of the circle, then what is the degree measure of angle AOC ?

    (A)   81°
    (B) 135°
    (C) 144°
    (D) 180°
    (E) 279°

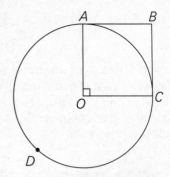

5. What is the area of the circle above with center *O* ?

    (1) The length of arc *CDA* is 27π.

    (2) The perimeter of *OABC* is 72.

(A) Statement (1) ALONE is sufficient, but statement (2) alone is not sufficient.
(B) Statement (2) ALONE is sufficient, but statement (1) alone is not sufficient.
(C) BOTH statements TOGETHER are sufficient, but NEITHER statement ALONE is sufficient.
(D) EACH statement ALONE is sufficient.
(E) Statements (1) and (2) TOGETHER are NOT sufficient to answer the question asked, and additional data are needed.

6. Mikaela pushes her bike up a 120 foot hill. If the front wheel of her bike has a radius of 3 feet, including the tire, how many complete 360° rotations will the front wheel of Mikaela's bike have made when she reaches the top of the hill?

    (A)   4
    (B)   5
    (C)   6
    (D)   7
    (E) 19

7. The length of the edge of a large circular pie plate is twice that of a small circular pie plate. What is the area of the larger plate?

    (1) The length of the edge of the smaller plate is 8π centimeters.

    (2) The area of the smaller plate is 16π square centimeters.

(A) Statement (1) ALONE is sufficient, but statement (2) alone is not sufficient.
(B) Statement (2) ALONE is sufficient, but statement (1) alone is not sufficient.
(C) BOTH statements TOGETHER are sufficient, but NEITHER statement ALONE is sufficient.
(D) EACH statement ALONE is sufficient.
(E) Statements (1) and (2) TOGETHER are NOT sufficient to answer the question asked, and additional data are needed.

8. Line segment *AB* lies in a plane and has a length of 5. If *A* lies inside Circle *X* with center *O*, does *B* lie inside Circle *X* ?

    (1) The radius of Circle *X* is 4.

    (2) The length of line segment *BO* is 2.5.

(A) Statement (1) ALONE is sufficient, but statement (2) alone is not sufficient.
(B) Statement (2) ALONE is sufficient, but statement (1) alone is not sufficient.
(C) BOTH statements TOGETHER are sufficient, but NEITHER statement ALONE is sufficient.
(D) EACH statement ALONE is sufficient.
(E) Statements (1) and (2) TOGETHER are NOT sufficient to answer the question asked, and additional data are needed.

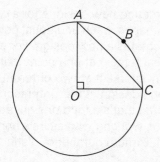

9. If the length of arc *ABC* in the figure above is 5π, what is the area of the circle?

(A) 20π
(B) 40π
(C) 60π
(D) 80π
(E) 100π

Total Revenue for the six
products sold by company Q

10. The circle graph above represents Company Q's total revenue as divided by revenue for each of its 6 products. If *O* is the center of the circle and if Company Q's total revenue is $12,500,000, then what is the revenue generated by product *E* ?

(1) $x = 72°$

(2) The total revenue generated by products A and F is twice as much as the revenue generated by product E.

(A) Statement (1) ALONE is sufficient, but statement (2) alone is not sufficient.
(B) Statement (2) ALONE is sufficient, but statement (1) alone is not sufficient.
(C) BOTH statements TOGETHER are sufficient, but NEITHER statement ALONE is sufficient.
(D) EACH statement ALONE is sufficient.
(E) Statements (1) and (2) TOGETHER are NOT sufficient to answer the question asked, and additional data are needed.

11. A landscaper wishes to dig a circular pond in a rectangular plot of land that is 4 feet in width. If the length of the plot is 3 times its width, and the area of the surface of the pond is to be $\frac{1}{3}$ the area of the plot, what must be the radius of the circular pond, in feet?

(A) $\sqrt{\dfrac{16}{\pi}}$

(B) $\dfrac{8}{\pi}$

(C) 4

(D) $\dfrac{16}{\pi}$

(E) $\dfrac{16}{\sqrt{\pi}}$

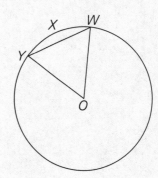

<u>Note</u>: Figure not drawn to scale

12. If sector *WOY* is $\frac{1}{4}$ of the circle with center *O* above, and the perimeter of triangle *YWO* is $20 + 10\sqrt{2}$, what is the length of arc *WXY* ?

(A) 5π
(B) 10π
(C) 20π
(D) 25π
(E) 100π

13. In the rectangular coordinate system, a circle is tangent to both axes. If the distance from the center of the circle to the origin is equal to w, what is the area of the circle, in terms of w ?

(A) $\dfrac{w^2}{9}\pi$

(B) $\dfrac{w^2}{4}\pi$

(C) $\dfrac{w^2}{3}\pi$

(D) $\dfrac{w^2}{2}\pi$

(E) $w^2\pi$

14. An artist is creating new designs for a wall by intersecting shapes. Each additional point of intersection creates a new design. For example, if two shapes intersect at one point that's one design, if they intersect at two different points, that's a second design, if they intersect at three different points, that's a third design, and so on. If the designer is working with a circle and a triangle, what is the maximum number of distinct designs she can make?

(A) 3
(B) 4
(C) 5
(D) 6
(E) 7

Check your answers on page 449.

3D FIGURES

You may see some questions involving basic three-dimensional objects on the GMAT. The questions generally involve **volume** or **surface area**.

Volume

You will need to know the formulas for the volume of a rectangular solid, a cube and a cylinder. These are easy to remember because you simply add the third dimension to the formulas for the area of a rectangle, a square, and a circle. Thus, the formulas are

> For a rectangular solid: $V = lwh$
>
> For a cube: $V = S^3$
>
> For a cylinder: $V = \pi r^2 h$

Surface Area

Surface area is the combined area of all the surfaces, or faces, of a solid. Calculating surface area is easy. Simply find the area of each face and add the areas all together.

The formula to find the area of a rectangular solid is $2(lw + lh + wh)$; the opposite faces of a rectangular solid have the same area, so once you've found the area of each of the three different types of faces (front/back, left/right, top/bottom), you can just double them.

Cubes have six equal faces, so you only have to find the area of one face and multiply it by six. The formula is $6s^2$.

Diagonal of a Rectangular Solid

A diagonal is the longest distance between any two corners of a rectangular solid. If you ever need to find a diagonal, the following formula is easy to remember because of its similarity to the Pythagorean theorem:

$$a^2 + b^2 + c^2 = d^2$$

Here, a, b, and c are the dimensions (length, width, and height) of the figure.

3D FIGURES DRILL

1. A small rectangular jewelry box has a capacity of 12 cubic inches. If the length, width, and height of a second jewelry box are all twice as big as those of the first box, what is the capacity of the second box, in cubic inches?

   (A) 18
   (B) 24
   (C) 48
   (D) 72
   (E) 96

2. A cylindrical canister is filled to half its capacity and set on its side on a flat surface. The canister contains 64π cubic inches of water, and the height of the water in this position is 4 inches. If the canister is set upright on its circular base on a flat surface, what is the height of the water, in inches?

   (A) 4
   (B) 6
   (C) 8
   (D) 12
   (E) 16

3. What is the total volume of rectangular solid S ?

   (1) The length of one of the faces of S is 5.

   (2) The surface area of one of the faces of S is 35.

   (A) Statement (1) ALONE is sufficient, but statement (2) alone is not sufficient.
   (B) Statement (2) ALONE is sufficient, but statement (1) alone is not sufficient.
   (C) BOTH statements TOGETHER are sufficient, but NEITHER statement ALONE is sufficient.
   (D) EACH statement ALONE is sufficient.
   (E) Statements (1) and (2) TOGETHER are NOT sufficient to answer the question asked, and additional data are needed.

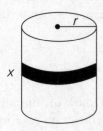

4. A rectangular band has been painted around the circumference of a tub, as shown above. What is the value of x, the width of the band?

   (1) The band and the base of the tub have the same area.

   (2) The radius of the tub is 5.

   (A) Statement (1) ALONE is sufficient, but statement (2) alone is not sufficient.
   (B) Statement (2) ALONE is sufficient, but statement (1) alone is not sufficient.
   (C) BOTH statements TOGETHER are sufficient, but NEITHER statement ALONE is sufficient.
   (D) EACH statement ALONE is sufficient.
   (E) Statements (1) and (2) TOGETHER are NOT sufficient to answer the question asked, and additional data are needed.

5. What is the surface area of the sphere shown above?

(1) The radius of the sphere is .5 meters.

(2) The sphere fits into a square box with a volume of 1 cubic meter.

(A) Statement (1) ALONE is sufficient, but statement (2) alone is not sufficient.
(B) Statement (2) ALONE is sufficient, but statement (1) alone is not sufficient.
(C) BOTH statements TOGETHER are sufficient, but NEITHER statement ALONE is sufficient.
(D) EACH statement ALONE is sufficient.
(E) Statements (1) and (2) TOGETHER are NOT sufficient to answer the question asked, and additional data are needed.

6. A right circular cone is inscribed in a hemisphere so that the base of the cone coincides with the base of the hemisphere. What is the volume of the hemisphere? (The formula for the volume of a sphere is $V = \frac{4}{3}\pi r^3$.)

(1) The height of the cone is 3.

(2) The area of the base of the cone is 9π.

(A) Statement (1) ALONE is sufficient, but statement (2) alone is not sufficient.
(B) Statement (2) ALONE is sufficient, but statement (1) alone is not sufficient.
(C) BOTH statements TOGETHER are sufficient, but NEITHER statement ALONE is sufficient.
(D) EACH statement ALONE is sufficient.
(E) Statements (1) and (2) TOGETHER are NOT sufficient to answer the question asked, and additional data are needed.

7. In a rectangular shoebox with dimensions 3 inches by 4 inches by 12 inches, Kelly is running a taut string from the corner nearest her to the farthest possible corner. What is the length, in inches, of the string, as measured from corner to corner of the box?

(A) 6
(B) 12
(C) 13
(D) 19
(E) 24

8. Sandbox B has three times the capacity of sandbox A. Sandbox A is filled to $\frac{1}{4}$ of its capacity, and sandbox B is filled to $\frac{1}{3}$ of its capacity. If all of the sand in box A is poured into box B, what fraction of sandbox B is filled?

(A) $\frac{1}{4}$

(B) $\frac{5}{12}$

(C) $\frac{7}{12}$

(D) $\frac{4}{3}$

(E) $\frac{13}{12}$

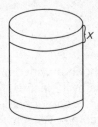

9. A soup can has a label around its circumference as shown above. What is the surface area of the label?

    (1) The height of the label is 3 centimeters.

    (2) $x = .25$

    (A) Statement (1) ALONE is sufficient, but statement (2) alone is not sufficient.
    (B) Statement (2) ALONE is sufficient, but statement (1) alone is not sufficient.
    (C) BOTH statements TOGETHER are sufficient, but NEITHER statement ALONE is sufficient.
    (D) EACH statement ALONE is sufficient.
    (E) Statements (1) and (2) TOGETHER are NOT sufficient to answer the question asked, and additional data are needed.

10. A cylinder with a radius of 5 stands upright in a closed rectangular box. If the volume of the cylinder is 100π, what is the minimum volume of the box?

    (A) 100
    (B) 200
    (C) 320
    (D) 400
    (E) 480

11. The inside dimensions of a rectangular wooden box are 5 inches by 12 inches by 13 inches. A cylindrical container is to be placed inside the box so that it stands upright and the ends of the container both touch the ends of the box. What is the volume of the cylindrical container?

    (1) The surface area of the cylindrical container is 48π inches.

    (2) The box lies so that its base has an area of 156 inches.

    (A) Statement (1) ALONE is sufficient, but statement (2) alone is not sufficient.
    (B) Statement (2) ALONE is sufficient, but statement (1) alone is not sufficient.
    (C) BOTH statements TOGETHER are sufficient, but NEITHER statement ALONE is sufficient.
    (D) EACH statement ALONE is sufficient.
    (E) Statements (1) and (2) TOGETHER are NOT sufficient to answer the question asked, and additional data are needed.

12. A cylinder with a diameter of x inches is half full of liquid and standing upright on its circular base. If the height of the liquid is 2 inches, what is the total capacity of the cylinder?

    (A) $2x\pi$

    (B) $4x\pi$

    (C) $\dfrac{x^2\pi}{4}$

    (D) $\dfrac{x^2\pi}{2}$

    (E) $x^2\pi$

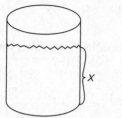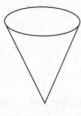

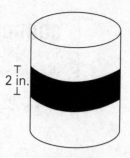

13. Water from the cylindrical glass above is poured into the cone cup shown above. Will all of the water from the glass fit into the cup?

    (1) $x = 5$

    (2) The length of the edge of the glass is equal to the length of the edge of the cup.

(A) Statement (1) ALONE is sufficient, but statement (2) alone is not sufficient.
(B) Statement (2) ALONE is sufficient, but statement (1) alone is not sufficient.
(C) BOTH statements TOGETHER are sufficient, but NEITHER statement ALONE is sufficient.
(D) EACH statement ALONE is sufficient.
(E) Statements (1) and (2) TOGETHER are NOT sufficient to answer the question asked, and additional data are needed.

14. A cylindrical can has a label wrapped completely around it, as shown in the figure above. If the surface area of the label is 12π inches, what is the area of the circular base of the can, in square inches?

    (A) 2π
    (B) 4π
    (C) 9π
    (D) 12π
    (E) 24π

Check your answers on page 449.

COORDINATE GEOMETRY

Some GMAT questions test your familiarity with the coordinate system. You should review the basics.

The coordinate grid consists of two perpendicular axes, *x* and *y*.

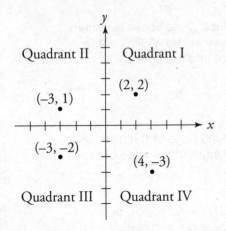

The horizontal line is the **x-axis** and the vertical line is the **y-axis**. The *x*-coordinate of any point tells you its horizontal position, while the *y*-coordinate tells you its vertical position. Every point in the grid has an *x*-coordinate and a *y*-coordinate and can be expressed in the form (*x*, *y*). The point where the axes intersect is called the **origin**. Its coordinates are (0, 0).

The *x*- and *y*-axes split the grid into four quadrants, starting with Quadrant I in the upper right and moving counterclockwise. All the points in Quadrant I have a positive *x*-coordinate and a positive *y*-coordinate (+, +). All the points in Quadrant II have a negative *x*-coordinate and a positive *y*-coordinate. (−, +). All the points in Quadrant III have a negative *x*-coordinate and a negative *y*-coordinate (−, −). All the points in Quadrant IV have a positive *x*-coordinate and a negative *y*-coordinate (+, −).

Slope

Slope is the steepness of a line. A line that goes up from left to right has a positive slope and a line that goes down from left to right has a negative slope. A horizontal line has a slope of 0 and a vertical line has no slope at all; it's undefined. You will need to know how to calculate the slope of a line.

$$\text{Slope} = \frac{Rise}{Run} = \frac{\text{Vertical Change}}{\text{Horizontal Change}} = \frac{y_2 - y_1}{x_2 - x_1}$$

In this formula, (x_1, y_1) and (x_2, y_2) are points on the line.

It doesn't matter which coordinate you call y_2 or y_1 as long as you use the corresponding x_2 and x_1.

If you are given two sets of points, you want to use the $\frac{y_2 - y_1}{x_2 - x_1}$ formula. If you are working with a graph, it's often easier to calculate the slope by taking the vertical change between any two points on the line and dividing it by the horizontal change between those points. This is called putting the *rise* over the *run*.

Line Equations

The other formula that involves slope that you need to know is the formula for the equation of a line.

$$y = mx + b$$

x, y = variables that stand for the coordinates of any point on the line.

m = slope of the line.

b = *y*-intercept = *y*-coordinate of the point (0, *b*) where the line crosses the *y*-axis.

Thus, the line with the equation $y = \frac{4}{3}x + 5$ crosses the *y*-axis 5 units above the origin and has a slope of $\frac{4}{3}$.

The *x*-**intercept** of a line is the point where the line crosses the *x*-axis. At the *x*-intercept, *y* equals 0, so to find the *x*-intercept, set *y* equal to 0 and solve for *x*. Thus, the *x*-intercept of the line above is $(-\frac{15}{4}, 0)$.

It is worth mentioning that the slopes of perpendicular lines are just the negative reciprocals of each other. So, a line that is perpendicular to the line represented by the equation above would have a slope of $-\frac{3}{4}$.

COORDINATE GEOMETRY DRILL

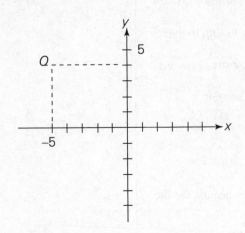

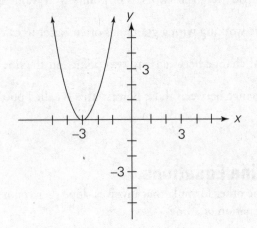

1. What are the coordinates of point Q in the figure above?

   (A) $(-5, 4)$
   (B) $(4, 5)$
   (C) $(5, -4)$
   (D) $(5, 4)$
   (E) $(4, -5)$

2. In the xy-plane, at what two point does the graph of $y = (x + p)(x - q)$ intersect the x-axis?

   (1) The graph intersects the y-axis at $(0, -12)$.

   (2) The difference of p and q is 11.

   (A) Statement (1) ALONE is sufficient, but statement (2) alone is not sufficient.
   (B) Statement (2) ALONE is sufficient, but statement (1) alone is not sufficient.
   (C) BOTH statements TOGETHER are sufficient, but NEITHER statement ALONE is sufficient.
   (D) EACH statement ALONE is sufficient.
   (E) Statements (1) and (2) TOGETHER are NOT sufficient to answer the question asked, and additional data are needed.

3. In the figure above, the graph is symmetric with respect to the vertical line described by the equation $x = -3$. If $y = 4$ when $x = -5$, what is the value of y when $x = -1$?

   (A) 0
   (B) 1
   (C) 2
   (D) 3
   (E) 4

4. In the xy-plane, does the point $(5, 12)$ lie on line l ?

   (1) The point $(-3, 7)$ lies on line l.

   (2) The point $(11, 26)$ lies on line l.

   (A) Statement (1) ALONE is sufficient, but statement (2) alone is not sufficient.
   (B) Statement (2) ALONE is sufficient, but statement (1) alone is not sufficient.
   (C) BOTH statements TOGETHER are sufficient, but NEITHER statement ALONE is sufficient.
   (D) EACH statement ALONE is sufficient.
   (E) Statements (1) and (2) TOGETHER are NOT sufficient to answer the question asked, and additional data are needed.

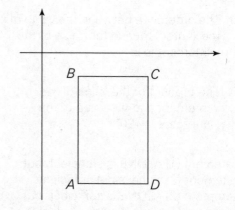

5. In the coordinate plane above, what is the area of rectangular region *ABCD* ?

    (1) *B* has coordinates (2, –1).

    (2) *C* has coordinates (7, –1).

(A) Statement (1) ALONE is sufficient, but statement (2) alone is not sufficient.
(B) Statement (2) ALONE is sufficient, but statement (1) alone is not sufficient.
(C) BOTH statements TOGETHER are sufficient, but NEITHER statement ALONE is sufficient.
(D) EACH statement ALONE is sufficient.
(E) Statements (1) and (2) TOGETHER are NOT sufficient to answer the question asked, and additional data are needed.

6. In the coordinate system, if a line has slope of –3 and passes through the point (–2, 7), what is the *x*-intercept of the line?

    (A) (–1, 0)

    (B) $(-\frac{1}{3}, 0)$

    (C) $(0, \frac{1}{3})$

    (D) $(\frac{1}{3}, 0)$

    (E) (1, 0)

7. If *c* and *d* are negative numbers, what are the coordinates of the midpoint of line segment *JK* in the *xy*-plane?

    (1) The coordinates of *J* are (1 – *c*, *d*).

    (2) The coordinates of *K* are (*c*, 1 – *d*).

(A) Statement (1) ALONE is sufficient, but statement (2) alone is not sufficient.
(B) Statement (2) ALONE is sufficient, but statement (1) alone is not sufficient.
(C) BOTH statements TOGETHER are sufficient, but NEITHER statement ALONE is sufficient.
(D) EACH statement ALONE is sufficient.
(E) Statements (1) and (2) TOGETHER are NOT sufficient to answer the question asked, and additional data are needed.

8. If point (*a*, –*b*) lies in quadrant III of the rectangular coordinate system, and *ab* ≠ 0, in which quadrant does point (*a*, *b*) lie?

    (A) None
    (B) I
    (C) II
    (D) III
    (E) IV

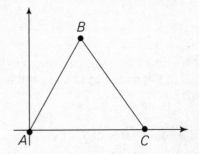

9. In the rectangular coordinate system above, if $AB < BC$, is the area of region ABC less than 45 ?

    (1) The coordinates of point B are (5, 12).

    (2) The coordinates of point C are (15, 0).

(A) Statement (1) ALONE is sufficient, but statement (2) alone is not sufficient.
(B) Statement (2) ALONE is sufficient, but statement (1) alone is not sufficient.
(C) BOTH statements TOGETHER are sufficient, but NEITHER statement ALONE is sufficient.
(D) EACH statement ALONE is sufficient.
(E) Statements (1) and (2) TOGETHER are NOT sufficient to answer the question asked, and additional data are needed.

10. Which of the following quadrants in the rectangular coordinate system contains points that satisfy the inequality $3x - 4y \geq 8$?

(A) All
(B) I, II, and IV
(C) I, II, and III
(D) II only
(E) None

11. If h is a line in the xy-plane, then what is the slope of h ?

    (1) The difference between the value of the x-intercept and the value of the y-intercept is 8.

    (2) The product of the value of the x-intercept and the value of the y-intercept is –20.

(A) Statement (1) ALONE is sufficient, but statement (2) alone is not sufficient.
(B) Statement (2) ALONE is sufficient, but statement (1) alone is not sufficient.
(C) BOTH statements TOGETHER are sufficient, but NEITHER statement ALONE is sufficient.
(D) EACH statement ALONE is sufficient.
(E) Statements (1) and (2) TOGETHER are NOT sufficient to answer the question asked, and additional data are needed.

12. Lines k and l lie in the xy-plane. Is the slope of line k greater than that of line l ?

    (1) The y-intercept of line l is less than the y-intercept of line k.

    (2) Lines k and l intersect at the point (4, –1).

(A) Statement (1) ALONE is sufficient, but statement (2) alone is not sufficient.
(B) Statement (2) ALONE is sufficient, but statement (1) alone is not sufficient.
(C) BOTH statements TOGETHER are sufficient, but NEITHER statement ALONE is sufficient.
(D) EACH statement ALONE is sufficient.
(E) Statements (1) and (2) TOGETHER are NOT sufficient to answer the question asked, and additional data are needed.

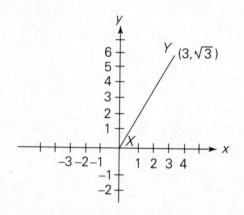

13. In the figure above with origin at point *X*, which of the following is the point on segment *XY* that is twice as far from *X* as it is from *Y*?

(A) (1, 2)

(B) (2, 1)

(C) $(1, \sqrt{3})$

(D) $(2, 2\sqrt{3})$

(E) (2, 4)

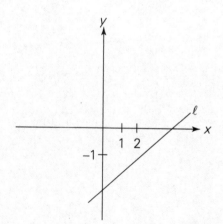

14. Which of the following is the equation of a line that is perpendicular to a line with slope $\frac{1}{2}$, *y*-intercept of –2, and *x*-intercept of 4?

(A) $2y + x = -4$
(B) $2x - y = -2$
(C) $2x + y = -2$
(D) $2y + x = -2$
(E) $2y - x = -4$

15. If ℓ is a line in the *xy*-plane, what is the *y*-intercept of ℓ?

(1) The *x*-intercept of ℓ is 4.

(2) The slope of ℓ is $-\frac{1}{2}$.

(A) Statement (1) ALONE is sufficient, but statement (2) alone is not sufficient.
(B) Statement (2) ALONE is sufficient, but statement (1) alone is not sufficient.
(C) BOTH statements TOGETHER are sufficient, but NEITHER statement ALONE is sufficient.
(D) EACH statement ALONE is sufficient.
(E) Statements (1) and (2) TOGETHER are NOT sufficient to answer the question asked, and additional data are needed.

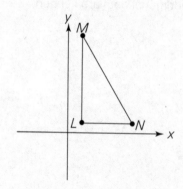

16. In the coordinate plane above, what is the area of *LMN*?

(1) *L* has coordinates (1, 3).

(2) *N* has coordinates (5, 3).

(A) Statement (1) ALONE is sufficient, but statement (2) alone is not sufficient.
(B) Statement (2) ALONE is sufficient, but statement (1) alone is not sufficient.
(C) BOTH statements TOGETHER are sufficient, but NEITHER statement ALONE is sufficient.
(D) EACH statement ALONE is sufficient.
(E) Statements (1) and (2) TOGETHER are NOT sufficient to answer the question asked, and additional data are needed.

17. In the *xy*-coordinate plane, line *p* passes through

the point $\left(\dfrac{3}{4}, -\dfrac{5}{2} \right)$. Is the slope of line *p* equal to

$\dfrac{2}{3}$?

    (1) Line *p* passes through the point (–3, –5).

    (2) Line *p* passes through the point (3, –1).

(A) Statement (1) ALONE is sufficient, but statement (2) alone is not sufficient.
(B) Statement (2) ALONE is sufficient, but statement (1) alone is not sufficient.
(C) BOTH statements TOGETHER are sufficient, but NEITHER statement ALONE is sufficient.
(D) EACH statement ALONE is sufficient.
(E) Statements (1) and (2) TOGETHER are NOT sufficient to answer the question asked, and additional data are needed.

Check your answers on page 449.

INSCRIBED FIGURES AND SHADED REGIONS

Inscribed Figures

Some geometry problems involve multiple geometric shapes that overlap or are inscribed in one another. The key to these problems is figuring out what the two shapes have in common.

Example

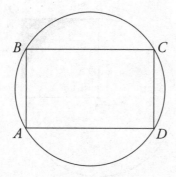

1. Rectangle *ABCD* has length 8 and width 6. What is the area of the circle?

   (A) 10π
   (B) 25π
   (C) 50π
   (D) 64π
   (E) 100π

You are asked to find the area of the circle, which means you need the radius. What do the two figures have in common that will help you find the radius of the circle? The diagonal of the rectangle is the diameter of the circle. If you draw in one of the diagonals it creates a 6:8:10 triangle, so the diameter of the circle is 10. That means that the radius is 5. Thus, the area of the circle is πr^2 or 25π and the correct answer is (B).

Shaded Regions

Sometimes the test writers will ask you to find the area of a weird-looking shaded region. To find it, subtract the non-shaded part from the total figure.

> Shaded Area = Total Area – Unshaded Area

Example

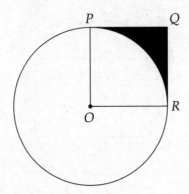

2. In the figure above, *OPQR* is a square. If *O* is the center of the circle, and the distance between point *P* and point *R* is $4\sqrt{2}$, what is the area of the shaded region?

    (A) $16 - 8\pi$
    (B) $16 - 4\pi$
    (C) $32 - 8\pi$
    (D) $32 - 2\pi$
    (E) $64 - 12\pi$

In this case the total area is the square and the non-shaded area is the sector. Start with the square. The problem says the distance between point *P* and point *R* is $4\sqrt{2}$. *OPQR* is a square and a square has four equal sides, so triangle *POR* is an isosceles right triangle with legs of 4. You now know that the area of the square is 4^2, or 16.

Now for the sector. A square has four right angles, so $\angle POR$ is 90°. That means that the sector is $\dfrac{90}{360}$ or $\dfrac{1}{4}$ of the area of the circle. The radius of the circle is four, so the area of the circle is πr^2 or 16π. That means the sector is $\dfrac{1}{4} \times 16\pi = 4\pi$. Thus, the area of the weird shaded region is $16 - 4\pi$, so the correct answer is (B).

For more about geometry problems, see *Cracking the GMAT,* 2016 Edition.

INSCRIBED FIGURES AND SHADED REGIONS DRILL

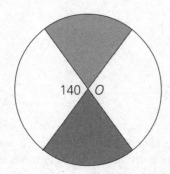

1. In the circular region with center O above, the radius is 6. What is the area of the shaded region?

   (A) 2π
   (B) 4π
   (C) 8π
   (D) 18π
   (E) 36π

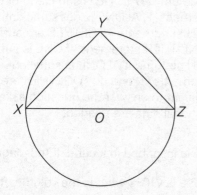

2. Triangle XYZ is inscribed in a circle with center O as shown above. What is the ratio of side XY of the triangle to the radius of the circle?

   (A) 1:1

   (B) $\sqrt{2}$:1

   (C) $\sqrt{3}$:1

   (D) 2:1

   (E) 3:1

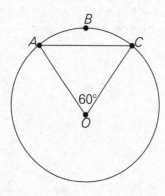

3. What is the area of the circle above with center O ?

   (1) The length of arc ABC is 3π.

   (2) The perimeter of triangle OAC is 27.

   (A) Statement (1) ALONE is sufficient, but statement (2) ALONE is not sufficient.
   (B) Statement (2) ALONE is sufficient, but statement (1) ALONE is not sufficient.
   (C) BOTH statements TOGETHER are sufficient, but NEITHER statement ALONE is sufficient.
   (D) EACH statement ALONE is sufficient.
   (E) Statements (1) and (2) TOGETHER are NOT sufficient to answer the question asked, and additional data are needed.

4. A new design is created by cutting a circle out of a circular piece of fabric. If the radius of the circular piece of fabric is 9 inches, and the circle that is cut out of it has a radius of 7 inches, then what fraction of the original circular piece of fabric remains after the cutout is removed?

(A) $\dfrac{32}{81}$

(B) $\dfrac{49}{81}$

(C) $\dfrac{32}{49}$

(D) $\dfrac{49}{32}$

(E) $\dfrac{81}{32}$

5. A square wooden table has a square glass inlay in its center, leaving a wooden border of uniform width around the glass. If the area of the glass is 16 square inches and the area of the border is 33 square inches, what is the width, in inches, of the border?

(A) 1
(B) 1.5
(C) 3
(D) 8
(E) 17

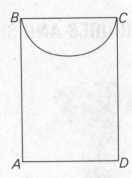

6. The figure above shows the mark a swinging door makes in a greenhouse. If arc *BC* is a semi-circle and *ABCD* is a rectangle, what is the area of the floor of the greenhouse?

(1) Arc *BC* is 6π feet.

(2) Each diagonal of *ABCD* is 20 feet.

(A) Statement (1) ALONE is sufficient, but statement (2) ALONE is not sufficient.
(B) Statement (2) ALONE is sufficient, but statement (1) ALONE is not sufficient.
(C) BOTH statements TOGETHER are sufficient, but NEITHER statement ALONE is sufficient.
(D) EACH statement ALONE is sufficient.
(E) Statements (1) and (2) TOGETHER are NOT sufficient to answer the question asked, and additional data are needed.

7. A sphere is inscribed in a cube. If the diagonal of the cube is $\sqrt{108}$, what is the volume of the sphere? (Volume of a sphere: $V = \dfrac{4}{3}\pi r^3$.)

(A) 4π
(B) 12π
(C) 18π
(D) 24π
(E) 36π

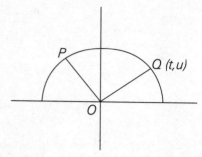

8. In the figure above, if ∠POQ is 90°, then what is the value of *t* ?

    (1) The value of *r* is $-\sqrt{3}$.

    (2) The *y*-coordinate of point *P* is 1.

(A) Statement (1) ALONE is sufficient, but statement (2) ALONE is not sufficient.
(B) Statement (2) ALONE is sufficient, but statement (1) ALONE is not sufficient.
(C) BOTH statements TOGETHER are sufficient, but NEITHER statement ALONE is sufficient.
(D) EACH statement ALONE is sufficient.
(E) Statements (1) and (2) TOGETHER are NOT sufficient to answer the question asked, and additional data are needed.

10. If, in the figure above, triangle *PQR* is an equilateral triangle, what is the area of the shaded region?

    (1) The perimeter of triangle *PQR* is 30.

    (2) The radius of the circle is $\dfrac{5\sqrt{3}}{3}$.

(A) Statement (1) ALONE is sufficient, but statement (2) ALONE is not sufficient.
(B) Statement (2) ALONE is sufficient, but statement (1) ALONE is not sufficient.
(C) BOTH statements TOGETHER are sufficient, but NEITHER statement ALONE is sufficient.
(D) EACH statement ALONE is sufficient.
(E) Statements (1) and (2) TOGETHER are NOT sufficient to answer the question asked, and additional data are needed.

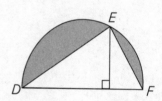

9. If arc *DEF* above is a semicircle, what is the area of the shaded region?

    (1) *DE* = 15

    (2) *EF* = 36

(A) Statement (1) ALONE is sufficient, but statement (2) ALONE is not sufficient.
(B) Statement (2) ALONE is sufficient, but statement (1) ALONE is not sufficient.
(C) BOTH statements TOGETHER are sufficient, but NEITHER statement ALONE is sufficient.
(D) EACH statement ALONE is sufficient.
(E) Statements (1) and (2) TOGETHER are NOT sufficient to answer the question asked, and additional data are needed.

Check your answers on page 449.

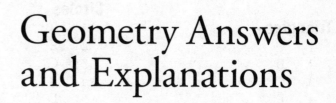

Geometry Answers
and Explanations

ANSWER KEY

Lines and Angles
1. C
2. A
3. E
4. B

Triangles
1. C
2. B
3. C
4. E
5. A
6. D
7. D
8. D
9. A
10. B
11. B
12. C
13. A
14. A
15. E

Quadrilaterals
1. B
2. C
3. D
4. E
5. C
6. D
7. C
8. E
9. E
10. C
11. A
12. D
13. D
14. A
15. C
16. A

17. B
18. B
19. C
20. B

Circles
1. B
2. E
3. C
4. A
5. D
6. C
7. D
8. B
9. E
10. A
11. A
12. A
13. D
14. D

3D Figures
1. E
2. A
3. E
4. C
5. A
6. D
7. C
8. B
9. E
10. D
11. C
12. D
13. E
14. E
15. C

Coordinate Geometry
1. A
2. C
3. E
4. C
5. E
6. D
7. C
8. C
9. A
10. B
11. C
12. C
13. D
14. C
15. C
16. E
17. D

Inscribed Figures and Shaded Regions
1. C
2. B
3. D
4. A
5. B
6. C
7. E
8. C
9. C
10. D

EXPLANATIONS

Lines and Angles

1. **C** This question is testing lines and vertical angles. There are 180° in a line, so $5w + 4w = 180$. Thus, $9w = 180$ and $w = 20$. $5w = z + 45$ by vertical angles. Substitute 20 for w and solve for z, which is 55.

2. **A** When 2 parallel lines are intersected by a third line, 2 kinds of angles are created: big angles and small angles. All the big angles are equal, all the small angles are equal, and any big angle plus any small angle equals 180. Therefore, $x + y = 180$. Statement (1) allows you to turn this equation into $3y + y = 180$, or $4y = 180$, so statement (1) is sufficient. Eliminate (B), (C), and (E). Statement 2 can be manipulated to yield $x + y = 180$, but this adds no new information to the problem, since you already know that $x + y = 180$. Therefore, statement (2) is insufficient.

3. **E** This question is testing lines and vertical angles. There are 180° in a line, so $w + z = 180$. You can cross multiply with the given equation and get that $z = 72$, which means that $w = 108$. Eliminate (B) and (C). Angle w and angle $2x$ are equal because they are vertical angles. That means that $x = 54$. $3(54) + 40 = 202$.

4. **B** The most difficult part of this problem is representing the information effectively. One solution is to use variables for the 3 missing angles between x and y. Label them p, q, and r (from left to right). The problem can then be restated as "what is $p + q + r$?" You can also restate the phrase "$\overline{OC}$ bisects $\angle AOF$" as "$20 + p = q + r + 30$", or $p - q - r = 10$. Statement (1) can similarly be rephrased as $p + q = r + 30$, or $p + q - r = 30$. However, while this equation can be combined with the first equation to solve for q, you will be unable to solve for $p + r$, so statement (1) is insufficient. Eliminate (A) and (D). Statement (2) can be rewritten as $q + r = 30$. If you add this equation to the first equation, you get $p = 40$. Since $q + r = 30$, $p + q + r = 70$. Statement (2) is sufficient.

Triangles

1. **C** Since $PQ = PR$, angles PQR and PRQ are equal. Statement (1) therefore tells you that both of these angles are 60°. If you draw the height of the triangle from point P down to QR, you form two 30:60:90 right triangles. However, since you have no information about the base or the height, statement (1) is insufficient. Eliminate (A) and (D). Statement (2) gives the base of the triangle, but tells you nothing about the height, or any of the angles, so it is also insufficient. Eliminate (B). If you put the two statements together, You have two 30-60-90 right triangles, each with a shortest side of 5. This tells you that the height of PQR is $5\sqrt{3}$. From there, you can find the area. Thus, statements (1) and (2) together are sufficient, and the answer is (C).

2. **B** This question is testing the third side of a triangle rule. The third side of a triangle must be less than the sum of the other two sides and greater than their difference. Therefore, the third side of this triangle must be less than 14 and greater than 6. Only 12 works, so the answer is (B).

3. **C** There are variables in the answers and the question says "in terms of," so Plug In. Let $s = 40$. There are 180° in a triangle, so the third angle in triangle XYW is 98. There are 180° in a line, so the missing angle in triangle YWZ must be $180 - 98 = 82$. $180 - (82 + 50) = 48$, so $t = 48$. You're looking for s, so your target is 40. Only (C) yields 40 when you Plug In 48 for t; the answer is (C).

4. **E** In a triangle, the shortest side is opposite the smallest angle, the medium side is opposite the medium angle, and the largest side is opposite the largest angle. Therefore, the question can be rephrased as "Is $x > z$? Statement (1) tells you only about x, so you know nothing about y. Eliminate (A) and (D). Similarly, statement (2) tells you only about y, so it is also insufficient. Eliminate (B). To test the two statements together, try some values for x and y. If $x = 61$ and $y = 61$, then $z = 68$, and $x < z$. However, if x is 59 and y is 69, then $z = 52$, and $x > z$. Therefore, statements (1) and (2) together are insufficient.

5. **A** This question is testing Pythagorean triplets. The triangle on the left is a 6:8:10 triangle, so the missing side is 10. The triangle on the right is a multiple of a 5:12:13 triangle, so the missing side is also 10. That means the triangle in the middle is an isosceles triangle. In any triangle, equal sides are opposite equal angles, so the angle adjacent to the 70° angle is also 70°, which means that x is 40°.

6. **D** If AB is parallel to EC, then triangles ABD and ECD are similar. Therefore, there is a constant ratio between any side of ABD and the corresponding side of ECD. Statement (1) tells you that $AE = 2$. Therefore, the ratio of AD:ED is 3:2. The ratio of AB to EC is also 3:2, so $AB = 3$. The same process can be used to find that BC is 1.5. From there, you can find the perimeter of $ABCE$, so statement (1) is sufficient. Eliminate (B), (C), and (E). Statement 2 also tells you that the ratio of side to side is 3:2, so statement (2) is also sufficient, and the answer is (D).

7. **D** The third side of a triangle must be greater than the difference and less than the sum of the other two sides. Therefore, AC must be greater than 3 and less than 7. Statement (1) tells you that AC is an odd integer. 5 is the only odd integer between 3 and 7, so statement (1) is sufficient. Eliminate (B), (C), and (E). Statement (2) tells you that triangle ABC is isosceles. So, your choices for AC are 2 and 5, but since AC must be greater than 3, only 5 will work. Therefore, statement (2) is also sufficient, and the answer is (D).

8. **D** In any triangle, equal sides are opposite equal angles. Therefore, angle WXY is 20°, angle YZW is 40° and angle WZX is a°. There are 180° in a triangle so angles, X, Y, and Z must add up to 180°. That means $2a + 20 + 20 + 40 + 40 = 180$, which means $2a = 60$.

9. **A** A good way to solve this is to Plug In numbers. For statement (1), suppose that $x = 100$ and $z = 95$. Then the base angles of the triangle will sum to 165, so z will equal 15. If you try $x = 150$ and $z = 45$, z will still equal 15, so statement (1) is sufficient. Eliminate (B), (C), and (E). For statement

(2), suppose $x = 120$ and $z = 75$. Then y will equal 15. But, if $x = 130$ and $z = 85$, then y will equal 35. Therefore, statement (2) is insufficient, and the answer is (A).

10.   **B**

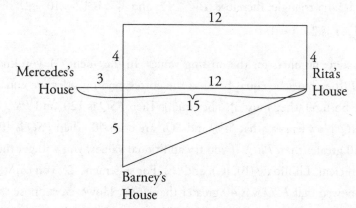

Start by drawing Mercedes's route as shown below. She travels 15 miles due east to get to Rita's house, but later travels 12 miles west to get to Barney's house, so her total horizontal distance is $15 - 3 = 12$ miles. She travels 4 miles due north from Rita's house, but later travels 9 miles due south to get to Barney's house so her total vertical distance is $9 - 4 = 5$ miles. Thus, a 5:12:13 triangle is formed and the distance from Barney's to Rita's house is 13 miles.

11.   **B**   The third side of a triangle rule states that the third side of a triangle must be less than the sum of the other two sides and greater than their difference. Thus, p must be between 6 and 12. Because p is an integer, it must be 7, 8, 9, 10 or 11. The question states that p is between 3 and 9, so that knocks out 9, 10 and 11, leaving 7 and 8 as the only possible values for p.

12.   **C**   In a right triangle, the Pythagorean theorem tells you that $a^2 + b^2 = c^2$. Any numbers you Plug In to the statements must fulfill this equation, as well as the statements, to be valid. For statement (1), if $a = 3$ and $b = 4$, then $c = 5$. But, if a and b are both 3.5, then c does not equal 5, so statement (1) is insufficient. Eliminate (A) and (D). Similarly, in statement 2, if $b = 4$ then $c = 5$ (this would also mean that $a = 3$). But, it could also be true that $b = 3$ and $c = 6$. Since you could use the Pythagorean theorem to find a valid solution for a, you have found 2 solutions for c, so statement (2) is insufficient. Eliminate (B). If you combine the two statements, it is still possible that if $a = 3$, $b = 4$, and $c = 5$. Now, you can try other values that fit the two statements, for example $a = 3.5$, $b = 3.5$, and $c = 5.5$. However $(3.5)^2 + (3.5)^2 \neq (5.5)^2$, so you are not allowed to use these numbers for a, b, and c. If you try a few other values for your variables, you will encounter the same problem. Only the values of $a = 3$, $b = 4$, and $c = 5$ will satisfy both the statements and the Pythagorean theorem. Note: there *is* another algebraic solution, which is $a = 15$, $b = (-8)$, and $c = 17$. However, the side of a triangle cannot be negative, so there is only one real solution to the problem. Since statements (1) and (2) together are sufficient, the answer is (C).

13.   **A**   This question is testing 30:60:90 triangles and Pythagorean triplets. If you name the 90° angle P, then triangle XPW is a 30:60:90 triangle, because its hypotenuse is twice one of its legs. That

means that XP is $10\sqrt{3}$. Thus, XY is $10\sqrt{3} - 16$, which is approximately 1. Triangle YPZ is a multiple of a 3:4:5 triangle; therefore, $PW = 12$, and WZ is $12 - 10 = 2$. Thus, the difference between WZ and XY is $2 - 1 = 1$.

14. **A** Plug In some numbers for the missing values. In statement (1), you know that RPS and RQS are both 20 (they must be equal because the corresponding sides are equal). Suppose that SPQ and SQP are both 30 (they must also be equal). Then PSQ is 120, and PRQ is 80, so PSQ is 40 greater than PRQ. Now let's say that SPQ and SQP are both 40. Then PSQ is 100, and PRQ is 60, so PSQ is still 40 greater than PRQ. If you try additional values, you will get the same result, so statement (1) is sufficient. Eliminate (B), (C), and (E). For statement (2), you can reuse your first set of values, which showed that PSQ was 40 greater than PRQ. However, suppose that RPS and RQS are both 30. Then PSQ will be 120, and PRQ will be 60, so PSQ will now be 60 greater than PRQ. Therefore, statement (2) is insufficient, and the answer is (A).

15. **E** This question is testing degrees of a triangle and of a line and vertical angles. Since $a = 40$, then angle VXW is 50, because there are 180° in triangle WVX. Because angle VXW is 50, the angle adjacent to b must be 40; that means that $b = 140$. Angle ZXU is 50° by vertical angles, which means that angle XZU is 40°. Angles ZXY, UYX and XZU must add up to 180, so $d = 20°$. There are 180° in a line, so $c + d$ must equal $180 - 50 = 130$. Because $d = 20$, then $c = 130 - 20 = 110$. Thus, $b + c = 250$.

Quadrilaterals

1. **B** The area of a rectangle is equal to length times width. The area of painting R, then, is $2 \times 6 = 12$. Apply the same formula to the area of painting S to get $12 = 4 \times w$. Solve for width w to get 3.

2. **C** There are 360 degrees in a quadrilateral. Statement (1) tells you that $x + y = 75$. Without knowing the measure of the unlabeled fourth angle, you cannot determine the measure of angle w. Therefore, statement (1) is insufficient. Eliminate (A) and (D). Statement 2 tells you that $y = 135$. Since there are 360 degrees in a circle, you can calculate that the unlabeled fourth angle of the quadrilateral is $360 - 135 = 225$. However, you know nothing about x and z, so statement (2) is insufficient. Eliminate (B). Combining the two statements gives you three of the four angles in the quadrilateral, enabling you to find angle w. Therefore, statements (1) and (2) together are sufficient, and the answer is (C).

3. **D** The area of a rectangle is equal to length times width, so the area of the mat is $16 \times 12\frac{1}{2} = 200$. The front and back of the mat have the same area, so the total, or combined area, is $200 + 200 = 400$.

4. **E** The area of a parallelogram is (*base*) (*height*). The height must be perpendicular to the base. Statement (1) gives you only one side, so statement (1) is insufficient. Eliminate (A) and (D). Statement

(2) also gives you only 1 side, so statement (2) is insufficient as well. Eliminate (B). Combining the two statements is also insufficient, because you do not know if *AB* and *AD* are perpendicular. If they were, the area would be 24, but if the are not, the area is less than 24. Therefore, statements (1) and (2) together are insufficient, and the answer is (E).

5. **C**   When dealing with unusual shapes, try breaking them up into simple shapes. Drop a line from *R* down to *PS*, such that the new line is parallel to *QP*. The figure now consists of a rectangle and a right triangle. If you can find the base of the rectangle and the base of the triangle, you can add them together to find the length of *PS*. Statement (1) gives you the base of the rectangle, but tells you nothing about the triangle; therefore, statement (1) is insufficient. Eliminate (A) and (D). Statement (2) enables you to use the Pythagorean theorem to find the base of the new triangle. However, you do not know the base of the rectangle, so statement (2) is insufficient. Eliminate (B). If you combine statements (1) and (2), you have the bases of both shapes, so you can find the length of *PS*.

6. **D**   To begin, note that that if the area of the figure is 64, and the figure is a square, its sides are 8. To find the area of square *I*, you need to know its sides. Statement (1) states that the area of rectangle *A* is 12. Since rectangle *B* must be equal to rectangle *A*, its area is also 12. To test statement (1), try different values for the length and width of rectangle *A*. If the length is 6 and the width is 2, then the sides of square *I* must be 6, and the sides of square *II* must be 2. If you add the areas of all four shapes together, you get 12 + 12 + 36 + 4 = 64, which works. However, if the length of rectangle *A* is 4 and the width is 3, then the sides of square *I* are 4, and the sides of square *II* are 3. Adding the areas together, you get 12 + 12 + 16 + 9 = 49, which is incorrect. You can try other combinations for the length and width of rectangle *A*, but the only one that works is 6 and 2. Therefore, statement (1) is sufficient. Eliminate (B), (C), and (E). Statement (2) tells you that the sides of square *II* are each 2. You can use this to find that the sides of square *I* are each 6. Therefore, statement (2) is also sufficient, and the answer is (D).

7. **C**   The diagonal of a square creates two equal right triangles with smaller angles of 45 degrees each. Such 45:45:90 triangles always have side ratios of 1:1:$\sqrt{2}$. Let *s* be the side of the square. The diagonal of the square is the hypotenuse of each triangle, so $s\sqrt{2} = 30$. Then $s = \dfrac{30}{\sqrt{2}} = 15\sqrt{2}$, so *s* equals a little more than 20. The perimeter equals the sum of the lengths of the sides, so a little more than 4 × 20. This is closest to 85. Alternatively, you could use the Pythagorean Theorem to find the side of the square.

8. **E**   The total area of the tabletop is equal to its length times width, or 14 × 16 = 224. To find the area that is not painted, take the total length, 16, and subtract the three strips of 2 inches each that run lengthwise, so 16 – (3)(2) = 10. Next, take the total width, 14, and subtract the three strips that run along the width, so 14 – (3)(2) = 8. Then the unpainted area equals 10 × 8 = 80. Subtract

this from the total area to find the painted area: 224 − 80 = 144. The fraction that is painted is $\frac{144}{224} = \frac{9}{14}$.

9. E   If the diagonals of a quadrilateral bisect each other, the quadrilateral is a parallelogram, which may or may not be a square. Therefore, statement (1) is insufficient. Eliminate (A) and (D). If the diagonals of a quadrilateral are perpendicular, the quadrilateral could be a parallelogram (which may or may not be a square) or a kite. Therefore, statement (2) is insufficient. Eliminate (B). If you combine statements (1) and (2), the quadrilateral must be a parallelogram, but is not necessarily a square. Therefore, statements (1) and (2) together are insufficient, and the answer is (E).

10. C   Plug In The Answers. Start with (C). Perimeter equals twice the width plus twice the length, so if the dimensions are $\frac{16}{3}$ by $\frac{32}{3}$, then the perimeter would be $\frac{32}{3} + \frac{64}{3} = \frac{96}{3}$, which reduces to 32. The question says the perimeter equals 32, so this is the correct answer and you need not try any of the others.

11. A   Tackle this question by plugging in values for the dimensions of the frame. You could start by making the frame 3 by 4. The total area of the figure is 12, so the area of the window alone is 6. If you make the dimensions of the window 2 by 3, the frame will have a uniform width of 0.5, and the ratio of the width to the length will be 2 to 3. Now make the frame 6 by 8. The total area of the figure is 48, so the area of the window alone is 24. If the dimensions of the window are 4 by 6, the frame will have a uniform width of 1, and the ratio of the width to the length will still be 2 to 3. Therefore, statement (1) is sufficient. Eliminate (B), (C), and (E). For statement (2), you can re-cycle the second set of numbers you plugged in for statement (1), and say that the ratio of the width of the mirror to the length of the mirror is 2 to 3. However, if you make the frame 9 by 12 (for example), the ratio of the width of the mirror to the length of the mirror will be 7 to 10. Therefore, statement (2) is insufficient, and the answer is (A).

12. D   The area of a trapezoid is the average of the two bases times the height. You are given the height, 6, and one of the bases, 4, so you need the other base. The distance from X to Y creates a right triangle with one side of 6 and a hypotenuse of 10. Use the Pythagorean Theorem, $a^2 + b^2 = c^2$, to solve for the other side. $6^2 + b^2 = 10^2$, so $36 + b^2 = 100$, $b^2 = 64$, and $b = 8$. Now you have both bases of the trapezoid, and the area equals $\frac{4+8}{2} \times 6 = 6 \times 6 = 36$.

13. D   If $ABCD$ is a parallelogram, then opposite angles must be equal, so $2x = 60$, and $x = 30$. The sum of adjacent angles must equal 180°, so $60 + y + 2y = 180$, or $3y = 120$ and $y = 40$. Then $x + y = 70$.

14. A   Writing equations is a good way to tackle this question. Call the side of the square x. The area of the square is x^2. The area of the rectangle is $(x + 40)(x − 20)$. Set these two equal to each other,

FOIL the right side, and you get $x^2 = x^2 + 20x - 800$. Subtract x^2 and add 800 to both sides to get $800 = 20x$. It's not necessary to solve any further; you can see at this point that it's possible to solve for x. Therefore, statement (1) is sufficient. Eliminate (B), (C), and (E). For statement (2), if you try the same process, you must say that the length of the rectangle is $2x$ and the width is $0.5x$. If you set the two areas equal to each other, you end up with $x^2 = x^2$! Therefore, statement (2) is insufficient, and the answer is (A).

15. **C** The patio and the wall have equal areas, so each one must comprise exactly half of the total area. The total area is $l \times w = 8 \times 6 = 48$, so the patio must have an area of $\frac{1}{2} \times 48$, or 24. The length and width of the patio have a ratio of 8 to 6. If you call the length and width of the patio a and b, you have $a \times b = 24$ and $\frac{a}{b} = \frac{8}{6}$. Rewrite the second equation as $b = \frac{6}{8}a$ and substitute this for b in the first equation to get $\frac{6}{8}a^2 = 24$. Solve this to get $a^2 = 32$, and $a = \sqrt{32}$. Factor out the perfect square 16 to get $a = 4\sqrt{2}$. Alternatively, try plugging in the answer choices for the length of the patio.

16. **A** Plug In values for the variables and test each answer choice. For example, let $l = 3$ and $w = 2$. Then $a = 6$ and $p = 10$. When you plug those values into (A), you get a true statement. None of the other choices result in a true statement, so (A) is correct. Alternatively, this can be solved algebraically. The formula for the area of a rectangle is $a = lw$. The formula for the perimeter of a rectangle is $p = 2l + 2w$. Solving for l in each equation yields $l = \frac{a}{w}$ and $l = \frac{p - 2w}{2}$. Set those equal to get $\frac{a}{w} = \frac{p - 2w}{2}$, or $2a = wp - 2w^2$. No other answer choice can be obtained by manipulating the equations that relate the variables.

17. **B** Statement (1) gives you information about the diagonals of the two squares. If you knew the length of CF, you would be able to find the perimeter of $CEFG$. However, the statement only gives you the relationship between the two diagonals, so it is insufficient. Eliminate (A) and (D). Statement (2) tells you that the length of CF is equal to the area of $CEFG$. If you say that x represents a side of $CEFG$, then the length of CF is $x\sqrt{2}$, and the area of $CEFG$ is x^2. Set these two equal to each other and solve to find that $x = \sqrt{2}$. From there, you can find the perimeter. Therefore, statement (2) is sufficient, and the answer is (B).

18. **B** The lengths of the sides of the rectangle are integers, so the only possible dimensions that yield an area of 12 are 1 by 12, 2 by 6, and 3 by 4. The diagonal of the rectangle creates two equal

right triangles, each with a hypotenuse of 5. The lengths of the sides must satisfy the Pythagorean Theorem, $a^2 + b^2 = c^2$. The only dimensions that do so are 3 by 4. The perimeter of a rectangle with length l and width w is given by $2l + 2w$. Either dimension can equal either the length or the width and still give a perimeter of $(2)(3) + (2)(4) = 14$.

19. **C** Solve this question by writing equations. For statement (1), you can say that the width is x and the length is $2x$, which means that the area is $2x^2$. However, you have no way to solve for x, so statement (1) is insufficient. Eliminate (A) and (D). Statement (2) gives you no information about the relationship between the length and the width, so you are forced to use two different variables. You could represent the information in statement (2) with the equation $xy = 2(x + y)$. However, you cannot solve for two variables with one equation, so statement (2) is insufficient. Eliminate (B). If you combine the two statements, you can replace y in the second equation with $2x$, and rewrite the equation as $x^2 = 6x$, which means that $x = 6$. Therefore, statements (1) and (2) together are sufficient, and the answer is (C).

20. **B** This question requires a little thought experiment. For statement (1), Suppose that carpet A had a length of 10 and a width of 2. Then carpet B would have a length of 5 and a width of 7, and the area of carpet B would be greater. However, suppose that carpet A had a length of 10 and a width of 9. Then carpet B would have a length of 5 and a width of 14, and the area of carpet A would be greater. Therefore, statement (1) is insufficient. Eliminate (A) and (D). The statement illustrates an important fact, which is that if two rectangles have the same perimeter, the one that is more like a square will have the greater area, and the area will be maximized when the rectangle is a square. Statement (2) tells you that carpet B is a square. It is important to note that this does not mean that rectangle A is <u>not</u> a square. There are two possibilities. The first is that rectangle A is a square. In this case, A and B will have equal areas. The second possibility is that rectangle A is not a square. In this case, the area of rectangle B will be greater. However, in neither case will the area of rectangle A be greater. Therefore, statement (2) is sufficient, and the answer is (B).

Circles

1. **B** This question is asking for the radius of the circle. The formula for circumference is $2\pi r$, so $2\pi r = 12\pi$, and the radius is 6.

2. **E** Draw the circle on the coordinate plane. Statement (1) tells you that every time line m moves up 1 it moves to the right 20. It could very well intersect Circle Q but since you have no idea of its location in the xy-plane (it could have a point at the origin or at $(0, 100)$), the statement is insufficient. Eliminate (A) and (D). Statement (2) tells you that the line crosses the x-axis to the left of the circle, but gives no other information about the line. Eliminate (B). Taken together, the two statements tell you the slope and a maximum for the x-axis, but it still isn't enough information. The line could intersect the x-axis at $(-100, 0)$, which would cause the line to not intersect the circle. It could also have a point at $(-4, 0)$, in which case it would intersect Circle Q.

3.   **C**   Statement (1) tells you the radius is 12, so the blue flag must lie outside the circle. Since the question asks about the red flag, the information isn't sufficient. Eliminate (A) and (D). Statement (2) tells you the distance between the blue and red flags. Drawing different options shows you that, though both flags can't lie inside the racetrack, either one could, or neither could. Eliminate (B). Taken together, the information tells you that the blue flag lies just outside the circle. The diameter of the circle is 24, so no matter where the red flag is placed, it must lie outside the circle.

4.   **A**   This question is testing the proportionality of a circle. Sector AOB + sector $BOC = \frac{3}{8} + \frac{2}{5}$ or $\frac{31}{40}$ of the circle, which means that sector AOC is $\frac{9}{40}$ of the circle. There are 360° in a circle, so angle AOC is $\frac{9}{40} \times 360 = 81°$.

5.   **D**   Statement (1) tells you the length of part of the circumference. Since you know that angle AOC is $\frac{1}{4}$ of the circle, 27π must be $\frac{3}{4}$ of the circumference. From this you can find the circumference (36π), the radius (18), and therefore the area (324π). The information is sufficient. Eliminate (B), (C), and (E). Statement (2) states that the perimeter of $OABC$ is 72. Because AO and OC are radii, they have equal lengths. $OABC$ must be a square, which means that each side is 18. Since a side is also the length of a radius, the information is sufficient to find the area.

6.   **C**   Questions about rotations are really about circumference. The radius of the wheel is 3 feet, so the circumference of the wheel is 6π, or 18.84 feet. Each rotation of the wheel equals one circumference, so if you divide the total distance traveled by the circumference, you get the number of rotations. $\frac{120}{18.84} = 6.37$, so there are 6 complete rotations.

7.   **D**   Statement (1) tells you the circumference of the smaller plate. Since you know the relationship between the small and large plates, you can determine the circumference of the large plate and therefore the area. The information is sufficient. Eliminate (B), (C), and (E). Statement (2) gives the area of the small plate. From this you can determine the radius and therefore the circumference of the small plate. Again, since you know the relationship between the circumferences of the two plates, you can figure out the area.

8.   **B**   Statement (1) tells you that the diameter of Circle X is 8. It is possible for AB, with a length of 5, to fit inside the circle. It is also possible that B lies outside the circle, which makes the information insufficient. Eliminate (A) and (D). Statement (2) tells you that the distance between points O and B is less than the radius, which means that B must lie inside the circle.

9. **E** Angle *AOC* is $\frac{90}{360}$ or $\frac{1}{4}$ of the total degrees of the circle, so arc *ABC* is $\frac{1}{4}$ of the circumference. Therefore, 5π equals $\frac{1}{4}$ of the circumference, which means the circumference is 20π. The formula for circumference is $2\pi r$, so $2\pi r = 20\pi$ and the radius of the circle is 10. The area of the circle is 100π.

10. **A** Statement (1) is sufficient. If $x = 72$, that's out of 360 total degrees in the circle, so you can find the fraction $\frac{72}{360} = \frac{1}{5}$. Since you know the total revenue, you can take $\frac{1}{5}$ of it and find what fraction E is of the total revenue. Eliminate (B), (C), and (E). Statement (2) gives you the relationship between E and two other products, but because you don't know their relationship to the total or to the other products, the information isn't sufficient.

11. **A** The length of the plot is 3 times its width, or 12 feet. Thus, the area of the plot is $12 \times 4 = 48$ feet. That means the area of the surface of the pound is $\frac{48}{3} = 16$ square feet. Thus, $16 = \pi r^2$, and the radius is $\sqrt{\frac{16}{\pi}}$.

12. **A** Because sector *WOY* is $\frac{1}{4}$ of the circle, angle *WOY* is $\frac{1}{4}$ the degrees of the circle, or 90°. Thus, triangle *WOY* must be a right triangle, and because its perimeter is $20 + 10\sqrt{2}$, it must be an isosceles right triangle with legs that equal 10 and a hypotenuse that equals $10\sqrt{2}$. The legs of the triangle are the radii of the circle, so the radius of the circle is 10. That means the circumference of the circle is $2\pi r$, or 20π. Because sector *WOY* is $\frac{1}{4}$ of the circle, arc *WXY* is $\frac{1}{4}$ of the circumference, or 5π.

13. **D** First draw the picture. The circle must be in the corner between the two axes in any of the 4 quadrants. A line that is tangent to a circle forms a 90° with the radius of the circle. Because all radii in a circle are equal, a square is formed by the radii that are perpendicular to each tangent point and the two axes. Thus the distance, *w*, from the center of the circle the origin is the diagonal of the square, which is also the hypotenuse of an isosceles right triangle. Now Plug In. If $w = 4\sqrt{2}$, that means the sides of the square and therefore the radii of the circle are 4. Thus, the area of the circle is πr^2, or 16π, which is your target. Now plug $4\sqrt{2}$ in for *w* in the answer choices. Only (D) yields 16π.

14. **D** This question is asking at how many points a circle and triangle can intersect. Draw the different designs, creating as many points of intersection as you can. As shown below, a circle and triangle can intersect at 1, 2, 3, 4, 5 or 6 different points.

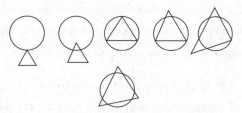

3D Figures

1. **E** The capacity, or volume, of a rectangular box with length l, width w, and height h is given by $V = lwh$. The first box has a capacity of 12, so $lwh = 12$. The dimensions of the second box are each twice those of the first, so the second box has length $2l$, width $2w$, and height $2h$. Then the capacity of the second box is $V = (2l)(2w)(2h) = 8lwh$. Since $lwh = 12$, $V = (8)(12) = 96$.

2. **A** The volume of a cylinder is equal to $\pi r^2 h$. If the canister is half full, then the total volume must be $(2)(64\pi) = 128\pi$. The height of the water when the cylinder is on its side must equal the radius of the cylinder, because the water will take up exactly half of the canister, which means it also must take up exactly half of the diameter of the cylinder. So $r = 4$, which gives $128\pi = \pi(4^2)h = 16\pi h$, and $h = 8$. Then the height of the canister while it is standing upright equals 8, and since the water occupies exactly half of the volume, it will take up exactly half of the height, or 4.

3. **E** Statement (1) tells you one dimension, but since you need three in order to find the volume, the statement is insufficient. Eliminate (A) and (D). Statement (2) tells you the area of one side, but since you need to multiply that by the third dimension, statement (2) is insufficient. Eliminate (B). Taken together, you know the surface area of one side, as well as the length of one edge, but it's unclear whether the edge is one of the two dimensions used in the surface area of one side.

4. **C** The band is actually a long rectangle that has been wrapped around the tub. In order to find x, which is the width of the band, you need the area of the band and the length of the band, which is the circumference of the tub. Statement (1) is not sufficient because you have no values for the length of the band or its area. Eliminate (A) and (D). Statement (2) does not tell you anything about the length or area of the band either. Cross off (B). When you combine the two statements, you can calculate the circumference of the tub, which gives you the length of the band. You can also calculate the base of the tub. Because the band and the base have the same area, this gives you the area of the band and you can solve for x. Thus, the answer is (C).

5. **A** Surface area is $4\pi r^2$. Statement (1) tells you the radius, which is sufficient to find the surface area. Eliminate (B), (C), and (E). Statement (2) tells you that the sphere fits into the square box, but it doesn't say whether it touches the sides of the box, in which case the diameter would be 1, or if it is smaller than 1. Statement (2) is insufficient.

6. **D** In order to find the volume of the hemisphere, you need its radius. Start by drawing the picture. Because the base of the hemisphere and the base of the cone coincide and because the cone is inscribed in the sphere, the height of the cone is a radius of the sphere. Thus, Statement (1) is sufficient. Eliminate (B), (C), and (E). Statement (2) gives you the area of the base of the cone. Because the bases of the cone and hemisphere coincide, they are equal. Thus, the area of the base of the hemisphere is 9π, which means its radius is 3. Statement (2) is also sufficient.

7. **C** This problem can be solved by using an extended version of the Pythagorean theorem, $a^2 + b^2 + c^2 = d^2$, where d is the diagonal of a rectangular box, and a, b, and c are the dimensions of the box. So in this case, $3^2 + 4^2 + 12^2 = d^2$, or $d^2 = 169$ and $d = 13$.

8. **B** Plug In values for the capacities of the sandboxes. Let sandbox B have a capacity of 36. Then sandbox A has a capacity of 12. Sandbox B is filled to $\frac{1}{3}$ (36) or 12. Sandbox A is filled to $\frac{1}{4}$ (12) or 3.

    When A is poured into B, there is 12 + 3 = 15 in sandbox B, so sandbox B is filled to $\frac{15}{36}$, which can

    be reduced to $\frac{5}{12}$. Alternatively, call a the capacity of sandbox A and b the capacity of sandbox B.

    Then $3a = b$, A contains $\frac{1}{4}a$, and B contains $\frac{1}{3}b$. If all of the sand in A is poured into B, then B

    contains $\frac{1}{3}b + \frac{1}{4}a$, or $\frac{1}{3}b + \frac{1}{4}\left(\frac{1}{3}b\right) = \frac{5}{12}b$.

9. **E** Statement (1) tells you that the height of the label is 3 centimeters. In order to find the surface area, you need the height of the label and the circumference of the can. Since you only know the height, this information is insufficient. Eliminate (A) and (D). Statement (2) says that $x = 0.25$, but this information is insufficient to find either the height of the label or the circumference of the can. Eliminate (B). Taken together, both pieces of information only refer to the height, not the circumference.

10. **D** The volume of a cylinder is given by $V = \pi r^2 h$, so $100\pi = \pi(5^2)h = 25\pi h$, and $h = 4$. The smallest box that can contain such a cylinder must have length and width equal to the diameter of the cylinder, so $l = 10$ and $w = 10$. The box must have a height equal to the height of the cylinder, so $h = 4$. A rectangular box has volume $V = lwh$, so $(10)(10)(4) = 400$.

11. **C** Statement (1) gives you the surface area of the cylinder, but not any information about the height or the radius of it. So it's insufficient. Eliminate (A) and (D). Statement (2) tells you the base of the box is 156 inches. Since the only 3 dimensions are 5, 12, and 13, the base must be 12 by 13. So the height is 5 inches. You know the height is 5 inches, but you know nothing about the circumference or radius. Eliminate (B). Taken together, you know the height of the container and the circumference, so the information is sufficient to find the volume.

12. **E** The volume of a cylinder is given by $V = \pi r^2 h$. If the diameter is x, then the radius must equal $\frac{x}{2}$. The cylinder is half full of liquid, so the total height of the cylinder must equal twice the height of the liquid, so the total height equals 4. Then $V = \pi\left(\frac{x}{2}\right)^2 (4) = \pi\frac{x^2}{4}(4) = x^2\pi$. Alternatively, try plugging in a value for x.

13. **E** Statement (1) tells you the height of the glass, but not the radius of the glass or anything about the cup. Eliminate (A) and (D). Statement (2) tells you that the circumferences of both containers are the same, but nothing about the height of either container. Eliminate (B). Taken together, you can Plug In for the radius, since the two are equal, but you still know nothing about the height of the paper cone cup.

14. **C** The surface area of the label is given by $A = lw$. The width equals 2, as given in the figure, and the length of the label equals the circumference of the can. The formula for circumference is $C = 2\pi r$, so $12\pi = (2)(2\pi r) = 4\pi r$, and $r = 3$. The area of the circular base is given by $A = \pi r^2 = \pi(3^2) = 9\pi$.

Coordinate Geometry

1. **A** Be careful not to mix up your x and y coordinates. Point Q is 5 units to the left of the y-axis and 4 units above the x-axis, so the correct answer is (A).

2. **C** Statement (1) tells you that when x is 0, y is −12. The function expanded out is $y = x^2 + (p − q)x − pq$, so pq must be 12. Because there are more than one factor pairs of 12, the information is insufficient. Eliminate (A) and (D). Statement (2) solves the middle of the quadratic equation, but says nothing about the product of p and q. Eliminate (B). Taken together, there are two equations: $p − q = 11$ and $pq = 12$. Two equations are sufficient to solve for both p and q, and thus for the line.

3. **E** The graph is symmetric to the line at $x = −3$ which means that the parts of the graph on either side of the line are mirror images of each other. Thus, if $y = 4$ when x is −5, or 2 units to the left of $x = −3$, y will also equal 4 when x is −1, or 2 units to the right of $x = −3$. Therefore, the correct answer is (E).

4. **C** Statement (1) tells you one point on the line, but this isn't sufficient information to determine if (5, 12) is on the line. Eliminate (A) and (D). The same is true for statement (2). Eliminate (B). Taken together, you can determine the slope of the line and then plug (5, 12) and one other point into the slope equation.

5. **E** Statement (1) only gives one point, which is insufficient information to find the area. Eliminate (A) and (D). Statement (2) is also insufficient because it only gives one point. Eliminate (B). Taking both statements together, you know the length of one side, but nothing else.

6. **D** At the *x*-intercept, *y* equals 0, so eliminate (C). Plug the slope and the point into the formula for the equation of a line to get $7 = -3(-2) + b$. Then solve for *b* to get the *y*-intercept, which is 1. Now you know that the equation of the line is $y = -3x + 1$. To find the *x*-intercept, set *y* equal to 0 and solve for *x*; *x* equals $\dfrac{1}{3}$, so the correct answer is (D).

7. **C** The question asks for the midpoint of line *JK*, which is represented by the expression $\left(\dfrac{x_1 + x_2}{2}, \dfrac{y_1 + y_2}{2} \right)$. So, to answer this question, the *x* and *y* coordinates for both points need to be given in the statements. Statement (1) gives that point *J* is at point $(1 - c, d)$, which can be inserted in the midpoint formula to yield $\left(\dfrac{1 - c + x_2}{2}, \dfrac{d + y_2}{2} \right)$. There are still unknown variables, so Statement (1) is not sufficient. Eliminate (A) and (D) and the remaining choices are (B), (C), and (E). Statement (2) gives information about point *K*, but, much like Statement (1), is insufficient to answer the question because there will be variables left over so (B) is also incorrect. Combined, the two statements will create a midpoint expression of $\left(\dfrac{1 - c + c}{2}, \dfrac{d + 1 - d}{2} \right)$. Now, all of the variables can cancel out, leaving the midpoint as $\left(\dfrac{1}{2}, \dfrac{1}{2} \right)$. This is sufficient, so the correct answer is (C).

8. **C** Because $ab \neq 0$, neither *a* nor $b = 0$, which means that point (a, b) lies within one of the quadrants. Eliminate (A). Point $(a, -b)$ lies in quadrant III, which means the values of *a* and $-b$ are both negative. That means that *a* is a negative number and *b* is a positive number. Therefore, point (a, b) must lie in quadrant II.

9. **A** Statement (1) lets you know that the height of the triangle is 12. Dropping a height from *B* shows that you have a smaller 5:12:13 right triangle. If the triangle were isosceles, then *BC* would be 13, and *AC* would be 10. Using the formula for area of a triangle, you know that the area would be $\dfrac{(10)(12)}{2} = 60$. Since $AB < BC$, you know that the base must also be bigger, which makes the area bigger than 60. The answer to the question is "no." Eliminate (B), (C), and (E). Statement (2) tells you the base of the triangle but nothing about the height.

10. **B**   First manipulate the inequality so that it is in $y = mx + b$ form. That gives you $y \le \frac{3}{4}x - 2$. Now you need two points so you can graph the line. The y-intercept is –2, so one point is (0, –2). If you Plug In 4 for x you get another point, (4, 1). You can now graph the line determined by the equation $y = \frac{3}{4}x - 2$. To determine which quadrants have points that satisfy the inequality, shade the side of the line that the inequality encompasses. To figure out which side this is, Plug In a point on one side of the line. If you plug that point into the inequality and it makes the inequality true, you shade the side of the line that included that point. If you Plug In a point that makes the inequality not true, you shade the side of the line that did not include that point. If you Plug In (0, 0), you get $0 \le -2$, which is not true. Therefore, shade the right side of the line and the inequality includes points in quadrants I, II, and IV and the correct answer is (B).

11. **C**   Line h is in the xy-plane, so to determine the slope, we need two points that line h crosses. Statement (1) gives the difference between the x and y intercept but that does not provide specific points on the line, so Statement (1) is not sufficient. Eliminate (A) and (D), which leaves (B), (C), and (E). Statement (2) gives the product of the x and y intercepts, but, again, this is not a specific value, nor is it enough information to determine specific points so eliminate (B). Now, look at both statements together. The only values of the x and y intercept that could both create a product of –20 and have a difference of 8 are 10 and –2. Since the points for the x and y intercept are now known, it is possible to solve for the slope. It doesn't matter which point has a value of 10 and which has a value of –2, as it will always result in the same slope. The correct answer is (C).

12. **C**   Statement (1) lets you know that line k touches the y-axis at a higher point than line l does. It doesn't say anything about the slope of either. Eliminate (A) and (D). Though statement (2) states at what point the two lines intersect, it also doesn't help you in terms of the slope. Eliminate (B). Now take the two statements together. If you draw a coordinate plane with one point at (4, –1) and two other points along the y-axis, as long as the y-intercept of line k is greater, the slope of line k will be smaller. Notice if the two y-intercepts are above $y = -1$, the slope of line k will be more negative. If they are below $y = -1$, line l will always be steeper, and therefore its slope will be greater.

13. **D**   Draw a perpendicular line from point Y to the x-axis. Call that point O. You now have a right triangle with a height of $3\sqrt{3}$ and a base of 3. Thus, triangle XYO is a 30:60:90 triangle with a hypotenuse of 6; the length of XY is therefore 6. The point on line XY that is twice as far from X as it is from Y must be 4 units away from X and 2 units away from Y. Triangle XYO divides into 3 different 30:60:90 triangles. Point $(1, \sqrt{3})$ is the apex of one 30:60:90 triangle with a hypotenuse of 2 and point $(2, 2\sqrt{3})$ is the apex of a second 30:60:90 triangle with a hypotenuse of 4. Therefore, point $(2, 2\sqrt{3})$ is the point on segment XY that is twice as far from X as it is from Y.

14. **C** Write the equation of the original line in $y = mx + b$ format. The equation of this line is $y = \frac{1}{2}x - 2$. A line that is perpendicular to that line will have a slope that is the negative reciprocal, so that line has the equation $y = -2x - 2$. Now, look at the answer choices. Rearrange the answer choices into $y = mx + b$ format to find out which one equals $y = -2x - 2$. The correct answer is (C).

15. **C** Statement (1) lets you know that one point on the line is (0, 4). This information is insufficient because without at least one other point on the line or the slope of the line, there is no way to know way to find the y-intercept. Eliminate (A) and (D). Statement (2) lets you know the slope of the line, but without a point the line passes through, there is not enough information. Eliminate (B). Putting the information together you know both the slope and a point on the line. This means you can figure out everything about the line, including the y-intercept.

16. **E** Statement (1) gives one coordinate point of the triangle, but since the area of a triangle is $\frac{1}{2}$ (base) (height), knowing one point is not enough information. Eliminate (A) and (D). Statement (2) does the same thing as Statement (1) with another point on the triangle. Eliminate (B). Taken together, you can figure out the length of one side of the triangle, but there is no information about the other side.

17. **D** Statement (1) gives you a second point on the line. Since you can find the slope with two points on a line, this information is sufficient. Eliminate (B), (C), and (E). Statement (2) also gives you a point on the line.

Inscribed Figures and Shaded Regions

1. **C** The angle opposite the 140° angle is also 140° by vertical angles, so the unshaded portion of the circle totals 280°. That means the two shaded angles add up to 360° − 280°, or 80°. There are 360° in a circle so the shaded area is $\frac{80}{360} = \frac{2}{9}$ of the circle. The area of the circle is 36π, so the shaded region is $\frac{2}{9} \times 36\pi = 8\pi$.

2. **B** The key to inscribed figures is figuring out what the two figures have in common. The height of the triangle is also the radius of the circle. All radii of a circle are equal, so $OY = OX$. Thus, triangle XOY is an isosceles right triangle with legs that each equal a, and a hypotenuse of $a\sqrt{2}$. Therefore the ratio of XY to the radius of the circle is $\frac{a\sqrt{2}}{a}$ which reduces to $\frac{\sqrt{2}}{1}$.

3. **D**   To find the area, you need the radius. Look at statement (1) first. Because angle AOC is a 60° angle, arc ABC is $\dfrac{60}{360}$, or $\dfrac{1}{6}$ of the circumference. That means that the circumference is 18π and therefore the radius is 9. That is sufficient to find the area. Eliminate (B), (C), and (E). For statement (2), lines OA and OC are radii and all radii are equal; therefore the angles opposite them are equal which means that angles OAC and OCA are 60°. That makes triangle OAC an equilateral triangle. Because its perimeter is 27, each of its sides, including the radii of the circle, is 9. Again, that is sufficient to find the area.

4. **A**   The original circular piece of fabric has a radius of 9, so its area is 81π. The radius of the cut-out circle is 7, which means its area is 49π. The part that is left behind is $81\pi - 49\pi$, or 32π, so the fraction that is left behind is $\dfrac{32\pi}{81\pi}$, or $\dfrac{32}{81}$.

5. **B**   The glass inlay plus the border equals the total area of the table. Thus, the total figure's area is $16 + 33 = 49$. To find the width of the border, subtract the length of the small square from the length of the large square. That gives you double the width of the border, so divide that by 2 to get the width of the border. The area of a square is side squared, so the length of the small square is 4 and the length of the large square is 7. Thus, the width of the border is $\dfrac{7-4}{2}$, or $\dfrac{3}{2}$.

6. **C**   Statement (1) gives enough information to figure out the length of BC, but since there is no information about AB it isn't sufficient. Eliminate (A) and (D). Statement (2) isn't sufficient information to find either the length or the width. Eliminate (B). Combine both statements. Knowing both the length of one side and the diagonal means that you can use Pythagorean theorem to solve.

7. **E**   First, draw the picture. The key to working with two figures together, is figuring out what the two figures have in common. The side of the cube is the diameter of the sphere, so use the super Pythagorean theorem ($a^2 + b^2 + c^2 = d^2$, where a, b and c are the sides of the rectangular solid and d is the diagonal) to determine the side of the cube. In the case of a cube, all the sides are equal so you can say $3s^2 = d^2$, where s is the side of the cube and d is its diagonal. $3s^2 = 108$. $s^2 = 36$. Thus, the side of the cube is 6, which means the radius of the sphere is 3. Using the volume of a sphere formula, you can determine that the volume of the sphere is 36π.

8.   **C**   First, redraw the picture on your scratch paper and draw a box to represent the 90° for $\angle POQ$. The first statement simply gives the x-coordinate of point P, which tells you nothing about point Q or the value of t. Eliminate (A) and (D). Statement (2) gives the y-coordinate of point P, which again tells you nothing about point Q or the value of t. When you combine the two statements, you know that the coordinates of point P are $(-\sqrt{3}, 1)$. Draw a line that is perpendicular to the x-axis from point P to the x-axis. This forms a 30:60:90 triangle with a height of 1 and a base of $\sqrt{3}$, which means that OP is 2. For the sake of reference, call the point where the semi-circle meets the x-axis on the left side point A, and the point where the semi-circle meets the x-axis on the right side point B. $\angle AOP$ is 30°, which means the angle between line OP and the y-axis is 60°. Therefore, because $\angle POQ$ is 90°, the angle between line OQ and the y-axis is 30° (90:60:30). That means that $\angle QOB$ is 60°. Now draw a line that is perpendicular to the x-axis from point Q to the x-axis. This forms another 30:60:90 triangle. OP and OQ are both radii and are therefore equal. Thus, OQ equals 2. Therefore, by the formula for 30:60:90 triangles, t = 1.

9.   **C**   To find the area of the shaded region, you need to subtract the area of triangle DEF from the area of the semicircle (shaded = total – unshaded). To find the area of the triangle you need its base and height and to find the area of the semi-circle you need the radius. When a triangle is inscribed in a circle so that the diameter of the circle coincides with one of the sides of the triangle, that triangle is by definition a right triangle. Thus, $\angle DEF$ is a right angle and triangle DEF is a right triangle. Statement (1) is insufficient because it simply gives one of the sides of the triangle. Eliminate (A) and (D). Statement (2) is insufficient because it simply gives one side of the triangle. Eliminate (B). When you combine the two statements, you now have 2 sides of a right triangle, so you can find the length of the third side with the Pythagorean theorem. ($15^2 + 36^2 = 39^2$, so side DF = 39.) With that, you have the radius and can find the area of the semicircle. You can use sides DE and EF as the base and height to find the area of the triangle. Thus you have everything you need to calculate the shaded region.

10.   **D**

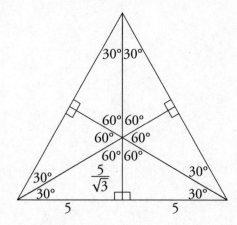

To find the area of the shaded region, you need to subtract the area of the circle from the area of the triangle (shaded = total − unshaded). Looking at statement (1), if the perimeter of the triangle is 30, then each side of the triangle is 10. If you draw an altitude from vertex Q to side *PR*, it divides the triangle into two 30:60:90 triangles and you learn that the height of the triangle is $5\sqrt{3}$. You already know that the base of the triangle is 10, so you can find the area of the triangle. To find the area of the circle you need the radius. If you draw an altitude from each vertex of the triangle to the opposite base, six 30:60:90 triangles are formed. (See illustration.) Because all these altitudes meet in the center of the triangle and because the circle is inscribed into the triangle, in each of these 30:60:90 triangles, the side across from the 30° angle is a radius of the circle. Because the base of the triangle is 10, in each of the 30:60:90 triangles the side across from the 60° angle is 5, which means that the side across from the 30° angle is $\dfrac{5}{\sqrt{3}}$, or $\dfrac{5\sqrt{3}}{3}$ when rationalized. This is the radius, so you can now find the area of the circle, which means that statement (1) is sufficient. Eliminate (B), (C), and (E). If you work backwards, statement (2) provides the same information as statement 1. If you have the radius of the circle, you can find its area. Because drawing an altitude from each vertex of the triangle *PQR* to the opposite base results in six 30:60:90 triangles as explained above, if the radius is $\dfrac{5\sqrt{3}}{3}$, using 30:60:90 triangles you can determine that half of the base of the triangle is 5 and that the whole base of the triangle is 10. Once you know the base of the triangle you can find the height by splitting the equilateral triangle into two 30:60:90 triangles as explained above. Statement (2) is also sufficient.

Verbal

Reading
Comprehension

READING COMPREHENSION

Reading comprehension questions make up roughly one-third of the questions on the Verbal section. The passages cover a variety of topics, but will generally come from the fields of social science, natural science, humanities, and business. You will see four reading passages on your test, and each passage will have three or four questions. The passages can appear at any point in the section, but all questions related to a passage will be presented together.

Reading Comprehension strikes fear into the hearts of many test takers because of the sudden influx of information on the screen and the pressure of a ticking clock. The good news is that the reading comprehension sections are like an open book test. Everything you need to know to answer the questions can be found in the text.

THE FORMAT

The passage appears on the left side of the screen and is usually too long to fit in the window, so you must use the scroll bar to read it completely. The questions appear on the right side of the screen, one at a time. After you answer the first question, another appears in its place. The passage remains so you can always refer to it.

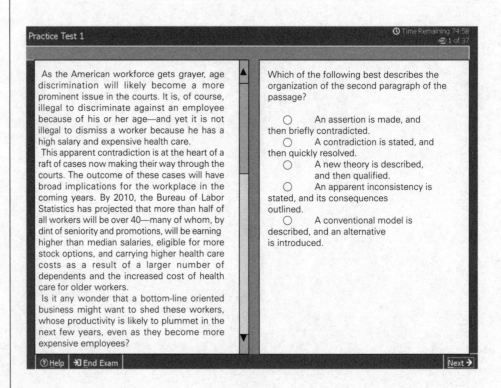

WORK THE PASSAGE

Because this part of the test is called Reading Comprehension, you may think you should read the whole passage carefully, understand all the details, and then try to answer the questions. That is what the test writers want you to do. They have deliberately provided passages that are dense, wordy, and boring so that you will get bogged down in the passage. What happens when you start out by reading the whole passage? You may

- zone out or even fall asleep (It has happened.)
- forget what you've read
- become bogged down in unnecessary details
- become confused by the answer choices, which may all appear to come from the passage

For all the reasons above, it's not such a great idea to start out by reading the whole passage. Also, sometimes the questions are all concentrated in one part of the passage, so if you read the whole thing you end up wasting a lot of time reading parts of the passage that won't be tested.

This does not mean that you get out of reading. It is reading comprehension, after all. However, you should do your detailed reading in response to specific questions, when it is most likely to pay off. At the beginning, you will simply read for the big idea.

Read for the Big Idea

Start out by skimming the passage. If you are having trouble, try reading the first two sentences of the first paragraph, the first sentence of subsequent paragraphs, and the final sentence of the whole passage. Your goal is not to understand every detail and nuance of the passage, but to get a sense of the main idea.

Trigger Words

As you are skimming, look for trigger words to help you get a sense of the main idea and structure of the passage. Some trigger words indicate that the author's ideas are **changing direction**. For example

- But
- Nonetheless
- Although
- Notwithstanding
- However
- Except

- Yet
- While
- Despite
- Unless
- Nevertheless
- On the other hand

Other trigger words indicate there will be no change in the direction of the paragraph in the passage. For example

- In addition
- By the same token
- Likewise
- Therefore
- Consequently
- Similarly
- For example
- Thus

When you work a passage read for the key ideas. Skim over the details. Look for the following and **note them on your scratch paper**:

Main Point/Thesis

Look for the author's main point or thesis statement, which is usually found in the first paragraph or at the end of the passage.

Author's Tone or Attitude

In many cases, the tone is neutral, but look for any positive or negative assessments of the subject and note them with a "+" or a "−".

Main Idea/Function of EACH Paragraph

Central ideas most often occur at the beginning or end of a paragraph. Make a brief note that describes the main idea of each paragraph. This will help you understand the passage as a whole.

After you've worked the passage, it's time to move on to the questions. Follow the basic approach on every reading comprehension passage.

THE BASIC APPROACH

Step 1: Work the passage

Read for the big idea. Make note of the main idea of the passage, the main idea of each paragraph, and the tone of the passage.

Step 2: Translate the question

If you don't understand what the question is asking, it's very difficult to answer it correctly. While some questions are pretty straightforward

1.   Which of the following best describes the organization of the passage?

others are not.

2.   The author's discussion of the traits that distinguish the economic system of Japan from the economic systems of Western countries is primarily concerned with explaining

That's why it's important to take the time to translate wordy, confusing questions into simple questions that are easier to answer. The question above could be translated to read

3.   What do the differences between Japanese and Western economic systems help explain?

Step 3: Find the information in the passage

Go back to the passage and read only what you need. Generally that will be a few lines above and below a lead word. A lead word is a word or phrase in the question that would be easy to spot if you scanned the passage looking for that word.

Example

The passage suggests which of the following about the fungus grown by the attine ants?

In this case you would look for "fungus" or "attine ants." Once you find your lead word, read a few lines above and below it to get the context.

Step 4: Answer in your own words

The only way to ensure you get a reading comprehension question correct is to answer the question in your own words **without looking at the answer choices**. The test is written for the person who reads the whole passage, glazes over, has no idea what he or she read, and picks an answer that looks familiar. Everyone has done that at some point. Unfortunately, the test writers know this and have planned traps with that in mind.

There are almost always answer choices that contain quotes or near quotes from the passage. If you force yourself to come up with your own answer, you are much less likely to fall for those traps.

Step 5: POE

Excelling at reading comprehension is all about POE. Look for an answer that matches the answer you stated in your own words. If you don't see it, don't panic. Go back to the passage. You might have looked in the wrong place, or you might have misread something.

Sometimes, however, you won't like any of the answers. In that case, your job is to pick the answer that is least bad. Look for little differences that make one answer worse than another to help you decide which ones to eliminate. Be sure to eliminate answers that are

- Not supported by the passage. Remember, this is an open book test. You should be able to point to the place on the screen where you found the right answer. Be especially wary of answers that make predictions. **Answers that make predictions are usually wrong.**
- Extreme. Answers that use words such as *always, must,* and *never* are usually wrong, unless supported by the passage.
- Contradictory to the passage. Again, this is an open book test. The correct answer cannot contradict the passage.
- Are true but don't answer the question. As mentioned previously, the test writers love to include answers that are from the wrong part of the passage for the tester who reads the whole passage, glazes over, and picks something that looks familiar.
- Half right. Some answers are only partially correct. Remember, a half bad answer is an all bad answer.

For general questions (passages that are about the passage as a whole), you should also eliminate answers that are

- **Too broad.** Answers should not go beyond the scope of the passage.
- **Too narrow.** The answer to a general question needs to be about the passage as a whole, not just part of the passage.
- **Extreme in tone.** The test writers deliberately pick authors who are not that worked up so that the passage will be more boring. Be very wary of answers that use extreme language to describe the tone of the passage, unless the passage really does support it.

Try the basic approach on a passage.

The wealth of morphological, phonetic, and word similarities among certain languages has led linguists to recognize the unity of the well-defined family of languages called the Aryan or Indo-European family. Yet even this latter term is largely a misnomer. This group of languages spreads over an enormous range virtually without interruption, reaching from Central Asia to the fringes of westernmost Europe. The westernmost terminus of the family is Celtic, while it's easternmost representatives were the Tokharian languages, a pair of tongues once spoken by the residents of the Tarim River Basin in Western China and unearthed in documents written more than a thousand years ago.

So remarkable and definite are the similarities among these languages that linguists are convinced they all derived from an earlier language spoken by some community in the prehistoric past. While we know that Latin began as a rustic dialect in the province of Latium, no one knows where proto-Aryan was first spoken. Some speculate that it was first used in Southern Russia, while still others point to the Iranian plateau as a potential cradle. Though some philologists believe that the Old Indic and Persian of the Avesta contain the most archaic features of Aryan found to date, this does not necessarily fix the habitat of these early Aryan-speaking peoples closer to Asia than to Europe. Consider Icelandic. Though this language has strayed far from its original source, it preserves many of the characteristics discarded by those who remained behind.

From the existing evidence, only one thing seems certain. By the time of Vedic hymns, the first recorded instance of Aryan, those tribes speaking this early language had already begun their widespread dispersal.

Start by working the passage. The main idea is that there is a family of languages with a common origin called the Aryan or Indo-European family. The tone of the passage is neutral or informative. Now look at each paragraph.

The trigger word "yet" early in the passage can help you see that the big idea of the first paragraph is that neither "Aryan" nor "Indo-European" is a good name for this family of languages. The big idea of the second paragraph is that the family of languages has a common source in the prehistoric past. The 3rd paragraph is essentially summing up, but it does mention that the languages have spread over a wide area.

You are now ready to try some questions. Most questions fall into one of two categories: specific or general. Most of the questions you will see are specific questions.

SPECIFIC QUESTIONS

Detail Questions

Detail questions ask you to retrieve a specific piece of information from the passage. Detail Purpose questions ask *why* the author has mentioned a specific piece of information. Here is an example of a detail purpose question.

1. The author mentions Icelandic in order to

    (A) provide support for the contention that early Aryan-speaking peoples did not necessarily live in Asia
    (B) provide another example of the archaic features found in the *Avesta*
    (C) provide evidence for the inception of proto-Aryan
    (D) counter the speculation that proto-Aryan was first spoken in Russia
    (E) provide an alternative explanation for the similarities found in early languages

First, translate the question. This question asks "Why does the author mention *Icelandic*?"

Now read what you need. Find the lead word, *Icelandic*. You don't typically need to go beyond the current paragraph when you read a few lines up and down, so read a few lines before the lead word to the end of the paragraph.

Answer in your own words. *Icelandic* is mentioned as an example of something. What does it exemplify? In the passage, the author says that early Aryan-speaking peoples did not necessarily live closer to Asia than to Europe. He then goes on to describe Icelandic as a language that has strayed far from its original source. So why does he mention Icelandic? To provide an example that shows that where people live does not necessarily indicate what language they speak.

Now check the answers. Choice (A) is pretty close. Keep it. Choice (B) does not match what you are looking for. Eliminate it. Choices (C) and (D) are both from an earlier (and wrong) part of the passage. Choice (E) doesn't match what you are looking for. Eliminate it. The correct answer is (A).

Infer/Imply/Suggest Questions

Although these questions may seem as though they ask you to go beyond what the passage says, the correct answer will always be directly supported by the passage. Treat these questions as you would any other specific question, ignoring the word "infer," "imply," or "suggest" when you translate them.

Example

2.   Which of the following does the passage imply about the Tokharian languages?

   (A)   They date to a far earlier period than does Celtic.
   (B)   They possess many of the same features as did the Old Indic and Persian of the *Avesta*.
   (C)   They were once spoken over a far greater range than they are today.
   (D)   They undermine the accuracy of the name "Indo-European" for their particular family of languages.
   (E)   They are remarkably similar to the languages spoken by current residents of the Tarim River Basin.

If you ignore the word *infer*, this question asks "What does the passage say about the Tokharian languages?" The lead word is *Tokharian*, so read roughly from the sixth line to the end of the first paragraph. Remember that the big idea of the first paragraph is that neither Aryan nor Indo-European is a good name for this family of languages. The passage says that the Tokharian languages are the easternmost representatives of the Indo-European family of languages and that they were once spoken in Western China. Now check the answers.

Choice (A) is not supported by the passage. Eliminate it. Choice (B) is from the wrong part of the passage. Eliminate it. Choice (C) is not mentioned in the passage and you don't even know if the languages are spoken today. The passage says they were *once spoken*. Eliminate it. Choice (D) is supported by the main idea of the first paragraph. Keep it. Choice (E) is not supported by the passage. The passage does not state if there even <u>are</u> any current residents of the Tarim River Basin. Eliminate it. The correct answer is (D).

EXCEPT Questions

These questions can be confusing because you are looking for the "wrong" thing. When you translate these questions, ignore the word "EXCEPT" and answer each choice "yes" or "no." The answer that is *incorrect* is the answer.

These questions can also be real time suckers because you really have 5 questions for the price of one. You have to go back to the passage to check each answer choice, and if you don't see it, you won't know if it's not there or if you're just not seeing it. If too much time is passing, don't be afraid to eliminate what you can, guess, and move on. Don't let yourself get bogged down.

Example

3.   According to the passage, all of the following characterize Indo-European languages EXCEPT

   (A)   similarities in the structure of words and in the sounds employed
   (B)   common origins in some prehistoric community
   (C)   widespread, intercontinental dispersal
   (D)   recorded instance of early use in ancient literature
   (E)   preservation of characteristics discarded by earlier speakers

You can translate this question to say "Which of the following are characteristics of Indo-European languages?" Now look at the answers.

Does the passage say anything about the languages having similarities in the structure of words and in the sounds employed? Yes. Line 1 says the languages have "morphological, phonetic and word similarities." Choice (A) is yes. Does the passage say the languages have common origins in some prehistoric community? Yes. Choice (B) is yes. Does the passage say that the languages are characterized by widespread, intercontinental dispersal? The first paragraph says the languages spread all the way from Ireland to China. Choice (C) is yes. Do the languages have recorded instances of early use in ancient literature? You saw in your reading about the Tokharian languages that they were written languages. In addition, the *Avesta* is mentioned as an example of Aryan. Because it is italicized, it is some kind of book, so (D) is yes. Do the languages have preservation of characteristics discarded by earlier speakers? The passage does mention this, but only in reference to Icelandic, not all the languages. This question asks about the whole family of languages, so (E) is no. The correct answer is (E).

GENERAL QUESTIONS

Most passages also ask one general question. General questions ask about the passage as a whole. They may ask about the author's main idea or purpose, the tone of the passage, or the structure of the passage.

Sometimes your very first question will be general, but you should still read to get the big ideas. If you read the whole passage, you may get bogged down into details and lose sight of the big picture.

Look at a general question from the same example passage.

4. Which of the following best describes the main purpose of the passage?

   (A) To account for the great diversity of language types
   (B) To consider the possible origins of one family of languages
   (C) To recognize and refute theories of the emergence of proto-Aryan
   (D) To counter one outdated notion of the connectedness of Indo-European languages
   (E) To pinpoint the earliest appearance of written Aryan

If you need to, go back to the passage and skim again. The purpose of the passage is to describe a family of languages with a common origin. Now check the answers.

Choice (A) is too broad. The passage only talks about one family of languages. Eliminate it. Choice (B) could work. Leave it in. Choice (C) is too specific and inaccurate. Although the passage mentions proto-Aryan, it is primarily about the origins of the Aryan family of languages. Eliminate it. Choice (D) contradicts the passage, which supports the connectedness of the Indo-European languages. Eliminate it. Choice (E) is too specific, so it goes too. The correct answer is (B).

PACING

Although the basic approach will help you work them more efficiently, reading comprehension questions take time. In fact, one way to improve your performance on reading comprehension is to improve your performance on sentence correction. If you can do the sentence correction questions more quickly, while maintaining accuracy, you'll have more time for reading comprehension. Adjust your approach to reading comprehension passages and questions according to where the passage appears in the Verbal section. Spend the time you need in order to get the early questions right, and spend less time on each successive passage.

Passage #1

- Passages early in the test matter most. Make sure you spend enough time to get the questions right
- Always go back to the passage. Make sure you can support your answer with proof or evidence. Spend as much time here as you need.

Passage #2

- The second passage counts less than the first, but it's still important to spend a good amount of time backing up your answers with evidence from the passage.
- Don't get stuck on killer questions.

Passage #3

- In order to establish a plan for the third and fourth passages, evaluate your strengths and weaknesses.
- If you excel at reading comprehension, invest the time to get these questions right.
- If reading comprehension is your weakest area, pick up the pace on the last two passages. Push through these questions to give yourself more time for the questions you are more likely to get right.

Passage #4

- The final passage affects your score the least. Spend more time here if this is your strongest area of the test and less if it is your weakest.
- If time is running out, dispense with working the passage. Go directly to the questions, and read only what you need to find the answers.
- If you only have a few minutes left in the section, eliminate answers that are extreme or that make predictions and guess from what's left. The few seconds it takes to eliminate these traps can help you get questions right and can make a difference in your score.

SOCIAL SCIENCE DRILL

Passage 1

The economic world has been buzzing for the last two years now as investors, homeowners, and trend analysts alike attempt to identify the causes, and ultimate effects, of the sub-prime lending mortgage crisis. Papers have been filled with headlines detailing the mass evictions, leading in particularly tragic cases to entire communities being reduced to little more than shanty towns. The onus today seems to be to find which people in which industry are to blame, but, in the end, untangling that knotted mess may prove impossible, and even were we to reveal an identifiable cause, would that help solve the current problems?

What is not drawing as much attention, but perhaps should be, is the effect that all of this has had not just on the value of the dollar internationally but domestically as well. The cost to rent an apartment has risen dramatically in most major metropolitan areas, as families that once owned homes are forced back into the rental market. The cost of student loans has also peaked sharply, with federal interest rates up to three times as high as the rates from a mere six years ago. Unfortunately for the many people affected by this, it seems unlikely that the rising cost of a college education will come to the attention of those at the highest levels until the country sees a decrease in the number of students receiving college degrees, at which point the solution may be out of our hands.

1. The passage most likely refers to student loans in order to

   (A) decry the unreasonable interest rates that are currently being charged by some unscrupulous lenders
   (B) argue that the economic problems evident in some sectors are not really as bad as they may appear superficially
   (C) underscore an earlier point regarding the widespread nature of some of the economic problems related to the housing crisis
   (D) support the claim that the country may eventually suffer from a lack of well-educated citizens
   (E) explain why the housing costs have risen so dramatically in certain major metropolitan areas in the United States

2. The author's attitude towards the economic problems discussed in the passage could most accurately be described as

   (A) frenzied ire
   (B) calculated scorn
   (C) reasoned frustration
   (D) modulated optimism
   (E) scholarly disdain

3. According to the author of the passage, the entity most likely to blame for the economic situation is

   (A) the unscrupulous lending industry that failed to recognize the potential pitfalls in the sub-prime lending scheme
   (B) ultimately of less import than is recognizing the far-ranging side effects and working to find a solution
   (C) also solely responsible for the present weakness of the dollar in overseas markets
   (D) only going to recognize the true effects of the mistakes that have been made once the results are irreversible
   (E) the public at large because it was the public that supported the sub-prime loans without learning what they entailed

4. The word *peaked* in the second paragraph most nearly means

   (A) reached an apex only to descend again
   (B) set a precedent for future valuations
   (C) quickly ascended in price
   (D) artificially inflated
   (E) caught nationwide attention

5. Which of the following techniques is used to further the point of the first paragraph?

   (A) Metaphor
   (B) List of adjectives
   (C) Ad hominem attacks
   (D) A rhetorical question
   (E) Synthesis

Passage 2

Recent investigations into how children acquire knowledge about the outside world have produced agreement on one point. Children are not the blank slates imagined by philosophers since Descartes. According to leading cognitive scientists, it appears that children possess some form of innate understanding about the physical world and its concepts, such as force, heat, matter, and weight. But while scientists agree that there is some sort of initial framework present in the minds of children through which observations about the outside world are filtered and then interpreted, there is considerable disagreement over how to characterize and describe these structures.

Some research suggests that children's innate knowledge is comprised of a number of abstract phenomenological principles. These principles provide abstractions of common events which a child can use to draw conclusions about the outside world. For example, a child might possess an inherent understanding of the force of gravity, which is represented in the child's mind by a basic principle: if something is not supported, it falls. From this simple principle, the child can then make a number of suppositions about how gravity works on objects in the world around him.

Other researchers believe that a child's mind comes equipped with a number of basic theories about common physical domains. These theories restrict both the type and number of viable inferences a child makes about the world, although these initial theories may then be amended by culturally acquired knowledge. Experiments have shown that when asked about the shape of the earth, very young children visualize it as a flat surface, usually a square or disc, resting on some form of support, with the inhabitants living on "top" of the surface. Such a perspective would be consistent with a child's basic experiences of the world. However, older children accurately describe the earth as a sphere floating in space, a picture that contradicts our intuitions about objects but is in accordance with the culturally and scientifically accepted views of the earth. Tellingly, none of the children in the experiment pictured the earth as a pyramid, a point, a line, or any of a number of other possible geometric forms.

6. The author's primary purpose is to

   (A) describe a new theory of cognitive development in children
   (B) present evidence that proves a recent theory correct
   (C) resolve a contradiction between two competing theories
   (D) advocate for further research into an important scientific field
   (E) detail two possible ways to define certain theorized traits

7. Which of the following is most similar to the "suppositions" a child might make about the world around him as detailed in the passage?

   (A) Because a child knows that an object that is not supported will fall, he infers that a certain stool will not be strong enough to hold his weight.
   (B) Because the child knows that she can walk on the floor, she deduces that she will not be able to walk on the ground.
   (C) Because a child knows that some objects are heavier than others, he concludes that he will be able to lift a small stone but not a large rock.
   (D) Because a child knows that a thrown object will fall back to earth, she realizes that she will break a window if she throws a baseball at it.
   (E) Because a child knows that a hot object is dangerous to touch, he figures out that raw food can be cooked on a stove.

8. The passage suggests that the "basic theories" possessed by children

   (A) are not necessarily immutable
   (B) are eventually abandoned
   (C) are soon replaced by cultural lessons
   (D) are restricted to a few domains
   (E) are learned responses to the world

9. The author of the passage mentions "a pyramid, a point, a line, or any of a number of other possible geometric forms" most likely in order to

(A) support an earlier assertion about the nature of certain mental models
(B) describe several other possible ways of visualizing the earth
(C) indicate how children who lacked an inherent theory about the world would respond
(D) question the validity of the experiment used by researchers
(E) suggest an area of further research into the way children perceive the earth

10. The author of the passage would most likely agree with which one of the following statements?

(A) It is more likely that children possess a number of basic theories about common domains than it is that they are equipped with abstract phenomenological principles.
(B) Researchers will eventually discover the way in which children acquire information about the outside world.
(C) Although the exact mechanism is in doubt, there is a consensus among scientists that children possess some form of innate mental framework for interpreting the outside world.
(D) Philosophical views about the nature of the human mind must be replaced by more accurate scientific theories based on experimental data.
(E) Children probably possess some sort of combination of the two viewpoints presented in the passage, using both abstract principles and theories about the world to acquire knowledge.

Passage 3

The bailout of the Chrysler Corporation by the federal government in 1979 was widely hailed as a success. Four years later Chrysler was profitable again, and proponents of the bailout claimed that it had saved Chrysler from bankruptcy without costing the taxpayers one penny. But a closer examination of the facts of the case leads to a more complicated picture.

In 1979 Chrysler was on the verge of bankruptcy. Thousands of workers had been laid off, creditors were unpaid and the senior management appealed to the administration of Jimmy Carter to provide more than $1 billion in tax rebates. The administration's proposal, however, was not for direct tax relief but rather for federal loan guarantees, which administration officials were initially estimating at a value of $750 million but which ultimately totaled more than $1.2 billion. When in 1983 Chrysler was profitable again, supporters of the bailout claimed that the taxpayers had saved Chrysler from bankruptcy without having spent a dime, since the federal government had not had to pay for any defaulted loans. Chrysler is supposed to pay the government the difference between the guaranteed rate the loans carry and the rate they would have carried had they been issued without the government guarantee.

This is, however, not entirely the case. In the early 1980s Chrysler was allowed, under the terms of the bailout, to issue federally guaranteed bonds at a rate of 10.35%. The Ford Motor Company, by contrast, was in better shape than Chrysler at the time, but was forced to issue bonds with a rate of 14.5%. It would seem then that Chrysler should have been paying the government a guarantee of at least 4%; in reality, however, Chrysler was only paying the government a guarantee of 1%. Further, the loss of jobs from cuts at Chrysler would have resulted in a reduction of payroll taxes to the federal government.

11. The purpose of the second paragraph is to

(A) provide an historical overview of a case
(B) offer insight into the strategies of Chrysler's management
(C) argue for the success of the bailout
(D) give a context for why the bailout failed
(E) argue against federal bailouts of private companies

12. The author of the passage is primarily concerned with which of the following?

(A) Arguing against federal bailouts of private companies
(B) Discussing the reasons for the bailout's failure
(C) Challenging the view that the bailout did not cost the federal government money
(D) Exploring the economics of government intervention in the economy
(E) Making the case that Chrysler is not a successful company

13. The passage suggests which of the following about the Ford Motor Company?

(A) It is a larger corporation than Chrysler.
(B) It currently is more profitable than Chrysler.
(C) It faced similar challenges to those Chrysler faced in the 1980s.
(D) It was handicapped by the high price of loans.
(E) It was more financially sound than was Chrysler in the early 1980s.

14. The author of the passage most likely considers the Chrysler bailout to be

(A) a model for future government interventions
(B) a warning to those who would support planned economies
(C) an example of an unsuccessful government bailout
(D) more costly than its supporters suggest
(E) a political decision that was unfair to the Ford Motor Company

15. Which of the following would be the most logical continuation of the last paragraph of the passage?

(A) These conditions indicate that the costs of government intervention are still felt more than 20 years after the initial bailout.
(B) Thus the bailout of Chrysler has more economic ramifications for the federal government than it might seem at first.
(C) However, these losses are more than offset by the gains in the economy that a resurgent Chrysler has produced.
(D) After the final reckoning, further government intervention in the marketplace would be a detriment to a free market economy.
(E) The Chrysler bailout provides a model for executives seeking to pursue other types of government intervention.

Passage 4

Published in 1961, *The Death and Life of Great American Cities* remains one of the most important texts in the field of urban planning. The author, Jane Jacobs, proposed that only by acknowledging the complex interplay between the residential, commercial, and industrial could we begin to develop cities that would not only be safe but also enjoyable. This thinking ran counter to many of the theories of the urban planning movements of the sixties and seventies, many of which advocated the separation of residential and commercial zones, and attempted to create orderly, efficient utopias. In doing so, however, they neglected the human element and many today feel that this is one of the major causes of the urban decay so prominent in many metropolitan areas.

As larger American cities attempt to combat crime and suburban flight, city leaders are reconsidering many of Jacobs's ideas and incorporating those ideas in sometimes unexpected ways. One prime example of this is The Grove, a shopping center in the Fairfax district of Los Angeles. Attached to the Farmer's Market, this sprawling commercial area resembles a village more than a mall, and intentionally so. There are outdoor seating areas, a pond, and many cafes mixed in with upscale shops. The question that remains, however, is whether this contrived community atmosphere will be able to replicate the dynamics of a naturally occurring neighborhood, and only time will provide the answer.

16. Which of the following best describes the relationship of the second paragraph to the first?

   (A) A generalization based on a previously stated hypothesis
   (B) The logical conclusion to the ideas proffered in the introductory sentences of the first paragraph
   (C) A description of a case study that hopes to demonstrate the efficacy of the ideas promoted in the first paragraph
   (D) A rebuttal of the claims made by the urban planners mentioned earlier in the passage
   (E) Suggestions that ought to be taken seriously by the aforementioned city planners and urban dwellers alike

17. In the second paragraph, the author refers to The Grove as an example of

   (A) an unnatural collection of buildings that hopes to create a new sense of community
   (B) successful city planning, based on the complex interplay of different aspects of human life
   (C) the kind of ineffective urban design that leads to suburban flight and downtown decay
   (D) a modern contrivance trying to piggyback on a time-honored community tradition
   (E) a highly suspect attempt to lull people into a false sense of community based on shopping

18. The primary purpose of the passage is to

   (A) urge the public to support zoning initiatives that would further the goals of planners such as Jacobs
   (B) lambaste short-sighted urban planners who neglect to consider the human element when planning a community
   (C) sympathize with people attempting to create a vibrant community without the requisite social support systems
   (D) cast doubt on the efficacy of some methods of urban planning while drawing attention to one more novel approach
   (E) educate readers about the potential pitfalls of developing a community without considering all relevant factors

19. According to the passage, the urban planners of the sixties and seventies would most likely respond to developments such as The Grove by

   (A) lauding the project's designers for their foresight in recognizing that neighborhood's need for an open-air place in which to gather
   (B) questioning the decision to place the new center so close to a previously established gathering and shopping area
   (C) warning that the mixture of dining and shopping establishments, combined with the disorganized layout, will lead to inefficiency
   (D) praising local residents for supporting an artificially-created community in an attempt to foster true relationships with neighbors
   (E) fearing that such a center will fail to recognize the complex interplay between the human users and the businesses that have been installed

20. Which of the following is most strongly supported about the theories of the urban planning movements of the sixties and seventies?

   (A) They did not attempt to address the relationship between residential and industrial aspects of life.
   (B) The actions they prompted did not all result in matching their intended outcomes.
   (C) They unintentionally led to more urban decay than would have existed in their absence.
   (D) The Farmer's Market is one of many areas they have influenced.
   (E) They failed to create an enjoyable atmosphere, and instead led to unsafe environments.

Passage 5

Although oft-maligned in modern culture, the pigeon once stood not only for speed and reliability but also for grace and beauty. Darwin himself became a pigeon fancier after beginning to work with the humble *Columba livia*, discovering them to be more fascinating than he had formerly believed. During the Victorian age, in fact, raising show pigeons was a popular hobby, with new breeds continuously arising as amateur (and not-so-amateur) ornithologists crossed animals in the hopes of creating ever more fantastic creatures. One of the most sought-after varieties was known as the Almond Tumbler, a name presumably derived from the color of the birds combined with the distinctive flight style. Over the course of many generations, this bird was so manipulated as to have a beak so small as to prevent the adult birds from feeding their offspring. And yet, it was wildly popular, drawing high prices at auctions and high prizes at competitions.

How then did an animal once so well-loved come to be so loathed? As recently as World War II, the military used pigeons to carry messages, but today, many people would kick a pigeon before they would feed one. Perhaps it is just a problem of population density, a lack of esteem for that which is ubiquitous. Pigeons have become our constant urban companions and, as such, have been transformed from symbols of peace, plenty, and prosperity, to representatives of disease and decay.

21. The primary purpose of this passage is to

   (A) convince the reader of the nobility of the pigeon, based on its history as a symbol of virtue
   (B) dissuade the reader from mistreating a once-majestic animal that has fallen from favor
   (C) rebut claims that the pigeon carries disease any more frequently than do other domestic animals
   (D) promote a renewal of pigeon fancying and a resurgence of breeds such as the Almond Tumbler
   (E) suggest that there might be more to the story of some urban wildlife than is commonly known

22. The case of the Almond Tumbler is most analogous to which of the following?

   (A) A strain of wheat that can be grown in plentiful quantities but loses much of its nutritional value in the process
   (B) Arabian horses that are able to run at phenomenal speeds due to centuries of careful breeding designed to enhance those physical attributes
   (C) Vitamins that were purported to provide all of the necessary nutrients but have since been found not to be very effective
   (D) The dachshund, a popular breed of dog that is nonetheless prone to severe back problems, due to weaknesses exacerbated by targeted breeding
   (E) The wild rock doves that are most commonly found nesting in the faces of cliffs far from human habitation

23. Based on the passage, which of the following statements about Darwin, if true, could be most effectively used to improve the popular view of pigeons today?

   (A) Darwin realized that the pigeon was a fascinating example of evolutionary adaptation.
   (B) Darwin understood that the pigeon's value as a messenger was superior to that of other birds.
   (C) Darwin's familiarity with pigeons led him to value aspects of the bird that he would never have otherwise noticed.
   (D) Darwin spoke at length about the need to treat all living things with great esteem.
   (E) Darwin learned to value peace, plenty, and prosperity as he became older.

24. According to the passage, the disparity between the Victorian and modern view of pigeons might be explained by

(A) the poor performance of those pigeon troops involved in espionage during World War II
(B) inherited problems common to some of the most popular breeds of fancy pigeons
(C) the fact that pigeons have become such a prosaic feature in many urban areas
(D) documented cases of diseases spread through human-pigeon contact
(E) the common belief that pigeons are filthy animals, living among us in squalor

25. In the context of the passage, the author uses the word "fancier" to describe

(A) the Victorian passion for ornately decorated possessions, which ultimately bled into the world of animal breeding, leading to ever more aesthetically pleasing, yet often physically feeble, strains
(B) the complicity of the scientific community in the suspect field of animal manipulation, performed for the benefit of the monied classes, often to the detriment of the animals chosen to be the subjects of their studies
(C) Darwin's interest in pigeons as part of a fashionable trend not confined to scientific pursuits but rather enveloping people from all different walks of life and stations in society
(D) the magnificence of *Columba livia*'s plumage as compared to that of the wild birds that have remained untouched by scientific advances and complex breeding programs, thus advocating an expansion of such programs
(E) Darwin's single-minded obsession with breeding an Almond Tumbler pigeon in order to study its flight patterns and physiology, in an attempt to demonstrate the superiority of certain breeds of pigeon

Check your answers on page 527.

HUMANITIES DRILL

Passage 1

Mass market history textbooks suffer from a number of deficiencies. Even with judicious editing and some stunning omissions, the typical high school history textbook is over one thousand pages long. Part of the problem lies in the publishers' desire to construct a book that appeals to as many regional markets as possible. In order to do so, the publisher must include details that have relatively little historical significance but evoke a degree of local pride in readers. But the sheer volume of information available in textbooks is not, in and of itself, the greatest difficulty with these textbooks. The most pressing problem is the textbook writers' philosophical approach to this information.

The manner in which most history textbooks treat the story of Columbus' "discovery" of America offers a telling example. First, there is a copious historical record indicating that a multitude of explorers had reached North America long before Columbus. This record consists of a diversity of sources, including genetic similarities between North American populations and populations in Africa, Asia, and Europe; homogenous social structures and art forms; and even oral histories and legends of various peoples. While historians argue over the value and reliability of this evidence, it is generally accepted that travelers from Siberia, Japan, China, Polynesia, West Africa, and Iceland most likely arrived in North America long before Columbus did. Textbook authors could simply present all of this evidence to students and let them come to their own conclusions about the discovery and settlement of America—in fact, that is how professional historians work. Instead, textbook authors decide to craft a simple narrative around certain historical events at the expense of the true complexities of history. By treating history as a series of settled facts instead of a sequence of ongoing debates and interpretations, textbook authors do a great disservice to both their students and to the educational process. In their quest to portray history as a story, textbook authors have unwittingly deprived the subject of some of its most vibrant and interesting aspects. It is no wonder that high school students in the United States rank history as one of their least favorite subjects.

1. The author of the passage is primarily concerned with

(A) recommending solutions to a problem
(B) debunking a long held perspective
(C) explaining the nature of a fault
(D) responding to an argument
(E) evaluating a proposed course of action

2. The "problem" mentioned in the first paragraph can best be described as arising from the pressure to

(A) create a product that will please as many customers as possible
(B) include as many relevant historical facts as feasible
(C) produce a text that will avoid containing controversial statements
(D) develop a book that contains a simple narrative
(E) arouse the interest of consumers from a particular region

3. The passage suggests in which of the following ways that the "philosophical approach" to historical information used by textbook authors compromises the teaching of history?

(A) By including far more information than is historically relevant, textbook authors make learning history a challenging process for students.
(B) By refusing to include a multitude of historical sources, textbook authors fail to provide teachers of history with an appreciation of the complexity of history.
(C) By presenting a vast amount of primary source data, textbook authors deprive students of the chance to approach historical studies the way professional historians do.
(D) By neglecting to introduce a certain degree of uncertainty to historical events, textbook authors have made the learning of history a less interesting process.
(E) By creating simple narratives out of the complex historical record, textbook authors have forced students of history to learn history the way most academics have.

4. The passage implies which of the following about high school history textbooks?

(A) Typical modern textbooks are much longer than were those of the past.
(B) Despite their size, many history textbooks still fail to include certain important historical details.
(C) High school history textbooks have not been submitted to a proper editing process.
(D) High school history textbooks are the only textbooks that tend to be tailored to local markets.
(E) No high school history textbook presents the complexities surrounding the discovery of America.

5. According to the passage, treating history as a series of debates and open questions could result in

(A) a narrative that more accurately portrays the general trends in history
(B) better educational performance from students in history classes
(C) more students deciding to pursue careers as professional historians
(D) students reaching more accurate conclusions about historical events
(E) history classes that are better at engaging their students

Passage 2

Though the term "literature" seems as though it would be simple to define, only a few moments of pondering the question "what is literature?" is required before one realizes how complex it really is. Imam Ja'far al-Sadiq, a Muslim philosopher who lived during the eighth century, A.D., wrote that, "Literature is the garment which one puts on what he says or writes so that it may appear more attractive." When viewed in this light, literature begins to resemble less a description of content itself than an artistic veil draped over content.

On the other hand, the term literature is cast in a harsher light when viewed as the twentieth century Russian thinker Roman Jakobson did; he declared that literature is "organized violence committed on ordinary speech." Jakobson thus suggests that the unstructured, conversational words that define ordinary speech are transmogrified into a particular arrangement on the page and, in so doing, become literature.

Another facet to consider is the public's perception of literature. While some may define cave paintings as literature, others would argue that they are merely graphic inscriptions that, though perhaps narrative, are not literary. Others may argue that banned books, such as *Go Ask Alice*, published in 1971 and excluded from many library shelves and schools, are not literature because the content cannot be universally appreciated. Because these questions remain unanswered and are largely subjective, in the final analysis, it may prove impossible to define the term "literature."

6. Which of the following best describes the main idea of the passage?

   (A) The question of "what is literature" has been answered differently by different cultures at different points in history.
   (B) Asking questions such as "what is literature" is an ultimately fruitless endeavor since there will never be consensus on the answer.
   (C) Literature is a little understood concept to this day because few scholars have thought to attempt to define it.
   (D) Attempts to answer the question "what is literature" are doomed to failure because literature has no defining characteristics other than the label, literature, itself.
   (E) A seemingly well-understood concept is shown to have been subject to much disagreement in the past and is expected to continue to be the subject of disagreement.

7. The author of the passage most likely mentions cave paintings in order to

   (A) prove that such merely graphic depictions have never been considered literature
   (B) provide an example of a type of artwork that has long been accepted as a form of literature
   (C) demonstrate that the definition of literature may require more than merely telling a story
   (D) emphasize that efforts to develop a definition of literature are destined for failure
   (E) underscore that content must be universally appreciated in order to be deemed literature

8. Based on the passage, about which of the following would Imam Ja'far al-Sadiq and Roman Jakobson be most likely to disagree?

(A) Literature is more concerned with aesthetic criteria than substance.
(B) Without the label "literature" the ugliness of most writing would be apparent.
(C) Literature is dangerous because of its inherently violent structures.
(D) Literature may have innate characteristics by which it may be recognized.
(E) Banned books are not literature because they are not universally appreciated.

9. Based upon the passage, which of the following is <u>NOT</u> an example of a work of art that could be considered literature?

(A) A comic book that tells the story of a Greek myth
(B) A court transcript of a trial for a double murder
(C) A play that recounts the dissolution of a marriage
(D) A dramatic retelling of a conversation between two world leaders
(E) A novel that has been unanimously praised by critics and readers alike

10. The author of the passage most likely mentions the book *Go Ask Alice* in order to

(A) illustrate one reason why a piece of writing may not be considered literature
(B) argue that banned books should not be considered literature because they are not universally appreciated
(C) counter a point of view that some works not widely considered literature should be reevaluated
(D) offer an alternative explanation for why some pieces of writing should be considered literature
(E) present another piece of evidence supporting Jakobson's theory of literature

Passage 3

Although the theory that all things in nature are conceived of the same elementary substance is now familiar to most philosophers, when Baruch de Spinoza proffered his version of this theory in the tense religio-political climate of seventeenth-century Europe, he met not only with censure but with threats and even exile. Cast out of the Jewish community in his youth due to heterodox ideas, Spinoza found himself once again reviled in his early adulthood, this time by many prominent members of Dutch society. One is forced to wonder how much of the isolation in this brilliant man's life was due to these imposed periods of solitude as opposed to being solely due to his philosophical goal of living a life of the mind.

For the modern scholar, it is imperative to recall that theories such as the one referred to above shook not only an individual's view of the world, but the entire political system and society in which these views were espoused. What was the cause of the French Revolution if not a changing view of the hierarchical system of medieval French society? During his life, then, Spinoza was to some extent another victim of the medieval mindset, struggling to live past its expiration date.

11. The author of the passage most likely refers to Spinoza's exclusion from the Jewish community of his youth in order to

    (A) condemn Dutch religious groups for their intolerant views and unwillingness to be open to new scholarship
    (B) support Spinoza's later decision not to leave his inheritance to members of his erstwhile family
    (C) juxtapose his treatment at the hands of his own people with his later treatment at the hands of the Dutch authorities
    (D) draw a parallel between Spinoza's earlier conflicts and his eventual decision to withdraw from Dutch society
    (E) underscore the utter isolation in which Spinoza was ultimately forced to pursue his scholarly research into the life of the mind

12. Which of the following, if true, would provide the best support for the author of the passage's statements regarding the French Revolution?

    (A) Many of the late eighteenth century's prominent philosophers claimed, after the end of the French Revolution, that the fighting had been inevitable due to a changing political climate around the world.
    (B) The Russian Revolution was based in large part on a changing philosophy regarding the status of commoners and its leaders attributed many of their initial theories on ideas inspired by the events leading up to the French Revolution.
    (C) Many writers in the years immediately before the outbreak of the French Revolution wrote pamphlets regarding the rights of man that were then used to garner popular support by the leaders of the Revolution.
    (D) Spinoza believed that war between factions within a country was an unfortunate side effect of living closely with other people, many of whom would necessarily have beliefs that differed from one's own beliefs.
    (E) Modern day France sets great store by its philosophers, asserting that it is through the ideas of the great thinkers that France is able to maintain a position of global prominence, and due to those ideas that it has such a rich history.

13. Based on the passage, which of the following statements about Spinoza's experience with members of Dutch society is most supported?

(A) Negative views of Spinoza led to more than emotional consequences.
(B) Spinoza was exiled by prominent members of Dutch society.
(C) Spinoza's treatment by members of Dutch society reminded him of his youth.
(D) Members of Dutch society believed that natural objects were unrelated to each other.
(E) Spinoza's attempts to blend in with Dutch society were thwarted.

14. Which of the following best describes the main idea of the passage?

(A) Spinoza was a martyr to old-fashioned ideas, who lived and died in undeserved obscurity, due to the narrow-mindedness of others.
(B) If the Dutch society of the seventeenth century had been more receptive, the course of history might have been dramatically different.
(C) The French Revolution was, at the most fundamental level, a fight to determine which idea would gain ascendancy.
(D) All tangible objects are made from the same universal substance, as shown by the seventeenth century philosopher Spinoza.
(E) Spinoza may be viewed as an example of someone who suffered for proposing ideas that were, at that time, unpopular.

15. The author of the passage's attitude towards Spinoza could best be described as

(A) unmitigated adoration
(B) tepid support
(C) academic respect
(D) woeful condemnation
(E) benign neglect

Passage 4

Many critics of popular culture claim that the modern information age has led the public to be more interested in the personal lives of entertainers than in their actual artistic abilities. Some have even gone so far as to posit that many of today's famous faces would be nowhere were it not for their personal scandals. This is not, however, the purely modern phenomenon that some believe it to be.

As far back as human records go, evidence can be seen of public figures indelibly linked, accurately or otherwise, with scandal. One notable example is Maria Callas. This glamorous Greek opera singer was almost as well known for her supposed temperamental outbursts, vitriolic rivalries, and tempestuous relationships as for her musical abilities. During her lifetime, many critics referred to her robust voice as inherently flawed, implying too that her fame was undeserved. Today, however, without Callas's undeniably vivacious personality clouding the picture, most critics agree that she was in fact an immensely talented singer of the first degree, ranging in her performances from dramatic soprano pieces such as *Die Walküre* to coloratura, *bel canto* pieces such as *I Puritani*, managing to excel at both. Such talent is truly undeniable, no matter what the personality of the performer.

16. The author of the passage mentions the operas *Die Walküre* and *I Puritani* in order to support the claim that

   (A) Callas's artistic temperament was unstable and thus fit for a wide range of roles
   (B) a truly talented artist must be able to perform in a wide range of styles
   (C) the ability to perform such diverse pieces demonstrated to her peers Callas's talent
   (D) whether Callas was a difficult person to work with is not the most important gage of her skill
   (E) Callas was the most versatile opera singer of the past century, temperamental or not

17. The critics would most likely respond to the author of the passage's claim that such talent is truly undeniable, no matter the personality of the performer by discussing

   (A) precise aspects of Callas's vocal technique that did not conform with the classical standards of vocal purity
   (B) evidence supporting claims that Callas was prone to walking out on performances when displeased with the management
   (C) claims that Callas's ability in coloratura roles was exaggerated by the singers' fans and friendly critics
   (D) scholarly papers asserting that *I Puritani* and *Die Walküre* are not as thematically different as some suppose
   (E) the personal scandals that dogged Callas's career from her earliest days in Greece until her death in Paris

18. The author of the passage's attitude toward Maria Callas could best be characterized as

(A) unbridled contempt
(B) wistful nostalgia
(C) scholarly disinterest
(D) passionate defense
(E) reasoned support

19. The organization of this passage could best be described as

(A) thesis, followed by antithesis, and concluded with synthesis
(B) thesis, corroborated by evidence, finalized with a conclusion
(C) a generalization narrowed into one specific example
(D) a widespread belief proven to be false with opposing examples
(E) a statement based on emotion followed by an argument based on logic

20. The passage could most reasonably be said to suggest

(A) that Callas is the prototypical example of a coloratura soprano, as seen in twentieth-century operas
(B) a refutation of the idea that the linking of scandals and celebrities is a solely modern phenomenon
(C) that modern opera requires its top singers to have an immense range of abilities
(D) that a performer's personality is irrelevant and should not even be addressed by critics
(E) a credible explanation of Callas's immense popularity even among those unfamiliar with opera

Passage 5

In 1775, James Adair published <u>History of the American Indians</u>, a work that historians have quoted as an insight into the characteristics of eighteenth-century Cherokee society. Residing with the Cherokee for over forty years, the British Adair was considered an expert on the subject. However, his depiction of events has lead to a false conclusion, a fault made by those who were not accurately pinpointing the timeline at which his observations were made.

Adair noted that the Cherokee were settling in towns with some distance between each other because "the land will not admit any other settlement." The conclusion drawn from this statement was that the deterioration of the Cherokee society was caused by a depletion of resources such as crops, acreage, and wildlife.

However, new findings suggest that it was outside stressors, such as warfare, that lead to the collapse. What, then, of Adair's assertion? A recent study noted that because Adair chronicled his experiences over a forty-year period, his quote could have referred to any interval within that span, not necessarily the final stage of the society. Furthermore, after carefully examining cartographical data, which depicted an abundance of land, anthropologists determined that the Cherokee society must have flourished until the French and Indian wars added unexpected pressure and also usurped precious time that could have been spent farming.

21. Which of the following most accurately expresses the main idea of the passage?

   (A) Critics of Adair have misconstrued the meaning of a quote he obtained from a Cherokee person.
   (B) Some historians have used Adair's work to form an unjustified conclusion.
   (C) The Cherokee built towns far from each other in order to minimize impact on the land.
   (D) Cartographical data provide evidence that one of Adair's claims is false.
   (E) The demise of the Cherokee people was caused by the French and Indian wars.

22. The author of the passage refers to the French and Indian wars in the final sentence in order to

   (A) counter the idea that all Native American tribes were pacifist
   (B) pin down the time at which the Cherokee society began its decline
   (C) suggest that it was war, not resource depletion that caused the Cherokee to settle in towns far from each other
   (D) lay the blame for the decline of the Cherokee on Europeans rather than Indians
   (E) support an alternative hypothesis that combats other historians' misinterpretation of Adair's quote

23. Which of the following best expresses the author of the passage's attitude toward the writing of James Adair?

   (A) Measured appreciation
   (B) Unbridled enthusiasm
   (C) Mild reservation
   (D) Hostile contempt
   (E) Scholarly disrespect

24. Which of the following does the author of the passage use as evidence to support the position that the French and Indian wars caused the decline of the Cherokee people?

   (A) Adair's *History of the American Indians*
   (B) A quote from a Cherokee person
   (C) The pattern of depletion of natural resources
   (D) Cartographical data
   (E) Hearsay

25. With which of the following statements would the author of the passage most likely agree?

   (A) The Cherokee brought about their own demise by settling in towns too close to one another.
   (B) It is impossible for a British academic to fully understand the plight of the Cherokee.
   (C) During the forty years Adair lived with the Cherokee, their settlement pattern probably did not change dramatically.
   (D) Once he has died, it is impossible to pin down exactly when an anthropologist may have received a quote.
   (E) James Adair should have been more careful in assigning meaning to quotations he received from Cherokee people.

Check your answers on page 527.

NATURAL SCIENCE DRILL

Passage 1

The spotted hyena, or *Crocuta crocuta*, found throughout sub-Saharan Africa, is, contrary to popular belief, one of nature's fiercest predators. Some early tribes mistook the hyena's distinctive call, which some have equated to hysterical human laughter, for the cries of lost souls, while many others associated the animal with the lords of the underworld. In modern movies, the hyena has most often been caricatured as a buffoon-like creature or a villain, preying on the weak. These beliefs have led to the common fallacy that the hyena is primarily a scavenger. The reality, however, is that hyenas are predators first and scavengers only through need.

Hyena physiology may look comical, but it is designed for pure power. It has been postulated that the jaws of a fully-grown hyena are potentially capable of exerting a bite force of 1,000 pounds, which would give it one of the most powerful grips in the animal world. The hyena's heart is equally powerful, enabling an adult to run at a steady rate of six miles per hour, with bursts of up to thirty miles per hour. In the wild, hyenas tend to hunt in packs led by a matriarch and have been known to bring down animals as large as the Cape buffalo. It seems that, in the case of the hyena, appearances can certainly be deceiving.

1. According to the passage, all of the following are characteristics of hyenas EXCEPT

   (A) a tendency to prey upon the weak
   (B) a hierarchical clan structure led by a single female
   (C) dynamic mandibular strength
   (D) vocalizations that some people find unnerving
   (E) a high level of endurance

2. Which of the following, if true, would most undermine the application of the argument presented in the final sentence of the passage to the hyena?

   (A) Many other animals that seem comical are as powerful as the hyena.
   (B) The hyena often walks in a manner that causes it to appear smaller than it is.
   (C) The jaws of hyenas are smaller than those of sharks, and the lion is a faster runner than the hyena over both short and long distances.
   (D) People who have observed a hyena attack concur that hyenas are fearsome predators.
   (E) Most people unfamiliar with popular beliefs about hyenas find the sight of the animal to be immediately intimidating.

3. The author of the passage would be most likely to agree with which of the following statements?

(A) The spotted hyena is the most powerful animal found in sub-Saharan Africa.
(B) It is possible for an animal to look less dangerous than it truly is.
(C) Animals that hunt in matriarchal packs are able to bring down bigger animals than lone hunters could.
(D) Early tribes often held mistaken beliefs regarding the animals that shared their territory.
(E) It is important to be able to run at least six miles an hour in order to bring down animals such as the Cape buffalo.

4. The passage best supports the claim that the author of the passage believes the hyena to be

(A) a commonly misunderstood deadly predator
(B) prone to scavenging for meals whenever possible
(C) associated with the lords of the underworld
(D) saddled with an inappropriate cry
(E) built more for speed than for endurance

5. The primary purpose of this passage is to

(A) argue that hyenas should not be depicted as scavengers in the modern media
(B) undermine the belief that hyenas sound like the souls of the lost
(C) describe the hyena's physiology and hunting style
(D) counter the popular notion that hyenas lack hunting prowess
(E) support the proposition that sub-Saharan animals be further studied

Passage 2

Since 1929, physicists have known that the universe is expanding. Most physicists hold that the entire observable universe was condensed into a tiny area of exceptional density and that this initial mass exploded outward in what is commonly referred to as the "Big Bang." The universe has been expanding steadily ever since this cataclysmic event and most physicists naturally assumed that this expansion must be gradually slowing down. Some theorists even predicted that the gravitational pull of the universe would cause the eventual contraction of the universe—the "Big Crunch." However, in 1998, a team of observers studying supernovae made a shocking discovery. Instead of slowing down, the expansion of the universe is accelerating. In fact, the acceleration appeared to have begun some 10 billion years ago. Later measurements of the cosmic microwave background and a survey of the distribution of galaxies seem to corroborate the initial finding that the expansion of the universe is indeed accelerating.

Cosmologists believe the most likely explanation for the acceleration of the universe's expansion is an entity known as dark energy. According to theory, dark energy should account for approximately two-thirds of the total cosmic energy density. It also is believed to be gravitationally repulsive and diffused throughout the areas of space unoccupied by galaxies. Although theoretically possible, dark energy, if it were found to exist, would provide theorists with a number of difficulties and perhaps even require an extensive rethinking of fundamental physics. Some cosmologists believe that the existence of dark energy implies the existence of subatomic particles more than thirty orders of magnitude smaller than the electron. Others have tinkered with Einstein's theory of relativity in an attempt to account for the perceived effects of dark energy.

Such drastic revisions to long-held tenets have encouraged some physicists to seek a more conventional solution to the accelerating universe enigma, one that does not invoke the specter of dark energy. These theories posit more mundane explanations, such as the aggregate gravitational effect of interstellar dust. Recently, four independent groups have found evidence of the integrated Sachs-Wolfe effect, a phenomenon linked to the presence of dark energy.

6. The passage is primarily concerned with

(A) defending an innovative theory
(B) comparing competing scientific theories
(C) detailing the ramifications of a finding
(D) describing a problem and its possible solution
(E) proposing a new approach to cosmology

7. The passage implies that the expansion of the universe

(A) has been continuing for approximately 10 billion years
(B) was assumed in most theoretical models of the universe
(C) will eventually slow down and stop, leading to a "Big Crunch"
(D) is thought to result from the initial conditions of the universe
(E) is continuing to accelerate at a constant rate

8. Which of the following is suggested by the passage as a reason dark energy provides an explanation for an accelerating expansion of the universe?

(A) Dark energy fills two thirds of the universe.
(B) Cosmologists believe that it is theoretically possible for dark energy to exist.
(C) The space unoccupied by galaxies creates a vacuum.
(D) A separating force can cause acceleration.
(E) Most of the universe is made up of particles larger than an electron.

9. The author of the passage most likely mentions the "evidence of the Sachs-Wolfe effect" in order to

(A) indicate mounting support for the existence of dark energy
(B) prove that more mundane explanations for the expansion of the universe are incorrect
(C) provide an example of a phenomena that will need to be rethought in light of the existence of dark energy
(D) show that most astronomers accept the existence of dark energy
(E) defend the attempts of more traditional astronomers to explain the universe's accelerating expansion

10. The author of the passage indicates that physicists have concluded that the universe is expanding by studying all of the following EXCEPT

(A) supernovae
(B) cosmic background radiation
(C) integrated Sachs-Wolfe effect
(D) interstellar dust
(E) placement of galaxies

Passage 3

The Arctic Circle comprises approximately 6 percent of the Earth's surface. Of the 21 million square-kilometer Arctic region, only about 8 million square kilometers is onshore; the rest of the area is located on continental shelves, which are covered by no more than 500 meters of water. Expeditions to the northern regions of Canada, Russia, and Alaska have discovered some 400 oil and gas fields within the Arctic Circle. These fields are capable of producing upwards of 200 billion barrels of oil and natural gas, a quantity representing about 10 percent of the world's known petroleum reserves. And yet, most of the Arctic Circle region remains unexplored. Some geologists believe that the expansive Arctic continental shelves may contain vast petroleum reserves.

Recently, a group of researchers from the United States Geological Survey completed an extensive survey of the Arctic region. The members of the Circum-Arctic Resource Appraisal (CARA) team sought to discover the possible petroleum reserves in all areas north of 66.56 degrees north latitude. Due to the relative lack of information on the Arctic Circle region, the CARA team was unable to employ the standard geological techniques of resource assessment, including discovery prospect modeling and deposit simulation. Instead, the scientists employed a probabilistic methodology to attempt to pinpoint areas of the Arctic Circle that had at least a 10 percent chance of harboring oil reserves in excess of 10 billion barrels. The model used by the researchers determined the probability that a certain location possesses significant oil reserves by considering certain geologic factors typically associated with oil fields, including rock type and formation, and the relative age of the geologic structures. The results of the CARA team's study indicate that 17 of the 25 Arctic Circle regions have a greater than 10 percent chance of holding oil reserves. Geologists on the team further conclude that over 70 percent of the estimated oil reserves in the Arctic Circle occur in just five of the regions, while over 70 percent of the probable natural gas reserves lay in just three of the regions.

11. The author of the passage is primarily concerned with

(A) critiquing a recent scientific study
(B) reporting the results of a geologic survey
(C) enumerating the world's potential remaining oil reserves
(D) advocating increased oil drilling in the Arctic Circle region
(E) describing a new geologic research methodology

12. According to the passage, the majority of the Arctic Circle region

(A) contains vast untapped oil reserves
(B) is located under water
(C) is found in the northern areas of Canada, Russia, and Alaska
(D) represents about 10 percent of the Earth's surface area
(E) lies to the north of 66.56 degrees latitude

13. The passage implies that the CARA team researchers employed a probabilistic methodology because

(A) the unexplored nature of the Arctic Circle region made a probabilistic method the most efficient way of searching a large land area
(B) the techniques of discovery prospect and deposit simulation had failed to turn up evidence of significant oil deposits
(C) the nature of the land area that they were exploring rendered standard resource assessment tools unusable
(D) more than half of the Arctic Circle region lies underwater, making it difficult to use typical geologic survey methods
(E) standard geologic resource assessment techniques are unsuited to areas with less than a 10 percent chance of containing oil reserves

14. The results of the CARA team's survey have which of the following relations to the views of the geologists mentioned in the first paragraph?

(A) The results of the survey conclusively prove that the beliefs of the geologists are true.
(B) The results of the survey corroborate the geologists' beliefs about petroleum reserves, but undermine their beliefs on natural gas reserves.
(C) The results of the survey indicate that the geologists' beliefs are likely to be true, although the survey indicates the oil is located in areas not predicted by the geologists.
(D) The results of the survey fail to confirm the beliefs of the geologists and indicate that the geologists are very likely mistaken about the quantity of oil reserves in the Arctic Circle.
(E) The results of the survey indicate that the suppositions of the geologists may be correct, although there is no definitive proof that the areas surveyed hold significant oil reserves.

15. It can be inferred that the CARA team's research revealed that

(A) 8 of the 25 Arctic regions surveyed contained no oil reserves
(B) oil companies should focus their prospecting efforts on no more than 8 of the regions studied
(C) the majority of oil and natural gas reserves lie in 8 different regions of the Arctic Circle
(D) if there are significant oil reserves in the Arctic Circle, it is likely that they are concentrated in a few areas
(E) the Arctic Circle region contains more oil deposits than it does natural gas deposits

Passage 4

Found along the coastlines of southern Australia and New Zealand, *Eudyptula minor* is the smallest species of penguin on record. Due to its diminutive size, it is often called the Little Penguin, though the residents of Australia call it the Fairy Penguin and those of New Zealand prefer the name Little Blue Penguin or even just Blue Penguin. The latter names are derived from the deep blue coloring of the penguins' backs, designed to enable the penguins to better blend in with the surrounding water when viewed in the ocean from above. Their white underbellies work in a similar manner, helping camouflage the penguins from undersea carnivores, which comprise the majority of the penguins' natural predators.

It is fortunate that the penguins have few natural enemies, as human encroachment into their territory has taken its toll. Due to their small size, Little Penguins are easy prey not only for now-feral introduced species such as foxes and ferrets but also for companion animals such as dogs and cats. On Phillip Island, the penguins draw huge crowds of tourists on a nightly basis and many of these visitors unknowingly expose the penguins to injury by taking flash photographs, which can damage the nocturnal birds' highly sensitive eyes. Moreover, during the day the penguins have been known to hide behind everything from benches to cars; an incautious human could easily hurt or even kill one of them without even knowing.

16. The primary purpose of the passage is to

(A) convey to the reader the plight of the Little Penguins of Australia and New Zealand
(B) educate the reader about the Little Penguin and some of the potential dangers that it faces
(C) argue that the governments of Australia and New Zealand must impose stricter animal import laws
(D) decry the thoughtlessness of those who visit the penguins' territory without taking proper precautions
(E) suggest that feral carnivores be prohibited from territory populated by the Little Penguins

17. The passage refers to foxes as an example of

(A) animals whose predations have caused untold harm to Australia's Little Penguin population
(B) native animals that are also in danger due to human encroachment on its territory
(C) companion animals that were imported into Australia by early settlers who were unaware of the native species' danger
(D) nocturnal animals that are unable to deal with the bright lights of flash photography
(E) non-native animals that have become part of the Australian ecosystem, preying on smaller animals

18. According to the passage, the tourists are most likely there in order to

(A) tour the pristine countryside of Phillip Island
(B) have the opportunity to handle a penguin
(C) view some of the native wildlife
(D) help protect the habitat of the penguin
(E) enjoy the diverse geography and mild climate

19. Based on the information in the passage, which of the following would be most analogous to the Little Penguin's distinctive coloring?

(A) The fur of the snowshoe hare changes from a mottled reddish-brown during the summer, so as to blend in with dry grasses, and white in the winter, to match the snow.
(B) A male peacock has more brightly colored plumes than does a female peahen, because the male must use its plumage to draw attention, in order to attract suitable mates.
(C) Some tropical frogs are able to alter the pigmentation in their skin, either to hide more effectively in the surrounding foliage or to mimic the markings on other frogs.
(D) Many varieties of sparrow are pale when viewed from below, making it more difficult for land predators to see the flying bird, but darker from above, obscuring the bird from birds of prey.
(E) The tiger, although widely known as a brightly colored, easily visible animal, is able to almost disappear among the long grass and shadows from which it typically hunts its prey.

20. The statement in the passage that the Little Penguin has few natural enemies provides support for which of the following inferences?

(A) The waters surrounding southern Australia and New Zealand host a relatively small number of predators.
(B) The Little Penguin is pleasant to observe, and most people on Phillip Island enjoy watching the penguin swim.
(C) Ferrets are the only animal on Phillip Island small enough to prey on young Little Penguins.
(D) The survival of the Little Penguin species would not likely be compromised solely by ocean predation.
(E) Human encroachment should be halted or prevented on Phillip Island.

Passage 5

Today's pet dog descended from wolves—wild
animals that shared the same habitat as human
hunter-gatherers and, eventually, became
domesticated companions at about 7,000 BC.
There are a few theories that explain the change
from savage creature to complimentary intimate.
One hypothesis suggests that when humans took
in abandoned wolf cubs, inbreeding and a new
generation of domesticated animals followed.
Another theory posits that scavenging wolves
would find carrion that had been discarded
by humans, which lead them to approach the
unfamiliar beings. As they got nearer, they fought
their instinct to flee, and that trait was passed
along to their descendents, making them more
suited for domestication.

Along with the domestication of wolves came
physical changes to the tame canine such as a
smaller build, a more compact jaw along with
diminutive teeth as compared to their feral
counterparts, alterations in fur coloring and
markings; a smaller brain and subsequently a
decrease in cranial capacity which did not allow
room for certain instincts that are essential in the
wild.

In an attempt to recreate the domestication of
these mammals, Dmitry Belyaev commissioned
an experiment with wild silver foxes that were
discerningly bred over four decades and, therefore,
displayed amiability towards humans that they
previously had not possessed.

21. Which of the following can be inferred regarding
Dmitry Belyaev?

(A) He succeeded in domesticating wild silver
foxes.
(B) He is one of the premiere researchers into
wolf genetics.
(C) He took in abandoned silver fox cubs and
bred them for amiability.
(D) His experiment emphasized one particular
trait in the breeding of silver foxes.
(E) His experiment lured scavenging foxes into
human camps.

22. According to the passage, which of the following
is a characteristic of domestic dogs that is not
found in wolves?

(A) Domestic dogs do not hunt primarily for food.
(B) Domestic dogs have striped fur.
(C) Domestic dogs lack instincts necessary for
survival in the wild.
(D) Domestic dogs fight their natural instincts to
flee humans.
(E) Domestic dogs have large teeth.

23. Which of the following best describes the organization of the first paragraph?

(A) It presents two explanations for a particular phenomenon, and then evaluates them.
(B) It poses a question and then suggests a possible answer.
(C) It describes several characteristics of a particular phenomenon.
(D) It offers a resolution to a controversy.
(E) It presents two hypotheses for a particular occurrence.

24. The author of the passage most likely mentions inbreeding in the first paragraph in order to

(A) suggest one way in which wolves raised by humans might have had descendents who became domesticated
(B) explain how domesticated dogs came to have smaller teeth
(C) describe the domestication experiments of Belyaev
(D) suggest a cause for diminished brain capacity in wolves
(E) offer an explanation for the scavenging behavior of wolves

25. The author of the passage implies that which of the following is true of undomesticated wolves?

(A) They have smaller brains than do domesticated dogs.
(B) They have an instinct to flee from humans.
(C) They lack certain instincts that are essential for survival in the wild.
(D) They typically abandon their cubs.
(E) They have compact jaw lines and diminutive teeth.

Passage 6

For many years, scientists have recognized a number of symbiotic relationships that develop between human and animal species. Typically, these relationships have been categorized as mutualistic, parasitic, or commensal in the cases of wild animals, and domestication in the cases of livestock and companion animals. Recent studies, however, suggest that there should perhaps be another category to describe those creatures that seem able to settle within human societies, benefiting from certain human behaviors while nonetheless remaining wild.

In order to more fully comprehend this phenomenon, commonly referred to as synanthropy, a new breed of scientists has developed. Traditionally, the fields considered most prestigious and thus most likely to draw financial support have been those centering on exotic and endangered animals, or those animals actively used as labor, companionship, or food stock by humans.

Species that can be characterized as having a synanthropic relationship with humans, however, fall into neither category, as they tend to be both common and local. Ironically, it is those very species with which humans must interact on a daily basis. So perhaps it is fortuitous that, at long last, curious individuals have begun to study those species on a more serious basis. Urban wildlife, such as rats and pigeons, may not draw the admiring looks that a cassowary or koala do, but most people living in metropolitan areas will interact with the former on a regular basis while never seeing the latter outside of a zoo.

26. According to the passage, the word "synanthropy" could best be defined as

   (A) a mutually beneficial relationship between two species
   (B) occurring less commonly than do parasitism and commensalism
   (C) a popular and well-funded branch of urban zoology
   (D) one type of symbiosis that occurs between humans and animals
   (E) the antithesis of the more common category of domestication

27. The author of the passage refers to the cassowary in order to

   (A) contrast its exoticism with the more familiar figures of rats and pigeons
   (B) refute the claim that exotic animals cannot also have a symbiotic relationship with humans
   (C) draw a parallel between the plights of exotic animals in other countries with those in the United States
   (D) underscore the need to support funding to protect animals whether they be prolific or not
   (E) demonstrate one example of an animal that is both urbanized and yet still endangered

28. According to the passage, all of the following studies would traditionally be likely to receive funding EXCEPT

(A) an experiment designed to monitor milk production in dairy cows in order to better regulate vitamin dosages
(B) a survey of the population of aye-ayes, a rare type of lemur found primarily in the rainforests of Madagascar
(C) a research group dedicated to mapping the location of raccoon habitats against areas of high human population density
(D) a joint venture between an animal shelter and correctional facility designed to measure the effect of animal companionship on prisoners
(E) tagging endangered California condors at birth and following them for years in order to monitor birth and death rates

29. The author of the passage's attitude towards the study of urban wildlife could best be characterized as

(A) reasoned advocacy
(B) impassioned support
(C) scholarly neutrality
(D) hesitant optimism
(E) mild censure

30. The author of the passage would be most likely to agree with which of the following statements?

(A) The fact that an animal does not appeal to our aesthetic sensibilities or to our sense of responsibility does not indicate that the animal is not worthy of legitimate scholarship.
(B) Pigeons, like rats, may live within human society but they have never become fully incorporated into the ecosystem of the city, remaining, instead, perpetual outsiders.
(C) If scientists were willing to dedicate their time to less glamorous pursuits, humans would be better able to coexist with the many other living organisms found on the planet.
(D) The governments of the world have a responsibility to support scientific studies of the plants and animals found within that government's area of dominion.
(E) It is more important to study the animal species that share our immediate territory than it is to study those that we are likely to see only inside of zoos.

Check your answers on page 527.

BUSINESS DRILL

Passage 1

In recent years, the amount of money spent on advertising has skyrocketed. Expenditures on advertising totaled 40 billion dollars in 1970, 56 billion dollars in 1980, and a staggering 110 billion dollars by 1988, representing more than two percent of the gross national product of the United States. Furthermore, corporations are spending more and more money on design, display, packaging, and marketing. While exact figures are not available, conservative estimates indicate that in 1988 businesses spent at least as much on these areas as they did on advertising. Among advertisers, it has become accepted wisdom that in a highly competitive market, corporations must spend more and more money on researching target consumers, attractive packaging and display, and compelling promotional activities.

The prodigious amount of money spent on the sales effort has generated some negative consequences. Because of the oversaturation of the market and the struggle for consumers' limited attention, the recent trend has been towards the concentration of power in a small number of giant corporations. Problematically, the monopolization of media capital has led to a situation in which many of the key producers of consumer goods also control the media through which their products are advertised. These conglomerates tend to have limited interests, which results in a restriction of the types of media content and information delivered to the average media consumer.

The concentration of advertising power in the hands of a number of large corporations grants these leviathans a high degree of influence over popular culture and society. While it is traditionally assumed that mass media content is designed for consumers, it is perhaps more accurate to say that the media content is actually geared towards the needs of advertisers. Consider that in 1981, newspapers and magazines brought in 30 billion dollars from their advertisers and a mere 7 billion dollars from their customers. This disparity in income shows who in fact the purveyors of media content are truly beholden to.

1. Which of the following titles would be most appropriate for the passage?

(A) Advertisers and Consumers: An Examination of Their Complicated Relationship
(B) Mass Media and Corporate Interests: An Inherent Conflict
(C) Monopolization and Its Effect On The Advertising Industry
(D) Money and Advertising: The Rising Costs of Promoting Consumer Goods
(E) Concentrated Power and Advertising: Undesirable Consequences of a Modern Trend

2. According to the passage, it can be inferred that in 1988, the amount of money spent on the "sales effort"

(A) represented approximately four percent of the gross national product of the United States
(B) was expended primarily on packaging, display, market research, and promotional efforts
(C) was no more than twice the amount of money spent on similar activities in 1980
(D) can be determined to represent exactly two percent of the United States' gross national product
(E) demonstrates that mass media conglomerates are more concerned about advertisers' interests than consumers' interests

3. Based on information in the passage, it can be inferred that the author of the passage would be most likely to agree with which of the following statements?

(A) Advertisers have more control over popular culture than they have ever had in the past.
(B) One adverse result of the increase in advertising has been the limiting of knowledge available to the typical citizen.
(C) There are no positive consequences of the concentration of media capital.
(D) If companies spent less money on advertising and marketing, media monopolization would not occur.
(E) Media companies do not consider the interests of their customers.

4. The author of the passage most likely mentions that "newspapers and magazines brought in 30 billion dollars from their advertisers" in order to

(A) illustrate a paradoxical relationship in the advertising world
(B) criticize a commonly occurring business practice
(C) point   a problem with a long held supposition
(D) refute an assertion about how typical businesses generate profits
(E) support an argument about the profitability of the media sector

5. According to the passage, it can be inferred that advertisers

(A) mostly agree that a corporation must expend a large amount of money on the sales effort in order to stay competitive
(B) are unaware of the negative consequences that have resulted from increased spending on advertising
(C) predict that corporations will continue to spend a higher and higher percentage of their revenue on advertising
(D) have a more prominent role in media corporations than they have had in the past
(E) are responsible for restricting the amount of information available to consumers

Passage 2

In 1980, Michael Porter released the seminal book *Competitive Strategy: Techniques for Analysing Industries and Competitors*, which shared his work on techniques that businesses can use to achieve and maintain dominance in their respective markets. According to Porter, an engineer who later became an economist, differentiation, cost leadership, and market segmentation are the foremost generic strategies for dominating the market. Strategic scope and strategic strength are two additional variables to the equation and help define the terms under which the three previous conditions are to be analyzed. Porter contends that scope is considered a "demand-side" variable that illustrates the size and makeup of the desired market. On the other hand, strategic strength is deemed a "supply-side" factor as it addresses the competency of the company itself. To help others visualize his theory, Porter created a diagram that depicts the overlapping of these specifications.

In the concluding summary of his research, Porter points out that, surprisingly, companies with both high and low market share are both profitable; the companies that suffer most in that respect are those that fall in the middle. Porter explains that the companies with high market share are those that have utilized cost leadership while the companies with low market share have taken advantage of market segmentation to hone in on a small but financially rewarding niche. Companies in the middle range, however, inevitably are those that lack a generic strategy and, therefore, are not as profitable.

6. The main purpose of the passage is to

   (A) offer evidence of a recently emergent trend in business modeling
   (B) argue that utilization of cost leadership is the best indicator of profitability for a company
   (C) describe a business study and discuss one of its unexpected findings for companies
   (D) show how following Porter's strategies can create increased market share for companies
   (E) disprove the traditional belief that one must increase market share to be profitable

7. Which of the following may be inferred based upon the discussion of market share in the passage?

   (A) There is not necessarily a direct relationship between market share and profitability.
   (B) No company in the middle range of market share is profitable.
   (C) Companies with higher market share are the most profitable companies.
   (D) No company that is not profitable is not a company in either the high or low ranges of market share.
   (E) If a company pursues a strategy of cost leadership, then it will gain high market share.

8. According to the passage, what is the distinction between the variables of strategic strength and strategic scope?

(A) Strategic strength is a demand-side variable as it concerns the strength of interest for a good or service in the market while strategic scope is a supply-side variable as it concerns the size and complexity of the companies that respond to market demands.

(B) Strategic strength is a supply-side variable that focuses upon the aspects of the companies themselves that meet demand while strategic scope is a demand-side variable that addresses the make-up of the consumers of the goods and services supplied.

(C) Strategic strength is a more important variable for companies to consider than strategic scope as the former is internal to the company and thus controllable while the latter is external and thus more difficult for a company to control.

(D) Strategic scope is a more important variable for companies to consider than strategic strength as the characteristics of the company focused on by the latter are irrelevant if the company does not first consider the characteristics of the market within the former.

(E) Since it is a supply-side variable, strategic strength helps to define the terms under which differentiation, cost leadership, and market segmentation are to be analyzed while strategic scope, as a demand-side variable, does not.

9. Which one of the following is LEAST likely to be considered a supply-side variable?

(A) The ease of manufacture of the company's products
(B) The condition and quality of the company's facilities
(C) The productivity of the company's workforce
(D) The competitiveness of the company's industry
(E) The company's access to inexpensive resources

10. Which of the following, if true, would most undermine Porter's point in the second paragraph about companies with low market share?

(A) Many such companies also utilize cost leadership within their small but financially rewarding niche.
(B) Few such companies fail to take advantage of market segmentation.
(C) All such companies employ generic strategies at least as well as those with higher market share.
(D) Many such companies formerly had larger market share and have lost it due to failure to adapt to changes in demand-side variables.
(E) Porter's research excluded the majority of such companies since data on their profit-ability was unavailable.

Passage 3

A popular maxim in the business world states that leaders are supposed to "do the right thing" and managers are supposed to "do things right." There are a number of different management styles that can be effective; some managers rely on hard quantitative data, including detailed summaries of all business transactions and tables of numbers, while others focus more on qualitative data, such as reports from the field and recent trends in the financial world. Since the late 1960s, managers in the business world have had access to a new tool to aid them in decision-making. Advances in computer technology and modeling software led to the introduction of Data Support Systems (DSS). This new technology resulted from a combination of theoretical work carried out in the 1950s on how managers made decisions and technical innovations in computers systems achieved in the early 1960s. A wealth of literature has been produced on DSS since that time, detailing both practical applications and theoretical investigations into the subject.

Stephen Alter, an early innovator in the DSS field, outlined the three major characteristics of DSS. According to Alter, a DSS should be designed to facilitate the decision making process, to support rather than automate decisions, and to be able to quickly adapt to the changing needs of managers. Within this broad framework, programmers have developed a number of different data support systems. Some systems aid the manager by making a huge amount of data readily available. Others contain theoretical models pertaining to specific decision making scenarios. A data support system can be designed for managers who typically arrive at a decision independently or for those who wish to coordinate information among a number of individuals in order to arrive at a joint decision. A DSS can be more than just a simple tool for data mining or data warehousing. Advances in artificial intelligence capabilities have led to DSS that feature interactive query capabilities and are sophisticated enough to handle problems that are not clearly defined or clearly structured.

11. According to the passage, DSS have all of the following characteristics EXCEPT

   (A) application of theoretical models to specific problems
   (B) automation of the decision making process
   (C) provision of large amounts of information
   (D) facilitation of communication among managers
   (E) storage of data and information

12. The passage suggests which of the following about the introduction of DSS?

   (A) The development of DSS has radically changed the way managers make decisions.
   (B) At the time DSS was introduced, managers had few quantitative tools to aid in decision making.
   (C) The DSS was designed to help managers who relied mostly on quantitative analysis when making decisions.
   (D) The development of DSS would not have been possible prior to the 1960s.
   (E) Managers who use qualitative factors in decision making were not aided by the introduction of DSS.

13. Which of the following scenarios would most call for the use of a "sophisticated" DSS?

(A) A manager wishes to pinpoint which division in the company has the lowest sales figures.
(B) The manager of a marketing company needs to analyze a vast quantity of data on consumer spending habits.
(C) The manager of a sales company realizes that sales are down but is not sure of the cause.
(D) A manager wants to restructure the company and needs to find out which divisions can be eliminated.
(E) A manager wants to expand into a new market and needs a profile of potential consumers.

14. The passage provides support for which of the following statements?

(A) Managers who rely on qualitative judgments can be just as successful as those who rely on quantitative factors.
(B) Managers who employ DSS in their decision making process tend to be more successful than those who do not.
(C) A DSS will never be able to make decisions as well a human manager can.
(D) DSS are most effective when a manager is faced with a clearly defined problem that involves analyzing large amounts of data.
(E) The amount of literature produced on DSS has slowed since the early 1960s.

15. It can be inferred from the passage that all of the following are elements of effective decision making EXCEPT

(A) access to relevant information
(B) reliance on theoretical models
(C) incorporation of non-quantitative data
(D) coordination of actions among managers
(E) increased ease of communication

Passage 4

In most tourist towns in the United States, mom-and-pop businesses compete with larger, corporate conglomerates. On one side of the street, signs in the windows advertise that a souvenir store is family run, while the other side boasts of discount t-shirts with the city's name emblazoned on the front.

The competing approaches beg the question: What is the difference?

When studying both methods of operating a business, there are several factors to take into account. If one compares the relationship with the customer, mom-and-pops often prevail. Because they boast the benefit of forging a personal connection with their customers, travel guidebooks will often point out the family-operated stores so that tourists can participate in a distinctive experience. The larger stores often hire part-time staff who either do not live in the locale year-round and, therefore, do not embody the city's characteristic flavor or are not as personally invested in the products as an owner who started the company from the ground up.

However, a financial comparison can turn the tables in favor of the larger conglomerates. They can purchase in bulk and then slash prices, which is appealing to the average buyer. In addition, they can be more equipped to handle weighty expenses, such as taxes and liability insurance costs. When larger businesses are run by even more sizable corporations, the latter can spread its earnings and costs among several store locations and, therefore, average out any individual losses among the various sites.

16. The primary purpose of the passage is to

(A) explain a little-known discrepancy within business operations
(B) propose an alternative to the most common business model
(C) critique the methods of large conglomerates
(D) advocate more effective strategies for mom-and-pop businesses
(E) compare and contrast two different business approaches

17. The passage provides support for each of the following EXCEPT

(A) travel guidebooks can include retail information.
(B) some towns that do not attract tourists do not have mom-and-pop businesses.
(C) corporations can have higher average earnings than those generated by one of their stores.
(D) clothing can be decorated with regionally specific information.
(E) some consumers are attracted by lower prices.

18. Which of the following, if true, would best support the author of the passage's argument in the third paragraph?

(A) The owners of mom-and-pop stores started those stores.
(B) Part-time workers at any store rarely care about their store's products.
(C) Owners of stores usually live in the same town in which their stores are located.
(D) The owners of large conglomerates are personally invested in their products.
(E) Travel guidebooks never point out large conglomerates.

19. Which of the following can be inferred from the passage about large conglomerates?

(A) If an employee does not live in the locale of the store year-round, he or she does not embody the city's characteristics.
(B) If the owner started the company, that store will have as good a relationship with customers as do mom-and-pop stores.
(C) They can handle financial loss better than mom-and-pop stores can.
(D) They are usually run by even larger corporations.
(E) They are not mentioned in travel guidebooks.

20. The author of the passage implies which of the following about part-time staff who do not live in the store's locale year-round?

(A) They do not forge personal connections with their customers.
(B) They are not hired at mom-and-pop stores.
(C) They are not personally invested in the product.
(D) They do not embody the city's characteristic flavor.
(E) They represent the majority of employees at large conglomerates.

Passage 5

While Chester Barnard's assertions about management proved unconventional for the 1900s, they are sage guidelines that still remain relevant today. His book, <u>Functions of the Executive</u>, which was published in 1938, outlined a suggested corporate communication system and also set forth theories on authority and incentives.

His theory on authority depended on the direct report as well as the manager. Up until this time, certain schools of thought were focused on the actions of the higher-ranking employee; however, Barnard stressed that, in order to encourage a solid communication system, everyone had an equal part to play. In Barnard's view, the notion of authority is meaningless without a subordinate who responds accordingly. Therefore, it is the subordinate who determines the relationship, not the manager.

Another management tool that Barnard stressed, which is still applicable today, is found in his theory on incentives. He postulates that managers can use both economic incentives and persuasion to achieve their goal. Surprisingly, especially to those who value tangible rewards, his conviction is that persuasion is more powerful than material incentives. Barnard stresses that, despite the generic assumption, many employees would be delighted with nonmaterial rewards such as occasions for distinction, a pleasurable work atmosphere, and self-pride for one's labor. A study of today's most profitable companies would likely reveal that they employ much of Barnard's advice.

21. The primary purpose of the passage is to

(A) introduce a new perspective on business management
(B) propose an alternative interpretation of a classic business model
(C) critique the methods used by early management theorists
(D) discuss one author's theories on business management
(E) evaluate a proposed course of action

22. The passage suggests that which of the following is called into question by Barnard's theory on incentives?

(A) Work atmosphere is not a powerful incentive.
(B) Managers can use material incentives to achieve goals.
(C) Persuasion is correlated with self-pride for one's labor.
(D) Employees prefer occasions for distinction to a pleasurable work atmosphere.
(E) Many profitable companies rely on both material and persuasive incentives.

23. The author of the passage's attitude toward Chester Barnard's theories is best described as one of

(A) cautious endorsement
(B) respectful appreciation
(C) guarded disbelief
(D) wholehearted disapproval
(E) fanatical promotion

24. The passage suggests which of the following about Barnard's theory on authority?

(A) It focused on the actions of the manager.
(B) It depended more on the manager than on the subordinate.
(C) It viewed authority as necessary to a solid communication system.
(D) It placed as much importance on the role of subordinate as on the role of manager.
(E) It relied heavily on the schools of thought that preceded it.

25. The author of the passage implies that Barnard's guidelines are

(A) out-of-date in that they only apply to older corporations
(B) inaccurate in their description of material incentives
(C) relevant in today's corporate environment
(D) funded by profitable corporations
(E) too reliant on subordinate behavior

Passage 6

Although the Austrian school of economic thought, sometimes called the Vienna school, shares with neoclassical economics a focus on the actions of the individual actor, it distinguishes itself most from this more orthodox perspective with its influential Austrian Business Cycle Theory (ABCT).

ABCT represents an attempt by the school's theorists to explain the "boom and bust" cycle in modern economies. Proponents of the ABCT claim that economic recessions will not occur in a purely free market system because it is highly unlikely that a preponderance of business leaders and entrepreneurs will simultaneously engage in risky economic practices. Thus, economic downturns must instead result from unnatural interference with the economic system. The ABCT claims that this interference comes in the form of banks artificially manipulating interest rates. Economists from the Austrian school contend that banks, by creating new money, drive down interest rates, which fools investors into thinking that the supply of saved funds is larger than it actually is. This misapprehension of reality causes businesses and entrepreneurs to focus their energies on investment, which causes the economy to shift from emphasizing consumer goods to capital goods. For a short while, the economy booms. However, the investors soon find that their speculation was based on incorrect assumptions about the economy and has resulted in an increase in production for which there is no comparable demand from consumers. A recession then occurs as the economy attempts to correct itself after this period of wasteful investment.

ABCT has received a fair share of criticism. Most problematically, the theory requires businesspersons and entrepreneurs to continually act irrationally by making unsound investments during periods of low interest rates. However, ABCT and the Austrian school in general have remained influential in economic circles due to their emphasis on the time preferences of individuals. While neoclassical economists make use of the idea of time preferences in some economic analyses, the Austrian school makes time preferences a major focus of its theoretical investigations, leading to a number of interesting hypotheses about economic activities.

26. The author of the passage is primarily concerned with

(A) proposing a new theory of boom and bust cycles in economics
(B) questioning the validity of a discipline's theoretical focus
(C) drawing a key distinction between competing schools of economic thought
(D) providing an overview of a significant theory from an economic school
(E) contrasting two different theories about the nature of economic recessions

27. Which of the following statements about the Austrian school would the author most likely agree?

(A) It has generally been less influential than the neoclassical school in modern economics.
(B) Its theory on boom and bust cycles will eventually be falsified.
(C) Its focus on time preferences gives it an advantage over the neoclassical school of thought.
(D) It has been somewhat less conventional than has been the neoclassical school.
(E) Its theory of economic downturns is a more or less accurate description of reality.

28. It can be inferred from the passage that proponents of the ABCT believe that an economy in the midst of a recession

(A) would be characterized by artificially low interest rates
(B) must be subject to some form of market controls
(C) would be unlikely to recover unless banks raise interest rates
(D) would contain a high number of irrationally acting investors
(E) must correct itself by emphasizing the production of consumer goods

29. According to the passage, a major difference between the Austrian school and the neoclassical school is the Austrian school's

(A) focus on the actions of the individuals in the economic system
(B) attempt to explain an economy's boom and bust cycles
(C) emphasis on historical factors in its economic analyses
(D) endorsement of a purely free market economy
(E) ascription of irrational behavior to economic actors

30. It can be inferred from the passage that the author of the passage regards the ABCT as

(A) an interesting, though fatally flawed, theory of economic activity
(B) a theory that has not received its proper due from more mainstream economists
(C) a theory that lacks empirical support for its major assumptions about the actions of investors
(D) a more successful theory of economic cycles than those offered by the neoclassical school
(E) a theory that has managed to affect the thinking of other economists despite its flaws

40. It can be inferred that the critics mentioned in the final paragraph believed the excellent results of the two experiments had less to do with the innate decision-making of the subjects than with

(A) the excellent decision-making of Evanston and Cramer
(B) the expertise of Malcolm Gladwell, who originated the theory
(C) not choosing candidates who "looked the part"
(D) the use of videotape as a method of choosing candidates
(E) their unconscious use of visual stereotypes in making their selections

Check your answers on page 527.

For additional practice problems, log on to your online Student Tools and complete the Mixed Drill found there.

Reading
Comprehension
Answers and
Explanations

ANSWER KEY

Social Science		Humanities		Natural Sciences		Business	
1.	C	1.	C	1.	A	1.	E
2.	C	2.	A	2.	E	2.	A
3.	B	3.	D	3.	B	3.	B
4.	C	4.	B	4.	A	4.	C
5.	D	5.	E	5.	D	5.	A
6.	E	6.	E	6.	C	6.	C
7.	C	7.	C	7.	D	7.	A
8.	A	8.	D	8.	D	8.	B
9.	A	9.	B	9.	A	9.	D
10.	C	10.	A	10.	D	10.	E
11.	A	11.	D	11.	B	11.	B
12.	C	12.	C	12.	B	12.	D
13.	E	13.	A	13.	C	13.	C
14.	D	14.	E	14.	E	14.	A
15.	B	15.	C	15.	D	15.	D
16.	C	16.	D	16.	B	16.	E
17.	A	17.	A	17.	E	17.	B
18.	D	18.	E	18.	C	18.	A
19.	C	19.	C	19.	D	19.	C
20.	B	20.	B	20.	D	20.	D
21.	E	21.	B	21.	D	21.	D
22.	D	22.	E	22.	C	22.	A
23.	C	23.	A	23.	E	23.	B
24.	C	24.	D	24.	A	24.	D
25.	C	25.	C	25.	B	25.	C
				26.	D	26.	D
				27.	A	27.	D
				28.	C	28.	B
				29.	A	29.	C
				30.	A	30.	E

EXPLANATIONS

Social Science

1. **C** The sentence that is mentioned refers to the rising interest rates attached to some student loans and comes immediately after the sentence that mentioned rising housing costs. Both refer back to the first sentence in the second paragraph, suggesting that the effects of the sub-prime crisis reach much farther than the mortgage industry. Therefore, the problem with student loans is another example of a problem outside the realm of housing. Choice (A) is incorrect because the author is troubled by the rising interest rates but does not call them unreasonable. Choice (B) is incorrect because the passage makes no attempt to make the problem seem less severe. Choice (C) correctly identifies the problem with interest rates to the earlier point about general problem. Choice (D) is incorrect because it reverses the causality—the comment regarding potentially lowered college graduation rates supports the claim that this is a serious problem, not the other way around. Choice (E) is incorrect because the rising cost of housing serves as a fellow example of the widespread nature, not the result of the rising interest rates.

2. **C** The tone of the passage is clearly not positive, as the words *unfortunately*, *mess*, *tragic*, and *crisis* all indicate. Eliminate (D), since it's positive. Choice (A) is incorrect because the passage isn't *frenzied*—it includes facts and data without getting too emotional. Choice (B) is incorrect because the author comes across as sad more than scornful. Choice (E) has the same problem—there's no evidence for the passage being disdainful.

3. **B** The passage mentions the issue of blame in the first paragraph. First, it states that finding someone to blame is very important to a lot of people right now. It then suggests that finding the person to blame might not be possible, then asks if finding anyone to blame would really matter. That suggests that the author does not believe that it is necessary. Choice (A) is incorrect because the passage does not lay the blame at anyone's doorstep. Choice (B) is promising, because it recognizes the author's unwillingness to identify a culprit and belief that doing so is unnecessary. Choice (C) is incorrect because, while the passage does connect the housing crisis with international problems, it does not claim that the lending problems were the sole cause of the dollar's weakness. Choice (D) incorrectly connects this section about who is to blame with the concluding section about college attendance. Choice (E) again incorrectly identifies a specific culprit, which the passage does not do.

4. **C** The word *peaked* in the second paragraph is used to describe *the cost of student loans* and the passage gives that the cost is *three times as high as the rates from a mere six years ago* and that the peak was *sharp*. Therefore, a good phrase to describe the word *peaked* is "sharply rose in cost." Choice (A) contains outside knowledge with the phrase *only to descend again*, so eliminate (A). Eliminate (B) as the higher prices of student loans are not considered a *precedent for future valuations*. Choice (C) is a good paraphrase of "sharply rose in cost" so keep it. Choice (D) is another appeal to outside knowledge and does not match with "sharply rose in cost" so eliminate it. Choice (E) is a reversal of when the passage states the rising cost of tuition is unlikely to *come to the attention of those at the highest levels* and is a poor match to describe *peaked*, so it can be eliminated. The correct answer is (C).

5. **D** The easiest way to approach this is to check each of the answers against the first paragraph. There aren't really any comparisons so there can't be a metaphor, which eliminates (A). There is a list of nouns but no list of adjectives, so eliminate (B). Although the tone of the passage is unhappy, no one is really being attacked, so you can eliminate (C). There does appear to be a question at the end, so (D) looks good. And finally, although the passage itself does try to combine some ideas, the first paragraph really doesn't, eliminating (E).

6. **E** This is a primary purpose question which must be answered by considering the entire passage. The first paragraph states *But while scientists agree that there is some sort of initial framework present in the minds of children through which observations about the outside world are filtered and then interpreted, there is considerable disagreement over how to characterize and describe these structures.* The next two paragraphs then detail two possible ways of describing the structures. Choice (A) is incomplete because two theories are discussed, not one. Choice (B) doesn't work because neither theory is proved correct. Choice (C) is incorrect because no resolution is reached; neither theory is endorsed by the author. Choice (D) can be eliminated because it doesn't even mention the two theories.

7. **C** According to the second paragraph, one theory holds that children possess *abstractions of common events* which can be used to *draw conclusions about the outside world.* The sample principle given is *if something is not supported, it falls* so the correct answer will be close to this type of principle. Choice (A) is incorrect because the conclusion does not follow from the principle, so eliminate it. Choice (B) is also incorrect because the conclusion does not follow from the principle, so eliminate it. Choice (C) is the correct answer because the principle is that some objects are heavier than others, and the conclusion is that some stones will be lighter and some will be heavier, which follows directly from the principle. Choice (D) doesn't work because the principle is again about objects falling, but the conclusion is about using force to break something. Choice (E) is incorrect because the conclusion does not follow from the principle, so eliminate it.

8. **A** The answer to this question is near where the author discusses *basic theories* in the third paragraph. The author states *These theories restrict both the type and number of viable inferences a child makes about the world, although these initial theories may then be amended by culturally acquired knowledge.* Choices (B) and (D) are not mentioned in the passage, while Choice (E) contradicts the passage. Choice (C) is a trap because the author says the theories *may* be amended, but they do not have to be. The theories may be changed and are therefore not immutable; the correct answer is (A).

9. **A** This question asks why the author makes a particular statement. To answer it, read the third paragraph. The author describes the theory, stating that *These theories restrict both the type and number of viable inferences a child makes about the world....* Next, the author gives the results of an experiment used to support this theory. The question asks about certain shapes that the children didn't mention, which supports the author's earlier assertion that the theories *restrict both the type and number of viable inferences a child makes about the world.* None of the other choices is supported by the passage. While (E) might seem tempting, the author does not go so far as to suggest that further research in this area is needed.

10. **C** Use POE on this question. The author doesn't come out in favor of one theory or the other, so eliminate (A). Choice (B) sounds tempting, but there is nothing in the passage to support this firm assertion. Choice (D) goes too far; the author mentions that Descartes' idea was incorrect, but that is not the same as saying philosophical views in general must be replaced. Choice (E) is also not supported, as the author doesn't present any opinion as to which mechanism is correct. In the first paragraph, the author states *Recent investigations into how children acquire knowledge about the outside world have produced agreement on one point.* This agreement concerns the presence of *some sort of initial framework…in the minds of children.* Thus, the correct answer is (C).

11. **A** The second paragraph discusses the circumstances of the Chrysler bailout. Choice (A) adequately expresses this. Although the passage does mention management, the second paragraph covers more than management strategies, so (B) should be eliminated. The passage does not necessarily view the bailout favorably, so (C) is out. The author does not argue against bailouts in general, so (E) is out too. To say that the bailout failed is too extreme, so eliminate (D).

12. **C** The last sentence of the first paragraph contains the main idea of the passage—note the *But*, which indicates that it contradicts the previous sentence. The piece does not make a broader argument against federal bailouts, nor does it dispute that Chrysler is now a successful company, so (A) and (E) are out. Choice (D) is far too broad (the passage only discusses the Chrysler example) and the author does not state that the bailout is a failure, so eliminate (B).

13. **E** The passage does not say anything about the current state of the Ford Motor Company in the passage, so (A) and (B) are out. Although the loans Ford received were at a higher rate of interest, you don't know that Ford was handicapped in the early 1980s. Eliminate (D). You also know nothing from the passage about Ford's challenges in the 1980s, so eliminate (C). The passage says *The Ford Motor Company, by contrast, was in better shape than Chrysler at the time….* Choice (E) is a good paraphrase of this.

14. **D** The author's opinion of the bailout is somewhat negative, so the bailout would not be a good model; eliminate (A). Although the author's opinion is somewhat negative, both (B) and (C) are too strong, so they're out. You don't know what impact the decision had on Ford, so eliminate (E). The first and last paragraphs make the case that the bailout was more costly than was suggested.

15. **B** There is no statement in the passage about the ongoing costs of intervention, so eliminate (A). Choice (B) is a good completion of the ideas expressed in the final paragraph. There is no comparison in the passage between the gains and costs, so eliminate (C). The passage does not argue for or against such bailouts, so both (D) and (E) are too strong.

16. **C** The first paragraph introduces Jane Jacobs's ideas and mentions that those ideas were often ignored, perhaps to the detriment of the cities. The second paragraph, however, describes one attempt to incorporate her ideas in a part of Los Angeles. Choice (A) incorrectly identifies the second paragraph as generalization, instead of a specific example. Choice (B) is too strong—the author of the passage ends by commenting that it's still too early to know if this plan will work. Choice (D) is

also too strong—the author is not rebutting the planners. Choice (E) is too personal—the passage isn't trying to tell anyone what ought to happen.

17.   **A**   The author refers to The Grove as one example of an attempt to incorporate some of Jacobs's ideas into modern urban planning. Although the shopping area is described in generally positive terms, the author is still uncertain as to whether this created community will function in the intended way. Choice (B) incorrectly refers to the development as successful, even though the passage specifically states that the result of the experiment is still unknown. Choice (C) incorrectly associates The Grove, an example of Jacobs's style of planning, with the problematic planning mentioned in the first paragraph. Choice (D) is incorrect because the passage does not claim that The Grove is trying to rely on the success of nearby attractions. Choice (E) is too strongly negative—the author is uncertain as to whether the center will be a success, but there's no evidence that she finds it suspect.

18.   **D**   The first paragraph of the passage explains Jacobs's basic theory and then contrasts that with some of the more problematic developments from the past. In the second paragraph, the passage focuses on one development that appears to adhere more closely to Jacobs's ideals, though the author expresses some uncertainty about whether or not it will work. Choice (A) is incorrect because, while the author does seem to admire Jacobs, nothing in the passage suggests a call to arms, nor does it focus on zoning issues. Choice (B) incorrectly focuses on the misguided urban planners instead of Jacobs. Choice (C) is incorrect because it doesn't address the changing ideas at all. Choice (D) most accurately captures the passage as a whole, mentioning both the problems from the past and the possible new approach from the second paragraph. Choice (E) is incorrect because it focuses solely on the potential problems.

19.   **C**   The urban planners of the sixties and seventies, according to the passage, sought to create communities that were *orderly, efficient utopias*. In order to do so, they separated residential, commercial, and industrial zones. The Grove, on the other hand, is an example of the Jacobs-influenced type of planning that is becoming more popular. Therefore, the planners would probably worry that this new development would be a disorderly, inefficient non-utopia, since it violates all the rules that they felt were necessary. Choice (A) incorrectly has the planners supporting the development. Choice (B) incorrectly relates the planners' concerns to the proximity of the Farmer's Market instead of the mixture of different kinds of spaces. Choice (C) correctly identifies the planners' concerns, commenting on the mixture of establishments and possibility for disorganization. Choice (D) supports the development, while you need an answer that does not. Choice (E) incorrectly attributes Jacobs's fears about other developments to the planners.

20.   **B**   Inference questions require proof in the passage. The passage states that *the theories of the urban planning movements of the sixties and seventies…attempted to create orderly, efficient utopias, but neglected the human element, which many…feel…is one of the major causes of…urban decay.* Choice (A) is a memory trap, referring to Jacobs's ideas, and cannot be supported as something the other planners *did not attempt.* Choice (B) is supported by the passage, since areas impacted by *urban*

decay do not match the intended *utopias*. Choice (C) is unsupported, as the passage draws no such comparison between the amount of urban decay that *would have existed* without the theories. Choice (D) is unsupported recycled language, as the passage does not provide any information about the nature of the *Farmer's Market.* Choice (E) is too extreme to be supported, as the contrast between Jacobs's ideas and the theories of the sixties and seventies focuses on the methods of *urban planning,* and some results of the theories may have been enjoyable and safe.

21.   **E**   The passage gives a brief description of the pigeon's place in recent human history and then goes on to contrast that with modern perspectives of the birds. Choice (A) goes too far—the author doesn't give any indication of believing the pigeon to be noble. Choice (B) focuses too specifically on a side comment in the second paragraph. Choice (C) also focuses too specifically on a side comment—the passage is not primarily about disease. Choice (D) is too strong—the passage isn't really promoting any specific action. Choice (E) remains neutral and informational, as does the passage.

22.   **D**   The Almond Tumbler is described as a breed of pigeon that was very popular during the Victorian era. The passage also mentions that the selective breeding used to create that particular kind of bird also led to tiny beaks that kept parent birds from feeding their babies. Therefore, the best analogy would be another animal that is popular even though it has problems due to its design. Choice (A) is incorrect because it leaves out the aspect of popularity. Choice (B) is only positive and you need something that's also negative. Choice (C) is not about something that has been bred for a specific purpose, nor does it deal with popularity. Choice (D) correctly refers to a popular animal with a common health problem. Choice (E) does not refer to pigeons that have been bred by humans.

23.   **C**   The task of this question is to apply *statements about Darwin* to something that would *improve the popular view of pigeons today,* which is *a lack of esteem for that which is* [widespread]. Regarding Darwin, the passages states that he found pigeons *to be more fascinating than he had formerly believed,* so the credited response should show some element of how Darwin's opinion changed that could change the current negative view of pigeons, which is based on their widespread presence. Choice (C) is the credited response because it shows how *familiarity* can be applied to finding *value in aspects...that...would never have* [been] *noticed.* Choice (A)'s reference to evolution contains outside information about Darwin that would not be likely to change opinions about pigeons. Choice (B)'s extreme statement about the *superior...value* of *messenger...pigeons* is also unlikely to change opinions. While treating *all living things with great esteem* is tempting and recycles the word *esteem* from the passage, (D) can be eliminated because it does not provide a way to address a view of pigeons based on their widespread presence. Choice (E) can also be eliminated because the recycled language *peace, plenty, and prosperity* fails to address the current view about pigeons.

24.   **C**   The last part of the passage discusses some of the author's thoughts on why pigeons have become unpopular. It suggests that *[p]erhaps it is just a problem of population density, a lack of esteem for that which is ubiquitous.* In other words, there are just too many pigeons living right around people for the animals to seem exotic and interesting. Choice (A) refers to the earlier comment linking pigeons to World War II. The passage did not, however, mention whether or not the pigeons were

successful. Choice (B) refers to the earlier discussion of the Almond Tumbler whose genetic problems did not, however, seem to deter Victorian fanciers. Choice (D) refers to pigeons spreading disease. Although the passage refers to this belief obliquely, nowhere does it come out and state whether or not the author believes this to be true. Choice (E) may be plausible, but it's not supported by the passage. The last line states that people do view pigeons in this light, but does not attribute this as a cause of the common prejudice. Choice (C) is the closest match to what the passage actually says.

25. **C** The word *fancier* is used in the following sentence: *Darwin himself became a pigeon fancier after beginning to work with the humble Columba livia, discovering them to be more fascinating than he had formerly believed.* The passage then goes on to discuss the widespread popularity of pigeon breeding during the Victorian era. Therefore, the author is using Darwin's personal interest to introduce the broader topic of the Victorian fascination with the pigeon. Choice (A) incorrectly focuses on *ornately decorated possessions* in general, rather than on pigeons specifically. Choice (B) incorrectly describes a negative opinion of the scientific community of the time; the passage never indicates that the author has strongly negative feelings about Victorian scientists. Choice (C) mentions Darwin's interest in connection with the passage's discussion of the widespread Victorian interest in pigeons; keep it. Choice (D) incorrectly focuses on the *plumage*, or feathers, of the pigeon and compares it favorably to that of other birds. The passage does not support that comparison. Choice (E) is too strong—nothing in the passage indicates that Darwin was obsessed with pigeons in general, much less with the Almond Tumbler, which is mentioned at a later point in the passage.

Humanities

1. **C** This question asks for the primary purpose of the passage, so the right answer should encompass the entire passage. In the first paragraph, the author mentions a few problems with history texts, and then states that the major problem is the textbook authors' *philosophical approach* to history. The second paragraph then describes this approach and why it is problematic. Choice (A) is incorrect because although the author mentions a solution at the end of the second paragraph, this is not the primary purpose. Also, there are not multiple *solutions* mentioned. Choice (B) doesn't work because the author isn't debunking anything; he is exposing a problem with a perspective. Also, nothing in the passage supports the idea that the viewpoint is *long held*. Choice (D) is incorrect because the author makes an argument of his own and does not respond to one. Choice (E) is incorrect because no evaluation is offered. Choice (C) best describes the purpose of the passage and is therefore the correct answer.

2. **A** In the lines referenced, the author states *Part of the problem lies in the publishers' desire to construct a book that appeals to as many regional markets as possible.* Thus, the pressure is to *appeal to as many regional markets as possible.* Choice (B) is incorrect because it contradicts the passage—many of the facts lack historical relevance. Choice (C) is not mentioned, and while (D) is listed as a problem, it is not a *pressure* faced by publishers. Choice (E) is incorrect because the publishers want to appeal

to a large number of regions, not a particular region. Choice (A) is about this pressure and is therefore the correct answer.

3. **D** To answer this question, read the second paragraph to see what the author indicates is problematic about the *philosophical approach*. The following lines explain the nature of the author's complaint: *textbook authors decide to craft a simple narrative around certain historical events at the expense of the true complexities of history. By treating history as a series of settled facts instead of a sequence of ongoing debates and interpretations, textbook authors do a great disservice to both their students and the educational process. In their quest to portray history as a story, textbook authors have unwittingly deprived the subject of some of its most vibrant and interesting aspects.* The only choice that matches this information is (D), making it the correct answer.

4. **B** Look for the parts of the passage where the author discusses high school history textbooks. Right in the beginning, the author states, *Mass market history textbooks suffer from a number of deficiencies. Even with judicious editing and some stunning omissions, the typical high school history textbook is over one thousand pages long.* Choice (A) mentions length, but the author never discusses textbooks of the past, so eliminate it. Choice (C) is incorrect because the author says the books exhibit *judicious editing.* No other textbooks are mentioned, so (D) is not supported. The passage states that *most* textbooks treat the discovery in a certain way, but not all. This makes (E) too extreme. Because the author states that the books have *stunning omissions*, some significant details must have been left out, making (B) the correct answer.

5. **E** In the last paragraph, the author states, *By treating history as a series of settled facts instead of a sequence of ongoing debates and interpretations, textbook authors do a great disservice to both their students and the educational process. In their quest to portray history as a story, textbook authors have unwittingly deprived the subject of some of its most vibrant and interesting aspects.* This implies that treating history as a series of debates and open questions could make history more vibrant and interesting. Choice (A) is incorrect because the author doesn't believe that history should be taught as a story. Nothing in the passage supports (B) or (C) at all. Choice (D) is incorrect because, although the passage states that students can reach their own conclusions about history, it doesn't say that these conclusions will be more *accurate*. Only (E) refers to the possibility of making history more interesting, so (E) is the correct answer.

6. **E** The passage states that literature, though an apparently simple concept, is in fact a divisive one about which there is no consensus. Choice (A) may be true, but misses the point that even today people cannot define it. Choice (B) is close, but too strong since the passage only states that it *may* be impossible to define, not that it never will be defined. Choice (C) is unsupported; there is no evidence that scholars have not thought about it. Choice (D) is unsupported; this is only the view of Imam Ja'far al-Sadiq, not necessarily of the author.

7. **C** The passage states that some consider cave paintings literature and others do not. Choice (A) is not supported by the passage as some do consider them literature. Choice (B) is also not supported as the passage never states for how long they have been considered literature. Choice (D) may be true, but it is extreme and not related to the discussion of cave paintings. Choice (E) is not related to cave paintings.

8. **D** Roman Jakobson states that literature imposes a structure upon *unstructured, conversational* words, while Imam Ja'far al-Sadiq merely states that literature is a veil draped over words; thus, Jakobson believes that language has identifiable characteristics while Imam Ja'far al-Sadiq believes that the only thing that makes something literature is the label *literature*. Choice (A) is unsupported because Imam Ja'far al-Sadiq does not believe that there is one thing called *literature* and Jakobson argues that literature is defined by structure. Choice (B) is unsupported because neither discusses literature as being fundamentally ugly. Choice (C) is too strong because neither suggests that literature is dangerous. Choice (E) is unsupported because neither expresses an opinion of banned books.

9. **B** The passage offers definitions of literature such as writing that has been offered as literature, application of organization to ordinary speech, or narratives. Choice (A) is a narrative. Choices (C) and (E) are offered as literature. Choice (D) is ordinary speech that has been organized and structured.

10. **A** The passage states that some people do not consider banned books literature because they are not universally appreciated. Choice (A) fits with this. Choice (B) may seem quite tempting, but is unsupported because the passage does not attribute this viewpoint to the author. Choice (C) is unsupported because the author does not argue for a reevaluation of *Go Ask Alice*. Choice (D) is unsupported because *Go Ask Alice* is offered as an example of a book that is not considered literature. Choice (E) is unsupported because that *Go Ask Alice* is not related to Jakobson's theory of literature being organized ordinary speech.

11. **D** The author mentions that Spinoza was exiled from the Jewish community *due to heterodox ideas* before discussing the fact that Spinoza was again effectively exiled from Dutch society as an adult, for the same kinds of unusual ideas. Choice (A) is an emotional appeal as well as an appeal to outside knowledge. While it is a common practice for someone exiled from a religious group to *condemn… for their intolerant views*, this is not the purpose of including that piece of information in the text, so eliminate it. Choice (C) is incorrect because it contrasts Spinoza's two experiences when in fact they are described as similar. Choice (B) brings up Spinoza's family and an inheritance, neither of which was mentioned in the passage. Choice (E) goes too far; although the passage refers to Spinoza living in isolation, it does not say that his isolation was complete.

12. **C** The passage asks: *What was the cause of the French Revolution if not a changing view of the hierarchical system of medieval French society?* As a rhetorical question, this is intended to support the previous comments claiming that novel ideas once had the power to overthrow a society. To support this claim, the correct answer needs to assert that this is so. Choice (A) might look appealing but it relies solely on the post-facto claims of people. Choice (B) might also look good at first, but it

also relies on the claims of individuals, made after the end of the French Revolution. Choice (C), the correct answer, instead links action previous to the French Revolution to events that took place during the fighting, and connects both to the promotion of new ideas. Choice (D) brings up Spinoza and, while he may be the primary topic of the passage, he's not really relevant to the causes of the French Revolution. Choice (E) incorrectly refers to ideas in modern day France, which doesn't really relate directly to the French Revolution.

13.   A   Begin to address this question by determining what the passage states about *Spinoza's experience with members of Dutch society*, which is that *Spinoza found himself…reviled…by prominent members of Dutch society*, leading to one of the *imposed periods of solitude* the passage references. Thus, (A) is supported, since an *imposed…solitude* is *more than* an *emotional* [consequence]. While the passage refers to *exile*, it does not say who was responsible for the exile, so (B) can be eliminated for insufficiently linking these two ideas. The passage compares *Spinoza's treatment by members of Dutch society* with *his youth* in order to draw a comparison about the way Spinoza was treated, so the memory trap in (C) cannot be supported as the passage does not state that his treatment *reminded him of his youth*. While the passage supports that Spinoza's ideas were not well received in *Dutch society*, it would be extreme to state the opposite, that people believed *natural objects were unrelated*, so eliminate (D). Choice (E) presents an unsupported memory trap because saying that Spinoza was *reviled* does not indicate that he tried to *blend in*.

14.   E   The passage is basically just a quick summary of who Spinoza is and what happened to him, so the main idea needs to stick to that. Choice (A) is rather too strong for the wording of this passage, which is more academic than anything else. Choice (B) incorrectly focuses on Dutch society instead of Spinoza. Choice (C) incorrectly focuses on the French Revolution. Choice (D) focuses on the idea mentioned in the opening line, used more to introduce the philosophers than anything else.

15.   C   The passage is fairly neutral, though the author makes her admiration for Spinoza clear when she refers to him as a *brilliant man*. Choice (D) is negative, while (B) and (E) are too mild—the author isn't neglecting Spinoza and her support isn't *tepid*. Choice (A), on the other hand, is too strong—the author does like Spinoza, but the passage isn't strongly worded enough to merit the description of *unmitigated adoration*.

16.   D   The passage states, just before the line in question, that *most critics agree that she was in fact an immensely talented singer of the first degree* and then goes on to explicitly state that (*s*)*uch talent is truly undeniable, no matter what the personality of the performer*. Thus, the operas mentioned are intended to support that author's claim regarding Callas's talent, without regard to her personality. Choice (A) incorrectly links Callas's ability to perform a wide range of pieces with her temperament, something that the passage does not do. Choice (B) goes too far—the author never extends judgment to other singers in this passage. Choice (C) incorrectly refers to Callas's peers—although this statement could be true, it is not supported by the passage, which only mentioned modern critics. Choice (E) goes too far—although Callas is described as versatile, nowhere does it state that she was the most versatile.

17. **A** The critics of Callas, according to the passage, claimed that her voice was *inherently flawed* while the author of the passage believes that Callas's wide-ranging abilities demonstrate her brilliance. If the critics wanted to support their claims, the best thing they could do is explain exactly why Callas's voice was flawed. Choice (B) focuses on Callas' personality, rather than her voice, which is the topic under discussion. Choice (C) would go against the author's claims, but it simply disagrees without providing any support other than an opposing opinion. It also fails to address the critics' initial claims regarding Callas's voice. Choice (D) incorrectly focuses on whether or not there are thematic differences between the two operas under discussion instead of on Callas's actual vocal ability. Choice (E) addresses the scandals rather than the vocal ability.

18. **E** Although the author is clearly a fan of Maria Callas, she is also careful to at least acknowledge some of the criticisms of the performer. Therefore, the correct answer will be positive but not excessively so. Choices (A) and (C) are not positive and can immediately be discarded. Choice (B) is incorrect because the passage is not really reminiscing about anything. Choice (D) is a bit too strong, leaving (E) as the correct answer.

19. **C** The passage starts out by stating that those who believe that focusing on famous scandals is somehow a new development are incorrect. It then goes on to discuss Maria Callas as an example of a celebrity from the past who was as well-known for her scandals as her talent. Choice (A) includes a synthesis, which never really takes place. Choice (B) does not address the change of focus. Choice (D) incorrectly refers to multiple opposing examples. Choice (E) refers to an argument based on emotion, which is not present.

20. **B** Choice (A) incorrectly identifies Callas as a prototypical example, something that the passage never mentions. Choice (C) takes the attribute identified with Callas (the ability to sing a wide-range of pieces) and incorrectly applies it to all top singers, an application that the passage does not support. Choice (D) goes too far—although the author clearly states that Callas' talent outweighs any claims regarding her personality, nowhere does that passage assert that the personality of the performer is therefore irrelevant. Choice (E) mentions people unfamiliar with opera, while the passage does not.

21. **B** The main idea of the passage is that the quote Adair used did not, as some historians have interpreted it, imply that over-concentrated settlement lead to the decline of the Cherokee. Choice (B) best expresses this. There is no mention of Adair's critics in the passage, so (A) cannot be correct. Choice (C) may be true based on the second paragraph, but it is not the main idea of the passage. Cartographical data is used as evidence that wars, not over-settlement, caused the demise of the Cherokee, but it is a detail in the passage, not its main idea, so (D) can be eliminated. Similarly, (E) is suggested at the end of the passage, but it is used to support the main idea of the passage.

22. **E** Nowhere in the passage is it suggested Native Americans are pacifist, so the final sentence cannot counter that idea, so you can eliminate (A). The author's issue with the timeline is when in Adair's 40 years with the Cherokee did he obtain the quote about settlement patterns, but the wars don't help to resolve that issue, so (B) cannot be correct. The author suggests it was war rather than resource depletion that caused the demise of the Cherokee, but not that war caused them to settle in

towns far from each other, so (C) is probably not the correct answer. Nothing in the passage suggests an assignment of blame for the French and Indian wars, or for anything for that matter, so eliminate (D). For (E), the *historians' misinterpretation of Adair's quote* is that it reflected a change in Cherokee settlement policy after they had witnessed the beginning of their decline. The author's alternative hypothesis is that they had settled in that manner since before the beginning of the decline, and that the decline was brought about by the French and Indian wars. So the notion that the French and Indian wars were the primary cause of the decline supports the author's alternative hypothesis.

23.   **A**   Choice (A), in accord with the terms *insight* and *expert* in the first paragraph, would be a good description of the author's attitude towards Adair. The tone of the passage is academic, so (B) is too extreme. The author thinks that a group of historians that misinterpreted Adair's quote made an error, but not Adair himself, so you can eliminate (C). Nothing in passage suggests hostility or disrespect, so neither (D) nor (E) is correct.

24.   **D**   The statement that the French and Indian wars caused the Cherokee's decline comes in the first sentence of the final paragraph. The evidence is in the last sentence of the same paragraph: *...carefully examining cartographical data...[led to the conclusion that] Cherokee society must have flourished until the French and Indian wars....*

25.   **C**   The purpose of the passage is to combat the idea that the quote supports the notion that close settlement brought about the demise of the Cherokee, so (A) is incorrect. The author seems to generally value Adair's work; there is nothing to suggest she thinks Adair could not have understood anything, so (B) can be eliminated. Choice (C) highlights the contrast between the passage's author and the historians she takes issue with. The other historians interpret the quote to mean that the Cherokee had recently realized a former manner of settlement was unsustainable, so they changed in a futile attempt to survive. The author suggests that their settlement pattern did not change—what did change was the arrival of the French and Indian wars. Keep this choice. For (D), in this case, it appears difficult to determine the exact time of the quote, but to say that it is impossible is an overgeneralization. The author suggests that other historians have misinterpreted the quote that Adair got, not Adair himself, so (E) is incorrect.

Natural Sciences

1.   **A**   Check each of the answers against the passage to see which one is not mentioned or is untrue. Choice (A) is mentioned in the first paragraph, but as part of a list of mistaken beliefs about the hyena. Hold on to this choice. Choice (B) is true—the second paragraph describes hyenas as living *in packs led by a matriarch*, or dominant female. Eliminate it. Choice (C) is also true—*mandibular* is just another word for the jaw, and the passage definitely commented on the hyena's impressive jaw strength. Choice (D) is true—the beginning lines referred to the famous *laugh* of the hyena that some people mistook for *the cries of lost souls*. Choice (E) is also true—the second paragraph mentions the hyena's ability to run at high speeds for both short and prolonged periods.

2. **E**   The task of this question is to *undermine* the argument that *in the case of the hyena, appearances can certainly be deceiving*. This argument is a contrast between the appearance and reality of the hyena, so the credited response needs to show a weakening of that contrast. Choice (A) fails to weaken the argument because it only applies the argument to *other animals*, rather than weaken the application to the hyena. Choice (B) strengthens the argument by providing another way in which the hyena has a deceptive appearance. Choice (C) may at first appear tempting as it compares the hyena to animals that may be more impressive in some manner, but it can be eliminated since it fails to weaken the contrast between the hyena's appearance and reality. Choice (D) may at first appear tempting since it refers to *people who…concur that hyenas are fearsome*, but can be eliminated because [observing] *a hyena attack* may be the cause of their opinion, not a lack of contrast between the hyena's appearance and reality. Choice (E) weakens the argument, because it indicates that *people* who do not already have the belief that hyenas are *comical* see the animal as *intimidating*.

3. **B**   Check each answer against the passage to see which one is best supported. Choice (A) goes too far—the passage says that the hyena is powerful, and that it is one of nature's fiercest predators, but it does not say it is the absolute strongest. Choice (B) is true—the passage acknowledges that the hyena looks comical but points out that it is nonetheless a very dangerous predator. Choice (C) incorrectly makes a generalization based on the one example given in the passage. Choice (D) also makes a generalization about tribal beliefs based solely on the two examples given in the passage. Choice (E) combines the separate comments regarding the hyena's running abilities with its ability to bring down an animal as large as the Cape buffalo.

4. **A**   Once again, check the answers against the facts in the passage. In the concluding lines, the passage states that it is possible for appearances to be deceiving; this comes immediately after a description of the hyena's strength and hunting prowess. Therefore, (A) looks promising. Choice (B) is incorrect because the first paragraph countered the belief that hyenas are scavengers, claiming that they scavenge only when necessary. Choice (C) incorrectly associates the beliefs of the author with the beliefs of some early tribes. Choice (D) incorrectly uses the word *inappropriate*; although the passage referred to the cry of the hyena as *distinctive*, nowhere did it call the cry *inappropriate*. Choice (E) is incorrect because the passage states that the hyena is built primarily for power, not speed.

5. **D**   The passage, as a whole, is about misunderstandings surrounding the hyena. Choice (A) is incorrect because, although the passage does point out that this is a misconception, nowhere does it say that the practice should be discontinued. Choice (B) is incorrect because the comment comparing the hyena's cry to the calls of the lost souls is found in the very beginning and is not relevant to the second paragraph. Choice (C) goes too far—the passage gives only very basic information about hyena physiology, not a detailed description. Choice (D) matches the summary from above fairly well, since it focuses on the common mistaken perceptions of the hyena. Choice (E) is incorrect because the passage does not address any other sub-Saharan animals.

6. **C** This question requires you to understand the author's primary purpose. The first paragraph introduces evidence that indicates the universe's expansion is accelerating. The second and third paragraphs present the ramifications of this discovery for physicists. The author is not defending a theory, as the passage does not describe that the theory is under attack. Thus, (A) should be eliminated. The author mentions a few theories, but the primary purpose of the passage is not to compare them, as (B) states. Choice (D) is close, but the author is not discussing a *problem* but rather a new finding. Choice (E) is incorrect because the author isn't proposing a new approach but instead describing what other theorists have proposed.

7. **D** The answer to this question is found in the first paragraph. The author states *the universe has been expanding steadily ever since this cataclysmic event and most physicists naturally assumed that this expansion must be gradually slowing down.* The cataclysmic event referred to is the origin of the universe in the Big Bang. This statement supports (D). Choice (A) is wrong because the passage indicates that the acceleration of the expansion has been occurring for 10 billion years, not simply the expansion. No information supports (B) because the author doesn't mention *most models* of the universe. Choice (C) indicates a view held by some physicists, but it is not necessarily true and thus cannot be inferred. Choice (E) is wrong because it is not stated that the acceleration is at a constant rate.

8. **D** In order to answer this question, determine what the passage states about how *dark energy* helps to explain *an accelerating expansion of the universe*, which is that *dark energy…is believed to be gravitationally repulsive*—In other words, that it applies a repelling force of some kind. The recycled language in (A), (B), and (E) fails to provide an *explanation* for acceleration, so those choices can be eliminated. Choice (C) provides a consideration that, if true, may explain how dark energy prevents a contraction of the universe, but can be eliminated because it does not explain acceleration. Choice (D) is supported because it clarifies the connection between a *repulsive* force and *acceleration*.

9. **A** In the final paragraph, the author indicates that some physicists are looking for a more conventional explanation of the acceleration, one that does not include dark energy. However, the author states that some researchers have found evidence that tends to support the existence of dark energy, making (A) the correct answer. Choice (B) is too extreme in its use of the word *prove*. Choice (C) is incorrect because the evidence mentioned by the author supports the existence of dark energy. It doesn't require a rethinking because of dark energy. Choice (D) is out of scope because the author doesn't mention *most astronomers*. Choice (E) should be eliminated because the evidence supports dark energy, not the more traditional theories.

10. **D** For this question, it is necessary to pick the choice that is not supported by the passage. The line that states *team of observers studying supernovae made a shocking discovery* supports (A). Choices (B) and (E) are supported by the line *later measurements of the cosmic microwave background and a survey of the distribution of galaxies seem to corroborate the initial finding that the expansion of the universe is indeed accelerating.* Choice (C) is supported by the end of the last paragraph. Only (D) is not mentioned as an indicator of dark energy. Instead, the dust is offered as a counter explanation.

11.   **B**   This is a primary purpose question, so you need to use the entire passage to answer the question. The author introduces some facts about the Arctic Circle region and states that some geologists believe it contains oil. Next, the author describes the results of a recent investigation into the region. The author does not critique the study, so (A) is incorrect. Nor does the author list out the world's remaining reserves, so (C) is incorrect. The passage does not advocate anything, which means that (D) can be eliminated. Although the passage does mention a methodology, it doesn't state that it is *new*, nor is the methodology the primary focus of the passage. Eliminate (E). Only (B) matches the scope and focus of the passage.

12.   **B**   The answer to this question is in the first paragraph. The author states, *Of the 21 million square kilometer Arctic region, only about 8 million square kilometers is onshore; the rest of the area is located on continental shelves, which are covered by no more than 500 meters of water.* Thus, about 13 million square kilometers of the region, more than half the total area, is underwater, making (B) the correct answer. Choice (A) is incorrect because the passage states that geologist *believe* there to be vast reserves, but this hasn't been proven. Nothing in the passage supports (C); parts of the Arctic are in those countries, but not the *majority*. Choice (D) contradicts the passage, which says that the entire Arctic Circle is 6 percent of the Earth's area, not 10 percent. Choice (E) is a trap; the question asks about the *majority of the Arctic Circle*. The passage states that the survey was done above that latitude, but does not say that the majority of the Arctic Circle is above that latitude.

13.   **C**   The answer to this question is in the second paragraph. The author states, *Due to the relative lack of information on the Arctic Circle region, the CARA team was unable to employ the standard geological techniques of resource assessment, including discovery prospect modeling and deposit simulation. Instead, the scientists employed a probabilistic methodology….* So, the nature of the region made the standard tools unusable, as (C) states. Nothing says it was the *most efficient* way to search, as (A) says. The passage says the standard methods couldn't be used, not that they failed, so (B) is out. The reason given for the probabilistic method is not that the region is underwater; it is that the region is unknown. Eliminate (D). Choice (E) is not mentioned at all.

14.   **E**   To answer this question, first find out what the beliefs of the geologists are. The first paragraph says, *Some geologists believe that the expansive Arctic continental shelves may contain vast petroleum reserves.* Next, look at the results of the survey: the results *indicate that 17 of the 25 Arctic Circle regions have a greater than 10 percent chance of holding oil reserves.* Thus, the results are in line with the geologists' beliefs. That makes (D) wrong. However, the results do not *conclusively prove* the geologist beliefs, because the results only indicate a likelihood of oil. So (A) is too extreme. Choice (B) can be eliminated because the results do not *undermine* the geologists' beliefs about natural gas reserves—the results support those beliefs. Choice (C) is wrong because the results indicate the oil is in the Arctic region, which is where the geologists believe it to be. Choice (E) is correct because the results indicate the geologists may be right, but the results are still only probabilistic in nature, so they do not definitively prove the geologists correct.

15. **D** Of the CARA team's research, the author says, *Geologists on the team further conclude that over 70 percent of the estimated oil reserves in the Arctic Circle occur in just five of the regions, while over 70 percent of the probable natural gas reserves lay in just three of the regions.* The correct answer must be true based on this information. Choice (A) is incorrect because the text says that 17 of the regions have a greater than 10 percent chance of oil reserves, meaning the other 8 have a less than 10 percent chance. But they still might contain oil, so (A) is wrong. Nothing in the passage states what oil companies should do, so (B) is not correct. Choice (C) is not necessarily true. Seventy percent of the oil lies in five regions, and 70 percent of the gas lies in three, but they do not necessarily have to be different regions. Nothing in the text compares the amounts of gas and oil, so (E) is not supported. Choice (D) is true because the survey indicates that the majority of reserves are in at most less than half of the regions.

16. **B** The passage begins by describing the Little Penguin itself then goes on to describe some of the problems faced by the penguins. Choice (B) best captures this. Choice (A) is incorrect for two reasons: because the passage does not imply that the Little Penguins are in serious trouble and because the scope is too narrow. Choice (C) is incorrect because the passage does not discuss government action. Choice (D) is incorrect because the passage as a whole is not about the problems posed by tourists. Choice (E) is incorrect because the problem of feral animals is only mentioned as supporting evidence, not as the main idea.

17. **E** The fox is given as an example of one of the imported species of animal that now preys on the Little Penguins. Choice (A) is incorrect because it goes too far—although the passage refers to the fox as a predator, it does not specify how much danger it poses for the penguins. Choice (B) incorrectly identifies the fox as a native species. Choice (C) incorrectly refers to the fox as a companion animal. Choice (D) incorrectly attributes the problem that the penguins have with bright lights to the foxes. Choice (E) is the closest paraphrase of the given information.

18. **C** The passage states that the tourists are drawn by the penguins and sometimes *expose the penguins to injury by taking flash photographs.* Therefore, they must want to see and photograph the penguins, making (C) the correct answer. Choice (A) is incorrect because the passage does not mention the countryside. Choice (B) is incorrect because the passage does not mention handling the penguins. Choice (D) is incorrect because the passage does not connect the tourists with protecting the penguins. Choice (E) incorrectly focuses on the land and weather instead of the penguins.

19. **D** The penguin is described as being white on its underbelly, to help it blend in with the sky, and dark on its back, to help it blend in with the ocean. Therefore, the best analogy will also feature an animal with different colored coverings to help it blend into different settings. Choice (A) is about changing color for camouflage, and it describes a seasonal change, whereas the penguins' coloration is permanent. Choice (B) does not describe an example of camouflage. Choice (C), like (A), describes a change in coloration based on need. Choice (E) corrects a misconception regarding camouflage. Only (D) describes an animal that is seen differently from different angles, in order to blend in more accurately.

20. **D** The passage states that *it is fortunate that the penguins have few natural enemies*, which follows a discussion about *coloring*, which [helps] *camouflage the penguins* and protect them from *carnivores*. Thus, while the statement about *few natural enemies* may seem to state a lack of natural predators, it more directly implies that the penguins are relatively safe from whatever natural predators exist due to color-based defenses. Therefore, (A) can be eliminated, and (D) is supported. Choice (B)'s memory trap about people observing the penguin contains elements which cannot be proven, such as *enjoy watching the penguin swim*. Choice (C) makes the unsupported extreme statement that *ferrets are the only* predator *small enough* to harm the penguins' young. Choice (E) may seem tempting, as the passage carries a negative tone towards human *encroachment*, but can be eliminated because much of the human impact discussed regards changes that have already occurred and cannot be *halted or prevented*.

21. **D** Although Belyaev's experiment increased the amiability of the foxes, the passage does not say that they were domesticated, so eliminate choice (A). Nor does it say Belyaev is a premiere researcher, so eliminate (B). The abandoned cubs and scavenging are mentioned as theories about the domestication of wolves, not in regard to Belyaev's experiment, so eliminate (C) and (E). But the experiment did increase the amiability of the foxes through discerning breeding, and therefore the correct answer is (D).

22. **C** To say that domesticated dogs never hunt goes too far, so eliminate choice (A). Similarly, although the passage says that dogs have alterations in markings, it does not say their fur is striped. Eliminate (B). Choice (C) is supported by the end of the second paragraph, which says *decrease in cranial capacity which did not allow room for certain instincts that are essential in the wild…* The wolves, not the dogs, are described as fighting their instinct to flee and as having larger teeth, so eliminate (D) and (E).

23. **E** Be sure to apply the vague language in the answer choices to the specifics of the passage. The first paragraph presents two possible explanations for the domestication of wolves. There is no evaluation of the two possible explanations for wolf domestication, nor is there a question or controversy posed in the first paragraph. This rules out (A), (B), and (D). Choice (C) does not take into account the two theories offered.

24. **A** Inbreeding is discussed in the first paragraph as a possible explanation for domestication. Teeth and brain capacity are mentioned in the second paragraph (and dogs, not wolves, have smaller brain capacity) so (B) and (D) are out. Belyaev is mentioned in the third paragraph, so eliminate (C). Scavenging relates to the second theory, while inbreeding refers to the first theory mentioned, so (E) is out.

25. **B** Domesticated dogs have smaller brains and more compact jawlines than wolves, so (A) and (E) are out. Dogs also lack certain survival instincts, so (C) is out too. Although some wolf cubs are abandoned, to say that wolves do this typically is too extreme; eliminate (D). At the end of the first paragraph, part of the process of domestication is described as *they fought their instinct to flee*. This implies that undomesticated wolves had a natural instinct to flee.

26. **D**   In the passage, synanthropy is defined as wild animals living among humans and benefitting from some human behavior. It is contrasted with the more well-known types of symbiosis, such as parasitism, commensalism, and mutualism. Choice (A) is incorrect because the passage does not say that humans benefit from the presence of these wild animals. Choice (B) is incorrect because, while it is a newer category, the passage does not compare the frequency with which these phenomena occur. Choice (C) is incorrect because the passage does not specify whether the field is well-funded. Choice (D), the correct answer, correctly identifies synanthropy as another type of symbiosis as described in the first paragraph. Choice (E) is incorrect because the passage does not directly compare synanthropy and domestication.

27. **A**   The cassowary is mentioned in the last sentence, grouped with the koala, in contrast to animals such as the rat and pigeon. This refers back to the previous comment, that the non-exotic animals may not be as superficially appealing as subjects of research but they might be more useful. Therefore, the cassowary is being used as an example of an exotic, endangered animal. Choice (A) correctly recognizes this connection and is the correct answer. Choice (B) is incorrect because the passage does not mention what kind of relationship the cassowary has with humans. Choice (C) is incorrect because the passage does not specify where these animals are from. Choice (D) incorrectly refers to funding, which is not relevant to this part of the passage. Choice (E) is incorrect because the passage does not specify whether or not the cassowary is urbanized.

28. **C**   The author claims that the areas of animal research that have traditionally been well-funded are those that deal either with exotic, endangered animals, or with those animals that are used as labor, companions, or food stock. Since the question asks which study would *not* be well-funded, you're looking for the one that does not fall into either category. Choice (A) deals with dairy cows (food stock), so eliminate it. Choice (B) deals with a rare animal, so eliminate that too. Choice (C) deals with raccoons, which are wild but not rare—hold on to it. Choice (D) deals with companion animals—eliminate it. Choice (E) is also about an endangered animal—eliminate it.

29. **A**   Although the tone of the passage is fairly neutral, you do get the impression that the author supports the study of urban wildlife from the last few sentences, referring to this new field of study as *fortuitous*. Therefore, you want a mildly positive answer. Choice (C) is neutral and (E) is negative, so you can eliminate those immediately. Choice (B) is too strong. Choice (D) isn't as good as (A) because the passage isn't really hesitant; the author is definitely optimistic, just in a mild way.

30. **A**   In order to determine which answer the author would agree with, it's best to compare each answer with the information given in the passage. Choice (A) matches with the concluding comments about pigeons and rats—they may not be as pretty but we interact with them, so it might be wise to study them. Choice (B) is incorrect because the passage does not refer to pigeons as *perpetual outsiders*, but as wild animals that live among us. That's a little bit too much of a value judgment for the GMAT. Choice (C) is also a value judgment—the author does refer to the more prestigious fields as those more likely to get funding but nowhere does he advise scientists as to which field they should enter. Choice (D) refers to governments, which are never mentioned in the passage.

Choice (E) goes a step further than the passage does. Although the author supports studying local animals, nothing in the passage indicates that doing so is more important than is studying other, more exotic animals.

Business

1. **E** The title should reflect the main idea of the passage. The first paragraph describes a trend towards increasing spending on advertising. The next two paragraphs describe negative consequences of this trend, including concentration of power and monopolization of the industry. Choice (A) is a tempting choice, but it doesn't address the problems the author mentions in the passage. Choice (B) doesn't mention advertising at all, which is a prime focus of the passage. Choice (C) misstates the relationship presented in the passage; the passage is about the effect of monopolization on society, not the advertising industry. Choice (D) refers to the first paragraph but not the rest of the passage.

2. **A** The *sales effort* referred to is described in the first paragraph. Here, the author states that corporations spent *a staggering 110 billion dollars by 1988, representing more than two percent of the gross national product of the United States. Furthermore, corporations are spending more and more money on design, display, packaging, and marketing. While exact figures are not available, conservative estimates indicate that in 1988 businesses spent at least as much on these areas as they did on advertising.* The 110 billion represents 2% of the gross national product. In addition, the corporations spent *at least as much* on the other areas, meaning approximately another 110 billion. The total expenditures would be around 220 billion, which would be 4% of the gross national product. None of the other answer choices are supported by the passage.

3. **B** Choice (A) is not supported in the passage because the author never talks about the degree of *control* advertisers had in the past. Although the passage has a negative tone towards increasing advertising, (C) goes too far in saying that there are *no positive consequences.* Choice (D) also goes beyond the information in the passage. The author does not explicitly say that the only cause of media monopolization is an increase in money spent on advertising. Choice (E) is not correct because the author says that media companies cater to their advertisers, but that is not the same as saying they do not *consider* the interests of others. The author says *these conglomerates tend to have limited interests, which results in a restriction of the types of media content and information delivered to the average media consumer,* which makes (B) the correct answer.

4. **C** The question asks why the author mentions a certain fact. Read the lines before and after that reference to get the context. *While it is traditionally assumed that mass media content is designed for consumers, it is perhaps more accurate to say that the media content is actually geared towards the needs of advertisers....This disparity in income shows who in fact the purveyors of media content are truly beholden to.* Thus, the author is trying to show that the traditional assumption is wrong; media content is not for consumers but for advertisers. Choice (A) is incorrect because there is no paradox. Choice (B) is incorrect because the passage does not criticize a commonly occurring practice, but instead says that the practice is not what people think it is. Choice (D) is too broad with *typical*

businesses, rather than simply newspapers and magazines. Choice (E) does not express the purpose of the line at all.

5.   A   Choice (A) is supported in the first paragraph, where the author says, *Among advertisers, it has become accepted wisdom that in a highly competitive market, corporations must spend more and more money on researching target consumers, attractive packaging and display, and compelling promotional activities.* None of the other choices are supported by the passage.

6.   C   The author introduces Porter's study in the first paragraph and then mentions a "surprising" finding in its concluding summary. Choice (A) is unsupported because the passage does not make clear whether this is a *trend*. Choice (B) is too strong; even though the passage says that the companies with high market share utilized cost leadership, it does not say that they are the most profitable. Choice (D) is unsupported as the passage does not explain how market share increases. Choice (E) is unsupported because the passage is purely descriptive; it does not try to prove or disprove anything.

7.   A   The passage says that the most profitable companies are those that successfully use cost leadership and market segmentation. Choice (B) is too strong; the passage only states the middle range companies are *not as profitable*. Choice (C) is unsupported because the passage never states whether the high or low range companies are more profitable. Choice (D) is confusing; however it is too extreme because it claims that if a company is not profitable, then it must be in either the high or low range of market share. Choice (E) is also too strong; the passage never states that a mere pursuit of cost leadership will result in higher market share.

8.   B   The passage states that strategic strength is a supply-side variable because it describes the strategic strength of the company while strategic scope is a demand-side variable because it only describes the depth of the market. Choice (A) switches the two variables. Choices (C) and (D) are unsupported because the passage never states which variable is more important. Choice (E) contradicts the passage; strategic scope also helps to define terms.

9.   D   A supply-side variable relates to the competency of the company itself and thus must not focus on something outside of the company. Choices (A), (B), (C), and (E) all relate to the internal characteristics of the company. Choice (D) relates to the market, therefore, the correct answer is (D).

10.   E   In the second paragraph, Porter explains that companies with lower market share are profitable due to market segmentation. In order to undermine this, it must be shown that his research does not support this conclusion. Choice (A) does not undermine it; the passage does not say that companies could not use both strategies. Choice (B) does not undermine it, since *few* does not speak to what most such companies do. Choice (C) does not undermine it because even if this were true, Porter's point could still also be true. Choice (D) merely contradicts Porter's research; a mere disagreement with a premise does not undermine a conclusion.

11. **B** The passage states that *the three major characteristics of DSS* include *to support rather than automate decisions*. Thus, DSS should not automate the decision making process. Choice (A) is supported by the lines *Others contain theoretical models pertaining to specific decision making scenarios*. Choice (C) is found when the passage states *Some systems aid the manager by making a huge amount of data readily available*. Choices (D) and (E) are supported in the lines *…wish to coordinate information among a number of individuals in order to arrive at a joint decision. A DSS can be more than just a simple tool for data mining or data warehousing.*

12. **D** To answer this question, read the first paragraph where the author talks about the *introduction of DSS*. The author states that, *This new technology resulted from a combination of theoretical work carried out in the 1950s on how managers made decisions and technical innovations in computer systems achieved in the early 1960s*. Thus, DSS could not have resulted until the technical innovations occurred. None of the other choices are supported by the passage.

13. **C** According to the passage, *sophisticated* DSS can handle problems that are *not clearly defined or clearly structured*. The right answer, therefore, must contain a problem of this type. Choice (A) represents a simple, quantitative question, which is clearly defined. Choice (B) involves analyzing vast amounts of data, which the passage states is a feature of many DSS, not just the sophisticated ones. In (C), the manager is unsure of the cause, so the problem is not clearly defined. This would be the best scenario for a sophisticated DSS. Choice (D) presents the manager with a clearly defined problem while (E) involves compiling data, a task suited to most DSS.

14. **A** To answer a vague question such as this one, use process of elimination on the answer choices. The author discusses quantitative and qualitative-based decisions in the beginning of the first paragraph, which states, *There are a number of different management styles that can be effective; some managers rely on hard quantitative data…while others focus more on qualitative data….* Since the authors allow that both can be effective, (A) is the correct answer. Choice (B) is not supported, since success is not discussed in the passage. There is no support for Choice (C) anywhere in the passage. Choice (D) is incorrect, since the passage implies that *sophisticated* DSS can handle more vague tasks. Choice (E) contradicts the passage, which says *A wealth of literature has been produced on DSS since that time.*

15. **D** Check the passage to find evidence of each quality. Choice (A) matches with the line *…aids the manager by making a huge amount of data readily available*. Choice (B) is supported by the line *Others contain theoretical models pertaining to specific decision making scenarios*. Choice (C) is based on *There are a number of different management styles that can be effective; some managers rely on hard quantitative data…while others focus more on qualitative data*, while (E) is supported by the line *coordinate information among a number of individuals*. Nothing in the passage, however, discusses *coordination of actions*.

16. **E** The primary purpose should sum up the passage in its entirety. The author introduces two competing business models, then compares the businesses in two different contexts. First, the business models are compared in the context of the relationship with the customer; second, the models are

compared in a financial context. Choice (A) addresses a discrepancy, which does not match the passage. Choice (B) addresses the most common business model, which is not mentioned in the passage. Choice (C) addresses a critique, which does not match the passage. Choice (D) addresses more effective strategies, which are not mentioned in the passage. Choice (E) correctly describes the passage and is the correct answer.

17. **B** Here you are looking for a choice that is NOT supported by the passage. Choice (A) is supported by *travel guidebooks will often point out the family-operated stores.* Choice (C) is supported by information in the final sentence of the passage. Choice (D) is supported by *t-shirts with the city's name emblazoned on the front.* Choice (E) is supported by *slash prices, which is appealing to the average buyer.* The passage does not discuss mom-and-pops in towns other than tourist towns.

18. **A** In the third paragraph, the author argues that mom-and-pop stores have better relationships with their customers than do large conglomerates. One reason given for this is that the large stores hire staff members who are not as personally invested as is an owner who started the company. To strengthen this argument, show that the personal investment does apply to mom-and-pop stores. Choice (A) correctly links owning a store, and therefore having a personal investment in the store, to mom-and-pop stores. Choice (B) addresses workers at any store, which is irrelevant to the author's argument. Choice (C) addresses owners of any type of store, which is irrelevant to the author's argument. Choice (D) links personal investment to large conglomerates, which could weaken the author's argument. Choice (E) addresses travel guidebooks, which are irrelevant to the author's argument.

19. **C** The final paragraph discusses how large conglomerates outperform mom-and-pop stores when it comes to financial operation. The last two sentences provide support for the fact that they can deal with expense, cost, and individual store loss better than mom-and-pop stores can. Choice (A) presents a conditional statement that is not supported, since the passage only says this is true for part-time employees. Choice (B) is not supported by any information in the passage. Choice (C) is supported by the passage. Choice (D) describes what usually occurs, and the passage does not address the frequency with which large businesses own other large businesses. Choice (E) is not supported by any information in the passage.

20. **D** The third paragraph suggests that if one is a part-time staff member who does not live in the locale year-round, then he or she does not embody the city's characteristic flavor. Choice (A) is not supported by any information in the passage. Choice (B) addresses whether they are hired at mom-and-pop stores, which is not mentioned in the passage. Choice (C) discusses another possible characteristic of part-time staff, but not necessarily of those who do not live in the locale year-round. Choice (D) is supported by the passage. Choice (E) is not supported by any information in the passage.

21. **D** The primary purpose should sum up the entirety of the passage. The author begins by introducing Chester Barnard and his work. The following two paragraphs detail two theories Barnard put forth. Choice (A) discusses a new perspective, which does not match the passage. Choice (B)

discusses an alternative interpretation, which does not match the passage. Choice (C) addresses a critique, which does not match the passage. Choice (D) correctly matches the passage. Choice (E) addresses a proposed course of action, which does not match the passage.

22. **A** The author says Barnard's conviction that persuasion is more powerful than material incentives is *surprising*. He then goes on to list those things that, *despite the generic assumption*, would delight employees, including a pleasurable work atmosphere. It can then be inferred that the generic assumption is that a pleasurable work atmosphere is not a useful incentive. Choice (A) is supported by information in the passage. Choice (B) presents a fact that Barnard does not dispute. Choice (C) presents an inference from the passage that Barnard does not dispute. Choice (D) presents a comparison that is not made in the passage. Choice (E) presents a possible inference from the passage that Barnard does not dispute.

23. **B** The attitude of the author can be determined by looking at the descriptive language used. The author calls Barnard's theories *sage* and *relevant*. At no point does the author criticize or write negatively about Barnard. Choice (A) includes caution, which is not expressed by the author. Choice (B) correctly describes the positive attitude expressed by the author. Choices (C) and (D) both describe negative attitudes. Choice (E) includes fanaticism, which is too extreme.

24. **D** The second paragraph states that Barnard held that *everyone had an equal part to play* and that *the notion of authority is meaningless without a subordinate*. The schools of thought that came before his focused on the manager; his focused on both the subordinate and the manager. Choices (A), (B), and (C) describe the theories that came before Barnard's. Choice (D) is supported by information in the passage. Choice (E) is not supported by the passage, since Barnard's theory was contrary to those that came before.

25. **C** The author states that the guidelines *remain relevant today* and are likely used by *today's most profitable companies*. Choice (A) is contrary to the passage. Choice (B) is not supported by the passage, since the author views Barnard's guidelines as accurate. Choice (C) is supported by information in the passage. Choice (D) is not supported by any information in the passage. Choice (E) is not supported by the passage, since the author does not critique Barnard's guidelines.

26. **D** The first paragraph states that the Austrian school distinguishes itself with a theory. The next paragraph briefly describes this theory, and the final paragraph mentions a criticism of it, but notes that the theory is still influential. This best matches (D). Choice (A) is wrong because the author is not proposing a *new* theory. Choice (B) does not match the passage at all. Choice (C) is incorrect because the passage doesn't primarily focus on distinctions; the second and third paragraphs are devoted to describing the theory and one of its problems. Choice (E) is wrong because there is no contrast with another theory.

27. **D** To answer this question, use the lead words *Austrian school,* which occurs in the beginning of the passage. The author states that it *distinguishes itself most from this more orthodox perspective.* This implies that the neoclassical school is more orthodox and the Austrian school less orthodox. Only (D) matches this information. Choice (A) is wrong because the author does not state that the school is less influential, only that it is less orthodox. The author makes no predictions about the future, so (B) is too extreme. While the author states that the school's focus on time preferences leads to some interesting hypotheses, this is not the same as saying the school itself has an *advantage* over the neoclassical school. Thus, (C) should be eliminated. The author does not give his or her opinion of the theory's truthfulness; therefore, (E) is inaccurate.

28. **B** The answer to this question is in the second paragraph, where the author talks about *proponents of ABCT.* The passage says these proponents *claim that economic recessions will not occur in a purely free market system.* Thus, if an economy is in the midst of a recession, the system must not be a purely free market system. Choice (A) is wrong because the passage indicates that a recession is started when interest rates are manipulated. It is not stated in the passage what the rates are in the midst of recession, as the question asks. Choice (C) is not correct because the passage does not state how the economy recovers from a recession. Choice (D) also refers to a situation that helps begin the recession, but it is not clear from the passage that investors make unsound decisions during the recession. Choice (E) is wrong because the author does not state in the passage how the economy *must* correct itself.

29. **C** The third paragraph most directly compares the Austrian school and the neoclassical school. It states that *while neoclassical economists make use of the idea of time preferences in some economic analyses, the Austrian school makes time preferences a major focus of its theoretical investigations….* The focus on time preferences is reflected in (C), which mentions an emphasis on *historical factors.* Choice (A) is contradicted in the first paragraph. Choice (B) cannot be the answer because the author never states that the other school doesn't have its own theory of boom and bust cycles. Choice (D) is not supported by the passage. The theory holds that recessions do not occur in a pure free market system, but that is not the same as an endorsement of such a system. Choice (E) is mentioned as a part of the theory, but nowhere in the passage does the author say that this is a contrast with the neoclassical school.

30. **E** This question asks for the author's general opinion of ABCT. In the first paragraph, the author calls the theory *influential.* However, the author also mentions the criticism that the theory has received and discusses one of its *problematic* aspects. Choice (A) goes too far in calling the theory *fatally* flawed. The author allows that the theory is subject to criticisms, but does not say that these criticisms sink the theory. Nothing in the passage supports the idea that the theory has not received its *proper due,* as (B) says. In fact, the author describes the theory as influential. The author does not discuss empirical support at all, so (C) is not supported. Nor does the author state which school's theory is *more successful,* so (D) is incorrect.

Sentence
Correction

SENTENCE CORRECTION

The sentence correction questions on the GMAT supposedly test your knowledge of English grammar. The English language has hundreds of grammar rules, but luckily, the test writers only test a limited number of them. You should spend your time reviewing the most commonly tested errors.

If you are like most people, you will try to answer the sentence correction questions "by ear." Unfortunately, this can get you into trouble, because most people speak incorrectly a lot of the time. That means that many things that sound right are actually wrong, and many things that are wrong sound right. The test writers know this and plan traps with that in mind.

Even if you have a good ear, you'll do better on the sentence correction questions if you go by the rules (some of which are hard and fast grammar rules and some of which are style preferences of the test writers) and not by the sound. If you know the rules and recognize the cues for when those rules are being tested, you will be able to work sentence correction questions more quickly and efficiently.

THE FORMAT

Each question presents a sentence with part or all of the sentence underlined. Each answer choice represents a different version of the underlined portion. Your job is to pick the answer choice that makes the best sentence according to the rules of grammar and the test writers' twisted logic.

The first answer choice always repeats the underlined portion of the original sentence, so if the sentence is correct as written, select (A). You should bear in mind that 20% of the sentence correction questions are correct as written.

1. Each team of business students <u>are responsible for creating a marketable business plan</u>.

    (A) are responsible for creating a marketable business plan
    (B) are responsible to create a marketable business plan
    (C) is responsible for creating a business plan that is able to be marketed
    (D) is responsible for creating a marketable business plan
    (E) is responsible to create a marketable business plan

The 2/3 Split

Notice that two of the answers start with *are* and that the other three start with *is*. This is a "2/3 split." When it is present, the 2/3 split often tells you what grammar rule is being tested and can help you with Process of Elimination. The split can appear in any part of the answer choices: beginning, middle or end. Look for it, because once you know which side of the split is correct, you can eliminate approximately 50% of the answer choices!

BASIC APPROACH

Most sentence correction questions have more than one error. The key is to identify one of the errors being tested and eliminate all the answer choices that have that error. Then look for a second and/or third error and repeat the process until you have only one choice left.

Avoid the temptation to rewrite the sentence in your head before looking at the answer choices, and try to avoid reading the entirety of every answer choice. Instead, vertically scan the choices looking for 2/3 splits or other patterns, then use POE.

Use the previous question as an example.

Step 1: Identify an error

Look for

- a 2/3 split in the answer choices
- other differences or patterns among the answer choices
- the common types of errors

The 2/3 split in the example is between *is* and *are*. One is singular and one is plural, which means you are being tested on subject-verb agreement.

Step 2: Use POE

Eliminate all answer choices that contain the error.

The subject of the sentence is *each*, which is singular, so eliminate (A) and (B).

Step 3: Identify an error in the remaining choices

Look for another grammatical error in the remaining answer choices. Once again, compare the answer choices and look for differences.

If you visually compare the remaining answer choices you may notice that (C) and (D) say *responsible for creating* and (E) says *responsible to create*.

Step 4: Use POE

Eliminate the remaining choices that contain the secondary error.

The correct idiom is *responsible for*, so eliminate (E).

Step 5: Keep going until only one answer choice remains

If you visually compare the remaining answer choices, you may notice that (C) says *business plan that is able to be marketed* and (D) says *marketable business plan*.

Which is better? There is no grammar rule that makes one better than the other, but the test writers consider (C) too wordy. Choice (D) is shorter and simpler, so the correct answer is (D).

Style Points

Sometimes you may have to choose between two or more answers that are grammatically correct. When that happens, keep the following in mind:

- Avoid answers that *unnecessarily* change the meaning of the original sentence. They are incorrect, although there may be rare times when the intended meaning of the original sentence is obscured by bad grammar.
- Choose the shortest and simplest answer, especially if two answers are both grammatically correct. Short and simple is good; wordy and awkward is bad.
- Use the active voice, especially if you have a choice. Answers in the passive voice can sometimes be correct, but never in the presence of an equally grammatically correct answer choice in the active voice.
- Avoid redundancy and repetitive answers.
- Watch for verbs that end in *-ing*. They are often wrong. This should not be your first line of defense, because words that end in *-ing* are sometimes correct. However, if you have to choose between two answers that are both grammatically correct, go with the one without the *-ing* verb.
- Stay away from answer choices that include the word *being*. It is a weak verb that is wrong 99.9% of the time.

THE BIG SIX

The test writers concentrate on a handful of errors: The Big Six. Learn these rules and the cues for recognizing them.

- Subject-Verb Agreement
- Verb Tense
- Pronouns
- Parallel Construction
- Misplaced Modifiers
- Idioms

SUBJECT-VERB AGREEMENT

The Rule: A singular subject requires a singular verb. A plural subject requires a plural verb.

Because the rule is so basic, the test writers try to find ways to trick you into missing subject-verb errors. You should look out for the following:

- Extra words, especially prepositional phrases, between the subject and the verb
- Compound subjects
- Singular pronouns (e.g., each or anyone) as subjects
- The following (all of which are singular) as subjects:
  - Abstract nouns (e.g., justice or wealth)
  - Collective nouns (e.g., the jury or the family)
  - Gerunds (e.g., walking or singing)
  - Infinitive nouns (e.g., to forgive or to err)
  - Singular nouns that end in –s (e.g., economics or species)

The ID

- Look for changing verbs (for example, *is* vs. *are*) in the answer choices
- Look for an agreement error in the original sentence

2. <u>Attempts to maintain the current level of funding for museums, though impressive</u>, has not resulted in the continuation of financial backing for the coming year.

    (A) Attempts to maintain the current level of funding for museums, though impressive

    (B) The attempt to maintain the current level of funding for museums, though impressive

    (C) Maintaining the current level of funding, though an impressive attempt

    (D) The impressive attempts to maintain the current level of museum funding

    (E) Attempts to maintain the level of funding for museums currently, though impressive

You may notice that the subject of the original sentence, *attempts*, does not agree with the verb *has*. That means you're being tested on subject-verb agreement. If you don't notice this, you may notice a 2/3 split in the answer choices. Two of the answers say *attempt* and three of them say *attempts*. When you look for the verb that goes with *attempt/attempts* you discover it is *has*, which is singular. *Has* is not underlined, which means it is correct; therefore, the correct subject is *attempt* or something else that is singular. Eliminate (A), (D), and (E). Choice (C) unnecessarily changes the meaning of the original sentence. It also uses an *-ing* word, something the test writers are not fond of, so the correct answer is (B).

SUBJECT/VERB AGREEMENT DRILL

1. Efforts to gain bipartisan support for an economic stimulus package, a goal of a number of members of Congress, <u>has not resulted in less bickering between the Democratic and Republican members of the House</u>.

    (A) has not resulted in less bickering between the Democratic and Republican members of the House
    (B) has not reduced the amount of bickering between Democratic and Republican members of the House
    (C) has not made a significant reduction in the amount of bickering that exists between the Democratic and Republican members of the House
    (D) have not significantly reduced the amount of bickering between the Democratic and Republican members of the House
    (E) have not been significant in the reduction of the bickering between the Democratic and Republican members of the House

2. In the last decade, the number of environmental pollutants released into the <u>atmosphere, which harm the environment and raise the global temperature, have</u> declined dramatically.

    (A) atmosphere, which harm the environment and raise the global temperature, have
    (B) atmosphere, harming the environment and thereby raising global temperatures, have
    (C) atmosphere, that harms the environment by raising global temperatures, have
    (D) atmosphere which harms the environment in that they raise the global temperature, has
    (E) atmosphere that harm the environment by raising global temperatures has

3. <u>Eight out of ten mortgage holders also owe money to at least one credit card company.</u>

    (A) Eight out of ten mortgage holders also owe money to at least one credit card company.
    (B) Out of every ten, eight mortgage holders also owes money to at least one credit card company.
    (C) Money is owed to credit card companies by eight out of ten mortgage holders.
    (D) Eight out of ten mortgage holders also owes money to at least one credit card company.
    (E) Out of every ten mortgage holders, money is also owed to credit card companies by eight.

4. Playwright Samuel Beckett, whose well crafted works, unsympathetic examination of the human condition, and theatrical techniques, <u>were given recognition by critics, and also served to influence many writers, that included Edward Albee and Paula Vogel whose writing styles differed from his own</u>.

    (A) were given recognition by critics, and also served to influence many writers, that included Edward Albee and Paula Vogel whose writing styles differed from his own
    (B) recognized by critics, also influenced many writers, including Edward Albee and Paula Vogel, whose writing styles differed from his own
    (C) was recognized by critics, and also served to influence many writers, which included Edward Albee and Paula Vogel, whose writing styles differed
    (D) was recognized by critics, was also influential to many writers, who included Edward Albee and Paula Vogel who had a different writing style from his own
    (E) were given recognition by critics, also influencing many writers, including Edward Albee and Paula Vogel whose writing styles were different from that of his own

5. According to various ecological surveys, <u>the number of chlorofluorocarbons that has been released</u> into the atmosphere have decreased significantly since the 1970s.

(A) the number of chlorofluorocarbons that has been released into the atmosphere have decreased significantly since the 1970s

(B) the number of chlorofluorocarbons released into the atmosphere has decreased significantly since the 1970s

(C) there has been a decrease in the number of chlorofluorocarbons released into the atmosphere since the 1970s

(D) a decreasing number of chlorofluorocarbons have been released into the atmosphere since the 1970s

(E) chlorofluorocarbons have been decreasing in the number by which they have been released in the atmosphere since the 1970s

6. Since the early 1980's, when proton pump inhibitors were first marketed, the number of patients newly diagnosed with acid-related diseases <u>have increased from 1 million a year to nearly 20 million a year, a number that is about twice that of colitis</u> patients.

(A) have increased from 1 million a year to nearly 20 million a year, a number that is about twice that of colitis patients

(B) have increased from 1 million a year to nearly 20 million a year, a number that is about twice colitis patients

(C) has increased from 1 million a year to nearly 20 million a year, which is about twice the number of patients diagnosed with colitis

(D) has increased from 1 million up to nearly 20 million a year, which is about double the number of patients diagnosed with colitis

(E) has increased from 1 million up to nearly 20 million a year, about twice the patients who have colitis

7. Although the listening audience of satellite radio <u>amount to a number lower</u> than one percent of the terrestrial radio audience, radio station owners mounted a lawsuit last year to prevent the merger of two satellite radio behemoths.

(A) amount to a number lower
(B) amount to fewer
(C) amounted to less
(D) amounted to lower
(E) amounted to a lower total

8. Rheumatologists believe that the number of individuals suffering from gout in the United States can be estimated <u>to 1 million to 2 million provide</u> evidence for the need for a better treatment option.

(A) to be 1 million to 2 million provide evidence
(B) at 1 million to 2 million and providing evidence
(C) to be 1 million to 2 million which provides evidence
(D) as being 1 million to 2 million, and that it provides evidence
(E) over 1 million to 2 million people, provide evidence

9. Declining prices for homes and businesses, <u>the underlying assets of the mortgages that banks issued, is</u> going to force a number of financial institutions to declare bankruptcy in the coming years.

(A) the underlying assets of the mortgages that banks issued, is

(B) which are the underlying assets that banks issue is

(C) the mortgages that comprise the underlying assets that are issued by banks, is

(D) which banks issue as assets to issue mortgages, are

(E) the underlying assets of the mortgages that banks issued, are

10. <u>An e-mail by the superintendent of schools, sent out the same year as the first of the charter schools were opened</u>, revealed that the school board was opposed to the public financing of these schools.

(A) An e-mail by the superintendent of schools, sent out the same year as the first of the charter schools were opened
(B) An e-mail by the superintendent of schools, sent out in the same year of the opening of the first charter school,
(C) An e-mail by the superintendent of schools, sent out in the same year that the first charter school was opened
(D) The superintendent of schools sent an e-mail in the same year as the first of the charter schools that
(E) The superintendent of schools sent a letter in the same year of the opening as the first of the charter schools that

11. Viola Spolin's therapeutic style and methods—the recreational use of games, the ability to unlock the individual's capacity for creative self-expression, the focus on being part of an ensemble —<u>was as fresh an idea among her contemporaries as it is considered unique in present day theater</u>.

(A) was as fresh an idea among her contemporaries as it is considered unique in present day theater
(B) were as fresh to her contemporaries as they are to present day artists
(C) has been as fresh an idea to her contemporaries as they are to present day artists
(D) had been as fresh to her contemporaries as they are considered to be unique to present day theater
(E) have been as refreshing to her contemporaries as they would be to present day theater

12. The degree to which the values of stocks traded on the New York Stock Exchange (NYSE) and the other world exchanges—the JASDAQ security exchange in Japan, the EUREX in Germany, the JSE securities exchange in South Africa—<u>fluctuates was determined from</u> perceptions of worldwide investors of the health of the world economy.

(A) fluctuates was determined from
(B) fluctuates were determined as a result of
(C) fluctuates was determined through
(D) fluctuate was determined by
(E) fluctuate was determined because of

13. Efforts to increase recycling among consumers, a major goal of many American communities throughout the past decade, <u>has not abundantly reduced the number of plastic water bottles being discarded annually into landfills</u>.

(A) has not abundantly reduced the number of plastic water bottles being discarded annually into landfills
(B) has not been abundant in reducing the number of plastic water bottles that have been discarded annually into landfills
(C) has not made an abundant reduction in the number of plastic water bottles that has been discarded annually into landfills
(D) have not reduced the abundant number of plastic water bottles that has been discarded annually into landfills
(E) have not reduced the abundance in the number of plastic bottles that have been discarded annually into landfills

14. Many state tax codes, such as the Homestead Credit in Wisconsin, <u>offer tax relief that enable lower income families with little money to pay for rent to be able to</u> receive money back at the end of the year.

(A) offer tax relief that enable lower income families with little money to pay for rent to be able to
(B) offer tax relief that enables lower income families with little money to pay for rent to
(C) offers tax relief; that enables a family with less money to pay for rent to
(D) offers tax relief, which enable lower income families with little money to pay for rent to have the ability to
(E) offers tax relief, enabling lower income families with little money to be able to

15. The decline in students' performances on statewide tests <u>has been documented by a number of researchers, but what is more difficult to determine are</u> the root cause of this decline, the reason for the lack of equality between school systems, and the degree to which teachers can be held accountable.

(A) has been documented by a number of researchers, but what is more difficult to determine are
(B) has been documented by a number of researchers, but what is more difficult to determine is
(C) have been documented by a number of researchers, but what is more difficult to determine are
(D) is documented by a number of researchers, but what has been more difficult to determine are
(E) are documented by a number of researchers, but that which is more difficult to determine is

16. A major investment bank's <u>adjustment of interest rates on mortgages held by individuals is both a recognition of the depth of the financial crisis and an attempt to balance its books</u>.

(A) adjustment of interest rates on mortgages held by individuals is both a recognition of the depth of the financial crisis and an attempt to balance its books
(B) adjustment of interest rates on mortgages held by individuals both recognize the depth of the finance crisis and attempt to balance their books
(C) adjustment of interest rates on mortgages held by individuals is a recognition both of the depth of the financial crises as well as an attempt to balance its books
(D) adjusting interest rates on mortgages to individuals is a recognition both of the depth of the financial crisis and an attempt to balance its books
(E) adjusting interest rates on mortgages held by individuals both recognize the depth of the financial crisis and attempt to balance its books

17. Out of this season's obsession with all <u>things political have grown a market for official memorabilia and trinkets that are flooding</u> the shops with t-shirts, bumper stickers, and lapel pins.

(A) things political have grown a market for official memorabilia and trinkets that are flooding
(B) things political has grown a market for official memorabilia and trinkets that is flooding
(C) things that are political has grown a market for official memorabilia and trinkets that floods
(D) political things have grown a market for official memorabilia and trinkets that are flooding
(E) political things has grown a market for official memorabilia and trinkets that floods

18. While <u>all financial institutions face a similar crisis, those investment houses that hold a significant number of subprime mortgage loans and the insurance companies that underwrite credit swaps obviously dictates</u> the types and amounts of assistance required to fix the problem.

(A) all financial institutions face a similar crisis, those investment houses that hold a significant number of subprime mortgage loans and the insurance companies that underwrite credit swaps obviously dictates

(B) each financial institution faces a similar crisis, the investment houses holding a significant number of subprime mortgage loans and the insurance companies that underwrite credit swaps obviously dictate

(C) all financial institutions face a similar crisis; the financial investment houses that have a significant holding in subprime mortgage loans and the insurance companies that underwrite credit swaps obviously dictates

(D) each financial institution faces similar crises, the investment houses that hold a significant number of subprime mortgage and each of the insurance companies that underwrite credit swaps obviously dictates

(E) all financial institutions face similar crises, those investment houses that have a significant holding in subprime mortgage loans and those insurance companies that underwrite credit swaps obviously dictate

19. Taiwanese eat a cuisine unique to the island's history; the country's cuisine is basically Chinese <u>to which has been added Polynesian, Portuguese, and even Dutch influences</u>.

(A) to which has been added Polynesian, Portuguese, and even Dutch influences

(B) added to which is Polynesian, Portuguese, and even Dutch influences

(C) to which Polynesian, Portuguese, and even Dutch influences have been added

(D) with Polynesian, Portuguese, and even Dutch influences having been added

(E) and, in addition, Polynesian, Portuguese, and even Dutch influences have been added

20. The type of alliances <u>formed by businesses in pursuit of their various objectives are</u> one critical component of great leadership decisions.

(A) formed by businesses in pursuit of their various objectives are

(B) formed by business in pursuit of their various objectives is

(C) forming businesses in pursuit of their various objectives are

(D) formed by businesses in pursuit of their various objectives is

(E) formed by businesses in pursuit of their various objective are

21. <u>Despite some initial lack of enthusiasm, the work of William Faulkner, comprised of a series of elegant short stories and a number of blockbuster, overpoweringly complicated novels,</u> remains among the most revered in the American literary canon.

(A) Despite some initial lack of enthusiasm, the work of William Faulkner, comprised of a series of elegant short stories and a number of blockbuster, overpoweringly complicated novels,

(B) Despite some initial lack of enthusiasms, the works of William Faulkner, comprised of a series of elegant short stories and a number of blockbusters, overpoweringly complicated novels,

(C) Despite some initial lack of enthusiasm, the works of William Faulkner, comprised of a series of elegant short stories and a number of blockbuster, overpoweringly complicated novels,

(D) Despite some initial lack of enthusiasms, the work of William Faulkner, comprised of a series of elegant short stories and a number of blockbusters, overpoweringly complicated novels,

(E) Despite some initial lack of enthusiasm, the works of William Faulkner are comprised of a series of elegant short stories and a number of blockbuster, overpoweringly complicated novels,

22. <u>After leaving the ranch, the herd of longhorns, the historic cattle of Texas whose image grace everything from coffee mugs to velvet paintings, heads out into the sunset.</u>

(A) After leaving the ranch, the herd of longhorns, the historic cattle of Texas whose image grace everything from coffee mugs to velvet paintings, heads out into the sunset.
(B) After leaving the ranch, the longhorns who formed a herd, the historic cattle of Texas whose image grace everything from coffee mugs to velvet paintings, heads out into the sunset.
(C) After leaving the ranch, the herd of longhorns, the historic cattle of Texas whose image graces everything from coffee mugs and velvet paintings, heads out into the sunset.
(D) After leaving the ranch, the herd of longhorns, the historic cattle of Texas whose image grace everything from coffee mugs to velvet paintings, head out into the sunset.
(E) After leaving the ranch, the herd of longhorns, the historic cattle of Texas whose images grace everything from coffee mugs to velvet paintings, heads out into the sunset.

23. When Orion, whose anthropomorphic image is among the easiest to locate for amateur astronomers, sets at night, <u>the challenges remaining in the night sky are the province of those hardy souls who have spent hours training themselves to identify the subtler and more elusive constellations</u>.

(A) the challenges remaining in the night sky are the province of those hardy souls who have spent hours training themselves to identify the subtler and more elusive constellations
(B) the challenges remaining in the night sky is the province of those hardy souls who have spent hours training themselves to identify the subtler and more elusive constellations
(C) the challenge remaining in the night sky are the province of those hardy souls who have spent hours training themselves to identify the subtler and more elusive constellations
(D) the challenge remaining in the night sky are the province of those hardy souls who have spent hours training themselves to identify the subtler and more elusive constellations
(E) the challenges remaining in the night sky are the province of those hardy souls who has spent hours training themselves to identify the subtler and more elusive constellations

24. In the legal world, members of the jury <u>is sometimes considered to be the trier of questions of fact</u>, while the judge is the trier of questions of the law.

(A) is sometimes considered to be the trier of questions of fact
(B) is considered the trier of questions of fact
(C) are considered the triers of questions of fact
(D) is considered as the trier of questions of fact
(E) are considered to be triers of questions of fact

Check your answers on page 605.

VERB TENSE

Verb tense questions are usually easy to correct once you decide which tense to use. In most cases, verb tense should be consistent throughout the sentence.

The Rule: Sentences should use only one tense (past, present, or future) unless the meaning of the sentence requires a shift.

You can use other verbs in the sentence (particularly those that are not underlined) to help you decide which tense to use. You can also look for time cues such as *Last year* or *Next summer* to help you decide on the correct tense.

The ID

- Look for changing tenses (for example, did vs. do) in the answer choices.
- Look for multiple tenses in the original sentence.

1. Until Jackie Robinson made his debut in a Brooklyn Dodgers uniform in 1947, African Americans <u>were prohibited to play</u> for any Major League baseball team.

   (A) were prohibited to play
   (B) have been prohibited from playing
   (C) have been prohibited to play
   (D) had been prohibited to play
   (E) had been prohibited from playing

You know that you are being tested on verb tense, because there are three different tenses in the answer choices: *were* (past tense), *have been prohibited* (present perfect) and *had been prohibited* (past perfect).

The **present perfect tense** describes an action that occurred at an indefinite time in the past or one that started at an indefinite time in the past and continues up to and through the present.

You can recognize this tense when you see the helping verbs *has* or *have* followed by the past participle. For example

I *have never read* a book by Jackie Collins.
Michael *has been studying* for the GMAT since birth.

The **past perfect tense** describes an action that happened in the past before some other action that was also in the past.

You can recognize this tense when you see the helping verb *had*. For example

Kelly *had been studying* for the GMAT, until she won the lottery.

In the past, Kelly won the lottery. Before that (in the distant past) she was studying. Now, she is probably on a beach in Hawaii, but the present tense is not stated explicitly in the sentence; it is just implied.

In the Jackie Robinson example above, you need the past perfect tense, because you are trying to express the idea that something happened in the past (African-Americans were prohibited from playing) before something else that also occurred in the past (Jackie Robinson came along). *Had been* is correct so eliminate (A), (B), and (C).

You may notice that (D) says *prohibited to* and (E) says *prohibited from*. The correct idiom is *prohibited from*, so the correct answer is (E).

VERB TENSE DRILL

1. The country's willingness to withdraw its troops <u>have fostered the hope that there will be peace eventually</u>; however, most experts indicate there will be continued hostilities in the region.

   (A) have fostered the hope that there will be peace eventually
   (B) has fostered the hope that there will eventually be peace
   (C) fostered the hope for peace eventually
   (D) had fostered the hope for there eventually being peace
   (E) fostered the hope for there being peace eventually

2. Sales of the new vehicle are not what they should be, because the car has an idiosyncratic appearance <u>which prevented</u> more conservative consumers from buying it.

   (A) which prevented
   (B) that has been preventing
   (C) which has prevented
   (D) having prevented
   (E) that prevents

3. Of all the scandals of the 1984 election season, <u>maybe none is more controversial as</u> the one that ended the 30-year political career of the senator from Alaska.

   (A) maybe none is more controversial as
   (B) maybe it is none that was more controversial than
   (C) perhaps none was more controversial than
   (D) it may be that none is more controversial as
   (E) perhaps it is none that is more controversial than

4. Once they had completed preliminary testing of the soil at the excavation site, the archaeologists <u>did not doubt whether the skeleton found was</u> a reptile from the Mesozoic era.

   (A) did not doubt whether the skeleton found was
   (B) have no doubt whether the skeleton found was that of
   (C) had no doubt that the skeleton found was that of
   (D) have no doubt whether the skeleton found was
   (E) had not doubted that the skeleton found was

5. His tour of the new outdoor mall, erected in the newly revitalized urban center, led Mayor Webster to recall an America <u>in which segregation had existed in now currently multi-ethnic neighborhoods</u>.

   (A) in which segregation had existed in now currently multi-ethnic neighborhoods
   (B) when segregation existed in areas now that are multi-ethnic
   (C) when segregation had existed in current multi-ethnic areas
   (D) when segregation existed where there were neighborhoods now multi-ethnic
   (E) in which segregation existed in what are now multi-ethnic neighborhoods

6. A 1964 ordinance in the city of Pittsburgh <u>increased the number of people who had been allowed to occupy a single-family dwelling</u> in a residential neighborhood.

   (A) increased the number of people who had been allowed to occupy a single-family dwelling
   (B) increased the number of people who are allowed to occupy a single-family dwelling
   (C) increases the number of people who have been allowed to occupy a single-family dwelling
   (D) increased the number of people who had been occupying a single-family dwelling
   (E) increases the number of people allowed for occupation in a single-family dwelling

7. A foreign consortium wants to mine copper and gold in a small town near the home of the sockeye salmon in Bristol Bay; the question is <u>whether the sockeye salmon will return to the bay and spawn their young after the area is</u> disturbed by miners.

   (A) whether the sockeye salmon will return to the bay and spawn their young after the area is
   (B) if the sockeye salmon will return to the bay to spawn them after the area has been
   (C) if the sockeye salmon will return to the bay and spawn their young once the area is
   (D) whether the sockeye salmon will return to the bay to spawn their young once the area has been
   (E) whether the sockeye salmon will return to the bay to spawn them once the area is

8. A PhD student at the University of Portsmouth has identified an ancient ancestor of the modern grasshopper, a species of the family Proscopiidae <u>existing concurrently with those that did</u> in the Cretaceous period, approximately 115 million years ago.

   (A) existing concurrently with those that did
   (B) existing concurrently with those that were
   (C) that existed concurrently with those that had
   (D) that existed concurrently with other grasshoppers
   (E) that had existed concurrently with other grasshoppers

9. Although home foreclosures last month <u>totaled a higher sum</u> than 1 in every 464 U.S. households, some economists believe the market could stabilize by early 2009.

   (A) totaled a higher sum
   (B) totaled more
   (C) totaled higher
   (D) totals more
   (E) totals a sum higher

10. In order to counter the tepid audience response, the producers have hired a composer known for his rousing musical numbers; his songs <u>have been designed to engage the audience, and they are</u>.

    (A) have been designed to engage the audience, and they are
    (B) are designed to engage the audience, and they have
    (C) had been designed to engage the audience, and they have
    (D) are being designed to engage the audience, and have
    (E) are designed to engage the audience, and they do

11. Although shortening <u>was first developed as a cheaper alternative to the lard needed to make candles, it had been marketed as food</u> when the prevalence of electricity decreased the demand for tapers.

    (A) was first developed as a cheaper alternative to the lard needed to make candles, it had been marketed as food
    (B) was developed first as a cheaper alternative to the lard needed to make candles, it was marketed as food
    (C) was first developed as a cheaper alternative to the lard needed to make candles, it was marketed as food
    (D) was developed first as a cheaper alternative to the lard needed to make candles, marketing as food
    (E) developed as a cheaper alternative to the lard needed to make candles first, it was marketed as food

12. Although some doctors believe that the drug can have positive effects when taken sporadically, most agree that the medicine is effective only if it is administered in a single, concentrated dose.

(A) only if it is administered in a single, concentrated dose
(B) if it was administered only in a single and concentrated dose
(C) if it would only be administered in a concentrated dose, singly
(D) only if it would be administered in a singly concentrated dose
(E) if it is administered only in a dose concentrated singly

13. A study conducted at Cedar-Sinai Medical Center indicated that if heart surgery patients participate in group therapy and talked about their surgeries, they will feel less pain and recover quicker than do those who are isolated.

(A) talked about their surgeries, they will feel less pain and recover quicker than do
(B) talk about their surgeries, they have felt less pain and will recover more quickly than do
(C) talk about their surgeries, they feel less pain and recover more quickly than
(D) talked about their surgeries, they feel less pain and recover quicker than
(E) talk about their surgeries, they felt less pain and will recover quicker than do

14. At least one recent poll has indicated that in the past few months, many pregnant teenagers have chosen to give birth to their babies rather than braving the lines of protestors at abortion clinics.

(A) have chosen to give birth to their babies rather than braving
(B) had chosen birth of their babies instead of braving
(C) have chosen birthing their babies instead of braving
(D) have chosen to give birth to their babies rather than brave
(E) had chosen birth of their babies rather than brave

15. What many think is a fancy drink is actually a very basic cocktail; a Batida is simply Cachaça or vodka to which has been added fruit juice and sugar.

(A) to which has been added fruit juice and sugar
(B) and, in addition, fruit juice and sugar are added
(C) with fruit juice and sugar having been added to it
(D) to which fruit juice and sugar have been added
(E) added to which is fruit juice and sugar

16. The mayor announced that the fire and subsequent rain caused more property damage than experts had predicted it to and city operations will be affected for several months.

(A) had predicted it to and city operations will be affected
(B) predicted it would and that it will affect city operations
(C) had predicted and that city operations would be affected
(D) predicted and that it will have affected city operations
(E) predicted them to and city operations would be affected

17. Medical experts predict that the number of unnecessary deaths in nursing homes will rise if the elderly resident ratio in public facilities were more numerous than ten residents for every one staff member.

(A) will rise if the elderly resident ratio in public facilities were more numerous than
(B) will rise if the ratio of elderly residents in public facilities is greater than
(C) should rise if the elderly resident ratio in public facilities was greater than
(D) would rise provided the ratio of elderly residents in public facilities is more than
(E) would rise if the ratio of elderly residents in public facilities is more numerous than

18. The council recommended <u>that support for the construction of the wind power farm, which could be the first of its kind in the area, is</u> raised as quickly as possible.

    (A) that support for the construction of the wind power farm, which could be the first of its kind in the area, is
    (B) support for the wind power farm's construction, the first of its kind in the area, be
    (C) construction funding for the wind power farm, which could be the first of its kind in the area, is to be
    (D) that support for the construction of the wind power farm, which could be the first of its kind in the area, be
    (E) support for the construction of the wind power farm, perhaps the first of its kind in the area, to be

19. At the time of his death, followers of Mahatma <u>Gandhi's have stated that he had</u> committed himself to the highest moral principles: truth, faith and nonviolence.

    (A) Gandhi's have stated that he had
    (B) Gandhi's state that he had
    (C) Gandhi's stated that he has
    (D) Gandhi had stated that he has
    (E) Gandhi stated that he had

20. As technology increases, teens <u>communicating primarily through media like those of email and text messaging have been becoming increasingly</u> ill-prepared for college.

    (A) communicating primarily through media like those of email and text messaging have been becoming increasingly
    (B) who communicate primarily through informal media like those of email and text messaging have been becoming more and more
    (C) who communicate primarily through such informal media as email and text messaging are becoming more and more
    (D) who communicated primarily through informal media such as those of email and text messaging are being increasingly
    (E) having communicated primarily through such informal media as email and text messaging are being increasingly

21. Of all the years in Einstein's life, <u>possibly none is more impressive than</u> 1905 when four of his ground-breaking papers were published in a prominent German physics journal.

    (A) possibly none is more impressive than
    (B) maybe none was more impressive as
    (C) possibly none was more impressive than
    (D) perhaps none is more impressive as
    (E) maybe none is more impressive than

22. Anthropology programs at some colleges have recently been separated into two categories, one that focuses on more objective and interpretive studies of the past and the other that <u>relied</u> on quantitative results that are based in theory.

    (A) relied
    (B) will rely
    (C) relies
    (D) relying
    (E) is relying

23. A tiger escaped his enclosure at the San Francisco zoo, <u>and it caused</u> some to question whether the height of the dry moat that separated the animal from his victim was adequate.

    (A) and it caused
    (B) and it causes
    (C) and caused
    (D) and causing
    (E) causing

24. Dorothy Parker's fiery personality was often mirrored in her caustic stories, which were brazen for the 1930s, a time period <u>in which women were more cautious about voicing their opinions</u>.

    (A) in which women were more cautious about voicing their opinions
    (B) where women were more cautious about voicing their opinions
    (C) in which women had been more cautious about voicing their opinions
    (D) when women would have been more cautious about voicing their opinions
    (E) when women had been more cautious about voicing their opinions

25. Much to the chagrin of citizens who enjoyed such performances as *The Sleeping Beauty* and *Carmen*, London's Royal Opera House was twice destroyed by fires, succumbed to flames in both 1809 and 1856.

(A) London's Royal Opera House was twice destroyed by fires, succumbed to flames
(B) London's Royal Opera House was twice destroyed by fires, succumbing to flames
(C) twice destroyed by fires, London's Royal Opera House succumbed to flames
(D) twice destroyed by fires, London's Royal Opera House succumbing to flames
(E) London's Royal Opera House has been twice destroyed by fires, succumbed to flames

26. The preeminent astronomer, Carl Sagan, posited that the expansion of the universe, with galaxies rushing ever outward away from each other, was caused by the Big Bang about 15 billion years ago.

(A) The preeminent astronomer, Carl Sagan, posited that the expansion of the universe, with galaxies rushing ever outward away from each other, was caused by the Big Bang about 15 billion years ago.
(B) The preeminent astronomer, Carl Sagan, posited that the expansion of the universe, with galaxies rushing ever outward away from each other, is caused by the Big Bang about 15 billion years ago.
(C) Carl Sagan, the preeminent astronomer, posited that the expansion of the universe was caused by the Big Bang about 15 billion years ago and the galaxies are rushing ever outward away from each other.
(D) The preeminent astronomer, Carl Sagan, posited that the Big Bang caused the expansion of the universe about 15 billion years ago, sending the galaxies rushing ever outward away from each other.
(E) The preeminent astronomer, Carl Sagan, posited that the Big Bang, causing the expansion of the universe about 15 billion years ago, sending the galaxies rushing ever outward away from each other.

27. Hunter-gatherers, those who gain sustenance from plants and animals, are generally known to have an abundant social life because they work approximately 15 hours a week, which leaves a significant amount of time for group gatherings.

(A) are generally known to have an abundant social life because they work approximately 15 hours a week
(B) are generally known to have an abundant social life because they worked approximately 15 hours a week
(C) are generally known to have been abundant socially because they work approximately 15 hours a week
(D) were generally known to have an abundant social life because they work approximately 15 hours a week
(E) were generally known to have an abundant social life because they worked approximately 15 hours a week

28. In Nathanial Philbrick's book, *Mayflower*, the author attempts to describe the challenges that Puritans faced as they struggled to recreate the English village that they left behind.

(A) Puritans faced as they struggled to recreate the English village that they left behind
(B) Puritans faced as they struggled to recreate the English village that they had left behind
(C) Puritans were facing as they struggled to recreate the English village that they left behind
(D) Puritans had been facing as they struggled to recreate the English village that they left behind
(E) were faced by Puritans as they struggled to recreate the English village that they left behind

Check your answers on page 605.

PRONOUNS

There are two types of pronoun errors you should look for on the test: agreement and ambiguity. Because pronouns are small words, you must read carefully to spot them.

The Rule: A pronoun must agree in number with the noun to which it refers (singular/singular, plural/plural).

The Rule: A pronoun must unambiguously refer to one noun.

Even if you think you know to which noun a pronoun refers, if it is not explicitly clear, that is considered an error.

The ID

- Look for changing pronouns (for example, *their* vs. *its*) in the answer choices.
- Be especially wary of *they* and *it*.

1. Each of the dogs now in the animal shelter <u>had been neglected by their former owner before they were abandoned</u>.

   (A) had been neglected by their former owner before they were abandoned
   (B) was neglected by its former owner before it was abandoned
   (C) was neglected by their former owner before they were abandoned
   (D) had been neglected by its former owner before it was abandoned
   (E) was abandoned, but before that they had been neglected by their former owner

You may notice that there is a 2/3 split between *their* and *its*, as well as a 2/3 split between *they* and *it*. That means you are being tested on pronoun agreement. Start with *their* vs. *its*. *Their/its* refers to the word *each*, which is singular. Therefore, *its* is correct and you can eliminate (A), (C), and (E).

The remaining two choices have two different verb tenses, so you are also being tested on verb tense. In this case, you need the past perfect tense, because in the distant past the dogs were neglected, after that (still in the past) they were abandoned, and now they are in the shelter. Therefore, *had been* is correct and the correct answer is (D).

PRONOUNS DRILL

1. Continuing a recent trend of support for the arts, the city council passed a resolution yesterday stating that <u>they would provide a fund to the historic theater for renovation</u>.

   (A) they would provide a fund to the historic theater for renovation
   (B) it would provide funding for the renovation of the historic theater
   (C) it would, for the purposes of renovating, grant funding to the historic theater
   (D) they would, with a grant for renovation, provide funding to the theater
   (E) it could, with funds, grant renovation to the historic theater

2. According to statements released by health officials, individuals <u>that inhale second-hand smoke on a regular basis face health risks almost as grave as those faced by direct smokers, and as a result many states have passed laws banning it</u> in public places.

   (A) that inhale second-hand smoke on a regular basis face health risks almost as grave as those faced by direct smokers, and as a result many states have passed laws banning it
   (B) who inhale second hand smoke on a regular basis are facing health risks almost as grave as those facing at direct smokers, and as a result many states are passing laws banning it
   (C) who inhale smoke on a regular basis face health risks almost as grave as those faced by direct smokers, and as a result many states have passed laws that ban smoking
   (D) who inhale smoke on a regular basis face health risks almost as grave as those facing direct smokers, with the result of many states having passed laws banning
   (E) that inhale smoke on a regular basis face health risks almost as grave as direct smokers, and as result many states have passed laws banning smoking

3. The Department of Agriculture has released studies indicating <u>that proper chicken egg refrigeration is important if they are to be consumed, as eating them if they have been improperly preserved</u> may lead to salmonella infection.

   (A) that proper chicken egg refrigeration is impo-rtant if they are to be consumed, as eating them if they have been improperly preserved
   (B) if chicken eggs are to be consumed, it is important for them to be properly refrigerated, as eating improperly preserved eggs
   (C) if chicken eggs are to be consumed, the refrigeration of them is important, as eating them if they have been improperly
   (D) that if chicken eggs are to be consumed it is important to refrigerate them properly, as eating improperly preserved eggs
   (E) the importance of proper chicken egg refrigeration, if they are to be consumed, because eating them if they have not been properly preserved

4. Professors at the college, <u>many of whom</u> have tenure, argue that the starting salary for most faculty positions is too low.

   (A) many of whom
   (B) of many of who
   (C) many of who
   (D) many of which
   (E) many that

5. The research team announced Tuesday <u>that they have identified a group of proteins that can reveal to them the biological age of an individual</u>.

   (A) that they have identified a group of proteins that can reveal to them the biological age of an individual
   (B) that they have identified a group of proteins that can reveal to them the biological age of all individuals
   (C) it has identified that a group of proteins that to it can reveal the biological age of an individual
   (D) that it has identified a group of proteins that can reveal the biological age to them of an individual
   (E) that it has identified a group of proteins that can reveal the biological age of an individual

6. While the term "desktop publishing" <u>is typically used to describe page layout skills, they are not limited to book publishing, and may extend</u> to skills and software used to create graphics for promotional items, signs, and trade show exhibits.

   (A) is typically used to describe page layout skills, they are not limited to book publishing, and may extend to skills
   (B) is typically used to describe skills of laying out pages, it is not limited to book publishing and may have extended
   (C) has typically used to describe skills used for laying out pages, it has not been limited to book publishing, and is extending
   (D) has typically been used to describe page layout skills, they are not limited to book publishing, and may extend
   (E) is typically used to describe page layout skills, the definition is not limited to book publishing only, and may extend

7. A new strategy for releasing the seals into the wild has been created; the question is <u>if marine biologists will be able to track the seals once they are back in</u> the ocean.

   (A) if marine biologists will be able to track the seals once they are back
   (B) whether marine biologists will be able to track it once they are back in
   (C) whether marine biologists will be able to track one after the seal has been returned to
   (D) if marine biologists will be able to track and follow the seals after the seals have been returned to
   (E) whether marine biologists will be able to track the seals once the creatures have been returned to

8. The emergency ward at the hospital has decreased the average wait time for patients <u>by not only increasing the number of nurses on staff but also by streamlining the paperwork that they must</u> complete.

   (A) by not only increasing the number of nurses on staff but also by streamlining the paperwork that they must
   (B) by not only increasing the number of nurses on staff, but it has also streamlined the paperwork they must
   (C) not only by increasing the number of nurses on staff but it also gave them less paperwork that they must
   (D) not only increasing the number of nurses on staff but also these patients have been given more streamlined paperwork to
   (E) by not only increasing the number of nurses on staff but also by streamlining the paperwork that patients must

9. The proper way to make confit of goose is <u>to boil them in their own fat and then allow the fats to set</u>.

   (A) to boil them in their own fat and then allow the fat to set
   (B) to boil the goose in its own fat and then allow the fats to set
   (C) if they are boiled in fats and then the fats are allowed to set
   (D) for them to be boiled in their own fats and then the fats are allowed to set
   (E) if the goose is boiled in fat and then their fat allowed to set

10. After announcing that <u>they had been bought out</u> by the larger corporation, the bank assured customers that all deposits would continue to receive full protection and that the daily operations of the firm would remain unchanged.

    (A) they had been bought out by the larger corporation
    (B) they were being bought out by the larger corporation
    (C) it was being bought out largely by the corporation
    (D) it had been bought out largely by the corporation
    (E) it had been bought out by the larger corporation

11. In 1773 the British Government passed the Tea Act, which allowed the British East India Company to sell tea directly to the American colonies and <u>exempting them from paying</u> British customs fees.

    (A) exempting them from paying
    (B) exempted it from paying
    (C) for exempting payment of British
    (D) that exempted them from paying
    (E) that they were exempted from the paying of

12. Due to improvements in modern technology, some people <u>who were once completely blind</u> have been able to undergo laser surgery and gain nearly perfect eyesight.

    (A) who were once completely blind
    (B) that once had been blind completely
    (C) that at one time were completely blind
    (D) who at one time were completely blind in the past
    (E) who, when they were completely blind at one time

13. As the prairies of the Midwest dried up due to drought and over-farming, many settlers of the time <u>where land was barren and homes</u> had been seized in foreclosure moved further westward in search of food and employment.

    (A) where land was barren and homes
    (B) where their land was barren and their homes
    (C) with more barren land and homes that
    (D) whose land was barren and whose homes
    (E) having barren land and homes that

14. Although the baseball team practiced more diligently that year than <u>their prior years</u>, in the end it still lost the championship to the opposing team.

    (A) their prior years
    (B) they had in prior years
    (C) in prior years
    (D) they had for any prior years
    (E) in their prior years

15. Although certain great apes have successfully
    been taught how to communicate with humans
    through sign language, it is considered by some
    researchers to be merely a clever trick done for a
    reward.

    (A) Although certain great apes have successfully
        been taught how to communicate with
        humans using sign language, it is considered
        by some researchers to be merely a clever
        trick for a reward.
    (B) Although certain great apes have been taught
        how to communicate with humans through
        sign language, some researchers consider
        these signs to be merely clever tricks done
        for a reward.
    (C) Certain great apes have been successfully
        taught how to communicate with humans
        using signs that are considered by some
        researchers to be merely clever tricks done
        as rewards.
    (D) Although certain great apes have been
        successfully taught how to communicate
        with humans, using sign language; causing it
        to be considered by some researchers to be
        merely a clever trick for a reward.
    (E) Although certain great apes have been taught
        how to communicate with humans, through
        sign language, which is considered by some
        researchers to be merely a clever trick done
        for a reward.

16. By extracting moisture from the humid air using
    its nasal passages and by collecting seeds from
    native grasses, giant kangaroo rats adapted well
    to the desert environment in the San Joaquin
    Valley before the encroachment of irrigated farms
    forced it to move to higher ground.

    (A) giant kangaroo rats adapted
    (B) giant kangaroo rats adapt
    (C) giant kangaroo rats were adapted
    (D) the giant kangaroo rat had adapted
    (E) the giant kangaroo rat adapts

17. Much like their counterparts in other countries,
    labor unions in the United States often support
    candidates for elected office that put the rights of
    workers above large corporations.

    (A) labor unions in the United States often
        support candidates for elected office that put
        the rights of workers above large corporations
    (B) labor unions in the United States often
        support candidates for elected office who put
        the rights of workers above large corporations
    (C) labor unions in the United States often
        support candidates for elected office that put
        the rights of workers above the rights of large
        corporations
    (D) labor unions in the United States often
        support candidates for elected office who put
        the rights of workers above the rights of large
        corporations
    (E) labor unions in the United States often
        support candidates for elected office where
        rights of workers are put above the rights of
        large corporations

18. Founded by Steven Wozniak and Steve Jobs in
    Cupertino, California, Apple Computers has grown
    to employ over 15,000 employees under his
    leadership as CEO, and the number of products
    offered at a given time has grown from one to
    over one-hundred.

    (A) Apple Computers has grown to employ over
        15,000 employees under his leadership as
        CEO
    (B) Apple Computers has grown to employ over
        15,000 employees under Jobs's leadership as
        CEO
    (C) Apple Computers growing to employ over
        15,000 employees under his leadership as
        CEO
    (D) over 15,000 employees are employed by
        Apple Computers under his leadership as
        CEO
    (E) over 15,000 employees are employed by
        Apple Computers under Jobs's leadership as
        CEO

19. While it was initially unclear whom was to blame for the assassination of Archduke Franz Ferdinand of Austria, evidence later surfaced that a group of Serbian military officers organized a conspiracy to exterminate the leader and cause a break-up of the Balkan states that would eventually lead to the First World War.

    (A) While it was initially unclear whom was to blame for the assassination of Archduke Franz Ferdinand of Austria
    (B) While it was initially unclear to whom was to blame for the assassination of Archduke Franz Ferdinand of Austria
    (C) While it was initially unclear who was to blame for the assassination of Archduke Franz Ferdinand of Austria
    (D) While it was initially unclear to who was to blame for the assassination of Archduke Franz Ferdinand of Austria
    (E) The blame for the assassination of Archduke Franz Ferdinand of Austria was initially unclear

20. When crafting a resume, one should include as many specific measurements of past performance as possible, such as sales figures or successful projects, in order to accentuate the positive and "put your best foot forward," as the saying goes.

    (A) one should include as many specific measurements of past performance as possible
    (B) one should include as many specific measurements of past performance
    (C) you should include as many specific measurements of past performance as possible
    (D) you should include as many specific measurements of past performance
    (E) people should include as many specific measurements of past performance

21. The Hawthorne Effect, named after a series of psychological experiments at the Hawthorne Works in Cicero, Illinois, describes a phenomenon in which the subject of a study or experiment, under the observation of researchers, often improve their behavior or performance simply because they are part of a study or experiment.

    (A) often improve their behavior or performance simply because they are part of a study or experiment
    (B) often improves their behavior or performance simply because they are part of a study or experiment
    (C) often improve his or her behavior or performance simply because they are part of a study or experiment
    (D) often improves his or her behavior or performance simply because he or she is part of a study or experiment
    (E) often, because they are part of a study, improve their behavior or performance

22. In an effort to off-set their potential losses from highly volatile technology stocks and protect short-term investors, the pension fund bought hundreds of thousands of dollars worth of municipal bonds and, in the process, diversified their portfolio.

    (A) In an effort to off-set their potential losses from highly volatile technology stocks and protect short-term investors, the pension fund
    (B) In an effort to off-set its potential losses from highly volatile technology stocks and protect short-term investors, the pension fund
    (C) In an effort to off-set their potential losses from highly volatile technology stocks and protect short-term investors, pension funds
    (D) The pension fund, in an effort to off-set their potential losses from highly volatile technology stocks and protect short-term investors,
    (E) The pension fund, off-setting their potential losses from highly volatile technology stocks and protecting short-term investors,

23. The public's general concern about the solvency of the Social Security Trust Fund <u>and their overall faith in the long-term growth of the stock market has</u> led to a rise in interest in Individual Retirement Accounts or IRAs.

(A) and their overall faith in the long-term growth of the stock market has
(B) and they have overall faith in the long-term growth of the stock market which has
(C) as well as their overall faith in the long-term growth of the stock market, has
(D) as well as overall faith in the long-term growth of the stock market, have
(E) and its overall faith in the long-term growth of the stock market have

24. Considered one of the most intelligent of the New World monkeys, <u>capuchins cleverly create an insecticide and crush millipedes, rubbing the remains</u> of the bugs over its back.

(A) capuchins cleverly create an insecticide and crush millipedes, rubbing the remains
(B) capuchins cleverly create an insecticide, they crush millipedes, and with such rub the remains
(C) capuchins use their cleverness to create an insecticide, crush millipedes, and rub the remains
(D) the capuchin cleverly creates an insecticide, crushes millipedes, and it rubs the remains
(E) the capuchin cleverly creates an insecticide, crushing millipedes and rubbing the remains

> Check your answers on page 605.

PARALLEL CONSTRUCTION

Parallel construction means that words in a sentence need to be similar in form to other words in that sentence. Words should share the same part of speech and phrases should have the same structure.

On the GMAT, parallel construction is primarily tested in two ways: lists and comparisons. Lists are somewhat easier, so start with lists.

Lists

The Rule: Items in a list must take the same form.

All the items in a list or series must be parallel, which means that items should share the same part of speech (nouns or verbs) and the forms of the nouns or verbs should match as closely as possible.

The ID

- Look for lists or series. (The test writers may use prepositional phrases to make it harder to identify which items are parts of the list.)

1. The two main goals of the Eisenhower presidency were <u>a reduction of taxes and to increase military strength</u>.

   (A) a reduction of taxes and to increase military strength
   (B) to reduce taxes and an increase in military strength
   (C) to reduce taxes and to increase military strength
   (D) a reduction and an increase in taxes and military strength
   (E) taxes being reduced and military strength being increased

You have a list so you know you're being tested on parallelism. The list in the original sentence has a noun (*reduction*) and a verb (*to increase*). You need two nouns or two verbs, so eliminate (A) and (B). Choice (E) contains the word *being*, so you can eliminate it as well. Choice (D) simply doesn't make sense. That leaves you with (C), which is, in fact, parallel. The correct answer is (C).

Comparisons

The Rule: In comparisons, items must be compared to like items.

In comparisons, the items compared must be similar. You must compare apples to apples and oranges to oranges. You can't compare apples to oranges.

The ID

- Look for the following comparison words:

    - Than
    - As
    - Like
    - Just as
    - Not only… but also

2. The rules of written English are more stringent <u>than spoken English</u>.

    (A) than spoken English
    (B) as spoken English
    (C) than those of spoken English
    (D) as those of spoken English
    (E) so than those of spoken English

The question contains the word *than*, so you know you are being tested on comparisons. The comparison in the original sentence is incorrect, because you cannot compare the rules (of written English) to (spoken) English. You must either compare rules to rules or English to English. Eliminate (A).

You may also notice that two of the answers say *than* and two of them say *as*. This change in small words means you are also being tested on idioms. The correct idiom is *more than* so eliminate (B) and (D). You can also eliminate (E), because *so than* is also an incorrect idiom. That leaves only (C), which is the correct answer.

Questions involving parallel construction can be some of the hardest ones on the sentence correction portion of the test.

PARALLEL CONSTRUCTION DRILL

1. The Industrial Revolution was a time of marked technological change that influenced nearly all aspects of society, and particularly methods of transporting goods, smelting iron, and <u>manufacturing</u> textiles.

    (A) manufacturing
    (B) manufactured
    (C) they manufactured textiles
    (D) had manufactured
    (E) the manufacture of

2. Citing recent rises in world temperature, climatologists argue that continued pollution of the atmosphere may cause sea levels to rise, glaciers to retreat, <u>changing precipitation patterns, and resulting in</u> greater occurrences of flooding and drought.

    (A) changing precipitation patterns, and resulting in
    (B) changing the patterns of precipitation, with the result of
    (C) changing precipitation patterns, that result with
    (D) and precipitation patterns to change, resulting in
    (E) and precipitation patterns to change, resulting with

3. Recent surveys indicate that an increasing number of commuters <u>have chosen to take public transportation rather than driving</u> to work in the gridlock of city traffic.

    (A) have chosen to take public transportation rather than driving
    (B) have chosen taking public transportation rather than to drive
    (C) choose to take public transportation rather than drive
    (D) choose to take public transportation rather than driving
    (E) choose to take public transportation instead of driving

4. Unlike dark roofs, which absorb the sun's rays and thus emit many dangerous greenhouse gases, <u>using white roofs is more environmentally friendly as they instead reflect the sun's rays and as a result give</u> off fewer greenhouse gases.

    (A) using white roofs is more environmentally friendly as they instead reflect the sun's rays and as a result give
    (B) white roofs reflect the sun's rays, and as a result are more environmentally friendly as they give
    (C) using white roofs is more environmentally friendly as they instead reflect the sun's rays and as a result are giving
    (D) the use of white roofs is more environmentally friendly as they instead reflect the sun's rays, and as a result give
    (E) white roofs reflect the sun's rays and as a result are more environmentally friendly as they have given

5. The recent startup of the Large Hadron Collider in Switzerland has raised concerns among critics about both the risk of <u>releasing dangerous hypothetical particles called strangelets and the risk of creating a black hole that could potentially destroy the earth</u>.

    (A) releasing dangerous hypothetical particles called strangelets and the risk of creating a black hole that could potentially destroy the earth
    (B) releasing dangerous hypothetical particles called strangelets and risking the destruction of the earth by creating a black hole
    (C) the release of dangerous particles called strangelets and the risk of destroying the earth with a potential black hole
    (D) dangerous hypothetical particles called strangelets being released and the risk of creating a black hole that could potentially destroy the earth
    (E) dangerous hypothetical particles called strangelets being released and the risk of a black hole being created that could destroy the earth

6. Under the No Child Left Behind Act, public school systems are required either to meet established standards, or <u>that they provide</u> eligible children the opportunity to transfer to higher-performing local schools.

(A) that they provide
(B) to provide
(C) they should provide
(D) for providing
(E) it should provide

7. Wind turbines may be a visual blight upon the rural landscape, but proponents of alternative energy sources point out that <u>wind power causes much less environmental damage than using fossil fuels</u>.

(A) wind power causes much less environmental damage than using fossil fuels
(B) wind power causes much less environmental damage than fossil fuels do
(C) using wind power causes much less environmental damage than fossil fuels do
(D) using wind power causes less environmental damage as it does for fossil fuels
(E) to use wind power causes much less environmental damage as for fossil fuels

8. The recent increase in the number of tourists has caused overcrowding in the small town, <u>to lead to more traffic jams, and provokes</u> concerns among some residents that the quiet village atmosphere is being jeopardized.

(A) to lead to more traffic jams, and provokes
(B) leading to more traffic jam and provokes
(C) leading to an increase in traffic jams and provoking
(D) to lead to an increase in traffic jams and provoke
(E) to lead to an increase in traffic jams and provoked

9. The board voted Monday to purchase new offices overseas and <u>if the executives had received positive evaluations they would be promoted</u>.

(A) if the executives had received positive evaluations they would be promoted.
(B) receiving positive evaluations would be a promotion for the executives.
(C) promoting executives having received positive evaluations.
(D) promote the executives who had received positive evaluations.
(E) the executives to be promoted for having received positive evaluations.

10. Due to the impending blizzard, officials have ordered <u>all illegally parked cars to be towed and that the owners be</u> fined.

(A) all illegally parked cars to be towed and that the owners be
(B) that all illegally parked cars be towed and the owners
(C) that all illegally parked cars should be towed, with the owners being
(D) the towing of all illegally parked cars and the owners to be
(E) all illegally parked cars towed, with their owners

11. Experts examining trends in the housing market predict that the number of annual home foreclosures will continue to increase while <u>the number of new home sales will continue to decrease</u>.

(A) the number of new home sales will continue to decrease
(B) those of new home sale decrease
(C) it decreases for new home sales
(D) those of new home sales decrease
(E) there are decreases for the number of new home sales

12. Recent surveys indicate that eating a nutritious diet and exercising regularly are priorities for most people in the United States, like those of most other countries.

    (A) like those of most other countries
    (B) as those of most other countries
    (C) just as most people of other countries do
    (D) as do most people of other countries
    (E) as they are for most people in other countries

13. Earthquakes are the sudden result of energy release in the earth's crust, and can cause ruptures in the ground, the liquefaction of soil, flooding surrounding areas, and the occurrence of tsunamis.

    (A) flooding surrounding areas
    (B) flood surrounding areas
    (C) the flooding of surrounding areas
    (D) surrounding areas that are flooded
    (E) surrounding areas to be flooded

14. Recognized as one of history's most influential scientists, Paul Dirac helped to revolutionize the field of physics; his contributions to the theory of quantum electrodynamics were more valuable than were almost any other physicists of his time.

    (A) than were almost any other
    (B) than were those of almost any other
    (C) than almost any
    (D) than almost any other
    (E) as were those of almost any

15. Dallol, Ethiopia is one of the world's hottest places, with a recorded annual temperature of 94 degrees Fahrenheit, which is higher than in any other country on earth.

    (A) which is higher than in
    (B) which is higher than it is in
    (C) and higher than that of
    (D) higher than that of
    (E) higher than in

16. The proposal by the federal government to bail out two of the nation's largest lending institutions could lead to greater market stability and decreasing the probability of worldwide economic recession.

    (A) decreasing the probability
    (B) the probability decreased
    (C) the probability decreasing
    (D) the decreasing of probability
    (E) decrease the probability

17. Concerned that natural disasters may result in the disruption of basic services for an extended period of time, the Federal Emergency Management Agency recommends stockpiling food and water, storing extra batteries for flashlights and radios, and, when possible, connect a back-up generator to the electrical system.

    (A) and, when possible, connect a back-up generator to the electrical system
    (B) or, when possible, connect a back-up generator to the electrical system
    (C) and connecting, when possible to the electrical system, a back-up generator
    (D) and connect a back-up generator to the electrical system whenever possible
    (E) and, when possible, connecting a back-up generator to the electrical system

18. One of the duties of the Securities and Exchange Commission is to guarantee that individual or small investors have the same information about the financial health of a company as do the large, institutional investors.

    (A) as do the large, institutional investors
    (B) as does the large, institutional investors
    (C) like the large, institutional investors have
    (D) in addition to the large, institutional investors
    (E) as the large, institutional investors

19. The Great Depression, and the New Deal reforms that were enacted subsequently, resulted in regulations in the stock market, programs to help senior citizens during retirement, <u>saving Americans from poverty with an agency</u>, and insurance protecting bank deposits.

(A) saving Americans from poverty with an agency
(B) an agency to save Americans from poverty
(C) agencies saving from poverty Americans
(D) to save Americans from poverty with an agency
(E) savings of Americans from poverty with an agency

20. Many small businesses cannot afford to enroll their employees in group health insurance plans, <u>threatening the health of hundreds of thousands of Americans and leading</u> to a movement among advocacy groups for governmental intervention in the healthcare system.

(A) threatening the health of hundreds of thousands of Americans and leading
(B) threatening the health of hundreds of thousands of Americans and lead
(C) threaten the health of hundreds of thousands of Americans and lead
(D) which threatens the health of hundreds of thousands of Americans and leading
(E) despite threatening the health of hundreds of thousands of Americans and leading

21. <u>While the two differ greatly in size, population, and geography, the gross domestic product of the state of New Jersey in the United States is roughly equivalent to the entire country of Pakistan.</u>

(A) While the two differ greatly in size, population, and geography, the gross domestic product of the state of New Jersey in the United States is roughly equivalent to the entire country of Pakistan.
(B) While the two differ greatly in size, population, and geography, the gross domestic product of the state of New Jersey in the United States is roughly equivalent to that of the entire country of Pakistan.
(C) While the two differ greatly in size, population, and geography, the state of New Jersey in the United State has a gross domestic product roughly equivalent to the entire country of Pakistan.
(D) While they differ greatly in size, population, and geography, the state of New Jersey in the United State has a gross domestic product roughly equivalent to the entire country of Pakistan.
(E) While the two differ greatly in size, population, and geography, the state of New Jersey in the United States and the country of Pakistan have gross domestic products that are roughly equivalent.

22. Despite improvements in building materials and construction methods, many recently built houses in the small coastal town of Swansboro, North Carolina are still likely to suffer significant structural damage <u>on the event of a strong hurricane while only a couple are properly insured against</u> such damage.

(A) on the event of a strong hurricane while only a couple are properly insured against such damage
(B) in the event of a strong hurricane while few are properly insured against such damage
(C) on the event of a strong hurricane while few are properly insured against such damage
(D) when a strong hurricane hits, at the same time only a couple are properly insured against such damage
(E) in the event of a strong hurricane despite only a few being properly insured against such damage

23. The company announced that its gross margin improved in the second quarter largely due to contracts it renegotiated with several of <u>their suppliers and if other vendors would agree to renegotiate the trend would continue</u>.

(A) their suppliers and if other vendors would agree to renegotiate the trend would continue
(B) their suppliers and that other vendors need to agree to renegotiate for the trend to continue
(C) its suppliers and if other vendors would agree to renegotiate the trend would continue
(D) its suppliers and that other vendors need to agree to renegotiate for the trend to continue
(E) the company's suppliers and if other vendors would agree to renegotiate the trend would continue

24. Proponents of cloud computing, the idea that all computer software programs can exist on a centralized, shared server, or a "cloud," rather than on each individual machine, argue that it will free users from the tether of individual computers, save companies time and money when updating their software, and <u>it will encourage</u> developers to focus on integrated products that work well together in the "cloud."

(A) it will encourage
(B) it encourages
(C) will encourage
(D) encourage
(E) encouraging

25. Experts predict that the cost of crude oil will continue to increase steadily, <u>and acknowledging</u> that variable factors such as weather, international relations, and overall supply make precise forecasting difficult.

(A) and acknowledging
(B) but acknowledging
(C) and they had acknowledged
(D) however also acknowledging
(E) although they also acknowledge

26. Some may argue that the classical masterpieces Beethoven composed towards the end of his life, when he was deaf and could only feel the vibrations of the piano's pedals, <u>were greater than his earlier years</u>.

(A) were greater than his earlier years
(B) which are greater than those of earlier years
(C) are greater than earlier years
(D) are greater than those of his earlier years
(E) had to be greater than in those earlier years

> Check your answers on page 605.

MISPLACED MODIFIERS

Modifiers are words or phrases that describe other words in a sentence. For the sake of clarity, a modifier must go right next to the thing it describes.

The Rule: A word or phrase that describes something should go right next to the thing it modifies.

On the GMAT the modifier is usually an introductory phrase. You should always check for misplaced modifiers when you see an introductory phrase. If the whole sentence is underlined, you should also check for misplaced modifiers.

The ID

- Look for introductory phrases.
- Look for the whole sentence underlined.

1. Eaten in the Mediterranean countries, <u>northern Europeans viewed the tomato with suspicion, for they</u> assumed it had poisonous properties because of its relationship to deadly nightshade.

    (A) northern Europeans viewed the tomato with suspicion, for they
    (B) northern Europeans were suspicious of the tomato, and they
    (C) the tomato was viewed with suspicion by northern Europeans, who
    (D) the tomato was suspicious to northern Europeans, and it was
    (E) the tomato was viewed with suspicion by northern Europeans, it being

There is an introductory phrase, so check to see if the introductory phrase is describing the correct thing. Northern Europeans were probably *not* eaten in the Mediterranean countries, so eliminate (A) and (B).

When you scan the remaining answer choices, you may notice that (E) contains the word *being*. Eliminate it.

You may know that only people can be suspicious and that inanimate objects are suspect. If so, eliminate (D).

If not, you may notice that in the original sentence, northern Europeans viewed the tomato with suspicion for, meaning because, they assumed it had poisonous properties. In (D) the tomato was suspicious <u>and</u> it was assumed it had poisonous properties. The causal relationship between the two ideas has been removed in (D), unnecessarily changing the meaning of the original sentence. Thus, the correct answer is (C).

MISPLACED MODIFIERS DRILL

1. Making a legacy for himself as a President who wanted to have the last word on any decision, <u>the phrase "the buck stops here" was coined by Harry S. Truman.</u>

   (A) the phrase "the buck stops here" was coined by Harry S. Truman
   (B) phrasing "the buck stops here" was coined by Harry S. Truman
   (C) "the buck stops here" was a phrase coined by Harry S. Truman
   (D) Harry S. Truman coined the phrase "the buck stops here"
   (E) Harry S. Truman's phrase "the buck stops here" was coined

2. <u>Hunted for their decent size and succulent meat, which ranges from 420 to 1,210 pounds, wildebeests are</u> the most popular prey for lions in the wild.

   (A) Hunted for their decent size and succulent meat, which ranges from 420 to 1,210 pounds, wildebeests are
   (B) Hunted for their decent size and succulent meat, wildebeests range from 420 to 1,210 pounds, who are
   (C) Hunted for their decent size and succulent meat, ranging from 420 to 1,210 pounds, wildebeests are
   (D) Hunted for their succulent meat and decent size, wildebeests range from 420 to 1,210 pounds, who are
   (E) Hunted for their succulent meat and decent size, which ranges from 420 to 1,210 pounds, wildebeests are

3. <u>Working to support their families and pay off their homes, it is unfortunate that many people become embroiled in a constant struggle with their credit card companies, in which they agonize over making minimum payments and witness their monthly fees rise astronomically.</u>

   (A) Working to support their families and pay off their homes, it is unfortunate that many people become embroiled in a constant struggle with their credit card companies, in which they agonize over making minimum payments and witness their monthly fees rise astronomically.
   (B) Working to support their families and pay off their homes, many people become embroiled in an unfortunate struggle with their credit card companies, agonize over making minimum payments and witnessing their monthly fees rise astronomically.
   (C) Despite their work to support their families and pay off their homes, it is unfortunate that many people become embroiled in a constant struggle with their credit card companies, in which they agonize over making minimum payments and witness their monthly fees rise astronomically.
   (D) Unfortunately, to agonize over making minimum payments and to witness their monthly fees rise astronomically, many people who are working to support their families and pay off their homes become embroiled in a constant struggle with their credit card companies.
   (E) Working to support their families and pay off their homes, many people become embroiled in an unfortunate struggle with their credit card companies, agonizing over making minimum payments and witnessing their monthly fees rise astronomically.

4. Consumed on a daily basis in many unexpected foods, such as cereal and bread, <u>United States citizens are beginning to wonder if corn may be contributing to an increase in their national average weight</u>.

(A) United States' citizens are beginning to wonder if corn may be contributing to an increase in their national average weight

(B) United States' citizens are beginning to wonder if an increase in its national average weight may be due to corn

(C) the national average weight of United States' citizens may be due to corn, one wonders

(D) corn may be contributing to an increase in the national average weight of United States' citizens

(E) one wonders if the increase in the national average weight of United States' citizens may be contributed by corn

5. <u>Published every year since 1818, the Farmers' Almanac contains forecasts about the weather, the most recent astronomical calendar, and humorous advice on household interests, such as cooking and gardening.</u>

(A) Published every year since 1818, the Farmers' Almanac contains forecasts about the weather, the most recent astronomical calendar, and humorous advice on household interests, such as cooking and gardening.

(B) Published every year since 1818, the Farmers' Almanac contained forecasts about the weather, the most recent astronomical calendar, and humorous advice on household interests, such as cooking and gardening.

(C) Published every year since 1818, forecasts about the weather, the most recent astronomical calendar, and humorous advice on household interests, such as cooking and gardening are all contained in the Farmers' Almanac.

(D) Every year since 1818, the published Farmers' Almanac contained forecasts about the weather, the most recent astronomical calendar, and humorous advice on household interests, such as cooking and gardening.

(E) Every year since 1818, forecasts about the weather, the most recent astronomical calendar, and humorous advice on household interests, such as cooking and gardening were all contained in the Farmers' Almanac.

6. Even though they do not sting or bite, <u>many people are surprised to learn that cicadas are benign creatures because they appear threatening</u>.

   (A) many people are surprised to learn that cicadas are benign creatures because they appear threatening
   (B) many people are surprised to learn that cicadas are benign creatures, who appear threatening
   (C) surprising to many people is to learn that cicadas are benign creatures because they appear threatening
   (D) cicadas appear threatening, therefore, many people are surprised to learn that they are benign
   (E) cicadas appear threatening, which causes many people to be surprised when learning that they are benign

7. <u>The painter James Whistler used dark colors to emphasize the melancholy mood of his works, best known as a tonalist, and</u> played on haunting shadows in his most well-known piece, "Whistler's Mother."

   (A) The painter James Whistler used dark colors to emphasize the melancholy mood of his works, best known as a tonalist, and
   (B) The painter James Whistler, used dark colors to emphasize the melancholy mood of his works, being a tonalist, and
   (C) The painter James Whistler, best known as a tonalist, used dark colors to emphasize the melancholy mood of his works, and
   (D) The painter James Whistler, best known as a tonalist, used dark colors to emphasize the melancholy mood of his works, which he
   (E) The painter James Whistler, best known as a tonalist, used to emphasize the melancholy mood of his works with dark colors, and just

8. Before waging war on Britain in 1812, <u>the list of grievances produced by the United States included its claim that Britain had disregarded the former's established neutrality</u>.

   (A) the list of grievances produced by the United States included its claim that Britain had disregarded the former's established neutrality
   (B) the list of grievances produced by the United States included their claim that Britain had disregarded the former's established neutrality
   (C) the United States produced a list of grievances, including its claim that Britain had disregarded the former's established neutrality
   (D) the United States produced a list of grievances, including their claim that Britain had disregarded the former's established neutrality
   (E) the United States produced their list of grievances, including their claim that Britain had disregarded the former's established neutrality

9. Of the three Brontë sisters, <u>people are usually more familiar with Charlotte who wrote *Jane Eyre*, a popular required reading novel in the high school repertoire</u>.

   (A) people are usually more familiar with Charlotte who wrote *Jane Eyre*, a popular required reading novel in the high school repertoire
   (B) people are usually most familiar with Charlotte who wrote *Jane Eyre*, a popular required reading novel in the high school repertoire
   (C) Charlotte, who wrote *Jane Eyre*, is usually most familiar to people, a popular required reading novel in the high school repertoire
   (D) Charlotte is usually more familiar to people, writing *Jane Eyre*, a popular required reading novel in the high school repertoire
   (E) Charlotte is usually most familiar to people for writing *Jane Eyre*, a popular required reading novel in the high school repertoire

10. Wary of potential predators, including humans, and prone to high levels of anxiety, <u>Australian wildlife biologists must practice patience when attempting the spot the platypus</u>.

(A) Australian wildlife biologists must practice patience when attempting the spot the platypus

(B) Australian wildlife biologists must practice patiently when they attempt to spot the platypus

(C) the platypus can only be spotted by Australian wildlife biologists who practice patience

(D) biologists of Australian wildlife must practice patiently when attempting to spot the platypus

(E) the platypus is most often spotted by Australian wildlife biologists willing to practice patience

11. <u>Baffling students of the law year after year, property rights are, to this day, based primarily on a complex hierarchical system, much of which was developed in Europe during the Middle Ages.</u>

(A) Baffling students of the law year after year, property rights are, to this day, based on a complex hierarchical system, much of which was developed in Europe during the Middle Ages.

(B) Still baffling students of the law year after year, the complex hierarchical system that is still the primary basis of property rights had been developed in Europe during the Middle Ages.

(C) Property rights, baffling students of the law year after year, were primarily based, to this day, on a complex hierarchical system developed in Europe during the Middle Ages.

(D) Baffling students of the law year after year, Europe is where the complex hierarchical system of property rights that still forms their basis today was developed, during the Middle Ages.

(E) The complex hierarchical system on which property rights are still primarily based was developed in Europe during the Middle Ages, baffling students of the law year after year.

12. Used as writing surfaces for hundreds of years, <u>medieval scribes preferred certain animal skins over others</u>.

(A) medieval scribes preferred certain animal skins over others

(B) animal skins were viewed as preferable to medieval scribes

(C) medieval scribes preferred using certain animals skins to others

(D) animal skins were used by medieval scribes, who preferred some skins to others

(E) medieval scribes, preferring certain animal skins to others

13. Grown in specific climates under various conditions, <u>coffee is now available in many different styles, like organic, shade-grown, and a multitude of geographically-based varietals</u>.

(A) coffee is now available in many different styles, like organic, shade-grown, and a multitude of geographically-based varietals

(B) coffee is now available in many different styles, such as organic, shade-grown, and regional varietals

(C) many different styles of coffee, including organic, shade-grown, and geographic varietals, are all available now

(D) many different styles of coffee, like organic, shade-grown, and geographic varietals, is now available

(E) coffee in styles such as organic, shade-grown, and geographic varietals are now available

14. <u>Believed by some to be one of the most powerful market forces in the world today, much of the global commerce that is now conducted involves the European Union at some point during the full transaction.</u>

(A) Believed by some to be one of the most powerful market forces in the world today, much of the global commerce that is now conducted involves the European Union at some point during the full transaction.
(B) Because it is believed by some to be one of the most powerful market forces in the world today, most transactions of global commerce involve, at some point during the full transaction, the European Union.
(C) The European Union is involved at some point by much of the global commerce being conducted and is believed by some as one of the most powerful market forced in the world today.
(D) Global commerce often involves the European Union at some point during a full transaction, leading some to believe it to be one of the most powerful market forces in the world today.
(E) Much of the global commerce that is conducted today at some point involves the European Union, believed by some to be one of the most powerful market forces in the world today.

15. Filled with allegorical images and fiercely sought after by museums and private collectors alike, <u>Hieronymous Bosch painted disturbing images that continue</u> to influence not only the art world but also the film industry.

(A) Hieronymous Bosch painted disturbing images that continue
(B) Hieronymus Bosch's disturbing painted images continuing
(C) the disturbing images painted by Hieronymus Bosch continue
(D) the images, painted by Hieronymus Bosch, continue disturbing
(E) Hieronymus Bosch, whose disturbing paintings continue

16. Rarely fatal, though extremely dangerous nonetheless, <u>herpetologists studying rattlesnake venom must exercise caution</u>, lest the unwary handler find him or herself the subject of a later cautionary tale.

(A) herpetologists studying rattlesnake venom must exercise caution
(B) the study of rattlesnake venom requires caution on the part of herpetologists
(C) caution on the part of herpetologists is necessary when studying rattlesnake venom
(D) rattlesnake venom must be studied with caution, even by herpetologists
(E) studying rattlesnake venom requires herpetologists to be cautious

17. <u>Bred in captivity and thus unable to hunt live prey</u>, the zookeepers knew that the rare Sumatran tiger would most likely be incapable of surviving in the wild.

(A) Bred in captivity and thus unable to hunt live prey
(B) Because they were bred in captivity and are unable to hunt live prey
(C) Having been bred in captivity and thus unable to hunt live prey
(D) Although it had been bred in captivity and was unable to hunt live prey
(E) Because it had been bred in captivity and was unable to hunt live prey

18. <u>Many geologists fear that California, subject to earthquakes due to the positioning of the coastal tectonic plates,</u> may someday become too unstable along the coast to support large urban populations.

(A) Many geologists fear that California, subject to earthquakes due to the positioning of the coastal tectonic plates,
(B) California, subject to earthquakes due to the positioning of the coastal tectonic plates, is feared by many geologists, who
(C) California is subject to earthquakes because of its positioning above coastal tectonic plates and the fear of many geologists
(D) Many geologists fear that California is subject to earthquakes because of their position above coastal tectonic plates and
(E) California, feared by many geologists because of their position above coastal tectonic plates and thus subject to earthquakes,

19. Once valued as a rare commodity due to the prohibitive costs involved in their production, consumers are now able to purchase books from non-traditional vendors at increasingly low prices.

(A) consumers are now able to purchase books from non-traditional vendors at increasingly low prices
(B) books are now available for purchase from non-traditional vendors at increasingly low prices
(C) consumers are now able to purchase books from non-traditional vendors at increasing low prices
(D) books are now available for purchase from non-traditional vendors at increasing low prices
(E) consumers can now purchase books from non-traditional vendors at increasingly low prices

20. Thought by some to prey on unsuspecting and vulnerable individuals, the government is still researching the structure of sub-prime mortgages in order to determine the best way to address some of the problems that they have caused.

(A) the government is still researching the structure of sub-prime mortgages
(B) the structure of sub-prime mortgage industry is being researched by the government
(C) the government are still researching the sub-prime mortgage industry's structure
(D) sub-prime mortgages, and the structure of that industry, are being researched by the government
(E) the government is still researching the structure of the sub-prime mortgage industry

21. Shunned by literary critics for decades, as something fit only for youthful consumption, the graphic novel is now gaining recognition both as an art form and as a legitimate literary genre.

(A) the graphic novel is now gaining recognition both as an art form as
(B) the art form of the graphic novel is now gaining recognition, as is its reality
(C) the graphic novel, gaining recognition not only as an art form but also
(D) graphic novels are gaining recognition both as a form of artistic work and
(E) recognition of the graphic novel is gaining, both as an art form and

22. Sleeping, suspended in the leafy canopy, early explorers little expected the explosive speed that a sloth is capable of attaining when necessary.

(A) Sleeping, suspended in the leafy canopy, early explorers
(B) Watching them sleep, suspended in the leafy canopy, early explorers
(C) Suspended in the leafy canopy, watching it sleep, early explorers
(D) Early explorers, watching it sleep suspended in the leafy canopy,
(E) Suspended in the leafy canopy, watching them sleep, early explorers

23. Played in Belgrade, the famous game between Ivan Nikolic and Goran Arsovic lasted for 20 hours and 15 minutes and it was the longest time for a chess game ever recorded.

(A) Arsovic lasted for 20 hours and 15 minutes and it was
(B) Arsovic lasted for 20 hours and 15 minutes,
(C) Arsovic, which lasted for 20 hours and 15 minutes, was
(D) Arsovic lasted for 20 hours and 15 minutes, being
(E) Arsovick, lasted for 20 hours and 15 minutes, and was

Check your answers on page 605.

IDIOMS

Idioms are fixed expressions that are common in English. There's really no rule that applies to these expressions—conventions of English simply demand that certain words go together.

The Rule: Know your idioms!

Idioms frequently appear as secondary errors on sentence correction questions. They are very hard to spot unless you know them backwards and forwards.

The ID

- Know your idioms!
- Look for changes in small words, usually prepositions, in the answer choices.

1. Some students of literary criticism consider the theories of Blaine <u>to be a huge advance in modern critical thinking and question</u> the need to study the discounted theories of Rauthe and Wilson.

   (A) to be a huge advance in modern critical thinking and question
   (B) as a huge advance in modern critical thinking and question
   (C) as being a huge advance in modern critical thinking and questioned
   (D) a huge advance in modern critical thinking and question
   (E) are a huge advance in modern critical thinking and questioned

Some of the answer choices say *to be* and some say *as*. These changes in small words indicate you are probably being tested on idioms. If you know your idioms, you will know that the idiom tested here is *consider*. In real life, it's fine to say *consider to be*. For example: I consider George to be a great guy.

On the GMAT, however, nothing comes after the word *consider* except that which is considered. In other words, in order to be correct, the example would have to say: I consider George a great guy.

Thus, for the literary criticism example above, the correct construction would be

> *Some students of literary criticism consider the theories of Blaine a huge advance…*

Any answer choice that has extra words in front of *a huge advance* is incorrect. Thus, the correct answer is (D).

IDIOMS DRILL

1. Recently, <u>so in demand has salt been that supermarket employees have placed signs near the</u> <u>cash registers</u> asking customers not to purchase more than two bags per trip.

   (A) so in demand has salt been that supermarket employees have placed signs near the cash registers
   (B) supermarket employees have placed signs near the cash registers because salt has been so in demand
   (C) supermarket employees have placed signs near the cash registers which means that salt has been so in demand
   (D) salt has been that in demand so supermarket employees have placed signs near the cash registers
   (E) salt has been so in demand that supermarket employees have placed signs near the cash registers

2. Trevor Baylis, an accomplished British swimmer who fell just short of qualifying for the 1965 Olympics and later worked as a stuntman, is also a brilliant mind <u>who is credited as</u> the invention of the wind-up radio.

   (A) who is credited as
   (D) that credited as
   (C) that is credited with
   (D) who is credited with
   (E) who is credited with having

3. Sadly, revered authors sometimes succumb to tragic endings, <u>but perhaps none was more distressing as that of Sylvia Plath who</u>, in 1963, successfully erased her own existence while her children were sleeping in the next room.

   (A) but perhaps none was more distressing as that of Sylvia Plath who
   (B) but perhaps none was more distressing as that of Sylvia Plath whom
   (C) but perhaps none was more distressing than that of Sylvia Plath who
   (D) and perhaps none is more distressing than Sylvia Plath who
   (E) and perhaps it is none that is more distressing than Sylvia Plath who

4. <u>Depending on if its infrastructure</u> can hold up the dilapidated building for another year, the city council may hold a special place in the budget for future repairs instead of immediately giving several million dollars to the mayor, though his arguments were sound.

   (A) Depending on if its infrastructure
   (B) Depending on if their infrastructure
   (C) Depending on whether its infrastructure
   (D) Whether it depends on infrastructure, just that it
   (E) It's depending that the infrastructure

5. <u>Not so much as one employee retained his job when three banking firms announced that they were declaring bankruptcy.</u>

    (A) Not so much as one employee retained his job when three banking firms announced that they were declaring bankruptcy.
    (B) Not so much as one employee retained their jobs when three banking firms announced their bankruptcy.
    (C) Even not as much as one employee retained his job when three banking firms announced their bankruptcy.
    (D) Declaring bankruptcy, not one employee retained his job when three banking firms make the announcement.
    (E) As much as employees retain their jobs, not one did when three banking firms announced that they were declaring bankruptcy.

6. A recent study concluded that as more time progresses <u>between these two civil wars</u>, it is less likely that the second will ever occur.

    (A) between these two civil wars
    (B) between one civil war and the next
    (C) which is between two civil wars
    (D) through civil wars which fall between
    (E) through civil wars

7. The Jamaican Senate has determined <u>that the prime minister be tasked with appointing thirteen members to its panel</u>, while the opposition's leader can only appoint eight.

    (A) that the prime minister be tasked with appointing thirteen members to its panel
    (B) that the prime minister is tasked with appointing thirteen members to its panel
    (C) the prime minister is tasked with appointing thirteen members to it's panel
    (D) thirteen members' appointment to the panel be tasked with the prime minister
    (E) he is tasked with appointing thirteen members to its panel—the prime minister

8. It is common knowledge that Edith Wharton viewed her surroundings, <u>social stigmas and frequent faux pas, as being wrought with fodder for her novels</u>, particularly *The House of Mirth*.

    (A) social stigmas and frequent faux pas, as being wrought with fodder for her novels
    (B) being wrought with social stigmas and frequent faux pas, fodder for her novels
    (C) which were wrought with social stigmas and frequent faux pas, as fodder for her novels
    (D) wrought with social stigmas and frequent faux pas, being fodder for her novels
    (E) wrought with social stigmas and frequent faux pas; fodder for her novels

9. <u>As contrasted to humans who use lungs for their respiratory function, insects</u> have sacs and tubes which transport oxygen to their tissues, dramatically decreasing the need for an advanced circulatory system.

    (A) As contrasted to humans who use lungs for their respiratory function, insects
    (B) As contrasted to humans who use lungs for its respiratory function, insects
    (C) As contrasted with humans who use lungs for their respiratory function, insects
    (D) In contrast to humans who use lungs for one's respiratory function, insects
    (E) In contrast to humans who use lungs for their respiratory function, insects

10. Although minors <u>are prohibited by federal law to purchase alcohol, legislators have passed a number of laws in recent years designed to combat certain types of marketing that</u> are seen as directed towards juveniles.

(A) are prohibited by federal law to purchase alcohol, legislators have passed a number of laws in recent years designed to combat certain types of marketing that

(B) are prohibited from purchasing alcohol by federal law, legislators had passed an amount of laws in recent years designed to combat certain types of marketing which

(C) are prohibited from purchases of alcohol, by federal law, legislators have passed a number of laws in recent years designed to combat certain types of marketing which

(D) are prohibited by federal law to purchase alcohol, legislators are passing an amount of laws in recent years designed to combat certain types of marketing that

(E) are prohibited by federal law from purchasing alcohol, legislators have passed a number of laws designed to combat certain types of marketing that

11. There is clearly a difference, <u>whether based on an actual physiological change or a purely psychological basis, between the effects of taking a placebo from the effects of taking no</u> medication at all.

(A) whether based on an actual physiological change or a purely psychological basis, between the effects of taking a placebo from the effects of taking no

(B) based either upon actual physiological changes or on purely psychological bases, in the effects of taking a placebo and the effects of not taking

(C) whether based upon an actual physiological change or upon a purely psychological basis, in taking a placebo and not taking

(D) whether based on an actual physiological change or on a purely psychological basis, between the effects of taking a plaecbo and the effects of taking no

(E) either based on actual physiological changes or upon purely psychological bases, between taking a placebo or taking no

12. The kangaroo rat, <u>contrary with what its name might suggest, is found not in Australia</u> but in North America.

(A) contrary with what its name might suggest, is found not in Australia

(B) in contrast from the suggestion of their name, are found not in Australia

(C) contrary to what its name might suggest, is found not only in Australia

(D) in contrast with the suggestion of their name, are found not only in Australia

(E) contrary to what its name might suggest, is found not in Australia

13. The Grizzly Bear, or *Ursus arctos horribilis,* <u>was recently believed by zoologists to be seriously endangered, but today its numbers had moved</u> out of the danger zone and into relative safety.

(A) was recently believed by zoologists to be seriously endangered, but today its numbers had moved

(B) was recently believed by zoologists to be seriously endangered, but today its numbers are moving

(C) were recently believed by zoologists as seriously endangered, but today their numbers are moving

(D) was recently believed by zoologists as seriously endangered, but today its numbers have been moving

(E) were recently believed by zoologists to be seriously endangered, but today their numbers have moved

14. <u>As an increasing number of women have the opportunity of attending institutes of higher learning, the balance between male and female students is shifting</u> away from favoring men towards an equal distribution and, in some cases, even towards favoring women.

   (A) As an increasing number of women have the opportunity of attending institutes of higher learning, the balance between male and female students is shifting
   (B) As an increasing number of women have the opportunity to attend institutes of higher learning, the balance between male and female students is shifting
   (C) As an increasing amount of women has the opportunity to attend institutes of higher learning, the balance between male and female students are shifting
   (D) As an increasing amount of women has the opportunity of attending institutes of higher learning, the balance between male and female students is shifting
   (E) As an increasing number of women have the opportunity to attend institutes of higher learning, the balance between male and female students are shifting

15. <u>Although the plaintiff had been planning to call Mr. Hoff as a witness, she failed to secure a sworn record of his testimony</u> during the pre-trial discovery, leading the judge to grant the defendant's motion for summary judgment.

   (A) Although the plaintiff had been planning to call Mr. Hoff as a witness, she failed to secure a sworn record of his testimony
   (B) Even though the plaintiff was planning on calling Mr. Hoff as a witness, having failed to secure a sworn record of her testimony
   (C) Although the plaintiff has been planning to call Mr. Hoff as a witness, failing to secure a sworn record of her testimony
   (D) Even though the plaintiff was planning on calling Mr. Hoff as a witness, she was failing to secure a sworn record of his testimony
   (E) Although the plaintiff had planned on calling Mr. Hoff as a witness, she had failed to secure a sworn record of his testimony

16. Penguins can be found not only in arctic climes, <u>they can also be found in more moderate zones</u>.

   (A) they can also be found in more moderate zones
   (B) but also in more moderate zones
   (C) but they can also in more moderate zones
   (D) and in more moderate zones
   (E) but in more moderate zones as well

17. Judges, <u>trained to distinguish a question based on a matter of law and a question based on an interpretation of facts, are often empowered</u> to either decide a case independently or pass the decision-making on to a jury.

   (A) trained to distinguish a question based on a matter of law and a question based on an interpretation of facts, are often empowered
   (B) having been trained to distinguish between a question based on a matter of law from a question based on an interpretation of facts, are often empowered
   (C) trained to distinguish between a question based on a matter of law and a question based on an interpretation of facts, are often empowered
   (D) trained to distinguish a question based on a matter of law and a question based on an interpretation of facts, were often empowered
   (E) having been trained to distinguish between a question based on a matter of law from a question based on an interpretation of facts, were often empowered

18. Just as the giraffe, once known as the _cameleopard_, was once believed to be imaginary, the platypus was not taken seriously by the scientific community at first.

(A) Just as the giraffe, once known as the _cameleopard_, was once believed to be imaginary, the platypus was not taken seriously by the scientific community at first.
(B) Just as the giraffe, known at one time as the _cameleopard_, was once believed to be imaginary, so too was the platypus not taken seriously by the scientific community at first.
(C) Not only was the giraffe, known at one time as the _cameleopard_, believed as imaginary, but the platypus was also not taken seriously by the scientific community at first.
(D) Not only was the giraffe, which was once known as the _cameleopard_, believed as imaginary, so too was the platypus not taken seriously by the scientific community at first.
(E) Just as the platypus was not taken seriously by the scientific community at first, neither was the giraffe, known at first as the _cameleopard_ and once believed as imaginary.

19. Literary critics, always hoping to discover the next great modern novelist, are sometimes too quick to praise a new work based on not only the content of the novel but on the name or persona of the author.

(A) are sometimes too quick to praise a new work based on not only the content of the novel but on the name
(B) are sometimes too quick to praise a new work not because of the content of the novel but due to the name
(C) is, some of the time, too quick to praise a new work because of not the content of the novel but the name
(D) is sometimes too quick to praise a new work based not only on the content of the novel but also on the name
(E) are sometimes too quick to praise a new work based not on the content of the novel but on the name

20. The use of performance-enhancing drugs, though prohibited by all major sporting authorities, is still rife among professional and amateur athletes.

(A) drugs, though prohibited by all major sporting authorities, is still rife among
(B) drugs are prohibited in all major sporting authorities, yet are still rife among
(C) drugs, prohibited by all major sporting authorities, are still rife between
(D) drugs is prohibited by all major sporting authorities but are still rife between
(E) drugs, though prohibited in all major sporting authorities, is still rife among

21. Alternative medicine, although mocked by some as "quackery," are gaining repute and are considered by others as a more holistic approach to health.

(A) are gaining repute and are considered by others as a more holistic approach
(B) is gaining repute with those who consider it is a more holistic approach
(C) is gaining repute; its supporters consider it to be a more holistic approach
(D) are gaining repute and supporters, who consider it as a more holistic approach
(E) is gaining repute; its supporters consider it a more holistic approach

22. Swimming and sunbathing by the public is prohibited on stretches of private beach by landowners; however, the land extending up to the mean high tide line is in fact publicly owned and is open to everyone according to the public trust doctrine.

(A) Swimming and sunbathing is prohibited on stretches of private beach by landowners; however, the land
(B) Landowners, prohibiting the public to swim and sunbathe on stretches of private beach, even though the land
(C) Landowners often prohibit the public from swimming and sunbathing on stretches of private beach; however, the land
(D) Swimming and sunbathing by the public, prohibited on stretches of private beach by landowners, are, however, part of the land
(E) Landowners often prohibit swimmers and sunbathers from stretches of private beach; however, the land

23. Supreme Court decisions, while binding on all United States courts, leave room for interpretation; it is therefore <u>important for lawyers and judges to be able to distinguish between *dicta*, which refers to the written material detailing the opinions of the prevailing justices, from holdings which refers to the binding decisions of law</u>.

(A) important for lawyers and judges to be able to distinguish between *dicta*, which refers to the written material detailing the opinions of the prevailing justices, from holdings, which refers to the binding decisions of law

(B) important that lawyers and judges be able to distinguish between *dicta*, which refers to the written material detailing the opinions of the prevailing justices, and holdings, which refers to the binding decisions of law

(C) important for lawyers and judges to be able to distinguish *dicta*, that refers to the written material detailing the opinions of the prevailing justices, and holdings, that refer to the binding decisions of law

(D) important that lawyers and judges are able to distinguish *dicta*, referring to the written material detailing the opinions of the prevailing justices, from holdings, referring to the binding decisions of law

(E) important that lawyers and judges to be able to distinguish between *dicta*, which refers to the written material detailing the opinions of the prevailing justices, from holdings, which refers to the binding decisions of law

24. A grand tour of Europe, once the cherished prerogative of the monied classes, has since become impractical for most <u>Americans; this change has been attributed to reasons such as increased costs and decreased vacation time</u>.

(A) Americans; this change has been attributed to reasons such as increased costs and decreased vacation time

(B) Americans, a change that was attributed for reasons such as increased costs and decreased vacation time

(C) Americans, and this change had been attributed to reasons like increased costs and decreased vacation time

(D) Americans, which has been attributed as reasons such as increased and decreased costs and vacation time

(E) Americans; this change is attributed to reasons like increased costs and decreased vacation time

25. <u>Some psychologists argue that working full-time is incompatible to effective child-rearing, while others</u> assert that it is possible to pursue both paths without either area suffering.

(A) Some psychologists argue that working full-time is incompatible to effective child-rearing, while others

(B) Some psychologists, arguing that working full-time is incompatible with effective child-rearing, but others

(C) Working full-time is incompatible to effective child-rearing, according to some psychologists; others

(D) Some psychologists argue that working full-time is incompatible with effective child-rearing, while others

(E) Working full-time is incompatible to effective child-rearing, according to some psychologists, although others

26. Of the admirable advances Europe has made in the past few years, the encouraged use of the euro across almost all nations in the continent has to be the more impressive.

   (A) the encouraged use of the euro across almost all nations in the continent has to be the more impressive
   (B) the encouraged use of the euro across almost all nations in the continent was the most impressive
   (C) the encouraged use of the euro across almost all nations in the continent was impressive
   (D) more impressive was the encouraged use of the euro across almost all nations in the continent
   (E) the impressive continent's use of the euro across almost all its nations was most encouraging

27. Gliding, rather than actually flying, through the air, the flying squirrel is somewhat misnamed, like the flying fish; neither animal is actually capable of flight but early explorers based the animals' names on perceived, rather than actual, reality.

   (A) the flying squirrel is somewhat misnamed, like the flying fish
   (B) the flying squirrel is somewhat misnamed, like flying fish are
   (C) flying squirrels, like flying fish, is somewhat misnamed
   (D) flying squirrels and flying fish, both somewhat misnamed
   (E) the flying squirrel is somewhat misnamed, as is the flying fish

28. Among mammals, generally known for bearing live young, monotremes are unusual because they lay eggs that are then incubated outside the body.

   (A) Among mammals, generally known for bearing live young, monotremes are unusual because they lay eggs that are then incubated outside the body.
   (B) Between mammals, generally known for bearing live young, monotremes are unusual for instead laying eggs which they incubate outside the body.
   (C) Monotremes are unusual among mammals because they lay eggs that they incubate outside the body, instead of bearing live young.
   (D) Most mammals bear live young but monotremes are unusual for laying eggs, that they incubate outside the body.
   (E) Aside from mammals, generally known for bearing live young, the monotreme unusually lays eggs that they incubate outside the body.

29. <u>Native to the grassy plains of central North America, wild bison today find themselves in unusual and diverse places such as San Francisco's Golden Gate Park and Catalina Island due to wildlife protection efforts or, as in the latter case, the efforts of past Hollywood producers.</u>

(A) Native to the grassy plains of central North America, wild bison today find themselves in unusual and diverse places such as San Francisco's Golden Gate Park and Catalina Island due to wildlife protection efforts or, as in the latter case, the efforts of past Hollywood producers.

(B) Native to the grassy plains of central North America, the wild bison today finds itself in unusual and diverse places like San Francisco's Golden Gate Park and Catalina Island due to wildlife protection efforts or, as in the latter case, the efforts of past Hollywood producers.

(C) The wild bison, native to the grassy plains of central North America, today finds itself in unusual and diverse places like San Francisco's Golden Gate Park and Catalina Island due to wildlife protection efforts or, as in the latter case, the efforts of past Hollywood producers.

(D) Wild bison, native to the grassy plains of central North America, today find themselves in unusual and diverse places such as San Francisco's Golden Gate Park and Catalina Island due to wildlife protection efforts or, like the latter case, the efforts of past Hollywood producers.

(E) Native to the grassy plains of central North America, wild bison today find themselves in unusual and diverse places such as San Francisco's Golden Gate Park and Catalina Island due to wildlife protection efforts or, like the latter case, the efforts of past Hollywood producers.

30. <u>Among the many breeds of dogs that have developed over the last two centuries, some have been bred for specific tasks like herding or guarding</u> owners.

(A) Among the many breeds of dogs that have developed over the last two centuries, some have been bred for specific tasks like herding or guarding owners.

(B) Between the many breeds of dogs that were developed over the last two centuries, specific tasks have been bred into some, such as herding or guarding owners.

(C) Many breeds of dogs have developed over the last two centuries, some for specific tasks like herding and guarding owners.

(D) Over the last two centuries, many breeds of dogs have been developed, some for specific tasks such as herding or guarding owners.

(E) Among the many breeds of dogs that had developed over the last two centuries, specific tasks such as herding or guarding owners have been bred into some.

Check your answers on page 605.

MIXED DRILL

1. In order to better differentiate its product from generic brands, the cereal company first hired a marketing firm that specializes in creating campaigns to build brand awareness and <u>then retools its factory to produce a variety of different shapes of cereal</u>.

   (A) then retools its factory to produce a variety of different shapes of cereal
   (B) retools its factory to produce a variety of different shapes of cereal
   (C) then retooled its factory to produce a variety of different shapes of cereal
   (D) then will retool its factory to produce a variety of different shapes of cereal
   (E) then produces a variety of different shapes of cereal through retooling its factory

2. The Kyoto Protocol, a politically divisive environmental treaty <u>and important as a vehicle by which to gain international consensus on stabilizing greenhouse gas emissions as well, signify</u> the cooperation of many different authors.

   (A) and important as a vehicle by which to gain international consensus on stabilizing greenhouse gas emissions as well, signify
   (B) as well as an important vehicle for gaining international consensus on stabilizing greenhouse gas emissions, signifies
   (C) and also a vehicle of gaining important international consensus on the stabilization of greenhouse emissions is signifying
   (D) an important vehicle in international consensus on stabilizing greenhouse gas emissions and have signified
   (E) and as international consensus important to stabilizing greenhouse gas emissions too, signifies

3. Britain's representative government, in which citizens vote for lawmakers to uphold their wishes, functions on the belief that if people were unhappy with their circumstances, <u>they have more of an impetus to make their voices heard</u>.

   (A) they have more of an impetus to make their voices heard
   (B) they would have more of an impetus to make their voices heard
   (C) they will have more of an impetus to make their voices heard
   (D) it would have more of an impetus to make its voice heard
   (E) it will have more of an impetus to make its voice heard

4. The board of directors questioned the commitment of the CFO <u>because, in its opinion, she spent</u> too much of her time focused on her personal assets, rather than those of the company.

   (A) because, in its opinion, she spent
   (B) because, in their opinions, she spent
   (C) because spending in their opinion
   (D) due to, in its opinion, she is spending
   (E) although, in its opinion, she spent

5. Each of the books assigned to the AP English class—*To Kill A Mockingbird, The Adventures of Huckleberry Finn,* and *The Scarlet Letter*—were complex and well-regarded novels, very different from the books the students read in their spare time.

(A) Each of the books assigned to the AP English class—*To Kill A Mockingbird, The Adventures of Huckleberry Finn,* and *The Scarlet Letter* —were complex and well-regarded novels

(B) *To Kill A Mockingbird, The Adventures of Huckleberry Finn,* and *The Scarlet Letter* —each of them books assigned to the AP English class—were complex and well-regarded novels

(C) The books assigned to the AP English class—*To Kill A Mockingbird, The Adventures of Huckleberry Finn,* and *The Scarlet Letter* —were all complex and well-regarded novels,

(D) Complex and well-regarded novels—*To Kill A Mockingbird, The Adventures of Huckleberry Finn,* and *The Scarlet Letter*—each a book assigned to the AP English class, was

(E) Complex and well-regarded novels—*To Kill A Mockingbird, The Adventures of Huckleberry Finn,* and *The Scarlet Letter*—every one of the books assigned to the AP English class were

6. Members of a society are expected to abide with the laws of that society, as famously articulated in Rousseau's *The Social Contract*.

(A) a society are expected to abide with
(B) a society are expected to abide by
(C) societies are expected to abide with
(D) a society is expected to abide by
(E) societies is expected to abide with

7. Much of the often misunderstood theories about the purpose of the pyramids have led to the formation of a panel of Egyptologists, hoping to educate the public about the true history of the building of the ancient structures and their functions in the societies that worked so hard to create the marvels.

(A) Much of the often misunderstood theories about the purpose of the pyramids
(B) Much of the often misunderstood theories relating to the purpose of the pyramids
(C) Much of the often misunderstood theories and the purposes of the pyramids
(D) Many of the often misunderstood theories about the purpose of the pyramids
(E) Many of the often misunderstood theories relating to the purpose of the pyramids

8. Believed to be one of the first widely read female authors of the Western world, Christine de Pizan's masterwork, *The Book of the City of the Ladies,* was written in 1405 and is a history of the Western world from the woman's point of view.

(A) Believed to be one of the first widely read female authors of the Western world
(B) Written by one of the first widely read female authors of the Western world
(C) One of the first widely read female authors of the Western world, as some believe
(D) Written by what some believe as one of the first widely read female authors of the Western world
(E) Believed by some as one of the first works by a widely read female author in the Western world

9. Researchers have attempted to find evidence to explain why some of the statues, called moai, located on Easter Island were adorned with headwear made of red volcanic rock while other statues did not.

(A) did not
(B) do not
(C) were not
(D) should not
(E) are not

10. <u>Seen gathering for hours</u>, gaining momentum steadily and looming ever closer, the towns in the valley feared the worst from the impending hurricane.

   (A) Seen gathering for hours
   (B) Although seen gathering for hours
   (C) After they were seen gathering for hours
   (D) Having been seen gathering for hours
   (E) Having seen it gathering for hours

11. The domestic chinchilla is a diminutive creature, <u>especially as compared with their wild counterparts, found</u> high in the Andes.

   (A) especially as compared with their wild counterparts, found
   (B) as opposed to their wild counterparts, which can be found
   (C) particularly when compared to its wild counterpart, found
   (D) as compared against its wild counterparts that can be found
   (E) unlike its wild counterparts, who can only be found

12. Alexander MacKenzie, a Scottish-Canadian explorer, discovered what he termed "Disappointment River" because it did not flow into Alaska's Cook Inlet <u>which he hoped</u>.

   (A) which he hoped
   (B) which was being hoped for
   (C) which is what he hoped
   (D) as he hoped
   (E) as he had hoped

13. The jazz band's music transcends generational barriers by attracting people of all ages, <u>with the fusing of both modern funk and Dixieland styles</u>.

   (A) with the fusing of both modern funk and Dixieland styles
   (B) in that it fuses both modern funk and Dixieland styles
   (C) for it fuses both modern funk and Dixieland styles
   (D) when they fuse both modern funk and Dixieland styles
   (E) by the fusion that is of both modern funk and Dixieland styles

14. Babylon was the largest city in the world for hundreds of years, until 32 B.C. when it was conquered by Cyrus the Great, then king of Persia, <u>who, diverting the waters of the Euphrates, marched his invading army in the city on dry ground like</u> the river had never existed.

   (A) who, diverting the waters of the Euphrates, marched his invading army in the city on dry ground like
   (B) who, when the waters were diverted, marched his invading army in on dry ground like
   (C) who had diverted the waters of the Euphrates, marching his invading army in on ground dried to be as if
   (D) who diverted the waters of the Euphrates and then marched his invading army into the city on dry ground as if
   (E) diverting the waters of the Euphrates and marching his invading army in on ground dried as if

15. Although the word "sanguine" primarily means cheerfully optimistic, it can also mean reddish or ruddy.

   (A) it can also mean
   (B) it is also something
   (C) it is also
   (D) that is also a thing that is
   (E) it is also in reference to something

16. Electrons, elementary particles that exist in orbitals around the positively charged nucleus of an atom, seem similar in many ways to ordinary particles however exhibiting surprising wave-like characteristics.

   (A) seem similar in many ways to ordinary particles however exhibiting
   (B) are to ordinary particles very similar however exhibit
   (C) are in many ways similar to ordinary particles that have been known to exhibit
   (D) seem similar in many ways to ordinary particles which exhibit
   (E) are in many ways similar to ordinary particles but also exhibit

17. The velocity and inertia of the earth counter the force of gravity, thus maintaining the earth in orbit rather than allowing it to crash into the sun, as meteors do.

   (A) thus maintaining the earth in orbit rather than allowing it to crash into the sun, as meteors do
   (B) thus maintaining the earth in orbit and not allowing it to crash into the sun, as meteors
   (C) thus maintaining the earth in orbit instead of allowing it to crash into the sun, like meteors
   (D) and maintain the earth in orbit but do not allow it to crash into the sun, as is done by meteors
   (E) and maintain the earth in orbit, unlike meteors that crash into the sun

18. As did other wealthy aristocrats of her day, Marie Antoinette regarded luxury to be normal, rather than regarding it as unfair excess at the expense of the populace.

   (A) As did other wealthy aristocrats of her day, Marie Antoinette regarded luxury to be normal, rather than regarding it as
   (B) Marie Antoinette regarded luxury, as other wealthy aristocrats of her day, as normal, rather than as
   (C) Marie Antoinette regarded luxury to be normal, like other wealthy aristocrats of her day, rather than as
   (D) Marie Antoinette, like other wealthy aristocrats of her day, regarded luxury as normal, rather than as
   (E) Luxury to Marie Antoinette, like other wealthy aristocrats of her day, was regarded as normal rather than

19. Majestic, even breathtaking, tourists often find it difficult to believe that Angkor Wat once sat abandoned, lost to the encroaching wilderness for hundreds of years.

   (A) tourists often find it difficult to believe that Angkor Wat once sat abandoned
   (B) Angkor Wat, difficult for tourists to believe, once sat abandoned
   (C) tourists often have difficulty believing as Angkor Wat once sat abandoned
   (D) Angkor Wat once sat abandoned, much to the surprise of modern tourists,
   (E) Angkor Wat once sat abandoned, much to the disbelief of modern tourists who were

Check your answers on page 605.

Sentence
Correction
Answers and
Explanations

ANSWER KEY

Subject/Verb Agreement

1. D
2. E
3. A
4. B
5. B
6. C
7. C
8. C
9. E
10. C
11. B
12. D
13. D
14. B
15. B
16. A
17. B
18. E
19. C
20. D
21. A
22. E
23. A
24. C

Verb Tense

1. B
2. E
3. C
4. C
5. E
6. B
7. D
8. D
9. B
10. E
11. C
12. A
13. C
14. D
15. D

16. C
17. B
18. D
19. E
20. C
21. C
22. C
23. E
24. A
25. B
26. D
27. A
28. B

Pronouns

1. B
2. C
3. D
4. A
5. E
6. E
7. E
8. E
9. B
10. E
11. B
12. A
13. D
14. C
15. B
16. D
17. D
18. B
19. C
20. C
21. D
22. C
23. E
24. E

Parallel Construction

1. A
2. D
3. C
4. B
5. A
6. B
7. B
8. C
9. D
10. B
11. A
12. E
13. C
14. B
15. D
16. E
17. E
18. E
19. B
20. A
21. E
22. B
23. D
24. D
25. E
26. D

Misplaced Modifiers

1. D
2. E
3. E
4. D
5. A
6. D
7. C
8. C
9. E
10. E
11. A
12. D
13. B
14. E
15. C
16. D
17. E
18. A
19. B
20. E
21. A
22. D
23. B

Idioms

1. E
2. D
3. C
4. C
5. A
6. B
7. A
8. C
9. E
10. E
11. D
12. E
13. B
14. B
15. A
16. B
17. C
18. B
19. E
20. A
21. E
22. C
23. B
24. A
25. D
26. B
27. E
28. A
29. A
30. D

Mixed Drill

1. C
2. B
3. B
4. A
5. C
6. B
7. B
8. B
9. C
10. E
11. C
12. E
13. C
14. D
15. A
16. E
17. A
18. D
19. D

EXPLANATIONS

Subject-Verb Agreement

1. **D** The main verb of this sentence is *has not resulted*, and its subject is *Efforts*. Because *Efforts* is not underlined, it is correct, which means that the verb *has not resulted* must be conjugated in the plural to match the plural quantity of *Efforts*. Eliminate (A), (B), and (C) because these choices all contain the helping verb *has*. Choice (D) conjugates the verb correctly with the phrase *have not significantly reduced* and follows the verb with a direct object *the amount of bickering*. Choice (E) conjugates the helping verb *have* correctly but introduces a passive construction with the phrase *have not been significant*. The correct answer is (D).

2. **E** In this sentence, the main verb of the sentence does not agree with the subject. The subject of the sentence is *number* and therefore the verb should be *has*. Eliminate (A), (B), and (C). Choice (D) creates another subject-verb agreement problem because the verb *harms* is incorrectly used with the subject *pollutants*. The correct answer is (E).

3. **A** The sentence is correct as written. In (B) and (D), the subject *eight mortgage holders* does not agree with the singular verb *owes*. Choice (C) creates a passive construction with the phrase *by eight out of ten mortgage holders*. Likewise, in (E), *by eight* is a passive construction. The correct answer is (A).

4. **B** The sentence uses the relative pronoun *that* to refer to writers. However, one cannot use *that* to refer to people. Eliminate (A). Choices (C) and (D) both contain a subject-verb agreement error with their use of the word *was*. The subject for *was* is the plural list of the well crafted works, unsympathetic examination of the human condition and the theatrical works. Choice (E) contains the awkward passive phrase *were given recognition by critics*. The correct answer is (B).

5. **B** The subject is *the number,* which is singular and requires the verb *has decreased*. Choices (A) and (D) both state that the number of chlorofluorocarbons *have decreased*. Eliminate them. Choice (C) includes an awkward construction with the phrase *there has been a decrease*. In (E) the phrase *the number by which they have been released* is a passive construction. The correct answer is (B).

6. **C** The subject is *number* which is singular, and therefore requires the verb *has*. Choices (A) and (B) both have this error and should be eliminated. In (D) and (E) the *up to* is redundant with the verb *increased*.

7. **C** The verb in the underlined part of the sentence is *amount* and its subject is *audience*. The main verb in the sentence, however, is *mounted*, which is in the past tense, and *amount* must be conjugated in the past tense to achieve verb parallelism. Eliminate (A) and (B) because they both have *amount*. Choice (C) corrects the idiom error in the underlined portion of the sentence, changing *a number lower* to *less*. Choice (D) repeats *lower*, so it can be eliminated. Choice (E) also repeats *lower* so it can be eliminated as well. The correct answer is (C).

8. **C** The verb in the underlined portion of this sentence is *provide* and its subject is *number*. The word *number* is not underlined, so it is correct as written and *provide* must be conjugated to reflect a singular quantity, becoming *provides*. Eliminate (A) and (E) because they contain *provide*. Choice (B) changes *provide* to the participle *providing* which removes any finite verb from the clause, so it can be eliminated. Choice (C) correctly conjugates *provides* and also includes a necessary relative pronoun *which* in order to refer squarely back to its subject *number*, as well as changing the *to* at the beginning of the underlined portion to *to be*. Choice (D) changes the *to* to *as being* as well as introduces an ambiguous *it* as the subject of *provides*, so it can be eliminated. The correct answer is (C).

9. **E** The subject for the verb *is* is *declining prices*. Since *declining prices* is plural, the verb should be *are*. Eliminate (A), (B), and (C). Choice (D) incorrectly states that banks issue homes and mortgages as assets. The correct answer is (E).

10. **C** The verb in the underlined portion of this sentence is *were opened*, and its subject is *first*. It appears that *were opened* was conjugated for *charter schools*, but *charter schools* is actually a part of a prepositional phrase, signaled by the word *of*, meaning *were opened*'s real subject is *first*, which is singular instead of plural. Eliminate (A). Choice (B) slightly changes the meaning of the sentence by changing *were opened* into a noun—*opening*—so (B) can be eliminated. Choice (C) correctly conjugates *were opened* as *was opened*. Choice (D) changes the meaning of the sentence by eliminating *were opened* altogether, so (D) can be eliminated. Choice (E) not only changes *were opened* into *opening* but also adds an improper idiom with *as*, so (E) can be eliminated. The correct answer is (C).

11. **B** *Style and methods* is the compound subject of the sentence, and the main verb is *was*. Therefore the verb must be plural. Eliminate (A) and (C) because the verbs *was* and *has been*, respectively, are singular. Choice (B) conjugates *was* correctly, changing it to *were*. Choice (D) introduces an improper idiom with *considered to be unique*, so (D) can be eliminated. Choice (E) conjugates the verb *would be* in the wrong tense, so (E) can be eliminated. The correct answer is (B).

12. **D** The main verb of the sentence is *fluctuates* and its subject is *values*. As *values* is plural, the verb *fluctuates* must also be conjugated to reflect this. Eliminate (A), (B), and (C) because they all contain *fluctuates*. Choice (D) correctly conjugates the verb as *fluctuate* as well as correctly completes the passive construction *was determined* with *by* instead of *from*. Choice (E) completes the passive construction incorrectly with *because of*, so it can be eliminated. The correct answer is (D).

13. **D** The verb for the subject *efforts* should be the plural *have*. Choices (A), (B), and (C) all contain this error and should be eliminated. In (E), *the number* is singular, which creates a subject-verb agreement error with the plural verb phrase *have been discarded*. The correct answer is (D).

14. **B** The verb for the subject *relief* should be the singular *enables*. Eliminate (A). The subject of the main verb *offer* is *state tax codes*, creating a subject-verb agreement problem in (C), (D), and (E) which all ascribe the singular verb *offers* to tax codes. The correct answer is (B).

15. **B** The verbs in the underlined portion of the sentence are *has been documented*, *is more difficult*, and *are*; their subjects are *decline*, *what*, and *root cause*, respectively. Of these, the verb *are* is not conjugated for its singular subject, *root cause*, and should be changed to reflect the singularity of *root cause*. Eliminate (A), (C), and (D). Choice (B) correctly changes *are* to *is*. Choice (E) changes *has been documented* to a present tense *are documented*, which changes the meaning of the sentence. Eliminate (E). The correct answer is (B).

16. **A** The main verb of this sentence is *is* and its subject is *adjustment*. Since both *adjustment* and *is* are singular, they are in agreement, and this sentence is correct as written. Choice (B) incorrectly changes the verb from *is* to *recognize* and *attempt*. Choice (C) uses an improper idiom, pairing *both* with *as well as* instead of *and*. Choice (D) changes the noun *adjustment* into a gerund *adjusting* and changes *held by* to *to*, thereby changing the meaning of the sentence. Choice (E) changes *adjustment* to *adjusting* and changes the verb *is* to *recognize* and *attempt*. Choice (A) is the correct answer.

17. **B** The sentence creates a subject-verb agreement error by ascribing the verb *have* to the singular subject *market*. Choices (A) and (D) both have this error and should be eliminated. Choices (C) and (E) have a subject-verb agreement error with the usage of the singular verb *floods* for the plural *memorabilia and trinkets*. The correct answer is (B).

18. **E** The singular verb *dictates* is incorrectly ascribed to the plural noun construction *investment houses… and insurance companies*. Eliminate (A), (C), and (D). In (B) *the investment houses holding* is not parallel with *the insurance companies that underwrite*. The correct answer is (E).

19. **C** The verb in the underlined portion of the sentence is *has been added* and its subject is *influences*. Since *influences* is plural and *has been added* is singular, the two are not in agreement. Eliminate (A) and (B). Choice (C) correctly conjugates *has been added* as *have been added*. Choice (D) changes the perfect passive verb *has been added* to a past, passive participle *having been added*, so (D) can be eliminated. Choice (E) features redundancy with the words *and* and *in addition*, so (E) can be eliminated. The correct answer is (C).

20. **E** The main verb in this sentence is *are*, and its subject is *type*. Since *type* is singular and *are* is plural, the two are not in agreement. Eliminate (A), (C), and (E). Choice (B) has the plural pronoun *their* referring back to the singular noun *business*. As these two words do not agree, (B) can be eliminated. Choice (E) correctly conjugates *are* as *is* and keeps the word *businesses* as it is. Choice (E) is the correct answer.

21. **A** The main verb of this sentence is *remains* and its subject is *work*. Since both *remains* and *work* are singular, they are in agreement and this sentence is correct as written. Choice (B) incorrectly changes *enthusiasm* to *enthusiasms*, so eliminate (B). Choice (C) changes *work* to *works*, putting *remains* and *work* out of agreement, so (C) can be eliminated. Choice (D) also changes *enthusiasm* to *enthusiasms* so (D) can be eliminated. Finally (E) also changes *work* to *works*, so (E) can be eliminated. The correct answer is (A).

22. **E** The verbs in this sentence are *grace* and *heads*, and their subjects are *image* and *herd*, respectively. As *image* is singular and *grace* is plural, these two words are not in agreement. Eliminate (A), (B), and (D). Choice (C) contains an improper idiom *everything from coffee mugs and velvet paintings*, so (C) can be eliminated. Choice (E) correctly conjugates *graces* and uses the proper idiom *everything from coffee mugs to velvet paintings*. Choice (E) is the correct answer.

23. **A** The verbs in the underlined portion of this sentence are *are* and *have spent*, and their subjects are *challenges* and *hardy souls* respectively. As these verbs and subjects agree in quantity, the sentence is correct as written. Choice (B) incorrectly changes *are* to *is*, so (B) can be eliminated. Choice (C) incorrectly changes *challenges* to *challenge*, so (C) can be eliminated. Choice (D) also incorrectly changes *challenges* to *challenge*, so (D) can be eliminated. Choice (E) incorrectly changes *have spent* to *has spent*, so (E) can be eliminated. The correct answer is (A).

24. **C** The main verb in the underlined portion of the sentence is *is* and its subject is *members*. As *members* is plural and *is* is singular, the two words are not in agreement, and since *members* is not underlined, *is* needs to be changed to agree with it. Eliminate (A), (B), and (D) for this reason. Choice (C) correctly pluralizes *trier* to *triers* to make it agree with *members*, as well as changes *is* to *are*. Choice (E) introduces an improper idiom, adding an incorrect *to be* after the word *considered*, so (E) can be eliminated. The correct answer is (C).

Verb Tense

1. **B** The underlined verb, *have fostered*, is a present perfect verb. The subject of this sentence, *the willingness*, is in the third person, so the word *have* is not the correct tense. Eliminate (A). Choice (B) doesn't repeat the mistake, and neither does it make any new ones; keep it. Choice (C) makes a new error: it puts the word *eventually* after the verb, though customarily adverbs come before verbs. Eliminate (C). Choice (D) not only uses the incorrect tense, *had fostered*, but also uses the word *being*, which is the wrong tense. Eliminate (D). Finally, (E) repeats the same mistake as (C); eliminate it. The correct answer is (B).

2. **E** The underlined verb, *prevented*, is a simple past tense verb. However, the sentence earlier featured *has*, which is a present tense verb. That makes the simple past an incorrect choice, since the two actions occur at the same time. Eliminate (A) and any answer that repeats the mistake: (C) and (D). Now examine (B): *has been preventing* is a present perfect verb. It's the incorrect tense; eliminate (B). Choice (E) corrects the error and does not make any further errors, so the correct answer is (E).

3. **C** The election season occurred in 1984, which is in the past. The verb in the sentence should therefore be in the past tense. The current verb, *is*, is in the present tense. Eliminate (A) and any answer that repeats the mistake. This includes (B), (D), and (E). Examine (C) just to be sure. Choice (C) corrects the errors and does not make any new errors. The correct answer is (C).

4. **C** The non-underlined portion of the sentence indicates that *they had completed preliminary testing.* This verb form, *had completed*, is a past perfect verb tense. It tells us that the second verb in the sentence will be in the simple past. The underlined verb is *did not doubt*, which is in the simple past, making it correct. However, there is another problem. The word *whether* is only used to indicate a choice between two things. This sentence doesn't offer any such choice, so eliminate (A) and any answer that repeats this error, including (B) and (D). Look at the verb in (C), *had*. It's a main verb here (not a helping verb) and is therefore in the past tense. No new mistakes, so keep (C). Choice (E) uses the verb *had doubted*, which is past perfect tense, and therefore is incorrect. Eliminate (E). The correct answer is (C).

5. **E** The underlined verb is *had existed*, which is the past perfect tense. However, that verb is being contrasted with *now currently multiethnic neighborhoods*, which is present tense. This is incorrect. Eliminate (A) and (C) as it repeats the error. Choice (B) changes *in which* to *when*, but the word before *in which*—*America*—isn't a time. Therefore, eliminate any answer containing *when*: (B) and (D). The correct answer is (E).

6. **B** Choice (A) says that the number of people *had been allowed* . Because the ordinance is still being used in the present, this verb tense is incorrect. Eliminate (A) and (D), which uses the construction *has been occupying*. Now, compare the remaining answers. Choice (B) fixes the original error and does not make any new errors, so keep (B). Choices (C) and (E) for changing *increased* to *increases*, which is the present tense. Since the ordinance was passed in 1964, the underlined verb, *increased*, is correct. Eliminate (C) and (E). The correct answer is (B).

7. **D** The original sentence ends with the verb *is*. However, since the sentence is referring to something that happened in the hypothetical past, this is incorrect. Eliminate (A) and (E), as it repeats the error. Now, compare the other answer choices. Recall first that *whether* is used to indicate a choice, while *if* is used to indicate a conditional situation. Because there is a choice between two things, eliminate (B) and (C). Choice (D) ends in *has been* (present perfect). This fixes the original error and does not create any new errors. The correct answer is (D).

8. **D** Because the family Proscopiidae lived in the Cretaceous period, the word *existing*, which is a present participle, is the wrong tense. Eliminate (A) and (B). Now, compare the remaining answer choices. Choice (C) uses a pronoun while (D) more clearly restates the word *grasshoppers*, which is both more specific and avoids confusion. Eliminate (C) and keep (D). There is no reason to suspect that something happened before the Cretaceous period, which would require the use of the past perfect. Eliminate (E) for using the construction *had existed*. The correct answer is (D).

9. **B** The underlined phrase *totaled a higher sum* is followed by the phrase *than 1 in every 464 U.S. households*. This is an incorrect idiom, so eliminate (A) and (C). Choice (B) corrects this error with the use of the word *more* and does not make any new errors, so keep (B). Since the home foreclosures were totaled last month, the simple past will suffice. The underlined verb, *totaled*, is correct; eliminate (D) and (E) for changing it to *totals*, which is in the present tense. The correct answer is (B).

10. **E** Because this composer has been hired to do a job in the present, the verb tense should reflect that. *Have been* and *had been* are present perfect and past perfect, respectively, so eliminate (A) and (C). Now, compare the remaining answer choices. The only difference between (B) and (E) is *have* and *do*. Because the songs are engaging the audience right now, the present tense is preferred. Eliminate (B) but keep (E). Choice (D) is impossible; if the songs are still being designed, then they can't have engaged the audience yet. Eliminate (D). The correct answer is (E).

11. **C** The verb in the underlined portion, *had been marketed*, is past perfect. This occurred at the same time as *was developed*, which is simple past. Eliminate (A), which violates this rule. Now, evaluate the other answer choices. Choices (B) and (C) only differ in one way: the placement of the word *first*, which is an adverb. Because adverbs are typically placed before verbs, eliminate (B). Choice (C) corrects the original error and does not make any new errors, so keep (C). Choice (D) changes the verb to *marketing*, which by itself isn't a full verb; eliminate (D). Because the word *shortening* is a noun referring to a substance, it cannot take action. Therefore, the passive voice, *was developed*, is necessary. Eliminate (E) for active voice. The correct answer is (C).

12. **A** Because the non-underlined portion of the sentence reads *the medicine is effective*, it's in the present tense. Choice (A) is present tense, *is administered*, so keep it. Eliminate (B) for *was administered*, which is the past tense. Choice (C) offers the conditional verb, *would only be administered*, inside an *if*-clause. That's incorrect, so eliminate (C). Choice (D) repeats the same mistake, so eliminate that too. Choice (E) says *in a dose concentrated singly*, which is incorrect usage. Eliminate (E). The correct answer is (A).

13. **C** The non-underlined portion of the sentence reads *if heart surgery patients participate in group therapy*. The word *and* tells us that the next word, *talked*, is incorrect, since *participate* is present tense. Eliminate (A). Choice (B) reads they have felt less pain, which is present perfect. However, there's no reason to change the present tense. Eliminate (B). Lastly, the remaining answers use either *quicker* or *quickly*. Since this word is describing *recover*, which is a verb, eliminate anything that's not an adverb. That means *quicker* is wrong, so eliminate (D) and (E). Furthermore, (E) also uses *felt*, which is simple past. The correct answer is (C).

14. **D** The sentence as written mixes an infinitive, *to give*, with a gerund, *braving*. Eliminate (A). Since the non-underlined portion of the sentence reads *in the past few months*, the present perfect tense, *have indicated*, is correct. Eliminate (B) and (E). Because the remainder of the underlined portion is a comparison, it should be grammatically parallel. Choice (C) uses *instead of*, which isn't a formal comparison. Eliminate (C). The correct answer is (D).

15. **D** Because the addition of *fruit juice and sugar* occurred in the near but unspecified past, the present perfect tense is necessary. Eliminate (A). Choice (B) has the verb in the present tense, so eliminate (B). Choice (C) says having been added; the *-ing* form changes it from a verb to a participle. Eliminate (C). Lastly, because *fruit juice and sugar* are the subject of the verb, it's plural. Eliminate (E). The correct answer is (D).

16.   **C**   Since the question is in the hypothetical future, the word *will* is inconsistent, so eliminate (A). Now, look at the remaining answer choices. Since *the fire and subsequent rain caused more property damage*, which is past tense, the prediction of such damage necessarily occurred in the past of the past, which is known as past perfect. This requires the word *had*. Eliminate (B), (D), and (E). Choice (C) corrects the original error and makes no new errors. The correct answer is (C).

17.   **B**   Because of the non-underlined verb *predict,* this sentence is established in the present tense from the beginning. Therefore, the verb *were* in the underlined portion is in the wrong tense, especially since it's part of a conditional *if* clause. Eliminate (A) and any others that repeat the error, including (C), for the verb *was*. Compare the other answer choices. Choice (B) corrects this error and makes no new errors, so keep (B). The words *predict that* are typically followed by the simple future tense *will*. Therefore, eliminate (D) and (E). The correct answer is (B).

18.   **D**   The word *recommended* in the non-underlined portion of the sentence means to use the subjunctive tense, which requires that *recommended* be followed by the word *that*. Eliminate (B), (C), and (E). Choice (A) states that support *is raised as quickly as possible*, but the subjunctive mood requires the use of the infinitive form of the verb without the "to"; i.e. *be raised as quickly as possible*. The correct answer is (D).

19.   **E**   19. The two halves of this sentence imply a change in time. The *followers have stated* something about Gandhi's life prior to his death, which calls for simple past. Eliminate any answer that doesn't use *stated*—(A), (B), and (D). Examine the other answer choices. That something they stated was Gandhi's commitment to *the highest moral principles*, which occurred before the past, and is therefore past perfect. Therefore, eliminate (C). Choice (E) corrects the original error and makes no new errors, so keep (E). The correct answer is (E).

20.   **C**   The phrase *as technology increases* indicates present tense. Choices (A) and (B) use the present perfect tense, so eliminate them. Choices (D) and (E) use past tense for *communicated*, so eliminate them. Eliminate (A) and (B) because they use the word *like* instead of the words *such as* to indicate examples. The correct answer is (C).

21.   **C**   The underlined portion of the sentence has an error in verb tense (*is*) because the sentence refers to 1905, which is in the past, so eliminate (A), (D), and (E). Choice (B) is in the past tense, however, it has the incorrect idiom for comparison (*as instead of than*). Choice (C) is both in the present tense and has the correct idiom for comparison (*than*). The correct answer is (C).

22.   **C**   The underlined word contains an error in verb tense. *Focuses* is present tense, therefore, the next action verb (*relied*) must parallel the same present tense (*relies*). The only answer choice in the present tense which also matches the correct verb form is (C), the correct answer.

23.   **E**   The underlined portion of the sentence, *and it caused*, indicates an independent clause. The problem, however, is that *it* has an unclear antecedent; it's unclear whether the *zoo*, the *enclosure*, or the *tiger* caused one to question. Eliminate (A), as well as any choice that repeats the error, including (C). Choice (B) is in the present tense, which is incorrect; eliminate (B). Choice (D) provides an

and before *causing*, indicating another participle that unfortunately does not exist; eliminate (D). Choice (E) corrects the original error and makes no new errors, so the correct answer is (E).

24. **A** The sentence is correct as written because the simple past form of the verb (*were*) is accurate. Choice (B) also uses the simple past tense (*were*) but incorrectly uses *where* to refer to a time period. Choices (C) and (E) use the past perfect (*had been*), but the correct tense is the simple past (*were*). Choice (D) also uses the incorrect verb tense (*would have been*). In this sentence, *when* and *in which* are interchangeable. The correct answer is (A).

25. **B** The underlined portion of the sentence contains two past-tense verbs without a conjunction joining them. Therefore, you can eliminate (A) and (E), which contain the error. Choices (C) and (D) confuse the meaning of the sentence by introducing the phrase *twice destroyed by fires* in the wrong spot. Choice (B) corrects the original error by using the *-ing* form of succumb which is appropriate to make it a present participle phrase describing the Royal Opera House. The correct answer is (B).

26. **D** There are two underlined verbs. *Posited* is the same in all five choices and cannot be eliminated. The second, *was caused*, is passive voice. Barring an actual error in the grammar, any instance of the active voice is preferable to a use of the passive voice. For questions of this nature, you can generally eliminate choices that use the passive voice. Eliminate (A), (B), and (C). Choice (E) is active, but cuts the verb altogether, leaving the subject, *the Big Bang*, as a fragmented clause. Therefore, eliminate (E). The correct answer is (D).

27. **A** The sentence is correct as written. Choices (B), (D), and (E) all contain verbs in the past tense (*were* and *worked*), which change the meaning of the sentence. Choice (C) is wordy and confusing. The correct answer is (A).

28. **B** Because the settlers left their English village prior to recreating it, the past perfect tense is needed. *Left* is past tense, therefore, eliminate (A). In (C), *were facing* is the incorrect verb form because the actions were not happening at the same time. In (D), *had been facing* is the incorrect verb form because the actions weren't continuous. And in (E), regardless of the change to the beginning of the phrase, *left* is still the incorrect verb tense. Choice (B) uses the past perfect tense (*had left*). The correct answer is (B).

Pronouns

1. **B** The sentence has a pronoun error, using *they* to refer to *city council*. *City council* is a collective noun, so it is singular. Thus, the proper pronoun is *it*. Eliminate (A) and (D). Using *could* changes the meaning of the sentence, so eliminate (E). Between (B) and (C), (B) is the more concise answer, whereas (C) is quite jumbled. The correct answer is (B).

2. **C** The sentence incorrectly uses *that* to refer to *individuals*. Eliminate (A) and (E). Choice (D) uses passive voice with *the result of many states having passed*. So eliminate (D). Choice (B) uses the ambiguous pronoun *it*. The correct answer is (C).

3.   **D**   The sentence incorrectly uses the pronoun *they* to refer to *chicken egg refrigeration,* which is singular, so eliminate (A) and (E). Choices (B) and (C) use an improper idiom. The correct idiom is *indicating that,* so eliminate (B) and (C). Choice (D) properly uses the word *them* to refer to plural *chicken eggs,* so the correct answer is (D).

4.   **A**   In order to answer this question, you must ascertain whether to use *whom, who, which,* or *that.* The pronoun refers to people, so use *who* or *whom.* Eliminate (D) and (E). The remaining split is between *who* and *whom.* To test which pronoun you need, replace *whom* and *who* with other objective and subjective pronouns that have a more obvious correct use. You would correctly write "many of them," not "many of they," so in this instance you need to use the objective case of the pronoun, or *whom.* Eliminate (B) and (C). The sentence is correct as written and the answer is (A).

5.   **E**   The sentence incorrectly uses *they* to refer to *research team,* which is a collective noun, so a singular pronoun is required. Eliminate (A) and (B). Choice (D) also uses the plural pronoun *them* to replace *team,* so (D) is incorrect. Choice (C) is in passive voice, so the correct answer is (E).

6.   **E**   The sentence incorrectly uses *they* to refer to *desktop publishing.* Eliminate (A) and (D). Choices (B), (C), and (D) differ in their respective uses of *extended, extending,* and *extend.* The rest of the sentence is in present tense, so the use of past tense in (B) is incorrect. Choice (C) changes the meaning of the sentence to indicate that the definition is currently extending its range.

7.   **E**   The sentence incorrectly uses *if* instead of *whether.* When there are only two possible options, *whether* is idiomatically preferable to *if,* so eliminate (A) and (D). The remaining three choices differ in their use of pronouns. Choice (B) incorrectly uses *it* to replace *seals,* and *they* is ambiguous, as it could refer to either the marine biologists or the seals. Choice (C) somewhat ambiguously uses *one* to replace *seals,* and thus contains a pronoun error. The correct answer is (E).

8.   **E**   Because *they* could refer to either nurses or patients, *they* is an ambiguous pronoun. Eliminate (A), (B), and (C). Choice (D) switches to passive voice in the second half of the underlined portion, whereas (E) maintains parallelism and keeps the sentence in the active voice. The correct answer is (E).

9.   **B**   Since *goose* is singular, the pronoun referring to goose should also be singular. Choice (A) uses them, which is plural; eliminate (A). Choice (B) uses the correct pronoun and makes no further errors, so keep (B). Eliminate (C) and (D) for the same error (*they* and *them,* respectively). Choice (E) uses the word *their,* which is plural, to refer to *goose,* so eliminate (E). The correct answer is (B).

10.   **E**   The sentence incorrectly uses *they* to refer to *bank.* The correct pronoun is *it.* Eliminate (A) and (B). Using *largely* changes the meaning of the sentence to indicate the degree to which the bank had been bought out, rather than the size of the corporation that was bought out the bank. Eliminate (C) and (D). The correct answer is (E).

11. **B**   This sentence has both a verb tense and a pronoun error. The pronoun *them* is referring to *the British East India Company*, which is singular, so the correct pronoun is *it*. Eliminate (A), (D), and (E). The verb *exempting* must parallel the verb *allowed*, so (A) and (C) are incorrect for that reason. Choice (B) is both concise and logical and is the correct answer.

12. **A**   The sentence is correct as written. The pronoun *who* correctly refers to *people*, so eliminate (B) and (C). *Once* is idiomatically preferable to *at one time*, so eliminate (D) and (E). The correct answer is (A).

13. **D**   The first issue in this sentence is whether to use *where*, *with*, or *whose*. The prepositions both refer to *settlers of the time*, and because *settlers* are not a place it is inappropriate to use *where*. Eliminate (A) and (B). Choice (C) uses the term *more barren*, but because no comparison exists this term is ambiguous. Eliminate (C). Choice (E) creates a modifying phrase that would need to be set off by commas. The correct answer is (D).

14. **C**   The original sentence uses the pronoun *their*. The pronoun refers to *the baseball team*, which is singular, and thus should not be replaced by a plural pronoun. Eliminate (A). Choice (E) also uses the possessive pronoun *their*, so (E) is also incorrect. The remaining choices are split between using *they* and omitting the pronoun altogether. The pronoun *they* is also plural and inappropriately refers to *the baseball team*, so (B) and (C) are incorrect. Choice (C) draws the appropriate contrast and contains no pronoun errors, so (C) is the correct answer.

15. **B**   The original sentence contains the ambiguous pronoun *it*. It is not clear whether *it* refers to the fact that apes have been taught to communicate at all, or if *it* refers to the signs made by apes. Eliminate (A). Choice (D) repeats the error by using *it* ambiguously, so (D) is incorrect. Choice (C) indicates that the *tricks are done as rewards,* rather than *for rewards,* so it is incorrect. Choice (E) is an incomplete sentence fragment, so eliminate it. The correct answer is (B).

16. **D**   The non-underlined portion of the sentence uses the pronouns *its* and *it*, therefore the noun *giant kangaroo rats* should be singular. Therefore, eliminate (A), (B), and (C). In (B), *adapt* is also incorrect, as it is the wrong verb tense. This sentence describes two actions that took place in the past, in sequence, so the past perfect *had adapted* is needed. In (C), *were adapted* is the wrong verb tense. In (E), the pronoun error is corrected, but *adapts* is the incorrect verb form. Choice (D) is correct because *the giant kangaroo rat* agrees with *its* and *it* and because the correct past perfect form of the verb is used.

17. **D**   Since that word is describing *candidates for elected office*, the word *who* is the correct pronoun, so eliminate (A), (C), and (E). Choice (B) compares the *rights of workers* to *large corporations*, which is incorrect. Eliminate (B). Choice (D) uses the correct pronoun and does not make any further errors, so the correct answer is (D).

18. **B** The sentence is incorrect as written because *his* is an ambiguous pronoun—it's not clear which founder is referred to. Therefore, eliminate (A). In (C), a verb form error is introduced by changing *has grown* to *growing*. In (D) and (E), a modifier error is introduced by removing *Apple Computers* from its place at the beginning of the clause. Choice (B) corrects the ambiguous pronoun error.

19. **C** In the initial sentence, *whom* is the incorrect pronoun choice. Because the group to blame for the assassination is the actor in this sentence, the subject pronoun *who* should be used instead of the object pronoun *whom*. Therefore, eliminate (A) and (B). Choice (D) adds the preposition *to*, creating a new error. Choice (E) rewrites the clause completely so that it doesn't fit with the rest of the non-underlined sentence. The correct answer is (C).

20. **C** In the original sentence, *one* does not agree with *your*, therefore (A) and (B) are incorrect. Choice (C) corrects the error. Choice (D) omits the necessary *as* to complete the *as…as* idiom. In (E), *people* does not agree with *your*. The correct answer is (C).

21. **D** The original sentence is incorrect because both the verb *improve* and the pronouns *their* and *they* do not agree with the noun *subject*. Choice (B) corrects the verb but not the pronoun. Choice (C) corrects one pronoun but not the verb and the other pronoun. Choice (D) makes all the corrections. Choice (E) changes the order of the sentence but repeats the pronoun errors. The correct answer is (D).

22. **C** In the non-underlined portion of the sentence, the pronoun *their* is used to refer to the noun, which is originally written as *pension fund*. However, the pronoun *their* is a plural pronoun, so it must match with a plural noun, so the *pension fund* needs to be written as *pension funds*. Eliminate (A). Choice (B) changes the underlined pronoun from *their* to *its* which is no longer parallel, so eliminate (B). Choice (C) makes the appropriate change, so keep (C). Choice (D) and (E) both make the same plural noun error, so eliminate them both. The correct answer is (C).

23. **E** The word *their* refers to the word *public*. However, *their* is plural while *public* is singular. Eliminate (A) as well as (C), which repeats the mistake. Another plural pronoun, *they*, has been added to (B), which makes it wrong for the same reason; eliminate (B). The comma in (D) is unnecessary, so eliminate (D). Choice (E) corrects the original error, so the correct answer is (E).

24. **E** *Capuchins* does not agree with the pronoun *its* in the later, nonunderlined portion of the sentence, so eliminate (A). Choices (B) and (C) repeat the error by the use of *capuchins,* so eliminate these choices. Choice (D) introduces the pronoun *it*, which is unnecessary and creates a structure that is not parallel, so (D) is incorrect. The correct answer is (E).

Parallel Construction

1. **A** The sentence is correct as written. The words *transporting, smelting,* and *manufacturing* are all items in a list, and thus all need to be in the same form in order for the sentence to remain parallel. *Manufactured* is past tense, and not in the gerund form, so eliminate (B), (C), and (D). Notice too that (C) contains the ambiguous pronoun *they*. Of the remaining (A) and (E), only (A) maintains parallelism in the sentence.

2. **D** The phrase *changing precipitation patterns* is the third item in a list, and must remain parallel to the other items in the list. Because the other items in the list are written as *to rise,* and *to retreat,* the correct form of the third item is *to change.* Eliminate (A), (B), and (C). The final split is between *resulting in,* and *resulting with.* The correct idiom is *resulting in,* so the correct answer is (D).

3. **C** The underlined portion contains an incorrect comparison: *to take* is not parallel to *driving,* so eliminate (A), as well as (D) and (E), which repeat the error. Choice (B) is also not correct: *to drive* is not parallel to *taking.* Using *take* and *drive* makes the sentence parallel, so the correct answer is (C).

4. **B** The sentence incorrectly compares *dark roofs* to *using white roofs.* Nouns can only be compared to other nouns, so this is a parallelism error. Therefore, eliminate (A) and (C) which repeats the error. Choice (B) correctly compares *dark roofs* to *white roofs,* and makes no other errors, so retain this choice for now. Choice (D) makes another parallelism error, incorrectly comparing *dark roofs* to *the use of white roofs,* so eliminate this answer. Choice (E) corrects the comparison, but incorrectly uses the verb *have given.* In order to maintain agreement with the verb *absorb* it is necessary to use the present tense *give,* so (E) is incorrect. The correct answer is (B).

5. **A** The sentence is correct as written. *Dangerous particles being released* is in the passive voice, so (D) and (E) should be eliminated. Choice (B) is incorrect because *risk of releasing* is not parallel to *risking the destruction of.* Choice (C) is similarly incorrect because *risk of the release* is not parallel to *risk of destroying.* Only (A) maintains parallelism, so the correct answer is (A).

6. **B** The original sentence construction indicates that schools systems have a choice *to meet* or *provide.* The verb *provide* should be parallel to *to meet,* so (A) is incorrect. Choices (C) and (E) repeat the original error and can be eliminated. Choice (D) changes the verb form to *providing,* which is still not parallel to *to meet,* so eliminate (D). The correct answer is (B).

7. **B** The sentence lacks parallelism because it incorrectly compares the noun *wind power* to the gerund phrase *using fossil fuels.* Eliminate (A). Choices (C) and (D) reverse the order of words, but repeat the original error by comparing *using wind power* to *fossil fuels,* and *using wind power* to *it.* Choice (E) incorrectly compares the action *to use wind power* to *fossil fuels,* and contains the incorrect preposition *for.* The correct answer is (B).

8. **C** The sentence provides a list outlining two results of the overcrowding, and the two results should be in parallel form. However, *to lead to* is not parallel to *provokes,* so answer (A) contains an error. Choices (D) and (E) repeat the original error, and can be eliminated. Choice (B) incorrectly uses *provokes* instead of *provoking.* Only (C) maintains parallelism, so the correct answer is (C).

9. **D** The sentence provides a list of two things that the board voted to do. The first decision, *to purchase an overseas office*, should be parallel in form to the second decision *if executives had received positive evaluations they would be promoted*. The sentence lacks parallelism and is passive, so (A) is incorrect. Both (B) and (C) use the gerund form of verbs, so that you have *to purchase* listed with *having received* or *receiving*, neither of which is parallel. Choice (E) similarly lacks parallelism so it is incorrect. The correct answer is (D).

10. **B** The sentence mixes two constructions by using *all…to be towed* and *be fined*. Because the second half does not use the infinitive form *to be fined*, the sentence lacks parallelism. Eliminate (A). Choice (C) contains a similar error, as it uses *be towed*, and *being fined*. Choice (D) is equally lacking in parallelism, as it contains *towing* and *to be fined*. Choice (E) also lacks parallelism, and the use of *with* in this case is idiomatically incorrect. The correct answer is (B).

11. **A** The sentence is correct as written. *Those* is ambiguous because it does not refer to anything specifically, so eliminate (B) and (D). *It* is similarly ambiguous, so eliminate (C). The two remaining, (A) and (E), differ in how they order the words. The sentence is listing two possible future trends in the housing market, and the two things should be listed in parallel form. The non-underlined portion of the sentence uses *continue to increase*, and only (A) uses the parallel construction *continue to decrease*. The correct answer is (A).

12. **E** The sentence incorrectly compares a verb phrase, *are priorities for most people in the United states* to a noun phrase, *those of most other countries*. Actions should only be compared to other actions, so this sentence is not parallel: eliminate (A). Choice (B) merely changes the comparison word to *as*; it does not correct the error, so eliminate this answer. While (C) contains a verb phrase, the construction *are priorities for most people…as most people of other countries do* is not parallel, so eliminate this choice. Choice (D) contains a similar construction: *are priorities for most people…as do most people* is also not parallel, so eliminate it. Choice (E), with the parallel construction *are priorities for most people…as they are for most people*, is correct.

13. **C** The non-underlined portions of the sentence list three other possible outcomes of earthquakes in the following forms: *ruptures in, liquefaction of* and *occurrence of*. In order to maintain parallelism, the underlined portion must be a noun. Eliminate (A). Choices (D) and (E) are not parallel; *surrounding areas* does not match *ruptures, liquefaction*, and *occurrence*. Eliminate (D) and (E). Choice (B) changes the meaning of the sentence. The correct answer is (C).

14. **B** The sentence improperly compares the value of Dirac's *contributions* to *physicists of his time*. In order to correct the parallelism error, use *those of almost any,* so that the sentence properly compares the value of Dirac's contributions to the value of contributions made by other physicists. Eliminate (A), (C), and (D). Idiomatically, *more valuable* must be completed by *than*, rather than *as*, so (E) should be eliminated. The correct answer is (B).

15. **D** The sentence is comparing the average temperature in Ethiopia to the average temperatures of other countries, so the word *that* creates a parallelism error between the *recorded annual temperatures* of Ethiopia and *in any other country on earth*. Eliminate (A) and (E). Choices (C) and (D) differ only in that (C) incorrectly uses *and* to introduce a contrast. Eliminate (C). Between the remaining choices, (D) is more concise and is therefore correct.

16. **E** The sentence lists two possible outcomes of the bailout: *greater market stability* and *decreasing the probability of worldwide economic recession*. These are items in a list, and thus should be in parallel form. Listing *the probability* first creates a parallelism error, so (B) and (C) are incorrect. The remaining choices are split between *decreasing* and *decreased*. Only *decreased* is parallel to *greater*, so the correct answer is (E).

17. **E** The sentence contains a list of three elements that should be parallel. The first two verbs are *stockpiling* and *storing*, so the third should be *connecting*. Choices (A), (B), and (D) all use *connect*, so eliminate them. Choice (C) uses the correct verb form, but the revision changes the meaning of the sentence. The correct answer is (E).

18. **E** The comparison that is made between the types of investors is not parallel. The verb *do* is added incorrectly. Eliminate (A). Choice (B) contains the unnecessary verb *does*. Eliminate (C) and (D) because they change the meaning of the sentence with incorrect word choices. Choice (E) is in the correct, parallel form.

19. **B** The items listed that came as a result of the New Deal are mostly nouns (*regulations, programs,* and *insurance*) except for *saving* in the underlined portion. Eliminate (A). Choice (B) corrects the error while (C) and (E) introduce nouns (*agencies* and *savings*) but rewrite the rest of the sentence in an incorrect way. Choice (D) does not change to a noun form. The correct answer is (B).

20. **A** In the second part of the sentence, the verbs *threatening* and *leading* are in parallel form, therefore (A) is correct. The verbs in (B) and (D) are not parallel. In (C), the verbs are parallel but are not in the right form to match the first part of the sentence. Choice (E) changes the meaning of the sentence entirely by adding the word *despite*.

21. **E** In the original sentence, the gross domestic product of New Jersey is literally being compared to the *entire country of Pakistan*, not the GDP of Pakistan. When making comparisons, the things being compared must be parallel. The original sentence also contains a misplaced modifier, as the phrase *While the two…geography* is actually modifying the *gross domestic product of the state of New Jersey* instead of the state itself. Eliminate (A), (B), (C), and (D) as they all repeat one of these errors. Choice (E) corrects both errors and is the correct answer.

22. **B** The original sentence contains two errors. The first is the idiom usage of *on the event*, which should be *in the event*. The second is parallelism between *many* and the wordy *only a couple*. Eliminate (A). Choice (C) maintains the idiom error while (D) maintains the parallelism error. Choice (E) uses the passive construction *being* and changes the meaning of the original sentence. The correct answer is (B).

23.   D   The original sentence contains a list: *the company announced that...and if*, which is not parallel, so eliminate (A), and also (C) and (E), which repeat the error of *if*. Choice (B) is parallel, but contains the pronoun *their*, which does not agree with the noun *company*, so eliminate this answer. Choice (D) uses the parallel construction *and* that, and has the correct pronoun *its*, so this answer choice is correct.

24.   D   A list of items, in this case verbs, must be parallel in form. *Free* and *save* should match *encourage*. Choice (D) is the only answer that fixes this error. While (A) and (C) use the word *encourage*, they also add extraneous words. The correct answer is (D).

25.   E   The first half of the sentence notes that *experts predict*. The second half of the sentence notes that several factors *make precise forecasting difficult*. Therefore, a transition word showing contrast is needed. The word *and* is incorrect, which means (A) and (C). In (B), though *but* is an accurate transition, the word acknowledging wouldn't serve as the subject of the clause without changing its meaning. Eliminate (B). Choice (D) repeats the mistake and can be eliminated. Choice (E) corrects the original error and makes no further mistakes, so the correct answer is (E).

26.   D   The parallelism error in this sentence is the lack of a reference to *masterpieces* in the underlined phrase *were greater than his earlier years*. Eliminate (A) and (C) because they do not have any reference to the *masterpieces*. Choice (B) introduces an unnecessary relative pronoun *which*, so it can be eliminated. Choice (D) correctly changes the tense of *were* to *are* and introduces *those* to refer back to the *masterpieces* earlier in the sentence. Choice (E) changes the verb *were* to *had to be* and introduces an incorrect prepositional phrase *in those earlier years*, so (E) can be eliminated. The correct answer is (D).

Misplaced Modifiers

1.   D   The first part of the sentence describes Truman so the words directly after the comma should be *Harry S. Truman*, not *the phrase*. Therefore, eliminate (A), (B), and (C), which repeat the error. Choice (D) has *Harry S. Truman* after the comma, and makes no other errors, so retain this answer choice.   Now look closely at (E)—it's not describing Harry S. Truman but, rather, *Harry S. Truman's phrase*. The phrase didn't make a legacy for himself as President; Harry S. Truman did, so eliminate (E). The correct answer is (D).

2.   E   As currently written, *from 420 to 1,210 pounds* describes the *size*, so the position of that phrase next to the word *meat* is incorrect. Therefore, eliminate (A) and (C), which repeats the error. Choice (B) has the pronoun *who*. Since *who* can only be used to refer to people, this pronoun does not agree with *wildebeests*, so eliminate (B). Choice (D) also contains *who*, so eliminate this answer as well. Choice (E) positions *from 420 to 1,210 pounds* next to the word *size* and makes no other errors, so this answer choice is correct.

3. **E**   The beginning phrase should modify *many people*, which means that the latter should come right after the former. Therefore, eliminate (A) and (C). Choice (B) introduces a parallelism error (*agonize* is not the same format as *witnessing*). In (D), the verb choice (*to agonize* and *to witness*) does not compliment the rest of the sentence, making it a fragment. Choice (E) fixes the modifier error and is the correct answer.

4. **D**   Don't be fooled by the added phrase *such as cereal and bread*. As currently written, *consumed on a daily basis* modifies *United States' citizens*, implying that the citizens are the ones consumed. Therefore, eliminate (A) and (B), which repeats the error. Choice (C) incorrectly indicates that *the national average weight* is what is *consumed on a daily basis*, so eliminate this answer. Choice (D) correctly indicates that *corn* is what is consumed, so retain this answer. Choice (E) incorrectly indicates that *one* is what is *consumed on a daily basis*. The correct answer is (D).

5. **A**   The sentence is correct as written. The beginning phrase modifies the next words *the Farmers' Almanac*, avoiding any misplaced modifier errors. Eliminate (C) and (E) because they contain misplaced modifiers for the reason mentioned above. Eliminate (B) because it switches to the past tense (*contained*); the sentence should stay in the present tense because the Farmers' Almanac is still in publication. Also, *published every year* is present tense in this sentence, so it retains the parallelism. Finally, eliminate (D) because it is in past tense, and the placement of *published* makes the sentence awkward. The correct answer is (A).

6. **D**   The original sentence has a misplaced modifier error. Because *many people* immediately follows the modifying phrase, it sounds as though they do not sting or bite. *Cicadas* needs to follow the modifying phrase so eliminate (A), (B), and (C). The difference between (D) and (E) is that the latter's structure is more confusing and awkward. The correct answer is (D).

7. **C**   As currently written, the phrase *best known as a tonalist* incorrectly modifies the noun *works*, so eliminate (A). Choice (B) makes a similar error: the *works* are still referred to as *a tonalist*. Choice (C) places the phrase *best known as a tonalist* so that it correctly modifies *the painter James Whistler*, and makes no other errors, so keep this answer. Choice (D) presents nonsensical meaning via the construction *his works, which he played on haunting shadows*, implying that the painted works are played, so eliminate this answer. Eliminate (E) because it uses *just*, which is unnecessary and changes the meaning of the sentence. The correct answer is (C).

8. **C**   The original sentence has a misplaced modifier. The first phrase (*before waging war on Britain in 1812*) needs to immediately be followed by the noun it's modifying (*the United States*). Therefore, eliminate (A) and (B). Also eliminate (D) and (E) because those answers replace *its* with *their*. The United States is a collective noun and, therefore, should be accompanied by *its*. The correct answer is (C).

9. **E**   The sentence as written begins with the phrase *of the three Brontë sisters*, which incorrectly modifies *people*, the noun immediately after the comma. Therefore, eliminate (A) and (B), which repeats the error. Choice (C) correctly places *Charlotte* next to the modifying phrase *of the three Brontë sisters*,

but incorrectly refers to the noun *people* as *a popular required reading novel.* Choice (D) uses the quantity word *more,* which compares exactly two items, and is incorrect in a sentence about *three Brontë sisters.* Choice (E) places *Charlotte* next to the modifying phrase *of the three Brontë sisters* and makes no other errors, so this answer choice is correct.

10. E As written, the introductory phrase *wary of potential predators* incorrectly modifies *Australian wildlife biologists,* so eliminate (A), (B), and (D), which repeat that error. The use of the phrase *can only be spotted* in (C) changes the meaning unnecessarily, so eliminate this answer. Choice (E) correctly places *the platypus* next to the phrase *wary of potential predators,* and makes no other errors, so this is the correct answer.

11. A There is a descriptive phrase followed by a comma and a noun, so check for a misplaced modifier. Here, the noun given is indeed the one being modified. Choices (B) and (D) keep the format but change the noun, making the sentence incorrect. Eliminate them. Choices (C) and (E) change the format, though (E) still has a modifier error so eliminate (C) and (E). The correct answer is (A).

12. D This sentence has a misplaced modifier. As written, the medieval scribes are being used as writing surfaces. Choices (A), (C), and (E) repeat this error. Choice (B) incorrectly compares animal skins to medieval scribes, leaving only (D), the correct answer.

13. B This sentence begins with an introductory phrase followed by a comma and a noun, so you should check for a modifier error. There is none however, since the noun that follows the phrase is the correct one. Eliminate (C) and (D) based on this, since they change to the incorrect *many different styles of coffee.* The answer choices also alternate between using *such as, like,* and *including*—in this case, the correct usage is *such as* because the phrase is introducing a list of examples and *like* is only used for comparisons. Eliminate (A). Choice (E) has a major error: the subject *coffee* doesn't agree with the verb *are*—eliminate it. The correct answer is (B).

14. E As written, this sentence has a misplaced modifier: *much of global commerce* can't really be *one of the most powerful market forces.* Eliminate (A). Unfortunately, the rest all change the format, so find new errors. Choices (B) and (D) both use *it,* often a sign of danger. In both answers, *it* is ambiguous and could refer to global commerce or the European Union. Eliminate them. Choice (C) uses an incorrect idiom, saying *believed…as* instead of the correct usage, *believed…to be.* The correct answer is (E).

15. C As written, this sentence has a misplaced modifier as: Hieronymus Bosch himself wasn't filled with allegorical images—his paintings were. Choice (A) is wrong and (E) repeats the error; both can be eliminated. Choice (B) changes the form of *continue* to *continuing* but that leaves the rest of the sentence lacking a verb. Eliminate it. Choice (D) moves *disturbing,* which changes the meaning. The correct answer is (C).

16. D As written, this sentence has a misplaced modifier: *herpetologists* aren't generally fatal but *rattlesnake venom* might be. Choices (A), (B), and (C) all have this error and can be eliminated. Choice (E) replaces *herpetologists* with *studying,* which isn't really a noun nor is it fatal. The correct answer is (D).

17. **E** As written, this sentence has a misplaced modifier. *Zookeepers* aren't supposed to be the subject of the introductory phrase about being bred in captivity—*the rare Sumatran tiger* is. Choices (A) and (C) both have this error and can be eliminated. Choice (B) adds a pronoun, but *they* can only refer to the *zookeepers*, so that's not any better. Eliminate it. Choice (D) adds the word *although* at the beginning, which changes the meaning. The correct answer is (E).

18. **A** This sentence is correct as written. Choices (B), (C), and (E) all change the order to make *California* the subject from the very beginning. Choice (B), however, changes the subject to *geologists* by using the word *who*, which doesn't match the non-underlined portion. Choice (C) also changes the subject of the non-underlined portion, this time to *the fear of geologists*. Eliminate it. Choice (E) keeps California as the subject but changes the pronoun to *their*, and that would have to refer to *geologists* who are definitely not *position[ed] above coastal tectonic plates*. Choice (D) keeps the original format but repeats the pronoun error in (E). The correct answer is (A).

19. **B** As written, this sentence has a misplaced modifier error: *consumers* were not once a *rare commodity*. The noun after the comma needs to be *books*, not *consumers*. Eliminate (A), (C), and (E). Choice (D) incorrectly changes *increasingly* to *increasing*, which changes the meaning. The correct answer is (B).

20. **D** As written, this sentence has a misplaced modifier: *the government* isn't what's preying on people. Choices (A), (C), and (E) all contain that error and can be eliminated. Choice (B) incorrectly refers to the *sub-prime mortgage industry* in the singular, while the non-underlined portion uses the word *they*, signaling to use a plural noun. The correct answer is (D).

21. **A** This sentence is correct as written. The introductory phrase is correctly modifying *the graphic novel* and the comparison between graphic novels as an *art form* versus a *literary genre* is parallel. Choices (B) and (E) incorrectly change the subject of the introductory phrase. Choice (C) incorrectly removes the verb *is*, making the sentence incomplete. Choice (D) incorrectly describes plural *graphic novels* as a singular *art form*. The correct answer is (A).

22. **D** As written, this sentence has a misplaced modifier error: the *early explorers* weren't the ones *sleeping* in the trees. Choices (A), (B), (C), and (E) all contain this error, even when they try to fix it by adding in pronouns. Only (D) makes it clear that the explorers were watching the sloth, which was sleeping. The correct answer is (D).

23. **B** Two independent clauses should be connected either by a semicolon or a comma and a conjunction. While the underlined portion of the sentence contains a conjunction, *and*, it lacks a comma. Eliminate (A). Choice (B) corrects the original error and does not make any further errors, so keep (B). Choice (C), if read in context, says that *the famous game…was the longest time*; eliminate (C). Choice (D) incorrectly uses *being* as a participle; eliminate (D). Choice (E) uses an unnecessary *and*; eliminate (E). The correct answer is (B).

Idioms

1. **E** The correct idiomatic construction is *so [blank] that [blank]*. Choice (A) is phrased in passive voice so eliminate it. Choices (B) and (C) allow for a misplaced modifier. In those sentences, *asking customers not to purchase more than two bags per trip* is now modifying the salt instead of the signs. Choice (D) alters the idiomatic construction by switching *so* and *that*. Choice (E) maintains the correct idiom.

2. **D** The correct idiom is *credited with*, so eliminate (A) and (B). Choice (C) has the correct idiom, but replaces *who* with *that*. Always use *who* when referring to people. Choice (E) adds an extra unnecessary word, which changes the meaning of the sentence. Choice (D) contains the correct idiom and is the correct answer.

3. **C** The original sentence has an idiom error. The correct idiomatic structure in a comparison is *[blank] is more than [blank]*. Therefore, eliminate (A) and (B) which have *as* instead of *than*. Choice (D) is incorrect because, while the idiom is fixed, it introduces a verb error (*is* instead of *was*), a pronoun error (by removing *that of*), and uses the wrong conjunction (*and* instead of *but*). Choice (E) uses the wrong conjunction and the wrong verb tense. Choice (C) uses the correct idiomatic structure and keeps the correct verb tense (*was*).

4. **C** The original sentence has an error because *depending on if* is not the correct idiom. *If* should only be used for conditionals; when two options are available, use *whether*. Therefore, eliminate (A) and (B). Choices (D) and (E) are jumbled and force the rest of the sentence to be incorrect grammatically. Choice (C) contains the correct idiom, *depending on whether*. The correct answer is (C).

5. **A** The sentence is correct as written. *Not so much as* is a correct idiomatic expression. Choice (B) retains the expression but inserts a pronoun error (*their* instead of *his*). Choice (C) doesn't keep the meaning of the original sentence. Choice (D) has a misplaced modifier and makes it sound as though the employee declared bankruptcy, instead of the firm. In choice (E), *as much as* is a correct idiom, but the sentence then becomes wordy and confusing. The correct answer is (A).

6. **B** The correct idiomatic construction is *between [blank] and [blank]*. Choice (A) is incorrect because it is unclear to which civil wars *these* is referring. Choices (C) and (D) change the meaning of the sentence and are incorrect grammatically. Choice (E) uses an incorrect phrase to describe the time that has elapsed during these two events, *through* instead of *between*. Choice (B) uses the correct idiomatic structure and is the correct answer.

7. **A** Though the original sentence may sound awkward, it is indeed correct as written. The sentence correctly uses the subjunctive tense for *determined that...be tasked*. The idiomatic construction here is *tasked with*. Choice (B) replaces *be* with *is*, resulting in an incorrect subjunctive tense structure. Choice (C) eliminates *that*, has *is* instead of *be*, and also fiddles with the possessive pronoun *its*. Choices (D) and (E) eliminate *that*. The correct answer is (A).

8. **C**   The correct idiomatic construction is *viewed as*. In this case, Wharton viewed her surroundings as fodder for her novels. Choices (A), (B), and (D) do not maintain this idiom. In addition, (A) uses *social stigmas and frequent faux pas* to modify surroundings, which is not the intended effect of the sentence. It also adds *being*, which is not needed. Choices (B), (D), and (E) are all sentence fragments. The correct answer is (C).

9. **E**   As written, the sentence has an idiom error. *As contrasted to* is not a correct idiom, so eliminate (A) and (B). *As contrasted with* is also not a correct idiom so eliminate (C). *In contrast to* is a correct idiom, but the difference between the last two choices is that (D) has a pronoun error (*one's*). Humans is plural, so the correct matching pronoun is *their*, making the correct answer (E).

10. **E**   This question is testing the correct idiom for *prohibited*. The correct phrasing is *prohibited from* an action. As written, this sentence incorrectly says *prohibited…to purchase*. Eliminate (A) and (D). Comparing (B), (C), and (E), one major difference is the placement of the phrase *by federal law*; (B) moves it to after *alcohol*, making it sound as if someone is trying to purchase alcohol by means of federal law, which changes the meaning (and doesn't really make sense either). Between (C) and (E), the easiest difference to work with is probably *that* versus *which* at the end of the underlined portion. In order to use *which*, you have to have a comma, and there's no comma in (C). The correct answer is (E).

11. **D**   This sentence is testing the idiom for the word *difference*. The correct formation is *difference between…and….* This sentence instead says *difference…between…from*. The beginning of the underlined portion isn't grammatically relevant to the idiom, so you can just ignore it for now. The important part is towards the end, where it compares taking placebos to not taking medication. For the correct formation, the word *between* must be first, then the word *and* connecting the two possibilities. Choices (B) and (C) are both missing the *between* so eliminate them. Comparing (D) and (E) shows that (E) incorrectly uses the word *or* instead of *and*. The correct answer is (D).

12. **E**   This sentence is testing a couple of idiomatic constructs: *contrary to* and *not…Australia*. Both phrases are completely underlined though, and some of the answers give alternative pairs. Just remember: the keys are to have a proper construction and not to change the meaning. As written, the sentence says *contrary with*, which is incorrect. Eliminate it. Choice (D) repeats the same basic mistake—changing *contrary* to *in contrast* doesn't help, since they both need to be followed by *to*. Choice (B) must also be wrong then—*from* still isn't *to*. The only difference between (C) and (E) is at the very end. Choice (C) adds the word *only* after *not*, changing the meaning of the sentence. The correct answer is (E).

13. **B** The idiomatic error in this sentence is an improper use of the pluperfect tense, as the underlined part of the sentence reads *today its numbers had moved*. Since *today* refers to the present and *had moved* refers to the past, the words are not in agreement. Eliminate (A). Choice (B) correctly changes *had moved* to *are moving*. Choice (C) incorrectly changes *its*, which refers to Grizzly Bear, to *their*, so (C) can be eliminated. Choice (D) introduces the passive voice by changing *had moved* to *have been moving*, so (D) can be eliminated. Choice (E) also changes *its* to *their* so (E) can be eliminated. The correct answer is (B).

14. **B** The sentence has an idiom error: *opportunity of attending* should be *opportunity to attend*. Eliminate (A) and (D). Look at the remaining answers to see there's a split between *number* and *amount* at the very beginning. The word is being used to describe *women* and women are countable, so the correct word to use is *number*. Eliminate (C). Comparing (B) and (E), the difference is at the end of the underlined portion. Choice (B) says *is shifting* while (E) says *are shifting*. The verb refers to the *balance*, which is singular, so eliminate (E). The correct answer is (B).

15. **A** The sentence is correct as written. The first difference that stands out in the answers is the alternation between *although* and *even though*; unfortunately, the only difference between them is stylistic, not grammatical, so that's not really something fixable. The verbs are changing in tense, from *had been planning* to *was planning* to *had planned*. Check the rest of the sentence for other verbs and time cues. Logically, this action needs to take place before she *failed* or possibly simultaneously. Choice (B) incorrectly makes it sound like the failure happened first, and can therefore be eliminated. Choice (C) removes the *she* from before the failure and changes the verb to *failing*. That makes the sentence incomplete, so (C) can be eliminated too. Choices (D) and (E) both have simultaneous verbs. Choice (D) sounds kind of weird but that doesn't always mean an answer is wrong, so look for more errors. Comparing the remaining three, there's another difference after the word *planning*: (A) says *to* while (D) and (E) say *on*. The correct idiom is *planning to* so (D) and (E) can be eliminated. The correct answer is (A).

16. **B** The idiomatic error in this sentence is *not only…they can also*, instead of the correct *not only…but also*. Eliminate (A), (D), and (E), since these do not contain the proper idiom. Choice (B) correctly changes *they can also* to *but also*. Choice (C) incorrectly changes *they can also* to *but they can also*, so (C) can be eliminated. The correct answer is (B).

17. **C** The word *distinguish* is a tip-off that this sentence is testing idioms. There are two possible formations that are correct: *distinguish between…and* or *distinguish…from*. Choice (A) confuses the two, saying *distinguish…and*. Eliminate it. Choice (D) says the same and can also be eliminated. Choices (B) and (E) change the *and* to *from* but add *between*, making the *from* incorrect. Eliminate them. The correct answer is (C).

18. **B** The idiomatic error in this sentence is an improper pairing of *just as…was* instead of the correct *just as…so too*. Eliminate (A) and (E) for this reason. Choice (B) correctly pairs *just as…so too*. Choice (C) changes the idiom to *Not only…but the platypus was also*, instead of the correct *not only…but*

also, so (C) can be eliminated. Choice (D) changes the idiom to the incorrect *Not only...so too*, so (D) can be eliminated. The correct answer is (B).

19. **E**   The idiomatic error in this sentence is *not only...but on* instead of the correct *not only...but also*. Eliminate (A). Choice (B) incorrectly changes the idiom to *not because of...but due to*, so (B) can be eliminated. Choice (C) incorrectly changes the idiom to *because of not...but*, so (C) can be eliminated. Choice (D) correctly changes the idiom to *not only...but also*, but also incorrectly changes the verb *are*, whose subject is *Literary critics*, to is, so (D) can be eliminated. Choice (E) removes the idiom entirely and changes the formula to a parallel construction, *based not on...but on*. The correct answer is (E).

20. **A**   The idiom in this sentence is *prohibited by*, which is correct as written. Choice (B) incorrectly changes the verb *is*, whose subject is *use*, to *are* and removes the concessive *though*, so (B) can be eliminated. Choice (C) also changes the verb *is* to *are* without changing its subject, so (C) can be eliminated. Choice (D) removes the concessive *though* and correctly adds *is* to the beginning of the underlined portion of the sentence, but still incorrectly changes the verb *is* to *are*, so (D) can be eliminated. Choice (E) incorrectly changes the idiom *prohibited by* to *prohibited in*, so (E) can be eliminated. The correct answer is (A).

21. **E**   The idiomatic error in this sentence is an improper pairing of *considered...as* instead of simply using *consider*. Eliminate (A) and (D). Choice (B) incorrectly adds *is*, making the idiom *consider it is*, so (B) can be eliminated. Choice (C) incorrectly adds *to be*, making the idiom *consider it to be*, so (C) can be eliminated. Choice (E) correctly changes *considered* to *consider* and adds nothing to *consider*. Choice (E) is the correct answer.

22. **C**   The idiomatic error in this sentence is *prohibited on* instead of the correct *prohibited from*. Eliminate (A) and (D). Choice (B) incorrectly uses *prohibiting...to* instead of *from*, so (B) can be eliminated. Choice (C) correctly arranges the sentence, making the subject of *prohibit from Landowners* and the direct object of *prohibit from* the verbal concepts *swimming and sunbathing*. Choice (E) does correctly use *prohibit...from* but makes the direct object of *prohibit is swimmers and sunbathers* instead of the verbal concepts swimming and sunbathing, so (E) can be eliminated. The correct answer is (C).

23. **B**   The idiomatic error in this sentence is *between...from* instead of the correct *between...and*. Eliminate (A) and (E). Choice (B) correctly changes *between...from* to *between...and* and correctly changes *to be able* to the subjunctive *be able* which is commanded by the verb *it is...important*. Choice (C) removes *between* but does not use the other possible idiom *distinguish...from...*; instead it incorrectly uses *distinguish...and...*, so (C) can be eliminated. Choice (D) incorrectly changes the verb *to be able* to *are able*, instead of rendering it in the subjunctive mood as *be able*, so (D) can be eliminated. The correct answer is (B).

24. **A**   The idiom in this sentence is the phrase *such as*. Since *such as* introduces examples, it is used correctly in this sentence. Choice (B) incorrectly changes *attributed to* to *attributed for*, so (B) can be eliminated. Choice (C) incorrectly uses the comparative phrase *like* instead of *such as*, so (C) can be

eliminated. Choice (D) incorrectly changes *attributed to* to *attributed as*, so (D) can be eliminated. Choice (E) incorrectly uses the comparative phrase *like* instead of *such as*, so (E) can be eliminated. The correct answer is (A).

25. **D** The sentence contains an idiom error. The correct idiom is *incompatible with*, so eliminate (A), (C), and (E). Comparing (B) and (D), the first difference is between *arguing* and *argue*. In this case, using *arguing* would remove the only verb in the first half of the sentence. The sentence has to be parallel with the later phrase *assert that*, so you have to have a verb here. Eliminate (B). The correct answer is (D).

26. **B** This idiom error has to do with a quantity word (*more* versus *most*). When describing something of the highest kind, the correct form is *the most*. Therefore, eliminate (A) and (D), which repeats the error. Choice (B) uses *the most*, so keep this answer choice. Choice (C) is incorrect because it doesn't use a quantifiable word at all. Also eliminate (E) because the meaning of the sentence has changed—now the continent is *impressive* and the use of the euro was *encouraging*. The intention of the original sentence is to say that the *encouraged* use of the euro was *impressive*. Therefore, (B) is correct.

27. **E** The sentence as written incorrectly uses the word *like*, which is only used to compare things, not actions. In this case, the proper idiomatic word is *as* because the animals themselves aren't being compared—the way people refer to them is. Eliminate (A) and (B), which incorrectly use *like*. Choice (C) pairs the singular verb *is* with the plural subject *squirrels*, so eliminate this answer. Choice (D) incorrectly omits any verb. Choice (E) uses *as* and makes no other errors, so this is the correct answer.

28. **A** This sentence is correct as written: it contrasts *monotremes* and their egg-laying ways with other *mammals* that bear live young. Choice (B) changes *among* to *between*, which is used to describe exactly two items, not many. Eliminate (B). In (C), the construction *monotremes are unusual among mammals because they lay eggs* is ambiguous: *they* could refer to either *mammals* or *monotremes*, so eliminate this answer. Choice (D) changes the meaning of the sentence by omitting to mention that *monotremes* belong to the category of mammals. Choice (E) changes *among* to *aside from*, which changes the meaning of the sentence. In (E), the plural pronoun *they* does not agree with the singular noun *monotreme*. The correct answer is (A).

29. **A** This sentence is correct as written: the introductory phrase *native to the grassy plains* correctly modifies the noun *wild bison*. Choices (B) and (C) can be eliminated because they use *like San Francisco's Golden Gate Park and Catalina Island* rather than *such as San Francisco's Golden Gate Park and Catalina Island*; the phrase gives examples so the proper idiom is *such as*. Choices (D) and (E) incorrectly use *like the latter case* at the end of the sentence. The sentence is comparing an action to another action (*due to wildlife protection* and *[due to] the efforts*), so the word *as* should be used. The correct phrase is *as in the latter case*, so eliminate (D) and (E). The correct answer is (A).

30. **D** This sentence uses *like* at the end. In this case, the correct idiom is *such as* because the sentence is listing examples, not comparing things. Therefore, eliminate (A) and (C), which repeats the error. Choice (B) incorrectly uses *between*—there are more than two breeds of dog, so the proper word is *among*. Eliminate (B). Choice (D) correctly uses *such as* and makes no other errors, so keep this answer. Choice (E) creates a misplaced modifier issue—the introductory phrase *among the many breeds of dogs* is now modifying *specific tasks*. The correct answer is (D).

Mixed Drill

1. **C** As written, the actions of the cereal company are not in parallel form: the present tense verb *retools* does not match the past tense verb *hired*. Eliminate (A) and (B), which repeats the error. Choice (C) correctly matches *hired* with *retooled*, so keep this answer. Choice (D) incorrectly uses the future tense *then will retool*, which is not parallel, so eliminate this answer. Choice (E) incorrectly uses the present tense *produces*, which is not parallel to *hired*. The correct answer is (C).

2. **B** The subject of the sentence is the *Kyoto Protocol*. The sentence ascribes the verb *signify* to the Kyoto Protocol creating a subject-verb agreement error. Eliminate (A). Similarly, (D) includes a subject-verb agreement error by using *have signified* for the singular noun the *Kyoto Protocol*. In (C), the verb phrase *is signifying* is awkward. In (D), the use of the words *and* and *too* creates a redundancy error. Therefore, the correct answer is (B).

3. **B** This sentence uses the subjunctive mood with an *if* clause, which means that the sentence should use the conditional form *if they were...they would...* However, the sentence incorrectly uses the simple present tense *have*, making a verb tense error. Eliminate (A). Choice (B) correctly uses the conditional verb form *would have*, so retain this answer. Eliminate (C) because it incorrectly uses the future tense *will have*. Choices (D) and (E) incorrectly use the singular pronouns *it* and *its* to refer to *people*, so eliminate these answer choices. The correct answer is (B).

4. **A** The sentence is correct as written. The pronoun *its* may seem awkward because some may assume it is a pronoun referring to the plural noun, *directors*. However, it refers to the *board of directors* which is a singular, collective noun. Choices (B) and (C) are incorrect because *their* is a plural pronoun and does not agree with the singular, collective noun *board of directors*. Eliminate (D) because the present verb *is spending* does not match the time sense of the sentence reflected by the past tense verb *questioned*. Finally, (E) is incorrect because *although* changes the meaning of the sentence. The correct answer is (A).

5. **C** The sentence has a subject-verb agreement problem. The verb *were* does not agree with the singular subject *each*. Eliminate (A) and (B). In (D), the plural subject *novels* does not agree with the singular verb *was*. In (E), if the hyphenated potion of the text is taken out, what is left is an awkward construction that notes the novels as both plural and then singles them out individually. Choice (C) simply states that the books were all complex and well regarded novels. The correct answer is (C).

6. **B**   The sentence has an idiom error. The correct idiomatic phrase is *abide by*. Eliminate (A), (C), and (E). The big difference is now the *is* versus *are* difference. Both of these start with the phrase *a society*, which is singular, so you can eliminate (D). The correct answer is (B).

7. **D**   The sentence is incorrect as written because the quantity word *much* is used when the noun it refers to (*theories*) is countable. *Many* should be used instead. Eliminate (A), (B), and (C), which repeat the error. Choice (D) contains the correct quantity word *many* and makes no new errors, so keep this answer. Choice (E) offers the unnecessarily wordy construction *theories relating to*, which is not as concise as *theories about*. Choice (D) is the correct answer.

8. **B**   As written, this sentence has a misplaced modifier error: the book, *The Book of the City of the Ladies* isn't believed by anyone to be an author—*Christine de Pizan* is. Choices (A) and (C) repeat that error and can be eliminated. Choices (B) and (D) both change the introductory phrase to clearly refer to a written work, but (D) uses the incorrect idiom *believe as* instead of the correct form, *believe to be*. Choice (E) repeats that idiom error. The correct answer is (B).

9. **C**   The sentence compares the statues that were topped with the headwear with the statues that were not topped with headwear. Therefore, to maintain parallel structure, the verbs used must match. Choices (A), (B), and (D) all contain verbs that do not match *were*. Also, eliminate (E) because it changes the tense of the verb. The correct answer is (C).

10. **E**   As written, this sentence has a misplaced modifier: *the towns* aren't *gathering for hours*, the *hurricane* is. Choices (A), (B), and (D) all contain that error, so eliminate them. Choice (C) adds in the pronoun *they* but that just clarifies that the initial part of the sentence is referring to *the towns*. Eliminate (C). The correct answer is (E).

11. **C**   The sentence contains a pronoun error. The sentence is trying to compare *the domestic chinchilla* to the wild chinchilla. Choices (A) and (B) incorrectly use the pronoun *their* to refer to *the domestic chinchilla*. Eliminate them. Look at the other choices. The correct idiom is *compared to*. Choice (D) uses *compared against*, which is incorrect. Eliminate it. The next thing to check is the parallel structure. Choice (E) adds the word *only*, which changes the meaning of the sentence. It also compares the singular *domestic chinchilla* to plural *counterparts*. The correct answer is (C).

12. **E**   This sentence has a tense error. As the sentence is written, MacKenzie *hoped* before he *discovered*, therefore the verb form should be past perfect (*had hoped*). Eliminate (A). Choice (B) uses the verb *was being hoped*, which is still not past perfect. Choices (C) and (D) use the simple past *he hoped*, which is also not past perfect, so eliminate these answers. Choice (E) uses the past perfect form *he had hoped*, so this is the correct answer.

13. **C**   Establish the relationship between the first half of the sentence and the second half of the sentence. Implied is a cause-effect: the jazz band's cross-generational popularity is due to the fusing of old and new musical styles. Choice (A) doesn't indicate a cause-effect relationship, so eliminate (A). Eliminate (B) because there is no comma necessary before a *that* clause. Choice (C) corrects the original error and doesn't make any further errors, so keep (C). Choice (D) is incorrect because

when doesn't show a cause-effect relationship. Choice (E) is incorrect because *by the fusion* doesn't indicate a cause-effect relationship. The correct answer is (C).

14. **D** The first thing to recognize is that the king of Persia did all of these things in the past. Eliminate (A) for the word *diverting*, which is present tense. Eliminate (E) for repeating the mistake. Next, at the end of the underlined portion is *like* or *as if*. Since what follows is a clause, *like* is incorrect (like is a preposition, followed only by nouns). Eliminate (B). Choice (C) changes both underlined verbs to wrong verb tenses—*had diverted* is past perfect, and *marching* is present participle. Eliminate (C). The correct answer is (D).

15. **A** The sentence as written does not appear to have any errors, so keep choice (A). Since *sanguine* is an adjective, it can't be *something*, which means (B) is an incorrect comparison. Eliminate it. Choice (C) is lacking the word *mean*, so it's also an incorrect comparison; eliminate (C). In (D), the word *that* is repeated twice, and *thing* is unnecessary; eliminate (D). Choice (E) uses five words, *is also in reference to*, that could be more efficiently stated in a single verb, *mean*. Eliminate (E). The correct answer is (A).

16. **E** The verb tense *exhibiting* in the original sentence is not parallel to the other verbs *exist* and *seem*, so eliminate (A). Choice (B) is idiomatically incorrect: the correct idiom is either *similar to* or a comparison with *are to...is to...* (as in *X are to Y what A is to B*), so eliminate this choice. Choice (C) makes a verb tense error: *have been known to exhibit* is wordy and not parallel to the time sense of the rest of the sentence. Furthermore, this choice changes the meaning of the sentence: it is the *electrons* which exhibit surprising characteristics, not the *ordinary particles*. Choice (D) also changes the meaning of the sentence: it is the *electrons* which exhibit surprising characteristics, not the *ordinary particles*. Choice (E) is parallel in verb tense, has the correct idiom, and preserves the original meaning that the *electrons* which exhibit surprising characteristics, so this choice is correct.

17. **A** The sentence is correct as written. The underlined portion contains two instances of parallelism: *maintaining* and *allowing* are parallel, and the comparison of the actions *crash into the sun, as meteors do* is also parallel. Choices (B) and (C) are incorrect because they omit the final *do,* so the comparison is not parallel. Choice (D) is incorrect because the verbs in the comparison, *to crash* and *is done,* are not parallel. The comparison in (E) is incorrect because *maintain the earth in orbit* is not parallel to *meteors that crash into the sun.* The correct answer is (A).

18. **D** The sentence contains an idiom error: *regard...to be* is incorrect, so eliminate (A), and also (C), which repeats the error. Choice (B) incorrectly compares a verb phrase to a noun: *regarded luxury, as other wealthy aristocrats*. Choice (D) correctly compares *Marie Antoinette* to *other wealthy aristocrats*, and contains the correct idiom *regard...as*, so retain this answer choice. Choice (E) incorrectly compares *luxury to Marie Antoinette* to *other wealthy aristocrats*, so eliminate this choice. The correct answer is (D).

19. **D**   An obvious error in this sentence is the misplaced modifier *Majestic, even breathtaking*, placed right before the word *tourists*. Since the modifier is not underlined, the underlined portion must be changed to have the modifier closest to the word it describes—Angkor Wat. Eliminate (A) and (C). Choice (B) introduces another misplaced modifier with the phrase *difficult for tourists to believe* placed right after *Angkor Wat*, so (B) can be eliminated. Choice (D) correctly places *Angkor Wat* after the modifier at the beginning of the sentence. Choice (E) adds another modifying phrase *who were* making the tourists *lost to the encroaching wilderness* instead of *Angkor Wat*, so (E) can be eliminated. The correct answer is (D).

Critical Reasoning

CRITICAL REASONING

For the purposes of our discussion of these questions, we find it easiest to refer to them simply as "arguments." That's because each question is composed of a short argument, a question about the argument, and five answer choices.

PARTS OF AN ARGUMENT

The key to answering most argument questions is breaking the argument down into its parts. Three connected parts make up an argument. The first two, the **conclusion** and **premises**, are stated explicitly in the argument, while the third part, the **assumption**, is unwritten.

Conclusion

The conclusion is the main point or central claim of the argument. It is what the author is trying to make the reader believe. Sometimes, you will see indicator words that will help you find the conclusion.

These include

- Therefore
- Clearly
- Thus
- So

- Hence
- Consequently
- In conclusion

The best way to identify the conclusion of the argument is to determine what the author is attempting to convince the reader is true.

Premises

The premises of the argument are the reasons, statistics, or evidence provided support the conclusion. Even if you disagree with the premises provided as support for a conclusion, you must accept them as true for the purposes of the GMAT.

Once you have found the conclusion, find the information in the argument that justifies the conclusion. Sometimes, the author will provide extraneous information that does not justify the conclusion.

To make sure you have correctly identified the premises, ask yourself what information the author has provided the justify why the conclusion is true. Sometimes you will see indicator words that can help you find the premises.

These include

- Since
- Because
- As a result of
- Suppose

Assumptions

Assumptions are the unstated premises the author may rely on to prove his or her conclusion. They are facts or evidence that are not explicitly stated in the passage, but that must be true in order for the argument to be well reasoned.

To identify the assumption(s) of an argument, look for a gap in reasoning between the conclusion and the premise(s) that are used to justify the conclusion. If there is a gap in the reasoning between the conclusion and premise, that is an assumption in the argument. Oftentimes, it is easiest to identify the assumption of an argument by examining the stated facts of the conclusion and determining which of those facts are not stated as a premise in the argument.

Break down this example.

1. Cream cheese contains 50 percent fewer calories per tablespoon than does butter or margarine. Therefore, a bagel with cream cheese is more healthful than is a bagel with butter on it.

First, find the conclusion. The word "therefore" indicates that the conclusion is "a bagel with cream cheese is more healthful than is a bagel with butter on it."

Why is that true? The argument says that "cream cheese contains 50 percent fewer calories per tablespoon than does butter or margarine." This sentence justifies the conclusion, so it is the premise of the argument.

Now look for any assumptions in the argument by examining the stated facts in the premise and conclusion. The premise of the argument was about the calories per tablespoon of cream cheese in comparison to the calories in butter of margarine. The conclusion shifted the language to indicate that, because of the fewer calories, a bagel with cream cheese is "more healthful" than one with butter or margarine. Therefore, the assumption in this argument is the gap in reasoning between something with less calories being more healthful.

To fill the gap, it must be true that a food with fewer calories per set amount is more healthful than a food with more calories per that same set amount. It also must be true that people use similar quantities of butter, margarine, or cream cheese on a bagel, proving that the combination of bagel and cream cheese has fewer calories than a combination of bagel and butter. These assumptions are not explicitly stated in the passage and are necessary for the argument to be valid, so they are the assumptions.

COMMON FLAWS

If you can identify the three parts of the argument, you can also start to identify the most commonly used flaws. These flaws contain their own standard assumptions, so if you learn to recognize these flaws you can quickly break down an argument into its parts to find the information you need. There are four types of common flaws: Causal, Analogy, Sampling, and Statistical.

Causal Flaws

Causal arguments are the most common type of flaw you will see on the GMAT. In a causal argument, the premise states that two things happened, and the author concludes that one of the things caused the other. The assumption in a causal argument is that there was no other cause or that the cause-effect relationship wasn't reversed. For example:

> 2. A study indicated that adults who listen to classical music regularly are less likely to have anxiety disorders. Clearly, classical music helps calm the nerves and lower anxiety.

The conclusion of the argument is that classical music calms the nerves and lowers anxiety. The premise of the argument is that a study found that adults who listen to classical music regularly are less likely to have anxiety disorders. The assumption of the argument is that listening to classical music caused the people in the study to have lower anxiety levels.

However, the fact that these two things are correlated does not mean that one caused the other. This is a causal flaw. The people in the study could have been experiencing lower anxiety levels for another reason, like a new medication.

Another option is that the cause-effect relationship is reversed. Perhaps calmer people are more predisposed to listen to classical music because it reflects their mood.

Thus, the author's assumption that listening to classical music reduces anxiety is a flaw of the argument.

Analogy Flaws

In an analogy argument, the author uses evidence about one thing to reach a conclusion about another. These arguments assume that the two things are similar enough to sustain a comparison. For example:

3. Contrary to opponents' charges that a single-payer health care system cannot work in a democratic nation such as the United States, an overhaul of the American health-care system is necessary. Opponents of the single-payer system in the United States should remember that Canada, a nation with a strong democratic tradition, has run a viable single-payer health-care program for many years.

The conclusion of the argument is that the United States needs to change the health-care system and a single-payer system is a good strategy. The premise of the argument is that a single-payer system works in Canada, which is also a democratic nation. The assumption is that the United States and Canada are similar. This assumption is not valid because differences in the populations and economies of the two countries mean that policies that work in one country won't necessarily work in the other.

Sampling Flaws

An argument that contains a sampling flaw reaches a conclusion based on evidence about a subset of a group. They usually involve surveys or polls. The assumption in sampling arguments is that the people in the sample represent the larger population. For example:

4. Contrary to popular belief, Vinot High School students overwhelmingly approve of the school administrative staff. We know this to be true because the student council expressed admiration for the principal and her staff in the council's editorial for the school paper.

The conclusion of the argument is that the students approve of the school administration. The premise of the argument is that the students like the school administration because the student council expressed admiration for the principal and her staff in the school paper. The assumption is that the student council represents the beliefs of the entire student body, or at least a majority of them.

This is an example of a sampling flaw. What if, for example, the student council is composed of sycophants who want to get favorable college recommendations from members of the administration? The author's assumption that the student council represents the entire student population is not necessarily supported, which renders the author's conclusion invalid.

Statistical Flaws

Arguments with statistical flaws hinge on questionable interpretations of numerical data. Most often, the author confuses percentages with actual values, by assuming that a change in percentage translates into a change in numbers. Here's an example:

> 5. Ninety percent of the population of Prelandia lived in rural areas in 1800. Today, only 20 percent of the population lives in rural areas. Clearly, more people lived in the countryside two centuries ago.

The conclusion of the argument is that more people lived in the countryside two centuries ago. The premise is that in 1800 ninety percent of the population lived rurally, and only twenty percent live in rural areas today. The author is assuming that because the percentage of people living rurally decreased, the actual number of people must have decreased as well.

This is an example of a statistical flaw. If, for example, the total population of the country in 1800 was 100, 90 of them lived in rural areas. If the total population of the countries today is 1,000, then 200 (20%) live in rural areas. In this case, more people live in the countryside now. Thus, the author's assumption that the number of people in the countryside decreased because the percentage of people living in the countryside decreased is invalid.

THE BASIC APPROACH

There are several different question types on arguments questions. Your approach to each question depends on what type of question you are dealing with. However, the basic approach is the same for all argument questions.

Step 1: Identify the question

Always read the question first so that you know what type of question you are doing and what your approach will be.

Step 2: Work the argument

For the most common question types, this means breaking the argument down into its conclusion, premises and assumption.

Step 3: Predict what the answer should do

In many cases, you will be able to come up with your own answer or at least think about what the right answer should do before you go to the answer choices. This will help you avoid trap answers.

Step 4: Use POE to find the answer

Aggressively eliminate answers that don't fit your prediction of what the answer should do. If you're having trouble deciding between two answers choices, look for a reason that one choice is better than another.

Here's a list of the argument question types you'll see on the GMAT. This chapter will show you to how to approach each of them.

- Assumption
- Weaken
- Strengthen
- Inference
- Resolve/Explain
- Evaluate the Argument
- Identify the Reasoning

WEAKEN QUESTIONS

Weaken questions are very common on Critical Reasoning. These question types will ask you to pick the answer choice that, if true, would weaken the argument.

Step 1: Read and identify the question

Weaken questions are easily identifiable as they usually contain words such as *weaken, undermine, cast doubt,* or *flaw.*

Step 2: Work the argument

Break the argument down into conclusion and premise(s). Once that is done, be on the lookout for common flaws or differences in the language used between the conclusion and the premise to find the assumption of the argument.

Step 3: Predict what the answer should do

The easiest ways to weaken an argument are to find reasons why the assumption is wrong and to provide information that makes the conclusion false.

So, consider the conclusion and think about all the reasons that it could be incorrect. Once you have identified a handful of reasons, move on to Step 4.

Step 4: Use POE to find the answer

POE: Consider each answer choice individually and decide if the inclusion of the new information discredits the conclusion or the assumption. Typically, incorrect answer choices for weaken questions:

- Are irrelevant (outside the scope or bring in unnecessary information).
- Strengthen the argument. These are common because the test writers know that in the heat of the moment it's easy to forget whether you are strengthening or weakening.
- Don't weaken the argument as much as another answer.

Weaken (and strengthen) questions are the only questions in the arguments section in which strong language is good. On a harder question, you may have more than one answer that could weaken the argument and you have to go with the one that most strongly discredits it. Try the example below.

1. Party leaders feared that the recent addition of conservative planks to the party platform would diminish the popularity of the party among younger voters. Some predicted that the number of party members younger than 25 would decline, or, at best, stay the same. This fear, though, has proven to be unfounded: of all party members, the percentage younger than 25 is greater than ever. Rather than hurt the party, conservatism has helped attract more young voters to the party.

   Which of the following, if true, would most seriously weaken the author's conclusion?

   (A) Many party leaders are uncomfortable with the political direction the party is taking, for both political and ideological reasons.
   (B) Party candidates continue to suffer defeats when running on the party platform.
   (C) The number of party members older than 25 declined significantly after the announcement of the new conservative platform.
   (D) In the last election, the ratio of voters under the age of 25 who voted for the party to all voters under the age of 25 increased.
   (E) Over half the population of potential voters under the age of 25 never vote.

The question says *weaken* so this is a weaken question. Break down the argument. The conclusion is "rather than hurt the party, conservatism has helped attract more young voters to the party." The premise is that after the addition of conservative planks, "of all party members, the percentage younger than 25 is greater than ever." Now, try to identify the assumption using common flaws or gaps in language between the conclusion and premise.

This argument has a causal flaw. The author assumes that the greater number of younger members in the party is due to the conservative planks and not some other factor.

There is also a statistical flaw. The author assumes that because there is a greater percentage of younger members in the party, there is a greater number of younger members in the party.

You need an answer that discredits one of those assumptions or provides other information to dispute the conclusion. Examine the answer choices. Choice (A) is irrelevant, as the political direction the party is taking is not at issue, so eliminate (A). Choice (B) is also irrelevant. The issue is whether or not conservatism increased the number of young voters in the party, not that candidates continue to be defeated running on the party platform. Eliminate (B). Choice (C) attacks the statistical assumption by providing another reason for the greater percentage of younger party members: the number of party members older than 25 decreased, thereby increasing the percentage of members younger than 25 without the actual number of younger members increasing. Keep (C). Choices (D) and (E) are both also irrelevant. The argument is discussing younger voters who are *in* the party, not younger voters who voted *for* the party, or who never voted. Eliminate (D) and (E). The correct answer is (C).

WEAKEN DRILL

1. Switching to electric cars will not improve the environment, despite the fact that such cars produce no harmful emissions. The electricity to run them would still need to be generated from power plants, the majority of which burn such fossil fuels as coal, oil, and natural gas. Any reduction in fossil fuel demand at gas stations resulting from the replacement of internal combustion engines with electric ones would be reversed by a commensurate demand for more energy from our nation's power plants.

   Which of the following, if true, would most weaken the above argument?

   (A) The nation's power grid would need a massive restructuring if it is to generate the energy needed to power vehicles that run on electricity.
   (B) Electric vehicles are significantly more energy-efficient than their gasoline-powered counterparts.
   (C) Coal is a far less environmentally-friendly way to generate energy than is natural gas.
   (D) Studies indicate that most drivers would be reluctant to switch from gasoline-powered to electric vehicles.
   (E) Hybrid vehicles offer a more practical short-term alternative than do vehicles that run solely on electricity.

2. Numerous studies examining the potential hazards of cell phone radiation have not proven conclusively that it poses any long-term risks to human health. In fact, the majority of handsets released over the past couple of years have had a much lower SAR (Specific Absorption Rate) than even federal guidelines in the United States mandate. Since the FCC guidelines are stricter than those in Europe, it follows that cell-phone users in America have little reason to worry about exposure to handset radiation.

   Which of the following, if true, most undermines the above argument?

   (A) Cell-phone users in the U.S. make more phone calls than do their European counterparts.
   (B) Radiation from cell phones is not the biggest risk factor associated with their use.
   (C) U.S. cell-phone users average more minutes per conversation than do users in other countries.
   (D) A majority of wireless phone users in America spend more time with their handsets held to their heads than the FCC deems safe, even for phones with the lowest SAR levels.
   (E) Europeans are less concerned about wireless phone radiation than are Americans.

3. In generations past, women and their suitors spent relatively little time together before getting married. Arranged marriages, in which the partners were not previously acquainted, were commonplace. Most other marriages resulted from brief courtships, during which the future bride and groom spent little time alone together. Yet, marriages in modern-day society, in which partners date and even cohabitate for years, are much more likely to end in divorce than those of previous generations. Despite all the self-help books, "relationship experts," and emphasis on romance, modern marriages are clearly lacking the quality of those in decades past.

Which of the following would least weaken the above argument?

(A) Life in modern society places more challenges to marriages than did life in previous societies.
(B) Divorce was more socially objectionable in past societies.
(C) Most modern couples seek counseling before considering divorce.
(D) The quality of modern marriages is only slightly better than that associated with marriages of generations past.
(E) While a majority of marriages in past generations stayed intact, discreet extramarital affairs were more common than they are in contemporary society.

4. Flimco Solutions has instituted a bold plan to dramatically reduce its "carbon footprint," that is, the amount of nonrenewable energy it expends, by allowing two-thirds of its Salemville workforce to work from home up to 24 hours per week. By allowing its employees this telecommuting option, the company estimates that its carbon emissions will be significantly reduced because workers will not have to drive back and forth between their homes and Flimco headquarters.

Which of the following, if true, would most threaten the success of Flimco's plan?

(A) Most of the employees drive fairly late-model cars, many of which attain higher-than-average gasoline mileage.
(B) Some employees will need special accommodations in order to be able to do their jobs efficiently from their homes.
(C) A majority of Flimco's employees travel to and from work on a light-rail system that runs every 15 minutes, regardless of ridership.
(D) Flimco Corporation offered a similar option to its workers but many of them chose not to telecommute.
(E) Some of Flimco's workers live in homes that are not energy efficient, and would expend more nonrenewable energy maintaining the climate in their homes telecommuting than they would if they left their residences to work elsewhere.

5. The merger between Minion County's Yin Cablevision and Lemming County's Yang Cable Systems will provide a much-needed boost to Lemming County's economy. The reason is that Lemming County businesses will now have more than twice as many potential viewers to which to advertise, thanks to Minion County's denser population, which is twenty percent larger than Lemming County's.

Each of the following undermines the above statements EXCEPT

(A) The majority of Minion County residents already encounter frequent advertisements from most Lemming County businesses, via radio and print media.
(B) The merger between Yin and Yang came about because a growing number of Minion County residents do not subscribe to cable television.
(C) Most Minion County residents who watch cable television tune in to premium channels that do not show commercials.
(D) Many of the channels offered by Yang Cablevision broadcast programming are from out of state networks that do not accept advertising from outside of their respective areas.
(E) Rates to advertise on the merged networks' channels will increase significantly, beyond the budgets of most area advertisers.

6. A key study of Bleak County residents has revealed that over forty percent of them spend more than a third of their salaries just to pay their housing costs. With electricity, natural gas, and home heating oil prices expected to rise by more than 10 percent over the next six months, it's clear that many property owners will wind up homeless this coming winter.

Which of the following, if true, would most undermine the above conclusion?

(A) Most of the homes in Bleak County are non-owner-occupied investment properties, leased as rentals.
(B) Many of the county's homeowners are considering the purchase of solar hot water systems.
(C) Energy prices may rise only slightly once they reach an increase of about 10 percent.
(D) Bleak County was recently cited as one of the most environmentally-friendly counties in the area.
(E) The coming winter is not expected to be as harsh as was the previous one.

7. Socialized medicine cannot work in the United States, especially given the current challenges to the economic climate. More than half of American households already report feeling overwhelmed by expenses and are fearful of losing their incomes. Funding such a massive program would require significant increases in taxes, adding profusely to the formidable financial burden faced by individuals. Keeping the current, employer-sponsored healthcare system will keep taxes low, protecting our nation's economy.

Which of the following, if true, would most weaken the above statements?

(A) Many Americans enjoy sizable tax breaks for medical and related expenses.
(B) A system of socialized medicine would reduce the financial burden the current healthcare system places on employers, resulting in significant domestic job creation and wage increases.
(C) A majority of profitable, private health insurers have indicated that they expect to increase their payrolls in the next quarter.
(D) Pharmaceutical companies have less incentive to develop innovative new drugs under systems of socialized medicine.
(E) Most citizens of the United States are dependent on their employers for health coverage, and could not otherwise afford comparable coverage under the current system.

8. Although the human resources department at C.W. Industries spent more than $100,000.00 last quarter hiring a team of efficiency consultants, that was money clearly not well spent. The current quarter has been the company's least profitable in its 20-year history.

Which of the following most undermines the above conclusion?

(A) Changing market conditions negatively affected C.W. Industries' competitors, a select minority of whom also hired efficiency consultants but saw a noticeably better return on investment.
(B) The reduced profit was not significant enough to induce the company to lay off any of its current workers, although several senior managers opted for negotiated buyout packages.
(C) The company's revenue rose sharply in the previous quarter, but profits were lower than analysts had expected.
(D) C.W. Industries' stock price was only modestly impacted by the decrease in profit.
(E) The drop in both output and profit was due largely to a learning curve mounted by the line workers as they became acclimated to more efficient production methods.

9. Canning is one of the safest methods of food preservation. Its decades-old, high-heat process kills microorganisms that would otherwise cause food-borne illnesses. Meanwhile, the integrity of the can keeps out contaminants while extending the shelf life of the contained food to at least two years.

Which of the following, if true, would most weaken the conclusion above?

(A) Canned food is not as nutritious as fresh or frozen food.
(B) Meat products stored in cans have the same shelf life as do canned vegetable products.
(C) The canning process may affect the flavor of meat or vegetables.
(D) Food stored in cans for more than two years should be discarded.
(E) The materials lining the inside of many cans pose a potential contamination threat to their contents.

10. School vouchers, government funds granted to families to pay for their childrens' education, promote integration in Clink County's schools. Since parents can select the schools to which they send their sons and daughters—and use the voucher money to pay the costs—families can break free of the racial and ethnic limitations of their own communities when making educational decisions.

Which of the following, if true, casts the most doubt upon the above conclusion?

(A) Lower-income families are more likely to benefit from school voucher programs than are their middle or upper-income counterparts.

(B) Parents would not be willing to transport their children to schools more than five or ten miles from home.

(C) A significant number of public-school teachers are opposed to school vouchers.

(D) Many schools in the county have been known to discriminate against admitting students on the basis of race and ethnicity.

(E) Voucher programs have not been successful in several counties adjacent to Clink County.

11. Recent data show that two-thirds of ex-convicts from state prisons commit at least one serious new crime within three years of their release. Meanwhile, despite longer sentences and increased numbers of inmates, yearly figures show no decrease in criminal offenses. Since the penal system has proven so ineffective, we would be wise to reduce our prison populations significantly, saving millions in taxpayer dollars while not suffering any discernible increase in criminal activity.

Which of the following exposes a flaw in the above proposal?

(A) Many ex-convicts have been unable to find suitable employment.

(B) The prison system deters significant numbers of convicts from criminal activity merely by barring them from society.

(C) Criminals serving longer sentences are more likely to be reformed than those serving shorter ones.

(D) Violent crimes have increased more slowly than have property crimes.

(E) Inadequate policing is to blame for the persistence of criminal activity.

12. Despite formidable increases in health care costs over the past decade, it is evident that the quality of that care is in serious decline. A study of the average length of a hospital stay shows a dramatic regression over the same ten-year period, even among patients with serious illnesses. This trend suggests that many patients are being discharged before their conditions warrant.

The above conclusion would be most weakened if it were true that

(A) There has been a growing shortage of beds in hospitals and infirmaries.
(B) Patients who pay higher premiums for their health care are less likely than those who do not spend shorter amounts of time in a hospital.
(C) People whose medical conditions do not warrant serious treatment are not typically hospitalized as long as those who suffer from more serious ailments.
(D) Advances in medical care over the past ten years have significantly shortened average recovery times.
(E) Physicians are having more trouble keeping up with patient workloads than they did in the previous decade.

13. Exploration of outer space is a waste of time and taxpayer money. It makes little sense to squander hundreds of millions of dollars exploring such trivialities as the existence of water or microbial life on other worlds when there are more important issues plaguing our own planet, not least of which is the future of our own fragile environment.

The reasoning above overlooks the possibility that

(A) Space research is more costly than environmental research.
(B) Space programs can yield important discoveries applicable to the Earth's climate and natural resources.
(C) Human travel to other planets is scientifically feasible.
(D) There is only a scant probability of sentient life elsewhere in the universe.
(E) Environmental research has gotten more attention in recent years.

14. Despite the popularity of bottled water and consumer claims that it tastes better than water from a tap, a study by a reputable media outlet has found that there is no health benefit to drinking bottled water. Five bottles of water from different national brands were tested alongside a sample of tap water from a city drinking fountain. After analyzing the samples for disease-causing bacteria—including *E. coli*—a University of New Hampshire microbiologist found no significant difference between the tap water and its bottled counterparts. Clearly, drinkers of bottled water are wasting their money; tap water is just as healthy.

Which of the following does the most damage to the above conclusion?

(A) Proper pipe maintenance is important to ensure the quality of home drinking water.
(B) Many people claim that there is a discernible difference between the taste of tap water and that of its bottled counterparts.
(C) *E. coli* is found in comparable concentrations in both expensive and lower-priced brands of bottled water.
(D) Bacteria are not the only significant health hazard found in drinking water.
(E) The fountain water tested was a representative sample of that found in a typical household.

15. A major automaker recently announced that, due to budgetary constraints, it was cutting spending on new technology development. The firm's vice president praised the cost-saving measures, stating that they would enable the company to meet its fiscal obligations for the rest of the year and thus remain profitable. Analysts applauded the move as well, reasoning that it would allow the automaker to remain competitive amidst a tightening consumer climate.

Which of the following, if true, would most weaken the analysts' expectations?

(A) Consumers have significantly less interest in purchasing cars lacking innovative features than in purchasing those without.
(B) Many new technologies require intense marketing efforts to stimulate consumer demand.
(C) Automotive technology development is not always cost-effective.
(D) Vehicle safety is an even bigger concern for consumers than are vehicle aesthetics.
(E) A rival automaker has announced personnel reductions in its research and development.

16. It is clear that celebrities, despite their wealth, are more troubled on average than are people who are not famous. This is evidenced by the high concentration of movie and television stars seen regularly on Wilshire Boulevard in Beverly Hills, an exclusive city in Los Angeles County. There, they are often spotted walking into and out of the facilities of many well-known psychiatrists and plastic surgeons.

Which of the following would LEAST weaken the author's claims?

(A) Many "B-movie" actors cannot afford to hire plastic surgeons.
(B) Ordinary citizens often forgo mental-health treatment and cosmetic surgery for financial reasons.
(C) Troubled people are no more likely to pursue plastic surgery than are their emotionally stable counterparts.
(D) People of modest financial means are much less likely to be seen walking in exclusive areas.
(E) Patients of psychiatrists differ from those not seeking such treatment primarily in terms of awareness of their own emotional vulnerabilities.

17. A new study finds that social skills are a better predictor of future earnings than are test scores. Analyzing data from a 20-year longitudinal study, a university sociologist tracked 11,000 students from 10th grade through ten years after high-school graduation. She found that students described by teachers as motivated, conscientious, and outgoing earned an average of $3,200 more annually than did those with comparable test scores but poorer social skills.

Which of the following, if true, does most to undermine the findings of the above-mentioned study?

(A) Analytical skills, which are also crucial to life success, were not considered by the authors of the study.

(B) Students regarded favorably by their teachers tend to have more self esteem and confidence in their own abilities than do other students.

(C) Many successful entrepreneurs did not do well in academic settings.

(D) Some teachers are biased in their attitudes toward particular students.

(E) Children who have older siblings tend to acquire sophisticated language skills more quickly than do those whose siblings are closer in age.

18. Allegations of healthcare discrimination against women are false. Federal antidiscrimination laws, which govern all employer-sponsored health insurance plans, mandate that female and male workers receive comparable health insurance coverage, in addition to equal pay for equal work. The laws are both specific and stringent, allowing few exceptions for age or even prior health conditions.

Which of the following, if true, would most weaken the above argument?

(A) Employers are beginning to offer fewer healthcare coverage options for their workers.

(B) Costs for health insurance premiums have been rising faster than inflation.

(C) Many workers continue with otherwise less desirable employers and jobs because of health insurance benefits, which would cost far more for those individuals to purchase outside of a group insurance plan.

(D) Insurance plans often charge higher premiums for subscribers with pre-existing health conditions than for subscribers without such conditions.

(E) With recent changes in the economy, a growing number of individuals are losing their group health insurance and having to purchase individual coverage, which is not affected by federal antidiscrimination laws.

19. Static stretching, a warm-up technique used by sports enthusiasts that entails holding a stretch for up to 30 seconds, can actually weaken muscles. In a university study, athletes produced less power from their leg muscles after static stretching than they did after not doing so, while other research has found that such stretching reduces muscle strength by up to 30 percent. Stretching muscles while moving, however, a method known as dynamic stretching, has been shown to increase power, flexibility and range of motion. Therefore, athletes can reduce their risk of injury by switching from static to dynamic stretching before physical activity.

Which of the following, if true, does the most to undermine the above argument?

(A) Dynamic stretching is more complex than is static stretching, and thus more likely to be done incorrectly, resulting in a greater likelihood of injury.

(B) Stretching does not relieve muscle soreness as effectively as does a mineral bath.

(C) Holding a stretching position for more than 30 seconds does not result in greater muscle benefit.

(D) Cooling down after strenuous physical activity has also been shown to reduce muscle injury.

(E) The quality of training that athletes receive is the most important factor in injury prevention.

20. Converting vinyl records to CD or other digital formats makes little sense. Vinyl records, played on a high-quality, well-maintained turntable integrated with a top-grade audio system produce a more natural sound than do their digital counterparts, since the latter use computer code to store and reproduce audio signals. Since human ears are, in fact, analog hearing devices, music enthusiasts will get the most realistic listening experience if they switch from CDs to vinyl records.

Which of the following, if discovered to be true, would do most to weaken the above statements?

(A) Most people who listen to music do not have access to high-end sound systems.

(B) Music enthusiasts are not always willing to pay top dollar for brand-name turntables.

(C) Analog audio systems are more expensive than are digital audio systems.

(D) Vinyl records are not nearly as portable or convenient as are digital music clips, which can be stored by the thousands on a keychain-sized device.

(E) Many individuals are unable to discern any difference in fidelity between digital and analog music sources.

21. Buildings constructed from clay or mortar are more sensitive to earthquakes than are those built with bricks, stones, or cement blocks. Architecture and even construction quality are not as big determining factors as are the building materials themselves. This is evident in the aftermath of the recent earthquake in the region of Clavamacchia. A much higher number of adobe structures were destroyed during that event than were those built with brick or stone.

Which of the following, if true, would most seriously call into question the argument above?

(A) The earthquake damage in the regions south and west of Clavamacchia was inconsistent, with most of the damage occurring within Clavamacchia.
(B) It takes more training to construct buildings with cement blocks than it does to construct those made from adobe.
(C) Nearly all of the clay structures still standing had been designed and built by skilled masons, while the majority of those that were destroyed had not.
(D) The last time an earthquake struck the region had been eighty years prior, a seismic event that flattened nearly all of the structures in the region.
(E) Tornado and wind damage to buildings can often resemble that done by earth tremors.

22. Demand for innovative wireless technology has accelerated rapidly. One of the hottest niche markets has been the development of wireless applications, special software that can be installed on phones or other handheld devices and used to perform all kinds of tasks, from organizing data to providing satellite-based navigation to playing multimedia files. It is clear that tech-minded persons interested in a lucrative career should consider learning to write and distribute such software.

Which of the following, if true, would cast the most doubt on the statements above?

(A) There are a number of competing software platforms for handheld devices, each requiring different programming skills to produce applications.
(B) Projected worldwide growth for handheld software applications is not expected to be outstripped by the projected global supply of programmers.
(C) Development tools that allow people with low-level technical skills to create and market wireless applications have become increasingly available.
(D) Some wireless devices are more likely to be passing fads than are other wireless devices.
(E) Programming for handheld devices requires continuous updating of one's knowledge and technical skills.

23. "Run-flat" tires, which have internal bracing systems that allow the tires to be driven for up to 150 miles upon puncture, offer distinct safety advantages over conventional tires. For one thing, a car equipped with such tires is less likely to be in an accident following a puncture, since the tires will continue to support the vehicle until it can be driven to a repair facility. In fact, the tires perform so well that drivers are often unaware that any damage has occurred. Another advantage is that a driver will not have to exit a vehicle to replace a faulty tire under potentially dangerous conditions. For safety considerations alone, all drivers should switch to run-flat tires.

Which of the following, if true, would do the most to undermine the above statements?

(A) Run-flat tires cost significantly more than conventional pneumatic tires.
(B) A large number of automotive service centers do not sell or repair run-flat tires.
(C) Standard inflatable tires offer a smoother ride experience than do their run-flat counterparts.
(D) Most cars sold with run-flat tires as standard equipment do not come with spare tires.
(E) Most vehicles with run-flat tires do not have tire-pressure monitoring systems to warn drivers of tire damage that they would not otherwise notice.

24. More than 95% of Web pages on the World Wide Web, according to a recent survey, do not conform to current HTML standards. The code that makes up those pages has long been deprecated, or declared invalid, by the W3C (Worldwide Web Consortium). Some of the newer Web browsers do not display those pages sufficiently, if at all. Therefore, to ensure the greatest level of accessibility to all Web site visitors, page designers should update all of their pages to be in line with current Web standards.

Which of the following, if true, most undermines the above reasoning?

(A) Updating the billions of pages on the World Wide Web would be an enormous and expensive undertaking.
(B) Not all Web designers can afford to buy the latest Web-publishing software.
(C) The majority of people who use the World Wide Web care little about standards, preferring to view pages through popular browsers that can correctly render most Web sites.
(D) A growing number of users are accessing Web pages via handheld devices, for which many Web sites have not yet been optimized.
(E) Web standards are subject to review and change over time.

25. New home buyers looking for an affordable alternative to site-built homes should look to prefabricated construction, which is more cost effective, efficient, and environmentally friendly than is conventional construction. One advantage is that complete sections of a home are assembled at a factory site, under controlled conditions, without the inconvenience and weather disruptions associated with traditional, site-built methods. Meanwhile, many builders repurpose salvaged materials, further adding to the cost savings.

Which of the following, if true, offers the best support for an argument against the purchase of prefabricated housing for the reasons stated by the author?

(A) Conditions in some housing markets have substantially reduced the prices of existing homes to below those of new residences.
(B) Owners of prefabricated houses are not significantly happier with the design of their homes than are owners of traditionally built homes.
(C) Prefabricated construction methods are not available in many regions.
(D) Densely populated regions are not always conducive to the logistics of prefabricated construction techniques.
(E) Supplementary costs, including site preparation, transportation of prefabricated components, and local contractor fees can add significantly to the price of a prefabricated home.

26. A farmer wishes to reduce the number of flies on his farm by preventing the fly larva from transitioning into adult flies. He plans to raise chickens that will eat fly larva before they have a chance to become flies. When the chickens are grown they will be slaughtered and sold.

If true, which of the following casts the most serious doubt on the farmer's plan?

(A) The farmer could make more money selling the chickens' eggs than slaughtering them.
(B) The manure of one chicken can support more fly larva than a single chicken can consume.
(C) Chickens farmers often must use antibiotics preventively to keep their chickens healthy.
(D) Farmers in Australia have tried a similar approach using foxes to combat rabbit infestation, and they have almost all failed.
(E) Chickens need many more calories than can be provided by fly larva alone.

27. CFO: The average cost of a workers' compensation claim at our warehouses is $1,900. A new training program would significantly lessen the chance of a worker filing a claim. Though the training program would be beneficial for many reasons, it would cost $2,200 per person, so it cannot be justified.

If true, which of the following statements reveals the most serious weakness in the CFO's logic?

(A) The probability of a workers' compensation claim being filed is less for female workers than it is for males.
(B) A significant percentage of the cost of the new training program is to bring in outside consultants, the cost of which is rapidly rising.
(C) Workers who complete only a portion of the new training program have an increased chance of filing a worker's compensation claim relative to those who complete the program.
(D) Often, when a workers' compensation claim is filed, the cost to the company of worker's compensation insurance increases.
(E) The training program focuses on prevention of injury, since attention is too often applied to remedying a problem after it has occurred instead of preventing it before it occurs.

28. Recently, several wildlife photographers working in the African savanna have been killed in attacks by large predators. In looking for ways to stay safe from large predators, some wildlife photographers have suggested traveling with a flock of birds, since the birds stop singing when large predators are approaching.

Which of the following statements casts the most serious doubt on the effectiveness of the photographers' proposal?

(A) The approach of common, small, herbivorous animals causes birds to stop singing.
(B) Native tribes of the savanna have long associated the silence of birds with the approach of predators.
(C) Remaining inside specially made vehicles can reduce the risk posed by a large predator attack.
(D) Attempts to develop technologies to detect approaching predators have thus far been futile.
(E) As predators approach, they ruffle the long grasses of the savanna, alerting birds to their movement.

Check your answers on page 721.

STRENGTHEN QUESTIONS

Along with assumption and weaken questions, strengthen questions are one of the most common question types for Critical Reasoning. Strengthen questions will ask you to find the statement that, if true, would most strengthen the argument.

Step 1: Read and identify the question

Strengthen questions are easily identifiable as they usually contain words such as *strengthen, support,* or *justify.*

Step 2: Work the argument

Break the argument down into conclusion and premise(s). Once that is done, be on the lookout for common flaws or differences in the language used between the conclusion and the premise to find the assumption of the argument.

Step 3: Predict what the answer should do

The easiest ways to strengthen an argument are to find additional reasons why the assumption is correct and to provide information that validates the conclusion.

So, consider the conclusion and think about all the reasons that it could be proven true. Once you have identified a handful of reasons, move on to Step 4.

Step 4: Use POE to find the answer

POE: Consider each answer choice individually and decide if the new information bolsters or provides reasons why the conclusion or assumption is true. Typically, incorrect answers for strengthen questions:

- Are irrelevant (outside the scope or bring in unnecessary information).
- Weaken the argument. These are common because the test writers know that in the heat of the moment it's easy to forget whether you are weakening or strengthening.
- Don't strengthen the conclusion or assumption enough in comparison to another answer choice.

Strengthen (and weaken) questions are the only questions in the arguments section in which strong language is good. On a harder question, you may have more than one answer that could strengthen the argument and you have to go with the one that most strongly supports it. Try the example on the next page.

1. The mayor of City *X* wishes to increase voter turnout for the next city council election. A recent poll of registered voters in neighboring City *Y* showed a high level of dissatisfaction with that city's voting facilities. Based on this result, City *X*'s mayor proposed a dramatic update of his city's voting facilities to increase turnout at the next election.

    Which of the following statements, if true, most strongly supports the mayor's plan?

    (A) A majority of respondents in City *Y*'s poll had voted in favor of a tax cut in the previous election.
    (B) City *Y*'s voter turnout rates increased as the result of the publicity the recent poll generated.
    (C) A City *X* poll of registered voters revealed that their behavior is not strongly influenced by their perception of voting facilities.
    (D) Even the best polling methods have difficulty capturing voter opinions accurately.
    (E) The City *Y* poll showed that voters who are satisfied with voting facilities are more likely to vote.

The question says *most strongly supports,* so this is a strengthen question. Break down the argument into its conclusion and premise(s).

This argument describes a plan to increase *turnout at the next election* by updating *voting facilities in City X.* The conclusion here is that the plan will work or there is nothing wrong with the plan. Thus, the conclusion here is that updating the voter facilities in City *X* will increase voter turnout. The premise for the conclusion to update voting facilities to increase turnout is the result of a poll of voters in a different city, who expressed their dissatisfaction with the voting facilities of their city. Now, try to identify the assumption of the argument using the common flaws or gaps in the language between the conclusion and the premise.

This argument has an analogy flaw. The author assumes that the voters of City *X* are similar to the voters of City *Y* and feel the same way about the voting facilities in their city.

There is also a causal flaw. The author assumes dissatisfaction with voting facilities is the reason voters did not vote in City *X*.

An answer choice that strengthens this argument will either support one of the assumptions or provide information to support the conclusion of the argument. Evaluate each answer choice individually, looking for answer choices that strengthen the argument. Choice (A) is beyond the scope of the argument as tax cuts are not part of the conclusion or premise, nor would information about tax cuts strengthen the argument, so eliminate (A). Choice (B) is also out of scope. The issue is not publicity, but whether or not updating voter facilities will increase voter turnout, so eliminate (B). Choice (C) actually weakens the argument, so eliminate (C). Choice (D) is about the effectiveness of polling, which is both out of scope and serves as an argument for weakening the conclusion, so eliminate (D). Choice (E) supports the assumption that dissatisfaction with voting facilities is the reason people didn't vote in City *X*, thus strengthening the argument. The correct answer is (E).

STRENGTHEN DRILL

1. Businesses other than banks require credit in order to meet expenses. But in an environment in which there is a lack of trust, banks are often unwilling to lend to other banks. Therefore the government should guarantee loans between banks to help non-bank businesses survive.

   Which of the following would most strengthen the conclusion above?

   (A) There currently is not an environment lacking trust between banks.
   (B) If banks lend to other banks, then they will lend to non-bank businesses as well.
   (C) Non-bank businesses also make loans to each other.
   (D) Banks may only lend up to a certain percentage of deposits held.
   (E) The government guarantee has never previously been offered.

2. In order to boost employee retention, Maggie Maid Service has developed a plan to boost morale. It plans to offer childcare, improve parking, and subsidize continuing education.

   Which of the following, if true, would offer the best support for the success of the company's plan?

   (A) Maggie Maid Service's competitors are offering childcare.
   (B) Few of Maggie Maid Service's employees are working on furthering their education.
   (C) The job market is particularly competitive for the maid service industry.
   (D) Maggie Maid Service has recently suffered a number of employee losses.
   (E) A survey has revealed that parking has been a source of employee dissatisfaction among Maggie Maids.

3. KaleeCo has compared the loss in productivity it experiences from employee sick days to the loss experienced by its competitor, Devron. Although they have the same number of employees working the same hours, KaleeCo had on average twice the loss of productivity due to sick days that Devron had. KaleeCo officials concluded that Devron's employees made additional productivity gains on other days to compensate.

   Which of the following, if true, offers the most support of the conclusion drawn by KaleeCo officials?

   (A) Some of the days categorized as sick days by KaleeCo employees were actually personal days.
   (B) The employees of Devron were actually no healthier than the employees of KaleeCo.
   (C) The overall productivity of KaleeCo is equal to that of Devron.
   (D) KaleeCo was more profitable than Devron last quarter.
   (E) KaleeCo and Devron are in the same industry.

4. Some anthropologists believe that South America was first settled by Pacific Islanders who first traveled there by boat. But a new group disagrees with this theory. They point out that the Bering Land Bridge would have allowed settlers to travel from Asia to North America and from there on to South America, and thus the boat theory is unlikely.

   Which of the following statements, if true, most supports the group that dissents from the boat theory?

   (A) It is far more difficult for groups to travel by boat than to walk over land.
   (B) The settlement of South America via the Bering Land Bridge would have taken more time than the settlement of South America by boat.
   (C) The settlement of South America by boat is a relatively untested theory.
   (D) The Bering Land Bridge was later submerged by water.
   (E) If the Bering Land Bridge were submerged, it would have been impossible for settlers from Asia to reach South America by land.

5. Purebred dogs, such as German shepherds, often display congenital defects. German shepherds in particular tend to display a defect known as hip dysplasia. Itzak's dog displays no hip dysplasia, and therefore is not a German shepherd.

Which of the following, if true, most strengthens the argument above?

(A) No dog that is not a German shepherd displays hip dysplasia.
(B) Not all dogs display hip dysplasia.
(C) Some dogs do not display hip dysplasia.
(D) All German shepherds display hip dysplasia.
(E) Some German shepherds do not display hip dysplasia.

6. In a recent poll, Candidate A polled a 60% favorable rating while Candidate B polled only a 50% favorable rating. Therefore Candidate A is sure to win the election.

Which of the following, if true, would best support the conclusion above?

(A) Candidate A has raised more money than Candidate B.
(B) Candidate A is the incumbent.
(C) Elections are won by the candidate with the higher favorability rating.
(D) There are only two weeks until the election.
(E) Poll results generally reflect how voters will vote on election day.

7. To finance a construction program, Ameeville is considering raising the sales tax by 4%. This plan is clearly flawed. There will be no additional revenue for the city, as consumers will merely reduce their spending by at least 4%.

Which of the following, if true, most strengthens the argument above?

(A) Consumers are at liberty to determine the amounts they spend.
(B) Consumers are opposed to additional taxes.
(C) The construction program has broad support.
(D) The construction program is unpopular among consumers.
(E) The proposed tax will raise more than enough money for the construction, should consumer spending remain the same.

8. The migration of birds is not fully understood, but one prominent theory posits that migratory birds are able to find their direction by sensing the magnetic field of the earth. Recently, some scientists have posited that the magnetic field generated by high-tension power lines can interfere with this guidance system. This appears not to be the case, however, since there are no greater reports of birds losing their way near high-tension power lines than there are far from high-tension power lines.

Which of the following, if true, best refutes the claim that the magnetic field generated by high-tension power lines interferes with the guidance system of migratory birds?

(A) Scientists have a full understanding of the workings of the internal guidance system of migratory birds.
(B) There have been consistent, accurate records kept of lost migratory birds both near and far from high-tension power lines.
(C) The theory that power lines can interfere with the guidance system of migratory birds is widely accepted.
(D) After installing high-tension power lines, work crews recorded changes in the magnetic field of the earth near those power lines.
(E) The best current high-tension power lines produce less of a magnetic field than did previous high-tension power lines.

9. After extensive testing, the Dvorak motor company released a new, fuel-efficient automobile. Some customers complained, however, that the air conditioning failed to work after two or three uses. Dvorak claimed that the malfunction was due to operator error, since they had extensively tested the system before releasing it.

Which of the following, if true, would most support Dvorak's claim?

(A) None of the complaining customers live in especially hot regions.
(B) All of the cars in question were made on the same day, in the same plant.
(C) All of the customers in question had previously owned cars.
(D) Dvorak previously addressed problems with the car's transmissions in its testing.
(E) Dvorak's testing included endurance testing of the air conditioning under normal conditions.

10. The country of Sondinia has speakers of three different languages: Erlene, Elba, and Elena. The speakers of Elba wish to have their own state within the country, but do not live in only one state. Therefore it is clear that there can be no state made that will contain only speakers of Elba.

Which of the following statements, if true, would most support the conclusion above?

(A) The Elba speakers have never had a state of their own.
(B) There are more speakers of Erlene than Elba.
(C) Any Elba state should be composed of one and only one current Sondinian state.
(D) The Elena community is opposed to an Elba state.
(E) The Elba are the least numerous of the three language communities.

11. Fluoride is added to municipal drinking water to aid in dental health; the compound acts to prevent tooth decay. Nevertheless, other dentifrice is required to maintain healthy teeth.

Which of the following, if true, would most strongly support the position above?

(A) Regular removal of food particles is required in combination with fluoride fortification to maintain healthy teeth.
(B) Tooth decay has decreased in some areas where fluoride has been added to the water.
(C) Studies have shown that rinsing with a fluoride mouthwash can be beneficial for dental health.
(D) The level of fluoride has varied from municipality to municipality.
(E) Before the addition of fluoride to drinking water, more people flossed regularly.

12. The governor of State X recently announced a plan to put computers in schools. He noted that math scores in State X had been declining, and stated that the plan will reverse the trend.

The conclusion above would be most strongly supported if which one of the following were inserted into the argument as an additional premise?

(A) Students in State X have more hours of math instruction now than 10 years ago.
(B) A polling firm recently showed that education was a top concern of the residents of State X.
(C) Studies have shown that students who use computers regularly achieve higher test scores than do students who do not use computers.
(D) Studies have shown that students who use computers regularly score more highly on the math portions of standardized tests than students who do not.
(E) Studies show that students who rely on computers for calculations do not learn to make those calculations themselves.

13. The average turnout for elections in Kailand is 34% of the voters. Since polls show that there has been more interest in this election than in previous ones, this election should have a turnout in excess of 34%.

Which of the following, if true, most supports the conclusion of the argument above?

(A) The candidates for this election have spent more than in any other election.
(B) There are more registered voters now than in previous elections.
(C) Turnout always rises for elections that have above-average interest from the voters.
(D) The polls are from a company that has never worked in Kailand before.
(E) Recently Kailand changed to a new optical scanning voting machine.

14. Kimberly Pharmaceutical has conducted tests on a new drug. Of the subjects tested, none has had a serious side effect. Therefore the new drug likely has no side effects.

Which of the following, if true, most strengthens the argument above?

(A) All of the subjects tested were women.
(B) None of the subjects had ever been part of a previous drug study.
(C) The drug will be quite profitable for Kimberly Pharmaceutical.
(D) If a drug has no serious side effects, it is likely that the drug has no side effects.
(E) The study was conducted in several states with subjects of all different age groups.

15. Subcontracting is the practice of hiring another firm to complete some task on behalf of a client. If a subcontractor can do the job more cheaply than the main firm, the main firm should hire the subcontractor to do that work and thereby increase its profits.

Which of the following, if true, most strengthens the argument above?

(A) The main firm will be able to charge the client more than the cost of the subcontractor.
(B) The main firm's primary goal is to increase its profits.
(C) The subcontractor will not become resentful of the main firm keeping the profit.
(D) The subcontractor's work might not be as good as the main firm's work.
(E) The client will be unaware of the use of the subcontractor.

16. Tofu is made from soy beans, which contain large quantities of complete protein—protein consisting of all the amino acids that are essential for humans. A serving of tofu sometimes provides as much protein as a serving of chicken or beef. Nevertheless, animal sources such as chicken and beef are a better source of protein for humans than is tofu.

Which of the following statements most strengthens the above argument?

(A) Foods containing incomplete protein are often supplemented with the deficient amino acid to create a complete protein.
(B) Soy protein in the form of tofu is no more difficult for the human body to digest than other forms of protein.
(C) Certain components of chicken and beef allow protein to be more easily utilized by the human body.
(D) People who consume a lot of tofu often don't consume any animal protein for moral reasons.
(E) Other soy foods, such as edimame and tempeh, are easier for the human body to digest than tofu.

17. Profits from sales of propane canisters for camping stoves vastly exceed those for the stoves themselves. Valleys and Rivers Outdoor Equipment cannot sell their propane canisters as cheaply as their competitors can. Thus, Valleys and Rivers Outdoor Equipment is developing a new camping stove that will only accept a newly designed Valleys and Rivers Outdoor Equipment propane canister, which will be sold at the same price as the old canisters.

Which of the following most strongly suggests that the company's plan to sell more propane canisters will be effective?

(A) The research and development group at Valleys and Rivers Outdoor Equipment is also looking for new ways to package its propane such that it could be sold more cheaply.
(B) Customers buying their first camping stove tend to buy the least expensive model available.
(C) A competing camping supply company has announced plans to release a similarly priced stove that will also use only their own proprietary propane canisters.
(D) In user groups around the world, campers preferred Valleys and Rivers Outdoor Equipment camping stoves to others they had used.
(E) Sales of camping stoves are expected to increase dramatically in coming years.

18. In a recent NIH-funded study, 36 men—the experimental group—drank two glasses of red wine every night for three months. After the three month period, the men in that group had higher HDL cholesterol levels than 36 men who didn't drink any red wine—the control group. The scientists hypothesized that the increased HDL levels were due to the presence of flavonoids in the wine.

Of the following statements, which one, if true, offers the strongest support for the conclusion that some component in the red wine was responsible for the rise in HDL levels among the experimental group?

(A) The amount of wine consumed by the experimental group is within the bounds of what the FDA considers healthy intake.
(B) Outside of the experiment, few drinkers consume wine in a regular pattern of two glasses every night.
(C) Increased HDL cholesterol levels are considered healthy for the heart.
(D) The experimental and control groups had similar HDL levels before the three month period began.
(E) A second experiment failed to find a similar increase in HDL cholesterol levels when subjects consumed alcohol in various other beverages.

Check your answers on page 721.

ASSUMPTION QUESTIONS

Assumption questions are one of the most common question types on Critical Reasoning. To answer assumption questions, find the assumption in the argument presented by looking for the common flaws or gaps in logic between the conclusion and premise.

Step 1: Read and identify the question

Assumption questions can be identified by words such as *assumption, assume, presupposition, relies on, depends on,* or *necessary.*

Step 2: Work the argument

Break the argument down into conclusion and premise(s). Once that is done, be on the lookout for common flaws or differences in the language used between the conclusion and the premise to find the assumption of the argument.

Step 3: Predict what the answer should do

The correct answer will be an assumption made by the argument. So, if you can effectively identify the assumption based on the conclusion and premise(s), look for an answer choice that is similar in meaning.

Step 4: Use POE to find the answer

POE: Consider each answer choice individually and determine if the answer choice is an assumption in the argument. Common incorrect answers for assumption arguments:

- Are irrelevant (outside the scope or bring in unnecessary information)
- Weaken the argument
- Use extreme language

Extreme language answers are those that contain words such as *always, never, everyone, must,* or *cannot.* Strongly worded answers are usually wrong on assumption questions unless the conclusion is very strong.

If you have trouble choosing between two answers, try to determine which of the answer choices best fills the gap in logic between the conclusion and the premise(s). Try the example on the next page.

1. Educational theorists have long hypothesized that an interest in culture and the arts, especially music, has a positive impact on academic performance. A recent study of high school seniors confirms this theory. A test measuring proficiency in a broad range of academic disciplines was administered to high school seniors in major cities in the northeastern United States. The average score of students who attended schools that offered classes in art history and music appreciation was significantly higher than that of students who attended schools without such cultural enrichment programs.

    Which of the following is an assumption in the argument presented above?

    (A) At the schools offering art history and music appreciation classes, such classes were open to underclassmen, as well as juniors and seniors.
    (B) Enrollment in the art history and music appreciation classes was restricted to students who had previously demonstrated an interest in culture and the arts.
    (C) Students attending schools with cultural enrichment programs, whether they participated in such a program or not, possessed a higher average level of interest in culture and the arts than did students at other schools.
    (D) Among students attending schools offering cultural enrichment classes, those enrolled in such classes performed better on the test than did those not enrolled in such classes.
    (E) Students attending the schools that did not offer enrichment programs had no other opportunities to develop interest in culture and the arts.

The question contains the word *assumption*, so it is an assumption question. Break the argument down to determine the conclusion and premise(s). The conclusion is that an *interest in culture and the arts...has a positive impact on academic performance*. The premise of the argument is that *the average score of students who attended schools that offered classes in art history and music appreciation was significantly higher than that of students who attended schools without such cultural enrichment programs*. Now, identify the assumption(s) of the argument by keeping a lookout for the common flaws and gaps in the logical reasoning between the conclusion and premise.

This argument has a causal flaw. The argument states that an interest in the arts caused higher test scores; therefore, the assumption is that higher test scores were due to the cultural enrichment programs. However, it is possible there is another reason for the higher test scores.

This argument also contains a sampling flaw. The assumption for the sampling flaw is that the students in the study are representative of all students and that all students will have the same experience.

Now check the answers, looking for an answer choice that is similar in meaning to the assumptions identified.

Choice (A) is out of scope. The fact that underclassmen were able to take the classes has no bearing on whether the classes caused the scores to increase or whether the students in the study were representative of all students, so eliminate (A). Choice (B) is also out of scope. Previous interest in the arts doesn't matter for the purposes of this argument, so eliminate (B) as well. Choice (C) is a strong possibility to be the correct answer. The argument requires the assumption of this answer choice to link an interest in culture with the better test scores by students at those schools, so keep (C). Choice (D) has too strong language and actually strengthens the argument by providing evidence that people with an interest in the arts scored better than those without such interests. Eliminate (D). Choice (E) has no bearing on whether the higher scores were due to the classes or whether the students in the study were representative. As such, it is out of scope and eliminate (E). The correct answer is (C).

ASSUMPTION DRILL

1. With dwindling aid to public colleges and universities, accelerating tuition increases, and tightening credit conditions, area students and their families will be forced to make compromises in their educational pursuits. Many prospective students may forego college altogether. As a result, the state will face a significant shortage of skilled workers over the next decade.

   Which of the following is an assumption underlying the statements above?

   (A) A college education is necessary to produce skilled workers.
   (B) Unless trade schools see an increase in their enrollments, there will not be enough skilled workers.
   (C) Community colleges are less likely to produce graduates with skills than are state colleges.
   (D) On-the-job training programs are not as effective as those found at technical schools.
   (E) Workers with skills will be able to secure bigger salaries in the coming decade.

2. The local library in Midgeville has long been a source of knowledge and art for the town's residents. Many of them, especially the town's teens and seniors, spend long hours at the facility—reading newspapers, viewing art exhibits, watching documentary films, and attending educational events. Now that the mayor has instituted large budget cuts that will significantly shrink the library's funding, the people of Midgeville will clearly be culturally deprived.

   Which of the following exposes a presupposition regarding the author's reasoning in the statements above?

   (A) Midgeville's library has a culturally-diverse selection of books.
   (B) Bridgeville's library, which is a half-mile away in a town bordering Midgeville, has a more extensive program of art, media, and events than Midgeville's does, and is open to residents of all adjacent municipalities.
   (C) Midgeville residents will see fewer documentary films once the library's funding is cut.
   (D) Few of the town residents who visit the library prefer to bring their own books and newspapers to read.
   (E) The residents of Midgeville have no other significant source of cultural enrichment aside from the local library.

3. According to the "many-worlds" theory, an infinite number of parallel universes is continuously being generated, with a new set occurring whenever the probability of an event exceeds zero. A simple illustration of how the theory works can be seen in the following example: if a person stifles an impulse to shout aloud at an inappropriate moment, the person actually does and does not shout, splitting into many people, each of whom occupies a distinct but identical parallel universe—save for the fact that she shouts in some of those universes and not in others. However, this theory is almost certainly wrong. Consider that we rarely see or even hear about such odd behavior, despite the assertion that such events are constantly occurring.

Which of the following is a key assumption in the above argument?

(A) People do not commit highly irrational acts in more than a few parallel universes.
(B) Highly irrational acts would not be sparsely distributed through a multitude of parallel universes, making their witness in any particular one likely.
(C) The theory of parallel universes is accepted equally among traditional and quantum physicists.
(D) Most people have irrational impulses that they must work to curb.
(E) The "many-worlds" theory takes a thorough understanding of physics to comprehend.

4. Retailers that hold special sales on grocery items are unwittingly driving down their profits, because sale items are sold at greatly-reduced profit margins. As a result, consumers become accustomed to buying those particular items only when they are sold at a discount. Thus, retailers should consider other incentives if they want to increase their profits.

Which of the following is an assumption underlying the above statements?

(A) Shoppers going to retailers to purchase sale items do not buy a significant number of other items not offered at a discount.
(B) Discounted items are equal in quality to those not discounted.
(C) Customers will not buy a rival product if it is not offered at the same level of discount as a sale item.
(D) There are few alternate incentives retailers can use to attract customers to their outlets.
(E) Special sales do not generate publicity for retailers.

5. The city's recent enforcement of two-hour parking in its business district is unfair to residents. The restrictions require drivers to move their vehicles after 120 minutes or face a $75.00 fine. It is merely a ploy to take money away from local citizens while not benefiting them in any perceivable way.

Which of the following is an assumption upon which the above conclusion depends?

(A) Revenue from collected fines is not used by the city to improve parking-enforcement technology.
(B) The restrictions do not free up parking spaces that residents use when running necessary errands.
(C) The parking restrictions were ratified without a public referendum.
(D) Visiting drivers are just as likely to be ticketed as city residents.
(E) The city will have to hire new parking enforcement officers to ensure that the new restrictions are observed.

6. Public health screenings, particularly those that provide cholesterol and blood pressure diagnostics, are highly effective toward reducing future health-care costs. Since the screenings are free of charge and take place in convenient locations, such as shopping centers, people who might ordinarily not be inclined to consult with health professionals will now receive essential information about potential health problems earlier than they otherwise would.

The statements above assume which of the following?

(A) More people would prefer to receive a health screening at a shopping mall than at a physician's office.
(B) Store owners will receive a boost in business as a result of the screening booths set up in or near their retail locations.
(C) The quality of care received at public screenings is superior to that of most municipal health clinics.
(D) Cholesterol screenings are more important than most other diagnostic measures of human health.
(E) A majority of people who do not regularly seek the aid of medical professionals, but who receive health data from free screenings, will follow up on those results.

7. The new "Aqua-Brite" water-filtration system is a worthwhile investment for any home because its patented, double-layer purification chamber removes 99.9% of chemical additives, especially chlorine. Since long-term chlorine ingestion has been linked to heart disease, strokes, and even certain kinds of cancer, use of the Aqua-Brite system will serve to protect the health of household members who rely upon it.

Which of the following is a necessary presupposition in the above argument?

(A) Residential plumbing systems do not contain trace amounts of lead.
(B) Bottled water is not a safer alternative to tap water.
(C) The system will not need frequent replacement of component parts.
(D) All homes have unsafe levels of chlorine in their tap water.
(E) Chlorine in drinking water does not kill significant levels of bacteria that would otherwise prove highly toxic to humans.

8. The imposition of caps on executive salaries and bonuses, while a well-intentioned reaction to the current woes besetting the financial system, will only make economic matters worse. The present crisis may indeed be rooted in the questionable actions of some exorbitantly-compensated corporate leaders, but now—more than ever—competent managers are needed to restore the health of the nation's troubled markets.

Which of the following is an assumption upon which the above argument depends?

(A) Few business leaders with adequate talent are unopposed to the recommended salary and bonus caps.
(B) Talent is negatively correlated with compensation.
(C) Limits on executive compensation will turn away leaders with enough talent to stem the economic crisis.
(D) The solutions currently proposed will only work if executives are paid more than they receive presently.
(E) Incompetent managers are less opposed to compensation limits than are those with more talent.

9. Nations that support democracy will at last see their patience pay off in the next year or two, and should refrain from active interference in Country A's politics. Its ailing leader, Monvez Shiquez, will not likely survive beyond the next eighteen months. Since a growing number of the country's citizens oppose Shiquez's dictatorial policies, democracy is almost certain to arise once he is gone.

Which of the following is necessary to reach the above conclusion?

(A) Potential successors to Shiquez are relatively inexperienced with democratic principles of leadership.
(B) The country's citizens who oppose Shiquez's policies comprise a small but well-organized minority.
(C) A democratic successor to Country A's current leader will be found immediately upon Shiquez's departure.
(D) Opposition to a dictator's policies necessarily means support for democracy.
(E) Political interference from outside nations should be avoided except under extreme circumstances.

10. Despite the popularity of vitamin and mineral supplements, people taking them are not giving themselves any significant nutritional advantage. Vitamins and minerals derived from fresh fruits and vegetables have far more potency than those processed in pill form. Not long ago, in fact, the Surgeon General recommended that people consume five servings of fruit and vegetables each day.

Which of the following is an assumption upon which the above conclusion is based?

(A) Vitamin supplements offer no health benefit.
(B) Meats and fish do not contain healthy levels of vitamins and minerals.
(C) Frozen vegetables and fruits are not an adequate source of vitamin nutrition.
(D) It would take an enormous amount of fresh fruits and vegetables, consumed on a daily basis, to offer a worthwhile health advantage.
(E) People who consume vitamins and minerals in pill form would still consume significant amounts of fresh fruits and vegetables, whether or not they take vitamin and mineral supplements.

11. Switching from the current, five-day workweek to a four-day one would provide a significant benefit to both employers and their workers who commute, because employees would spend less time traveling between their homes and workplaces. Since many commuters report feeling fatigued from their travels, businesses would see a boost in productivity simply by tacking on additional hours to each remaining workday and reducing their employees' number of trips to and from work.

Which of the following is necessary to reach the above conclusion?

(A) Increased productivity results in lower fatigue.
(B) Travel by rail is less tiring than travel by motor vehicle.
(C) Corporate managers would be reluctant to consider employee workweek reductions without commensurate cuts in commuter reimbursements.
(D) Longer hours spent at the workplace do not contribute significantly to worker fatigue.
(E) Telecommuting does not offer a better option for increasing productivity than does reducing the number of days in the workweek.

12. Thanks to rapid advancements in digital technology, businesses now communicate more efficiently than they ever have before. Wireless phone, Internet, and email technology presently allow quicker correspondence between team members, managers, and vendors than was possible even just a few years ago.

The above conclusion depends upon which of the following assumptions?

(A) Managers and workers know how to use all of the features supported by the latest communications technology.
(B) Most businesses plan to upgrade their communications technology in the next six months.
(C) The new technology has not contributed to a surplus of unnecessary yet time-consuming correspondence.
(D) Team members without access to the latest digital technology are at a significant disadvantage to those who have such access.
(E) Wireless Internet coverage has seen sporadic improvement over the past several years.

13. According to a recent university study, smiling and relating well to others may strengthen one's immune system. 700 older adults who got along well with their relatives, neighbors, and friends were less likely to report physical limitations or health problems than were adults who did not get along well with others. Clearly, reducing conflict can go a long way toward improving one's overall health.

Which of the following is an assumption underlying the statements above?

(A) None of the study participants had pre-existing health conditions prior to the study.
(B) People who get along well with others are not less likely to reveal their own health problems than are those who do not get along well with others.
(C) Most of the study participants did not need or use prescription drugs.
(D) Conflict-resolution courses were available to all study participants.
(E) Diet and exercise have less effect on one's overall health than does the quality of one's relationships.

14. Secondhand smoke is not a threat to human health, despite what some prominent media sources proclaim. While it is true that Italian researchers found an 11.2 percent decrease in acute coronary events among people aged 35 to 64 following a nationwide ban on smoking in public places, it is also true that the heart-attack rate had been falling at an annual rate of 6 percent before the ban went into effect. Meanwhile, the rate continued to fall at that same 6 percent rate in the years following the ban. It is obvious that the public smoking ban had no significant or lasting effect on cardiovascular health.

Which of the following is necessary to reach the above conclusion?

(A) Managers of public places in the country had not placed significant restrictions on where people could smoke in the years before the ban took effect.
(B) Heavy smokers were forced to reduce their nicotine intake as a result of the ban.
(C) Patrons would rather eat at restaurants that ban smoking than at those that do not.
(D) Alcohol consumption declined sharply in the years following the ban's adoption.
(E) Heart attack rates in Italy were not already lower than those of other European nations before the ban took effect.

15. Environmentalists fear that a looming global economic slowdown will thwart efforts to curb carbon emissions. Since complying with strict environmental regulations would impose a significant financial burden on many businesses and industries, most will balk at the prospect and not reduce their respective carbon footprints. Governments, meanwhile, will be reluctant to impose environmental restrictions, for fear of suppressing economic growth.

Which of the following represents a necessary presupposition with regard to the environmentalists' fears?

(A) Governments, whether local or federal, will not raise taxes on already financially-burdened populations.
(B) There are no cost-cutting measures that businesses could implement to help them survive a compromised economic climate.
(C) Tax cuts alone will not stop industries from resisting efforts to curb carbon emissions.
(D) A worldwide economic slowdown would not significantly reduce energy demand and industrial output, both of which are linked to high levels of carbon emissions.
(E) High levels of economic growth are impossible to achieve with any level of reduction in global energy consumption.

16. Despite the lingering popularity of alternative health treatments for musculoskeletal injuries, such as acupuncture and chiropractic manipulation, it is quite clear that the curative prowess of such so-called remedies is questionable. In a recent survey of people who had tried at least one of those remedies, more than seventy percent of respondents reported that the therapies had little, if any, curative impact. People with such injuries are, thus, well-advised to forego alternative therapies in favor of traditional, interventive methods of treatment.

The above argument assumes that

(A) Other alternative therapies, such as aromatherapy, are not more effective than acupuncture or chiropractic medicine.
(B) Traditional methods of treatment have a higher success rate than that of alternative therapies.
(C) The survey participants had no reservations about the therapy methods they chose prior to receiving treatment.
(D) No respondent had used any form of traditional treatment prior to the survey.
(E) A combination of traditional and alternative therapies is the most optimal way to treat musculoskeletal ailments.

17. Employees who understand how their roles fit into the "big picture" of a business or organization are more motivated to do their jobs well. Corporate leaders wishing to improve worker morale should thus consider the "participatory" style of management, in which workers are given an individual piece of a project to carry out, replete with its own explicit goals and responsibilities.

Which of the following illuminates an assumption underlying the statements above?

(A) Workers with responsibilities are more motivated than those without.
(B) Few employees are inclined to participate in any phase of a project without being granted express rights and responsibilities.
(C) Managers using less interactive leadership methods are not as effective as those who use such methods.
(D) Having responsibility for a segment of an enterprise helps employees grasp where they fit within an organizational structure.
(E) Corporate managers should involve subordinates in all levels of decision-making.

18. A diet including a variety of both fish and shellfish can improve cardiovascular and neurological health, particularly because such sources of food contain beneficial oils and essential fatty acids. Due to industrial marine pollution, however, the FDA has warned that eating more than twelve ounces of seafood per week can expose a person to potentially toxic levels of mercury or PCBs. One viable solution for those wishing to add the benefits of a diet rich in seafood, while minimizing the health risks, is to consume pharmaceutical-grade fish oil pills instead of eating fish directly.

Which of the following is necessary to reach the above conclusion?

(A) Quotas on catching species of fish known to be high in contaminant levels have produced mixed results.
(B) Oils in pill form are as abundant in health-enhancing substances as are the foods from which the oils emanate.
(C) There are no other viable sources of healthy oils besides those derived from fish.
(D) The FDA warnings are strict enough to limit potential health problems among those wishing to consume fish and fish products.
(E) Pharmaceutical-grade fish oil pills do not contain unsafe levels of marine toxins.

19. People who claim that popular music lyrics are detrimental to teens are being as hypocritical as they are unreasonable. Many such gainsayers are adults who came from generations whose music was also criticized, in its day, for having potentially harmful lyrics. People who make such condemnations must have forgotten what it was like to be young; historically, youth culture has typically been seen as threatening in its own time.

Which of the following is necessary to reach the above conclusion?

(A) Youth culture will always be perceived as threatening by most adults.
(B) Drug use was as big a problem in past generations as it is now.
(C) Those who criticize popular music were approving of their own generation's music.
(D) Modern popular music is just as good as that of previous generations.
(E) Most listeners are able to hear music lyrics clearly enough to make sense of them.

20. Manager: A bachelor's degree should be a prerequisite for applicants to this position, so that interviewers won't waste time and resources interviewing candidates that lack the necessary intelligence for the job.

On which of the following assumptions does the manager's argument depend?

(A) An applicant will be a good candidate for the position if he has a bachelor's degree.
(B) A candidate's intelligence is of more importance than his interpersonal skills.
(C) Any candidate without a bachelor's degree lacks the necessary intelligence for the position.
(D) The only function of a bachelor's degree is to test one's intelligence as it relates to potential employers.
(E) The intelligence of applicants is the primary factor in making hiring decisions at this firm.

21. The slow advancement of the technology used in golf balls is a reflection of the demand which manufacturers aim to meet. Only golfers active in competition tournaments are willing to pay the high price necessary to justify the research and development costs needed to generate an innovative golf ball. Therefore, the technology that manufacturers pursue is limited to that which is deemed permissible for competition golf tournaments.

The above conclusion rests upon which of the following assumptions?

(A) The slow pace of technological advancement is a consequence of golf ball manufacturers not wanting to manufacture different products for different national markets.
(B) Unless the market for balls for competition golfers expands, the market for golf balls for non-competing golfers will not expand.
(C) Innovative golf balls are more likely to be developed by small, young manufacturing companies than by industry giants.
(D) There is not a strong demand for non-competition-permissible golf balls generated by competition golfers.
(E) The authorities who determine what is permissible in competition golf tournaments are not necessarily up-to-date on cutting-edge technological improvements.

22. Crenkotown, USA has a large population of Korean-Americans. Some of them make a living by delivering otherwise hard to find comforts of home to their fellow country men and women. In Crenkotown, between 1957 and 1971, commercial deliverers of kimchi—a staple Korean food—increased from 12 to 25. However, during the same time period the number of Koreans living in Crenkotown stayed roughly constant. Therefore, it is unlikely that many more Crenkotownies had kimchi delivered in 1971 than in 1957.

The conclusion rests on which of the following assumptions?

(A) In 1971, most Korean-Americans living in Crenkotown purchased kimchi deliveries from a commercial delivery service.
(B) In 1971, almost all of those who wanted kimchi delivered were within the range of a delivery service.
(C) Not all of the kimchi available for delivery in Crenkotown in 1971 was of the same variety or quality.
(D) None of the commercial operations that started delivering kimchi after 1957 serviced areas in Crenkotown that didn't formerly have delivery service.
(E) Per capita demand for kimchi among Korean-Americans in Crenkotown went unchanged from 1957 to 1971.

23. Measuring the productivity of service workers is a fairly simple matter, mathematically speaking. Simply divide the number of service operations they provide in a day by the amount of time worked in a day to arrive at a numerical representation of their productivity.

Which of the following is NOT an assumption made in the above argument?

(A) The number of times a service worker accomplishes a task is the only behavior that should be taken into account when calculating productivity.
(B) Tracking the number of service operations a service employee does in a given time period is an easy task.
(C) All the operations of a given service worker are of equal value, as far as calculating productivity is concerned.
(D) The quality with which an operation is carried out is irrelevant to the calculation of productivity.
(E) The number of mistakes made in performing operations should not be considered when calculating a worker's productivity.

24. Activist: To reduce the burden to taxpayers and to reduce the number of dogs put to death each year, the town animal shelter should stop accepting dogs that people can no longer care for.

Shelter Manager: That would be unfortunate because it would mean a dramatic increase in the number of stray dogs around town.

On which of the following does the manager's conclusion depend?

(A) All of the dogs for which the shelter is unable to find an owner are put to death.
(B) Dogs whose owners can't care for them wouldn't find a new home without the shelter.
(C) The shelter houses more and spends more on dogs than it does cats.
(D) The shelter releases all dogs that it does not kill.
(E) The shelter is not a no-kill shelter, one that never puts dogs to death.

25. City X depends on two highways, A and B, for all traffic entering and leaving the city. The population of City X has increased to such an extent that the city will soon be forced to build a third highway running into and out of the city to accommodate the increased number of drivers.

Which of the following is an assumption on which the argument depends?

(A) Much of the population enters and leaves City X at similar times of the day.
(B) Building a third highway will not increase City X residents' drive times.
(C) The population of City X has been increasing at the same rate in recent years.
(D) Residents of City X who own cars greatly outnumber those who do not own cars.
(E) Most new families in City X own only one vehicle.

26. A courier has two possible routes to take for a certain delivery. One route is significantly shorter, in miles, but the speed limit along that route is much lower. The courier determines that it will take a shorter amount of time to drive the longer route.

Which of the following is an assumption on which the courier's conclusion depends?

(A) A different delivery requires the courier to take the longer route.
(B) The proportional difference in miles between the two routes is more than made up for by the proportional difference in speed limits.
(C) The courier's vehicle gets better gas mileage than do most vehicles.
(D) The courier prefers to drive more direct routes with fewer stop lights.
(E) The courier would not drive over the speed limit on either route.

27. In the future, live sound engineers hope to be able to identify the best equalization for each type of microphone. Once the appropriate frequencies have been changed, there will be no more feedback during live performances.

The argument above is based on which of the following assumptions?

(A) Live sound engineers only use certain types of microphones.
(B) Feedback is the only problem encountered during live performances.
(C) Most microphones require different levels of equalization.
(D) Every instance of feedback results from incorrect frequency equalization.
(E) In the future, live sound engineers will use more advanced types of equalization tools.

28. Yoga can help strengthen muscles and increase flexibility. Because muscle strength is more important to most people, yoga teachers should choose to focus primarily on exercises that strengthen muscles.

Which of the following is an assumption on which the argument depends?

(A) Some yoga exercises are better for beginning students, while others are more appropriate for advanced practitioners.
(B) Different teachers are able to interpret yoga poses in different ways.
(C) Even if a practice has two benefits, teachers should focus on the one that the majority of people find important.
(D) If an exercise is designed primarily to strengthen muscles, that exercise will not also increase flexibility.
(E) Yoga teachers are not concerned with the desires of their students.

Check your answers on page 721.

INFERENCE QUESTIONS

Inference argument questions ask you to make some sort of determination about the argument. It is a common mistake to believe that these questions are asking for something that exists outside of the information presented in the passage. However, this is not the case. The correct answer for any GMAT question must always be able to be determined based on the information given. So, inference questions are really asking what must be true based on the information presented.

Step 1: Read and identify the question

Inference questions can be easily identified by the inclusion of words such as *infer, imply, must be true, supports,* or *conclusion* in the question stem.

Step 2: Work the argument

To answer this type of question, it is still useful to determine the conclusion, premise, and assumption. However, oftentimes the correct answer to an inference question is contained within strongly worded language in the passage.

Step 3: Predict what the answer should do

Because the answer is stated in the passage, it is dangerous to try and predict the answer. Instead, use the information in the passage to answer the question directly.

Step 4: Use POE to find the answer

POE: Consider each answer choice individually and determine if the answer choice can be determined to be true based on the information presented in the passage. POE is an important tool for inference questions, so eliminate any choice that isn't necessarily true based on the information in the passage. Incorrect answer choices for inference questions:

- Go beyond the information given. Any answer that brings in new information, requires outside knowledge or needs additional assumptions should be eliminated.
- Contradict information in the passage.
- Could be true, but cannot be proven using facts in the passage. These may appeal to some sort of common knowledge about a subject. If it is not mentioned in the passage, it cannot be considered true.
- Are too extreme. Unless the passage really does support an extreme statement, be wary. Correct inference answers frequently use wishy-washy words such as *can, might,* or *sometimes.*

Take a look at the example on the next page.

1. According to a recent study, fifteen corporations in the United States that follow a credo of social responsibility are also very profitable. Because of their credos, these fifteen corporations give generously to charity, follow stringent environmental protection policies, and have vigorous affirmative action programs.

Which of the following can be correctly inferred from the information above?

(A) Following a credo of social responsibility helps to make a corporation very profitable.
(B) It is possible for a corporation that follows a credo of social responsibility to be very profitable.
(C) A corporation that gives generously to charity must be doing so because of its credo of social responsibility.
(D) Corporations that are very profitable tend to give generously to charity.
(E) Corporations that have vigorous affirmative action programs also tend to follow stringent environmental protection policies.

The question stem contains the word *inferred*, so this is an inference question. Take the time to quickly identify the conclusion and premise. However, because this is an inference question pay particular attention to understanding what the argument is saying. Look at the answer choices and use POE aggressively.

Choice (A) is an assumption that one might make about the argument. The argument doesn't indicate that following the credo *made* the corporations profitable. It simply indicates that there are 15 corporations that follow credos and are profitable. Eliminate (A).

Choice (B) has to be true. If there are 15 corporations that follow credos of social responsibility and are very profitable, then it is *possible* for a corporation that follows a credo of social responsibility to be very profitable. Keep (B).

Choice (C) does not have to be true. There is nothing in the argument that indicates that all corporate giving must be due to a credo of social responsibility. Also notice the extreme language: "must be doing so." Eliminate (C).

Choice (D) is out of the scope of the argument. No information is given about whether or not *very profitable* corporations *tend to give generously to charity* or not. All that is given is that there are 15 profitable corporations that gave generously to charity, so eliminate (D).

Choice (E) is also out of the scope of the argument. No information is given that connects corporations with *vigorous affirmative action programs* to those that follow *stringent environmental protection policies*. All that is presented is that the 15 corporations in the study have both vigorous affirmative action programs and follow stringent environmental protection policies. Eliminate (E).

INFERENCE DRILL

1. When choosing a digital camera, it is important to consider each model's design, options, and limitations. For the serious photographer inte-rested in superior image quality, it is best to choose a camera that has fixed-length or interchangeable lenses. On the other hand, those who have neither the need nor the means to tote bulky equipment may be satisfied with the compactness and portability of cameras that have folded-optics systems.

   Which of the following can reasonably be concluded from the above statements?

   (A) Cameras with fixed-length lenses are too bulky for anyone but the professional photographer.
   (B) Serious photographers are concerned primarily with superior image quality.
   (C) Despite claims to the contrary, traditional film cameras are still the best choice for professionals.
   (D) Cameras with folded optics systems generally do not produce images as high in quality as those with interchangeable lenses.
   (E) Price should not be a primary factor in determining whether to buy a particular camera.

2. Although manned spaceflight to Mars is not out of the question, it does raise some important considerations. Extended time in space means extended time in weightlessness, which is linked to bone loss, muscle atrophy, cardiovascular problems, and other serious health issues. For example, astronauts who spent 28 days on Skylab, a space station that orbited the Earth back in the 1970s, required approximately 10 days to return to their normal, pre-mission condition. It bears noting that a one-way trip to Mars alone would take approximately eight months, using current technology.

   If the above statements are true, which of the following must also be true?

   (A) As long as astronauts receive proper training, they will be at reduced risk of health complications arising from time spent in space.
   (B) Scientists have not made progress on the development of viable artificial-gravity systems.
   (C) Travel to and from the Moon does not entail significant enough risk to prevent such a mission from occurring.
   (D) No Mars missions should be scheduled until simulated gravity systems are fully developed.
   (E) Travel to Mars could adversely affect the health of those undertaking such a journey.

3. Ultraviolet radiation from the sun can damage not only eyelid skin but also the cornea and conjunctiva, which are the clear outer parts of the eye. UV exposure also contributes to the development of cataracts. Blue-blocking sunglass lenses, which are typically yellow or orange, may make distant objects easier to see, especially in low light. However, such lenses may also make the hues in traffic lights difficult to discriminate. Meanwhile, not all blue-blocking lenses offer adequate UV protection.

Which of the following can be properly inferred from the above statements?

(A) Ultraviolet radiation is the most serious threat to eye health.
(B) Eyelid skin is more sensitive to direct sunlight than are other parts of the human face.
(C) Blue-blocking lenses should not be used when driving.
(D) Some sunglasses may leave their wearers vulnerable to eye problems.
(E) No amount of sun exposure can be considered safe.

4. Corncob Industries has instituted an employee shuttle program to provide a free transportation option to its workers who would otherwise need to commute via public transit or automobile. To help subsidize the program, the company cut its cafeteria budget, and now requires employees who choose to eat company-provided meals to pay nominal fees for its previously complimentary foods and beverages. Meanwhile, no additional benefit programs have been created.

From the above statements, it can be reasonably concluded that

(A) Corncob employees who use the company shuttle generally do not have more convenient transportation options.
(B) Fewer Corncob workers have used the company cafeteria since the shuttle program began.
(C) Some workers who still commute to Corncob on their own are unhappy about the shuttle program.
(D) More Corncob employees have begun bringing their own meals since the shuttle program began.
(E) The shuttle program is not truly free for any Corncob worker, since it affects another employee perquisite.

5. Although they cost up to three times as much as standard engine oils, synthetic motor oils resist viscosity breakdown, that is, a degradation of their lubricating and engine-protection abilities, longer than do standard motor oils. They also maintain maximum lubrication over a wider variety of temperatures than their conventional counterparts. That allows for up to 66% longer durations between oil changes, as well as significantly more protection at engine startup, when most engine-wear is believed to occur.

If the above statements are true, then which of the following must also be true?

(A) Cars that use synthetic motor oils will last longer than cars that use standard motor oil.
(B) The benefits of certain kinds of motor oil may compensate for their added cost.
(C) Drivers who use synthetic motor oils care more about their cars than do drivers who use conventional oils.
(D) Blended motor oils, which fuse standard and synthetic oils, offer considerably less engine protection than does purely synthetic motor oil.
(E) Treatments or additives for standard motor oil do not offer a viable alternative to synthetic oils.

6. One proven way for a product's marketing to succeed is for that product to be the first in a particular category. The product becomes the top because it defines the category—so much so that people may refer to the particular item by its brand name rather than by its category, be that facial tissue or photocopies. As such, a brand's success is due primarily to its being first in the market rather than via its company's marketing abilities.

The claims above, if true, most strongly support which of the following statements?

(A) Corporations stand to gain more value from brand names than from the quality of their products.
(B) No amount of marketing expertise can supersede the importance of product ranking.
(C) Marketers should focus more on creating new product categories than on creating new products.
(D) The best-selling products are those that are the first in their respective categories.
(E) Products that are the first of their kind have, in at least some instances, sold better over time than rival products.

7. Access to capital is only one of several factors necessary to business success. Proper pricing structure is equally essential, so as to furnish consistently a particular product or service for less than one's costs. Further complicating this scenario is that many startup companies must compete with established businesses that can offer lower prices for the same products and services.

If the above statements are true, then it must be true that

(A) Price competition is a more common way to drive out market rivals than is a battle over product superiority.
(B) Recently-formed companies have higher operating costs than do established companies.
(C) Established businesses can drive competitors out of a given market by offering lower prices than those competitors can.
(D) Length of time serving a particular market may correlate with capital or cost advantages.
(E) Startup companies cannot usually acquire capital quickly enough to compete with their established rivals.

8. Distance learning offers a potentially lucrative option for learning institutions. Money that would otherwise be spent on classroom space, parking facilities, climate control, and other particulars associated with providing a location-specific service can be diverted to marketing and quality control, two crucial factors that can drive new business.

Which of the following can be correctly inferred from the statements above?

(A) The costs associated with offering distance learning are lower than those of other instruction methods.
(B) Online classes are more convenient for both instructors and students than are classes held at specific geographic locations.
(C) Distance learning does not require climate control or parking facilities.
(D) Most types of instruction can be effectively conducted in an online setting.
(E) Computers and Internet access are uniformly available to people in the developed world.

9. The interplay between what a given item is worth and its price is hardly based on logic. This is especially true of fashion, luxury, or other nonessential items. Designer clothing, for example, becomes worth what it is priced, as opposed to being priced what it is worth. When that price is set high, the product's value is perceived accordingly, even when its quality is no higher than that of less expensive rivals.

The statements above suggest that

(A) People consistently make logical choices when shopping for essential items.
(B) Designer clothing is not an indispensable item.
(C) The higher a product's price, the more that product is worth.
(D) Low-priced items are usually of the same quality as high-priced items.
(E) People are not logical when they shop for clothing.

10. In the context of finance, speculation involves assuming the risk of loss in return for the uncertain prospect of financial gain. It is only in the absence of risk that one may call a particular financial strategy an investment. Therefore, as long as a monetary transaction involves potential capital loss _____.

The above statements are structured to lead to which of the following as a conclusion?

(A) that investment cannot be considered sound.
(B) it should not be attempted without consulting a financial services professional.
(C) it is not an investment but an act of speculation.
(D) it cannot be considered an instance of speculation.
(E) it may be regarded as an investment if it rises in value.

11. Returning to school at an advanced age is not unusual. Many people, including seniors and retirees who have enjoyed full lives and careers, find that studying and thinking critically come just as readily to them as those skills did decades prior. Furthermore, since people in their 50s and beyond do not need to "find themselves," they are better able to focus and commit to their coursework than many of their younger peers.

The author of the above statements suggests that

(A) Young people have more need to discover where their interests truly lie than do their older counterparts.
(B) Additional schooling offers new career opportunities for people regardless of age.
(C) Older university students have less hectic schedules than do younger students.
(D) Book learning is not a suitable alternative to college study for seniors and retirees.
(E) Most colleges and universities do not discriminate against applicants on the basis of age.

12. Casino gambling may inherently involve risk, but different games offer different levels of risk. Blackjack, for example, gives players the most favorable odds of winning, but that is contingent upon ability. As such, a novice gambler has less chance of losing money by shooting craps, a casino game offering the next-highest odds, than by taking a place at a blackjack table.

The author of the above statements suggests that

(A) Only expert players should participate in blackjack games.
(B) The game of craps does not require as much skill as blackjack does.
(C) Slot machines require considerably less skill than do all other casino games.
(D) Seasoned blackjack players would be well advised to avoid shooting craps.
(E) Poker offers better odds for the skilled player than does roulette.

13. Investment newsletters can be a handy guide to stock market profits or a waste of cash. Either scenario depends not only on the quality of newsletter you choose but also on whether you are willing to put in the time and effort required to follow its advice properly.

From the above statements, it can be inferred that

(A) Investment newsletters may not garner profits for people who heed their recommendations properly.
(B) Following a newsletter's advice properly may result in steady, long-term profits.
(C) The better the quality of a particular investment newsletter, the higher its subscription price is likely to be.
(D) Some investment newsletters have subscription costs that are beyond the reach of many investors.
(E) Laypersons should not invest money in the stock market without seeking some level of financial advice.

14. A group of university researchers has found that gender bias continues to affect social interactions. The experimenters had both men and women perform a perceptual task, involving objects that had distinctively masculine or feminine qualities. Meanwhile, to keep the experiment's purpose concealed, each participant's performance was rated by a single evaluator. When men proved competent at a task involving, for example, a tire-iron, their success was attributed more often to ability; when women did the same, however, their success was often attributed to luck. Conversely, when a feminine object was involved in the task, neither the women's nor the men's success was attributed to ability.

The above statements suggest that

(A) women who are good at perceptual tasks will have their abilities go under-appreciated
(B) a tire-iron cannot be perceived as having feminine qualities
(C) having only one person rate another can hide the purpose of an experiment
(D) successful women are often regarded as having more masculine qualities than are their less successful peers
(E) more men performed the task competently than did women

15. According to Howard Gardner's Theory of Multiple Intelligences, human intellectual ability is not limited to the verbal, visual-spatial, and logical/mathematical tasks measured by traditional IQ tests. Rather, Gardner's theory posits that humans manifest at least eight separate intelligences, including not only the aforementioned three but also interpersonal, intrapersonal, bodily-kinesthetic, musical, and naturalistic intelligence. Support for his theory comes, in part, from the observation that when particular parts of the human brain are compromised, isolated and specific deficits in cognitive function occur while other mental capabilities remain unaffected.

Which of the following may correctly be inferred from the above statements?

(A) Verbal intelligence does not correlate with logical/mathematical ability.
(B) A brain-altering substance or injury may affect one's ability to speak coherently while simultaneously impairing that person's ability to play a violin concerto.
(C) Visual-spatial performance is guided primarily by brain regions distinct from those used to solve crossword puzzles.
(D) IQ tests are not useful measures of human intellectual ability.
(E) People who are especially good at sports are not as prolific in mathematical matters.

16. A major study has found that an experimental drug developed to reduce unhealthy amounts of low-density lipoprotein, or "bad cholesterol," should not only be approved but should also be prescribed to healthy individuals. In fact, the study was cut short after just eighteen months when it was found that levels of HDL cholesterol, otherwise known as high-density lipoprotein or "good cholesterol," were boosted in all participants, whether or not they had high levels of LDL, or low-density lipoprotein. While it is true that the study was funded by the drug's manufacturer, there is little reason to believe that the results were manipulated, given that the study was quite large in scope and sample size.

From the above statements, it can be inferred that

(A) small-scale study results are more difficult to influence than are large-scale study results
(B) drug companies that sponsor research are reluctant to release results that contradict their expectations
(C) cholesterol drugs benefit healthy individuals as much as they do those with cardiovascular issues
(D) natural remedies are usually discouraged by physicians in favor of drug treatments
(E) research not sponsored by corporate interests is unlikely to be biased

17. Automatic transmissions do not provide the level of fuel economy that their manual-shift counterparts do, because the preset gear sequences of the former cannot match the quickness of human judgment. A skilled driver who pays sharp mind to tactile and auditory cues, in addition to the visual information provided by dashboard gauges, is able to coax optimum functioning from a car's engine, ensuring that it neither overworks nor under-performs.

Which of the following can be reasonably concluded from the above statements?

(A) Cars equipped with automatic transmissions are more likely to experience engine wear than those equipped with standard-shift systems.
(B) Some drivers obtain unexceptional economy from manual-shift transmissions.
(C) Formal training is essential to attain maximum performance from a manual-shift transmission.
(D) Advances in automatic-transmission technology will not put such systems on par with their manual counterparts.
(E) Professional drivers derive more fuel economy from their cars than do nonprofessionals.

18. When considering an applicant for potential employment, it is essential to identify the "overachiever," a candidate whose resume and personality traits indicate a pattern of solving problems with prodigious amounts of persistence and effort. Although such individuals may seem desirable to an organization, given their strong desire for upward mobility, the time will ultimately arise when they and their employers find that hard work alone will not supplant the "big-picture" thinking needed to resolve the complex issues regularly engaging upper management.

The above statements suggest that

(A) high achievers are not "big-picture" thinkers
(B) candidates for high-level job positions often claim to be harder workers than their achievements might suggest
(C) the most effective leaders are not necessarily those who expend maximal effort
(D) upward mobility requires persistence and effort
(E) hard work impedes resolution of complex issues

19. The typical worker changes career paths as many as seven times over the course of her working life, frequently starting over with a new employer, sometimes in a completely different field. That is reason enough to pursue a liberal arts education, because it provides students with cultural breadth, strong communication skills, discipline to work well alone as well as with others, and effective problem-solving abilities.

The above statements suggest that

(A) People who expect to change careers frequently are those best served by a liberal arts education.
(B) A trade-school education does not provide an adequate environment for students to develop problem-solving skills.
(C) Advanced degrees have become a prerequisite for some entry-level positions.
(D) A broad background in arts and culture is considered an asset to some employers.
(E) Specializing in a particular discipline or profession does not provide adequate job security over the long run.

20. Publicly-traded companies must answer to shareholders whenever quarterly profits decline. In an effort to avoid a significant decline in profit, corporate leaders too often rely on familiar approaches, evaluating potential strategies on the basis of what has worked before rather than trying something new. However, creativity requires an environment that facilitates long-term thinking, risk-taking, and openness to untested ideas.

If the above statements are true, then which of the following must also be true?

(A) Privately-held companies are more innovative than their publicly-held counterparts.
(B) A company's need to gain a competitive advantage is hampered by the division of its ownership.
(C) Innovation can contribute to a reduction in corporate proceeds.
(D) Stock-market investors are frequently short-sighted.
(E) Some corporations hide losses in an effort to prevent shareholders from selling.

21. One way of determining whether a job candidate is telling the truth has to do with his or her willingness to divulge negative information during the interview process. If, for example, a candidate admits to being fired from a previous job, having a less-than-stellar attendance record, or possessing a below-average typing speed, that may be interpreted as a sign that she is telling the truth, particularly regarding any favorable information she divulges about herself or her work history.

The above statements support which of the following as a conclusion?

(A) Candidates who do not reveal negative aspects of their personalities or work histories are not being truthful.
(B) Self-deprecation is ultimately self-serving.
(C) Interviewees often use reverse psychology to gain the trust of influential people.
(D) Candidates with stellar credentials are probably lying about those qualifications.
(E) Unfavorable character traits can prove beneficial in some situations.

22. Among the benefits to owning an upright piano are economy, compactness, and quality sound. Although the resonance comes from the rear of the instrument, the typical upright has a lid that allows the tones to emanate from the top. Meanwhile, thanks to technological advancements in factory-set key action, new uprights now come close to their baby-grand counterparts in overall feel and response. Since the needs of most players do not warrant concert-pianist key action, an upright makes a worthy alternative to an electronic or digital piano.

If the above statements are true, it can be inferred that

(A) concert pianists do not regard upright pianos as acceptable practice instruments
(B) old upright pianos have inadequate key response
(C) grand pianos are too bulky for most households
(D) the typical pianist may find little justification for owning a baby-grand piano
(E) digital pianos cost less than upright pianos

23. Through "pay-per-click" advertising, also known as PPC, an Internet advertisement appears in designated sections of a results page when a person enters certain keywords into a search engine. While many Web users ignore such results, given that those listings look different from the non-sponsored results listed in the main body of the page, people who do see PPC ads will be pre-qualified sales prospects, given that such ads are specific to the keywords entered by the person seeing them. PPC offers advertisers control over their budgets, since only ads for the highest bidders on specific keywords appear at the top of a search results page.

Which of the following conclusions is most supported by the statements above?

(A) Most Web users do not consider paid search-engine results legitimate.
(B) The visibility of some kinds of Internet advertising is inversely proportional to the revenue spent on such advertising.
(C) Companies that do not offer products or services online will not derive a significant benefit from PPC advertising.
(D) Print and broadcast advertising is not as effective for online businesses as is PPC advertising.
(E) PPC advertisers may be forced to choose between spending more than they intended or missing potential sales opportunities.

24. Greg: The dramatic rise in illegal immigration in the last decade is evidenced by the fact that 7 of every 10 small business owners reports knowingly employing, or knowing a small business owner who knowingly employs, an illegal immigrant.

Jackson: But the statistics show that 10 years ago, approximately 8% of small businesses employed an illegal immigrant, with 1 in 12 doing so. So if the average small business owner knew 20 other small business owners, it is unlikely that he would not have known one who employs an illegal immigrant.

Jackson's argument is designed to support which of the following conclusions?

(A) If more than 8% of small businesses employ an illegal immigrant, the 7 of 10 figure Greg cites must be too high.
(B) The current percentage of small businesses employing an illegal immigrant must be greater than it was a decade ago.
(C) If statistics show that 8% of small businesses employed an illegal immigrant, the actual percentage is likely much higher.
(D) That 7 of 10 small business owners know someone who employs an illegal immigrant does not demonstrate that illegal immigration has increased in the last 10 years.
(E) It is unlikely that the owners Greg cites would have openly acknowledged breaking the law.

Check your answers on page 721.

EVALUATE-THE-ARGUMENT QUESTIONS

Evaluate-the-argument questions ask the test taker to determine which of the answer choices would provide information that would help evaluate the information provided in the argument.

Step 1: Read and identify the question

Evaluate-the-argument questions can be identified because of the inclusion of words such as *evaluate* or *assess* in the question stem.

Step 2: Work the argument

Break the argument down into conclusion and premise(s). Next, determine the assumption by looking for common flaws and gaps in the language between the conclusion and premise.

Step 3: Predict what the answer should do

The correct answer will be one that helps evaluate the portion of the argument that is the subject of the question. So consider what information could be presented that could possibly help in that evaluation.

Step 4: Use POE to find the answer

POE: Consider each answer choice individually and determine whether that information helps to evaluate the portion of the argument in question.

The format of these questions can be confusing. Sometimes the answers are in question form. If they are, turn the questions into statements and then evaluate them based on the question being asked.

Common incorrect answers for these types of questions are irrelevant, either because they're outside the scope or because they bring in unnecessary information.

Try the example on the next page.

1. Ergonomically designed computer keyboards tend to lose their "play"—the responsiveness of the keys—more quickly than do traditional keyboards. A software designer has suggested that it is in fact the curvature of the key rows and not increased typing speed that is to blame. Due to the bent shape of the board, it is more difficult for the average user to clean between the keys, resulting in a gradual deadening of the spring mechanisms.

    The answer to which of the following questions will most likely yield significant information that would help to evaluate the software designer's hypothesis?

    (A) Do traditional keyboards and ergonomically designed keyboards utilize the same plastics?
    (B) Does sprinkling a keyboard with dust impede the spring action beneath the keys?
    (C) Does a keyboard with deadened play make typing more difficult?
    (D) Do computer manufacturers receive more complaints about ergonomically designed keyboards than about traditional keyboards?
    (E) Are software designers more likely than other users to utilize their keyboards when working?

This is an evaluate-the-argument question as indicated by the word *evaluate* in the question stem. Break down the argument to find the conclusion and the premise.

The conclusion is that the *curvature of the key rows and not increased typing speed* causes the loss of play of ergonomically designed keyboards. The premise of the argument is that *it is more difficult for the average user to clean between the keys, resulting in a gradually deadening of the spring mechanisms.*

Now, look for the assumptions of the argument using the common flaws and identifying gaps in the language between the conclusion and premise. There is a causal flaw here. The author assumes that the dirty keyboard, and not some other factor, is causing the dead keys.

Now look at the answer choices. Because the answer choices are written as questions, turn each one into a statement before evaluating it.

Choice (A) reads *traditional keyboards and ergonomically designed keyboards utilize the same plastics.* This information is out the scope of the argument. Eliminate (A). Choice (B) reads *sprinkling a keyboard with dust impedes the spring action beneath the keys.* This strengthens the argument by supporting the assumption that the dirty keyboard is to blame. Keep (B). Choice (C) reads *a keyboard with deadened play makes typing more difficult.* This answer choice does not help to evaluate the argument. Eliminate (C). Choice (D) reads *computer manufacturers receive more complaints about ergonomically designed keyboards than about traditional keyboards.* This is also out of scope, so eliminate (D). Choice (E) reads *software designers are more likely than other users to utilize their keyboards when working.* This is out of scope as well so eliminate (E). The correct answer is (B).

EVALUATE DRILL

1. A bakery in neighborhood X sells cakes that are very intricately created using a rare method that a bakery in nearby town Y used in previous years. Because of its complexity, the baking method is unlikely to have developed independently in both bakeries. One food critic theorized that the bakers at neighborhood X's bakery must have learned the method from the bakers at town Y's bakery.

   The answer to which of the following questions would be most useful in evaluating the critic's theory?

   (A) Do bakers ever leave their own bakeries in order to socialize with other bakers?
   (B) Are baked goods ever brought from bakery to bakery?
   (C) Do bakers in town Y's bakery still employ the same method to create cakes?
   (D) Do food critics personally travel to local bakeries to sample their baked goods?
   (E) Does the bakery in neighborhood X sell any other types of baked goods?

2. Following several years of decreasing sales, a large retailer decided to restructure its management staff. The managers had previously been assigned to one store location only; after the restructuring, each manager was assigned to a new store location every other month. After the restructuring, sales increased and the retailer concluded that the restructuring led to the increased sales.

   Which of the following would be most useful to establish in evaluating the conclusion that the restructuring of the management staff caused the increase in sales?

   (A) whether the retailer had to hire additional staff during the restructuring
   (B) whether other retailers implemented a similar restructuring
   (C) whether the management staff increased during the restructuring
   (D) whether the customer base of the retailer increased during the restructuring
   (E) whether the ratio of managers to non-managers increased during the restructuring

3. A magazine office uses an outdated, easily broken fax machine. The office staff is considering replacing the machine with a newer fax machine that is less prone to breakdowns and easier to operate.

   Which of the following would be most useful for the office staff to establish in evaluating whether to replace its current fax machine?

   (A) whether the office will soon be moving to a new location
   (B) whether the number of received faxes is predicted to remain the same
   (C) whether the office will soon be converting to a paperless fax-through-e-mail system
   (D) whether the office will also replace its copy machine if it replaces its fax machine
   (E) whether the number of pages faxed at one time is predicted to remain the same

4. An encyclopedia is considering a proposal to include an article on a start-up company in its collection. One of the criteria in the encyclopedia's guidelines is that the subject of the proposed entry show a demonstrated importance and be referenced in third-party, unsolicited press. The proposed article includes six links to press references, none of which were solicited, and all of which are in established magazines and newspapers.

   The answer to which of the following would be most useful for the editors of the encyclopedia in evaluating whether to accept the proposed entry on the start-up company?

   (A) Are there other start-up companies included in the encyclopedia?
   (B) Does having more than one press reference indicate the subject's importance?
   (C) How long has the start-up company been in existence?
   (D) Do most encyclopedia readers already know about the start-up company?
   (E) Was the proposed article written by an employee of the start-up company?

5. A training company was hired by a large brokerage firm to provide in-house training on a new software program. In order to maximize efficiency and cut costs, the brokerage firm demanded that the training company remove those trainers who spent the longest amounts of time in one-on-one sessions with brokerage employees.

The answer to which of the following would be most useful in evaluating the brokerage firm's choice of which trainers to remove?

(A) Are the most efficient trainers asked to assist the brokerage employees who have the most difficult questions?
(B) Do the trainers also provide training to other brokerage firms?
(C) Would the trainers who were removed be re-assigned to other projects?
(D) Are the brokerage employees able to access training after the in-house trainers leave?
(E) Would the brokerage firm lose clients if its employees increase their fees?

6. A certain apple orchard typically has a large yield mid-season, while the number of apples decreases near the end of the season. The apples picked early in the season are larger and brighter, and those picked late in the season are smaller and duller. A pie maker who uses the orchard's apples claims that her profits will increase near the end of this year's season.

Which of the following would be most useful in evaluating the pie maker's claim?

(A) comparing this year's predicted profits to last year's profits
(B) calculating the number of apples needed to make each pie
(C) determining whether smaller, duller apples make better-tasting pies
(D) comparing this season's pie quality to last season's pie quality
(E) determining whether the characteristics of the apples affect the price of pies

7. Bicycle riders have recently made fixed-gear bicycles very popular. These bicycles have no brakes and are therefore assumed to be much more dangerous. An editorial writer claims that fixed-gear bicycles are the cause of a recent increase in the number of bicycle accidents.

The answer to which of the following would be most useful in evaluating the editorial writer's argument?

(A) Are fixed-gear bicycles ridden in the same types of streets and under the same conditions as are regular bicycles?
(B) Are the regular bicycle riders who are involved in accidents familiar with the bicycle rules and regulations?
(C) Do more bicycle riders wear helmets this year than last year?
(D) Are car drivers becoming more aggressive when confronted with bicycles on the road?
(E) Are fixed-gear bicycles more expensive than regular bicycles?

8. Certain pesticides used two decades ago contained agents now known to cause cancer. However, a study conducted ten years ago showed no increased incidence of cancer in people exposed to the pesticide.

The answer to which of the following would be most useful in evaluating the results of the study?

(A) Two decades ago, were there pesticides that did not contain the cancer-causing agents?
(B) Is the pesticide still in use today?
(C) How long does it take for cancer to develop?
(D) Are some cancers caused by things other than pesticides?
(E) Ten years ago, were there countries that did not use pesticides?

9. The Robertson division of the police department has brought more suspects in for questioning than has any other division this year. The police chief claims that, of all the divisions, Robertson is doing the most to reduce crime in the city.

Which of the following, if established, would be most useful in evaluating the police chief's claim?

(A) whether any other district has released more suspects after questioning than Robertson has
(B) whether the police chief has accurate data on the numbers of suspects questioned and subsequently charged in each division
(C) whether crime is increasing in most major cities in the country
(D) whether the Robertson division has questioned a majority of suspects in the city
(E) whether there exists a correlation between the number of suspects questioned and the number of crimes committed

10. Consuming high levels of potassium can reduce some of sodium's harmful effects. Because many foods are naturally high in potassium, there is no reason to take potassium supplements.

The answer to which of the following would be most useful in evaluating the argument above?

(A) Are potassium supplements widely available?
(B) Do most people experience sodium's harmful effects?
(C) Are there any disadvantages to consuming high levels of potassium?
(D) Do many foods contain high levels of both potassium and sodium?
(E) Are there advantages to consuming high levels of sodium?

11. Farmers get water at subsidized rates that are much lower than the increasingly high prices fetched on the open market. Some farmers are debating whether to continue irrigating their crops and sell their produce or to let the crops die and sell their irrigation water to needy cities and other farms.

Which of the following would be most useful to determine in order to evaluate the farmers' current debate?

(A) whether farmers will get water at subsidized rates in the future
(B) whether produce prices will increase if some farmers let their crops die
(C) whether irrigation water needs to be filtered and purified before drinking
(D) whether their crops, if allowed to die, can easily be replanted the following year
(E) whether the price of water will continue to increase at its current rate

12. Some species of bombardier beetles have vestigal flight wings but cannot fly. Some researchers argue that the wing remnants must have a function, although that function is still unknown.

Which of the following, if determined, would be most useful in evaluating the researchers' argument?

(A) Can the function of the wing remnants be discovered?
(B) Are there any other winged insects that are unable to fly?
(C) Can the species which prey on the beetle fly?
(D) Did the beetle's ancestors have the ability to fly?
(E) Does each characteristic of a life form serve a purpose?

13. Researchers discovered that Sumatran tigers share three DNA markers that are not found in any other type of tiger. Based on this discovery, the researchers concluded that there are two distinct species of tigers, one comprised solely of Sumatran tigers and the other comprised of all other types of tigers.

The answer to which of the following would be most useful in evaluating the researchers' conclusion?

(A) Are Sumatran tigers in danger of extinction?
(B) Do any of the other types of tigers have genetic markers that are specific to that type of tiger?
(C) Are all types of tigers susceptible to similar genetic disorders?
(D) Do Sumatran tigers have external markings that distinguish them from other types of tigers?
(E) Are all types of tigers descendants of the same species?

14. A clothing manufacturer prides itself on offering the lowest prices in its industry. The machines it uses, however, are very old and in need of expensive repairs or replacement. If the manufacturer cannot maintain its low prices, it will lose much of its market share. The company owners are considering taking out a loan in order to replace the oldest machines.

The answer to which of the following would be most important for the company owners to determine while evaluating their options?

(A) Do the newer machines require expensive parts and continued maintenance?
(B) Do the company's competitors use newer machines?
(C) Is most of the company's inventory sold to local retailers?
(D) Have other clothing manufacturers taken out loans in order to buy equipment?
(E) Are the company's employees in favor of replacing the oldest machines?

15. There is a demonstrated correlation between a healthy diet during childhood and good grades. On a small island near Denmark, there are no fast food restaurants and many local, organic farmers who sell their produce to families on the island. The high school students on the island have some of the highest grades in the world. Clearly, their grades are a result of their healthy childhood diets.

The answer to which of the following would be most useful in evaluating the argument?

(A) Do residents of other islands maintain healthy diets?
(B) How many high school students live on the island?
(C) Have the majority of high school students lived on the island since childhood?
(D) Do the adults on the island leave the island to go to work?
(E) Do the high school students work on farms?

16. Baseball bats transfer less power to the ball upon contact after years of use. A high school teacher, who coaches the school's baseball team, hypothesizes that the cause of the reduction of power transfer is the build-up of dirt and dust on the surface of the bat rather than a change in the material of the bat.

The answer to which of the following could help determine whether the teacher's hypothesis is correct?

(A) Do bats of different length and weight lose power at different rates?
(B) Do bats made of aluminum or wood lose power faster?
(C) Are wood or metal bats used for the high school team?
(D) Do new and old bats transfer different amounts of power to a ball?
(E) Does smearing various substances on a bat result in less power transfer?

17. Speaker: High schools should not increase the amount of time students spend in math and science classes. Although students need to achieve greater competency at math and science by the time they graduate, the plan to increase classroom math and science time has a major drawback: the additional time for math and science classes is necessarily cut from fine arts class time, which is important for students' development.

To evaluate the speaker's argument, knowledge of which of the following would be most valuable?

(A) Whether students who take extra math and science or students that take fine arts classes fare better in gaining admission to highly-selective colleges and universities.

(B) Whether students whose studies are largely confined to math and science develop the communication skills they will need after graduation.

(C) Whether there are certain scientific subjects that, even with the extra time allotted to math and science, could not be taught to the high school students.

(D) Whether there are fine arts teachers who could teach math and science.

(E) Whether students could be better educated in math and science without putting more class time into the subjects.

Check your answers on page 721.

IDENTIFY-THE-REASONING (DIALOGUE) QUESTIONS

There are two types of questions included under the category of Identify-the-Reasoning. There are dialogue questions and bolded phrase questions. The common bond is that both question types relate to *how* the author makes his or her argument. Let's first look at a dialogue question.

Step 1: Read and identify the question

These arguments can be identified by the words *technique, strategy,* or *method* used in reference to one of the speakers in the argument.

Step 2: Work the argument

There will be at least two speakers in dialogue questions. Find the conclusion and premise for each speaker. However, keep in mind that the conclusion for one of the speakers may not be explicitly stated because that speaker may just be responding to the other. Only worry about finding the assumption for the speaker that the question asks about.

Step 3: Predict what the answer should do

Think about how the two arguments relate to one another and try to formulate your own answer.

Step 4: Use POE to find the answer

POE: Consider each answer choice individually and eliminate answers that:

- Are only partially correct.
- Describe something the argument outside of the scope of the argument.

Try the example on the next page.

1. Poppy: High taxes have a chilling effect on the economy. When individuals and corporations are taxed, they have less money to spend. Demand for products and services is reduced, causing unemployment to increase. Taxes must be lowered.

    Lilly: But you must also consider that taxes generate funds for the government. If taxes are lowered, the government will be forced to borrow more money, thus reducing the amount of credit available. Unable to borrow money easily, businesses and individuals will be forced to limit their purchases.

    Lilly objects to Poppy's argument by

    (A) claiming that Poppy has exaggerated the adverse effects of high taxes
    (B) indicating that Poppy has based his argument on insufficient evidence about the effects of taxes on the economy
    (C) noting that Poppy has failed to adequately define the term "taxes"
    (D) demonstrating that the danger of reducing taxes is far more severe than the threat of maintaining them at current levels
    (E) suggesting that the economic benefits of easy credit outweigh the danger of unemployment

The question is asking what method Lilly uses or *how* she objects to Poppy's argument, so this is an Identify-the-Reasoning question.

Break down Poppy's argument and find his conclusion and premise. His conclusion is that *taxes must be lowered* and his premise is that *High taxes have a chilling effect on the economy.*

Now, look at Lilly's argument. Her conclusion, though not explicitly stated, is that taxes shouldn't be lowered. Her premise is *If taxes are lowered, the government will be forced to borrow more money, thus reducing the amount of credit available. Unable to borrow money easily, businesses and individuals will be forced to limit their purchases.*

The question asks how Lilly objects to Poppy's argument. So examine how she does this. Lilly begins by stating *But you must also consider.* The implication is that Poppy has not considered all the facts. Therefore, Lilly objects to Poppy's argument by stating that he hasn't considered all the information on this issue. Now look at the answer choices.

Choice (A) states that Lilly claims that Poppy has exaggerated the adverse effects of high taxes. This is not supported by the passage, so eliminate (A). Lilly does indicate that Poppy has based his argument on insufficient evidence about the effects of taxes on the economy, so keep (B). Lilly does not note that Poppy has failed to adequately define the term taxes, so eliminate (C). Choice (D) is too extreme as Lilly does not compare the levels of danger of reducing taxes and keeping them at their current rates. Eliminate (D). Only Poppy mentions unemployment, so it is not correct to state that Lilly compares unemployment to the benefits of easy credit, so eliminate (E). The correct answer is (B).

IDENTIFY-THE-REASONING (BOLDED PHRASES) QUESTIONS

Questions with bold-face phrases are the second type of question included under the category of Identify-the-Reasoning. For these questions, identify what part of the argument each bold-face phrase represents. The bold-face phrase can never be an assumption, because assumptions aren't stated.

Step 1: Read and identify the question

Identify these questions by the bolded phrases or words such as *role, function,* or *purpose.*

Step 2: Work the argument

Find the conclusion and the premises. It is unnecessary to find the assumption for these question types as the bolded phrases are not assumptions.

Step 3: Predict what the answer should do

Decide whether each bolded phrase is a conclusion or a premise. Note that the answer choices may use words other than "conclusion" and "premise" to describe the conclusion and premise.

Step 4: Use POE to find the answer

POE: Consider each answer choice individually and use POE. Common incorrect answers for this type of question are ones that:

- Are only partially correct.
- Describe something outside the scope of the argument.

Try the example on the next page.

2. Although computer manufacturer *X* has experienced decreasing sales in the last quarter, **stockholders should not sell their shares of the company**. The stock price of a financially troubled company can rise dramatically once those problems are solved. Last year, **the stock price of steel manufacturer *Y* rebounded after the company reduced its accounts receivable backlog**.

The bolded phrases play which of the following roles in the argument above?

(A) The first phrase contains the author's conclusion and the second phrase contains unrelated information.

(B) The first phrase states a position and the second phrase provides evidence to undermine that position.

(C) The first phrase states a premise on which the conclusion is based and the second phrase provides the conclusion.

(D) The first phrase states the conclusion and the second phrase supports the conclusion with an analogy.

(E) The first phrase offers advice and the second phrase draws a contrast between two companies.

The bolded phrases and the word "role" signify that this is an Identify-the-Reasoning question so find the conclusion and premise and determine the roles of the bolded phrases.

The conclusion of the argument is *stockholders should not sell their shares of the company*. The premise is *the stock price of steel manufacturer Y rebounded after the company reduced its accounts receivable backlog*.

Thus, the first bolded phrase is the conclusion and the second bolded phrase is the premise.

Now, check the answers.

Choice (A) is incorrect because the second phrase did not contain unrelated information, so eliminate (A). Choice (B) is incorrect because the second phrase did not provide evidence to undermine the position in the first phrase, so eliminate (B). Choice (C) is incorrect because the first phrase is not a premise, so eliminate (C). Choice (D) works as a premise supports the conclusion and the author did use an analogy, so the second part of the answer choice is as accurate as the first. So keep (D). Choice (E) is incorrect because the second phrase didn't draw a contrast; it made a comparison, so eliminate (E). The correct answer is (D).

ID REASONING DRILL

1. Harvey: Providing a government subsidy to individual firms is bad policy under any conditions. If the firm is a large business, then government subsidies would be unnecessary, because the firm should already be large enough to realize the economies of scale needed to make it competitive; in that case, subsidies would be wasted. If the firm is small, then government subsidies would be unavailing, because small firms would be unable to compete in global marketplaces in which they did not command economies of scale; in this case, subsidies would be wasted as well. Thus, government subsidies are always unwise.

Zane: What about medium-sized firms? If the firm is able to achieve some but not all typical economies of scale, government subsidies might make the difference between being narrowly uncompetitive and being able to sell successfully in world markets. Thus, government subsidies might sometimes be effective.

Zane responds to Harvey's argument by

(A) demonstrating that Harvey fails to prove a necessary premise about the relationship between economies of scale and competitiveness
(B) noting that Harvey's argument requires inconsistent definitions of key terms
(C) raising an alternative excluded by Harvey's discussion in order to indicate that Harvey's conclusion is flawed
(D) providing an example of an instance in which Harvey's premises must lead to a contradictory outcome
(E) accepting Harvey's conclusion as valid and then showing that it need not depend on Harvey's premises

2. **Media coverage of complex news events often oversimplifies**. The causes of this strong tendency include the inherent challenge of explaining the larger context in which events occur, the need to provide coverage across a wide range of issues, the emotional power of images, and the short time allotted to news relative to entertainment by ratings-conscious broadcasters. This has helped give rise to "soft news," in which events are covered by talk shows. The format of such shows, however, lends itself most strongly not to a complex factual explanation of events but instead to the creation of a narrative that engages our sympathy and emotions—a story about the event in which there are "good guys" and "bad guys," heroes, villains, and victims. **The power of such narratives may well have helped increase support among the American public for 1990s-era U.S. intervention in Somalia, Bosnia, and Kosovo.**

How is the relationship between the two bolded sentences best described?

(A) The first is an assessment of a phenomenon and the second is a description of specific examples of this phenomenon.
(B) The first is an evaluation of a general trend and the second is a reason for this trend.
(C) The first is a judgment of a relationship and the second is an instance in which this judgment is shown to be correct.
(D) The first is a statement evaluating a phenomenon and the second is an observation of a possible result of that phenomenon.
(E) The first is a claim about a particular issue and the second is an assessment of the accuracy of that claim.

3. There is a thriving industry designing "table top" map-and-unit pieces games that simulate historical battles, such as the clashes of the Napoleonic Wars or the far-flung battles of World War II. **Authors of historical simulation games have to address far greater issues than mere historical accuracy**. Designing such a simulation must, by its very nature, entail grappling with profound philosophical questions of causality and history. How great should be the role of random chance when determining the outcomes of a simulated battle? How much weight should be accorded to quantitative advantage of numbers rather than qualitative advantages in organization and technique? How critical is the role of individual leadership in determining the outcome of these enormous conflicts? How should the game account for the inability of each side to know precisely the actions of the other? **What appears to be a simple way to while away the afternoon replaying Waterloo is actually to engage in an implicit meditation on destiny, chance, historical agency, knowledge, and free will.**

The relationship between the two bolded statements is best described as

(A) The first is a conclusion about the status of an industry and the second is a supporting example drawn from an analogous situation.
(B) The first is an assessment of the challenge facing individual firms and the second is a characterization of an industry.
(C) The first is a descriptive statement of a situation and the second is an evaluation of the possible larger implications of that situation, using a specific example.
(D) The first is an assertion of a difficulty confronting members of a profession and the second is an evaluation of the solution.
(E) The first is a characterization of a kind of production difficulty and the second is an explanation of the specific origins of that difficulty.

4. Russell Sage was a highly prominent nineteenth-century railroad tycoon and financier; **after his death, Sage's wealth established a non-profit foundation for the improvement of public social conditions**. Sage was also at the center of perhaps that era's most notorious lawsuit, *Laidlaw versus Sage,* which made him a figure of public revulsion. An aggrieved man entered Sage's office and quietly told him that he had a satchel full of dynamite, which he would detonate unless Sage promised to pay him over $1 million. While continuing to speak in a calm conversational tone to the explosive-toting man, Sage walked over to the office door, where a clerk named Laidlaw stood waiting to speak to the Wall Street titan. Sage casually turned Laidlaw around, holding him so that Laidlaw's body was directly between Sage and the bomber. At this point, the bomber detonated the dynamite. Laidlaw's body took the brunt of the blast intended for Sage, leaving Laidlaw with severe, life-long injuries; Sage was unharmed. Sage, a man of vast personal wealth, never compensated Laidlaw in any way and repeatedly fought court efforts to force him to do so. After his death, Sage's wealth established a non-profit foundation for the improvement of public social conditions. **This demonstrates that every effort at societal betterment merely serves to conceal some private crime.**

The functions of the bolded sentences can best be described as

(A) The first states a general principle and the second gives a specific example of its application.
(B) The first gives a specific example of a phenomenon and the second provides a flawed generalization about that phenomenon from that particular instance.
(C) The first describes an example of an action and the second logically generalizes based on that example.
(D) The first cites a historical instance of an activity and the second assesses its future effects.
(E) The first establishes an initial claim contradicted by the rest of the paragraph and the second presents the valid, corrected conclusion.

5. Gene: The movie *A Flame This High* was a tremendous failure. Critics unanimously considered it incoherent and derivative, poorly acted, and shoddily directed, while the subject matter caused a public controversy. The lead actress was unable to land a starring role in any subsequent studio film, the screenwriter never sold another script, and the director was never asked to make another movie. Despite an enormous marketing campaign, other films released at the time easily eclipsed its box office.

Roger: It is inaccurate to call the film a failure. Theatrical release box office revenue, foreign ticket sales, and DVD sales more than recouped the costs of production and marketing, resulting in a net profit.

Roger responds to Gene's argument by

(A) advancing an unproven assumption about the main sources of film revenue
(B) asserting a contrary conclusion by failing to present relevant evidence that Gene's account of the film's effect on the principals' career paths was untrue
(C) refuting Gene's characterization of the film's revenue relative to contemporaneous competing releases
(D) implicitly invoking another measure of a film's success in order to make a comparable assessment of a particular movie's standing
(E) reaching an opposite conclusion by utilizing a different measure to determine whether a film can be accurately termed a failure

6. Norman: Advertising or branding imagery depends on making a lasting impression with consumers, which requires employing images that resonate with the audience. The most powerful such images draw on fundamental character types or figures, such as found in childhood story books, myths, legends, and fairy tales. These are therefore the most effective brand images.

Otto: On the contrary, effective branding can tap contemporary concerns, such as technology or the environment, using potent archetypes drawn from the natural or technological worlds. Advertising campaigns that utilize images drawn from the animal world or from the realm of technology strike a chord with consumers and hence are powerful means of branding.

Otto's response to Norman's argument is flawed as a refutation because it

(A) proposes a diametrically opposed end, to be reached by similar means
(B) mistakenly treats Norman's claim that a particular method is the most effective means of achieving an end as a claim that it is the only such means
(C) posits an inconsistent mechanism with which to evaluate Norman's specific proposition
(D) assumes the validity of Norman's ends even though disagreeing about the means by which to accomplish them
(E) argues that Norman's conception of appropriate means is overly broad

7. <u>Johann</u>: Great civilizations are necessarily founded on strict hierarchy and order. Beethoven's symphonies, which have stood the test of time and are considered great to this day, can be realized only through the subordination of individual musicians' performances to the control and guidance of the conductor.

   <u>Steve</u>: Yet some of the greatest works of jazz, which even decades later command critical acclaim, can be brought to life only through the freely improvised interplay of the musicians' performances, spontaneously responding to each other's actions.

   The reasoning of Steve's response is subject to legitimate criticism because it

   (A) incorrectly treats Johann's claim that something is a cause as an assertion that it is the only cause
   (B) generalizes inappropriately from Johann's specific claim to a wider conclusion
   (C) provides a purported counter-example that actually supports Johann's claim
   (D) needlessly accepts Johann's questionable implicit claim that music is an appropriate proxy indicator of civilization and that what is true of one is true of the other
   (E) introduces additional factors irrelevant to the argument as constructed

8. <u>Victor</u>: The project with which you were involved failed, despite the fact that abundant resources, time, and personnel were committed, and the outcome itself was not subject to chance provided that the project was executed according to proper specifications. I personally examined the project's specifications and judged them to be correct. The only remaining possibility is that the project failed due to your negligence or misdeeds.

   <u>Reed</u>: That is an unjust accusation, because you are also presupposing that you would be able to assess, without error, your own ability to determine the correct specifications.

   Reed responds to Victor's argument by

   (A) providing an alternative conclusion by demonstrating that the facts presented by Victor are in error
   (B) proving the opposite of Victor's conclusion by exploiting an ambiguity in a key term
   (C) offering a counter-example to demonstrate that Victor's conclusion need not depend on his premises
   (D) undermining the validity of Victor's conclusion by positing additional independent causes of the project's success
   (E) reaching a contrary conclusion through identifying a necessary assumption by which Victor's conclusion would follow from his premises

9. Diana: Men in positions of political leadership are biologically, culturally and psychologically prone towards particular types of displays of aggression and confrontation, contributing in international politics to a tendency for crisis escalation, saber-rattling, and even outbreaks of war.

Etta: But women leaders of India and Israel, for example, have taken their countries to war, too.

Etta's refutation of Diana's argument is flawed because it

(A) treats Diana's argument that something is a cause of a phenomenon as though it claimed it were the only such cause
(B) fails to provide necessary counter-examples of male leaders who didn't lead their countries to war
(C) overlooks the fact that both counter-example women leaders were elected
(D) assumes that women leaders' behavior is shaped by something other than biology, culture, and psychology
(E) presupposes that the women leaders selected as counter-examples had no other choice than to go to war

10. Wilson: Dietary plans based on the simple reduction of calories usually fail. The body will respond to a sharply lower caloric intake by decreasing its metabolic rate. Exercise serves the function of forcing the body to maintain or enhance its mobilization of energy from the body's own reserves, the energy stored in body fat tissue. Thus, exercise alone is the sure route to weight loss.

Marisa: I don't see why that must be true. Although dieting alone is unlikely to work well, exercise also increases appetite, since the body will seek to replace the expended calories. For this reason, even if one chooses exercising over dieting as a strategy, careful control of one's eating habits remains necessary if one hopes to realize sustained weight loss.

Marisa responds to Wilson's argument by

(A) proposing that a method previously critiqued as flawed is actually superior to its alternative
(B) contradicting Wilson's conclusion by articulating and refuting an assumption necessary for that conclusion
(C) denying the validity of the conclusion by questioning the existence of the claimed causal mechanism by which it would follow
(D) explaining that the inadequacy of one method of solving a problem does not establish that another method is therefore sufficient
(E) providing an alternative means by which Wilson's conclusion would follow even if the premises were false

11. **Modern viewers of most classic films may find it difficult to muster a complete appreciation of these older works**. For many classics, however, this reflects not how much we have left these old films and their times behind but rather how much these old films remain ever with us in our modern cinema vocabulary. We are unable to be dazzled by a film's accomplishment precisely because what was fresh and wholly original has since become clichéd and conventional. **The famous film *Citizen Kane* contains a swooping camera shot in which the camera pulls back and back and finally out through a window—exhilarating for original audiences, precisely because it was the first such instance of this cinematic invention.** Now, the casual modern viewer is scarcely likely even to notice it. Perhaps he might even dismiss it as corny, unaware that he was witnessing the very birth of this Hollywood staple.

The relationship between the two bolded sentences would best be described as

(A) The former is a conclusion and the latter is a particular example intended to prove the conclusion through analogy.
(B) The former is a point supported by the rest of the paragraph and the latter presents a case when the opposite may be true.
(C) The former is a recommendation and the latter is an example illustrating a key assumption.
(D) The former is a judgment of a situation and the latter is a concrete example proving the validity of that judgment.
(E) The former is a generalized assessment and the latter is a specific instance that would support the assessment, provided the example is representative of the larger group.

12. The majority of restaurants fail within the first three years. **One apparently effective means of minimizing the risk of business failure is to operate a franchise establishment of a larger, well-established chain of restaurants.** The logic is that the pre-existing brand name, national marketing, economies of scale, and standardization of procedure work to insulate the new establishment from important potential sources of failure. Commonly, business analysts buttress this argument by citing a certain famous survey of franchise owners, in which the vast majority reported satisfaction with their franchise arrangement and cited it as a reason for their success. **The problem, however, is that the survey in question polled only those owners who still remained affiliated with the franchise years after they first purchased their franchise rights, thereby excluding all those whose businesses had failed or who had grown dissatisfied and quit.**

The relationship between the first bolded sentence and the second is

(A) The former is an assessment of a business plan and the latter demonstrates that this assessment is untrue.
(B) The former is a conclusion about a business strategy and the latter points out a flaw in methodology that raises doubts about the factual support for that conclusion.
(C) The former is a premise of an argument about business organization and the latter provides evidence about a situation analogous to that form of business organization.
(D) The former is a judgment about the feasibility of a business model and the latter is an objection to the deductive logic behind the model.
(E) The former is a statement supported by the rest of the passage, while the latter is an example of specific supporting evidence.

13. **One method of generating powerful insights for business planning for important unexpected market events is the use of strategic simulations.** These "war games" allow business planners to pose hypothetical "what if" scenarios for future market conditions in the wake of major changes. The explicit consideration of different possible market outcomes prompts business planners to reflect on their optimal responses under such circumstances and to assess their likely ability to implement these plans. In this way, planners consider which capabilities their companies would need to create and which resources they should devote to such purposes, giving rise to novel insights into planning for the unknown and unanticipated. **At the same time, however, in order to design a hypothetical market scenario in the first place, the designers of strategic market simulations must presume that they understand the essential characteristics and probable consequences of particular changes.**

The functions of the two bolded statements are

(A) The former explains a business method while the latter provides an example of its successful application.
(B) The former describes a particular technique and the latter provides an alternative procedure.
(C) The former describes an approach to solving a problem and the latter provides an observation that highlights a potential paradox in the proposed solution.
(D) The former is a judgment supported by the rest of the passage and the latter demonstrates a key supporting point.
(E) The former provides a conclusion about a business procedure and the latter states an irrelevant fact.

14. **In surveys taken at the height of economic booms, business managers consistently report high levels of optimism.** Historically, however, economic booms are almost invariably followed by busts, sharp downturns in the economy. When this occurs, businesses that had been seized by optimism about future prospects of unbroken growth are often found to have greatly over-expanded. Under the new conditions of market turmoil, these businesses are at great risk of failure, precisely because of their prior unfounded optimism. **Thus, pessimism is clearly the smarter attitude.**

The relationship between the two bolded sentences is best described as

(A) The former is a conclusion, while the latter is an assumption that contradicts that conclusion.
(B) The former is a description of a particular example of a phenomenon, while the latter is a conclusion that necessarily follows.
(C) The former is the principal point supported by the rest of the paragraph, while the latter illustrates an exception.
(D) The former is an assessment of a relationship, while the latter is an accurate implication of that relationship.
(E) The former is a description of a correlation, while the latter is a flawed conclusion.

15. Contained in a memo from the Marketing Department at Momentum Motors

Over the last two years, women have gone from under 20 percent of all purchasers of our "Conquista" model to nearly half of all "Conquista" buyers. Starting two years ago, we began a new marketing campaign to emphasize features of the car that our research showed women buyers would prefer. We made significant advertising buys in women's magazines and ran extensive commercials during shows with heavily female audiences. In addition, we sought to circulate among sales staff a list of recommended methods to communicate the benefits of "Conquista" ownership in ways that women would not find condescending—a frequent problem, according to consumer surveys that show women often feel "talked down to" in auto dealerships. **That is why more women today buy the "Conquista" than ever before.**

The relationship between the two bolded statements is best described as

(A) The first is a conclusion explained by the rest of the paragraph and the second is a supporting example.
(B) The first is an assessment of a market outcome and the second is a judgment about the implications of that outcome.
(C) The first is a statement about the causes of a market shift and the second is a correct assessment of the extent and origins of that shift.
(D) The first is a factual observation about a changing market situation and the second is a flawed conclusion about both the causes and character of that change.
(E) The first is a description of a recent alteration in the market and the second is a flawed evaluation of the expected future consequences of that alteration.

16. Charles: Symbiosis is a mutually beneficial relationship between species. Mitochondria are the components within our cells that provide the chemical energy that powers cellular activities. However, rather than having evolved within our cells, mitochondria are thought to have once been completely separate and independent microorganisms. They live within our cells, in effect receiving shelter in exchange for the "rent" of power generation. Thus, sustained interspecies symbiosis is possible, even vital for life as we know it.

Magnus: The truth is that the symbiosis you have described actually originated as a specialized form of biological conquest. Mitochondria were once free-living bacteria that were then wholly engulfed by the earliest eukaryotic organisms, reduced to mere components within a superior species, and remain so subordinated to this very day. Even today, they maintain their own DNA completely separate from our own.

Magnus' response is flawed as a refutation of Charles' argument because it

(A) fails to address the issue of whether mitochondria represent an example of sustained interspecies symbiosis
(B) assumes without direct evidence that all symbiosis originated as biological conquest
(C) never specifies the mechanisms by which mitochondria retain their separate genetic identities
(D) treats Charles' argument as though it were about individual cells rather than entire species
(E) simply contradicts Charles' argument without providing a necessary alternative logic for the argument itself

17. Nancy: Evolutionary biology teaches that enduring affection for others rests most solidly when it relies on some definite shared genetic inheritance. For this reason, the love of a mother for her child will, in almost every case, be greater and longer-lasting than the love of that woman for her husband, which relies merely on an emotional affinity. The foundation of common genetics creates the mother-child love, which then makes the mother willing to care for the child.

Clio: You misunderstand the nature of lasting love, which frequently does arise entirely from emotional affinity. Consider an adoptive mother: caring for a child creates a strong emotional affinity, which in turn creates a lasting mother-child love, without any genes in common. Thus, there is no reason that a husband-wife bond must be any weaker than a mother-child bond.

Clio responds to Nancy's argument by

(A) presenting a counter-example to disprove Nancy's claim that common genetic inheritance can create lasting love
(B) seeking to refute Nancy's argument by providing a counter-example in which some claimed intermediate causal mechanisms were reversed, implying an alternative conclusion
(C) stating a contending general theory and demonstrating that it better explains the original examples
(D) proposing a hypothetical means to conduct comparative testing of the claimed relationships
(E) reasoning by analogy to call into question the original conclusion

18. **In economics, the term "moral hazard" refers to the consequences when an actor is protected against the risk of negative outcomes, and so chooses to take on more risk than he would have in the absence of such protection**. As a result, even a praiseworthy attempt to shield someone from the worst-case scenario can perversely so decrease incentives to exercise care that such a bad outcome becomes more likely. Banks that believe they will receive a government bailout if they lend unwisely will have less reason to conduct their lending activities with due prudence. At the same time, attempts to avoid moral hazard completely can also give rise to unfortunate results. The Federal Reserve remained largely passive during the Great Depression, even as bank failures swept the country and the national economy seized up, sparking massive unemployment. **One explanation for this seemingly inexplicable inactivity was that Federal Reserve officials were so intent on avoiding bailing out irresponsible banks that they simply failed to appreciate the much greater hazard posed by prolonged economic crisis**.

The two bolded sentences are related in such a way that

(A) the former defines a troubling phenomenon and the latter poses a possible instance in which the phenomenon was avoided at great cost
(B) the former explains an economic term and the latter illustrates it through an historical example
(C) the former posits a general principle of economics and the latter supports it through an historical analogy
(D) the former is the conclusion demonstrated by the rest of the passage while the latter is a supporting opinion
(E) the former is a premise establishing a key concept and the latter is the necessary logical conclusion demonstrating its successful application

Check your answers on page 721.

RESOLVE/EXPLAIN QUESTIONS

Resolve/explain questions contain a seemingly contradictory pair of facts. This question will ask you to choose the answer that resolves the paradox. In other words, choose the answer that explains how both facts can simultaneously be true.

Step 1: Read and identify the question
Identify these questions by words such as *resolve* and *explain*.

Step 2: Work the argument
To answer these questions, you don't need to find the conclusion, premise, or assumption. All you need to do is find pieces of information that are potentially in conflict with each other. Look for words such as but, yet, and however to help identify that conflict.

Step 3: Predict what the answer should do
To try and predict what the answer will do, put the conflict into your own words that asks the question that the correct choice will answer.

Step 4: Use POE to find the answer
The correct answer will provide additional information that explains how both facts could be simultaneously true.

POE: Consider each answer choice individually and determine if that answer reconciles the apparent conflict. Common incorrect answer choices are ones that:

- Don't clear up the conflict.
- Make the conflict worse.
- Address only one side of the conflict; i.e., explain why one of the facts is true, but not the other.

Try the example on the next page.

1. In September of last year, the number of people attending movies in theaters dropped precipitously. During the next few weeks after this initial drop the number of filmgoers remained well below what had been the weekly average for the preceding year. However, the total number of filmgoers for the entire year was not appreciably different from the preceding year's volume.

    Which of the following, if true, resolves the apparent contradiction presented in the passage above?

    (A) People under the age of 25 usually attend films in groups, rather than singly.
    (B) The gross income from box office receipts remained about the same as it had been the preceding year.
    (C) For some portion of last year, the number of people attending movies in theaters was higher than it had been during the previous year.
    (D) The number of people attending movies in theaters rises and falls in predictable cycles.
    (E) The quality of films released in September and October of last year was particularly poor.

The question contains the word *resolve* which is a good indication that this is a resolve/explain question. So, look for the conflict in the argument.

The conflict here is *How could the total number of filmgoers for the entire year be the same as the previous year, when the numbers for September were so low?* Now look for an answer that explains that paradox.

Choice (A) does not address the conflict or provide any way that the conflict could be resolved, so eliminate (A). The conflict mentioned in the passage is about attendance, not about money, so (B) does not resolve the conflict. Eliminate (B). Choice (C) explains the conflict. If there was a period of time last year that counteracted the low period in September, that could explain why attendance this year was the same as last year. Keep (C). Choice (D) is close, but it does not specifically explain this situation by stating that there was a high period that counteracted the low period in September. Eliminate (D). Choice (E) only explains one of the facts. It gives a possible explanation of why attendance was low in September, but it does not explain why attendance for the whole year was close to the previous year's attendance. Eliminate (E). The correct answer is choice (C).

For more information on critical reasoning questions, see *Cracking the GMAT, 16th Edition.*

RESOLVE/EXPLAIN DRILL

Questions 1 and 2 are based on the following:

In a recent experiment, half of the participants, the experimental group, consumed a popular energy drink. The other half of the participants, the control group, did not consume the drink. The experimental group showed more signs of sticky blood, a risk for blood clots, than did the control group. Researchers attributed these negative effects to an organic acid that is one of the primary ingredients of the drink.

1. Which of the following, if true, best supports the conclusion that an ingredient of the drink caused the detrimental results described?

   (A) The experimental group members consumed more of the drink than most consumers do.
   (B) Prior to the experiment, no one in either group showed any signs of sticky blood.
   (C) Federal food regulators consider the amount of the drink consumed by the individuals in the experimental group to be safe.
   (D) Some of the proteins that make up the organic acid referred to in the conclusion must be consumed for adequate nutrition.
   (E) In a second experiment in which participants consumed the energy drink, there was no control group of participants who did not consume the drink.

2. Which of the following, if true, is the best explanation of how the energy drink might cause the observed effect?

   (A) According to an analysis by the government, the drink contained high levels of the organic acid.
   (B) The energy drink contains caffeine, which raises the energy levels of consumers.
   (C) The consumers in the experimental group did not notice any adverse reactions to the drink.
   (D) The organic acid contained in the drink can be metabolized relatively quickly.
   (E) A high level of the organic acid increases clotting factors in the blood.

3. A report that a crop of spinach from a major grower had become contaminated apparently did not alarm consumers. Few consumers made plans to change their spinach buying habits after hearing the report. Despite this, after the report came out in late August, spinach sales in supermarkets dropped drastically in the first two weeks of September.

Which of the following, if true, is the best explanation of why spinach sales dropped?

   (A) Because only a small amount of spinach was contaminated, and because that spinach was traced and destroyed, public officials did not believe the contaminated spinach posed a major health threat.
   (B) The report appeared in all the major news outlets, including online.
   (C) Many supermarket chains removed spinach from their shelves in late August in an effort to prevent potential lawsuits.
   (D) Although another grower reported that a crop of squash had become contaminated, the report about the spinach did not mention that fact.
   (E) Due to a dramatic increase in the number of food-safety warnings in recent months, consumers have become increasingly indifferent to such warnings.

4. In a troubled economy, experienced drivers with no moving violations are more likely to lose their cars due to failure to make car payments, than due to accidents in which the vehicle is totaled. Despite this, most banks and finance companies require borrowers to have collision insurance, although they do not require insurance against disability or loss of employment.

Which of the following, if true, best explains the banks' insurance requirements?

(A) Insuring against accidents is generally more expensive than insuring against disability or loss of employment.
(B) Many people don't like to consider the possibility that they may lose their jobs.
(C) Loss of employment or disability of the driver does not affect the value of a vehicle to a bank or finance company.
(D) Some people are more sympathetic to a driver who loses his car due to an accident than to one who loses it due to failure to make payments.
(E) Most employers do not insure their employees against a temporary loss of income due to injuries from a car accident.

5. Although experts predicted an increase in the demand for soybeans, no such increase has occurred in recent years. Despite this, soybean growers increased their profits last year by 8 percent over the level of the previous year, even though prices and production amounts have remained stable during the last 4 years.

Each of the following, if true about last year, helps explain the rise in profits EXCEPT:

(A) Growers were able to save money on costly artificial irrigation, because the amount of rainfall in soybean-growing areas was greater than it had been the previous year.
(B) Oil prices dropped by more than 15%, which enabled soybean growers to harvest their crops more cheaply.
(C) Soybean growers stopped paying laborers an hourly wage and started paying them based on the amount harvested, which resulted in a savings on wages paid.
(D) Several small soybean growers formed a conglomeration of soybean producers which began to buy supplies at discounted group rates.
(E) Although their overall consumption of soybeans decreased, many countries that are large consumers of soybeans increased their production of soybean oil.

6. A consortium of small business owners is lobbying against proposed federal legislation that would require businesses to provide health insurance for their employees. Observers are surprised by this opposition, because the legislation exempts small businesses from the provision.

Which of the following, if true, best explains why the consortium is against the proposed legislation?

(A) Service companies, which typically employ more employees per dollar of revenues than do other types of businesses, make up the majority of small businesses.
(B) Some states already require businesses to provide health insurance for their employees.
(C) It is not known how many companies would be exempt from providing health insurance under the proposed law.
(D) Small businesses must offer benefits that are comparable to those of their larger competitors, who won't be exempt from the law, in order to attract and retain workers.
(E) There is no requirement for businesses to provide health insurance for their employees under current federal law.

7. A man riding a burro down into a canyon passed a sign that read "30" on the side facing him and "32" on its back. The man deduced that the next sign would indicate he was halfway to the bottom of the canyon. However, when he reached the next sign it read "29" facing him and "33" on its back.

Which of the following, if true, would be the best explanation for the discrepancy above?

(A) The facing numbers on each sign indicate distance to the bottom of the canyon, not distance from the top.
(B) The numbers on the signs were in miles, not kilometers.
(C) The signs are intended for the use of hikers, not burro riders.
(D) A sign was missing between the two signs the man encountered.
(E) A vandal had reversed the numbers on the next sign.

8. The diet industry is booming, and according to experts, it will continue to do so. In the United States this year, although the number of adult dieters has decreased, the total number of diet products sold has actually increased.

If true, all of the following could explain the concurrent increase in diet products and decrease in number of adult dieters EXCEPT:

(A) This year, more of the diet products that were manufactured in the United States were exported to other countries than were the year before.
(B) The number of men who have begun to diet during this year is greater than the number of women who have stopped dieting during this same period.
(C) During this year, the number of non-dieters who have begun using diet pills is greater than the number of people who have stopped dieting.
(D) The people who have continued to diet are using more diet products than they have in the past.
(E) During this year, the number of teenagers who have begun dieting is greater than the number of adults who have stopped dieting.

9. Researchers were surprised by the results of an experiment in which human subjects were asked to identify a geometric pattern embedded in a network of abstract shapes and then identify a second pattern that had the same characteristics as the first. Although researchers expected the opposite result, the highest expenditure of energy in the neurons of the brain was discovered in the subjects who performed the least successfully in the experiments.

Which of the following, if true, best accounts for the paradox above?

(A) Athletes, whose energy expenditure is lower when they are at rest, perform better than others in identifying a geometric pattern that has the same characteristics as the first.
(B) The recognition of geometric patterns was more enjoyable to those who performed better in the experiment than to those who did not perform as well.
(C) The neurons of the brain don't react as much when a subject is attempting to recognize geometric patterns than when the subject is participating in deductive reasoning.
(D) A different study has provided evidence that more energy-efficient neural connections are found in those people who are better at geometric pattern recognition.
(E) When a design that duplicates the geometric pattern found in the original network is identified, the energy expenditure of the subjects' brains increases.

10. An experiment was done in which adult virgin female rabbits were exposed to foster rabbit pups for 14 days. The rabbits did not show any maternal responsiveness to the pups. However, when their olfactory bulbs were surgically removed, the rabbits demonstrated maternal behavior within 3 to 13 days of pup exposure.

Which of the following theories best explains the results described above?

(A) The odor of rabbit pups inhibits the development of maternal responsiveness in female rabbits that did not give birth to them.
(B) Virgin female rabbits are less affected by olfactory clues than are female rabbits that have given birth.
(C) Rabbit pups produce more scent in the presence of a female rabbit that did not bear them than they do in the presence of a female rabbit that did bear them.
(D) Rabbit pups have a more acute sense of smell than do adult female rabbits.
(E) A female rabbit that has not given birth shows maternal behavior toward rabbit pups more slowly than does a female rabbit that has given birth.

Check your answers on page 721.

MIXED DRILL

1. A new disease called Probibeleosus has emerged in Oceania. Though non-fatal, Probibeleosus leads to disfigurement, reduced mobility and chronic pain. Medical researchers have thus far discovered two variants of the disease which they have labeled Probibeleosus-A(P-A) and Probibeleosus-B (P-B). Sex partners and siblings of those with P-A are four times as likely as the general population to have P-A. Sex partners of those with P-B are no more likely than the general population to have P-B, but siblings of those with P-B are over eight times more likely to have the disease than the average person.

   Which of the following statements is best supported by the above information?

   (A) Vulnerability to P-B is more likely hereditary than is vulnerability to P-A.
   (B) Of those with P-A, their parents would be no more likely than average to have the condition.
   (C) Somewhere between one-in-eight and one-in-four people in Oceania have either P-A or P-B.
   (D) The sex partners of those who do not have P-A are less likely than average to have P-A.
   (E) Those who have never had sex are less likely to have P-B than P-A.

2. Economic interdependence has long been heralded as a source of international peace and cooperation, even in the face of continued tensions. **Trading nations would be tamed, with too much to lose if crisis erupted into war and severed the complex webs of commerce on which countries' prosperity had come to rely**. Despite this, the combatants of the two World Wars were each other's leading trade partners. High levels of trade and investment between Britain and Germany did little to avert those catastrophic events. **Some historians even argue that pre-WWI German leadership underestimated British resolve and disastrously pursued a harder line, lulled into thinking that the British would back down rather than risk a disruption of trade**. At the same time, the intuitive logic of the proposition that trade breeds peace seems compelling, and the historical record is equally rich in examples of states whose relations have warmed as trade has grown. It is difficult to imagine post-WWII reconciliation between France and Germany in the absence of renewed and deep trade ties.

   The relationship between the two bolded excerpts could best be described as

   (A) The former is a general principle explaining state behavior and the latter is an example of the behavior thus predicted.
   (B) The former is an example of a counter-intuitive outcome and the latter is the proposed relationship between two phenomena.
   (C) The former is a claim about the plausibly foreseeable effects of an aspect of international relations and the latter is an attempt to prove this claim by applying it to an analogous situation.
   (D) The former is a proposition predicting state response to a given phenomenon and the latter is a paradoxical instance in which the opposite result may have proved true.
   (E) The latter is a past case of a predicted phenomenon in action and the former is a set of parameters necessary for it to occur.

3. IgE antibodies protect against parasitic infection by attaching themselves to foreign invaders, serving as flags for other immunological cells, which then destroy and expel the tagged parasite. Allergies occur when IgE antibodies recognize a benign substance—an allergen, such as pollen—as a foreign invader and tag it for destruction, triggering the body's immunologic response system.

Which of the following statements, if true, reveals the most serious flaw in a pharmaceutical company's plan to develop a new allergy drug that would function by preventing IgE antibodies from attaching to allergens?

(A) The drug would be prophylactic only, and would not be able to stop an allergy attack once it had begun.

(B) Scientists have thus far been unable to discover how the body produces the IgE antibodies that attach to allergens.

(C) The drug would be unable to differentiate between allergens such as pollen and parasites such as ringworm.

(D) Scientists don't yet understand what makes some ethnic groups more susceptible to IgE-induced allergies and other groups less.

(E) Due to funding requirements for research, development, and testing, the company would have to raise a great deal of capital, and then the drug still wouldn't be available for several years.

4. Medical students at Middle State University recently formed a union in order to negotiate with the university's administration for health insurance. Since law students have also traditionally not been provided health insurance, and since any campus group is permitted to unionize, Middle State's law students should also form a union in order to negotiate for health insurance.

Which one of the following statements most strengthens the above argument?

(A) There is a university operated clinic on the Middle State campus that treats students for free.

(B) Unionization has been effective for student groups negotiating for benefits such as health care.

(C) The health insurance provided by universities to student groups often doesn't cover visits to psychiatrists or dentists.

(D) The average law student is less concerned with health than the average medical student and therefore will use the health care system less.

(E) Because starting salaries for lawyers are higher than they are for doctors, it is less risky for law students to take on additional debt to pay for health insurance.

5. Oil is often traded as a future commodity before it is produced. If oil production is predicted to fall, the price of oil futures generally rises; if production is predicted to rise, prices generally fall. A hurricane is moving into the Gulf of Mexico, and meteorologists are predicting it will hit active off-shore oil rigs there in the next 48 hours, causing extensive damage and taking them off line for years. Since these rigs generate a significant percentage of world oil production, prices of oil futures will surely rise today.

Which of the following statements, if true, casts the most doubt on the above conclusion?

(A) Most of the production in the Gulf of Mexico comes from rigs off the coast of Texas, on the west side of the Gulf.
(B) Meteorologists are also predicting a second hurricane will make landfall in Mexico later in the week.
(C) Future prices for oil have been more volatile this year than in years past.
(D) The United Nations has announced the lifting of a trade embargo on an oil producing nation in the Persian Gulf.
(E) Traders of oil futures rarely come into physical contact with the barrels of oil they buy and sell.

6. *Prince of Meat*, a fast food restaurant, has relied on revenues from soft drinks to cover slight losses on each hamburger it sells. Recently, the government ended subsidies that had made the sweetener in the soft drinks *Prince of Meat* sells cheaply available. As a result, consumers will be unwilling to pay prices for soft drinks that are any higher than the wholesale price that the restaurant pays for them.

Which of the following statements is best supported by the above information?

(A) Although government subsidies have made sugar substitutes cheaply available, the impact of those sweeteners on public health has yet to be determined.
(B) If *Prince of Meat* cannot sell a hamburger for more than the cost of producing it, it must either stop selling them or take losses if it does.
(C) Customers never purchase hamburgers without also buying a soft drink.
(D) Customers would continue to pay the same price for hamburgers if *Prince of Meat* purchased lower quality beef, so a profit can be made on hamburger sales.
(E) Although soft drink sales to children have typically been very strong, they are presently declining.

7. Responding to customer complaints of high pressure sales techniques being used to sell add-ons such as printers and warranties, a computer company began rewarding its sales agents more for customer satisfaction and less for sales of add-ons. After implementing this change, the company saw increases in both customer satisfaction and sales of add-ons.

All of the following statements could have contributed to the increase in sales under the new reward system, EXCEPT:

(A) Sales agents began to listen more carefully to the stories of repeat customers and consequently were able to sell them relevant add-ons.
(B) After learning that the company had changed its policies in response to their complaints, the customers who had complained recommended the company to their friends, who bought computers and add-ons.
(C) Agents who sold add-on warranties to systems often delayed forwarding the orders to the warranty department, even until after the computers were being used by customers.
(D) Some customers came to trust and like the agents they bought their systems from, so when they needed an add-on, they went back to them instead of to another company.
(E) Customers of other companies that had become wary of their high-pressure sales tactics were attracted to positive reviews of the company's changed policies and eventually become customers.

8. Consumer Advocate: Your finance company operates almost exclusively in low-income urban neighborhoods. The company specializes in "payday" loans, which entail extremely high rates of interest and steep surcharges for what may be only a week or two of lending. Such loans generate returns many times exceeding the industry average, extracted precisely from those who can afford it least and possess the fewest alternatives, and are not consistent with ethical business practices.

Executive: We are serving a population that otherwise is persistently unable to procure credit for life needs. Banks are generally unwilling to make small-scale loans for such short terms, and seldom have a retail storefront presence in inner-city neighborhoods. Our company is in fact providing an important product to a community that stands in dire need of financial services that they cannot easily find elsewhere.

The executive's response to the consumer advocate's criticisms

(A) proposes an alternative general principle under which the company's current fee structure would be ethically justified
(B) disproves the advocate's conclusions by assuming an ethical standard based solely on market outcomes
(C) provides information to confirm why customers would use their services but does not present an explicit justification for the company's fee structure
(D) seeks to redirect the advocate's moral condemnation to other financial institutions' similar practices.
(E) correctly assumes that the criticisms are based on a failure to understand key facts about the company's market and customer base.

Questions 9–10 are based on the following:

Some have argued that open-access fisheries will always be subject to more exploitation than are private fisheries. The reasoning is that each fisherman will be more likely to overfish open-access fisheries because he alone reaps the benefits, while the costs of mitigating measures to prevent the collapse of over-exploited fisheries is borne by all. Despite this, one study of 250 common-access fisheries and 103 private fisheries showed that the open-access fisheries were less exploited than the private ones.

9. In relation to the claim above, the answer to which of the following questions would be most valuable in assessing the significance of the study above?

   (A) Were the fisherman who used the common-access fisheries as prosperous as those who used the private fisheries?
   (B) Did any of the fishermen in the study have a preference for using common-access fisheries over private fisheries?
   (C) Did any of the fishermen in the study fish only common-access fisheries, and no private fisheries?
   (D) Did the private and open-access fisheries in the study have an equivalent level of marine life before any of them were used for fishing?
   (E) Did any of the fishermen in the study use both common-access and private fisheries?

10. Which of the following, if true and known by the fishermen, is the best explanation for the results of the study?

   (A) There are more common-access fisheries than there are private ones.
   (B) It is more difficult to measure the cost of overfishing that is attributable to any particular fisherman in common-access fisheries than in private ones.
   (C) If one fisherman were to overfish a common-access fishery even slightly, the other fishermen are more likely to do so even more, with the result that the ultimate costs to each fisherman outweigh the benefits.
   (D) Both the costs and benefits of overfishing fall to the individual user in private fisheries.
   (E) An individual fisherman would obtain a competitive advantage if he or she were able to catch more fish than other fishermen by overfishing common-access fisheries.

11. A new U.S. magazine will feature reviews, descriptions and discussion of high-end audio equipment. The publishers plan to draw wealthy readers who would consider purchasing such equipment, and thus appeal strongly to advertisers of luxury goods.

All of the following support the publishers' plan, EXCEPT:

   (A) Readers interested in high-end audio equipment tend to be wealthy heads of households who make purchasing decisions.
   (B) A magazine published and distributed in Europe dedicated to high-end audio equipment has succeeded commercially.
   (C) Advertising space in publications geared toward the wealthy tends to sell for significantly higher prices than does advertising space in other publications.
   (D) Those interested in high-end audio equipment tend to devote little leisure time to hobby reading.
   (E) There are no magazines currently in distribution in the U.S. that cover high-end audio equipment.

12. One food writer wrote that reducing the amount of animal products in one's diet can contribute to better health and well-being. Based on this claim, some people are completely eliminating meat from their diets in order to be healthier.

The argument above relies on which of the following assumptions?

(A) Increasing the amount of vegetables and grains in one's diet can contribute to better health.
(B) There will be no corresponding increase in the amount of dairy products in the diets of those who are eliminating meat.
(C) Most food writers believe that some amount of animal products is necessary to a healthy diet.
(D) Not all healthy lifestyles require a vegetarian diet.
(E) Many people who do not eat animal products make decisions for health reasons.

13. Studies reveal that a daily exercise regimen helps stroke survivors regain dexterity in their extremities. Being given an exercise routine and having a consultation with a doctor about the exercise routine have been shown to be effective mechanisms to get patients to exercise daily.

From the above information, which of the following statements can be reasonably inferred?

(A) A stroke survivor that is given a detailed exercise plan and consults her physician about the plan will regain full dexterity in her extremities.
(B) If a stroke survivor is not given an exercise plan and does not consult with a doctor, she will not regain dexterity in her extremities.
(C) Stroke survivors who are given an exercise routine and consult with a doctor about that routine will sometimes regain dexterity in their extremities.
(D) Being given an exercise routine and having a consultation with a doctor about the routine is the best way to help a stroke survivor regain dexterity in their extremities.
(E) Only being given an exercise routine is necessary to regenerate dexterity in the extremities of seniors who have suffered a stroke.

14. The makers of amplifiers are concerned primarily with the needs of the professional musicians who purchase their equipment. Therefore, makers of amplifiers focus on gear that will sound best played at high volumes during live performances.

Which of the following is an assumption made in drawing the conclusion above?

(A) Amateur musicians only purchase gear that professional musicians recommend.
(B) Improvements in amplifier design result only from long testing processes involving studio musicians.
(C) The makers of amplifiers rely heavily on certain regional markets for the majority of their revenue.
(D) Musicians rarely keep informed about new, improved amplifier designs.
(E) Professional musicians do not need equipment that will not be played during live shows.

15. Obtaining technological superiority to competitors used to lead to sustained increased profits because a firm could offer consumers a better product than could its competitors or a similar product at a lower price or with a greater profit margin. Today, however, technological innovation occurs at such a rapid pace that technological superiority is increasingly tenuous. Paradoxically, obtaining technological superiority is more advantageous than ever before.

Which of the following, if true, most helps to resolve the above paradox?

(A) Potential investors and employees perceive technological advantage as evidence of a company's solid foundation.
(B) Potential investors and employees are increasingly aware of the tenuousness of technological advantage.
(C) Acquisitions of small, new companies are often made by older, larger companies in order to bolster their image.
(D) When it was easier to maintain a technological advantage, it was also easier to reap profits from that advantage.
(E) The rapid pace of innovation makes it difficult for a company to compare its technological sophistication with that of its competitors.

16. A professor of anthropology recently published a study titled "The Decline of Agriculture among Indigenous Tribes of Brazil," in which she argues that much agricultural knowledge among the native people of Brazil has been lost over the last 30 years. Her analysis must be correct, since compared to 20 interviews of Brazilian natives made 30 years ago, her interviews of 20 natives taken during her recent trip to Brazil clearly show the contemporary natives to be much less knowledgeable about agriculture.

Which of the following demonstrates the most serious logical weakness in the above analysis?

(A) The agricultural methods used by natives of Brazil could be less knowledge-intensive than the methods used by natives in other countries.
(B) The title of the study could bias readers toward the professor's hypothesis before reading the study.
(C) The interviewees could be selected to support the professor's hypothesis.
(D) A reader not familiar with native Brazilian agricultural techniques might not agree with the professor's assessment of the natives' farming ability.
(E) There could be other factors in determining the skill of a farmer besides agricultural knowledge.

Check your answers on page 721.

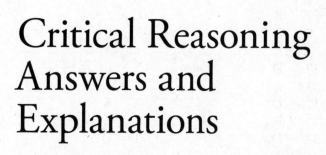

Critical Reasoning
Answers and
Explanations

ANSWER KEY

Weaken

1. B
2. D
3. C
4. C
5. D
6. A
7. B
8. E
9. E
10. D
11. B
12. D
13. B
14. D
15. A
16. A
17. B
18. E
19. A
20. A
21. C
22. C
23. E
24. C
25. E
26. B
27. D
28. A

Strengthen

1. B
2. E
3. C
4. A
5. D
6. C
7. A
8. B
9. E
10. C
11. A

12. D
13. C
14. D
15. A
16. C
17. D
18. D

Assumption

1. A
2. E
3. B
4. A
5. B
6. E
7. E
8. C
9. D
10. E
11. D
12. C
13. B
14. A
15. D
16. B
17. D
18. E
19. C
20. C
21. D
22. D
23. B
24. B
25. A
26. B
27. D
28. C

Inference

1. D
2. E
3. D
4. E
5. B
6. E

7. D
8. A
9. B
10. C
11. A
12. B
13. A
14. C
15. C
16. A
17. B
18. C
19. D
20. C
21. E
22. D
23. E
24. D

Evaluate

1. B
2. D
3. C
4. B
5. A
6. E
7. A
8. C
9. E
10. D
11. D
12. E
13. B
14. A
15. C
16. E
17. E

ID Reasoning

1. C
2. D
3. C
4. B
5. E
6. B

7. D
8. A
9. B
10. C
11. A
12. B
13. A
14. C
15. C
16. A
17. B
18. A

Resolve/Explain

1. B
2. E
3. C
4. C
5. E
6. D
7. A
8. B
9. D
10. A

Mixed Drill

1. A
2. D
3. C
4. B
5. D
6. B
7. C
8. C
9. D
10. C
11. D
12. B
13. C
14. E
15. A
16. C

EXPLANATIONS

Weaken

1. **B**   Choices (A), (C), and (E) all deal with issues that are irrelevant to the argument. Choice (D), meanwhile, is out of scope, because even if drivers didn't want to switch to electric cars, the argument is only concerned with the environmental impact that would occur if they did. Choice (B) directly affects the conclusion; if electric cars are significantly more energy-efficient than gasoline-powered ones, then less fossil fuel would be needed to run them.

2. **D**   The argument concludes that American cell-phone users don't have to worry about radiation exposure because handsets sold in the U.S. are under stricter radiation guidelines than those sold in Europe. Choice (A) only talks about a greater number of phone calls, but offers no information on how long those calls are. Choices (B) and (E) are out of scope; both other risk factors and lack of concern are irrelevant. Choice (C), meanwhile, only mentions longer average phone calls, with no information on the frequency of those calls. However, if (D) were true, then Americans would still be risking radiation exposure, regardless of the level of handset emissions.

3. **C**   Choice (A) weakens the conclusion by pointing out an alternative to *bad quality* as a cause of higher modern divorce rates. Choice (B) undermines the conclusion by suggesting that unhappy marriages in past generations may have stayed intact for reasons other than quality. Choice (C), in contrast, leaves open the possibility that modern marriages may not be as good as those of previous eras; just because couples are seeking counseling doesn't mean they're staying together. Meanwhile, (D) may sound negative on modern marriages, but *only slightly better* still means they're better; eliminate it. Finally, regarding (E), if marital partners in past generations were unfaithful to their spouses, that would weaken the conclusion.

4. **C**   The company's projected emissions reduction makes a number of assumptions, including that employees commute in carbon-emitting automobiles. Choice (A) doesn't provide enough information on how fuel efficient the workers' cars are. Choice (B), meanwhile, has nothing to do with carbon emissions. However, if (C) is true, then most Flimco employees do not drive their cars to work even when they do come to the office, so letting those people work from home will not make a significant difference in carbon emissions. Choice (D), on the other hand, is out of scope, while (E) is not strong enough, since it only refers to some of Flimco's employees.

5. **D**   To locate the correct answer, cross out anything that inhibits the number or effectiveness of new advertising opportunities for Lemming County businesses. If (A) is true, then Minion County residents are already aware of what those businesses have to offer. Choice (B), meanwhile, suggests that cable subscribership is falling among Minion County's population, while (C) points out that the merger will not bring Lemming County businesses significantly more advertising opportunities. Choice (D), however, does not affect the conclusion, because Yang Cablevision is already in Lemming County. Meanwhile, (E) poses budgetary problems for anyone wishing to advertise on the merged networks.

6.   A   The argument assumes that Bleak County residents own the homes they occupy. If (A) were true, then it negates that assumption, so hang onto it. As for (B), you don't know whether those home-owners will actually buy solar hot water systems, nor do you know whether those systems will result in significant energy savings. Choice (C) does little to weaken the argument, since it suggests that costs will still rise, while (D) is irrelevant, since the study cited in the argument already tells you that housings costs are high. Meanwhile, (E) does not provide enough information as to the degree of harshness of the prior winter or for the coming one.

7.   B   The argument cites the current financial burden faced by many Americans, assuming that a switch to socialized medicine will not significantly compensate for any expenses it incurs. Choice (A) does not tell you whether the medical tax breaks it mentions will be discontinued, so eliminate it. Choice (B), on the other hand, indicates that socialized medicine could have a significantly posi-tive financial effect, so keep it. Choice (C), in contrast, is out of scope, while (D) doesn't focus on cost. Finally, (E) only tells you how the current system works; coverage under socialized medicine could prove more affordable for citizens.

8.   E   Be careful of the twists in the question. You need to weaken the argument, which means—in this case—to defend C.W.'s hiring of efficiency consultants. Choice (A) is out of scope, while (B), (C), and (D) have no impact on the author's conclusion. On the other hand, if (E) were true, then the payoff from hiring the consultants could be delayed but still potentially rewarding.

9.   E   The argument claims that canning is safe because it kills microorganisms and external contami-nants, assuming that nothing with regard to the cans themselves poses a health threat. Choice (A) is about nutrition, not safety, so eliminate it. Choice (B), meanwhile, tells you that canning and other foods have similar shelf lives, but doesn't mention a safety threat specific to canning, so eliminate that one, too. Eliminate (C) also, since that one's not about safety. Choice (D) tells you to discard two-year-old canned goods, but you don't know whether that's for safety reasons. That leaves (E), which addresses a potential health threat from canning.

10.   D   The argument assumes that vouchers subvert discrimination. Choice (A) doesn't challenge that assumption, while (B) is out of scope. Choice (C), meanwhile, is irrelevant, since you don't know whether those teachers opposed to vouchers have any say in school admissions. Choice (D), on the other hand, poses a potential discrimination problem; parents may try to enroll their children in a particular school but be turned down for racial or ethnic reasons. Finally, (E) does not necessarily apply to Clink County.

11.   B   The conclusion assumes that prisons aren't keeping the number of offenses from increasing. Choice (A) doesn't challenge that assumption, but (B) does, so keep the latter. Choice (C), meanwhile, is out of scope. Besides, it doesn't tell you the extent to which criminals serving longer sentences are better reformed than those serving shorter ones; the difference may be insignificant. Finally, (D) is irrelevant and (E) is out of scope.

12. **D** The conclusion overlooks the potentially positive side of shorter hospital stays. Choice (A) does not challenge the assumption that shorter stays mean a decrease in the quality of hospital care, so eliminate it. Choice (B), on the other hand, suggests that the assumption could be true, so eliminate it too. Choice (C) does not address the overall trend of shorter hospital stays, so it's out of scope. However, if (D) were true, then the shorter stays could be a sign of better quality care; keep it. Finally, (E) would only strengthen the author's conclusion. The correct answer is (D).

13. **B** The argument overlooks the environmental upside of space research. Eliminate (A), since it only strengthens the author's conclusion. Choice (B), however, points out an environmental benefit, so keep it. Choices (C) and (D), meanwhile, are out of scope, and (E) is irrelevant.

14. **D** The argument assumes, among other things, that the water types tested were representative samples, and that bacteria pose the only significant health threat to drinking water. Eliminate (A), because even if it were true, it could be that most home plumbing systems are properly maintained. While you're at it, cross off (B), since that one has to do with taste and not health. Choice (C) only compares different kinds of bottled water, so toss that one, but keep (D), since it clearly challenges a major assumption in the argument. Choice (E) strengthens the argument.

15. **A** The automaker and the analysts both assume that technology development is not an important factor in profits. Choice (A), however, challenges that assumption, so keep it. Choice (B), in contrast, is out of scope, and (C) strengthens the automaker's and analysts' reasoning; eliminate those two. Choices (D) and (E) are both irrelevant.

16. **A** This is a "LEAST-weaken" question, so cross off anything that challenges the author's assumptions. Choice (A) is out of scope, so keep it. Each of the remaining choices, however, negates a key assumption in the argument. The author assumes that money is not an issue when it comes to pursuit of mental-health treatment, desire for plastic surgery means a person is troubled, the people seen on Wilshire Boulevard are a random sample of all people, and pursuit of mental health treatment is not a sign of greater emotional maturity. Choices (B) through (E) address and negate all of those assumptions.

17. **B** The study findings assume that being motivated, conscientious, and outgoing are traits that can be accurately identified by teachers, and that teachers' feelings toward students have no significant impact on the success of those students. Choices (A), (C), and (E) are all out of scope, but if (B) were true, then the causal assumption that certain traits lead to success would be weakened (teachers' feelings = success). While (D) could also potentially weaken the argument, the word *some* makes it less effective at undermining the conclusion than is (B).

18. **E** The argument assumes that all women get their health coverage from employers and that the anti-discrimination laws that apply to that coverage are enough to guard against healthcare discrimination in general. Neither (A) nor (B) necessarily applies to women, so eliminate those. Choice (C), meanwhile, is out of scope, and (D) doesn't specify whether women are singled out more often for preexisting conditions than men are. Choice (E), if true, would leave women outside the protection of federal antidiscrimination laws affecting health coverage.

19. **A** The argument assumes that just because dynamic stretching is more effective than static stretching is in increasing power, range, and flexibility, dynamic stretching entails less injury risk. Choice (A) challenges that assumption, so keep it. Choices (B) through (E), on the other hand, all deal with issues that are out of the scope of the argument.

20. **A** The argument assumes, among other things, that because vinyl records sound better than CDs or digital clips when played on optimum equipment, people will have regular access to that kind of equipment. If (A) were true, however, it would negate that assumption. On the other hand, even if (B) were true, people might still have access to high-end equipment, whether or not they'd pay high prices for brand names. Similarly, regarding (C), people may find ways to get high-end audio equipment, whether or not it's more expensive. Besides, (C) doesn't tell you how much more expensive analog systems are than their digital counterparts. Choice (D) is out of scope. As for (E), whether or not *many individuals* can tell the difference in quality may have some bearing on the argument, but (E) is not as strong as (A).

21. **C** The author assumes that structural integrity is determined less by design and building quality than by the type of construction materials used. Choice (A) is irrelevant, while (B) is out of scope. Choice (C), on the other hand, tells you that of the clay structures still standing, most were built by skilled people, so hang onto that one. Neither (D) nor (E) is within the scope of the argument.

22. **C** The conclusion assumes that demand for particular services means that those services will have a high market value, and that learning their technical foundations is needed to offer those services. Choice (A) neither addresses nor challenges those assumptions, while (B) actually strengthens the author's argument. However, if (C) were true, then the wireless application market could become saturated, particularly with relatively unskilled people. Choices (D) and (E) are both out of scope.

23. **E** In asserting the safety of *run-flat* tires, the author assumes that people whose cars are so outfitted will know when their tires are damaged and get their cars serviced in time to avoid accidents. Choices (A) through (C) do not address safety, so they can be eliminated. As for (D), run-flat tires may be safe enough following a road hazard that no spare tire is needed. On the other hand, if (E) is true, then drivers may not realize their tires are damaged and thus drive them past the point of reliability.

24. **C** The author asserts that Web page accessibility is enhanced by adherence to Web code standards. That assumes, among other things, that people visiting standards-compliant pages have browsers modern enough to read those pages correctly, and that a significant number of Web visitors do not wish to access older, non-compliant pages. Choice (A) brings up a good-sounding objection, but it doesn't challenge the author's main assumptions. Choice (B) assumes that the latest Web-publishing software is needed to create standards-compliant pages. On the other hand, if (C) were true, then accessibility could be reduced, since many site visitors might not be able to view their favorite pages correctly. Choice (D) is out of scope and (E) is irrelevant.

25. **E** The author assumes that controlled conditions and use of salvaged materials make prefabricated construction more economical than other building methods. Choice (A) offers some argument against the author's conclusion, so keep it. Choice (B) is out of scope. Even if (C) were true, prefab construction could still be a more economical choice in areas where it is available. Choice (D), like (A), raises an objection that could affect the cost of prefab construction; keep it too. Choice (E) specifically addresses costs, so it weakens the author's argument more effectively than either (A) or (D) does.

26. **B** The farmer's stated purpose isn't making more money, rather it is reducing the number of flies, so (A) is incorrect. Choices (C) and (E) will both have to be addressed by the farmer, and may cause him additional costs, but they do not interfere with the plan as it is stated. The approach of Australian farmers may be similar, but it may also have critical differences; you cannot say that based on the failure of the Australian farmer, this farmer will also fail, so (D) is incorrect. However, if each chicken will produce more fly larva, via their manure, than each chicken can consume, the result of raising chickens will be a net *increase* in fly larva population, which means the farmer's plan will be counter-productive.

27. **D** The CFO's logic doesn't address sex differences, so (A) is not relevant. If (B) were true, that would make the training program even *more* expensive in the future, so that would strengthen the CFO's argument. For (C), you don't know if workers who complete part of the program have a greater or lesser chance of filing a claim than those who don't participate in the program at all, nor do you know if anyone would complete only part of the training, so you cannot draw conclusions based on that statement. Regarding (E), the CFO's logic addresses only the cost of the program, the cost of claims and the probability of workers filing claims, so a statement about the methods used is irrelevant. For (D), if a claim were to result in additional expenses in insurance, on top of the $1,900 quoted by the CFO, that would make the training program more attractive, since it would prevent even more costly claims.

28. **A** Looking at (A), if the approach of common plant-eating animals triggers the same warning as the approach of a lion, it would cause the photographers to run for cover much more often than necessary, making it harder for them to perform their job. This would weaken. Choice (B) is not relevant, unless it suggests that the technique is effective, in which case it strengthens the photographers' proposal. Choice (C) proposes a different way to deal with the threat, but it doesn't change the effectiveness of the original proposal. Similarly, (D) addresses an alternative approach —it doesn't have anything to do with the original proposal; if anything, it highlights a need for the photographers' proposal. Choice (E) describes the mechanism through which birds are alerted to the presence of the approaching predators, but it doesn't change the effectiveness of the proposal.

Strengthen

1. **B**   The conclusion of the argument is that the government should guarantee loans between banks to help non-bank businesses; the premises are that non-banks need credit and that in an environment lacking trust, banks won't lend to other banks. So to help the argument you need to bridge the gap, which is between banks lending to banks and banks lending to other kinds of businesses. Choices (A), (C), and (E) would all weaken the conclusion of the argument; eliminate them. Choice (D) is unrelated. Choice (B) makes the link between lending to banks and helping non-bank businesses.

2. **E**   To support Maggie Maid Service's plan, you need to show that morale will be boosted by the things it plans to do (childcare, parking, education). Maggie Maid Service's competitors are irrelevant, so eliminate (A). Choice (B) actually hurts the company's plan, so eliminate it. The specifics of the job situation for maids doesn't actually affect whether these steps will be effective, so eliminate (C) and (D). Choice (E) shows that Maggie Maid Service can address a source of dissatisfaction by improving parking.

3. **C**   The conclusion, that Devron employees made up the productivity on other days, requires you to assume that KaleeCo is at least as productive as Devron, and you are not given information about that in the argument. Whether the sick days were properly categorized, the profitability of the companies, the industry they're in—all of these things are irrelevant to the conclusion, so eliminate (A), (D), and (E). The actual health of the employees isn't actually related to sick days or profitability (you should only be concerned with loss of productivity from sick days, not who's healthier) so eliminate (B). Choice (C) tells you that the two companies are equally productive, so it's the strongest answer.

4. **A**   The new group believes that South America was not settled by boat, since there was a possibility it was settled by land. For this to be true, you need some evidence that the possibility of a land settlement would in some way invalidate the possibility of a boat settlement. Choice (A) gives you that. Choices (B) and (D) somewhat weaken that conclusion; (C) and (E) are not actually relevant to the conclusion.

5. **D**   The conclusion is that since Itzak's dog does not display hip dysplasia, it is not a German shepherd. For this to be true, then you must assume that all German shepherds do display hip dysplasia, which is what (D) states. Choice (E) invalidates that idea, so eliminate it. You know that (B) and (C) must be true from the passage, so they do nothing to strengthen the argument. Choice (A) is not relevant; Itzak's dog does not display hip dysplasia.

6. **C**   The conclusion is that A will win the election, based on the sole premise that A's favorability ratings are higher than B's. You need some evidence to connect favorability ratings to electoral success: (C) gives you that. Choices (A), (B), (D), and (E) are not relevant to the scope of the argument, dealing with things that are not clearly about favorability or winning elections.

7. **A**   The argument states that the proposed tax increase will derive no additional revenue, because consumer spending will fall. For this to happen, consumers must be able to control their level of spending, which is what (A) states. The opposition of consumers to either taxes or the program is not relevant, since the argument is about their spending, not their voting; eliminate (B), (C), and (D). The sufficiency of the tax is also irrelevant, so eliminate (E).

8. **B**   The conclusion you need to support is that power lines do NOT interfere with the guidance system of migratory birds. The evidence offered is that there are not more records of birds lost near power lines than far from them. For the argument to hold, you would need to know that the records, both near and far from the power lines, were reliable. Choice (B) gives you this assurance. The acceptance of the theory being refuted is not important, so eliminate (C). Nor is it necessary to understand everything about the guidance system, so eliminate (A). And for the purposes of the argument, it is not essential to prove the strength of the power line's magnetic field, so (D) and (E) can be eliminated as well.

9. **E**   Choices (A) and (B) might actually weaken Dvorak's claim that it was operator error, by indicating something about the cars as a group and eliminating the possibility that they were worked harder in a hot environment. Choice (C) might weaken the argument, indicating that the customers might be familiar with operating a car. Choice (D) is irrelevant to a discussion of air conditioning.

10. **C**   The reason given that the Elba will not have their own state is that they currently live in different states. The missing link is that the Elba state cannot be composed of pieces of different states. Choice (C) gives that missing link. Again, focusing on the link between the conclusion and premises shows that (A), (B), (D), and (E) are all out of scope, although they sound plausible.

11. **A**   The conclusion that additional dentifrice is required assumes that fluoride alone is not sufficient. Choice (A) states this. Choice (B) actually weakens the argument. Choices (C) and (D) are outside the scope of the argument, and (E) by itself does not make the connection between other types of teeth cleaning and dental health.

12. **D**   The missing link here is the connection between computers in schools and math scores. Choice (D) makes that connection. Choices (A) and (B) are not relevant to connecting computers and math; eliminate them. Choice (C) connects test scores and computers, but the argument requires a connection between computers and math scores specifically. Choice (E) weakens the conclusion.

13. **C**   To strengthen the argument you need to connect interest to turnout; Choice (C) does this. Spending is not mentioned, nor is the type of voting machine relevant, so eliminate (A) and (E). Choice (B) might seem tempting, but more registered voters is not important, because the argument is about an average, not a total. Choice (D) might actually undermine the argument; eliminate it.

14. **D**   Here the conclusion goes beyond the information given in the premises; the premise is that there are no serious side effects, and the conclusion is that there are no side effects whatsoever. You need to show that no serious side effects means no side effects at all. Choice (A) will actually undermine the validity of the study; eliminate it. Choices (B) and (C) are outside the scope; eliminate them.

Choice (D) shows that no serious side effects means no side effects at all. Choice (E) makes the study seem more credible, but offers no information about side effects, so eliminate it.

15. A The conclusion is that the firm will increase its profits through subcontracting, if the subcontractor can do the task more cheaply. This assumes that the main firm can still charge more than the cost of the subcontracting and pocket the difference. Choice (A) basically says this. Choice (B), although plausible, does not prove the wisdom of subcontracting; eliminate it. Choices (C), (D), and (E) are not particularly relevant to the scope of this argument; eliminate them.

16. C Incomplete proteins are irrelevant to the question, so (A) is not correct. Choice (B) argues that tofu is a good source of protein, which works against the conclusion in the question stem, so (B) is incorrect. If, as in (C), protein from chicken or beef is more easily used by the body than is protein from tofu, that strengthens the conclusion that chicken and beef are better sources of protein than is tofu. Choice (D) is an outside knowledge trap: whether people eat protein only from soy beans or only from animals or from a mix of the two is irrelevant to the argument's logic, which addresses only whether chicken and beef or tofu are a better source of protein. Choice (E) compares various sources of soy protein, but doesn't discuss animal protein, so it cannot strengthen the argument that animal protein is the better source.

17. D For (A), you don't know if the propane could be sold more cheaply than competitors', or even if it is feasible, so you don't know that (A) affects the company's plan at all. Since you don't know anything about the price of Valleys and Rivers Outdoor Equipment's stoves, or their competitors', (B) cannot be correct. The fact that a competing company is pursuing a similar plan says nothing about how effective Valleys and Rivers Outdoor Equipment's plan will be, so (C) is incorrect. If, however, as in (D), users like Valleys and Rivers Outdoor Equipment's stove better than their competitors', they will be likely to want to continue to use it, in which case they will have to by propane canisters from Valleys and Rivers Outdoor Equipment. Keep this choice. For (E), increased sales of camping stoves would apply to all companies, not just Valleys and Rivers Outdoor Equipment, and while it may be good for the company, it isn't due to the plan described in the question stem, so (E) is incorrect.

18. D You're looking for a statement that strengthens the conclusion that it was something in the wine that caused the wine drinkers to have higher HDL levels than the non-wine drinkers. Choice (A) is a true statement, but offers no support for the conclusion. Eliminate it. Choice (B) may also be true, but the conclusion (and question) is concerned only with what happened within the experiment, so (B) is irrelevant. Eliminate (B). Choice (C) is also true, but you're looking for the cause of increased HDL levels, not an effect of HDL levels, which is what (C) addresses. Eliminate (C). For (D), if the group that drank the wine had higher HDL levels prior to the experiment, the conclusion that the wine caused their higher levels would be weakened. Therefore, eliminating that possibility strengthens the conclusion that some component of the wine was responsible. Keep this choice. Choice (E) suggests that it is not the alcohol in red wine that has a causative effect, but alcohol isn't the only agent in red wine that could be the causal factor. If it were, (E) would weaken the conclusion since it wasn't the alcohol that caused the increased HDL levels.

Assumption

1. **A** The premises discuss financial problems that could potentially reduce college enrollment, but do not mention skills. Choice (A) bridges the gap between the premises and conclusion by citing a direct relationship between higher education and skills. Choice (B), in contrast, is out of scope, since it talks about trade schools, while (C) pits community colleges against state colleges. Choice (D) is irrelevant because it compares on-the-job training programs to those at technical schools. Meanwhile, (E) makes a prediction and is out of scope.

2. **E** Choice (A) is out of scope; it doesn't matter whether the library's books are as culturally-diverse as its other forms of media. Choice (B), in contrast, weakens the argument by pointing out another source of cultural enrichment for Midgeville residents. Choice (C) makes a prediction and is thus out of scope, while (D) is irrelevant. However, (E) is essential to the argument, since it suggests that a funding cut could hurt the most significant source of culture to the town's residents.

3. **B** Be careful here. Choice (A) is relevant but it weakens the author's argument; if people did not act strangely in most universes, then the "many worlds" theory could remain valid. Choice (B), on the other hand, clearly is necessary to reach the conclusion, because if weird acts were plentiful among different universes, you should see more of them occurring in whatever universe you happen to occupy. In contrast, (C), (D), and (E) are all irrelevant to the author's reasoning.

4. **A** In concluding that retailers lose profit by discounting certain goods, the author necessarily assumes that customers lured by sale items don't buy significant quantities of non-discounted items. Choice (A) addresses that assumption, so it's worth keeping. Choice (B), in contrast, is irrelevant, while (C), (D), and (E) all discuss things that are beyond the scope of the argument.

5. **B** In concluding that the increased fines are unfair, the author assumes that there are no potential benefits to city residents. Choice (A) doesn't discuss any positives for citizens, but (B) is essential to the author's conclusion; the tight restrictions don't even free up parking spaces that could otherwise benefit residents. Choice (C) is beyond the scope of the argument, while (D) and (E) do nothing to link the author's premises to her conclusion.

6. **E** The argument concludes that public screenings reduce future healthcare costs, assuming that the reason many people don't take preventive measures is that their access to health professionals is limited. Choice (A) is not essential to the author's conclusion; eliminate it. Choice (B) is more of a prediction than an assumption, so you can eliminate that one, too. Choices (C) and (D), meanwhile, may or may not be true, but neither is essential to the author's conclusion. On the other hand, (E) would have to be true before the author's argument could be validated, otherwise the screenings will not contribute to preventive measures that could reduce healthcare costs.

7. **E** The argument overlooks the potential health benefits of chlorine in drinking water, assuming that removing the chemical will only have a positive effect. Choice (A) cites another potential health hazard, but even if there is lead in tap water, it could still be beneficial to remove the chlorine.

Bottled water, meanwhile, is beyond the scope of the argument, so eliminate (B). Choice (C) is irrelevant and can also be eliminated, since parts replacement has nothing to do with health. As for (D), it goes too far; the author doesn't assume that all tap water has too much chlorine. That leaves (E), which is essential to the author's conclusion because it rules out chlorine's potential benefits.

8. **C** The author links compensation to talent, assuming that limits on executive pay are restrictive enough to discourage leaders with enough ability to tackle current financial problems. Choice (A) may be true, but it's not essential to the author's conclusion, while (B) works against it. Choice (C), on the other hand, bridges the gap between the premises and conclusion, so hang onto that choice. As for (D), since the argument suggests that the compensation limits are still in the proposal stage, we can't be sure that current executives aren't paid enough, so cross out that choice. Finally, (E) goes too far; it could be that all managers are opposed to pay limits, but that could also not be true. Neither scenario affects the argument much.

9. **D** The conclusion links opposition to a dictator's policies to support for democracy, but there is no evidence of such a connection in the argument's premises. Choice (A), if true, would weaken the argument, so you can eliminate that one. Choice (B), meanwhile, is out of scope. Choice (C) is too strong; the author doesn't go that far in making assumptions. In contrast, (D) would provide the additional evidence needed to connect the premises to the conclusion, so hang onto it. Finally, (E) is outside the scope of the argument.

10. **E** The argument assumes that, because they are not as potent as fresh fruits and vegetables, vitamins don't offer significant nourishment. Choice (A) is too strong; the author doesn't go that far. Choices (B) and (C), meanwhile, are beyond the scope of the argument. Choice (D) may or may not be true, and is also outside the argument's scope. Choice (E) would have to be true for the conclusion to be valid. Even if vitamins only have some of the nutritional benefits of fresh produce, they would still offer a dietary advantage to people who would not otherwise get such nutrients from food.

11. **D** The argument considers a reduction in fatigue that might occur if workers commuted less, but overlooks another potential source of fatigue that could be created by longer workdays. Choice (A) introduces a causal assumption that has nothing to do with the author's conclusion, so eliminate it. Choices (B) and (C), meanwhile, may be true but are out of scope. Choice (D), in contrast, would have to be true for the conclusion to be valid, so hang onto it. Finally, (E), like (B) and (C), is beyond the argument's scope.

12. **C** The argument assumes that immediate access is the primary factor affecting efficient communication. Choice (A) may seem necessary to the author's point, but it could still be possible to communicate quickly without knowing all of a technology's features. Meanwhile, (B) is irrelevant. Keep (C), because the latter rules out a possible negative consequence of the new technology. Choice (D) goes too far to be an assumption; it's possible that recent technology is just about as good as *the latest*. Finally, (E) is beyond the scope of the argument, because you can't know whether the coverage increased steadily or sporadically.

13. **B**   The author assumes that conflict and health are causally related. Choice (A) may look good, but it's not essential to this argument, since the study relies on anecdotal data that don't necessarily have a starting point. Choice (B), on the other hand, rules out an alternate explanation for the study results, so keep it. Choice (C), in contrast, is irrelevant, as is (D), which doesn't affect the correlation between conflict and health. Finally, (E) is beyond the argument's scope.

14. **A**   The author denies a connection between secondhand smoke and heart disease, assuming that the decrease in the heart attack rate before the ban had nothing to do with reduced exposure to cigarette smoke. Choice (A) rules out that possibility, so keep it. Choice (B), in contrast, could be true but is irrelevant to the argument. Choices (C) and (D), meanwhile, are out of scope, so eliminate those. Finally, (E) compares heart-attack rates in Italy to those of other nations, something out of the argument's scope.

15. **D**   The environmentalists assume that complying with regulations is the only way to reduce carbon emissions. Choices (A) and (B) are beyond the scope of the argument. Choice (C), if it were true, might strengthen the argument, but it's really out of scope. On the other hand, (D) rules out another way that carbon emissions might be reduced, justifying the environmentalists' fears, so hang onto it. Finally, (E) is too extreme.

16. **B**   Among the assumptions the author makes is that traditional methods are more effective than alternative ones, even though she offers no information about traditional medicine. Choice (A) is out of scope, but (B) addresses a key assumption, so keep it. Choice (C) is irrelevant, while (D) is not necessary to reach this argument's conclusion; whether or not the participants had used traditional therapies, none of them felt that their alternative treatments had worked. Meanwhile, (E) could be true, but it's well beyond the scope of the argument.

17. **D**   The author says that a macro understanding of a business improves morale, then concludes that giving workers full responsibility for part of a project leads to better morale. The argument assumes a link between *big picture* and responsibility for a project segment. Choice (A) may be true, but there could be other ways to motivate workers besides giving them responsibilities, so cross that one out. Choice (B), on the other hand, is too extreme, while (C) is a lot like (A) (there could be other effective management styles). Choice (D) addresses a key assumption, so keep that choice, but eliminate (E), as it is too strong.

18. **E**   The author recommends fish oil in pill form as a way of avoiding potential marine toxins, but provides no information as to whether the pills are free of such toxins. Eliminate (A), as it is irrelevant. Choice (B) sounds good, but is not necessary to support the author's conclusion; people may be willing to compromise some nutritive value if they can avoid toxins. Both (C) and (D) are beyond the scope of the argument. Choice (E), in contrast, directly addresses a key assumption.

19. **C**   The author claims that people who complain about pop music lyrics are hypocrites, but that can only be true if those people embraced their own generation's music, which, the author maintains, was also criticized in its time. Choice (A) may be true, but it has no impact on the argument.

Meanwhile, (B) is out of scope, since it talks about drug use and not lyrics. Choice (C), in contrast, is essential to the author's conclusion; keep it. Finally, (D) is irrelevant and (E) is not necessary to the author's conclusion, because the argument is about people who criticize the lyrics, which they may be familiar with via reading them rather than just hearing them.

20. C The assumption in the manager's argument is that a bachelor's degree is indicative of intelligence and anyone without a bachelor's degree does not have enough intelligence for the job. Look for an answer choice that reflects this. Choice (A) is not an assumption of the argument but an extension of the manager's thinking, so eliminate (A). Choice (B) makes a comparison about the importance of different skills that the manager does not address in the argument, so eliminate (B). Choice (C) is a good paraphrase, so keep it. Choice (D) discusses the merits of a bachelor's degree, but is not an essential assumption in the argument, so eliminate (D). Choice (E) can also be eliminated because it discusses the relative importance of factors in hiring decisions, which is not an assumption of the argument. The correct answer is (C).

21. D The question says nothing of nations or their markets; there is nothing to suggest that different products are needed for different markets, so (A) is not correct. The conclusion says that only technologies falling within the parameters for use in competitions are what manufacturers pursue; the effect on the non-competitive golfers' market is irrelevant; (B) should be eliminated. There is nothing in the question to suggest that it is easier for small, young companies to develop innovative balls, so the statement in (C) cannot be an assumption upon which the conclusion rests. The authorities who decide what is permissible for competitions may or may not be aware of new technologies, but only that there are limits on what is acceptable is relevant, so (E) is incorrect. If, however, competition golfers were willing to pay high prices for balls that are not allowed in tournaments, the manufacturers would have a market for such balls, which would contradict the conclusion of the question stem. Choice (D) articulates the assumption that such a market does not exist.

22. D Whether most or very few Korean-Americans living in Crenkotown purchased kimchi deliveries from a commercial delivery service in 1971 tells you nothing about the number that did so in 1957, so (A) is incorrect. Choice (B) is backwards: if in 1957 most were within range of a delivery service, that would justify the question stem's conclusion. But that it is true in 1971 tells you nothing about the situation in 1957, so (B) is out. Neither the type nor quality of kimchi is discussed in the passage, so (C) cannot be correct. Per capita demand could stay constant with more people ordering smaller deliveries, so (E) is not assumed. However, if any of the new operations serviced areas with people that previously wanted kimchi delivered but were unable to get it, an increase in the number of Crenkotownies that got deliveries would result. Therefore, the statement in (D) is an assumption on which the conclusion depends.

23. B Remember, this question asks which answer choice is NOT assumed. The question stem says that the number of times a worker accomplishes an operation is the only behavior that needs to be looked at, so (A) is an underlying assumption and is incorrect. For (B), the question only says that

the math is easy, not that tracking the tasks an employee does is easy. Therefore, (B) is not an assumption made. For (C), the question does assume, however irrationally, that all a worker's operations are mathematically equal, so (C) is a necessary assumption. The method described ignores quality of operations, so the statement in (D) is an assumption. And since the method also doesn't take into account a worker's mistakes, it does assume that mistakes should not be considered and (E) is incorrect.

24. **B** The manager's conclusion is regarding only what happens to dogs that the shelter doesn't accept; it has nothing to do with what happens after the dogs go to the shelter, so (A) is incorrect. Choice (B), however, if untrue, would mean that when owners can't care for their dogs any more, they could find new homes for them without the shelter. That would make the manager's claim that those dogs would end up as strays less credible, so (B) does state an assumption on which the manager's conclusion depends. Keep this choice. The conclusion is only concerning dogs (cats are irrelevant) so (C) is incorrect. Choice (D) is incorrect because there is nothing in the argument to suggest that there are only two options: kill or release. Choice (E) negates part of the activist's argument, but it isn't relevant to the manager's conclusion, so it is incorrect.

25. **A** In order to identify an assumption necessary to the argument that City X will have to build a third highway running into and out of the city because of the population increase, determine what the truth of that conclusion relies on. If the increased number of drivers does not affect traffic into and out of City X, then a third highway is not necessary. Because the argument concludes that a third highway is necessary, it assumes the traffic entering and leaving the city will increase as the population increases. Choice (A) correctly addresses the amount of traffic into and out of the city. Choice (B) addresses drive time, which is irrelevant to the amount of traffic. Choice (C) addresses the rate of the population increase, but does not make the link between population and traffic. Choice (D) addresses the proportion of the city's residents who own cars, which is irrelevant to the amount of traffic into and out of the city. Choice (E) addresses the number of vehicles per household, which is irrelevant to the amount of traffic.

26. **B** The courier's conclusion that it will take less time to drive the longer route assumes that the differences between the speed limits more than compensates for the differences between the lengths of the routes. If the speed limit does not increase by a factor that is greater than the factor by which the miles differ, then taking the longer route will not take less time. Choice (A) addresses a different delivery, which is irrelevant to the current decision. Choice (B) correctly addresses the relative difference between the speed limits and the distance. Choice (C) addresses gas mileage, which would affect both routes equally and is irrelevant to the length of time each route takes. Choice (D) addresses direct routes, which is irrelevant to the amount of time each route takes. Choice (E) addresses speeding, which is irrelevant to the current decision.

27. **D** The conclusion that there will be no more instances of feedback during live shows requires an assumption about the causes of feedback. The possibility that the appropriate equalization has been taken and feedback still occurs must be removed. Choice (A) addresses the types of microphones

engineers use, but the argument clearly refers to each type of microphone. Choice (B) states that feedback is the only problem with live shows, but this is not a necessary assumption to the argument. Choice (C) addresses the different needs of different microphones, but the argument clearly refers to equalizing each type of microphone. Choice (D) correctly limits the cause of feedback to equalization. Choice (E) addresses advanced types of tools, but this is not a necessary assumption to the argument.

28. C The argument draws the conclusion that teachers should focus on the yoga exercises that strengthen muscles, because that is what most people consider important. The assumption must link the things on which teachers should focus and the things people find important. Choice (A) states that there are different exercises for different skill levels, which is irrelevant to the argument. Choice (B) states that different teachers can interpret poses differently, which is irrelevant to what the teachers should be focusing on. Choice (C) correctly identifies the assumption that teachers should focus on the things people find important. Choice (D) addresses exercises designed to strengthen muscles, which are irrelevant to what teachers should focus on. Choice (E) weakens the argument by stating that yoga teachers have no interest in what their students find important.

Inference

1. D The statements separate the need for image quality from portability. Choice (A) goes beyond the information given, so eliminate it. Meanwhile (B) is too strong, because you can't know for sure whether serious photographers have image quality as their main concern; perhaps ruggedness or durability concerns them even more. Eliminate (C) as well, since, like (A), it's beyond the information given. However, (D) is clearly supported by the second and third sentences, so keep it. Finally, (E) is out of scope. The correct answer is (D).

2. E The passage discusses the negative consequences of extended periods in weightlessness and then points out that travel to Mars would require a highly-extended period. Eliminate (A), since the passage doesn't give you enough information to know whether proper training would help. Meanwhile, (B) is too strong; it's possible that there has been some progress on the artificial-gravity front. Choice (C), like (A), is beyond the scope of the passage, so eliminate that one, too. Choice (D) makes a recommendation, so it goes too far. Choice (E) is most supported by the statements and is the correct answer.

3. D The statements provide information about both the negative effects of UV exposure and the limitations of certain kinds of lenses. Eliminate (A), since it's too extreme. You can also discard (B), since it goes beyond the information given. Choice (C) makes a recommendation that goes too far, but (D) is in line with the author's statements. Finally, (E), like (A), is too extreme.

4. E The passage discusses how Corncob's shuttle program will derive its operating costs from reduction of another employee benefit, with the addition of no new benefits. That suggests that the program will cost all employees, regardless of whether they use the shuttle. Eliminate (A), (B), and (D)

because they're beyond the scope of the passage. Choice (C), meanwhile, is possible but cannot be known based only on the provided statements.

5. **B** The statements discuss the advantages of synthetic over standard motor oils. Choice (A) goes beyond the information given. Choice (B), however, has the conservative wording you like to see in an inference answer, so keep that one. Get rid of (C), since you can't generalize about drivers who use certain kinds of oil. Eliminate (D) and (E), since they're beyond the scope of the statements.

6. **E** The statements don't provide enough information to verify whether (A) is true, since all you know is that products first in their categories tend to have a marketing advantage over those that come later. Eliminate (B) as well, since it's too extreme, and cross out (C), since it gives advice and thus goes beyond the scope of the passage. Choice (D), meanwhile, goes too far; you don't know that all products first in their respective categories sell best. That leaves (E), which has moderate enough language to make it an acceptable inference.

7. **D** The statements discuss key factors to business success, but they don't provide enough information to know whether (A) is true. You can also eliminate (B), since you can't know that based only on the statements. Eliminate (C) because it's too extreme. Choice (D), on the other hand, is in line with the author's statements and uses conservative language, so keep it. Choice (E) goes beyond the scope of the statements.

8. **A** In discussing *money that would otherwise be spent*, the author implies that distance learning is less costly to provide than are other forms of education. That supports (A), so keep it. However, (B) goes beyond the information given and (C) is too extreme; it could be that distance learning requires at least some amount of climate control or parking facilities. You can also eliminate (D), since it is beyond the scope of the statements, as well as (E), since the author never suggests that.

9. **B** The author mentions nonessential items, then provides designer clothing as an example, suggesting that designer clothing is not essential. Eliminate (A), since it goes beyond the information given, but keep (B), since, as previously stated, it's suggested by the author. Choice (C), in contrast, discusses products in general, something outside the scope of the passage. Choice (D) is also out of scope, since the author never mentions quality. Finally, (E) is too extreme.

10. **C** The author states that *only...the absence of risk* constitutes an investment, so anything with a chance of financial loss would not be an investment. Eliminate (A), since it's too extreme, while (B) is outside the passage's scope. Keep (C), however, since it follows the author's reasoning. Eliminate (D), since it goes against what the author is saying. Eliminate (E), as well, since something that rises in value could have involved risk.

11. **A** The author states that older students *do not need to 'find themselves'* [and] *are better able to focus... than their younger peers*. That suggests that young people do need to *find themselves*. That supports (A). You can eliminate (B), since it's beyond the scope of the statements. Choice (C) is too extreme; the author never mentions schedules. Choice (D) goes beyond the scope of the passage and (E) also requires outside knowledge and is not implied by the author.

12. **B** The author tells you that blackjack's odds depend on a player's ability, suggesting that skill is involved. Then she adds that novices won't be as likely to lose money if they shoot craps, suggesting that no skill is involved in the latter. Eliminate (A), since it's too extreme, but keep (B), since it follows the author's logic. Choice (C) is outside the scope of the statements, as is (E). Choice (D) does not necessarily follow; shooting craps might still prove profitable for someone who is good at blackjack.

13. **A** The author discusses two essential facets of newsletter investing: the quality of the newsletter and one's willingness to follow its advice. Neither facet depends on the other, meaning that you could be willing to follow a low-quality newsletter and thus not earn profits. Keep (A), since it reflects that logic, but eliminate (B), since the author never mentions *steady* or *long-term* profits. Choice (C) is beyond the scope of the passage, as is (D), so eliminate both. Finally, (E) offers advice that goes beyond the author's statements.

14. **C** The author makes a conclusion about gender bias, so it's easy to miss a more subtle assertion, that single evaluators were used *to keep the experiment's purpose concealed*. Eliminate (A), since you can't generalize about all women from the results of a single study. Choice (B) can also be tossed, since it's both general and extreme. In contrast, (C) aligns with the aforementioned assertion about experimental secrecy, so keep it. Choice (D), like (A), goes beyond the scope of the study. Choice (E) requires more information than the statements provide.

15. **C** Gardner's theory, according to the statements, asserts that separate and distinct parts of the brain are used for particular cognitive activities. Choice (A) is too extreme; you can't know from the statements whether no correlation exists between any two intelligences. Choice (B) goes in the opposite direction of the author's statements, so eliminate that one, too. In contrast, (C) is in line with the author's logic and has moderate enough language (*primarily*) so keep it. Choices (D) and (E) both go beyond the scope of the passage.

16. **A** The argument brushes aside the notion that the research results were manipulated, citing the breadth of the study. That suggests that a small-scale study is not necessarily protected from bias or tampering. Keep (A), since that's in line with the author's reasoning, but eliminate (B), since it's beyond the passage's scope. Choices (C) and (D) are also out of scope, and (E) is too strong.

17. **B** The argument suggests that manual transmissions benefit more from *the quickness of human judgment*, describing how the traits of the *skilled driver* contribute to the *optimum functioning* of an engine. As such, the author implies that skill is required to get the most out of a car equipped with a manual transmission. Choice (A) is too strong, but (B) would have to be true, since not all drivers are necessarily skilled. Choice (C), like (A), is also too strong, while (D) and (E) are beyond the scope of the passage.

18. **C** The author tells you that hard work is not a substitute for *big-picture* thinking, suggesting that effectiveness is not necessarily proportional to effort. Choice (A) is extreme, so cross that one out. Choice (B) is outside the scope of the passage. Choice (C), however, is supported by the author's reasoning, so keep it. Choice (D) is not necessarily true, given the author's reservations about effort and managerial effectiveness. Finally, (E) is too extreme.

19. **D** The author uses career change to justify a liberal arts education, which has *cultural breadth* among its cited benefits. Choice (A) is too strong, given the word *best*. Choices (B) and (C) are beyond the scope of the passage. However, (D) seems in line with the author's reasoning, so keep it. Choice (E) is out of scope.

20. **C** The passage describes how stockholders may cause corporate leaders to be too conservative, because new ideas can take time to work and may result in a *significant decline in profit*. Eliminate (A) and (B), since they're too strong, but keep (C), which parallels the author's reasoning. Choice (D) is too extreme and (E) is out of scope.

21. **E** The passage discusses how willingness to reveal negative information suggests that a job candidate is being truthful. That said, (A) is too strong, while (B), (C), and (D) are all beyond the scope of the passage. Choice (E), however, is directly in line with the author's reasoning.

22. **D** The author discusses the benefits of upright pianos, noting that *since the needs of most players do not warrant concert-pianist key action, an upright makes a worthy alternative*. Choice (A) goes too far along those lines and (B) is extreme. Choice (C) is out of scope, but (D) agrees with what the author says about *the needs of most players*. Choice (E), like (C), is out of scope, so eliminate it.

23. **E** The passage states that PPC listings are ranked by the size of advertisers' bids, suggesting that a larger budget allows one businesses' ad to gain precedence over those of its competitors. Eliminate (A), since it's too strong; you don't know whether *most* Web users mistrust PPC ads. Cross out (B) as well, since it goes in the opposite direction of the author's logic. Choice (C) is outside the scope of the passage, as is (D). That leaves you with (E), which would have to be true, given the author's statements about ads with higher bids outranking other ads.

24. **D** The first thing to notice is that you don't know what correlation exists between how many small business owners know someone who employs an illegal immigrant and the prevalence of illegal immigration. Jackson's argument suggests that it is likely that 7 of 10 small business owners would know someone who employs an illegal immigrant even at the levels of illegal immigration seen 10 years ago. If more than 8% of small businesses employ an illegal immigrant, Jackson would say that it is likely that more than 7 of 10 would know someone who does so, so (A) is incorrect. Similarly, Jackson suggests that Greg's statistic doesn't necessarily point to a rise in illegal immigration, so (B) is incorrect. Neither (C) nor (E), about the accuracy of statistics, is called into question by Jackson; they are both irrelevant. Choice (D), on the other hand, is exactly what Jackson's argument points to—that 7 of 10 small business owners likely knew someone who employed an illegal immigrant 10 years ago, so the fact that 7 of 10 do now does not point to an increase.

Evaluate

1. **B**   The food critic theorized that the bakers at neighborhood X's bakery must have learned the cake-baking method from bakers at town Y's bakery. In order to evaluate this theory, determine whether the bakers had any exposure to the other bakery's cakes. Choice (A) makes it possible that the bakers from X and Y might have had contact, so hold on to this answer for now. Choice (B) correctly addresses whether the bakers might have seen the cakes, which is more relevant than (A). Eliminate (A) at this point. If the cakes were brought from one bakery to the other, it is possible that the baking method used to create the cakes was passed along as well. Choice (C) addresses the current bakers in town Y's bakery, who are irrelevant. Choice (D) addresses food critics, who are irrelevant. Choice (E) addresses other types of baked goods, not the cakes in question.

2. **D**   In order to establish that the restructuring of the managers caused the sales increase, eliminate other possible causes. Choice (A) addresses the hiring of additional staff, which is irrelevant. Choice (B) addresses other retailers, not the retailer in question. Choice (C) addresses an increase in staff, which is irrelevant. Choice (D) correctly addresses the number of customers, which can affect sales. If the customer base increased during the restructuring, the sales might have increased because of the increase in customers. Choice (E) addresses the types of staff, which is irrelevant.

3. **C**   In order to determine whether to replace its current fax machine, the office staff needs to consider whether the need for a fax machine is going to remain constant. Choice (A) addresses location, not the need for a fax machine. Choice (B) addresses the number of received faxes, but the number of sent faxes is not mentioned. If the total number of faxes both sent and received was going to decrease significantly, the office might decide not to replace its current machine; however, knowing just the number of received faxes is not enough to evaluate the replacement. Choice (C) correctly addresses an alternative to a fax machine. If the office converts to a paperless fax-through-e-mail system, a fax machine will no longer be necessary. Choice (D) addresses the copy machine, not the need for a fax machine. Choice (E) addresses the number of pages sent at one time, not the continued need for a fax machine.

4. **B**   In order to evaluate whether to accept the proposed entry, consider the criteria in the encyclopedia's guidelines. The proposed article has six press references that all conform to the criteria—they are in third-party publications and were not solicited. What the proposed article does not address is the importance of the start-up company. Choice (A) addresses other start-up companies, which are irrelevant. Choice (B) correctly addresses the importance of the start-up company, since it has six press references. Choice (C) addresses length of time, which is irrelevant. Choice (D) addresses readers, who are irrelevant. Choice (E) addresses the writer of the article, who is irrelevant.

5. **A**   In order to evaluate the removal of trainers who spend the longest amount of time in one-on-one sessions, determine whether the length of time spent is related to efficiency and cost. Choice (A) correctly addresses the relationship between the efficiency of the trainer and the length of time needed for one-on-one sessions. It takes longer to answer a difficult question than it does to answer

an easy question. If the most efficient trainers are asked to answer difficult questions, then the most efficient trainers are most likely to be removed under the demands of the firm. Removing them will then reduce efficiency. Choice (B) addresses other firms, which are irrelevant. Choice (C) addresses the removed trainers, whose future work is irrelevant. Choice (D) addresses the employees' access to training, which is irrelevant. Choice (E) addresses the firm's clients and fees, both of which are irrelevant.

6. **E** To evaluate the pie maker's claim that profits will increase near the end of the apple season, look for a relationship between profits and the smaller, duller apples picked late in the season. Choice (A) only addresses profits, and makes the irrelevant comparison between this year and last year. Choices (B) and (D) do not address profits. Choice (C) addresses the characteristics of the apples, but not profit. Choice (E) correctly makes the link between profits and the seasonal change in apples.

7. **A** In order to evaluate the argument that the lack of brakes on fixed-gear bicycles has caused an increase in bicycle accidents, look for information that rules out other possible causes for the increase in accidents. Choice (A) correctly introduces the possibility that different types of bicycles are ridden under different conditions, which, if true, would provide an alternate explanation for the increase in the number of accidents. It may be the conditions under which they are ridden that cause the accidents, not the fixed-gear bicycles themselves. Choice (B) discusses regular bicycle riders, who are irrelevant. Choice (C) addresses helmet use, which would affect riders of both types of bicycles. Choice (D) addresses car drivers, who would affect both types of bicycle riders. Choice (E) addresses cost, which is irrelevant.

8. **C** In order to evaluate the results of the study, determine whether the ten years that occurred between the pesticide use and the study was enough time for cancer to develop. Choice (A) addresses other types of pesticides, which are irrelevant. Choice (B) addresses today, which is irrelevant to the study's results. Choice (C) correctly addresses the amount of time it takes for cancer to develop, which affects whether the study could have detected cancer ten years after the pesticide use. Choice (D) addresses other causes of cancer, which are irrelevant to the study's results. Choice (E) addresses the lack of pesticides, not the link between pesticides and cancer.

9. **E** To evaluate the chief's argument that the Robertson division is doing the most to reduce crime because it has questioned more suspects than any other division has, determine whether there is a link between questioning suspects and reducing crime. Choice (A) is irrelevant; even if Robertson held more suspects after questioning, there is still no established connection to the amount of crime. Choice (B) addresses the police chief's data, but the premise of the argument still must be taken as fact, whether the chief's numbers match or not. Choice (C) addresses most major cities, which are irrelevant to the chief's argument. Choice (D) addresses the majority of suspects, but it is only known that the Robertson division has questioned the most. Establishing that Robertson questioned the majority of suspects in the city still does not make the link to reducing the amount of crime. Choice (E) correctly introduces the link between the number of suspects questioned and the amount of crime.

10. **D** In order to evaluate the argument that there is no reason to take potassium supplements because many foods are naturally high in potassium, determine whether there might be some other advantage to taking the supplements. Choice (A) addresses the availability of the supplements but not of the foods, so there is no basis for a comparison. Choice (B) addresses the harmful effects of sodium, not the sources of potassium. Choice (C) addresses the disadvantages of potassium, but those would affect both sources of potassium. Choice (D) correctly introduces a reason to take the potassium supplements. The argument presents potassium as a way to reduce the effects of sodium, but if the potassium source is also a source of sodium, then the supplements are a better choice. Choice (E) addresses the advantages of sodium, not the sources of potassium.

11. **D** To evaluate the farmers' debate, determine whether the decision would have consequences that would make one choice more cost-effective than the other. Choice (A) addresses the farmers' future rates, which are irrelevant to their current debate. Choice (B) addresses produce prices, which are irrelevant to their debate. The farmers who continue to irrigate and sell their crops would certainly benefit from higher produce prices, but those prices would have no impact on the farmers who decide to sell their water. Choice (C) addresses filtering the irrigation water, which is irrelevant to the farmers' debate. Choice (D) correctly introduces a long-term financial consideration. If crops can easily be replanted each year, then there is no financial reason to sell those crops instead of water. However, if certain crops require a heavy capital investment and must be carefully maintained for years, then the cost-effectiveness of selling irrigation water is lost. Choice (E) addresses the future price of water, which is irrelevant to the farmers' current debate.

12. **E** To evaluate the researchers' argument that the wing remnants must serve a function even if the function is as yet unknown, determine whether all aspects of insects have functions. Choice (A) addresses whether the function can even be discovered, but the researchers' argument does not depend on this. They claim that the function exists, not that it can necessarily be discovered. Choice (B) addresses other species, which are irrelevant to the researcher's argument. Choice (C) addresses the beetle's predators, which are irrelevant. Choice (D) addresses the beetle's ancestors, who are irrelevant to the researchers' argument. Choice (E) correctly addresses whether every aspect of the insects has a function, whether or not that function is known.

13. **B** To evaluate the researchers' conclusion that there are two species of tigers, one comprised of the Sumatran tigers, who share three DNA markers, and one comprised of all other types of tigers, who do not share those three DNA markers, determine whether the other types of tigers might each share some DNA markers not shared by any other types. It is possible that each type of tiger constitutes its own species. Choice (A) addresses extinction, which is irrelevant to the argument. Choice (B) correctly addresses the genetic material of the other types of tigers and raises the possibility that other types have their own genetic markers, just as the Sumatran tigers do. Choice (C) addresses susceptibility of all tigers to genetic disorders, which is irrelevant to determining species. Choice (D) addresses distinguishing Sumatran tigers from other types of tigers, which the argument has already done. Choice (E) addresses the origins of all tigers, which is irrelevant to determining current species.

14. **A** In order to evaluate the owners' decision, assess the possible effects on the company's most important criteria, which is maintaining its low prices. The loan will cover the cost of the replacement machines, but it is possible that there will be additional costs after the machines are replaced. Choice (A) correctly addresses a long-term cost that would be incurred if the machines were replaced. Choice (B) addresses the company's competitors, who are irrelevant. Choice (C) addresses where most of the company's inventory is sold, which is irrelevant to maintaining low prices. Choice (D) addresses other manufacturers, who are irrelevant to the company owners' decision. Choice (E) addresses the company's employees, who are also irrelevant to the decision.

15. **C** In order to evaluate the argument that their healthy diets as children affect the high school students' high grades, determine whether the high school students actually spent their childhoods on the island, where people maintain healthy diets. Choice (A) addresses other islands, which are irrelevant to the argument. Choice (B) addresses the number of students, which is irrelevant to the cause of their good grades. Choice (C) correctly addresses whether the students spent their childhoods on the island. If many students moved to the island after childhood, then the link between the island's healthy diet and high grades is weakened. Choice (D) addresses where adults work, which is irrelevant to the argument. Choice (E) addresses the work options for young adults on the island, which are irrelevant.

16. **E** Choices (A), (B), (C), and (D) all deal with issues other than the teacher's hypothesis. The hypothesis says the build-up of dirt and dust on the bat is responsible, so the correct answer should involve materials on the surface of the bat. Choice (A) is about bats of different sizes. Choice (B) is about bats of different materials. Choice (C) is about which bats the team uses. Choice (D) would test the *premise* of the question stem—that old bats transfer less power than do new bats, but not the teacher's hypothesis.

17. **E** Nothing in the speaker's argument implies that admission to colleges is the goal of the proposed change, so (A) cannot be correct. Choice (B) is too extreme. The suggestion is not to confine students to math and science, just to transfer some time from fine arts classes to math and science classes. For (C), surely there are certain subjects, quantum mechanics comes to mind, that high school students won't be taught, but that doesn't mean that what they would be taught with the extra time would be any less valuable. Nothing suggests a teacher shortage, so (D) is incorrect. For (E), students could learn math and science better without transferring extra time to those subjects, then they could take fine arts classes too.

Identify-the-Reasoning

1. **C** Harvey argues that large firms do not need subsidies to compete, so subsidies would be wasted, while small firms would remain uncompetitive even with subsidies, so subsidies would again be wasted. He never considers the issue of firms of intermediate size. Zane raises this unconsidered third possibility to point out the possibility that Harvey's conclusions might not apply in such an instance. This is best expressed in (C). Zane rejects Harvey's conclusion, contrary to (E), never makes (B)'s claim that Harvey uses inconsistent definitions, and never demonstrates anything about the link between economies of scale and competitiveness, (A). Choice (D) overstates the case, since it is not clear that an intermediate-size firm must necessarily contradict Harvey's conclusion, only that it may.

2. **D** The first statement says that media coverage often oversimplifies the complexity of news events, while the second statement notes that some believe that the particular ways the media oversimplify had the historical effect of increasing popular support for foreign interventions. This matches (D). Choice (A) might be tempting, but the specific examples are of the possible results of oversimplified media coverage, not the coverage itself.

3. **C** The first bolded statement describes the need for historical simulation authors to address issues beyond simple historical accuracy. The second statement makes a more sweeping claim that playing a Waterloo simulation carries with it profound implications about human nature, fate, etc. This corresponds with (C). Choice (E) might be tempting, but the second statement does not explain the origins but instead discusses the consequences.

4. **B** The first statement provides a description of the attempt to apply Sage's wealth in a publicly beneficial way. Since this is a specific example, eliminate (A). The body of the paragraph then illustrates that Sage himself would appear to have personally acted in a morally reprehensible fashion. The second statement draws a sweeping and logically flawed conclusion from the particular case of Sage's posthumous use of his wealth to rehabilitate his image to all such attempts to dedicate large fortunes to public improvement. Since this is a flawed conclusion, eliminate (C), (D), and (E).

5. **E** Gene argues that the film was a failure, referring to various aspects of its popular and critical reception. Roger argues that the film was a success, explicitly referring not to the issues raised by Gene but to the film having earned a net profit. This corresponds to (E). Roger did not make a claim about the main sources of revenue or the film's revenue compared to other films at the time, so eliminate (A) and (C). Contrary to (D), the assessment was contrasting rather than comparable. Choice (B) is inaccurate in that failing to present evidence disproving Gene's specific factual claims would not disprove such claims.

6. **B** Norman contends that effective branding requires images that strongly appeal to consumers and hence storybook imagery is the most effective. Otto's response seeks to deny this by noting that animal and technology imagery are also effective. However, Norman merely claimed that storybook imagery was the most effective tool, not the only effective tool. This corresponds to (B). No evaluative mechanism, different end, or narrower means was proposed, so eliminate (A), (C), and (E). Although (D) correctly describes the format of Otto's response, the flaw in the refutation does not lie in the format, but in the error of equating the best means with the only means.

7. **D** Johann claims that all great civilizations must depend on strict control, but his example is not a civilization but a great piece of music. Steve responds by providing a counter-example of great music that depends on artistic freedom, which rebuts the argument only if one also accepts the premise that what is true of music is also true of civilization. This is best stated in (D). Steve's counter-example is relevant and undermines Johann's conclusion, eliminating (C) and (E). It does not generalize to a wider conclusion, contrary to (B), and correctly identifies Johann's claim that order is the only cause of great civilization, contrary to (A).

8. **E** Victor notes that the project failed, despite the sufficient resources devoted to it and the fact that success would then necessarily follow if the project had been performed to proper specifications. He then asserts that he had assessed the specifications as correct, concluding that this leaves only error or sabotage by Reed. Reed denies this, observing that such an explanation would follow only if one also assumes that Victor's assessment of the specifications is itself without error. This corresponds with (E). The argument is about independent causes of failure, not success, contrary to (D). Reed demonstrates no factual errors, terminology ambiguity, or counter-examples, eliminating (A), (B), and (C).

9. **A** Diana argues that, for biological, cultural, and psychological reasons, male leaders tend to choose certain types of confrontation, which increases the chance of conflict and war. (The claim itself is fairly vague: male leaders *tend* to do this, which *contributes* to conflict.) Etta attempts to rebut this by pointing to specific instances in which female leaders have gone to war; however, Diana's claim was merely that men are likely to do this, not that only men would do so. This corresponds to (A). Because Diana never said that *all* men would do this, male counter-examples would not rebut this, invalidating (B). The methods and motives of women leaders are irrelevant to Diana's argument, invalidating (C), (D), and (E).

10. **D** Wilson argues that simply reducing one's food intake is unlikely to lead to weight loss, since the body reduces its metabolism in response. He concludes that exercise alone, with its ability to force the body to use up fat-stored energy, leads to weight loss. Marisa responds by disagreeing, noting that, while diet alone is unlikely to work, exercise builds appetite, too; thus, some degree of food intake control is necessary, whatever strategy one chooses. This matches (D). Choice (A) overstates her argument, since she never says dieting is superior. Marisa never explicitly identifies and refutes an assumption, invalidating (B). Because Marisa does not argue that exercise doesn't entail using the body's fat reserves, (C) does not match. Contrary to (E), Marisa contradicts Wilson's conclusion, not the premises.

11. E The first bolded passage states an assessment that most classic films won't be fully appreciated by modern viewers. The second bolded passage provides an example from a single famous film of a particular sequence that within its historical context was extraordinary but will not seem so to modern sensibilities. If that example is, in fact, representative of a general problem, this would strongly support the conclusion. This is best described by (E). Choice (D) overstates the case, because the claim was about most classic films, and one particular example, however famous, does not prove it true for most. Choices (A), (B), and (C) inaccurately report the function of the example, while (C) also claims the first passage is a recommendation.

12. B The first bolded statement says that franchising seems to be an effective business strategy to avoid the high failure rate of new restaurants, while the second statement points out a serious flaw in the statistical evidence often used to bolster this point. This corresponds with (B). The survey design flaw does not of itself actually disprove the effectiveness of franchising, invalidating choice (A), which is otherwise tempting. The evidence is not from an analogous case, not relevant to the deductive logic, and not supporting, contrary to (C), (D), and (E).

13. C The first statement explains that business planners can use strategic market simulations as a means of generating important insights into how to respond to unanticipated and novel changes. The second statement points out that the very task of designing hypothetical market scenarios presupposes that the novel, unpredictable event has a certain amount of recognizable predictability, which seems to be in tension with the other ideas behind the simulation approach.

14. E The first statement gives an example of a relationship between an event and the effects of that event, and the second statement leaps from a problem outlined about the relationship in the first sentence to an assertion that is not supported. So, look for an answer choice that reflects this idea. Choice (A) is incorrect because the first statement is not a conclusion. Choice (B) can be eliminated because the second statement is not a *conclusion that necessarily follows*. Choice (C) is incorrect because the second statement is not an exception, but rather an unjustified conclusion. Choice (D) is incorrect as the second statement is not an *accurate implication of that relationship*. Choice (E) is a good paraphrase of the relationship between the blanks, so it is the correct answer.

15. D The first statement says that women are a larger percentage of all buyers of the *Conquista* than two years ago. Since the first statement is a premise, (A) is out. The second statement argues that the marketing department's actions are the reason for this change, and that this means that more women buy the car now than before. The second statement is flawed for two reasons: it assumes that the marketing department's actions are the only possible cause of this change and it incorrectly assumes that if women make up a larger percentage of all buyers than before then they must have increased in actual numbers as well. Since the conclusion is flawed, eliminate (B) and (C). Since it is not an evaluation, eliminate (E) as well.

16. A Charles argues that symbiosis is possible and presents an example. Magnus attempts to refute this argument by noting the origins of the example, but does not address whether or how this would make it fail the definition of symbiosis, which depends on the effects of the relationship, not the

origins or causes. This corresponds with (A). Charles' conclusion rests on an example, not deductive logic, so there is no necessary alternative logic Magnus must supply, invalidating (E). Choices (B) and (C) are irrelevant to the question of whether symbiosis is possible, and (D) does not accurately describe Magnus' response.

17. **B** Nancy argues that lasting love flows primarily from common genetics rather than emotional affinity, utilizing the examples of mother-child love vs. husband-wife love. Common genes create mother love, which prompts care. Clio claims instead that emotional affinity is a powerful source of lasting love, putting forward the counter-example of adoptive mothers, whose care for the child creates an emotional affinity, which in turn creates lasting love even in the absence of common genes. Choice (B) best describes this. The counter-example does not disprove the claim that common genes *can* create lasting love, just whether it is substantially necessary, invalidating (A).

18. **A** The first bolded statement establishes the definition of *moral hazard*, a worrisome concept from economics, while the second bolded statement argues that one possible explanation for disastrous Federal Reserve inaction in the face of the Great Depression was too great a focus on avoiding moral hazard. This corresponds best to (A). Federal Reserve inaction was not an example of moral hazard but an attempt to avoid it, contrary to (B). Choice (C) is inaccurate in two aspects: moral hazard is not a general principle and the example is not an analogy. Choice (D) erroneously calls the first statement a conclusion, while (E) errs by calling the second statement a necessary logical conclusion that was then successfully applied.

Resolve/Explain

1. **B** The conclusion of this argument is that the organic acid in the drink caused the blood of the members of the experimental group to become sticky. This is based on the premise that those who consumed the drink showed signs of sticky blood and those who did not consume the drink did not. The author assumes there was no other cause for the sticky blood in the members of the experimental group, such as already having sticky blood before consuming the drink. Choice (B) supports the argument by stating that no one, including the members of the experimental group, had sticky blood at the beginning of the experiment. Choices (A), (C), (D), and (E) have no bearing on whether organic acid caused the sticky blood and are, therefore, irrelevant.

2. **E** The paradox here is: Why did those who consumed the energy drink show signs of sticky blood? Choices (A), (B), (C), and (D) don't explain how the organic acid leads to sticky blood. If, as stated in (E), the organic acid in the drink increases clotting factors in the blood, the acid could cause the blood to become stickier.

3. **C** The paradox here is *Why did spinach sales drop if few consumers planned to change their spinach buying habits?* Choice (C) explains that spinach was not available to buy in many supermarkets, which could explain the drop in sales. Choices (A) and (E) explain why few consumers planned

to change their buying habits, but not why spinach sales dropped. Choices (B) and (D) do not explain the drop in spinach sales either.

4.   C   The paradox here is: Why do banks and finance companies require insurance for collisions and not for disability or loss of employment, when drivers are more likely to lose their cars due to the latter? Choices (A), (B), (D), and (E) do nothing to resolve the paradox. However, (C) does explain the paradox, because banks and finance companies can repossess the vehicle in the case of loss of employment or disability, but in the case of an accident that totals the car, the property is lost.

5.   E   The paradox here is: Why did profits increase last year, when prices and production amounts remained stable and demand did not increase. This is an EXCEPT question, so ignore the word *except* and determine which answer choices explain the paradox. The one that doesn't explain it is the answer. Choices (A), (B), (C), and (D) all describe ways in which the soybean growers saved money, which explains how profits increased. Choice (E) gives a possible explanation of why demand did not increase, but does not explain why profits increased.

6.   D   The paradox here is: Why are small business owners against the proposed legislation when they would be exempt from it? Choices (A), (B), (C), and (E) provide no explanation for the opposition. Choice (D) states that the small business owners would have to provide the health insurance in order to compete with their larger counterparts; this explains why the small business owners are opposed to the legislation.

7.   A   The paradox here is: If the second sign indicated the halfway point to the bottom of the canyon, why are the numbers on the front and back of the sign not equal? Choices (B) and (C) are completely irrelevant to the discrepancy and do not explain it. Choices (D) and (E) do not work either, because even if a sign was missing or the numbers were reversed, there still would be no sign with equal numbers on each side. However, in (A), if the facing numbers are counting down to the bottom of the canyon and the reverse numbers are counting up, the numbers will never be equal even when the man is halfway to the bottom of the canyon.

8.   B   The paradox here is: How could the number of diet products sold increase when there are fewer adult dieters? Choices (A), (C), (D), and (E) all provide explanations for the increase by describing some kind of increase in demand for diet products that occurred despite the decrease in the number of adult dieters. In (B), while the gender of the adult dieters has changed, the number of adult dieters has actually increased instead of decreased. This contradicts the argument and does not explain the paradox.

9.   D   The paradox here is: Why did those who completed the experiment the least successfully expend the most amount of energy? Choices (A), (B), and (C) are irrelevant and don't explain the paradox. The information in (E) does not explain the paradox and, in fact, makes it worse. Choice (D) states that those who are more successful at the experiment are more energy-efficient, and therefore expend less energy.

10.   **A**   The paradox here is: Why do virgin female rabbits suddenly exhibit maternal behavior toward foster rabbit pups once their sense of smell has been deactivated and not before? Choice (A) explains the paradox, because if the female rabbits no longer have a sense of smell, the odor of the foster pups will no longer inhibit their maternal response. Choice (B) does not explain the contradiction, and in fact, makes it worse. Choices (C), (D), and (E) do not explain the paradox either.

Mixed Drill

1.   **A**   The passage only mentions sex partners and siblings of those with P-A. It is unknown how likely their parents would be to have P-A, so (B) is incorrect. There is no data in the question about the prevalence of either P-A or P-B, so (C) is incorrect. For (D), you know that the sex partners of those with P-A are more likely to have the disease, but you don't know anything about the sex partners of those who don't have the disease, nor does the question suggest that it is sexually transmitted, so (D) is incorrect. Again, there is nothing in the question stem that suggests either variant of the disease is sexually transmitted, so (E) is incorrect. Regarding (A), if siblings of those with P-B are much more likely to have the disease, while sex partners are no more likely than average, this suggests the disease is passed through genetics (i.e., it is hereditary). From the fact that sex partners and siblings of those with P-A have the same vulnerability, it seems likely that P-A is either environmental or contagious, but certainly not hereditary.

2.   **D**   The first excerpt lays out the reasons why economic interdependence would make trading states avoid crises and war, while the second presents an argument that in at least one instance trade may have perversely made war more likely. This corresponds most closely to (D). Choice (B) reverses the order and (A) misstates whether the outcome is as predicted. Choices (C) and (E) are descriptively inaccurate.

3.   **C**   While perhaps a limitation of the drug in question, that it is only prophylactic (preventative), does not mean it would not be effective or profitable, so (A) is incorrect. For (B) and (D), that scientists don't understand all the processes involved in allergic responses does not mean a drug couldn't be developed to treat them (in contrast, one could argue that science never fully understands any process!). Choice (E) reveals two obstacles for the company in question, but doesn't point to a flaw in the company's plan. In contrast, if the drug can't differentiate between allergens and parasites, it would prevent the IgE antibody from attaching to parasites and leave users vulnerable to parasitic infection.

4.   **B**   Choice (A) suggests that students have less of a need for health insurance, so it weakens the argument that law students should unionize to try to get health insurance. Eliminate (A). Choice (B), however, says that unionization is an effective strategy for students to get benefits, which strengthens the argument that the law students should unionize to try to get health insurance. Keep this choice. Choice (C) suggests a weakness in the health insurance law students might be negotiating for, so if anything, it weakens the argument and should be eliminated. For (D), if law students will

use their health insurance less, they have less motivation for negotiating for it, so (D) weakens the argument and should be eliminated. Choice (E) suggests that law students could more easily pay for their own health insurance, so again, they would have less motivation to negotiate for it, and the argument is weakened.

5. **D**   Without additional details of the meteorologists' predictions, you don't know whether the statement in (A) makes it more or less likely that the rigs will be hit, so by itself, this statement does nothing to weaken the argument. Similarly, without knowing anything about Mexico's oil production, (B) doesn't affect the argument's logic. Volatility (a measure of the magnitude of price fluctuation) doesn't tell you anything about whether the price will rise or fall, so (C) is incorrect. In (E), whether or not traders physically contact their oil, is irrelevant to the question. For (D), a trade embargo would reduce or eliminate a nation's ability to produce and trade oil, thereby reducing global supply and increasing prices. The end of an embargo, would increase supply and decrease price, potentially offsetting the price increase from the hurricane.

6. **B**   Choices (A) and (E) are irrelevant: neither public health nor sales to children are mentioned in the question stem. Choice (C) is unsupported by the stem; you know nothing of the behavior of individual customers. Similarly for (D), you don't know what customers would do if lower quality beef were used. The question stem suggests that *Prince of Meat* will no longer be able to make a profit on its soft drink sales, which were formerly relied upon to offset losses on hamburger sales. Thus, if *Prince of Meat* cannot profit on hamburgers, it will take a loss on each one it sells.

7. **C**   Choice (A) is a plausible scenario resulting in increased sales, so it is incorrect. Choice (B) would give the company more customers, which would help increase sales, so (B) is incorrect. Choice (C), on the other hand, wouldn't increase sales; if anything it would upset customers. Keep it for now. Choice (D) would give the company more business for their add-ons, so it is incorrect. Choice (E) also would provide more customers to the company and help to increase sales.

8. **C**   The advocate argues that the company makes immorally onerous loans to impoverished individuals without easy access to other credit. In reply, the company representative stresses the market features that make customers willing to pay the high fees, whose rationale he does not otherwise address. This is most consistent with (C). Choice (E) is incorrect since it is apparent that the advocate's description of the market facts was correct. Choice (B) might be tempting, but the executive never addresses, much less disproves, the conclusions. Choices (A) and (D) are invalid for similar reasons.

9. **D**   This is an evaluate-the-argument question, which means you need to turn the answer choices into statements and pick one that would either weaken or strengthen the argument if its answer were known. Choice (A) is irrelevant. Choice (B) is incorrect, because the preferences of the fishermen have no bearing on where they ultimately ended up fishing. Choices (C) and (E) are also incorrect

because where some of the fishermen fished is not relevant; only the ultimate condition of the fisheries matters. One way to strengthen an argument is to point out something that would weaken it and take that away as a possibility. If it were true that the common-access fisheries were already in better shape than the private fisheries before fishing occurred in either, that would detract from the study's assertion that the common-access fisheries were less exploited than the private ones. Choice (D), by stating (once it is turned into a statement) that the common-access and private fisheries had equivalent levels of marine life before they were fished, takes away the possibility of the common-access fisheries being in better shape from the beginning. This lends more credence to the study and, thus, weakens the author's conclusion.

10. C   The paradox here is: How could the common-access fisheries be in better shape when they had so many more users? Choice (A) is irrelevant and doesn't explain the paradox. Choices (B) and (D) don't explain the paradox either and (E) makes the paradox worse. Choice (C) resolves the paradox by explaining that the fishermen don't overfish because they know that if one of them overfishes, everyone else will too. If that happens, the fishery will become depleted and it will cost all of the fishermen more in the long run.

11. D   You are looking for a statement that does not support the idea that the new magazine will be successful. Choice (A) strengthens the publishers' plan because advertisers want to make contact with precisely *wealthy heads of households who make purchasing decisions.* Choice (B) suggests the model is sound since it has been successful elsewhere. Choice (C) suggests a strong revenue model. On the other hand, (D) suggests that the publication would fail to reach its intended audience, thus it probably would not *strongly appeal to advertisers of luxury goods.* Choice (E) suggests that the market is open to the benefit of the publishers.

12. B   The argument states that some people are eliminating meat from their diets because reducing the amount of animal products in one's diet can lead to better health. Meat is only one type of animal product, however. The argument assumes that by eliminating meat, the people are reducing the total amount of animal products in their diets. Choice (A) addresses increasing the amount of vegetables and grains, but the argument just deals with animal products. Choice (B) correctly addresses the people who are eliminating meat and states that those people are not increasing their consumption of dairy, which is another instance of using animal products. Thus, these people are actually reducing the amount of animal products in their diets. Choice (C) addresses most food writers, who are irrelevant to this argument. Choice (D) addresses healthy lifestyles, which are irrelevant to this particular argument. Choice (E) addresses the reasons behind not eating animal products, which is irrelevant to the argument.

13. C   This is an inference question, so evaluate the passage and then look for an answer choice that *can be reasonably inferred* from the information. The passage states that a *daily exercise regimen helps stroke survivors regain dexterity in their extremities* and that survivors who are *given an exercise routine* and who *have a consultation with a doctor* about the routine have been shown to be effective at getting *patients to exercise daily.* So it can be inferred that if a survivor is given a routine and consults with

a doctor, they are more likely to exercise daily, which will help them regain dexterity. Choice (A) is an example of extreme language. The phrasing *will regain full dexterity* is not promised in the information in the passage, as the passage only states that a routine and consultations may help a survivor exercise more. Eliminate (A). Choice (B) is also an example of extreme language. There is no way to discern from the information provided that a strong survivor would not regain dexterity without an exercise routine and a consultation, so eliminate (B). Choice (C) is a reasonable inference to make from the information in the passage so keep (C). Choice (D) also contains the extreme language *best way*. The information does not compare this method with any other method, so eliminate (D). Choice (E) is recycled language and does not address consulting with a doctor, so eliminate (E). The correct answer is (C).

14. **E** This argument assumes that there is a link between the needs of professional musicians and what the makers of amplifiers focus on. It is assumed that professional musicians need amplifiers that sound best played during live performances. Without this link, it is possible that professional musicians need amplifiers that are better suited to quieter practice situations. Choice (A) addresses amateur musicians, who are irrelevant to the argument. Choice (B) addresses how improvements in amplifier design come about, which is irrelevant to the argument. Choice (C) addresses revenue, which is irrelevant to the argument. Choice (D) addresses the musicians' knowledge of amplifier improvements, which is irrelevant to the musicians' needs and what the makers of amplifiers focus on. Choice (E) correctly identifies the assumption that professional musicians only need gear that will be used during live performances.

15. **A** Looking at (A), if investors and employees see technological superiority as evidence of a company's solid foundation, even if technological superiority is temporary, it will help that company attract funding and employees—a competitive advantage. For (B), if potential investors and employees know that technological superiority can quickly be lost, a company's technological advantage will be less likely to draw new investment or employees than if potential investors and employees were unaware of the tenuousness, so this would contribute to the paradox rather than help resolve it. Eliminate (B). Choice (C) is an outside knowledge trap. The answer says nothing about the technological sophistication of either type of company and so cannot help to resolve the paradox. Choice (D) is in agreement with the first sentence of the question stem; it does nothing to resolve the paradox. For (E), if a company is technologically superior to its competitors but doesn't know it, it will be more difficult for that company to take advantage its superiority. Hence, that superiority will be less valuable, so (E) would contribute to, not help resolve, the paradox.

16. **C** You are looking for a logical weakness in the analysis that concludes *the professors analysis that much agricultural knowledge among the native people of Brazil has been lost...must be correct*. Regarding (A), the study examines only natives of Brazil, so the knowledge other natives have is not relevant, and (A) is incorrect. Whether the title might bias readers may be a flaw in the study, but it is not a flaw in the analysis in the question stem, so (B) is incorrect. For (D), again, this is perhaps a problem in the study, but not in the logical analysis presented in the question stem, so (D) is incorrect. For (E), surely there are many skills a farmer needs, but the argument in the question stem is regarding only agricultural knowledge. So if other skills are important, it would demonstrate a weakness in the study, but not in the logic of the analysis. On the other hand, if the professor selected interviewees that she knew would confirm her hypothesis, then the analysis in the question stem—which says that the professor's conclusion that *much agricultural knowledge among the native people of Brazil has been lost... must be correct*, would be flawed. Rather than a loss of knowledge, it could be, for example, that the professor interviewed only members of a particular tribe that has urbanized, while others have remained rural and advanced their agricultural knowledge.

Analytical Writing Assessment (AWA)

ANALYTICAL WRITING ASSESSMENT (AWA)

The Analytical Writing Assessment (AWA) is the first section on the GMAT. It is designed to test your ability to express yourself in a cogent, well-organized manner. You will be asked to write an essay that is called the Analysis of an Argument essay, and you will have 30 minutes to write it. Your essay will be graded by a human and a computer on a scale from 0 to 6. The two grades will be averaged, rounded to the nearest half point and reported as a single score that is completely separate from your overall GMAT score.

Scoring

Both the human graders and computer grading program (known as the e-rater) look for certain features. The essay will be graded on organization and clarity, how well you address the questions, and your facility with the conventions of English. Don't worry about whether your ideas are original or creative; focus on writing a clear and organized essay. You are not expected to development a brilliant, sophisticated essay in 30 minutes. A well-organized, clearly structured essay that uses straightforward language will receive a good score.

Here's your basic approach.

Step 1: Brainstorm

Take a few minutes to come up with as many ideas as you can to support your position. Jot down your ideas on your scratch paper.

Step 2: Outline

Don't just start writing. Organization is one of the main grading criteria, so organize your ideas into a coherent outline. Use standard essay format: introduction, supporting paragraphs and conclusion. The brainstorming and outline steps should take a total of about 5 minutes.

Step 3: Write

Write the "bookends" (introduction and conclusion) first, and then go back and fill in the space between with your body paragraphs. This avoids the heartbreak of not finishing your essay because you ran out of time. Spend about 20 minutes writing your essay.

Step 4: Finish

Try to leave a few minutes to go back and read over your essay, making any necessary corrections.

WHAT TO EXPECT

For the essay you will be presented with an argument that is similar to those you have seen on assumption, weaken, and strengthen questions. Your job is to discuss how well reasoned the argument is. The argument is never well reasoned, so if you want a good score, don't praise the author's logic. However, you do need to have a "diplomatic tone." Be constructive, not destructive, in your criticism of the argument's flaws.

Remember, the way to attack an argument is to attack its assumptions, so identify the author's assumptions and explain why they are not necessarily true. You can also discuss how the argument could be strengthened. This does **not** mean describing what you would do in the situation presented or proposing a better solution to the problem described. It means detailing the facts or evidence the author would have to provide that would make his or her assumptions true.

To receive a high score, do the following:

- Identify the important features of the argument: conclusion, premises and assumptions.
- Critique the author's logic and assumptions, but not the conclusion. Show that the assumptions could be wrong or that some key term is not adequately defined.
- Suggest what evidence the author could provide that would make his or her assumptions true.
- Do NOT give your opinion of the truth of the conclusion. That is one of the most common mistakes on the argument essay. You get to discuss your opinion of the author's conclusion in the Issue essay, but if you do it here, you will hurt your score.

The Template

You don't have a huge amount of time, so you should know in advance how you will structure your essay. Here's a good way to write an Analysis of an Argument essay.

Introduction

Your introduction should quickly summarize the conclusion of the argument and state that the argument is flawed. Here's an example.

> The argument that (summary of the argument's conclusion) omits some important concerns that must be addressed to substantiate the argument.

It's that simple. Spend the majority of your time on the body paragraphs, supporting your position.

Body Paragraphs

Take the two to four strongest points you have brainstormed, and turn each into its own body paragraph. Be sure to use standard essay format and transition words between paragraphs.

Identify each assumption and explain why it is not necessarily true. Each assumption should get its own paragraph. You can give a few details or an example to support your assessment. You can also talk about what evidence is needed to make the assumption true. Try using constructions such as

> The argument assumes that (assumption). It is possible, however, that...

Conclusion

Write a strong conclusion paragraph that begins with a phrase that signifies your intention to conclude, such as "In conclusion..." and then summarize your critiques and suggest ways for improvement.

PRACTICE PROMPTS

The following appeared in a memorandum from the owner of Armchair Video, a chain of video rental stores.

> "Because of declining profits, we must reduce operating expenses at Armchair Video's ten video rental stores. Raising prices is not a good option, since we are famous for our special bargains. Instead, we should reduce our operating hours. Last month our store in downtown Marston reduced its hours by closing at 6:00 P.M. rather than 9:00 P.M. and reduced its overall inventory by no longer stocking any film released more than two years ago. Since we have received very few customer complaints about these new policies, we should now adopt them at all other Armchair Video stores as our best strategies for improving profits."

The following appeared in a letter to the Grandview City Council from a local business leader.

> "During last year's severe drought, when the water supply in the Grandview city reservoir fell to an extremely low level, the city council imposed much more rigid water-rationing rules. Just after these rules were imposed, however, industrial growth in the area declined. This clearly shows that the new rationing rules have hurt industry in Grandview. Therefore, to promote the health of the local economy, the city council should now stop water rationing."

The following appeared in a magazine article about planning for retirement.

"Because of its spectacular natural beauty and consistent climate, Clearview should be a top choice for anyone seeking a place to retire. As a bonus, housing costs in Clearview have fallen significantly during the past year, and real estate taxes remain lower than those in neighboring towns. Clearview's mayor promises many new programs to improve schools, streets, and public services. Retirees in Clearview can also expect excellent health care as they grow older, because the number of physicians in the area is far greater than the national average."